AMERICAN FOREIGN RELATIONS

Volume 1

A History · to 1920

FIFTH EDITION

THOMAS G. PATERSON

J. GARRY CLIFFORD

KENNETH J. HAGAN

HOUGHTON MIFFLIN COMPANY
Boston   *New York*

Editor-in-Chief: Jean L. Woy
Associate Editor: Leah Strauss
Project Editor: Aileen Mason
Editorial Assistant: Jane Lee
Associate Production/Design Coordinator: Jodi O'Rourke
Assistant Manufacturing Coordinator: Andrea Wagner
Senior Marketing Manager: Sandra McGuire
Senior Cover Design Coordinator: Deborah Azerrad Savona
Cover Design: Diana Coe/ko Design
Cover Art: British and Other Foreign Vessels off Yokohama, 19th century collection
of C. D. Wertheim, courtesy of Werner Forham/Art Resource, NY

The map on page 94 is reprinted from AMERICAN HISTORY ATLAS by Martin
Gilbert (London: Weidenfeld & Nicolson, 1968) by permission of Taylor & Francos
Books, Ltd.

Printed in the U.S.A.

Library of Congress Catalog Card Number: 99-71941

ISBN: 0-395-93886-4

1 2 3 4 5 6 7 8 9-FFG-03 02 01 00 99

for

Colin Graham Paterson

Carol Davidge

Vera Low Hagan

Thomas G. Paterson is professor of history emeritus at the University of Connecticut. Born in Oregon, he earned his B.A. from the University of New Hampshire (1963) and his Ph.D. from the University of California, Berkeley (1968). He has written *Contesting Castro* (1994), *On Every Front* (1992), *Meeting the Communist Threat* (1988), and *Soviet-American Confrontation* (1973), and he is co-author of *A People and a Nation* (1998, with Mary Beth Norton et al.). Tom has edited three books of original essays: *Explaining the History of American Foreign Relations* (1991, with Michael J. Hogan), *Kennedy's Quest for Victory* (1989), and *Cold War Critics* (1971). He has also edited *Major Problems in American Foreign Relations* (2000, with Dennis Merrill), *The Origins of the Cold War* (1999, with Robert J. McMahon), and *Imperial Surge* (1992, with Stephen G. Rabe). With Bruce Jentleson, Tom was senior editor for the four-volume *Encyclopedia of American Foreign Relations* (1997). A microfilm edition of *The United States and Castro's Cuba, 1950s–1970s: The Paterson Collection* appeared in 1999. He has served on the editorial boards of *Diplomatic History* and the *Journal of American History,* and he is a past president of the Society for Historians of American Foreign Relations. Recipient of a Guggenheim fellowship, Tom has also directed National Endowment for the Humanities Summer Seminars for College Teachers. A frequent speaker on American college campuses, he has also lectured in Canada, China, Colombia, Cuba, New Zealand, Puerto Rico, Russia, and Venezuela.

J. Garry Clifford teaches at the University of Connecticut, where he is a professor of political science and director of its graduate program. Born in Massachusetts, he earned his B.A. from Williams College (1964) and his Ph.D. in history from Indiana University. He has also taught at the University of Tennessee and Dartmouth College and has directed a National Endowment for the Humanities Seminar for High School Teachers at the Franklin D. Roosevelt Presidential Library. For his book *The Citizen Soldiers* (1972), he won the Frederick Jackson Turner Award of the Organization of American Historians. With Norman Cousins, he has edited *Memoir of a Man: Grenville Clark* (1975), and with Samuel R. Spencer, Jr., he has written *The First Peacetime Draft* (1986). Garry's articles have appeared in Gordon Martel, ed., *American Foreign Relations Reconsidered* (1994), Michael J. Hogan and Thomas G. Paterson, eds., *Explaining the History of American Foreign Relations* (1991), and in such journals as the *Journal of American History, Journal of Politics, Mid-America, American Neptune,* and *Diplomatic History.* He has served on the editorial board of *Diplomatic History* and also on the editorial board of the Modern War Series published by the University Press of Kansas. He frequently participates in American professional conferences and has also lectured in Russia.

Kenneth J. Hagan is an adjunct professor on the faculties of the U.S. Naval War College and the Naval Postgraduate School and professor of history and museum director emeritus at the U.S. Naval Academy in Annapolis. He previously taught at Claremont McKenna College, Kansas State University, and the U.S. Army Command and General Staff College. A native of California, he received his A.B. from the University of California, Berkeley (1958) and his Ph.D. from Claremont Graduate School (1970). Ken is the author of *This People's Navy: The Making of American Sea Power* (1991), a comprehensive history of American naval strategy and policy since the Revolution, and of *American Gunboat Diplomacy and the Old Navy, 1877–1889* (1973). His scholarship also includes two edited collections of original essays: *In Peace and War: Interpretations of American Naval History, 1775–1984* (1984) and *Against All Enemies: Interpretations of American Military History from Colonial Times to the Present* (1986). He frequently contributes articles to the journal *Naval History,* and lectures annually at the Canadian Forces College in Toronto. Besides regularly participating in panels at conferences in the United States, he has given papers on the history of naval strategy in Sweden, Greece, Turkey, France, and Spain. A retired captain in the naval reserve, he served on active duty with the Pacific Fleet from 1958 to 1963 and currently advises the Naval ROTC college program on its history curriculum.

Contents

Chapter 3
Extending and Preserving the Sphere, 1815–1848   85

Chapter 4
Expansionism, Sectionalism, and Civil War, 1848–1865   128

Chapter 7
Managing, Policing, and Extending the Empire, 1900–1914   632

Chapter 8
War, Peace, and Revolution in the Time of Wilson, 1914–1920   267

Maps and Graphs

Preface

Once again the advance of scholarly literature, the encouraging comments of instructors and students in history, political science, and international relations, and the passage of time have prompted us to revise *American Foreign Relations*. As before, in this fifth edition we engage influential approaches and interpretations, especially those articulated by younger scholars. We seek to explain foreign relations in the broadest manner as the many ways that peoples, organizations, states, and systems interact—economic, cultural, strategic, environmental, political, and more.

We continue to emphasize the theme of expansionism, explaining its many manifestations. We also show that on almost every issue in the history of American foreign relations, alternative voices unfailingly sounded among and against official policymakers. Americans have always debated their place in the world, their wars, their overseas commitments, and the status of their principles and power, and they have always debated the people of other nations about the spread of U.S. influence. We try to capture with vivid description and quotation the drama of the many debates.

A historical overview such as this one necessarily draws on the copious work of scholars in the United States and abroad. Their expertise informs this book throughout and helps lend it the authority instructors and students expect. Our "Further Reading" and "Notes" sections are one way to thank them for their books, articles, and conference papers. We have also appreciated their recommendations for text revisions and their suggestions for teaching the courses for which this book is intended. We thank them, too, for challenging us to consider the many different approaches and theories that have commanded attention in this field: world systems, corporatism, dependency, culture, psychology and personality, medical biography, lessons from the past ("thinking in time"), bureaucratic politics, public opinion, executive-legislative competition, gender, national security and power, impact on recipients of foreign aid, the natural environment, and ideology among them. This book also presents the findings of our own ongoing archival research and writing as we discover and rediscover the past.

The traditional topics of diplomacy, war, economic intercourse, and politics remain central to our presentation of the foreign-relations story, but we have made this edition more comprehensive by extending our discussion of the cultural dimensions of foreign relations: race-based and gender-based images of other peoples that condition the decisionmaking environment; the proliferation abroad of American mass culture (such as films and sports); the foreign response to "Americanization"; travel and tourism that help create a pool of knowledge about foreign places that promotes an expansionist consciousness; and "public diplomacy"—the presentation of a positive image of the United States abroad through propaganda, radio and television, and trade fairs. We have also expanded our coverage of relations with Native Americans and the frontier experience in the eighteenth and nineteenth centuries. Issues that spring from human interaction with the natural environment and the international conferences convened to deal with damage to the environment also receive more space in this edition. The post–Cold War declassification of documents in foreign archives—Russian, East German, Cuban, and Chinese among them—has helped us rewrite our treatment of the Korean War, Sino-American relations, the Cuban missile crisis, and the failure of détente in the 1970s. Because scholars have increasingly explored medical health as a factor in decisionmaking, we have integrated this subject—as in the lives of Woodrow Wilson, Franklin D. Roosevelt, John F. Kennedy, and Ronald Reagan.

In preparing this edition, we once again immersed ourselves in the memoirs, diaries, letters, speeches, recorded tapes, and oral histories of U.S. and international leaders. We often let them speak for themselves in the frankest terms, guarded and unguarded. We have sought to capture their anger and their humor, their cooperation and their competitiveness, their truths and their lies, their moments of doubt and times of confidence, their triumphs and setbacks. *American Foreign Relations,* in short, strives to capture the erratic pulse of international relations through peoples' struggles to plan, decide, and administer. We study not only the leaders who made influential decisions, but also the world's peoples who welcomed, resisted, or endured the decisions that profoundly influenced their lives. In this regard, we have drawn on the growing scholarship that studies non-state actors, including peace groups, African Americans, and international bodies such as the World Health Organization.

Each chapter opens with a significant and dramatic event—a "Diplomatic Crossroad"—that helps illustrate the chief characteristics and issues of the era. The introductory and concluding sections of each chapter set the themes. Illustrations—many of them new to this edition—from collections around the world, are closely tied to the narrative in image and caption description. The revised maps, graphs, and "Makers of American Foreign Relations" tables in each chapter provide essential information. The updated chapter bibliographies guide further reading and serve as a starting point for term or research papers. The "General Bibliography" at the end of the book is also a place to begin research or seek more information. The "General Bibliography" consists of three parts: first, general reference works, such as biographical dictionaries, atlases, statistics, encyclopedias, and bibliographies; second, overviews of U.S. relations with countries and regions, from Afghanistan to Zimbabwe; and, third, overviews of subjects, such as Air Force and air power, CIA and covert action, Congress, cultural relations, ethnic conflict, human rights, isolationism, Manifest Destiny, Monroe Doctrine, oil, refugees, slave trade and slavery, terrorism, and United Nations.

In the late 1970s, the People's Republic of China adopted a new system for rendering Chinese phonetic characters into the Roman alphabet. Called the Pinyin method, it replaced the Wade-Giles technique, which had long been used in English. Use of the Pinyin method is now common, and we use it in *American Foreign Relations.* Many changes are minor—Shantung has become Shandong and Mao Tse-tung has become Mao Zedong, for example. But when we have a possibly confusing Pinyin spelling, we have placed the Wade-Giles spelling in parentheses—for example, Beijing (Peking) or Jiang Jieshi (Chiang Kai-shek).

Instructors and students interested in the study of foreign-relations history are invited to join the Society for Historians of American Foreign Relations (SHAFR). This organization publishes a superb journal, *Diplomatic History,* and a newsletter; offers book, article, and lecture prizes and dissertation research grants; and holds an annual conference where scholars present their views and research results. Dues are very reasonable. For information, contact the SHAFR Business Office, Department of History, Wright State University, Dayton, OH 45435, or see SHAFR's web site at www.ohiou.edu/~shafr/shafr.htm. At this home page you will also find links to other sites related to American foreign relations.

Another informative web site is H-Diplo: Diplomatic History, found at www.h-net.msu.edu/~diplo. Besides presenting provocative online discussions on foreign-relations history, this site also provides research and bibliographic aids and an extensive list of links to other useful resources, including journals, newspapers, archives and presidential libraries, research organizations such as the National Security Archive, and government agencies such as the Central Intelligence Agency and Department of State.

Many colleagues, friends, students, and editors contributed to this edition of *American Foreign Relations* by providing research leads, correction of errors, reviews of the text, library searches, documents and essays, and editorial assistance. We give our heartiest thanks to John Burns, Alejandro Corbacho, Frank Costigliola, Michael Donoghue, Elizabeth Mahan, Elizabeth McKillen, Dennis Merrill, Marc O'Reilly, Chester Pach, Kenneth E. Shewmaker, Mark A. Stoler, Thomas Walker, Wang Li, and Imanuel Wexler. Jake Kawatski expertly prepared the comprehensive index. Houghton Mifflin's talented team merits the highest of praise: Jean L. Woy, editor-in-chief; Leah Strauss, associate editor; Aileen Mason, project editor; Jodi O'Rourke, production/design coordinator; Andrea Wagner, manufacturing coordinator; Pembroke Herbert, photo researcher; Patricia Herbst, copyeditor; and Deborah Karacozian, proofreader.

We are also eager to thank the many people who helped us in previous editions: Philip J. Avillo, Jr., Richard Baker, Ann Balcolm, Michael A. Barnhart, Kenneth J. Blume, Robert Beisner, R. Christian Berg, Richard Bradford, Kinley J. Brauer, Richard Dean Burns, Charles Conrad Campbell, Chen Jian, John Coogan, Carol Davidge, Mark Del Vecchio, Ralph Di Carpio, Justus Doenecke, Xavier Franco, Irwin Gellman, Paul Goodwin, James Gormly, Eric Hafter, Hope M. Harrison, Alan Henrikson, Gregg Herken, George Herring, Ted Hitchcock, Joan Hoff, Reginald Horsman, Michael Hunt, Edythe Izard, Holly Izard, Richard Izard, Leith Johnson, Burton Kaufman, Melville T. Kennedy, Jr., Thomas Lairson, Lester Langley, Thomas M. Leonard, Li Yan, Terrence J. Lindell, Martha McCoy, David McFadden, Charles McGraw, Matt McMahon, Robert McMahon, Shane Maddock, Elizabeth Mahan, Paul Manning, Herman Mast, Dennis Merrill, Jean-Donald Miller, Carl Murdock, Brian Murphy, R. Kent Newmyer, Arnold Offner, John Offner, Jerry Padula, Carol Petillo, David Pletcher, Salvadore Prisco, Stephen G. Rabe, Carol S. Repass, Wayne Repeta, Barney J. Rickman III, Michael Roskin, John Rourke, Kent M. Schofield, David Sheinin, Anna Lou Smethurst, Elbert B. Smith, Thomas G. Smith, Kenneth R. Stevens, Mark A. Stoler, William W.

Stueck, Jr., Duane Tananbaum, George Turner, Jonathan G. Utley, Wang Li, Kathryn Weathersby, Ralph E. Weber, Edmund S. Wehrle, Lawrence Wittner, Sol Woolman, and Thomas Zoumaras.

We welcome comments and suggestions from students and instructors.

T. G. P.
J. G. C.
K. J. H.

AMERICAN FOREIGN RELATIONS

CHAPTER

1

Embryo of Empire: Americans and the World Before 1789

French Snuffbox. *Benjamin Franklin's reputation as a representative of frontier America is captured in a contemporary French snuffbox. In this compliment the revered gentleman from Pennsylvania joins two other philosophers, Rousseau and Voltaire. (The Metropolitan Museum of Art, Gift of William H. Huntington, 1883. All rights reserved.)*

❖

DIPLOMATIC CROSSROAD

Jay, Franklin, Adams, and Negotiations for Independence, 1782

Two disgruntled Americans rode the same carriage from Versailles to the Parisian suburb of Passy on the afternoon of August 10, 1782. John Jay and Benjamin Franklin had just spent two frustrating hours with the French foreign minister, the Comte de Vergennes. These American peace commissioners, seeking to end the Revolutionary War for independence waged since 1775, had asked for French advice on two troublesome problems that had arisen in their concurrent negotiations with British and Spanish representatives. Because the Continental Congress had instructed them to make no decisions without the knowledge and counsel of the French, Jay and Franklin had asked Vergennes whether the United States should insist on explicit recognition of independence from England *prior* to a final peace treaty with the "mother country," and whether the western boundary of the new American nation should be the Mississippi River. On both points Vergennes and his secretary, Gérard de Rayneval, made suggestions that seemed to deny American interests. Do not worry about technicalities, Vergennes advised. If the British granted independence in the final treaty, as they were proposing, Americans should not make a fuss about formal titles during the negotiations. Regarding the western boundary, according to Jay, Vergennes and Rayneval hinted that "we [Americans] claimed more than we had a right to," and that Spain and England had valid claims to territory east of the Mississippi.[1]

Jay and Franklin wondered why their French ally proffered such negative advice. Jay was particularly suspicious, telling his older colleague that Vergennes was plotting to delay negotiations with England so that Spain, having captured West Florida, could acquire the whole Gulf Coast and additional territory to the north. Franklin agreed that Spain wanted to "coop us up within the Allegheny Mountains," but he did not think that the French were deliberately sacrificing American interests in order to gratify Spain.[2]

The discussion then became extremely animated, and when the carriage reached Passy, Franklin invited Jay inside his apartment to continue their conversation. "Have we any reason to doubt the good faith of the King of France?" inquired Franklin. "We can depend on the French," Jay rejoined, "only to see that we are separated from England, but it is not in their interest that we should become a great and formidable people, and therefore they will not help us to become so." Franklin asked on whom the United States should rely. "We have no rational dependence except on God and ourselves," Jay solemnly answered. The Pennsylvanian shot back: "Would you deliberately break Congress's instructions [on not negotiating separately]?" "Unless we violate these instructions the dignity of Congress will be in the dust," Jay asserted. The seventy-five-year-old Franklin pressed further: "Then you are prepared to break our instructions if you intend to take an independence course now." Jay stood up. "*If* the instructions conflict with America's honor and dignity I would break them—like this!" The dignified New Yorker threw his clay pipe hard into Franklin's fireplace. The pipe shattered.[3]

Nothing that occurred in the diplomacy of the next several weeks elevated John Jay's opinion of Europeans in general, or of the French and Spaniards in particular. In early September, Rayneval gave Jay his "personal ideas" to expedite peace negotiations with England as well as a boundary settlement with Spain. Again Rayneval urged the Americans not to press for the Mississippi. Jay correctly assumed that Rayneval reflected Vergennes's sentiments. A few days later Rayneval disappeared from Paris, sent on a secret mission to London. Jay became immediately suspicious. Paris buzzed with rumors. Even the usually unflappable Franklin became worried. Perhaps Rayneval's mission would bring the same arguments to the British that he was making to the Americans; perhaps France sought the role of arbiter in North America, supported British claims north of the Ohio River, and wanted to give Spain full control over the Mississippi. The next day Jay received from a British agent in Paris an intercepted French dispatch, in cipher, which urged a strong stand against American claims to the Newfoundland fisheries. Franklin cautiously pointed out that this dispatch, sent by a French envoy in America, did not necessarily reflect the views of Vergennes or King Louis XVI.

Jay had had enough. On September 11, without first even informing Franklin, Jay boldly sent his own secret emissary to London with the proposal that secret and separate negotiations for peace begin at once. The British jumped at the chance to split the Franco-American alliance. When he learned what his younger colleague had done, Franklin protested. But he went along.

By late October, when the third American peace commissioner arrived in Paris, private talks with the British had gone on for several weeks. John Adams had just successfully negotiated a commercial treaty with the Dutch. As a diplomat in Paris earlier in the war, he had come to distrust both the French and Franklin, a man of "cunning without wisdom" who seemed too cozy with Vergennes.[4] The cantankerous New Englander found it difficult to trust anyone, but he immediately found a kindred spirit in Jay, who apprised him of the state of the negotiations. He warned Jay that Franklin was hopelessly subservient to Vergennes. Like Jay, Adams thought that Vergennes opposed American expansion and kept "his hand under our chin to prevent us from drowning, but not to lift our heads out of the water."[5] Adams dallied for four days before making a courtesy call on Franklin. Once at Passy, Adams immediately launched into a lecture. Everything Jay had done was correct. Jay was right in his suspicions toward Vergennes. Jay was right to insist on prior independence, access to the fisheries, and extensive western boundaries. Adams waxed enthusiastic about the decision to ignore Vergennes and negotiate separately with the British on these issues. To do otherwise would be leaving "the lamb to the custody of the wolf."[6] His conscience unburdened, Adams returned to his apartment in the Hôtel du Roi.

Franklin hardly replied to Adams's outburst. Suffering from the gout, the old philosopher listened patiently and tolerantly to the person he later described as "always an honest man, often a wise one, but sometimes, and in some things, absolutely out of his senses."[7] Franklin agreed that the United States should remain firm on both the fisheries and the Mississippi boundary. Access to the Newfoundland fishing grounds was vital to New England's economy, while the "Father of Waters" stood as an indispensable highway for trans-Allegheny commerce. As for giving up the Mississippi, "a Neighbor might as well ask me to sell my Street Door," Franklin said.[8] What exercised

John Adams (1735–1826). Native of Braintree (Quincy), Massachusetts, graduate of Harvard, Boston lawyer, colonial rebel, and diplomat, Adams became president in 1797. Adams later likened his diplomacy in 1782 to that of "a Man running a race upon a right line barefoot treading among burning Plowshares, with horrid Figures of Jealousy, Envy, Hatred, Revenge, Vanity, Ambition, Avarice, Treachery, Tyranny, Insolence, arranged on each side of his Path and lashing him with Scorpions all the Way, and attempting at every Step to trip up his Heels." (The National Portrait Gallery, Smithsonian Institution)

"Blessed Are the Peacemakers." In this critical British cartoon of 1783 a Spaniard and a Frenchman lead George III by the neck while Lord Shelburne carries the "Preliminaries of Peace." The procession is commanded by an American wielding a whip and tugging a sulking, boorish Dutchman. (British Museum)

Franklin most was the failure to consult Vergennes. French loans had kept America solvent through six long years of war, and French ships and troops had contributed mightily to the decisive victory at Yorktown in 1781. Franklin valued the French alliance. "If we were to break our faith with this nation," he warned, "England would again trample on us and every other nation despise us."[9] Unlike his younger colleagues, Franklin did not believe that the French were dealing with Spain and England behind American backs. Franklin nonetheless recognized the importance of a united American front in negotiations. Always a pragmatist, he had written in his *Autobiography*: "So convenient a thing it is to be a *reasonable creature,* since it enables one to find or make a reason for everything one has a mind to do."[10] Franklin decided to be reasonable. Just prior to meeting with the British commissioners, he startled Jay: "I am of your opinion, and will go with these gentlemen in the business without consulting this [French] court."[11]

Franklin remained true to his word, and on November 30, 1782, England and the United States signed a "preliminary treaty" of peace. The terms, enumerated in a comprehensive treaty some ten months later, guaranteed American independence and provided generous boundaries. The historian Samuel Flagg Bemis has called the accord "the greatest victory in the annals of American diplomacy."[12]

The American decision to negotiate separately in 1782 was as symbolic as it was successful. By going to war with England, the colonies had sought to win their independence, enlarge their commerce, and expand their territorial domain. Patriot leaders hoped to attain these goals without getting entangled in European politics. One motive for independence was the desire to escape the constant wars and dynastic intrigues that characterized eighteenth-century Europe. But victory required help. France became America's ally in 1778, and in the next two years Spain and the Netherlands also joined the war against England. The war for American independence had evolved into a world war. The entanglements Americans hoped to avoid inevitably followed. At the critical moment in the peace negotiations, Jay and Adams rightly suspected that their French ally, although committed to American independence, did not share the expansive American vision of that independence. The two commissioners thereupon persuaded Franklin to pursue an *independent* course, take advantage of European rivalries, and extract a generous treaty from the British. In Adams's eyes especially, these American diplomats were maintaining American honor by breaking instructions that French diplomats had forced on a pliant Congress. It was an ironic moment. Americans said they pursued independence and empire not merely for selfish motives, but also for a more civilized mode of international relations, free from the monarchical double-dealing of European power politics. "Let Us above all things avoid as much as possible Entangling ourselves with their Wars or Politicks," wrote Adams in 1780. "America has been the Sport of European Wars and Politicks long enough."[13] To gain their ends, however, Franklin, Jay, and Adams employed the same Machiavellian tactics that they so despised in Europeans.

Reaching for Independence: Ideology and Commercial Power

The United States could not have won independence from England without assistance from France. Such was the inescapable fact of early American foreign relations. However much the patriots of 1776 wanted to isolate themselves from the wars and diplomatic maneuverings of Europe, European events provided them with the opportunity for national liberation.

The century-old rivalry between France and England for preeminence in Europe and control of North America provided the immediate backdrop for the American Revolution. Four wars fought between 1689 and 1763 were European in origin but had profound consequences in the New World. The most recent war, called the Seven Years' War in Europe (1756–1763) and the French and Indian War in America (1754–1763), had ensured the virtual elimination of French power from North America. By the Treaty of Paris (1763) the defeated French ceded Canada and the Ohio Valley to the British and relinquished Louisiana to the Spanish. Spain, in turn, gave up the Floridas to England.

For the most part colonial leaders cheered the victorious British war for empire. The Reverend Jonathan Mayhew of Boston envisaged the colonies as "*a mighty empire . . .* mighty cities rising on every hill, and by the side of every commodious port, mighty fleets . . . laden with the produce of . . . every other country under heaven; happy fields and villages . . . through a vastly extended territory."[14] Benjamin Franklin, then a colonial agent in England, had urged removal of the French from Canada. "The future grandeur and stability of the British empire lay in America," he wrote in 1760. "All the country from the St. Lawrence to the Mississippi will be in another century filled with British people."[15] Calculating that the American population, doubling every twenty-five years, would reach 32 million by 1865, a British visitor predicted that "this vast country will in time become the greatest and most prosperous empire that perhaps the world has ever seen."[16] According to the historian Gordon H. Wood, "this demographic explosion, this gigantic movement of people, was the most basic and the most liberating force working on American society during the latter half of the eighteenth century."[17]

As soon as the French and Indian War ended, however, London began to tighten the machinery of empire. A standing army of 10,000 men was sent to America for imperial defense. To pay for its upkeep, and to help defray the costs of the recent war with France, Parliament levied new taxes on the colonies. London now enforced mercantile regulations forbidding direct American trade with foreign ports in the West Indies. Even though the Treaty of Paris seemed to open the west to colonial settlement, an impressive Indian alliance under the Ottawa chief Pontiac united the western Indian nations, attacked British outposts, and raided settlements from the Great Lakes to Virginia during 1763. While ending Pontiac's uprising by peace treaty, the British ministry ineffectually sought control over the interior by issuing the Proclamation of 1763, which delineated the headwaters of rivers flowing into the Atlantic as a temporary boundary for colonial settlement. The Treaty of Fort Stanwix (1768) moved the line to the Ohio River, but settlers soon swarmed beyond the Ohio with "utter disregard for Indian rights," thus renewing conflict along the frontier from Pennsylvania to Kentucky by 1774.[18]

In response to London's apparent disregard for their interests, the colonials retaliated with petitions, economic boycotts, and sporadic outbreaks of violence. Parliament responded with more taxes. The Tea Act of 1773 led to the Boston Tea Party, which, in turn, triggered the Coercive Acts. Galling to expansionist Americans, the Quebec Act of 1774 made the Ohio Valley an integral part of Canada. Armed resistance exploded at Lexington and Concord in the spring of 1775, followed by battles around Boston. Then came an abortive American invasion of Quebec in December 1775. By this time John Adams and Benjamin Franklin were urging ties with the same "turbulent Gallicks" they had helped to defeat twenty years before.

As American leaders moved cautiously toward independence, the emerging republican ideology, which embraced the "rights of Englishmen" and the principles of representative government, also contained the roots of an independent foreign policy. Historical lessons seemed to point toward independence. Benjamin Franklin asked the central question: "Have not all Mankind in all Ages had the Right of deserting their Native Country? . . . Did not the Saxons desert their Native Country when they came to Britain?"[19] Americans specifically looked to their immediate colonial past. As British mercantile restrictions tightened in the 1760s, colonial leaders began to argue that the imperial connection with England was one-sided, and that Americans became constantly embroiled in England's wars against their will. Attacks by the French and Indians along the northern frontier usually had their origins in European quarrels, yet Americans nevertheless had to pay taxes, raise armies, and fight and die. Britain did not always seem to appreciate colonial sacrifices. The most telling example occurred in 1745 when New Englanders, through good luck and enormous exertion, captured the strategic French fortress of Louisbourg on Cape Breton Island. In the European peace treaty three years later, however, the British handed back Louisbourg in exchange for French conquests in India.

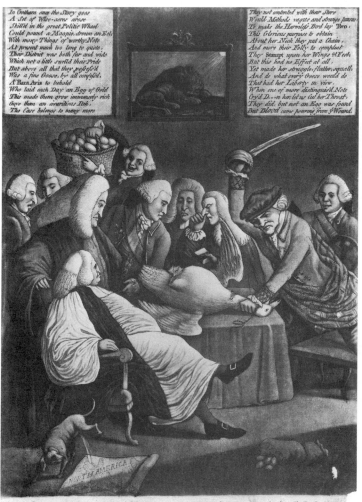

"The Wise Men of Gotham and Their Goose" (1776). This British cartoon satirized Britain's American policy as "folly." British politicians are killing the colonial goose that laid the golden eggs (in basket) while the plump king leans back in his chair and a dog urinates on a map of North America. (Library of Congress)

Americans had no wish to be pawns in England's colonial wars. Franklin exaggerated when he told Parliament in 1766 that the Americans had enjoyed "perfect peace with both French and Indians" and that the recent conflict had been "really a British war."[20] He was nonetheless expressing what one scholar has called "a deep-seated feeling of escape from Europe and a strong tendency, encouraged by European diplomacy, to avoid becoming entangled in European conflict, whenever it was to their interest to do so."[21]

Americans advocating independence also found arguments in recent British history. Many of the same English Whig writers whom Americans quoted in defense of "no taxation without representation" had also taken part in a great debate over the direction of British foreign policy during the first half of the eighteenth century. These Whigs had criticized British involvement in continental European wars. Since the European balance of power always seemed unstable, they argued that continental entanglements might improve the German territorial interests of the House of Hanover but certainly not those of England. Whigs distrusted England's German kings. "This great, this powerful, this formidable kingdom, is considered only as a province to a despicable electorate [Hanover]," William Pitt complained in 1743.[22] England's true interests, these Whigs emphasized, lay in expanding its commerce and empire. Political alliances had not "produced any advantage to us."[23] One pamphleteer posited a general rule: "A Prince or State ought to avoid all Treaties, except such as tend towards Commerce or Manufactures. . . . All other Alliances may be look'd upon as so many Incumbrances."[24] The similarity between these arguments for British isolation from Europe and the later American rationale for independence is striking. American leaders became familiar with the British debate. Benjamin Franklin, as a colonial agent in London, knew personally many of the Whig critics. American merchants, lawyers, and plantation owners visited England or studied there. In their desire to avoid British wars and British taxes, Revolutionary leaders not surprisingly appropriated British precepts.

Another source of American thinking on independence and foreign policy came in the writings of the French *philosophes*. As Enlightenment enthusiasts and advocates for the rising bourgeoisie, the *philosophes* launched an attack on all diplomatic and political practices that thwarted the proper rule of reason in international affairs. Traditional diplomacy had become synonymous with double-dealing, they argued, "an obscure art which hides itself in the folds of deceit, which fears to let itself be seen and believes it can succeed only in the darkness of mystery."[25] Like the English Whigs, the *philosophes* emphasized commercial expansion over standard power politics. Political barriers were artificial; commerce tied the "family of nations" together with "threads of silk."[26] Trade should be as free as possible, unfettered by mercantilism—a set of assumptions and laws that an imperial nation like Britain used to gain economic self-sufficiency by regulating trade between the mother country and subordinate colonies. Baron de Montesquieu, who believed that "the natural effect of commerce is to lead to peace," postulated that "everywhere there are gentle mores, there is commerce and that everywhere there is commerce, there are gentle mores."[27] More radical *philosophes* such as the Marquis de Condorcet wanted to take diplomacy out of the hands of princes and remove all obstacles to a direct expression of the popular will. "Alliances," wrote Condorcet, "are only means by which the rulers of states precipitate the people into wars from which they benefit either by covering up their mistakes or by carrying out their plots against freedom."[28] Diplomacy should be as simple as possible, consisting largely of commercial interchange between individual persons rather than governments. Such views impressed some Americans.

Although Americans never read or quoted the *philosophes* as often as they did the English Whigs, such continental ideas provided Revolutionary leaders with a missionary credo as they sought to win independence and an empire from the British Crown. Like John Winthrop's Puritans, they would not merely be benefiting themselves but also be erecting a model for the rest of the world. John Adams made this point when he told Vergennes in 1781 that "the dignity of North America does not consist in diplomatic ceremonials. . . . [It] consists solely in reason, justice, truth, the rights of mankind, and the interests of the nations of Europe."[29] Indeed, as the historian Anders Stephanson has argued, the Revolutionary generation believed itself "providentially assigned . . . to lead the world to new and better things," to create "an exemplary state *separate* from the corrupt and fallen world" while at the same time hoping to "push the world along by means of regenerative *intervention*."[30] Americans also shared with Europeans the belief that a single dominant power always carried forward civilization, and that historically such empires always moved, as the Reverend Thomas Brockway observed in 1784, "from east to west, and this continent is the last western state" wherein God is "erecting a stage on which to exhibit the great things of his kingdom."[31]

The movement for an independent foreign policy reached its climax with the convocation of the Second Continental Congress, following Lexington and Concord, in the summer of 1775. Some Americans who still wanted to remain within the British Empire held out hope that continued commercial opposition— no imports, no exports—would force Parliament and the king to negotiate. More radical delegates wanted to continue the war and declare independence. Benjamin Franklin proposed "articles of confederation" that would give Congress full power to make war and peace. John Adams called for construction of an American navy. Other advocates of independence urged the opening of American ports to foreign trade, arguing that only with protection from foreign navies could American merchant ships reach European ports. With their British market no longer available, the thirteen colonies needed commerce to survive. Foreign trade required foreign assistance. The argument for independence, made repeatedly behind the closed doors of Congress, became popularized on January 10, 1776, with the appearance of Thomas Paine's pamphlet *Common Sense*.

Tom Paine was an English Quaker who had come to America in 1774. While in England he had drunk deeply at the well of Whig dissent, and once in Philadelphia he became friends with those members of Congress who urged independence. Paine's pamphlet summarized their arguments. Opposing further petitions to the king, urging construction of a navy and the immediate formation of a confederation, emphasizing the need for foreign assistance, and calling for the opening of American ports to the rest of the world, Paine's celebrated call to "begin the world over again" also spelled out the benefits of an independent foreign policy. Reconciliation with England was no longer possible, and as Paine put it with some exaggeration, there was not "a single advantage that this continent can reap by being connected with Great Britain." On the contrary, "France and Spain never were, nor perhaps ever will be, our enemies as Americans, but as Our being subjects of Great Britain." American agricultural products, he emphasized, were "the necessaries of life and will always have a market while eating is the custom of Europe." For Paine and his American friends, "Our plan is commerce, and that, well attended to, will secure us the Peace and friendship of all Europe; because it is in the interest of all Europe to have America as a free port. . . . As Europe is our market for trade, we ought to form no partial connection with any part of it. It is the true interest of America to steer clear of European contentions."[32] After a declaration of

Thomas Paine (1737–1809).   This working-class Englishman found his way to Philadelphia in 1774, where he took a job as a journalist. "From shopkeepers, tradesmen, and attorneys," the British philosopher Adam Smith wrote after reading Paine's *Common Sense* (1776), Americans "are become statesmen and legislators . . . contriving a new form of government for an extensive empire, which, they flatter themselves, will become, and which, indeed, seems very likely to become, one of the greatest and most formidable that ever was in the world." The irascible Paine joined the Continental Army and later participated in the French Revolution. (National Gallery of Art)

independence, he predicted, Europe would compete for America's commercial favors. Paine assumed that a foreign nation would assist America to protect that trade. America would benefit, and so would the rest of the world.

Of course, part of what Paine wrote was more nonsense than "common sense," particularly his playing down of privileges that Americans enjoyed as part of the British Empire. After independence, Americans would miss British naval protection, British credit, and easy access to the British West Indies. The pamphlet nonetheless served as effective propaganda. *Common Sense* sold more than 300,000 copies, the equivalent of one copy for every ten persons living in the thirteen colonies in 1776. "With its idealism, its internationalism, and its hostility to power politics and reasons of state," one historian has written, Paine's pamphlet embedded "decidedly nontraditional—indeed, revolutionary—ideas in early American foreign relations."[33]

With the abortive invasion of Canada in the winter of 1775–1776 and the arrival of British reinforcements, it became obvious that some foreign help was imperative. Congress opened American ports in April 1776, but Paine's logic seemed irrefutable: No foreign power would openly aid the American rebels until independence was a declared fact. Virginia's Richard Henry Lee, on June 6, offered a resolution: "These United Colonies are, and of right ought to be, free and independent States."[34] Lee echoed Paine's thoughts. "No State in Europe," he explained to Patrick Henry, "will either Treat or Trade with us so long as we consider ourselves Subjects of G.B. . . . It is not choice . . . but necessity that calls for

Independence, as the only means by which foreign Alliances can be obtained."[35] Thomas Jefferson wrote the Declaration of Independence, and Congress endorsed it on July 4, 1776.

They next sought to secure foreign support. Congress designated a committee to prepare a "model treaty" to be presented to the French court of Louis XVI. The committee's so-called Plan of 1776, which Congress debated in August, would also serve as the basis for alliances with other countries. A final, amended version then accompanied Benjamin Franklin to France when he became American minister at the close of the year. John Adams drafted the Model Treaty. Like Paine, the lawyer from Braintree eschewed political entanglements. "I am not for soliciting any po-litical connection, or military assistance, or indeed naval, from France," he told a friend. "I wish for nothing but commerce, a mere marine treaty with them."[36] Adams's imprint on the Model Treaty became clear, for it was almost purely a treaty of commerce and navigation, which would permit American ships free entry into French ports while French military supplies entered American ports in ever-increasing quantities. Included also were elaborate rules protecting neutral com-merce in wartime. The Model Treaty suggested that the United States and France grant the nationals of each country the same "Rights, Liberties, Privileges, Immunities and Exemptions" in trade, but that if "his most Christian Majesty shall not consent" to such a novel idea, then the American commissioners should try to obtain a most-favored-nation clause, whereby American merchants would receive the same commercial benefits enjoyed by other nations.[37] In effect, as the historian John Crowley has noted, the treaty "intended to secure France as a de facto ally by encouraging it to violate the British monopoly of colonial trade and thereby draw it into war with Britain."[38]

Some of his closest friends in Congress, Adams later recalled, "thought there was not sufficient temptation to France to join us. They moved for cessions and concessions, which implied warranties and political alliance that I had studiously avoided."[39] Like most Americans in 1776, he feared that France, if offered politi-cal inducements, might demand Canada and access to the Newfoundland fisheries, both of which the new republic sought for itself. Somewhat naively, Adams and his colleagues convinced themselves that the ending of England's monopoly over North American commerce, accomplished through American independence, would by itself gain French support. Franco-American trade should be "ample Compensation to France for Acknowledging our Independence," Adams in-sisted.[40] The only political obligation in the Model Treaty came in Article VIII, which stipulated that America would not aid the British in any conflict between Britain and France.

The neutral-rights provisions of the Model Treaty deserve special attention. Although these commercial articles would not apply to the war against England, in which the United States was already a belligerent, they formed the basis of what later became America's historic policy of "freedom of the seas." Lifted almost word for word from earlier treaties signed by nations possessing small navies, these com-mercial clauses guaranteed the principles of "free ships, free goods" (that is, the neu-tral flag protected noncontraband cargoes from capture), the freedom of neutrals to trade in noncontraband between ports of belligerents, and a restricted and narrowly defined list of contraband (illegal cargo) exempting naval stores and foodstuffs from seizure. Regarding the neutral flag as an extension of territorial sovereignty on the high seas, Americans claimed broad freedom to trade in wartime, except in contraband articles and with places blockaded or besieged. Such principles of neutral rights were becoming increasingly accepted in the late eighteenth century, particularly among enlightened publicists and by countries lacking large navies. Although England had adopted liberal provisions in a few treaties, British diplomats grew understandably reluctant to endorse them as international law. If Britain went to war against an inferior naval force, for example, the British enemy might very well encourage neutral shipping to carry its commercial goods in order to protect its own vulnerable vessels from British warships. If neutrals could also supply an enemy nation freely, especially with naval stores, they could eventually undermine Britain's maritime supremacy. Americans, looking ahead to independence, envisaged future European wars and hoped, in the absence of political entanglements, to expand their commerce at such times. France, in the event of a naval war against the more powerful British, would benefit from American neutrality. Americans could fatten their pocketbooks and at the same time serve humanity by supporting more civilized rules of warfare. Or so Americans hoped.

The Model Treaty, then, introduced the main themes of early American foreign policy. It set forth the ideal of commercial expansion and political isolation. By specifically binding France against acquiring Canada, it also projected a continental domain for America beyond the thirteen coastal settlements. As the historian Peggy K. Liss has written, the Model Treaty underscored "the faith of the leaders of the new nation in the power of trade, and a concomitant desire to stay out of European struggles. . . . And it indicated a belief that freedom was on the wane everywhere but in mainland Anglo-America, that America, now liberty's home, must be maintained as 'an asylum for mankind.' "[41] To Benjamin Franklin fell the mission to determine whether Adams's "mere marine treaty" would secure French assistance.

Opportunity and Necessity: Alliance with France

Patriot leaders did not err in thinking that France would aid American independence. Indeed, in the years following the humiliating peace of 1763, when France had been stripped of its empire, the compelling motive of French foreign policy became *revanche*. The French foreign minister in the 1760s, the Duc de Choiseul, smacked his lips at England's colonial troubles. "There will come in time a revolution in America," he told the French king, "which will put England into a state of weakness where she will no longer be a terror in Europe. . . . The very extent of English possessions in America will bring about their separation from England."[42] Americans knew of this intense French preoccupation. "All Europe is attentive to the dispute," Franklin wrote from London in 1770, and "our part is taken everywhere."[43] Aside from strengthening the Bourbon Family Compact with Spain and sending secret observers to North America, France made no overt moves to intervene before Choiseul left office in 1770.

The decision to succor the Americans fell to Choiseul's successor, Charles Gravier, the Comte de Vergennes. Suave, polished, outwardly unemotional, Vergennes looked every inch the epitome of a successful diplomat of the ancien régime. In actuality, he could act impetuously (he had risked his diplomatic career by carrying on a secret liaison with a Franco-Turkish widow and then marrying her against the wishes of the French court). When the American colonies began their armed rebellion, he adopted the motto *Aut nunc aut nunquam* ("now or never").[44]

A perfect scheme for aiding the insurrectionaries short of war presented itself early in 1776 in the person of Pierre Augustin Caron de Beaumarchais. Confident that the Americans "must be invincible," the adventurous author of the *Barber of Seville* created a dummy trading house, Rodrigue Hortalez and Company, through which he could secretly ship military supplies to the American colonies.[45] The French court (and perhaps the Spanish as well) could provide secret financing. Vergennes jumped at Beaumarchais's idea. In a persuasive memorandum to the French king, Vergennes argued that American independence would "diminish the power of England and increase in proportion that of France." At the same time, British trade would suffer while French commerce gained. And, third, assistance to the Americans might permit France to recover "the possessions which the English have taken from us in America, such as the fisheries of Newfoundland. . . . We do not speak of Canada."[46] By May of 1776, before any American agent reached France and even before the Declaration of Independence, Paris took the plunge. The French Treasury quietly transferred 1 million livres (about $200,000) to Beaumarchais's "company." Charles III of Spain made a similar grant, and the first shipments of muskets, cannon, powder, tents, and clothing soon began to cross the Atlantic. By the time of Franklin's arrival in December 1776, then, French assistance already existed. Whether this assistance could be converted into recognition and a formal treaty remained to be determined.

Franklin took Paris by storm. Plainly dressed and wearing a comfortable fur cap, the seventy-year-old philosopher was already well known in France. *Poor Richard's Almanack,* with its catchy aphorisms, had run through several French editions, and Franklin's electrical experiments and philosophical writings had earned him honored membership in the French Academy. Parisians expected Franklin to be the personification of Rousseau's natural man, and he did not disappoint them. Disarmingly modest and soft-spoken, Franklin won friends everywhere. Because Franklin seemed "a very dangerous engine," the British ambassador reported that "we can postpone" but not "prevent" war with France.[47] Vergennes warmed to Franklin, whose kindly features soon appeared on medals and snuffbox covers. The elegant women of the French court adopted a *coiffure à la Franklin* in imitation of his omnipresent fur cap, and no social affair could be a success without his presence. Not without hyperbole, John Adams noted that the old Philadelphian was "so fond of the fair sex that one was not enough for him, but he must have one on each side, and all the ladies both old and young were ready to eat him up."[48] Franklin explained physics to Queen Marie Antoinette, played chess with the Duchesse de Bourbon, and even proposed marriage to the wealthy Madame Helvetius. She avoided Franklin's entangling alliance, but her "careless, jaunty air" and the fact that she kissed the "Good Doctor" in public scandalized Abigail Adams. "I was

Benjamin Franklin (1706–1790) at the Court of France. The elderly philosopher-journalist-humorist-politician-diplomat fascinated the snobbish court of France. Franklin's popularity grew to such proportions, according to the historian William Stinchcombe, that "out of disgust Louis XVI presented Vergennes with a chamber pot in which Franklin's face appeared on the bottom." (Courtesy of Kenneth M. Newman, Old Print Shop, New York City)

highly disgusted and never wish for an acquaintance with any ladies of this cast," she wrote.[49] Still, Franklin captivated his host country. Thomas Jefferson did not exaggerate when, on becoming minister to France in 1784, he said that he was merely succeeding Franklin, an American "*citoyen vertueux*" (virtuous citizen), for no one could replace him.[50]

Social popularity did not ensure diplomatic success, however. Vergennes might have recognized American independence prior to Franklin's arrival had not the successful British military campaign in New York in summer 1776 made the French court cautious. Recognition meant war with England, and the French hesitated to proceed without Spanish assistance. Spain was dragging its feet. Although French loans and supplies continued through 1776 and 1777, Vergennes avoided a formal commitment until there was a sure sign of American military success. "We are now acting a play which pleases all the spectators," observed one American in Europe, "but none seem inclined to pay the performers."[51] Then came Saratoga on October 17, 1777, a battle in which 90 percent of American arms and ammunition had come from French merchants. The defeat of "Gentleman Johnny" Burgoyne's troops in the forests of northern New York helped persuade England to send out peace feelers, with terms offering less than complete independence. Franklin was not averse to using the threat of reconciliation with England as a lever on Vergennes. A French diplomat asked Franklin what action was necessary to prevent Congress from coming to an agreement with England short of full independence. Franklin replied: The immediate conclusion of a treaty of commerce and alliance.

On February 6, 1778, Vergennes and Franklin affixed their signatures to two pacts. The first, a treaty of amity and commerce, gave the United States most-favored-nation privileges (which meant that America would enjoy any commercial favors granted by France to other countries). The two nations also accepted definitions of contraband and neutral rights that followed the articles of the Model Treaty.

The second pact, however, was a treaty of alliance, and it contained political commitments that departed from John Adams's original plan. Instead of the meager promise not to aid England if France entered the war for independence, Franklin had to agree not to make peace with the British without first obtaining French consent. Vergennes made a similar promise. Although Franklin managed to retain the prohibition against French territorial gains on the North American continent, the United States agreed to recognize any French conquests in the Caribbean and to guarantee "from the present time and forever" all French possessions in America and any others obtained at the peace table. France paid an equivalent price. According to Article II, "The essential and direct End of the present defensive alliance is to maintain effectually the liberty, Sovereignty, and independence absolute and unlimited of the said United States, as well in matters of Gouvernment as of commerce." Vergennes also guaranteed "from the present time and forever" American "Possessions, and the additions or conquests that their Confederation may obtain during the war, from any of the Dominions now or heretofore possessed by Great Britain in North America."[52] While France made no specific commitment to help the Americans conquer Canada, Vergennes seemed ready to guarantee whatever territories Franklin and his colleagues could wrest from England.

King George III (1738–1820). He ruled England from 1760 to 1820, progressively going insane. In 1787, for example, he alighted from his carriage in Windsor Park and addressed an oak tree as the king of Prussia. Although against leniency toward the rebellious Americans, the king appointed Lord Shelburne prime minister. Shelburne made a generous peace settlement. (Library of Congress)

The French alliance seemed to constitute the kind of political entanglement that Thomas Paine and John Adams had warned against. Certainly the stipulation prohibiting any peace without French consent, as well as the guarantee of territories, entangled American interests in the foreign policies of another nation. Congress had already retreated considerably from the principles of 1776 when it had instructed Franklin to seek an alliance with Spain in which the United States would assist Spain in conquering Florida and declare war against Portugal in return for diplomatic recognition and outright military assistance. Such a treaty did not materialize, but the instructions indicated the extent to which Congress, after two years without a major victory, might compromise its ideals for military help against Britain. Both Paine and Adams accepted the French alliance, Paine so enthusiastically that he named his next daughter Marie Antoinette after the French queen. Adams, after some initial hesitation, was soon calling the treaty "our Bulwark," "a Rock upon which we may safely build."[53] The treaty did fulfill the most important of Adams's original expectations—that the political and economic independence of the United States from England would be too great a prize for France to pass up. French and American interests coincided on the issue of independence. The French dreaded "the United British Empire" so much that they could not possibly "let slip the opportunity of striking one pistol at least" from "an enemy who constantly threatened them with two."[54]

The French diverged from their new allies on the extent of American independence. Notwithstanding vows of self-denial regarding Canada, Vergennes had no wish to replace Britain with a great American empire that might also eventually chase the French and the Spanish out of the New World. "[T]hey would not stop here," he said in 1775, "but would in process of time advance to the Southern Continent of America and either subdue the inhabitants or carry them along with them, and in the end not leave a foot of that Hemisphere in the possession of any European power."[55] The French made a commitment to American independence, not to American expansion.

The French commitment was tested at the very beginning of the alliance. When the Elector Maximilian of Bavaria died, on December 30, 1777, Joseph II of Austria promptly occupied and annexed that German principality. Frederick the Great of Prussia went to war on behalf of Bavarian independence. Austria urged France, allied to Austria since 1756, to join the War of Bavarian Succession against Prussia. The Austrian Netherlands would be France's reward, but Vergennes resisted temptation. A war for Flanders would require peace with England just when the opportunity for revenge seemed greatest. Toward Austria, therefore, Vergennes slyly assumed the role of benevolent mediator, hoping to keep Europe quiet in order to concentrate on the maritime war against England. This mediation of the *Kartoffelkrieg* ("Potato War"), so-called because the starving soldiers of Austria and Prussia spent the winter of 1778–1779 eating frozen potatoes, was successfully accomplished in 1779.

Ironically enough, Emperor Joseph resented French interference, and when the opportunity presented itself in the summer of 1781, he returned the French favor and offered to mediate between Britain and France. Russia also joined in the mediation offer. Since it came at a low point in the military struggle in America, Vergennes might have felt compelled to accept Austro-Russian mediation (the terms of which would *not* have recognized American independence) in 1781 had not English king George III stubbornly resisted any solution short of complete submission by the American colonies. The point is clear: France, whatever the entanglements and temptations of the European continent, was bent on defeating England by backing American independence. By the end of the war in 1783 France had expended some 48 million livres ($9.6 million) in behalf of American independence.

Nibbling and Piddling in Europe

Franklin had argued that "a virgin state should preserve the virgin character, and not go about suitoring after alliances, but wait with decent dignity for the application of others."[56] Congress, needing money and hoping for military assistance, ruled otherwise. Thus did American diplomats scurry to Berlin, Madrid, Vienna, St. Petersburg, Amsterdam, and other capitals in quest of alliances that never quite materialized. Frederick the Great had intimated that Prussia would recognize American independence if France did, but when William Lee arrived in Berlin, Frederick told his chief minister: "Put him off with compliments."[57] Fear of revolutionary principles, the danger of British retaliation, trading opportunities, and territorial ambitions closer to home—all made the European monarchies reluctant to challenge Britain. If only neutrals could identify their own interests with America and join the war, John Adams lamented: "Without it, all may nibble and piddle and dribble and fribble, waste a long time, immense treasures, and much human blood, and they must come to it at last."[58]

The Dutch exemplified the point. With institutions of representative government firmly entrenched in the Dutch Estates General, one might have expected the

Netherlands to be the first to recognize American independence. Not so. The burghers of Amsterdam were more interested in making money. Until Britain declared war on the United Provinces, in December 1780, the Dutch busied themselves by carrying naval stores from the Baltic to France, as well as using their West Indian island of St. Eustatius as an entrepôt for contraband trade with the Americans. These activities, plus a willingness to join Catherine the Great's League of Armed Neutrality in the year 1780, led to war with England, but the Dutch steadfastly refused to sign a treaty with the United States until October 1782, by which time the war had all but ended. John Adams, who negotiated the treaty of amity and commerce (following the Plan of 1776), could agree with a foreign visitor's assessment of Holland as "a land, where the demon of gold, crowned with tobacco, sat on a throne of cheese."[59] Although the Dutch treaty came too late to give military assistance in the war, Adams secured a loan of 5 million guilders in June 1782 from a consortium of Amsterdam bankers. This was the first of a series of Dutch loans, totaling some 9 million guilders ($3,600,000), that sustained American credit through the 1780s.

American efforts to join the Armed Neutrality of 1780 marked another episode in futile diplomacy. Organized by Catherine II of Russia, the Armed Neutrality also included Denmark, Sweden, Austria, Prussia, Portugal, and the Kingdom of the Two Sicilies. Its purpose was ostensibly to enforce liberal provisions of neutral rights ("free ships, free goods," no paper blockades, narrow definition of contraband) in trading with belligerents. Never very effective (Catherine herself called it *cette nullité armée* [armed nullity]), the league seemed to hold out some hope for the American cause. Because the Armed Neutrality's principles so closely resembled the Model Treaty, Congress immediately adopted its rules by resolution and sent a plenipotentiary to St. Petersburg to gain formal adherence to the league by treaty. It was an impossible mission. Aside from the obvious incongruity of a belligerent nation attempting to join an alliance of neutrals, it should have been apparent that Catherine, although no enemy of American independence, would not risk war with England by granting recognition prematurely. Her real purpose was to divert British attention while preparing to seize the Crimea from Ottoman Turkey. American envoy Francis Dana of Massachusetts returned "most heartily weary of the old world" after two long years in the Russian capital without ever being received officially.[60] Indeed, formal relations with Russia did not begin until 1809, when Catherine's grandson, Tsar Alexander I, received as American minister John Quincy Adams, who as a fourteen-year-old had been Dana's secretary during the abortive wartime mission. "Nobody here but princes and slaves," young Adams described Russia in 1781.[61]

Another ironic epilogue occurred. Once peace negotiations in Paris had established American independence in 1783, the Dutch government urged the United States to join the Armed Neutrality through a formal treaty with the Netherlands. At this point, however, with the war all but over, Congress reconsidered. In a resolution on June 12, 1783, Congress admitted that "the liberal principles on which the said confederacy was established, are conceived to be in general favourable to the interests of nations, and particularly to those of the United States," but there could be no formal treaty. The reason? "The true interest of these [United] states requires that they should be as little as possible entangled in the politics and controversies of European nations."[62] Thus, however much Americans desired freedom of trade for both profit and principle, they did not want to resort to political entanglements to achieve such an objective. They would have to face this dilemma again and again.

The most frustrating diplomacy of all occurred with Spain. Despite previous financial support for the embattled colonials, and notwithstanding the outwardly close alliance with France (the Bourbon Family Compact), the government of King Charles III was in no hurry to take up arms against England—especially if Spain could obtain its principal objective, the return of Gibraltar, by other means. In view of its own extensive colonial empire in the Americas, moreover, Spain was understandably less eager than France to encourage overseas revolutions. Not only might colonial rebellion prove to be a contagious disease, but a powerful American republic could threaten Spanish possessions as effectively as an expanding British Empire. Spanish foreign minister Count Floridablanca therefore hemmed and hawed, playing a double game by dickering with both France and England in the hope of regaining Gibraltar. Only by the Treaty of Aranjuez, signed on April 12, 1779, did Spain agree on war against England, and even then the alliance was with France, not with the United States. One article held enormous importance for American foreign policy. Because of Madrid's obsession with Gibraltar, France agreed to keep on fighting until they wrested that rocky symbol of Spanish pride from the British. According to the terms of the Franco-American alliance of 1778, the United States and France had pledged not to make a separate peace and to continue the war until England recognized American independence. Now France was promising to fight until Gibraltar fell. In this circuitous, devious fashion, without being a party to the treaty or even being consulted, the Americans found their independence, in the historian Samuel Flagg Bemis's notable phrase, "chained by European diplomacy to the Rock of Gibraltar."[63] And because the terms of Aranjuez remained secret, American diplomats could only guess at these new political entanglements.

Congress dispatched John Jay to Madrid in September 1779 to obtain a formal alliance. Described by the French as a "serious," "grave," "sedate young man" whose self-confidence "begat a not disagreeable vanity," the thirty-four-year-old New Yorker of Huguenot descent did not have an easy time of it.[64] Not once during his two-and-a-half-year stay did the Spanish court officially receive Jay. With Jay's mail opened and read and spies snooping everywhere, "only the lice in Spanish inns gave him a warm welcome."[65] Only rarely did Count Floridablanca deign to communicate with the American diplomat. Even more frustrating, Jay ran out of money and had to ask the Spanish for funds. Jay also suffered personal tragedy when his infant daughter died shortly after he and his wife, Sarah, arrived in Madrid. The Spanish count did give Jay some $175,000, but only to keep the American dangling while the count secretly negotiated with a British agent in the hope that Britain would accept outside mediation and cede Gibraltar. Even though the British prime minister, Lord North, privately vowed "to get rid of this d. . .d war," the Spanish ploy failed because George III remained as stubborn about Gibraltar as he did about American independence.[66]

John Jay (1745–1829). Graduate of King's College (now Columbia University), this upper-class New Yorker became one of America's most prominent diplomats. Before helping to negotiate the peace treaty with Great Britain, Jay represented the United States in Spain (1780–1782), where he met unrelenting frustration. Under the Articles of Confederation, Jay served as secretary of foreign affairs with a minuscule staff of only one secretary, part-time translators, and a doorkeeper-messenger. He later became chief justice of the Supreme Court (1789–1795). Sent by President George Washington on a special mission to Britain in 1794, Jay negotiated the controversial treaty that bears his name. (National Portrait Gallery, Smithsonian Institution)

At one point in the summer of 1781 Jay received instructions from Congress to give up the demand for navigation rights on the Mississippi River, if only Spain would recognize American independence and make an alliance. Such a message reflected the military dangers the colonists faced in the autumn of 1780, following the British capture of Charleston and successful invasion of the South. Although personally believing it "better for America to have no treaty with Spain than to purchase one on such servile terms," Jay obediently sought an interview with the Spanish foreign minister.[67] After several weeks Jay obtained an audience. The New Yorker made his proposal: a treaty relinquishing navigation rights on the Mississippi south of 31° north latitude, a Spanish guarantee to the United States of "all their respective territories," and an American guarantee to the Spanish king of "all his dominions in America."[68] Floridablanca refused. Had he accepted, the navigation of the "Father of Waters" and the boundary of West Florida—both destined to be troublesome issues in Spanish-American diplomacy—would have been settled to Spain's advantage. But Floridablanca preferred to gamble. Already Spanish troops from New Orleans had occupied West Florida, and possibly they could claim more territory between the Mississippi and the Alleghenies.

Rebuffed, Jay withdrew the concession on Mississippi navigation. He explained to Congress that if Spain refused to make an alliance during the war, the

United States should reassert its Mississippi claims in any final peace treaty. Congress endorsed his decision. "This government has little money, less wisdom, no credit, nor any right to it," he grumbled against Spain.[69] He had also begun to suspect, from conversations with the French ambassador in Madrid, that the French were encouraging Spain in its trans-Appalachian territorial ambitions. Indeed, by the end of his sojourn in Spain, John Jay had become, in the scholar Lawrence Kaplan's words, "an almost xenophobic American."[70] Jay's unpleasant experience in Spain and his suspicions of European intentions helped shape the American posture at the 1782 peace negotiations.

A Separate Peace: The Treaty of Paris

The surrender of Lord Cornwallis's army at Yorktown on October 19, 1781, precipitated serious peace negotiations. General Washington's French adjutant, the Marquis de Lafayette, wrote home: "The play is over. . . . the fifth act has just ended."[71] George III stubbornly tried to fight on, but the burgeoning public debt and war weariness finally caused the ministry of Lord North to fall early in 1782. The king reluctantly accepted a new ministry under the Marquess of Rockingham, committed to a restoration of peace but undecided as to what the terms should be.

The English sent an agent to Paris in April 1782 to sound out Benjamin Franklin. The emissary, Richard Oswald, seemed a curious choice, his chief qualifications being a previous friendship with Franklin and firsthand knowledge of America, derived in part from the slave trade. Franklin sized up Oswald quickly. After introducing the British envoy to Vergennes and saying that the United States would make no separate peace without French concurrence, Franklin privately intimated to Oswald the possibility of a separate peace if England granted complete independence and generous boundaries. Franklin even mentioned Canada. (He never told Vergennes about this goal.) The American did not demand Canada, for England might find such a stipulation "humiliating." A voluntary cession, however, would have "an excellent effect . . . [on] the mind of the [American] people in general."[72] Oswald promised to try to persuade his superiors in London. "We parted exceedingly good friends," Franklin wrote in his journal.[73]

Peace talks stalled for the next several weeks, as another cabinet crisis distracted the British. Not until Rockingham's death and Lord Shelburne's succession as prime minister on July 1 could the British agree on a negotiating position, and even then Shelburne had to proceed cautiously for fear of offending his prickly sovereign. During this interval, Franklin summoned his fellow peace commissioners, Jay and Adams, to Paris. Jay, delighted to escape Madrid, arrived by the end of June. Adams continued commercial negotiations in the Netherlands and did not reach the French capital until October 26.

The success of the separate negotiations, which began in October and ended on November 30, owed much to the conciliatory attitude of Shelburne. A believer in natural rights and *liberté du commerce* (free trade) through his friendship with French *philosophes*, the prime minister wanted to break up the French–American alliance, and by "encouraging the expansion of American territory and population, he now hoped to promote the growth of new markets for British goods to con-

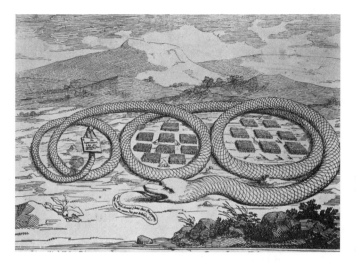

"The American Rattlesnake." Coiled around the armies of Burgoyne and Cornwallis, the American snake gloats over triumph in this cartoon of 1782:
> Britons within the Yankeean Plains,
> Mind how ye March & Trench,
> The Serpent in the Congress reigns,
> As well as in the French.

(Library of Congress)

quer."[74] The peace terms were thus exceedingly generous; as Vergennes later put it: "The English buy the peace more than they make it."[75] Not only was the United States granted complete independence, but also the new nation's extensive boundaries (the Great Lakes and St. Lawrence River to the north, Mississippi River to the west, 31° north latitude line across Florida to the south) far surpassed what Americans had won on the battlefield. Any chance of obtaining Canadian territory was probably foreclosed by eleventh-hour British naval victories in the Caribbean and the failure of a combined French-Spanish siege of Gibraltar in September 1782. Canada remained in the British Empire. This important result, according to the historian Reginald Stuart, meant that henceforth "American expansionism had a westward, but not a northward gaze."[76]

With the issues of independence and boundaries easily settled, the most heated dispute occurred over other articles of the treaty. Much wrangling focused on the Atlantic fisheries, without which, so Thomas Paine had declared, "independence would be a bubble."[77] The British argued that access to the fishing grounds off the Grand Banks of Newfoundland, as well as the right to dry and cure fish on Canadian shores, should be limited to members of the British Empire. The Americans disagreed. New England, where "Tom Cod," not George III, was king, had a stubborn advocate in John Adams, who claimed that the fisheries were "indispensably necessary to the accomplishment and preservation of our independence."[78] Many coins minted during the American Revolution had embossed images of cod on them. The Americans finally won their point, although the treaty ambiguously granted the "liberty" to fish, not the "right," thus perpetuating a controversy over which succeeding generations of diplomats (and succeeding generations of Adamses) battled for more than a century.

Sharpest disagreement came over the intertwined issues of Loyalists and pre-Revolutionary debts. The British, quite understandably, sought generous treatment for the thousands of colonials who had fled into exile for their loyalty to the Crown. The British negotiators wanted restitution of confiscated property, or at least compensation. The Americans adamantly disagreed, especially Franklin, whose own son

William, the former royal governor of New Jersey, had deserted to the British cause. Even the moderate Jay spoke of Loyalists as having "the most dishonourable of human motives" and urged that "every American must set his face and steel his heart" against them.[79] As to the 5 million pounds owed by Americans (mostly southern planters) to British merchants, Americans hesitated to repay obligations contracted prior to 1775. Adams found acceptable compromise language whereby British creditors would "meet with no lawful impediment" in collecting their lawfully incurred debts.[80] This particular clause helped gain the support of the British commercial classes for what was an otherwise unpopular treaty. As Adams put it, American concession on the debts prevented the British merchants "from making common Cause with the Refugees [Loyalists]."[81] The British, for their part, accepted an article in the treaty that forbade all further persecution of Loyalists and "earnestly recommended" to the states that properties seized during the war be restored. Because Congress could not dictate to the states under the Articles of Confederation (see below), both the British and American commissioners understood that the "earnest recommendations" might not be followed.

Americans enthusiastically greeted the preliminary peace terms, because they obtained so much. Some worried that the independent negotiations might strain relations with France. French foreign minister Vergennes actually issued no rebuke to the Americans for failing to consult, saying only that their gains "exceed all that I could have thought possible."[82] Then, after two weeks of silence, Vergennes wrote plaintively to Franklin: "You are wise and discreet, sir; you perfectly understand what is due to propriety; you have all your life performed your duties. I pray to you to consider how you propose to fulfill those which are due to the [French] King?"[83] Franklin thereupon delivered one of the most beguiling replies in the history of diplomacy. He admitted that the American commissioners had been indiscreet—guilty of a lack of *bienséance* (propriety)—in not keeping the French fully informed, but he hoped that this indiscretion would not harm the alliance. "The English, I just now learn," he told Vergennes, "flatter themselves they have already divided us." Franklin added that he hoped the British would find themselves "totally mistaken."[84] The French foreign minister said nothing more. In fact, he even agreed to an additional loan of some 6 million livres, which Franklin had requested earlier. France's chargé d'affaires in Philadelphia, however, remarked that "Great Powers never *complained* but . . . *felt* and *remembered*."[85]

Why did the French respond so mildly? Vergennes, with Paris honeycombed with spies, knew all along about the secret negotiations, even if the final terms seem to have startled him. He did not protest, because he understood that England was indeed trying to break up the Franco-American alliance, as Franklin's comment seemed to indicate. The separate American peace, moreover, offered Vergennes a way out of a sticky tangle with Spain. He could now tell the stubborn Spaniards that Gibraltar was no longer a practicable objective with the Americans effectively out of the war. To Vergennes the fact of American independence counted far more than Gibraltar, and although he would have preferred a treaty that left the United States more dependent on France, he was not displeased with what Jay, Adams, and Franklin had accomplished. In Lawrence Kaplan's phrase, "even if Vergennes was serving his country first, he served America well."[86]

The General P—s, or Peace.

Say what they will, I call this an honourable P—.

I call this a free and Independent P—.

Such English we confess your exceeding good nature, tho' we have wrangled you out of America you freely make P—, with us.

Come all who love friendſhip, and wonder and ſee,
The belligerent powers, like good neighbours agree,
A little time paſt Sirs, who would have thought this,
That they'd ſo ſoon come to a general P—?

The wiſe politicians who differ in thought,
Will fret at this friendſhip, and call it tonought,
And blades that love war will be ſtorming at this,
But ſtorm as they will, it's a general P—.

A hundred hard millions in war we have ſpent,
And America loſt by all patriots conſent,
Yet let us be quiet, nor any one hiſs,
But rejoice at this hearty and general P—.

Tis vain for to fret or growl at our lot,
You ſee they're determin'd to fill us a pot,
So now my brave Britons excuſe me in this,
That I for a Peace am oblig'd to write Piſs.

"The General P—s, or Peace." The peace signed, Britain, the Netherlands, the United States, Spain, and France have put down their arms. Who would have thought, read this English cartoon of 1783, "that they'd so soon come to a general P—?" (Library of Congress)

Peace negotiations between England and France, as well as England and Spain, took several months. The final Treaty of Paris was not signed until September 3, 1783. Except for some complications regarding Florida (Britain finally ceded all of Florida to Spain, whose military forces had captured West Florida in 1780–1781), the terms were precisely those of the preliminary treaty between England and the United States. America's diplomats had performed well in overcoming political entanglements and exploiting European rivalries. "Undisciplined marines as we were," said John Adams, "we were better tacticians than we imagined."[87] The historian Jonathan Dull's more restrained assessment suggests that American success "depended on a heavy dose of foreign help and abundant good luck" and "the moral of the American Revolution thus may be the unpredictability, the expense, and the danger of war."[88] Still, to obtain both independence and empire ranks as an impressive achievement.

Diplomatic Frustrations Under the Articles of Confederation

Americans were in an exuberant, expansive mood in 1783. They now had independence, and two years earlier all thirteen states had ratified the Articles of Confederation, giving them a new, if cumbersome, government. "We have the experience of the whole world before our eyes," wrote Noah Webster in the preface to his famous speller. "It is the business of Americans to select the wisdom of all nations . . . [and] to add superior dignity to this infant Empire and to human nature."[89] Nearly half the national territory, some 220 million acres of wilderness, lay across the Appalachian chain, and the flood of emigrants westward, fleeing from heavy taxes to lower ones, from poorer to better lands, became inexorable. More than 100,000 Americans settled in Kentucky and Tennessee alone in the years between 1775 and 1790. As Jay put it in 1785, "a rage for emigrating to the western country prevails . . . and the seeds of a great people are daily planting beyond the mountains."[90] For George Washington, roads and canals would turn the trans-Allegheny region into "a field almost too extensive for imagination."[91] A Spanish official in Louisiana complained that Yankees were "advancing and multiplying . . . with a prodigious rapidity."[92]

Peace also brought trading opportunities. Foreign ships could now enter American ports without fear of British retaliation. Americans could regain British markets for their agricultural exports, trade directly with other European countries, and develop as extensive and free a trade as possible with the rest of the world. The broad Atlantic would serve as both a highway of commerce and a barrier against European predators. So Americans dreamed.

Impressive trade expansion fueled American optimism in the 1780s. Some 72,000 tons of shipping cleared America's busiest port, Philadelphia, in the year 1789, compared with an average of 45,000 tons in 1770–1772. Boston's tonnage increased from 42,506 in 1772 to 55,000 in 1788. Clearances in Maryland and Virginia doubled in volume over the figures from 1769. Tobacco exports brought a favorable balance of more than $1 million a year in trade with France during the 1780s. By 1788 the Netherlands was importing more than $4 million annually of tobacco, rice, and naval stores from the United States.

Merchants proved enterprising in gaining new markets. The *Empress of China,* the first American ship to trade with Asia, set sail from New York in February 1784 and reached Guangzhou (Canton) some six months later. The cargo was ginseng, which the Chinese believed would restore sexual potency to the aged. Another pioneering vessel, the *Columbia,* left Boston in 1787, wintered on the Pacific coast of North America near Vancouver Island, and traded metal trinkets to the Indians for otter furs. The *Columbia* then voyaged to China, exchanged the furs for tea, and returned to Boston—the first American ship to circumnavigate the globe. Other ships soon followed. Thus began a curiously complicated trade, which often included a stop at the Hawaiian Islands to pick up sandalwood for Chinese consumers. The trade brought profits to New England merchants for more than thirty years. On its second voyage, in 1792, the *Columbia* entered the mouth of the river named after it and helped establish the American claim to Oregon. In December 1785, Elias Hacket Derby of Salem sent the *Grand Turk* to the French island of Mauritius in the Indian Ocean, beginning a lucrative trade with India and other Asian ports. In their search for profitable cargoes, as the historian Harold D. Langley has noted, "American captains made the first contacts with the regions in the Indian and Pacific Oceans at least a generation before they attracted the official diplomatic attention of the U.S. government."[93]

Spanish America also loomed as a new market in the 1780s. Shipments of wheat, flour, and some reexported manufactures went to Cuba, Venezuela, and Argentina, and in particular to Santo Domingo, which served as an entrepôt for New Orleans, where American smuggling flourished as never before. By 1785 the viceroy of Buenos Aires in Argentina was reporting numerous *bostoneses* vessels plying southern waters "on the pretext of whaling and probably with hidden intentions."[94] Although most of this trade with Latin America remained in the Gulf of Mexico and the Caribbean, by 1788 American whalers and China traders carrying contraband had reached the west coast of South America, where they took on pelts and specie for the Asian market.

Despite the expansion of trade, the instant prosperity that many Americans expected in 1783 did not materialize because the United States had to adjust from a wartime to peacetime economy and from a favored position within the British Empire to independent status in a world dominated by mercantilist restrictions. Because of commercial habits and British credit facilities, the bulk of American trade continued to be with England. In 1790, the earliest year for which full statistics are available, nearly half of all American exports went to England, and 90 percent of American imports originated in England. Fully three-fourths of America's foreign trade remained with the former mother country. Contrary to Paine's *Common Sense,* however, independence brought an end to privileges that had been part of the imperial connection. New England suffered when London prohibited American ships from trading with the British West Indies. Even with smuggling, the exports of Massachusetts in 1786 totaled only one-fourth of what they had been in 1774. As James Madison lamented in 1785: "We have lost by the revolution our trade with the West Indies, the only one which yielded us a favorable balance, without having gained new channels to compensate it."[95] Because each of the thirteen states had its own customs service and tariff schedules, moreover, American diplomats could not threaten commercial retaliation against England. George Washington complained: "One State passes a prohibitory law respecting some article, another State opens wide the avenue for its admission. One Assembly makes a system; another Assembly unmakes it."[96]

Indeed, as peacetime problems multiplied, structural weaknesses under the Articles of Confederation loomed as a major obstacle to successful diplomacy. Not only did the sovereignty of the individual states prevent a uniform commercial policy, but states' rights thwarted national power in other respects as well. Congress had raised a continental army and constructed a small navy during the war, but in

peace these "implied" powers collapsed; all naval vessels were sold or scrapped by
the end of 1784, and the army dwindled to a mere regiment. Congress remained
nominally in charge of foreign policy. Yet during the war this large body had
proven itself so faction-ridden and devoid of responsibility that it had given the
French foreign minister veto power over American peace commissioners, and thus,
in the words of one scholar, "eliminated itself from any prominent role in foreign
affairs for the remainder of the Revolution."[97] The legislative body took a forward
step in 1784 by creating a Department of Foreign Affairs and selecting John Jay as
secretary. Although Congress retained the basic powers of foreign policy—the right
to make war and peace, to send and receive ambassadors, to make treaties and alliances—it lacked the power to enforce its diplomacy. Individual states violated
the 1783 peace treaty with impunity. Diplomacy became an awkward, frustrating
affair.

Relations with England quickly deteriorated after 1783. In the first flush of
peace it had looked as though the United States might actually conclude a favorable commercial treaty with the British. Lord Shelburne's grand scheme of rapprochement would have continued the benefits Americans had enjoyed under the
Crown, including free access of American goods and ships to British and West
Indian ports. But Shelburne was soon forced from office for having given the
Americans too much, and his successors (even the liberal William Pitt, who became
prime minister in 1784) found commercial reciprocity with the United States a political impossibility. Mercantilist thinking still held sway in England. Pamphleteers
such as the Earl of Sheffield argued that the United States, if allowed to resume the
privileges of the British Empire without any of the responsibilities, would eventually outstrip Britain in shipping, trade, and the production of manufactured goods.
A restrictive policy, however, would allow England to increase its carrying trade,
particularly in the West Indies, where colonial shipping had long predominated.
Canada and Ireland could serve as alternative sources of provisions for the West
Indian planters.

Such mercantilist precepts became institutionalized in a series of orders in
council, according to which American raw materials and foodstuffs, but not manufactures, were permitted to enter the British home islands aboard American vessels, while Canada and the West Indies remained closed to American shipping. Such
restrictions, it was believed, would not hurt British exports to America. As Sheffield
prophetically observed: "At least four-fifths of the importations from Europe into
the American States were at all times made upon credit; and undoubtedly the States
are in greater want of credit at this time than at former periods. It can be had only
in Great Britain."[98] As for possible commercial retaliation, the British scoffed at the
likelihood that all thirteen "dis-united" states could agree on a uniform set of tariff
schedules. "Pish! . . . What can Americans do?" boasted one Briton. "They have
neither government nor power. Great Britain could shut up all their ports. . . ."[99]

The British refusal to evacuate the northwest forts also rankled. These fortified
posts, which ranged from Dutchman's Point on Lake Champlain to Mich-
ilimackinac on Lake Michigan (see map on page 27), strategically controlled the
frontier, including the fur trade. Indian tribes between the Great Lakes and the
Ohio River—the Six Nations of the Iroquois in the northeast, the Shawnees and

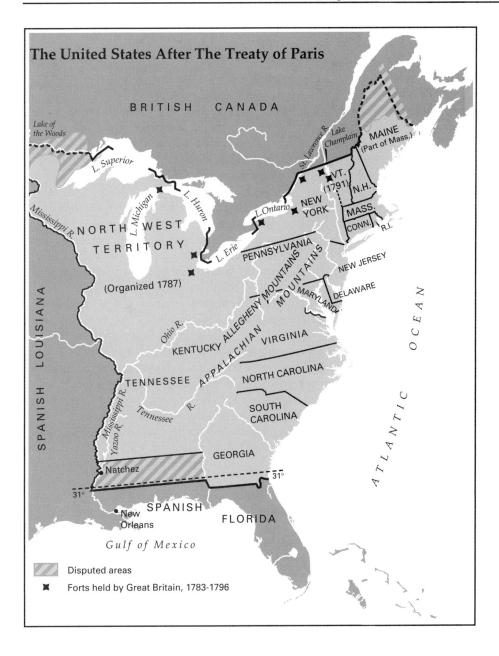

The United States After The Treaty of Paris

Disputed areas

✴ Forts held by Great Britain, 1783-1796

Algonquins in the northwest, and the Creeks, Cherokees, and Seminoles in the southeast—continued to resist white encroachment. Abandoned by the Paris treaty, "we are determined to pay no attention to the Manner in which the British Negotiators have drawn out the lines," vowed Creek leader Alexander McGillivray.[100] Indian claims to land above and below the Ohio remained valid under their previous treaties, Native Americans insisted.

Partly to placate the Indians and partly to protect Loyalists who had fled to the frontier, the British did not lower the Union Jack from the forts, despite their promise in Article II of the peace treaty to relinquish them with "all convenient speed." They later justified retention of the posts on the grounds that Americans themselves had violated the treaty by their failure to repay debts to British creditors and by the shabby treatment accorded Loyalists. The British adopted a "wait-and-see" policy in the west, holding the forts, encouraging the Indians, but avoiding overt provocation of the Americans by refusing Indian requests for troops to guarantee Indian territory. American shipping was thus effectively excluded from the Great Lakes after 1783, and new settlements were confined largely to Kentucky and Tennessee.

In 1786, British officials in Canada, thinking that the United States might soon dissolve because of the farmers' tax protest in western Massachusetts (Shays's Rebellion), entered into secret talks with separatist leaders in Vermont, luring them with special trade privileges along the Champlain–St. Lawrence water route. If the breakup did occur, Vermont could easily be attached to Canada, along with the lightly populated territories north of the Ohio.

Other issues troubled Anglo-American relations, including the disposition of slaves the British had carried off at the end of the war and a controversy over the Maine–New Brunswick boundary. Americans could only watch, helpless. With no army, no navy, no executive, no power to control the national commerce, the United States under the Articles of Confederation could do little to force British respect for the 1783 peace treaty. As the historian Julian Boyd has argued, British policies "may well have contributed more to the convoking and to the success of the Federal Convention of 1787 than many who sat in that august body."[101]

The thankless task of enduring humiliation fell to John Adams, who became the first American minister to the Court of St. James's in 1785. King George III scarcely concealed his contempt for the young republic, and his ministers imitated the monarch's lack of cordiality. When Adams protested British failure to send a minister to the United States, he was curtly asked whether there should be one envoy or thirteen. Adams could make no dent in British policy toward trade or the forts. The author of the Model Treaty saw the impossibility of free trade. "If we cannot obtain reciprocal liberality," he wrote in 1785, "we must adopt reciprocal prohibitions, exclusions, monopolies, and imposts."[102] British arrogance infuriated the New Englander. "If an angel from heaven," he noted sarcastically, "should declare to this nation that our states will unite, retaliate, prohibit, or trade with France, they would not believe it."[103] Adams repeated one message to Congress in dispatch after dispatch during his three frustrating years in England: Congress must have the power to regulate commerce; otherwise the British would not negotiate. As late as February 1788, when the new federal Constitution neared adoption, Adams assured John Jay, "that as soon as there shall be one [a national government], the British court will vouchsafe to treat with it."[104]

Diplomacy with Spain after 1783 fared little better. Just as the British refused to evacuate the Ohio Valley after the war, so did the Spanish try to retain control over the Southwest. Part of the problem stemmed from ambiguities in the peace treaty. According to Article VII of the Anglo-American treaty, the United States was guaranteed free navigation of the Mississippi "from its source to the ocean," and the northern boundary of Florida was set at 31° north latitude. Yet Spain had not agreed to either stipulation. British Florida prior to the war had extended northward to the Yazoo River, and Spain had no intention of yielding territory or encouraging American settlement by guaranteeing free navigation. Spanish troops continued to hold Natchez on the Mississippi. Like the British north of the Ohio, Spain made alliances with the Creeks and other Indian tribes and attempted to bribe frontier leaders, including General James Wilkinson, into a secessionist connection with the Spanish Crown. The most threatening move came in 1784 when Spain closed the mouth of the Mississippi to American commerce. Westerners exploded in violent protest, for control over the Mississippi meant the difference between a subsistence economy or one of agrarian expansion. George Washington, who visited the frontier territories that summer, reported: "The western settlers . . . stand as it were upon a pivot; the touch of a feather would turn them any way."[105]

Less powerful than the British and unprepared for a war on the frontier, the Spanish preferred to negotiate. Don Diego de Gardoqui arrived in New York in 1785. The crafty, charming envoy had instructions to obtain an American surrender on the Mississippi by dangling trade concessions with respect to Spain and the Canary Islands. Gardoqui also brought a Spanish offer to intercede with the Sultan of Morocco, whose pirates were seizing American merchant ships in the Mediterranean. Since such a treaty would obviously benefit the commercial Northeast at the expense of southern expansionists and western farmers, the Spanish envoy worked hard at flattering Secretary John Jay and the other easterners. Gardoqui gave splendid dinners with the best wines, acquired Spanish jackasses for General Washington, and squired Mrs. Jay to one festivity after another. "I am acting the gallant and accompanying Madame [Sarah Jay] to the official entertainments and dances," he reported, "because she likes it and I will do everything which appeals to me for the King's best interest."[106]

In 1786 Jay asked Congress for permission to negotiate a treaty whereby the United States would relinquish the *use* of the Mississippi River for twenty-five or thirty years while reserving the *right* to navigate until a time when American power would be sufficient to force Spanish concessions. Jay's request sparked heated debate in Congress. Dividing geographically, seven northern delegations voted to make the necessary concession, while the five southern delegations stood unanimously opposed. Although negotiations with Gardoqui continued in 1787, it became obvious to Jay that "a treaty disagreeable to one-half of the nation had better not be made, for it would be violated."[107] He told Congress that it must decide "either to wage war with Spain or settle all differences by treaty on the best terms available."[108] Congress did neither.

Spain resumed its intrigues with western leaders, and in 1788 it temporarily reopened the Mississippi River to American shipping after the payment of special duties. Although a definitive treaty did not come until 1795 (see Chapter 2), Spanish officials began in the mid-1780s to permit American immigrants to settle in Louisiana and Florida provided they take an oath of allegiance. The Americanization of Spanish borderlands thus commenced long before the United

**Thomas Jefferson
(1743–1826).** Before serving
as secretary of state (1790–1793)
and president (1801–1809), the
eloquent Virginia lawyer and graduate of the College of William and
Mary wrote the Declaration of
Independence and represented
the new nation as minister to
France (1784–1789). One French
diplomat remarked that Jefferson
preferred "to conquer without war."
("Thomas Jefferson" by John
Trumbull. © White House
Historical Association/Photo by
National Geographic Society)

States acquired those territories officially, eventually providing, as Thomas Jefferson prophesied, "the means of delivering to us peaceably, what may otherwise cost us a war."[109] In the short run, the Jay-Gardoqui talks consolidated a political alliance between the South and West and ensured a clause in the new Constitution that provided for a two-thirds majority for senatorial approval of treaties.

Relations with France also proved frustrating. France sustained Vergennes's view that a United States of limited territorial strength would remain a weak and dependent French client. Thomas Jefferson, who succeeded Franklin as minister to France in 1784, hoped that France could replace England as America's principal trading partner, and he worked very hard to convert the French to liberal commercial theories. Except for the opening of a limited number of French West Indian ports in 1784 and the negotiation of a consular treaty four years later, he ran into the same kind of mercantilist restrictions John Adams faced in England. Whenever Jefferson pressed for commercial concessions, he was always reminded of the outstanding Revolutionary debt of 35 million livres. The inability of Congress to retaliate distressed Jefferson. He momentarily thought of abandoning commerce and diplomacy and having the United States "stand, with respect to Europe, precisely on the footing of China."[110] Given political and economic realities in America, however, Jefferson understood that such isolation was impossible, so he advocated constitutional reform instead. "My primary object in the formation of treaties," he wrote in 1785, "is to take the commerce of the states out of the hands of the states, and to place it under the superintendence of Congress, so far as the imperfect provisions of our constitution will admit, and until the states by new compact make them more perfect."[111]

Another impetus to constitutional reform grew out of the dreary record of dealings with the Barbary "pirates" in the 1780s. The rulers of the North African states—Algiers, Tunis, Tripoli, and Morocco—had transformed piracy into a national industry. By capturing merchant ships, holding sailors and cargoes for ransom, and extorting protection money from nations willing to pay, the sultans nearly drove American shipping out of the Mediterranean. With Spanish assistance, the United States obtained a satisfactory treaty with Morocco in 1787, at the bargain price of only $10,000, but other negotiations proved fruitless. The young republic had neither the revenue to pay for protection nor the armed force to coerce the North African pirates. Thomas Jefferson asked for a fleet of 150 guns, which he hoped could become part of an international naval armada to enforce "a permanent peace" in the Mediterranean, but Congress took no steps toward constructing a navy.[112] Yankee sailors continued to languish in North African jails. John Jay saw a blessing in disguise: "The more we are ill-treated abroad the more we shall unite and consolidate at home."[113]

The New Constitution and the Legacy of the Founding Generation

Amid this troubled international setting, fifty-five delegates attended the Federal Convention in Philadelphia from May to September 1787. Although economic woes and Shays's Rebellion provided the immediate impetus for reform, the Founders had foreign relations in mind, too. The federal Constitution, approved by the Philadelphia assembly and ratified by the states over the next two years, eliminated most of the weaknesses that had plagued diplomacy under the Articles of Confederation. A central government consisting of an executive, a bicameral legislature, and a judiciary—all designed to balance one another—replaced the weak confederation of sovereign states.

Responsibility for negotiations rested with the president, who would make treaties "by and with the advice and consent of the Senate . . . provided two-thirds of the Senators present concur." The impunity with which the individual states had violated the 1783 treaty with England prompted Benjamin Franklin's proposal that treaties shall be "the Supreme Law of the land . . . any thing in the Constitution or laws of any State to the contrary notwithstanding."[114] Southerners, remembering the Jay-Gardoqui negotiations, hesitated to allow Congress too much power over commerce. In return for a constitutional prohibition against taxes on exports and a twenty-year moratorium on interference with the slave trade, however, southern delegates granted Congress the right to regulate imports by a simple majority. The way now seemed clear for commercial retaliation against England. The Constitution also provided for a standing army and navy, thus freeing national defense from dependence on requisitions from the various states. In every respect the United States had strengthened itself. "Tis done!" Benjamin Rush of Pennsylvania exclaimed. "We have become a nation. . . . We are no longer the scoff of our enemies."[115]

A heated discussion at Philadelphia erupted over the warmaking power. The early drafts of the Constitution granted Congress the power to "make" war. Delegates soon perceived, however, that both houses might lack sufficient knowledge and unity to act quickly in the event of attack. Congress might not even be in session. When someone suggested that the president be responsible, memories of an evil George III intruded. As delegate Elbridge Gerry of Massachussetts put it, he "never expected to hear in a republic a motion to empower the Executive alone to declare war."[116] Virginia's George Mason, in a telling phrase, advocated "clogging rather than facilitating war; but . . . facilitating peace." Fearful of executive tyranny, but not wanting to leave the country defenseless, Gerry and James Madison of Virginia proposed a compromise whereby Congress retained the power to "declare" war, while the president, as commander in chief, would still be able to "repel sudden attacks."[117] Since Congress was granted authority to raise and support armies and navies, call out the militia, make rules and regulations for all of the armed forces, and control all policy functions associated with national defense, it seems evident that the Philadelphia delegates intended to subordinate the executive on this issue.

The size of the federal republic also aroused debate at Philadelphia. According to classic political theory, particularly the writings of Montesquieu, republics stood the best chance of survival if the territory they occupied remained small. If the theory were accurate, a real disparity existed between the thirteen coastal states and the vast trans-Allegheny expanse stretching to the Mississippi. It took the thirty-five-year-old Virginia lawyer James Madison to articulate the philosophy of a growing republican empire. Not only did Madison draft much of the handiwork at Philadelphia, he also (along with John Jay and Alexander Hamilton) wrote the

James Madison (1751–1836). The Virginia-born politician graduated from Princeton, sat in the Continental Congress, and served in the state legislature before journeying to Philadelphia in 1787, where he earned the title "Father of the Constitution." In regular correspondence with Minister to France Thomas Jefferson, through whom Madison bought some 200 books on history and government, the young, shy public servant prepared himself exceptionally well for the constitutional convention. He later served as Jefferson's secretary of state (1801–1809) and was elected the fourth U.S. president (1809–1817). Madison believed strongly that economic coercion would compel European nations to make concessions to the Americans, especially on trade principles. (Library of Congress)

Federalist Papers, which exerted so much influence in the campaign for ratification of the new Constitution in 1787–1788. According to Madison, the greatest threat to a republic arose when a majority faction tyrannized others. Expansionism could benefit a republic by defusing the influence of factions, especially those that formed over economic issues. As Madison argued in *Federalist 10,* once you "extend the sphere" of government, "you take in a greater variety of parties and interests; you make it less probable that a majority . . . will have a common motive to invade the right of other citizens; or, if such a common motive exists, it will be more difficult for all who feel it to discover their own strength and to act in unison with each other."[118]

Although Madison's republican theories may not have necessitated continual expansion to ensure survival, the man who later as secretary of state presided over the huge Louisiana Purchase in 1803 welcomed westward expansion from the outset. Most delegates at Philadelphia did. Still, as the historian Michael H. Hunt has suggested, they had not yet answered a basic question—"whether domestic liberty could flourish alongside an ambitious and strongly assertive foreign policy."[119]

Congress's last official measure under the Articles of Confederation during the same summer of 1787 dealt with this very issue of westward expansion. With a bare quorum of eight states represented, the dying Congress enacted the Northwest Ordinance of 1787, which set up guidelines for governing the territories of the Old Northwest until they became ready for statehood. Its terms called for Congress to appoint a governor, secretary, and three judges, who would govern until the population of a territory reached 5,000, at which time the settlers would elect a legislature. The territorial legislature would then rule in conjunction with a council of five selected by the governor and by Congress. The governor retained veto power. As soon as the population grew to 60,000, inhabitants could write a constitution and apply for statehood on terms of equality with the original thirteen. Slavery was forbidden. The Founders at Philadelphia took cognizance of the new law, and stipulated, according to Article IV, Section 3 of the new Constitution, that "Congress shall have Power to dispose of and make all needful Rules and Regulations respecting the territory or other property belonging to the United States." A blueprint for an American colonial system was thus laid down. The same process that led to statehood for Ohio, Indiana, Michigan, Illinois, and Wisconsin continued into the twentieth century, including the admission of Hawai'i and Alaska as states in 1959.

Concurrent with these plans for organizing a territorial system, American commissioners negotiated with representatives of the Indians who still occupied these territories. At Fort Stanwix, New York, in 1784, and at Hopewell, South Carolina, in 1785–1786, officials signed treaties opening new lands for white settlement with emissaries claiming to represent the Iroquois, Choctaw, Chickasaw, and Cherokee nations. Although Native Americans later denied that those who had signed the treaties ceding lands had the authority to do so, the United States regarded these treaties as confirmation of its sovereignty over the trans-Allegheny interior. The Creeks, who did not sign the Hopewell treaties, continued to resist along the Georgia frontier until 1790. Although these treaties later became mechanisms for national expansion (or "licenses for empire," as the historian Dorothy

Jones phrases it), the military power to defend frontier settlements was conspicuously lacking under the Articles.[120]

When the esteemed George Washington took the oath of office as president on the balcony of Federal Hall in New York on April 30, 1789, he could look optimistically at the international prospects of the federal republic. Not only could Washington employ the new diplomatic tools fashioned at Philadelphia, but he and his compatriots could also make good use of the foreign-relations experiences of the past thirteen years. If the American Revolution and its aftermath produced nothing else, it provided the United States with a remarkable reservoir of leaders who had become sophisticated in world affairs. Diplomats like Jefferson, Jay, and Adams soon contributed their expertise to the new administration. Washington himself, as his wartime collaboration with the French attested, understood the intricacies of alliance politics, as did his wartime aide, Alexander Hamilton. Other "demigods" at the Philadelphia convention—Gouverneur Morris, Edmund Randolph, Rufus King, James Madison, to name but a few—would occupy important diplomatic posts in the new government.[121] Because intellectual and political leaders were often the same people in this era, and because domestic, economic, and foreign policies were inextricably related, the Revolutionary generation gave rise to a foreign-policy elite of exceptional skills.

The diplomatic goals of independence and expansion were both practical and idealistic. Adams's Model Treaty of 1776 had projected a vision whereby American commerce would be open to the entire world, thus diminishing one of the major causes of war and increasing American profits. Independence and extensive boundaries would protect a republican experiment that, in turn, could serve as a countervailing model for a world of monarchies. The Mississippi River, it seems, even had divine sanction. John Jay told the Spanish in 1780 that "Americans, almost to a man, believed that God Almighty had made that river a highway for the people of the upper country to go to the sea by."[122] Even more expansive, the geographer Jedidiah Morse predicted in 1789 that America would soon become the world's largest empire, including "millions of souls, west of the Mississippi."[123] Of course, before Americans could move beyond the Mississippi, the boundaries of 1783 had to be made secure.

The Revolutionary generation that looked westward held the optimistic belief, as one historian has put it, that "they could teach the peoples of the rest of the world to govern themselves in happiness and prosperity; they did not believe that the majority of other peoples were unteachable or expendable."[124] Yet as Americans moved across the Alleghenies, they entered "a cultural contact zone" of blurred boundaries and contested terrain, a frontier in which "no culture, group, or government can claim effective control or hegemony over others."[125] Agents of rival European empires, overlapping legal jurisdictions, alien customs and religions, and especially heterogeneous Indian populations with established linkages to European metropoles, all blocked the path of peaceful westward expansion. Over time, the Enlightenment belief in an innate general human capacity for progress gave way to the racist belief in Anglo-Saxon superiority over those whom Americans destroyed or dominated. As the historian Jay Gitlin has observed, "state and settlers alike" came to agree that "native political and cultural distinctiveness must disappear," and they debated how best to achieve this goal through "assimilation, removal, enslavement, or genocide."[126]

Americans wanted to obtain independence and empire without resort to European-style power politics. The attractions of American commerce proved insufficient to bring automatic aid and recognition; so Franklin in 1778 negotiated the alliance with France. The American preference for commercial treaties instead of political alliances did not diminish after 1778, however, and the commercial and neutral-rights provisions of the Model Treaty remained central to American foreign relations. Commercial treaties in the 1780s with Sweden, Prussia, and the Netherlands followed those principles. Minister to France Thomas Jefferson, in the historian Merrill Peterson's estimation, thought of himself as undertaking "nothing less than a diplomatic mission to convert all Europe to the commercial principles of the American Revolution."[127] Probably more than most Americans of his generation, Jefferson retained this faith in the efficacy of commercial power as a substitute for military power. Americans believed, however, that the emphasis on commerce did not exalt profits over principles. As Jefferson's friend James Monroe later wrote: "People in Europe suppose us to be merchants, occupied exclusively with pepper and ginger. They are much deceived. . . . The

Daniel Boone (1734–1820).   The legendary "pathfinder," "trailblazer," and "Indian fighter" who came to symbolize early westward expansion and the conquest of an ever-moving frontier is here depicted in Horatio Greenough's marble statue, *The Rescue Group* (1852), defending his family against an Indian attack. The adventurer, popularized in print and art, became a mythical folk hero. Born into a Quaker family in Pennsylvania, Boone moved from there to North Carolina and then to Kentucky, exploring the region in the early 1750s and founding Boonesboro. During the American Revolution, Shawnees captured Boone, but he escaped. Because of defective titles, he lost large tracts of his Kentucky lands, and in 1799 he and his wife Rebecca moved to Spanish Missouri, where he received a substantial land grant. After the Louisiana Purchase of 1803, Boone again suffered legal contests over his land holdings, some of which Congress restored to him in 1814. Boone experienced the multicultural complexities of the trans-Allegheny frontier. His son Daniel Morgan Boone married a French Creole, Constantine Philibert, whose daughters, Elizabeth and Eulalie, grew up in Creole Kansas City, spoke French, and became baptized Catholics. (Library of Congress)

immense majority of our citizens . . . are . . . controlled by principles of honor and dignity."[128]

The United States, of course, had been forced to compromise principle—to make the alliance with France to win independence. The value of the French alliance could not be downplayed. Without Comte de Rochambeau's army and Admiral de Grasse's fleet, Washington could not possibly have forced Cornwallis's surrender in 1781. Indeed, at the decisive battles around Yorktown, more French than American soldiers fought against the British. French loans of some 35 million livres had kept an impecunious Congress solvent during the war. To be sure, Vergennes wanted to limit American boundaries; French agents in Philadelphia used their influence with Congress to hamstring American diplomats abroad; and as late as 1787 the French chargé d'affaires predicted that America would break up and urged his government to plan the seizure of New York or Rhode Island before the British could act. Still, the French alliance had secured American independence, and the treaty remained valid in 1789, including the provision guaranteeing French possessions in the New World. Most Americans, according to the historian William Stinchcombe, "assumed that the alliance would officially end with the arrival of the definitive treaty of peace."[129] Not so.

The status of the French alliance notwithstanding, the eschewing of foreign entanglements remained a cardinal American tenet in the 1780s. "The more attention we pay to our resources and the less we rely on others," wrote Connecticut's Roger Sherman, "the more surely shall we provide for our own honor and success and retrieve that balance between the contending European powers."[130] Americans regarded the European balance of power as a "vortex of death and destruction, not a sensitive mechanism that could be made to work for neutral rights, free trade and world peace."[131] American diplomats abroad simply did not trust European countries. Europe had its own set of interests, America another. Even a Francophile like Jefferson could write: "Our interest calls for a perfect equality in our conduct towards [England and France]; but no preferences any where."[132] So wary were American leaders of foreign entanglements that they could contemplate political alliances only in the event of attack.

Americans, in short, sought fulfillment of their goals without war or foreign allies. The federal Constitution strengthened national power. With an abundant federal revenue came stronger national credit. A flourishing foreign commerce and the power to regulate that commerce, it was hoped, would provide an important diplomatic lever. American military power hardly existed. Europeans who visited America in the 1780s analyzed American speech patterns, described the flora and fauna, admired the landscape, but said little of military matters. The United States with its 3.5 million population seemed a slight threat to the 15 million British or 25 million French. The traditional Anglo-Saxon fear of standing armies, and the expense of naval construction, made Americans, even under the Constitution, slow to build a defense establishment. Even Hamilton, the most military-minded member of Washington's government, predicted that it would be fifty years before "the embryo of a great empire" developed military forces sufficient to tip the balance between competing European powers or between the Old World and the New.[133]

Without military power or a foreign ally, the United States might find it difficult to maintain its independence, claim and extend its boundaries, and expand its commerce.

FURTHER READING FOR THE PERIOD TO 1789

For the colonial period, see Frank W. Brecher, *Losing a Continent: France's North American Policy, 1753–1763* (1998); Marc Egnal, *A Mighty Empire* (1988); Felix Gilbert, *The Beginnings of American Diplomacy: To the Farewell Address* (1965); Lawrence S. Kaplan, *Colonies into Nation* (1972); Walter LaFeber, "Foreign Policies of a New Nation," in William A. Williams, ed., *From Colony to Empire* (1972); Douglas E. Leach, *Roots of Conflict* (1966); Peggy K. Liss, *Atlantic Empires* (1983); Max Savelle, *The Origins of American Diplomacy* (1967); Robert W. Tucker and David C. Henrickson, *The Fall of the First British Empire* (1982); and Richard W. Van Alstyne, *The Rising American Empire* (1960).

Revolutionary-era issues are treated in Samuel Flagg Bemis, *The Diplomacy of the American Revolution* (1957); John Crowley, *The Privileges of Independence: Neomercantilism and the American Revolution* (1993); Jonathan R. Dull, *A Diplomatic History of the American Revolution* (1985); Ronald Hoffman and Peter J. Albert, eds., *Diplomacy and Revolution: The French-American Alliance of 1778* (1981) and *Peace and the Peacemakers: The Treaty of 1783* (1986); Reginald Horsman, *The Diplomacy of the New Republic, 1776–1815* (1985); Lawrence S. Kaplan, ed., *The American Revolution and "A Candid World"* (1977); Isabel de Madariaga, *Britain, Russia, and the Armed Neutrality of 1780* (1962); Richard B. Morris, *The Peacemakers* (1965); Orville T. Murphy, *Charles Gravier, Comte de Vergennes* (1982); J. W. S. Nordholt, *The Dutch Republic and American Independence* (1986); Peter Onuf and Nicholas Onuf, *Federal Union, Modern World* (1993); Bradford Perkins, *The Creation of a Republican Empire, 1776–1865* (1993); Carl J. Richard, *The Founders and the Classics* (1994); Norman E. Saul, *Distant Friends* (1991) (on Russia); H. M. Scott, *British Foreign Policy in the Age of the American Revolution* (1990); William Stinchcombe, *The American Revolution and the French Alliance* (1969); Reginald C. Stuart, *United States Expansionism and British North America, 1775–1871* (1988); Richard W. Van Alstyne, *Empire and Independence* (1965); William Earl Weeks, *Building the Continental Empire* (1996); Peter Whitely, *Lord North* (1996); and Gordon S. Wood, *The Creation of the American Republic* (1969). See also essays on the 1783 peace in *International History Review* (August 1983).

Foreign relations under the Articles of Confederation and foreign-policy questions during the making of the Constitution are discussed in Richard Beeman et al., eds., *Beyond Confederation* (1987); Merrill Jensen, *The New Nation* (1950); Daniel G. Lang, *Foreign Policy in the Early Republic* (1985); Charles A. Lofgren, *"Government from Reflection and Choice"* (1986); Frederick W. Marks III, *Independence on Trial* (1986); Richard B. Morris, *The Forging of the Union, 1781–1789* (1987); Peter S. Onuf, *Statehood and Union: A History of the Northwest Ordinance* (1987); Jack N. Rakove, *The Beginnings of National Politics* (1979); Charles R. Ritcheson, *Aftermath of Revolution: British Policy Toward the United States, 1783–1795* (1969); Abraham Sofaer, *War, Foreign Affairs and Constitutional Power*, vol. 1, *The Origins* (1976); and J. Leitch Wright, *Britain and the American Frontier, 1783–1815* (1975).

For the frontier and relations with Indians, see Gregory Evans Dowd, *A Spirited Resistance* (1992); Frederick E. Hoxie, ed., *Indians in American History* (1988); Dorothy Jones, *License for Empire* (1992); and David M. Weber, *The Spanish Frontier in North America* (1992).

For individuals, see William H. Adams, *The Paris Years of Thomas Jefferson* (1997); Noble E. Cunningham, Jr., *In Pursuit of Reason: The Life of Thomas Jefferson* (1988); Jonathan R. Dull, *Franklin the Diplomat* (1982); Eric Foner, *Tom Paine and Revolutionary America* (1976); John Ferling, *John Adams* (1992); Don Higgenbotham, *George Washington and the American Military Tradition* (1985); James H. Hutson, *John Adams and the Diplomacy of the American Revolution* (1980); Lawrence S. Kaplan, *Jefferson and France* (1963); John Keane, *Tom Paine* (1995); Dumas Malone, *Jefferson and the Ordeal of Liberty* (1962); essays on Franklin, Hamilton, and Jefferson in Frank Merli and Theodore A. Wilson, eds., *Makers of American Diplomacy* (1974); Robert Middlekauff, *Benjamin Franklin and His Enemies* (1996); Edmund S. Morgan, *The Genius of George*

Washington (1980); George B. Shackelford, *Thomas Jefferson's Travels in Europe, 1784–1789* (1995); Gerald Stourzh, *Benjamin Franklin and American Foreign Policy* (1969); Esmond Wright, *Franklin of Philadelphia* (1986); and books on diplomatic leaders listed in Chapter 2.

See also the General Bibliography, the notes below, and Richard Dean Burns, ed., *Guide to American Foreign Relations Since 1700* (1983).

For a comprehensive survey of foreign-relations topics, see the articles in the four-volume *Encyclopedia of U.S. Foreign Relations* (1997), edited by Bruce W. Jentleson and Thomas G. Paterson.

NOTES TO CHAPTER 1

1. Quoted in Richard B. Morris, *The Peacemakers* (New York: Harper and Row, 1965), p. 307.
2. Quoted in Francis Wharton, ed., *The Revolutionary Diplomatic Correspondence of the United States* (Washington, D.C.: Government Printing Office, 1889; 6 vols.), V, 657.
3. Quoted in Morris, *Peacemakers*, pp. 309–310.
4. Quoted in John Ferling, *John Adams* (Knoxville: University of Tennessee Press, 1992), p. 257.
5. Quoted in Bradford Perkins, "The Peace of Paris," in Ronald Hoffman and Peter J. Albert, eds., *Peace and the Peacemakers: The Treaty of 1783* (Charlottesville: University Press of Virginia, 1986), p. 206.
6. Quoted in Morris, *Peacemakers*, p. 357.
7. Quoted in Albert H. Smyth, ed., *The Writings of Benjamin Franklin* (New York: Macmillan, 1905–1907; 10 vols.), IX, 62.
8. Quoted in Jonathan R. Dull, *A Diplomatic History of the American Revolution* (New Haven: Yale University Press, 1985), p. 147.
9. Wharton, ed., *Revolutionary Correspondence*, VI, 169.
10. Quoted in Richard B. Morris, *Seven Who Shaped Our Destiny* (New York: Harper and Row, 1973), p. 9.
11. Quoted in L. H. Butterfield, ed., *Diary and Autobiography of John Adams* (Cambridge: Harvard University Press, 1961; 4 vols.), III, 82.
12. Samuel Flagg Bemis, *The Diplomacy of the American Revolution* (Bloomington: Indiana University Press, 1957), p. 256.
13. Quoted in John Ferling, "John Adams, Diplomat," *William and Mary Quarterly*, LI (April 1994), 252.
14. Quoted in Marc Egnal, *A Mighty Empire* (Ithaca: Cornell University Press, 1988), p. 12.
15. Leonard W. Labaree, ed., *The Papers of Benjamin Franklin* (New Haven: Yale University Press, 1951— ; 39 vols. to date), IX, 7.
16. Quoted in Theodore Draper, *A Struggle for Power: The American Revolution* (New York: Times Books, 1996), p. 105.
17. Gordon H. Wood, *The Radicalism of the American Revolution* (New York: Knopf, 1992), pp. 133–134.
18. Kenneth M. Morisson, "Native Americans and the American Revolution," in Frederick E. Hoxie, ed., *Indians in American History* (Arlington Heights, Ill.: Harlan Davidson, 1988), p. 101.
19. Quoted in H. Trevor Colbourn, *The Lamp of Experience* (Chapel Hill: University of North Carolina Press, 1965), p. 129.
20. Labaree, *Franklin Papers*, XIII, 151.
21. Max Savelle, "Colonial Origins of American Diplomatic Principles," *Pacific Historical Review*, III (1934), 337.
22. Quoted in Felix Gilbert, *The Beginnings of American Diplomacy* (New York: Harper and Row, 1965), p. 25.
23. Quoted *ibid.*, p. 28.
24. Quoted *ibid.*
25. Quoted *ibid.*, p. 61.
26. Quoted *ibid.*, p. 57.
27. Quoted in David M. Fitzsimons, "Tom Paine's New World Order," *Diplomatic History*, XIX (Fall 1995), 573.
28. Quoted in Gilbert, *Beginnings*, p. 65.
29. Quoted in Jan W. Schulte Nordholt, *The Dutch Republic and American Independence* (Chapel Hill: University of North Carolina Press, 1982), p. 190.
30. Anders Stephanson, *Manifest Destiny and the Empire of Right* (New York: Hill and Wang, 1995), p. xii.
31. Quoted *ibid.*, p. 19.
32. Thomas Paine, *Common Sense* (New York: Wiley, 1942 ed.), pp. 26–32.
33. Quoted in Fitzsimons, "Paine's New World," 575.
34. Worthington C. Ford, ed., *Journals of the Continental Congress* (Washington, D.C.: Government Printing Office, 1904–1937; 34 vols.), V, 425.
35. Quoted in Richard Van Alstyne, *Empire and Independence* (New York: Wiley, 1965), p. 106.
36. Edmund C. Burnett, ed., *Letters of Members of the Continental Congress* (Washington, D.C.: Carnegie Institution, 1921–1936; 8 vols.), I, 502.
37. Ford, *Journals of the Continental Congress*, V, 768–769.
38. John E. Crowley, *The Privileges of Independence* (Baltimore: Johns Hopkins University Press, 1993), p. 58.
39. Charles Francis Adams, ed., *The Works of John Adams* (Boston: Little, Brown, 1850–1865; 10 vols.), X, 269.
40. Quoted in Ferling, "Adams," 232.
41. Peggy K. Liss, *Atlantic Empires* (Baltimore: Johns Hopkins University Press, 1983), p. 106.
42. Quoted in Claude H. Van Tyne, "French Aid Before the Alliance of 1778," *American Historical Review*, XXXI (October 1925), 27.
43. Quoted in Van Alstyne, *Empire and Independence*, p. 43.
44. Quoted in Morris, *Peacemakers*, p. 113.
45. Quoted in Orville T. Murphy, *Charles Gravier* (Albany: State University of New York Press, 1982), p. 233.
46. Quoted in Bemis, *Diplomacy of the American Revolution*, p. 27.
47. Quoted in H. M. Scott, *British Foreign Policy in the Age of the American Revolution* (London: Oxford University Press, 1990), p. 243.
48. Quoted in Van Alstyne, *Empire and Independence*, p. 163.
49. Quoted in Claude-Anne Lopez, *Mon Cher Papa: Franklin and the Ladies of Paris* (New Haven: Yale University Press, 1966), pp. 257–258.
50. Quoted in Labaree, *Franklin Papers*, XXX, lxv.

51. Quoted in Bradford Perkins, *The Creation of a Republican Empire, 1776–1865* (New York: Cambridge University Press, 1993), p. 30.

52. Gilbert Chinard, ed., *The Treaties of 1778 and Allied Documents* (Baltimore: Johns Hopkins University Press, 1928), pp. 51–55.

53. Quoted in Ferling, "Adams," 232.

54. John Adams quoted in James H. Hutson, "Early American Diplomacy," in Lawrence S. Kaplan, ed., *The American Revolution and "A Candid World"* (Kent, Ohio: Kent State University Press, 1977), pp. 56–57.

55. Quoted in Van Alstyne, *Empire and Independence*, p. 93n.

56. Quoted in Elmer Bendiner, *The Virgin Diplomats* (New York: Knopf, 1976), p. 63.

57. Quoted in P. L. Haworth, "Frederick the Great and the American Revolution," *American Historical Review*, IX (April 1904), 468.

58. Wharton, ed., *Revolutionary Correspondence, V*, 415.

59. Quoted in Morris, *Peacemakers*, p. 200.

60. Quoted in Norman E. Saul, *Distant Friends* (Lawrence: University Press of Kansas, 1991), p. 15.

61. Quoted in Greg Russell, *John Quincy Adams and the Public Virtues of Diplomacy* (Columbia: University of Missouri Press, 1995), p. 14.

62. Ford, ed., *Journals of the Continental Congress, XXIV*, 394.

63. Samuel Flagg Bemis, *A Diplomatic History of the United States* (New York: Holt, Rinehart and Winston, 1965; 5th ed.), p. 34.

64. Quoted in Murphy, *Gravier*, p. 328.

65. Esmond Wright, "The British Objectives, 1780–1783," in Hoffman and Albert, *Peace and the Peacemakers*, p. 6.

66. Quoted in Peter Whitely, *Lord North* (London: Hambledon Press, 1996), p. 175.

67. Quoted in Frank Monaghan, *John Jay* (Indianapolis: Bobbs-Merrill, 1935), p.136.

68. Quoted in Morris, *Peacemakers*, p. 242.

69. Quoted *ibid.*, p. 243.

70. Lawrence S. Kaplan, *Colonies into Nation* (New York: Macmillan, 1972), p. 135.

71. Quoted in Louis Gottschalk, *Lafayette and the Close of the American Revolution* (Chicago: University of Chicago Press, 1942), p. 331.

72. Quoted in Morris, *Peacemakers*, p. 263.

73. Quoted in Carl Van Doren, *Benjamin Franklin* (New York: Viking Press, 1938), p. 671.

74. Scott, *British Foreign Policy*, p. 327.

75. Quoted in Morris, *Peacemakers*, p. 383.

76. Reginald C. Stuart, *United States Expansionism and British North America, 1775–1871* (Chapel Hill: University of North Carolina Press, 1988), p. 26.

77. Quoted in Crowley, *Privileges*, p. 64.

78. Quoted in Mark Kurlansky, *Cod* (New York: Walker and Company, 1997), p. 100.

79. H. P. Johnston, ed., *Correspondence and Public Papers of John Jay* (New York: G. P. Putnam's Sons, 1890–1893; 4 vols.), II, 344.

80. Quoted in Mary Beth Norton *The British-Americans* (Boston: Little, Brown, 1972), pp. 175–176.

81. Quoted *ibid.*, p. 176.

82. Quoted in Murphy, *Gravier*, p. 393.

83. Wharton, ed., *Revolutionary Correspondence, VI*, 140.

84. Quoted in Esmond Wright, *Franklin of Philadelphia* (Cambridge: Harvard University Press, 1986), p. 318.

85. Quoted in Lawrence S. Kaplan, *Entangling Alliances with None* (Kent, Ohio: Kent State University Press, 1987), p. 86.

86. Kaplan, *Colonies into Nation*, p. 144.

87. Quoted in Morris, *Peacemakers*, p. 459.

88. Dull, *A Diplomatic History*, p. 163.

89. Quoted in Merrill Jensen, *The New Nation* (New York: Knopf, 1950), p. 105.

90. Johnston, ed., *Correspondence of John Jay, III*, 154.

91. Quoted in Richard Beeman, "James Madison and Visions of American Nationality in the Confederation Period," in Richard Beeman et al., eds., *Beyond Confederation* (Chapel Hill: University of North Carolina Press, 1987), p. 234.

92. Quoted in David M. Weber, *The Spanish Frontier in North America* (New Haven: Yale University Press, 1992), p. 274.

93. Harold D. Langley, "Trade as a Precursor of Diplomacy," in Joan R. Challinor and Robert L. Beisner, eds., *Arms at Rest* (Westport, Conn.: Greenwood, 1987), p. 40.

94. Quoted in Liss, *Atlantic Empires*, p. 112.

95. Quoted in Doron S. Ben-Atar, *The Origins of Jeffersonian Commercial Policy and Diplomacy* (New York: St. Martin's Press, 1993), p. 54.

96. Quoted in Samuel Flagg Bemis, *Jay's Treaty* (New Haven: Yale University Press, 1962), p. 34.

97. William C. Stinchcombe, *The American Revolution and the French Alliance* (Syracuse: Syracuse University Press, 1969), p. 169.

98. Quoted in Kaplan, *Colonies into Nation*, pp. 160–161.

99. Quoted in Frederick W. Marks III, *Independence on Trial* (Baton Rouge: Louisiana State University Press, 1973), p. 135.

100. Quoted in Gregory Evans Dowd, *A Spirited Resistance* (Baltimore: Johns Hopkins University Press, 1992), p. 93.

101. Julian P. Boyd, *Number 7* (Princeton: Princeton University Press, 1964), p. xi.

102. Quoted in Jerald A. Combs, *The Jay Treaty* (Berkeley: University of California Press, 1970), p. 24.

103. Quoted in Charles R. Ritcheson, *Aftermath of Revolution* (Dallas: Southern Methodist University Press, 1969), p. 44.

104. Quoted in Marks, *Independence on Trial*, p. 68.

105. John C. Fitzpatrick, ed., *The Writings of George Washington* (Washington, D.C.: Government Printing Office, 1931–1944; 39 vols.), XXVII, 475.

106. Samuel Flagg Bemis, *Pinckney's Treaty* (New Haven: Yale University Press, 1960; rev. ed.), p. 75.

107. Quoted in Richard B. Morris, *The Forging of the Union, 1781–1789* (New York: Harper and Row, 1987), p. 243.

108. Quoted in Marks, *Independence on Trial*, p. 31.

109. Quoted in Weber, *Spanish Frontier*, p. 281.

110. Quoted in Lawrence S. Kaplan, *Jefferson and France* (New Haven: Yale University Press, 1963), p. 23.

111. Quoted in Noble E. Cunningham, Jr., *In Pursuit of Reason* (Baton Rouge: Louisiana State University Press, 1988), p. 93.

112. Quoted in James R. Sofka, "The Jeffersonian Idea of National Security," *Diplomatic History, XXI* (Fall 1997), 534.

113. Quoted in Marks, *Independence on Trial*, p. 48.

114. Article VI of the Constitution.

115. Lyman H. Butterfield, ed., *Letters of Benjamin Rush* (Princeton: Princeton University Press, 1951; 2 vols.), I, 475.

116. Quoted in Jacob Javits, *Who Makes War: The President Versus Congress* (New York: Morrow, 1973), p. 13.

117. Quoted in Charles A. Lofgren, *"Government from Reflection and Choice"* (New York: Oxford University Press, 1986), p. 7.

118. Jacob E. Cooke, ed., *The Federalist* (Middletown, Conn.: Wesleyan University Press, 1961), p. 64.

119. Michael H. Hunt, *Ideology and U.S. Foreign Policy* (New Haven: Yale University Press, 1987), p. 21.

120. Dorothy Jones, *License for Empire: Colonialism by Treaty in Early America* (Chicago: University of Chicago Press, 1982).

121. Clinton Rossiter, *1787: The Grand Convention* (New York: Macmillan, 1966), p. 138.

122. Quoted in Paul A. Varg, *Foreign Policies of the Founding Fathers* (Baltimore: Penguin, 1970), p. 41.

123. Quoted in Reginald Horsman, "The Dimensions of 'An Empire for Liberty,'" *Journal of the Early Republic, IX* (Spring 1989), 6.

124. Reginald Horsman, *Race and Manifest Destiny* (Cambridge: Harvard University Press, 1981), p. 299.

125. Emily S. Rosenberg, "A Call to Revolution," *Diplomatic History, XXII* (Winter 1998), 65.

126. Jay Gitlin, "On the Boundaries of Empire," in William Cronon et al., eds., *Under the Open Sky* (New York: Norton, 1992), 72–73.

127. Merrill D. Peterson, "Thomas Jefferson and Commercial Policy, 1783–1793," *William and Mary Quarterly, XXII* (October 1965), 592.

128. Quoted in Ernest R. May, *The Making of the Monroe Doctrine* (Cambridge: Harvard University Press, 1975), p. 19.

129. Stinchcombe, *American Revolution*, p. 200.

130. Quoted *ibid.*, p. 205.

131. Peter Onuf and Nicholas Onuf, *Federal Union, Modern World: The Law of Nations in an Age of Revolutions, 1776–1814* (Madison, Wis.: Madison House, 1993), p. 162.

132. Julian Boyd, ed., *The Papers of Thomas Jefferson* (Princeton: Princeton University Press, 1950–1974; 19 vols.), *VIII*, 545.

133. Quoted in Hunt, *Ideology*, p. 25.

CHAPTER

2

Independence, Expansion, and War, 1789–1815

Leopard *Versus* Chesapeake 1807. *This naval encounter highlighted the impressment issue in Anglo-American relations and nearly caused war. After the incident, President Thomas Jefferson closed U.S. ports to the Royal Navy, only to find that British commanders haughtily anchored their ships in Chesapeake Bay. Preoccupied at the time by Aaron Burr's treason trial, Jefferson chose economic coercion over military retaliation. The British frigate* Shannon *later captured the ill-fated* Chesapeake *in 1813 outside Boston harbor following a battle in which the dying American captain, James Lawrence, uttered the now immortal words: "Don't give up the ship." The Royal Navy broke up and sold the vessel after the Napoleonic wars. (Watercolor by Irwin J. Bevan, courtesy of the Mariners' Museum, Newport News, Virginia)*

❖

DIPLOMATIC CROSSROAD

The *Chesapeake* Affair, 1807

At 7:15 A.M. on June 22, 1807, the thirty-six-gun American frigate *Chesapeake* weighed anchor from Hampton Roads, Virginia, and made sail under a pleasant southwesterly breeze. Commanded by Commodore James Barron, the *Chesapeake* was bound for the Mediterranean Sea, where it would replace the *Constitution* as flagship of the small naval squadron that protected American merchant vessels from the Barbary states. Nobody aboard expected trouble. The ship's crew numbered 329, several of whom had deserted the Royal Navy and enlisted on the *Chesapeake* under assumed names. Sick sailors, recovering from a drinking bout of the night before, were allowed by the ship's doctor to lie in the sunny air on the upper deck. Loose lumber cluttered the gun deck. Cables were not stowed. Four of the guns did not fit perfectly into their carriages. Only five of the powder horns used in priming the guns were actually filled. In fact, officers had not exercised the crew at the guns during the ship's fitting out in Hampton Roads. Barron set sail anyway. Already four months behind schedule, the ship and crew would have ample opportunity for gunnery practice during the long sea voyage.

At 9:00 the *Chesapeake* passed Lynnhaven Bay, where two seventy-four-gun British ships of the line, *Bellona* and *Melampus,* lay anchored. A rumor had circulated in Norfolk, Virginia, that the captain of the *Melampus* was threatening to seize from the *Chesapeake* alleged deserters, but if Barron had heard the story, he took no special precautions. Neither British ship stirred. Soon after midday the *Chesapeake* sighted another ship off Cape Henry, the fifty-six-gun ship H.M.S. *Leopard*. At approximately 3:30 P.M., when both vessels were some ten miles southeast of Cape Henry, the *Leopard* came about and hailed that the British captain wanted to send dispatches to the Mediterranean through the courtesy of the American commodore. The *Chesapeake* then hailed back: "We will heave to and you can send your boat on board of us."[1] At this point Barron made a serious mistake. According to naval custom, a captain should never permit a foreign warship to approach close alongside without first calling his crew to battle stations. The disorderly conditions on the *Chesapeake,* however, made it difficult to clear the guns quickly, and to Barron the idea of a British naval attack "was so extravagant that he might as well have expected one when at anchor in Hampton Roads."[2]

British lieutenant John Meade came aboard at 3:45 and handed Barron a copy of orders from Captain S. P. Humphreys, instructing him to search the *Chesapeake* for British deserters. Humphreys did not elaborate on his orders, except to "express a hope that every circumstance respecting them may be adjusted in a manner that the harmony subsisting between the two countries may remain undisturbed."[3] Barron replied correctly; he could never allow his crew to be mustered "by any other

James Barron (1769–1851). The commander of the *Chesapeake,* according to court-martial proceedings conducted in 1808, had not prepared his ship properly for battle with the *Leopard.* Many of his fellow officers thought Barron had prematurely surrendered. The U.S. Navy suspended Barron for five years without pay. He returned to service but was given only shore duty. Years later he killed his chief nemesis, naval officer Stephen Decatur, in a duel. (Library of Congress)

but their own officers. It is my disposition to preserve harmony, and I hope this answer . . . will prove satisfactory."[4] Meade returned to the *Leopard.* Barron now ordered the gun deck cleared for action.

The time was nearly 4:30. To prepare the frigate for battle required a full half hour. The sea was calm. The *Leopard* used the windward advantage to move closer. Captain Humphreys called through the hailing pipe: "Commodore Barron, you must be aware of the necessity I am under of complying with the orders of my commander-in-chief." Barron, now on deck where he could see the *Leopard's* ready guns, tried to gain time by shouting: "I do not hear what you say."[5] He ordered the men to their stations without drumbeat. The *Leopard* fired a shot across the *Chesapeake's* bow. Another shot followed a minute later. Then, from a distance of less than 200 feet, the helpless *Chesapeake* was pounded by an entire broadside of solid shot and canister. The Americans did not have time to carry lighted matches or loggerheads from below decks to their loaded guns before three full broadsides pummeled them. In ten minutes the *Chesapeake* was hulled twenty-two times. Its three masts badly damaged, the ship suffered three men killed, eight severely and ten slightly wounded, including Commodore Barron, who stood exposed on the quarterdeck throughout the barrage. Finally, not wanting to sacrifice lives needlessly, Barron ordered the flag struck. The Americans salvaged a modicum of honor by firing a lone shot at the *Leopard.* A lieutenant had managed to discharge the gun by carrying a live coal in his fingers all the way from the galley. The eighteen-pound shot penetrated the *Leopard's* hull but fell harmlessly into the wardroom. The battle had ended.

British boats again came alongside, and Captain Humphreys took only four sailors from the deserters and identifiable Englishmen aboard the *Chesapeake*. Of the four, three were undeniably Americans, deserters from the *Melampus* the previous March. Two of these, it turned out, both African Americans, had previously deserted from an American merchant ship and had voluntarily enlisted in the Royal Navy in 1806. The fourth deserter was a surly Londoner, Jenkin Ratford, who had openly insulted his former British officers on the streets of Norfolk. The British eventually hanged him from a Halifax yardarm; the three Americans received lesser punishment. A few days after the *Chesapeake* had limped back to Hampton Roads, another British warship off the Virginia Capes fired on an American cutter carrying Vice President George Clinton.

Americans exploded in anger when they heard about the attack on the *Chesapeake*. "This event has excited a universal Ferment," a British envoy reported.[6] Heretofore the Royal Navy's practice of impressing alleged British sailors from American merchant ships had caused much diplomatic wrangling. Just a few months earlier, President Thomas Jefferson and Secretary of State James Madison had rejected a treaty with England largely because it failed to disavow "this authorized system of kidnapping upon the ocean."[7] British warships constantly stopped and searched merchant vessels in American waters, and the previous year H.M.S. *Leander* had killed an American when firing a shot across a merchant ship's bow. But the *Chesapeake* affair lacked precedent: The British had deliberately attacked an American *naval* vessel, a virtual act of war.

Federalists and Republicans alike expressed shock. In the historian Henry Adams's words, "the brand seethed and hissed like the glowing olive-stake of Ulysses in the Cyclops' eye, until the whole American people, like Cyclops, roared with pain and stood frantic on the shore, hurling abuse at their enemy, who taunted them from his safe ships."[8] The citizens of Hampton Roads destroyed some 200 water casks ready for delivery to the thirsty British squadron in Lynnhaven Bay. The British threatened retaliation. An angry British admiral proposed a retaliatory attack on New York City that would "disable" Americans from going to war and "compel them to any treaty." Only "red hot [cannon] balls" can keep the British "from our Rivers & Bays," warned one American veteran of the Revolutionary War.[9]

Jefferson issued a proclamation on July 2 closing American waters to British warships. Two weeks later he told the French minister: "If the English do not give us the satisfaction we demand, we will take Canada."[10] Treasury Secretary Albert Gallatin believed that war with England would bring increased taxes, debts, and destruction but might also salvage "the independence and honor of the nation" and "prevent our degenerating, like the Hollanders, into a nation of mere calculators."[11]

The *Chesapeake* affair did not lead to war—at least not immediately. Jefferson chose, in the historian Bradford Perkins's phrase, "to play the part of a damper rather than a bellows."[12] First the president tried military preparations and diplomatic alternatives. Even before Congress convened late in the year, Jefferson moved energetically to strengthen U.S. defenses. Without public fanfare, the president called all naval and merchant vessels home, ordered naval gunboats to be readied, armed seven coastal fortresses, sent field guns to state militia, gave war warnings to all frontier posts, and informed state governors that he might call 100,000 militia members to federal service. In readying the ramparts, however, Jefferson discovered the inadequacy of U.S. defenses. The Navy Department, it turned out, could not even send a ship to the East Indies to call home American merchant ships because it lacked funds for such a voyage. Even Washington, D.C., seemed vulnerable to attack. Gallatin warned prophetically that the British could "land at Annapolis, march to the city, and re-embark before the militia could be collected to repel [them]."[13] When Congress met in December 1807, Jefferson persuaded reluctant Republicans to triple the size of the regular army—not to fight the British but to enforce embargoes against them; he similarly asked for inexpensive coastal gunboats in preference to oceangoing frigates.

Jefferson's diplomacy did not quiet the crisis. The British government might have settled the matter amicably if the Americans had asked only for an apology and reparations for the *Chesapeake* incident. Foreign Secretary George Canning told the American minister James Monroe exactly that, in July 1807, but Jefferson insisted that England abandon impressment altogether. Canning was willing to disavow the incident but not the practice. As it turned out, the British did not formally apologize for the *Chesapeake* attack until 1811, by which time America's wounded sense of honor and England's stubbornness made war almost unavoidable. The *Chesapeake* affair also advanced American thoughts about invading Canada, and the British, in turn, began to repair their alliances with Native Americans in the Ohio Valley. The British Indian agent Matthew Elliott openly encouraged the Shawnee chiefs Tecumseh and the Prophet to form a confederation of western Indians. In this way were maritime grievances linked to frontier friction. By 1812, most Americans could agree with South Carolina politician John C. Calhoun's declaration of a "second struggle for our liberty" that "will prove to the enemy and to the World, that we have not only inherited the liberty which our Fathers gave us, but also the will and power to maintain it."[14]

The French Revolution and American Alternatives

The *Chesapeake* affair came during the series of wars that engulfed Europe after 1789. The wars initially proved advantageous to the United States. The economic prosperity of the young republic depended on disposing of agricultural surpluses abroad on favorable terms, and war in Europe created new trading opportunities for neutral carriers. American exports amounted to $20,750,000 in 1792, the last year of peace between France and England; by 1796 exports had jumped to $67,060,000. War in Europe also gave the United States more diplomatic leverage with respect to territorial disputes in North America. Since England and Spain were embroiled with France, and both sides desired American trade, the administration of George Washington could proceed more forcefully in negotiating with Spain over the Mississippi and Florida, and with Great Britain over the still occupied northwest forts.

Makers of American Foreign Relations, 1789–1815

Presidents	Secretaries of State
George Washington, 1789–1797	Thomas Jefferson, 1790–1794
	Edmund Randolph, 1794–1795
John Adams, 1797–1801	Timothy Pickering, 1795–1800
	John Marshall, 1800–1801
Thomas Jefferson, 1801–1809	James Madison, 1801–1809
James Madison, 1809–1817	Robert Smith, 1809–1811
	James Monroe, 1811–1817

Yet Europe's battles also posed the danger that the United States might get sucked in. France might demand American assistance under the terms of the 1778 alliance. England and Spain might fight rather than concede territorial claims in North America. Even if the United States maintained neutrality, belligerent nations might still disrupt America's neutral commerce. Americans differed over the proper response to Europe's wars, and the ensuing debate over foreign policy helped give rise to national political parties. The political and economic stakes were high indeed.

George Washington, whether as plantation manager, military commander, or president, always sought the best counsel before making decisions. Although Vice President John Adams, Chief Justice John Jay, and Attorney General Edmund Randolph sometimes contributed recommendations, the making of foreign policy during Washington's first administration often resembled an essay contest between Secretary of State Thomas Jefferson and Secretary of the Treasury Alexander Hamilton. Hamilton usually won, sometimes by using unscrupulous tactics, and around his policies coalesced the first national political party in the United States, the Federalist party. Although historians correctly use the term "Hamiltonian" foreign policy, Washington tried to remain above partisanship and accepted Hamilton's advice because he thought it in the national interest. As Hamilton admitted, however, the popular Founding Father "was an *Aegis very essential to me.*"[15]

Hamilton dominated diplomacy because early in the Washington administration he had, as Treasury secretary, formulated and won congressional approval for a fiscal program with foreign-policy implications. By funding the national debt at par, assuming the Revolutionary debts of several states, and paying the arrears on the national debt owed abroad, Hamilton sought to attract financial support for the federal experiment from wealthier commercial interests. Such a program required revenue. Hamilton provided the necessary monies through a tariff on imports and a tax on shipping tonnage. The revenue laws, passed in July 1789, levied a tax of fifty cents per ton on foreign vessels in American ports and attached a 10 percent higher tariff on imports in foreign bottoms. Such navigation laws served to stimulate American shipping by discriminating moderately against foreigners, but not enough to curtail trade. Hamilton particularly opposed discriminatory measures against England, such as the bill sponsored by James Madison in 1791 that would have prohibited imports from countries that forbade American imports in American bottoms (as England did with respect to Canada and the British West Indies). In Hamilton's eyes, any interference with Anglo-American commerce spelled disaster. Fully 90 percent of American imports came from England, more than half in British ships; nearly 50 percent of American exports went to British ports. Revenue would dry up if trade were curtailed. National credit, said Hamilton, would be "cut up . . . by the roots."[16] This brilliant illegitimate son of a West Indian planter spent the better part of his tenure at the Treasury Department defending the sanctity of Anglo-American trade and hence Anglo-American diplomatic cooperation.

Opposition to Hamilton's definition of the national interest quickly developed, particularly among southern agrarian interests seeking new markets for grain, cotton, and tobacco on the European continent. Echoing Jefferson, who resented Hamilton's encroachment on his prerogatives, Madison raised questions in Congress. Unlike the Federalists, Madison wanted to use commercial discrimination as a lever to obtain trade and territorial concessions from England. As spokesmen for southern planters whose crops had long been shackled to British markets and British credit, Madison and Jefferson wanted to loosen Anglo-American patterns through favorable commercial treaties with other European states and by legislation favoring non-British shipping. Britain might retaliate, but, as Madison bragged: "The produce of this country is more necessary to the rest of the world than that of other countries is to America. . . . [England's] interests can be wounded almost mortally, while ours are invulnerable."[17] In particular, he calculated that the British West Indies, in the event of a European war, would starve without vital U.S. supplies. Even though Hamilton's supporters blocked Madison's navigation bill in the Senate, the mere threat of commercial reprisals induced the British to send their first formal minister, George Hammond, to the United States in October 1791. Washington thereupon returned the compliment by sending former governor of South Carolina Thomas Pinckney to the Court of St. James's.

The French Revolution of 1789 exacerbated what Jefferson called the "heats and turmoils of conflicting parties" over trade policy.[18] The initial phase of the French upheaval, with familiar figures such as Thomas Paine and the Marquis de Lafayette in positions of leadership, elicited almost universal approbation in America. Then came the spring of 1793 and news that King Louis XVI had been guillotined and France had declared war on England and Spain. While conservative Federalists recoiled at the republican terror in France, Jeffersonian Republicans cheered and began organizing popular societies in apparent imitation of the French Jacobin clubs. Caught up in the enthusiasm, Jefferson wrote: "rather than it [the French Revolution] should have failed I would have seen half the earth desolated; were there but an Adam and Eve left in every country, and left free, it would be better than it now is."[19] France and England became, in the historian Joyce Appleby's words, "symbols of two alternative futures or fates for the United States: England as the model of sober, ordered constitutional government . . . and France, presenting a vision of what a society of free men might be."[20]

Frightened Federalists suspected that the Jeffersonians sought to plunge the country into war on the side of France. Hamilton sneered that Jefferson and his friends harbored "a *womanish attachment to France and a womanish resentment against Great Britain.*"[21] The Jeffersonians, in turn, conjured up visions of plots by Federalists (or "Monocrats") designed "to make a party in the confederacy against human liberty."[22] In actuality, the rising political passions in 1793 obscured the fact that neither party placed the interests of France or England above those of the United States. Although Hamilton sometimes talked indiscreetly to British diplomats, he did so in the belief that the twin American goals of commercial and territorial expansion could be best achieved in close relationship with Great Britain. As for Jefferson's celebrated Francophilism, the French minister Pierre Adet commented in 1796: "Jefferson I say is American and as such, he cannot be sincerely our friend. An American is the born enemy of all the European peoples."[23] Even though the country remained officially neutral, it seemed inevitable that Americans would favor one side or the other in the symbolic struggle between "Jacobin and Angloman," between "revolutionary France and conservative England."[24]

Citizen Edmond Charles Genet (1763–1834). From Charleston to New York City, the French representative recruited Americans for anti-British activities, setting off political fireworks and complicating the nation's neutrality. (Albany Institute of History and Art)

President Washington's proclamation of neutrality on April 22, 1793, received the unanimous backing of his cabinet advisers. How to reconcile neutrality with the French alliance was another matter. In receiving France's new republican minister, Citizen Edmond Charles Genet, Jefferson refuted Hamilton's arguments that the 1778 treaties had lapsed with the death of Louis XVI. Jefferson thereby set two important diplomatic precedents: American respect for the sanctity of treaties and quick diplomatic recognition of regimes that had de facto control over a country. The thirty-year-old Genet eased his reception by not asking the United States to become a belligerent; he even offered new commercial concessions if American merchants would take over France's colonial trade with the West Indies.

Obstacles to Franco-American harmony quickly materialized. Genet outfitted some fourteen privateers—privately owned American ships, equipped in American ports for war under French commission. Before long they had captured more than eighty British merchant ships, some of them taken within the American three-mile coastal limit. Such activities openly violated neutrality regulations announced in August. British minister Hammond protested and Jefferson warned Genet, but pro-French juries often acquitted those Americans who were arrested. Genet infuriated Jefferson by promising that he would not send a captured British prize, *Little Sarah,* to sea as a privateer only a few hours before the vessel (renamed *Petite Démocrate*) slipped down the Delaware River to embark on a career of destroying commerce. Genet also conspired to capture Spanish-controlled Louisiana by means of an expedition comprising mostly American volunteers and led by the Revolutionary hero George Rogers Clark. Although the plan never reached fruition, the French envoy dramatically informed Paris: "I am arming the Canadians to throw off the yoke of England; I am arming the Kentuckians, and I am preparing an expedition by sea to support the descent on New Orleans."[25] Genet also encouraged pro-French editorials in the press of the nation's capital—Philadelphia at that time—hobnobbed with Republican leaders, and at one point appealed to the American people to disobey the president's neutrality proclamation. Washington grew furious, and even Madison admitted that Genet's "conduct has been that of a madman."[26]

The furor over Genet abated somewhat by late summer 1793, when an outbreak of yellow fever caused most government officials to leave Philadelphia. By this time Genet had made himself so obnoxious that the Washington administration agreed unanimously to ask the French government to recall its envoy. Even Jefferson considered Genet "hot headed, all imagination, no judgment, passionate, disrespectful & even indecent toward the P[resident]."[27] Meanwhile, Washington replaced Gouverneur Morris as American minister in Paris. The indiscreet Morris had proven himself a shrewd judge of the French Revolution but had alienated his hosts by befriending French aristocrats, at one point even aiding an abortive attempt to spirit the king and queen out of France. The nomination of James Monroe, a firm Virginia Republican, to replace Morris patched up quarrels temporarily, as did the arrival of Genet's successor, Joseph Fauchet, in February 1794. As for Genet, he never returned to France. By the time of his recall the French Revolution had moved decidedly to the left, the Jacobins having replaced the Girondins, and young Genet seemed likely to lose his head as well as his reputation. Washington relented and allowed Genet to remain in America, whereupon the once stormy Frenchman moved to New York, married the daughter of Governor George Clinton, and lived quietly until his death in 1834.

Commerce, Politics, and Diplomacy: Jay's Treaty

No sooner had the crisis with France eased than the country found itself on the edge of war with England. Seizure of American commerce on the high seas and threats of Indian attacks from Canada touched off a war scare in the winter and early spring of 1794. Indignation raged in Congress when it learned in late February that British cruisers, under a secret order in council (Admiralty decree) declaring foodstuffs contraband, had seized more than 250 American merchant ships trading with the French West Indies. These maritime actions, coupled with an inflammatory speech to the western Indians by Lord Dorchester, governor-general of Canada, posed a direct threat to the young republic. Congress responded, on March 26, 1794, by imposing a thirty-day embargo (later extended to sixty days) on all shipping in American ports bound for foreign destinations. Although ostensibly impartial, the legislation targeted England.

Cool heads sought to prevent a rupture. Fearful that the Republican majority in the House of Representatives would destroy trade and credit through permanent embargoes and thus cause war with England, Hamilton and other Federalists suggested a special mission to London. By a vote of 18 to 8, the Senate on April 18 confirmed the appointment of Supreme Court Chief Justice John Jay. Treasury Secretary Hamilton conceived the special mission and drafted the bulk of Jay's instructions. Only after strenuous argument from Edmund Randolph, who had replaced Jefferson as secretary of state, was a reference inserted to the possibility of sounding out Russia, Sweden, or Denmark about an alliance of neutrals. The Anglophilic Hamilton defused this threat, which might have induced England to make concessions on neutral rights, when he leaked to British minister Hammond the information that Washington's cabinet, ever wary of entanglements, had actually decided not to join a neutral alliance. Except for forbidding any agreement that contradicted obligations under the 1778 alliance with France, and prohibiting any commercial treaty that failed to open the British West Indies to American shipping, the special minister's instructions afforded him considerable discretion. Jay's concern for maintaining peace and commerce with Great Britain, moreover, stood almost as high as Hamilton's.

Amid much wine, dining, and expressions of "most sincere esteem and friendship" from the British foreign secretary, Lord Grenville, Jay negotiated the Treaty of Amity, Commerce, and Navigation, signed on November 19, 1794.[28] England, locked in deadly combat with France, found it prudent to conciliate the United States on North American issues but did not yield on the vital questions involving its maritime supremacy. Most important, Jay gained the British surrender of the northwest forts, which London had promised to relinquish in the 1783 peace treaty. This time the redcoats actually left.

Whitehall's abandonment of the West also aborted efforts to unite the Indians north and south of the Ohio River against American encroachment. When General Anthony Wayne defeated the Miami confederacy in the Battle of Fallen Timbers in August 1794, the British commander at nearby Fort Miami closed his gates to the retreating Indians. In the Treaty of Greenville (1795), the Indians ceded much of what soon became the states of Ohio and Indiana. Indeed, the towns of Dayton, Youngstown, and Cleveland sprang into existence within months. In return, the U.S. government formally recognized Indian sovereignty over unceded lands—"quietly to enjoy them, hunting, planting, and dwelling thereon so long as they please."[29] The agreement pacified the Ohio Valley for a decade.

Another British concession, the opening of the British East Indies to American commerce, held promise for future trade with Asia. Jay also obtained trade with the British Isles on a most-favored-nation basis. As for the British West Indies, however, the treaty limited American shipping to vessels of less than seventy tons and also forbade the American export of certain staples, such as cotton and sugar, to those islands. Other controversial matters, including compensation for recent maritime seizures, pre-Revolutionary debts still owed by Americans, and the disputed northeast boundary of Maine, would be decided by arbitration. In regard to neutral rights, Jay made concessions that violated the spirit, if not the letter, of America's treaty obligations to France. His accord stipulated that under certain circumstances American foodstuffs bound for France might be seized and compensation offered and that French property on American ships constituted a fair prize. In this case, then, "free ships" no longer meant "free goods." The commercial clauses were to remain in effect for twelve years, thus ensuring a "twelve year moratorium" on Republican efforts to discriminate against British trade.[30] Finally, the treaty said nothing about impressment and abducted slaves. "A bolder party stroke was never struck," Jefferson grumbled. "For it certainly is an attempt of a party, which . . . lost their majority in one branch of the legislature, to make a law by the other branch of the executive, under color of a treaty, which shall bind up the hands of the adverse branch from ever restraining the commerce of their patron nation."[31]

Jefferson's discontent notwithstanding, Jay's Treaty accelerated the nation's sovereignty. Faced with the loss of American trade, England had compromised on territorial issues in North America. London would no more surrender maritime supremacy in 1794 than it would in 1807, yet by avoiding war, the treaty sparked a

**George Washington
(1732–1799).** The esteemed
Virginia gentleman farmer and first
president always maintained a re-
gal, if not cold, countenance.
Thomas Jefferson became so angry over Jay's Treaty that he labeled Washington one of "the
apostates who have gone over to
the heresies, men who were Sam-
sons in the field and Solomons in
the council, but who have had
their heads shorn by the harlot
England." (National Portrait
Gallery, Smithsonian Institution/Art
Resource, N.Y.)

short-term trading boom with both England and Europe, "a golden shower," as
one merchant called it.[32] In the long run, it also linked American security and development to the British fleet, which provided "a protective shield of incalculable
value throughout the nineteenth century." In effect, Jay's Treaty bet on England
rather than France as "the hegemonic European power of the future."[33] In view of
the contempt England had shown American diplomacy since 1783, any concession
by treaty constituted real proof that the United States could maintain its independence in a hostile world. By inaugurating a critical period of relatively amicable relations between England and the United States, Jay's Treaty gave the United States
time in which to grow in territory, population, and national consciousness. By the
time war with Britain came in 1812, the United States had fought France and the
Barbary states and doubled in territorial size.

The treaty signed in November 1794 arrived in Philadelphia on March 7,
1795. The Senate had just dispersed, so Washington did not actually submit the
treaty for approval until early June. The senators debated in executive session, and
only by eliminating Article XII (the West Indian trade restrictions) could the Federalists secure a bare two-thirds vote of 20 to 10 on June 24. Complications prevented the president's immediate signature. While Washington pondered whether
he needed to resubmit the accord to England (without Article XII) before formally
ratifying it, a Republican senator leaked Jay's Treaty to the press. Critics quickly
charged that Jay had surrendered American maritime rights for minor British concessions, and that the French alliance had been betrayed. Antitreaty manifestos and
protest parades materialized in many towns and cities. In Philadelphia a mob hanged
John Jay in effigy and stoned the residence of the British minister. A would-be poet
called the treaty "truly a farce, fit only to wipe the national ---."[34]

Federalist leaders quailed at the onslaught. "If the President decides wrong, or
does not decide *soon*," wrote Senator Oliver Ellsworth of Connecticut, "his good
fortune will forsake him."[35] Seeking to quiet the clamor and to protect his reputation, Washington delayed formal ratification. He also became irked that the
British had resumed seizures of American vessels carrying foodstuffs to France.
Conferring almost exclusively with Randolph, he decided to wait for adequate
British explanations.

Always a deliberate man, Washington might have put off ratification indefinitely had not suspicions of treason intervened and thereby removed Edmund Randolph, the chief obstacle to normalizing relations with England. In March 1795, a
British man-of-war had captured a French corvette carrying dispatches from Minister Joseph Fauchet to Paris. Dispatch Number Ten recounted conversations in
which Randolph had allegedly sought from Fauchet money for Republican leaders
in Pennsylvania during the Whiskey Rebellion of 1794. The report of the conversations was confused and remains puzzling to scholars, but Foreign Minister
William Grenville sensed his opportunity and sent Dispatch Number Ten to Minister Hammond suggesting that "the communication of some of [the information]
to well disposed persons in America may possibly be helpful to the King's service."[36] Hammond showed the dispatch to Secretary of War Timothy Pickering, a
tall, pinch-faced New Englander and diehard Federalist. Convinced of Randolph's
treason, he deliberately but subtly mistranslated certain French passages in Number

Ten to make the evidence on Randolph look more incriminating. Then he wrote to Mount Vernon asking for a special meeting with Washington.

Washington arrived in Philadelphia in August, read Pickering's translation of Number Ten, and apparently pronounced his secretary of state guilty. He also decided to ratify Jay's Treaty. On August 18, 1795, the president put his official signature on the document. The next day he confronted Randolph. Washington handed him Fauchet's dispatch, pronouncing coldly, "Mr. Randolph! here is a letter which I desire you to read, and make such explanations as you choose."[37] The young Virginia Republican defended himself to no avail. Even though most scholars accept Randolph's innocence, he made the mistake of quarreling openly with the revered President Washington, and in the heated political atmosphere of 1795–1796 neither the Republicans nor the Federalists would take up his cause. Randolph resigned.

The Republicans, while avoiding any identification with the fallen Randolph, made one last effort in the House of Representatives to negate Jay's Treaty by trying to block appropriations for its implementation. During the House debates in March 1796, Republican leaders asked to see all official documents and correspondence relating to the treaty. In a precedent-setting decision, Washington refused, citing the need for secrecy and the fact that the Constitution authorized the Senate only to "advise and consent" on treaties. The debate raged on. Federalist Fisher Ames of Massachusetts evoked the fear of Indian warfare in the Northwest—"we light the savage fires"—if Congress rejected appropriations and British troops did not leave, and another Federalist wrote to his congressman: "If you do not give us your vote, your son shall not have my Polly."[38] A bare majority (51 to 48) of the House voted the necessary funds on April 30.

Pinckney's Treaty, France, and Washington's Farewell

One reason why the House, despite a Republican majority, voted appropriations for Jay's Treaty was the fear that its negation might jeopardize the more popular Pinckney's Treaty with Spain. This treaty (sometimes called the Treaty of San Lorenzo) obtained everything that the United States had sought from Spain since the Revolution, which especially delighted the South and West. Signed by Thomas Pinckney in Madrid on October 27, 1795, the agreement secured for American farmers free navigation of the Mississippi River and the right to deposit goods at New Orleans for transshipment. This privilege of deposit was stipulated to last for three years, renewable at either New Orleans or some other suitable place on the Mississippi (see map on page 62). Spain also set the northern boundary of Florida at 31° north latitude. The Senate approved the accord unanimously on March 3, 1796. With America's southeastern frontier now settled with Spain, some Republicans did not want to risk losing a similarly favorable settlement in the Northwest by voting against Jay's Treaty. "A rejection," one Republican warned, "would operate like a subtle poison, which . . . would quickly insinuate itself into the system, and affect the whole mass."[39] In the sense that they redeemed America's borderlands from foreign control, Jay's Treaty and Pinckney's Treaty stood together.

The popular treaty with Spain seems to have been a by-product of Jay's hand-iwork in England. When Thomas Pinckney arrived in Spain in June 1795, the Spanish knew of Jay's Treaty, but no one had yet seen the actual text. The Spanish foreign minister, Don Manuel de Godoy, feared a military alliance between England and the United States. Spain's lightly garrisoned outposts in North America already seemed vulnerable to American settlers moving across the Alleghenies, so an Anglo-American alliance would make Spanish territory indefensible. Better to make concessions to the grasping Americans and keep the peace. Godoy was in the process of extricating Spain from the war against France (effected in July 1795), and he hoped to renew the old alliance with France. He feared England's wrath after Madrid switched sides: hence his willingness to appease the Americans. Scholars have debated whether Godoy actually saw a copy of Jay's Treaty (and therefore knew that it was not a military alliance) before signing Pinckney's Treaty in October. The historian Arthur P. Whitaker has argued that Godoy did have an accurate text and thus Spain made a favorable treaty with the United States because it "had no stomach for dealing with the American frontiersman."[40] Godoy himself lamented: "You can't put doors on an open country [the United States]."[41] The historian Samuel Flagg Bemis has countered that Godoy did not know, thereby making European diplomatic considerations decisive. Whatever the reason, the war in Europe had diverted Spain's power and attention from North America. To use Bemis's famous phrase, this diplomatic episode probably ranks as a classic case of "America's advantage from Europe's distress."[42] European wars facilitated American expansion.

If diplomatic advantages from Spain followed logically from Jay's Treaty, the pact generated only trouble with France. James Monroe, who had assured the French that Jay's instructions precluded any violation of American obligations to the 1778 alliance, had to bear the brunt of French outrage over the surrender of "free ships, free goods." The only foreign diplomat to remain in Paris during the Reign of Terror, Monroe had ingratiated himself by hailing France's contributions to human liberty in a speech before the National Convention. When news of Jay's Treaty reached Paris, however, Monroe made the mistake of predicting that the treaty would be defeated. In July 1796, the angry French government announced that American ships would no longer be protected under the neutral-rights provisions of the 1778 treaty. To make matters worse, a disgruntled Washington ordered Monroe home in late August. French agents in America, meanwhile, stepped up their efforts to wean American policy from its pro-British orientation. Minister Pierre Adet, imitating his predecessors Genet and Fauchet, did his best to bring about "the right kind of revolution" by lobbying unsuccessfully in the House of Representatives against Jay's Treaty and openly backing Thomas Jefferson for the presidency.[43] Adet's electioneering efforts came to naught, however, and John Adams beat Jefferson by an electoral vote of 71 to 68.

The well-timed publication of Washington's Farewell Address on September 19, 1796, contributed to Adams's victory over Jefferson. To be sure, Washington, ever conscious of history's verdict, was setting down a testament that he hoped would have lasting effect. At the same time, the first president and Hamilton, who revised Washington's draft of the speech, had French intrigues very much in mind in making the famous warning: "Against the insidious wiles of foreign influence . . . the jealousy of a free people ought to be *constantly* awake."

Washington's valedictory stands as an eloquent statement of American diplomatic principles. It reiterated the "Great Rule" that "in extending our commercial relations" the United States should have "as little *political* connection as possible" with foreign nations. Like Thomas Paine, he posited the idea of American uniqueness. "Europe," said Washington, "has a set of primary interests which to us have none or a very remote relation. . . . Our detached and distant situation invites and enables us to pursue a different course." Then came perhaps his most memorable words: "'Tis our true policy to steer clear of permanent alliances, with any portion of the foreign world. . . . Taking care always to keep ourselves . . . on a respectable defensive posture, we may safely trust to temporary alliances for extraordinary emergencies."[44] Washington did not preclude westward expansion. Even though he seemed to fear a French connection more than a British linkage in 1796, the evenhandedness of his phraseology gave the Farewell Address an enduring quality. "Our countrymen," Jefferson commented in agreement, "have divided themselves by such strong affections to the French and the English that nothing will secure us internally but a divorce from both nations."[45]

The XYZ Affair and the Quasi-War with France

"My entrance into office," John Adams wrote, "is marked by a misunderstanding with France, which I shall endeavor to reconcile, provided that no violation of faith, no stain upon honor, is exacted. . . . America is not SCARED."[46] In July 1796, some four months after Jay's Treaty had officially gone into effect, the French decreed that they would treat neutral vessels the way neutrals permitted England to treat them—that is, "free ships" would not guarantee "free goods." Shortly thereafter, French privateers and warships began seizing American merchant vessels in the West Indies. By June 1797 the French had seized 316 ships. In addition, the five-man Directory that ruled France had refused to receive Charles C. Pinckney, the South Carolina Federalist whom Washington had sent to replace Monroe as American minister. Threatened with arrest, Pinckney fled to the Netherlands, thus presenting Adams with a complete diplomatic rupture. Rejecting suggestions of war from bellicose Federalists, the new president dispatched a special commission to negotiate outstanding differences with the French. To accomplish this delicate task, Adams named Pinckney, Federalist John Marshall of Virginia, and Massachusetts Republican Elbridge Gerry. Adams displayed his nonpartisanship by selecting Gerry, an old friend, only after Thomas Jefferson and James Madison had declined to serve.

The three U.S. envoys arrived in Paris in October 1797, whereupon they encountered perhaps the most fascinating, most unscrupulous diplomat of all time. The wily (the word was invented to describe him) Charles Maurice de Talleyrand-Périgord, formerly a bishop in the ancien régime, recently an exile for two years in

Talleyrand (1754–1838).
The wily French statesman ma-
jored in survival during the stormy
years of the French Revolution.
His attempt to solicit bribes from
U.S. envoys in the XYZ Affair, it
seems, stemmed in part from
losses he suffered in land specula-
tions when he was living in exile in
Pennsylvania in the early 1790s.
(Prints Division, New York Public
Library, Astor, Lenox and Tilden
Foundations)

the United States, had become French foreign minister that summer. Despite his firsthand acquaintance with Americans (indeed, he and Gouverneur Morris had once shared the same mistress in Paris), Talleyrand evinced little affection for the United States, a nation of mere "fishermen and woodcutters" that should not be treated "with greater respect than Geneva or Genoa."[47]

Maritime pressure offered a convenient way to persuade the Americans to acknowledge their commercial obligations to France under the treaty of 1778. The French still wanted Yankee ships to take over their carrying trade with the French West Indies, an impossible undertaking if the Americans refused to defend such commerce against the British. Talleyrand did not want open war, but as one of his diplomatic agents put it: "A little clandestine war, like England made on America for three years, would produce a constructive effect."[48] The war in Europe had begun to go well again for France under the young Corsican general Napoleon Bonaparte. American questions were not deemed urgent. If Talleyrand could string out negotiations with the U.S. commission, party divisions would reappear in the United States, and France could easily make a favorable settlement. "Nothing will disconcert or try them more than a cold and polite reception, rare, vague, and private discussions, and a far-distant prospect for results," another aide suggested.[49]

Three French agents, later identified in the American dispatches as X, Y, and Z, soon approached the commissioners on behalf of Talleyrand. The message, although indirect, seemed unmistakable. If the Americans expected serious and favorable negotiations, they should pay a bribe to the French foreign minister and arrange for a large loan to the French government. To the first request, Pinckney made his celebrated reply: "No; no; not a sixpence."[50] This initial attempt at bribery did not terminate negotiations. Conversations continued throughout the autumn and into the new year. Talleyrand apparently employed a beautiful woman to work her charms on Gerry and Marshall. "Why will you not lend us money?" she asked at one point. "If you were to make us a loan, all matters will be adjusted. When you were contending your Revolution we lent you money."[51]

Talleyrand's methods were common enough in European chancelleries. The Americans refused to pay because they had no instructions, not solely because they were indignant. Gradually, however, they lost patience. Marshall correctly observed that "this haughty, ambitious government is not willing to come to an absolute rupture with America during the present state of the war with England but will not condescend to act with justice or to treat us as a free and independent nation."[52] In January 1798, Marshall drew up a memorial, signed by Gerry and Pinckney, which recounted all American grievances against France, including the personal indignities that French agents gratuitously inflicted on the American commissioners. Talleyrand made no reply. The French issued new and harsher decrees that made a neutral cargo liable to capture if any part of it—even a jug of rum—had British origins. Marshall and Pinckney asked for their passports, although Gerry, a native of Marblehead, after vowing that he "would sooner be thrown into the Seine than consent to stay," did linger another three months in a futile attempt to negotiate.[53]

Rumors of French insolence began to filter back to the United States in early 1798. After receiving the first official dispatches from his three emissaries, Adams

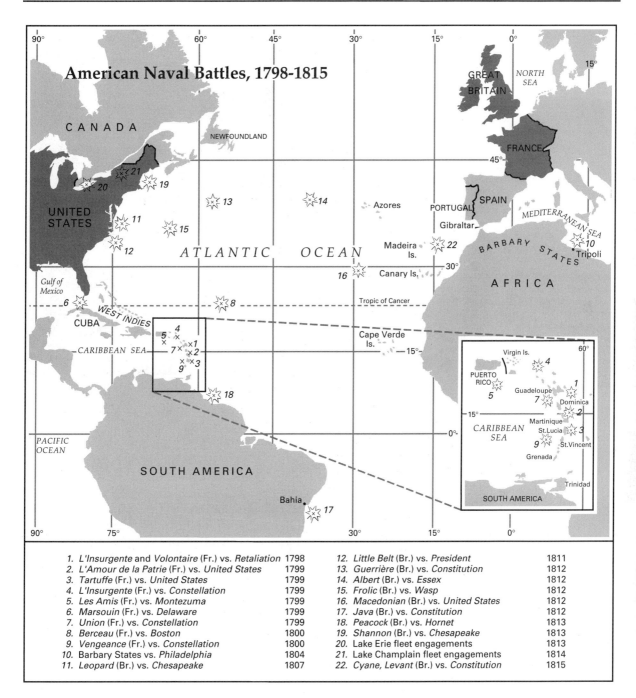

American Naval Battles, 1798-1815

1. *L'Insurgente* and *Volontaire* (Fr.) vs. *Retaliation*	1798	
2. *L'Amour de la Patrie* (Fr.) vs. *United States*	1799	
3. *Tartuffe* (Fr.) vs. *United States*	1799	
4. *L'Insurgente* (Fr.) vs. *Constellation*	1799	
5. *Les Amis* (Fr.) vs. *Montezuma*	1799	
6. *Marsouin* (Fr.) vs. *Delaware*	1799	
7. *Union* (Fr.) vs. *Constellation*	1799	
8. *Berceau* (Fr.) vs. *Boston*	1800	
9. *Vengeance* (Fr.) vs. *Constellation*	1800	
10. Barbary States vs. *Philadelphia*	1804	
11. *Leopard* (Br.) vs. *Chesapeake*	1807	
12. *Little Belt* (Br.) vs. *President*	1811
13. *Guerrière* (Br.) vs. *Constitution*	1812
14. *Albert* (Br.) vs. *Essex*	1812
15. *Frolic* (Br.) vs. *Wasp*	1812
16. *Macedonian* (Br.) vs. *United States*	1812
17. *Java* (Br.) vs. *Constitution*	1812
18. *Peacock* (Br.) vs. *Hornet*	1813
19. *Shannon* (Br.) vs. *Chesapeake*	1813
20. Lake Erie fleet engagements	1813
21. Lake Champlain fleet engagements	1814
22. *Cyane, Levant* (Br.) vs. *Constitution*	1815

Alexander Hamilton (1755–1804).   Hamilton served as General Washington's aide-de-camp during the Revolution and as the first secretary of the treasury. In the late 1790s, the pro-British Hamilton favored a muscular policy toward France. The fact that Hamilton would assume command of a wartime army helped restrain Adams from a military solution to the XYZ Affair. Hamilton died after he was shot in a duel with Aaron Burr. Talleyrand ranked "Napoleon, [William] Pitt, and Hamilton as the three greatest men of our age, and if I had to choose among the three, I would unhesitatingly give first place to Hamilton." (Library of Congress)

went before Congress on March 19. Pointing out that his peace overtures had been refused, the president asked for authority to arm merchant ships and for other defensive measures. Jeffersonian Republicans smelled a Federalist trap. The House of Representatives demanded that the president send it all relevant diplomatic correspondence. Adams, ignoring the precedent of Washington's refusal in the case of Jay's Treaty, sent all dispatches to the House, substituting the letters X, Y, and Z for the real names of Talleyrand's highwaymen. The country was soon aflame with the news. "Millions for defense but not one cent for tribute" (a phrase mistakenly attributed to Charles C. Pinckney) became a popular slogan, and crowds hailed John Marshall as a triumphant hero on his return to New York. Even the dour Adams aroused cheers when he promised Congress in June that he would never "send another minister to France without assurance that he will be received, respected, and honored as the representative of a great, free, powerful, and independent nation."[54] The outburst of anti-French passion astonished Jefferson, who acknowledged "such a shock on the republican mind, as has never been seen since our independence."[55]

The young republic nearly went to war with France. In the summer of 1798 Congress passed measures that amounted to "quasi-war." It declared all French treaties null and void, created a Navy Department, funded the construction of new warships, and increased the regular army. George Washington came out of retirement to lead the new forces, although effective command, at Washington's request, rested in the hands of the Inspector General Alexander Hamilton. Jeffersonians saw the army, in conjunction with the new Alien and Sedition Laws directed against pro-French radicals, as suppression of political opposition; the Federalists meant "to arm one half of the people, for the purpose of keeping the other in awe."[56] Nonetheless, Adams did not request, nor did Congress authorize, a declaration of war. The American navy received orders only to retaliate against attacking French warships and privateers. The quasi-war lasted more than two years, during which the U.S. Navy captured some eighty-five French vessels. The new frigates performed brilliantly, and such spectacular victories as that of the *Constellation* over *L'Insurgente* in February 1799 helped to deter the French from widening hostilities. Content with naval retaliation only, Adams correctly perceived that France, bogged down in campaigns in Europe and Egypt, would not respond with full-scale war or invasion. Adams lost interest in the army because "there is no more prospect of seeing a French army here, than there is in Heaven."[57]

Federalist partisans, including a majority of Adams's cabinet, were more warlike. Secretary of War James McHenry voiced exaggerated fears that the French might "convoy an army of ten thousand blacks and people of colour in vessels seized from our own citizens." This force might land on the defenseless parts of South Carolina or Virginia and spark a slave insurrection, he warned.[58] Hamilton (whose boundless ambitions President Adams attributed to a "superabundance of secretions") became particularly fascinated by a grand scheme promoted by Venezuelan revolutionary Francisco de Miranda, whereby the United States would undertake a joint expedition with Britain against both Spain and France in the Americas, thus securing the liberation of all Latin America, the acquisition of the Floridas and Louisiana for the United States, and military glory for Hamilton.[59] The idea of a British alliance intrigued Secretary Pickering, Treasury Secretary Oliver Wolcott, and other high Federalists. Miranda hurried to London in autumn 1798 to elicit British cooperation.

The scheme failed. Adams, always suspicious of British wiles, thought Miranda a "knight errant, as delirious as his immortal countryman, the ancient hero of La Manche."[60] The British, too, balked at aiding a new revolution, even one aimed at reducing French and Spanish power in the New World. Enough Anglo-American cooperation did occur during the quasi-war (British naval convoys for American merchant ships, a temporary softening of British maritime practices, cordial personal relations between Minister Rufus King and Foreign Secretary Lord Grenville) for the scholar Bradford Perkins to dub this period the "first rapprochement."[61] The point is clear, however: The Adams administration followed Washington's sage advice to avoid war with France or alliance with England.

The individual most responsible for stopping full-scale war, ironically enough, was the same Talleyrand who had initiated the crisis. Once he learned about the outraged American reaction to his bribery attempt, Talleyrand made it known throughout the summer and fall of 1798, especially through assurances to the American minister in the Netherlands, William Vans Murray, that France wanted peace. He promised Murray that any new envoy sent to make peace would "undoubtedly be received with the respect due to the representative of a free, independent, and powerful nation."[62] Adams had spoken those precise words before Congress in June 1798. To emphasize such assurances, the French repealed their decrees against American shipping and reined in their privateers.

Adams took the chance for peace. The president had received reports from his son John Quincy Adams, now American minister to Prussia, fully corroborating Murray's opinion that France was not bluffing and "a negotiation might be risked."[63] Always a solitary person, President Adams deliberated in private, shunned his cabinet, and, on February 18, 1799, sent a message to the Senate nominating William Vans Murray as minister plenipotentiary to France. Abigail Adams wrote from Massachusetts: "It comes so sudden, was a measure so unexpected, that the whole community were [*sic*] like a flock of frightened pigeons." She correctly ranked it as "a master stroke of policy."[64]

Federalist partisans, their appetites whetted for war with France, reacted mindlessly. "Had the foulest heart and the ablest head in the world, been permitted to select the most embarrassing and ruinous measure," Adams had done so, wrote one Massachusetts Federalist.[65] They threatened to block Murray's confirmation until Adams also nominated Chief Justice Oliver Ellsworth and William R. Davie of North Carolina, both Federalists, as additional plenipotentiaries. Secretary of State Pickering managed to delay departure of the three negotiators for several months. Adams eventually fired him. The president understood that his decision for peace meant political suicide, but he persisted anyway. Abigail wrote of her husband: "He has sustained the whole force of an unpopular measure which he knew would excite the passions of many, thwart the views of some, and shower down upon his head a torrent of invective."[66] Years later Adams himself declared: "I desire no other inscription over my gravestone than: 'Here lies John Adams, who took upon himself the responsibility of the peace with France in the year 1800.'"[67]

The American commissioners arrived in Paris in March 1800, and negotiations continued until the following autumn. Politics had again shifted in France. Napoleon Bonaparte had returned from Egypt, seized power in the coup d'état of 18 Brumaire, and had become first consul. Joseph Bonaparte, the future king of Spain, took charge of talks with the Americans. Although the war in Europe still raged fiercely, the new leadership had begun to think seriously of reconstituting France's empire in North America. Talleyrand won over Napoleon and told Spain that France's return to Spanish Louisiana would erect "a wall of brass forever impenetrable to the combined efforts of England and America."[68] Rebuilding the French empire required peace with Europe, and especially reconciliation with the United States. The Americans, according to Talleyrand, "will achieve a destiny we can no longer prevent, and the nation that hangs onto their friendship will be the last to retain colonies in the New World."[69] Napoleon's great victory at Marengo in June 1800 made a European settlement possible by assuring French control of territory in Italy, which Spain might accept in lieu of Louisiana. Only one day after the Franco-American Treaty of Mortefontaine was signed, the French and Spanish, on October 1, 1800, concluded secret arrangements whereby Napoleon promised Spain the Italian Kingdom of Tuscany, or its equivalent, in exchange for Louisiana. Although the American negotiators did not know about this Treaty of

San Ildefonso, the French desire for Louisiana played an important, if silent, role nonetheless in the Franco-American accord.

The Treaty of Mortefontaine, or Convention of 1800, amounted to a horse trade. The American negotiators had presented two basic demands: The French must nullify the 1778 treaties and pay some $20 million in compensation for illegal seizures of American cargoes. America, the French retorted, had itself invalidated the 1778 treaties by conceding maritime rights to the British in Jay's Treaty; thus French spoliations after 1795 were not illegal. The logjam broke when the Americans agreed to assume the claims of their own citizens, whereupon the French abrogated all previous treaties. Napoleon then suggested the insertion of a statement reaffirming American principles of neutral rights as enumerated in the Model Treaty and in the 1778 alliance. The Americans, seeing no entangling commitments, agreed. The formal signing of the treaty, on September 30, 1800, came amid much splendor and pageantry. Nearly 200 diplomats were treated to a deer hunt and huge banquet echoing with toasts to Franco-American harmony. Napoleon, that "most skillful self possest [*sic*] Fencing master," as Murray called him, was trying to lull the Americans until his plans for Louisiana jelled.[70]

The peace of Mortefontaine, followed by Thomas Jefferson's victory in the presidential election of 1800, ended the Federalist era in American diplomacy. The administrations of George Washington and John Adams, despite internal debate and external pressures, pursued a consistent foreign policy. Seeking to maintain independence and honor and to expand trade and territorial boundaries, the young republic at times seemed to veer in a pro-French direction and on other occasions tilted toward the British. At every juncture, however, Washington and Adams escaped being pulled into the European maelstrom by allying, in Adams's phrase, with "neither John Bull nor Louis Baboon."[71] Like Jay's Treaty before it, the peace of Mortefontaine avoided a war that hotheaded partisans had advocated. President Thomas Jefferson's Inaugural Address seemed to promise continuity. "We are all Federalists; we are all Republicans," he said. Slightly amending Washington's advice, the former Francophile pledged "peace, commerce, and honest friendship with all nations, entangling alliances with none."[72]

Napoleon's Ambition and Jefferson's Imperial Vision: The Louisiana Purchase

The new president showed an intense interest in American expansion westward. A few months after his inauguration Jefferson told fellow Virginian James Monroe: "However our present interests may restrain us within our limits, it is impossible not to look forward to distant times when our rapid multiplication will expand beyond those limits, & cover the whole northern if not the southern continent."[73] Jefferson primarily eyed the Mississippi Valley, but his vision also embraced the Pacific coast, the Floridas, Cuba, and a Central American canal. So long as Spain occupied America's borderlands, standing, in Henry Adams's phrase, like a "huge, helpless, and profitable whale," Jefferson advised patience.[74] The rapid expansion of the American frontier population, hungry for new land and numbering some

Thomas Jefferson (1743–1826). A Republican who in the heat of partisan politics saw his once close friendship with Federalist John Adams wounded, Jefferson became the third president, claiming that the United States was "the world's best hope." Jefferson's expansionist achievement in the Louisiana Purchase won favor with the American people, who reelected him in 1804. (Library of Congress)

900,000 inhabitants beyond the Alleghenies by 1800, would enable the United States to take over Spanish lands peacefully, "peice by peice [*sic*]."[75]

Then came rumors in summer 1801 about Spain's retrocession of Louisiana to France, along with news that England and France had made peace. Soon French ships were carrying an army to the New World, commanded by Napoleon's brother-in-law, Victor Emmanuel Leclerc, with orders to put down the black rebellion led by Toussaint L'Ouverture on Hispaniola (the island shared by Haiti and Santo Domingo in the Caribbean) and then, presumably, to occupy New Orleans, Louisiana, and perhaps the Floridas as well. Because he feared a slave rebellion, Jefferson initially encouraged the French "to reduce Toussaint," but the president grew alarmed at the size of French forces and then realized that "St. Domingo delays their taking possession of Louisiana."[76] With Spain no longer controlling the Mississippi, Pinckney's Treaty would become obsolete. Even if the French did not encroach on American territory, their control of New Orleans and commerce on the Mississippi might provoke western farmers either to wage war or secede from the Union. As Madison put it: "The Mississippi is to them [the westerners] everything. It is the Hudson, the Delaware, the Potomac and all the navigable rivers of the Atlantic States formed into one stream."[77] Jefferson seemed willing to consider a veritable revolution in American foreign policy. In a letter of April 1802 to Minister Robert Livingston in Paris, Jefferson warned that the day France took possession of New Orleans "we must marry ourselves to the British fleet and nation."[78] Although the president made sure that the warning became public knowledge in France, he did not directly approach the British.

The threatened Anglo-American alliance made little impact on France during 1802. Talleyrand baldly denied the existence of a retrocession treaty for several months (the Spanish king did not actually sign the order of transfer until October 1802), and then he refused to consider Livingston's offer to purchase New Orleans and West Florida. Napoleon, bent on reviving a grand French empire in America, redoubled his efforts to acquire the Floridas from Spain.

On October 16, 1802, the Spanish intendant of Louisiana suddenly withdrew the American right of deposit at New Orleans, in direct violation of Pinckney's Treaty. Most Americans suspected Napoleon's hand in the plot. The riflemen of Tennessee and Kentucky talked of seizing New Orleans before the French could take formal possession. Some Federalists suddenly found themselves supporting the West and urging war to embarrass Jefferson. Alexander Hamilton exhorted the administration "to seize at once on the Floridas and New Orleans, and then negotiate."[79] To calm the growing clamor and buy time for diplomacy, Jefferson, in January 1803, nominated James Monroe as special envoy to France and Spain, empowered to assist Livingston in purchasing New Orleans and Florida for $10 million. As the French minister reported to Talleyrand, the former governor of Virginia had "*carte blanche*" and would go to London if "badly received in Paris."[80] Congress provided additional diplomatic muscle by authorizing the president to call some 80,000 militia members into federal service. "If Mr. Monroe . . . should fail, we shall have noise, bustle, & Bloodshed," predicted army general James Wilkinson.[81] Monroe finally arrived in Paris on April 12, 1803. The previous day Talleyrand had astonished Robert Livingston by offering to sell all of Louisiana to the United States for $15 million.

New Orleans, 1803. The American eagle spreads its wings over the port of New Orleans at the mouth of the Mississippi River—a prize acquisition in the Louisiana Purchase. (Boqueto de Woieseri, *A View of New Orleans Taken from the Plantation of Marigny—November 1803,* oil on canvas, 58 1/2" x 7'6 1/2", 1803 [1932.18] Chicago Historical Society.)

Why did Napoleon sell Louisiana? The French failure in Haiti loomed large, an especially distressing defeat for Napoleon as Leclerc's 30,000-man army melted away, victim of guerrilla attacks and yellow fever. When Bonaparte learned in January that his brother-in-law had also succumbed to fever, he burst out: "Damn sugar, damn coffee, damn colonies."[82] In Napoleon's scheme of empire, he intended Louisiana as the source of supply for the sugar and coffee plantations of Haiti, but without Haiti, Louisiana became a liability. In the event of war, England could easily overrun Louisiana, and Napoleon was already thinking of war. In the historian Marshall Smelser's words, Napoleon "wished to get back to his glorious drums and trumpets, his drilling and killing of the fittest youth in Europe."[83] The sale price would fill French coffers in preparation for the next campaigns and at the same time eliminate American hostility.

The negotiations did not take long. "They ask of me a town . . . and I give them an empire," said Napoleon.[84] Monroe and Livingston had no compunction about violating their instructions; instead of paying $10 million for New Orleans, they pledged $15 million for New Orleans and an undefined empire that lay to the west of the Mississippi, including 50,000 new citizens of French-Spanish descent and about 150,000 Indians. The treaty, signed on April 30, 1803, stipulated that the United States received Louisiana on the same terms that Spain had retroceded the territory to France. Livingston, wondering if any of West Florida came with the purchase, asked Talleyrand what the precise boundaries were. The Frenchman replied vaguely, "You have made a noble bargain for yourselves, and I suppose you will make the most of it."[85] This enigmatic remark provided the basis for future

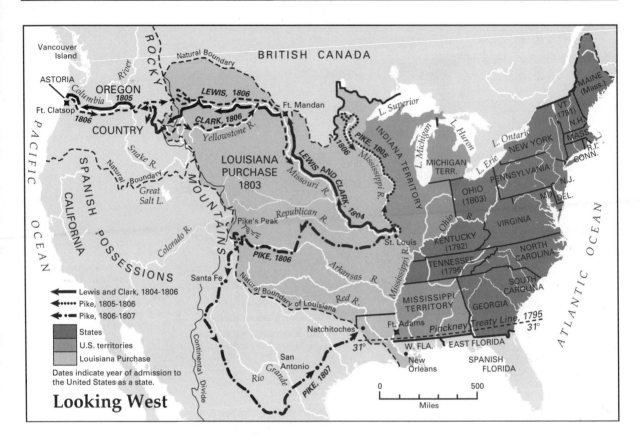

Looking West

Lewis and Clark, 1804-1806
Pike, 1805-1806
Pike, 1806-1807

States
U.S. territories
Louisiana Purchase

Dates indicate year of admission to the United States as a state.

American claims to Spanish territory in Florida and Texas. In fact, acquiring some 828,000 square miles of territory at three cents an acre seemed an enormous achievement. Livingston observed, "from this day the United States take their place among the powers of the first rank."[86] Bonaparte remarked: "This accession of territory affirms forever the power of the United States, and I have just given England a maritime rival that sooner or later will lay low her pride."[87]

The Senate still had to approve and ratify the treaty. Some Federalists, thinking that the addition of trans-Mississippi lands would tip the political balance toward agrarians, attacked the treaty. "We are to give money of which we have too little for land of which we already have too much," protested one Bostonian.[88] Another question, particularly bothersome to Federalist senator John Quincy Adams, asked whether the Constitution, under the treaty power, permitted the incorporation of 50,000 Creoles into the Union without their consent. The president, however, shedding his reputation as a strict constitutionalist, told Madison, "that the less we say about constitutional difficulties respecting Louisiana the better, and that what is necessary for surmounting them must be done sub silentio."[89] With the support of such prominent Federalists as Alexander Hamilton, Rufus King, and John Adams, the purchase passed the Senate 24 to 7 in October. The formal transfer of territory came at noon on December 20, 1803, in the Place d'Armée in New

Orleans. As the French flag fluttered down and the Stars and Stripes climbed upward, the United States officially doubled its territorial domain.

The Spanish borderlands continued to attract American diplomatic interest for the next several years. Claiming that Louisiana included West Florida, Jefferson sent troops in 1804 to the border area where American residents greatly outnumbered Spaniards and French. Only when persuaded that military action would "appear unjustifiable in the opinion of mankind and even of America" did the president back away from war.[90] He obtained $2 million from Congress to facilitate the possible purchase of Florida in 1806, despite one senator's querulous wail: "What next . . . why all the Globe—why this rage—Have we an inhabitant for every acre?"[91]

Although the maritime crisis with England soon forced Jefferson to defer expansion, other Americans probed the Spanish empire. In 1806–1807 an American military officer, Lieutenant Zebulon M. Pike, led a cartographic expedition up the Arkansas River into Spanish territory, failed to climb the mountain peak that bears his name, and was temporarily detained by Spanish troops for violating Spanish sovereignty. Impressed with the self-reliant inhabitants of New Mexico ("the bravest and most hardy subjects in New Spain"), Pike published an account of his travels that extolled the furs, precious minerals, and commercial attractions of Spanish settlements, thus envisioning what became the Sante Fe Trail in the 1820s.[92] At this time, too, Aaron Burr and sixty followers went down the Mississippi on flatboats, ostensibly to capture Texas from the Spanish, but more likely to set Burr up as the emperor of a secessionist Louisiana. Whatever the purpose of Burr's conspiracy, Jefferson had his former vice president arrested and took special care to keep the peace with Spain.

The most enduring example of Jefferson's "happy ability to combine an intense and lively scientific curiosity with political and national economic purposes" was his sponsorship of the Lewis and Clark Expedition (May 14, 1804–September 23, 1806).[93] Conceived by Jefferson even before he considered the acquisition of Louisiana, the trek was intended to find a useful route to the Pacific, to map the region, to study geography, and to develop fur trade with the Indians. Leaving St. Louis, the "Corps of Discovery" went up the Missouri, crossed the Continental Divide, and followed the Snake and Columbia rivers to the Pacific (Seaside, Oregon, today claims the "end of the trail"). Lewis and Clark returned along the same route, reaching St. Louis in September 1806. This epic exploration, which Jefferson took pains to publicize, helped the United States lay claim to lands in future negotiating, stimulated interest in the rich furs and abundant fauna of the Rocky Mountains, and suggested wrongly that the Missouri-Columbia route formed a convenient waterway for trade with China. Meriwether Lewis and William Clark became "the vanguard for an expanding intellectual frontier . . . engaged in a momentous contest for empires of the mind and flag, trading post and lodge."[94] John Jacob Astor chartered his American Fur Company in 1808, and with Jefferson's encouragement, Astor projected a line of fortified posts from St. Louis to the Pacific. Only Astoria, at the mouth of the Columbia River, was completed by the outbreak of war in 1812.

The acquisition of continental empire also planted "the seeds of extinction" for Indian culture because Jefferson wanted the Native Americans "either [to] incorporate with us as citizens . . . or remove beyond the Mississippi." If they insisted on

Stephen Decatur (1779–1820) Battles Muslims.   This popular engraving shows two American heroes and two Muslim enemies during the Barbary War of 1804. Stephen Decatur aims his pistol at a Tripolitan officer who had just killed his brother. An American sailor is shielding Decatur from a Muslim sailor about to slash Decatur with his sword. According to the historian Robert J. Allison, this engraving reflects the negative cultural images Americans had of the Muslim world in the eighteenth and nineteenth centuries—"where honest commerce was perverted into piracy by avaricious deys and pashas" and "women were debased in harems and seraglios, the victims of unrestrained sexual power." (U.S. Naval History Center)

"a sanctimonious reverence for the customs of their ancestors," he would banish the unassimilated to the trans–Mississippi region until white settlement overflowed those territories.[95] Jefferson's imperial vision embraced a pastoral society that was "distinctly egalitarian, democratic, and noncapitalist, avoiding both the savagery of the wilderness and the inevitable taint of the city."[96] He anticipated a loose confederation of possibly two republics, divided at the Mississippi, sharing a common language and tradition, shutting out Britain, Spain, and Native Americans. "The future inhabitants of the Atlantic and Mississippi States will be our sons," he wrote.[97] As one biographer puts it, Jefferson viewed western empire as "a self-renewing engine that drove the American republic forward." Indeed, he thought of the West much as "modern optimists think of technology, as almost endlessly renewable and boundlessly prolific," a "fountain of youth" that made "republicanism immune to the national aging process, at least for the remainder of the century."[98] Although a growing crisis with England soon interrupted his efforts at territorial expansion, his optimism remained undimmed. Shortly after leaving the White House in 1809, he prophesied "such an empire for liberty as she has never surveyed since the creation."[99]

If Jefferson sought to expand American institutions on land, he also wanted to protect American commerce on the high seas and repudiate any notion that "our government is entirely in Quaker principles and will turn the left cheek when the right has been smitten."[100] Jefferson eagerly employed the American navy in the Mediterranean to protect trade against the depredations of the Barbary states—Algiers, Tripoli, Tunis, and Morocco—which practiced piracy. The war with Tripoli lasted for years. A squadron consisting of the flagship *Constitution,* the frigate *Philadelphia,* and smaller vessels performed erratically but creditably under the com-

Building the Frigate *Philadelphia*.   Many Americans made their living from the sea. When foreign warships threatened their lucrative commerce, as in the 1790s and early 1800s, they prepared themselves for naval warfare. The citizens of Philadelphia raised the funds for the building of this American warship, launched in 1799. In a fall 1803 action against Tripoli on the Barbary coast, the ship fell into enemy hands. Later, in February 1804, a U.S. raiding party burned the vessel in Tripoli harbor. Other "gifts from seaport cities," as the historian G. Terry Sharrer has put it, went on to battle the British in the War of 1812. (Library of Congress)

mand of the feisty Commodore Edward Preble and his successor in the Mediterranean, Commodore Samuel Barron. In October 1803 the *Philadelphia* ran aground while chasing pirates outside the harbor of Tripoli. The captain of the ill-fated ship surrendered. "Would to God," fumed Preble, "that the Officers and crew of the *Philadelphia,* had one and all, determined to prefer death to slavery."[101] A few months later, Lieutenant Stephen Decatur heroically slipped into Tripoli harbor and burned the American frigate. In summer 1804 Preble's guns began to bombard the walled city, and in early 1805 a contingent of seven U.S. marines and 400 soldiers of fortune of various nationalities, led by Consul William Eaton, marched from Egypt across the Libyan desert and captured the port of Derna on the shores of Tripoli. The pasha of Tripoli cut a deal on June 10, 1805: He released the American prisoners for $60,000 in ransom. The extended encounter with the Barbary states disgusted most Americans, especially Eaton, who expressed astonishment that the sultan of Tunis, despite his harem of beautiful wives, preferred a "lusty Turk of thirty-three" as his lover, behavior which made "the most *depraved* of nature's children blush."[102] The prevailing American negative picture of the Muslim world, as conveyed by captivity narratives, poems, and other contemporary writings, emphasized the political and moral depravity of despotic Oriental power, "an inverted image of the world the Americans were trying to create anew," as one historian has put it. [103]

Americans had to wait until after the War of 1812 when two navy squadrons finally put an end to Barbary piracy. Nonetheless, Jefferson's vigorous defense of American rights in the Mediterranean helped set the United States on a course of projecting its naval presence throughout the world.

European Madhouse: Blockades, Neutral Trade, and Impressment, 1803–1807

Some two weeks after selling Louisiana to the Americans in spring 1803, Napoleon picked a quarrel with England over the island of Malta. War raged for twelve years, spreading over much of the world and ending only with the Congress of Vienna (September 1814–June 1815) and Bonaparte's lonely exile to St. Helena in the south Atlantic. The war transformed the United States into the world's largest neutral carrier. American shipping expanded at a rate of 70,000 tons annually, particularly between French and Spanish ports in the West Indies and French and Spanish ports on the European continent. Because such direct trade violated Britain's arbitrary Rule of 1756 (which decreed that trade not open to a nation in time of peace could not be opened in time of war), American merchants usually "broke" the voyage by stopping at a U.S. port and paying duties on the cargo, thus converting it to "free goods." The voyage would then continue until the "neutralized cargo" reached France or Spain. While direct American exports amounted to a steady $42 million annually in 1803–1805, the lucrative reexport trade soared from $13 million in 1803 to $36 million in 1804 to $53 million in 1805. A British diplomat angrily denounced the Americans, complaining that "there is not, thanks to our Tars, a single French or Spanish merchantman that now navigates these seas—& these Jews want to navigate for them."[104]

"John Bull Taking a Lunch." The Englishman enjoys a French warship for lunch. In a study of Republican rhetoric in 1811–1812, the scholars Ronald L. Hatzenbuehler and Robert L. Ivie have shown that congressional "war hawks" projected a diabolic image of John Bull, depicting the covetous British "trampling on America's rights and wresting independence from its citizens in order to sate a bestial appetite for control of world commerce." (Library of Congress)

For more than two years neither the British nor the French interfered seriously with American commerce. Indeed, British Admiralty courts, in the case of the American ship *Polly* (1800), had not disputed the legality of the "broken voyage." But on October 21, 1805, Lord Horatio Nelson's thick-hulled ships smashed the combined French and Spanish fleets off Trafalgar, thus establishing England's overwhelming control of the seas. Less than two months later Napoleon crushed the Russian and Austrian armies at Austerlitz, making him master of Europe. Neither the Tiger nor the Shark, each supreme in its own element, could fight the other directly. For the next several years commercial warfare dominated the struggle between England and France. In the ensuing web of blockades and counterblockades, America's neutral trade became inextricably ensnared.

The British decision in the *Essex* case, in May 1805, signaled trouble. British warships had captured the American merchant brig *Essex,* en route to Havana, Cuba, from Barcelona, after it had stopped (the "break" in the voyage) in Salem, Massachusetts. The British Admiralty judge reversed the *Polly* decision, claiming that the *Essex* had not paid bona fide duties on its cargo. Thereafter American shippers had to prove that importation of enemy goods into the United States was in good faith, not merely a legal subterfuge to bypass the Rule of 1756. Under the new doctrine of the "continuous" voyage, trade carried by a neutral between a belligerent colonial port and home port violated British maritime regulations. Soon British cruisers lurked outside American harbors, practically blockading the coastline.

The British followed up the *Essex* decision with an order in council of May 1806 calling for a complete blockade of Napoleonic Europe, from Brest to the Elbe River. Americans angrily denounced this declaration as a "paper blockade" because British cruisers ranged far out to sea and did not actually deny access to enemy ports. Napoleon, "fleetless but well supplied with parchment and sealing wax," retaliated in November with his Berlin Decree, which created a paper blockade of the British Isles.[105] The decree declared that any ship that had previously touched at a British port was a lawful prize and its cargo forfeit. The London government struck back with two more orders in council (January and November 1807), barring all trade with ports under French jurisdiction unless that shipping first passed through a system of British controls and taxes. England was in essence telling neutrals that they could trade with the continent of Europe only if they paid tribute first. Napoleon retaliated again, this time in the Milan Decree of December, which stated that any ship that paid taxes to the British, submitted to visit and search by British cruisers, or stopped at a British port, would be treated, ipso facto, as a British ship.

The French emperor was erecting what he called his "Continental System," a gigantic attempt to ruin England's export trade by closing off all European outlets. The Continental System never became fully effective, as Spain, Sweden, and Russia opened their ports to British goods at various intervals after 1807. John Quincy Adams likened the system to excluding "air from a bottle, by sealing up hermetically the mouth, while there was a great hole in the side."[106] Caught between French decrees and British orders in council, Yankee traders ran the risk of British seizure if they traded directly with French-controlled ports, whereas they incurred Napoleonic displeasure if they first submitted to British trade regulations.

"I consider Europe as a great mad-house," Jefferson lamented, "& in the present deranged state of their moral faculties to be pitied & avoided."[107] In the diplomatic protests that followed, American efforts aimed more at England than at France, because British maritime practices (particularly British warships operating in U.S. waters) more directly jeopardized American commerce. The British, so absorbed in the life-or-death struggle against Napoleon, hardly acted humbly or apologetically toward Washington. French seizures, although numerous, usually occurred in French ports and in the Caribbean and were often shrouded in official verbiage that smacked of misunderstanding and promised rectification. With the Americans, Napoleon was tricky and evasive but seldom arrogant.

Impressment, which rose to alarming proportions after 1803, and which exploded as an issue in the *Chesapeake* affair, helped focus resentment on England rather than France. With American shipping expanding rapidly, and with service on a British naval vessel resembling prison life, English seamen in increasing numbers jumped ship, took advantage of liberal American naturalization laws, and then enlisted in the American merchant marine. To cite one example, the vessel carrying the new British minister Anthony Merry to America in the autumn of 1803 lost fourteen men to desertion when the ship touched port. By 1812, according to official British claims, some 20,000 English sailors were manning American vessels, approximately one-half of all able-bodied seamen in the merchant marine. Since the Royal Navy required 10,000 new recruits annually to maintain full strength, the need to impress British deserters from American service became urgent. In carrying out impressment, however, British captains, "resorted to the scoop rather than the tweezers," and soon naturalized Americans by the hundreds were manning Royal Navy yardarms.[108] Altogether, according to James Monroe's figures in 1812, some 6,257 Americans suffered impressment after 1803, probably a more accurate estimate than the 1,600 conceded by the British.

The British could not accept any abridgment of a practice that they saw as vital to maritime supremacy. Americans admitted the British right to search for contraband or enemy personnel, but denied that this right justified the impressment of American citizens. "That an officer from a foreign ship," wrote Secretary of State James Madison in 1807, "should pronounce any person he pleased, on board an American ship on the high seas, not to be an American Citizen, but a British subject, & carry his interested decision . . . into execution on the spot . . . is anomalous in principle, . . . grievous in practice, and . . . abominable in abuse."[109]

Jefferson and Madison missed an opportunity to alleviate some of the controversy when they rejected the Monroe-Pinkney Treaty of December 1806. Jefferson had sent William Pinkney, an able Maryland lawyer, to join James Monroe in London in an attempt, similar to the Jay mission of 1794, to settle outstanding differences with England, including impressment and "broken" voyages, but any treaty had to contain an explicit British disavowal of impressment. The British would make concessions on broken voyages and the reexport trade, but not on impressment. The most London would concede was a separate note, attached to the final treaty, promising "observance of the greatest caution in the impressing of British seamen; . . . the strictest care . . . to preserve the citizens of the United States from any molestation or injury; and . . . immediate and prompt redress . . . of injury sustained by them."[110] The British clearly promised to mitigate in practice what they would not surrender in principle. Mindful of growing anti-American sentiment in England, and fearful of repercussions from Napoleon's recent Berlin Decree, Pinkney and Monroe opted for an accord that would give Americans more commercial benefits than they had enjoyed under the expiring Jay's Treaty.

Their treaty, signed on December 31, 1806, amounted to probably the best bargain that the United States could have extracted from England during the Napoleonic wars. Still, Jefferson refused to submit it to the Senate. He and Madison believed that the passage of time, plus the threat of American economic retaliation, would force the British to reconsider. Like John Adams in the Model Treaty of 1776, Jefferson and Madison thought that the attractions of American commerce, not to mention the rightness of American principles, would cause England to mend its ways. In the historian Robert Rutland's phrase, they were "old-fashioned men still dreaming that Hobbes was wrong and Locke was right."[111]

"Peaceable Coercions" and the Path to the War of 1812

Anglo-American relations deteriorated steadily following the abortive Monroe-Pinkney Treaty. The *Chesapeake* episode of June 1807 underscored the volatile nature of the impressment issue. "Never since the battle of Lexington," Jefferson wrote in July, "have I seen this country in such a state of exasperation as at present."[112] The president contemplated asking Congress for a declaration of war, but, owing partly to the country's lack of military and naval muscle, he sought another alternative. As he once put it, "those peaceable coercions which are in the power of every nation, if undertaken in concert & in time of peace, are more likely to produce the desired effect."[113] Congress passed the Embargo Act on December 22. One historian has described the legislation as "the greatest of all efforts to capitalize on the value of the American economy and to bend the Europeans by the policy of giving or withholding favor."[114] London did not flinch.

Evenhanded in principle, the embargo, in combination with a nonimportation measure against England, primarily targeted the British. The embargo banned the export of American goods anywhere, by sea or land, although coastal American trade continued with increasingly elaborate controls. Recorded American exports dropped 80 percent in 1808. American imports from Britain, not strictly enforced under the nonimportation act, decreased by 56 percent. The embargo effectively "stimulated manufactures, injured agriculture, and prostrated commerce."[115]

Domestic protest arose loud and shrill. John Randolph, pointing to the loss of shipping and declining agricultural prices, charged his fellow Virginians with attempting to "cure the corns by cutting off the toes."[116] Numerous vituperative epistles reached the White House, including one of August 1808: "Thomas Jefferson / You are the damdest / dog that God put life into / God Dam you."[117] Such dissent, when combined with widespread resistance to enforcement, caused Jeffersonians to despair. Albert Gallatin prefered "war itself than to display our impotence to enforce our laws."[118] According to one scholar, the embargo symbolized for Republicans what Vietnam later symbolized for the Nixon administration—"a test of both American domestic resolve and the credibility of a republican form of government."[119] In New England, where Yankee merchants and sailors had long depended on commerce for their livelihood, the economy suffered badly. Ships rotted in harbor and weeds grew on once busy wharves. Federalists accused Jefferson of conspiring with Napoleon in initiating the embargo, and the winter of 1808–1809 brought widespread rumors of secessionist conversations between New Englanders and British agents. "I did not expect a crop of so sudden and rank growth of fraud," wrote Jefferson, urging Congress to "legalize *all* means which may be necessary to obtain *its end*."[120] Despite the president's preference for war against England, his followers decided otherwise. On March 1, 1809, three days before Jefferson left the presidency, Congress replaced the embargo with the Non-Intercourse Act, thus freeing American exports to all ports except those controlled by England and France, and promising renewed trade with either belligerent if it respected American neutral rights.

Jefferson's embargo failed to deliver the desired diplomatic effect. The British government at first welcomed the measure, inasmuch as it removed quarrels over neutral rights and gave British shippers a virtual monopoly over trade with Europe. Nonimportation limited trade with Britain, but alternative markets for British goods conveniently appeared in Spain (which revolted against Napoleonic rule in 1808) and Spain's Latin American colonies. The French continued to seize American ships, even those that evaded the British blockade, using the argument that such ships had to be British in disguise because American law prohibited their presence on the high seas. Rising food prices in England, plus the decline of manufacturing sales, might have tempted the British to appease their best trading partner if the embargo had lasted longer. Actually, the rising prices had attracted the most American violators in the last months of the embargo. The historian Burton Spivak has concluded that "it was the winter evasions and not the March repeal that spoiled [Jefferson's] dream."[121]

The embargo also exacerbated sectional and party differences over foreign policy. New England Federalists argued that, absent the embargo, they could freely trade with other parts of the world where British restrictions did not apply. The embargo, not London, cut commercial ties with India, the East Indies, South America, and the Mediterranean. Southern planters, however, saw their prosperity dependent on selling their produce primarily in England and on the European continent. The British closing of continental markets hurt the South, and the British market itself became glutted. Tobacco and cotton prices fell below what it cost southerners to raise their crops. Thus Republicans grew more willing to support all "peaceable coercions," including the embargo, to force British concessions, and Federalists became more opposed to all restrictions on trade.

A face-saving substitute, nonintercourse actually favored the British more than the French. American ships could clear port ostensibly for a neutral destination such as Sweden but illegally take their cargo to Halifax in British Canada; vessels heading for French-controlled ports still had to face British blockade ships. The new president, James Madison, nonetheless hoped to use nonintercourse to modify British policy. He found a willing collaborator in British minister David M. Erskine. Married to an American, Erskine was the only British envoy in the early national period who developed cordial personal relations with his American hosts. When he came to Washington in 1806, he wanted very much to avoid war with America and, at Madison's urging, Erskine recommended repeal of the orders in council, provided that the United States keep nonintercourse against France. In April, Madison issued a proclamation lifting nonintercourse against Britain on June 10, the date that England, according to the Erskine agreement, would repeal its orders in council. More than 600 American vessels laden with two years' accumulation of goods promptly set sail for British ports. Huzzas echoed from Maine to Georgia.

The joy soon whimpered away. Foreign Secretary Canning repudiated the agreement and the "damned Scotch flunkey" who had negotiated it, for the foreign secretary had ordered Erskine to demand approval for the Royal Navy to seize American ships that violated the Non-Intercourse Act.[122] Canning, of course, allowed American ships still at sea to bring supplies to England. News of repudiation stunned Americans and angered Madison, who termed it a "mixture of fraud and folly."[123] The president quickly renewed nonintercourse, but the damage had been done. "We are not so well prepared for resistance as we were one year ago," Gallatin reported. "[Then] all or almost all our mercantile wealth was safe at home, our resources entire, and our finances sufficient. . . . Our property is now afloat; England relieved by our relaxations might stand two years of privations with ease; we have wasted our resources without any national unity."[124]

Canning aggravated matters further by replacing Erskine with Francis James ("Copenhagen") Jackson, a notorious diplomat whose mission to Denmark in 1807 had consisted of a brutal ultimatum followed by the British fleet's destruction of the Danish capital.[125] Jackson's instructions, in Henry Adams's phrase, were "to propose nothing whatever."[126] The bumptious Briton managed to offend almost everyone in Washington, and diplomacy went nowhere. "God damn Mr. Jackson," shouted one Kentuckian, "the President ought to . . . have him kicked from town to town until he is kicked out of the country. God damn him."[127] Madison finally declared Jackson persona non grata; London recalled him in April 1810, and a replacement did not arrive for nearly two years.

The Non-Intercourse Act expired in the spring of 1810. A complicated piece of legislation known as Macon's Bill Number Two replaced it. The new law ostensibly removed all restrictions on American commerce, including trade with England and France; it also empowered the president to renew nonintercourse against one belligerent if the other gave up its punitive decrees. Madison noted that "public attention is beginning to fix itself on the proof . . . that the original sin agst. Neutrals lies with G.B. & that whilst she acknowledges it, she persists in it."[128] Now came an opportunity for Napoleon. Without actually stopping the seizure of American ships, he promised repeal of the Berlin and Milan decrees against American commerce, provided only that the United States "shall cause their rights to be respected by the English."[129] The French pledged to lift their decrees on November 1, 1810. Whether or not Madison was trying to outfox Napoleon is a matter of scholarly debate, but the president assumed that the French promises were genuine. On November 2, 1810, without adequate proof that Napoleon had freed American shipping (he had not), the president proclaimed nonintercourse against Britain.

The British, quite understandably, refused to be blackmailed into lifting their blockade while Napoleon pretended to revoke his decrees. Not only did the British not repeal their orders in council, they enforced them even more vigorously. (Altogether the French confiscated 558 American vessels in the period 1803–1812, compared with 917 British seizures. In the years 1811–1812, however, French confiscations dwindled to a mere 34.) "The United States," wrote the new secretary of state, James Monroe, "cannot allow Great Britain to regulate their trade, nor can they be content with a trade to Great Britain only. . . . The United States are,

Tecumseh (1768–1813).
The Shawnee chief and his brother the Prophet sought but failed to block white expansion into Indian territory by forming a confederacy. During the War of 1812, Tecumseh joined the British army along the Canadian border. He died at the Battle of the Thames. (Library of Congress)

therefore, reduced to the dilemma either of abandoning their commerce, or of resorting to other means more likely to obtain a respect for their rights."[130]

Disputes with Native Americans on the frontier also contributed to Anglo-American animosities. Beginning in 1806 two remarkable Shawnees, Tecumseh and the Prophet, took advantage of a nativist religious revival to organize a Pan-Indian movement against further white expansion. When the U.S. government purchased 2.5 million acres of land from the Delaware, Potowatomi, Miami, and Eel River Indians in the Treaty of Fort Wayne in 1809, Tecumseh claimed the sale invalid because "all the lands in the western country was [sic] the common property of all the tribes." He pointedly asked Governor William Henry Harrison: "How can we have confidence in the white people when Jesus Christ came upon earth you kill'd and nail'd him on a cross."[131] Frontier leaders were quick to attribute conspiratorial designs to the British in Canada, where Tecumseh's followers received food and shelter (but not guns and ammunition, as Americans alleged).

On November 7, 1811, an armed clash occurred at Tippecanoe Creek in what is now Indiana. U.S. forces under Harrison barely defeated a superior Indian concentration. Americans simply assumed that the British were stirring up the tribes, which in fact they were not doing. In Congress and in the West people talked of taking Canada. As member of Congress from Kentucky Henry Clay put it: "Is it nothing to us to extinguish the torch that lights up savage warfare?"[132]

The United States thus moved inexorably, albeit haltingly, toward war in the winter and spring of 1812, not knowing that economic distress was finally causing Britannia to alter course. Beginning in autumn 1810, a depression hit the British, accompanied by poor harvests, unemployment, higher taxes, higher prices, and bread riots. British exports to the continent of Europe dropped by one-third from 1809 to 1811, and exports to the United States dropped by seven-eighths. Manufacturing interests began to put pressure on Parliament. On June 16, 1812, Britain scrapped the orders in council. Two days later, however, without knowing of this significant action, Congress declared war against England.

In All the Tenses: Why War Came

The close vote for war (79 to 49 in the House, 19 to 13 in the Senate) prompted one representative to exclaim: "The suspense we are in is worse than hell!!!"[133] Only 61 percent of voting senators and members of the House supported war, with most members from Pennsylvania and the South and West voting aye and most from the North and East voting nay. The vote followed partisan lines—81 percent of Republicans in both houses voted for war (98 to 23), and all Federalists voted nay (39 to 0).

Scholars have noted that had speedier transatlantic communications existed in 1812, war might have been prevented. True enough. But it does not follow that Americans went to war for imaginary, and therefore frivolous, reasons. The causes of the War of 1812 were numerous and compelling, and Madison gave a reasonably accurate listing in his war message of June 1. The president placed impressment first, spotlighting those hundreds of Americans "dragged on board ships of war of a foreign nation and exposed, under the severities of their discipline, to be exiled to the most distant and deadly climes, to risk their lives in the battles of their oppressors." Second, Madison mentioned British depradations against American commerce within sight of U.S. harbors, as well as "pretended blockades" that disregarded international law. Third, he charged that Britain's orders in council waged war on American trade in order to maintain "the monopoly which she covets for her own commerce and navigation." And last, Madison blamed the English for igniting "the warfare just renewed by the savages on one of our extensive frontiers."[134] Privately, without the need for presidential embellishment, Madison noted that Britain's conduct left the United States "no choice but between that [war] & the greater evil of a surrender of our sovereignty."[135]

Historians have speculated about the seeming contradiction between Madison's emphasis on maritime causes and the fact that a majority of war votes came from the agrarian South and West, not from the commercially minded Northeast. Part of the apparent paradox can be explained by noting economic self-interest: the West and South were wracked by depression in 1812; eastern merchants, even with British and French depradations, were still making profits. Jeffersonian farmers and people of the frontier, many dependent on the export trade, blamed falling agricultural prices on the British blockade. As John C. Calhoun of South Carolina argued: "They are not prepared for the colonial state to which again that Power is endeavoring to reduce us."[136]

Some scholars, echoing John Randolph's charge that the "war hawks" trumpeted a "whip-poor-will cry" for Canada, have listed land hunger or a desire for territorial expansion as major causes of the war.[137] "War hawks" did talk of adding Canada to the American union, but what "seemed territorial expansion," the historian Reginald Stuart has claimed, "actually arose from a defensive mentality, not from ambitions for conquest and annexation."[138] Westerners focused on Canada in part because of their belief that England was stirring up the Indians north of the Ohio River and because Canada was the only place to retaliate against British maritime practices. Matthew Clay of Virginia proclaimed, "We have the Canadas as much under our command as she [Great Britain] has the ocean; and the way to conquer her on the ocean is to drive her from our land."[139] Others urged an invasion of Canada because it had developed as an alternative source of supplies for the West Indies and as a mecca for American smugglers. Indeed, as the historian J. C. A. Stagg has emphasized, Canada had "the potential to destroy the very basis of Madison's diplomacy of commercial restriction: his assumption that the British empire was dependent on the United States for 'necessaries.'"[140]

National honor served as another unifying force for war. Commercial coercion had not worked. In the historian Norman Risjord's words, "submission to the orders in council presaged a return to colonial status; war seemed the only alternative."[141] The real issue, wrote one Virginian in 1812, "went beyond" certain rights of commerce, "it is now clearly, positively, and directly *a question of . . .* whether the U. States are an independent nation."[142] Indeed, these younger, "energized" Republicans, as the historian Steven Watts has called them, "ceased worrying whether war would corrupt the republic. Rather, they grew convinced that it *must* absorb the shock of violent conflict to prove its worth."[143]

England realized too late that the United States might actually fight. Preoccupied by the war against Napoleon and by economic dislocation and general unrest at home, the British were poorly served by Minister Augustus Foster, who fraternized too much with Federalists and did not take Madison's bellicose hints seriously. Usually inattentive to American relations anyway, British politicians became even more inward-looking at the close of 1810, when the aged George III finally went incurably insane on the death of his favorite child. Several months were taken up with political debate over the accession of the Prince Regent, who was mistakenly thought to favor repeal of the orders in council. Later, in the spring of 1812, a lunatic assassinated Prime Minister Spencer Percival, thus delaying for another month the decision to lift the orders against American shipping. These distractions notwithstanding, perceptive reporting by U.S. diplomats in England might have shown the signs that pointed to eventual repeal. The capable William Pinkney had departed England in despair in February 1811, however, and chargé d'affaires Jonathan Russell simply discounted the effect of protests and petitions on Parliament. Russell's last dispatches, which reached the United States on May 22, 1812, held out no promise that England would repeal its decrees. Not knowing that

Henry Clay (1777–1852). The powerful Kentucky politician and presidential aspirant served several terms in the House of Representatives and Senate. A "war hawk" in 1812, Clay helped negotiate the Treaty of Ghent that ended the war. As President John Quincy Adams's secretary of state (1825–1829), Clay negotiated twelve treaties to facilitate U.S. foreign trade. As expansionism and the issue of slavery in the territories threatened the Union, Clay helped compose the Compromise of 1850, which allowed California statehood without slavery and a territorial government in New Mexico without a ban on slavery. (Corcoran Gallery of Art)

Britain had repealed the orders in council, Madison made his decision for war in defense of American commerce, honor, and sovereignty.

Why did the United States not declare war against France as well? In a preliminary vote on June 12, a Federalist proposal to place France and England on the same belligerent footing just failed to pass, 17 to 15. The suspicious Federalists, citing Madison's false claim that France had repealed the Berlin and Milan Decrees, subsequently charged that the declaration of war against England was made in collusion with Napoleon. Not so. Madison and his Republican colleagues had no love for Napoleonic France. Indeed, it seemed a choice between "a ruthless tyrant, drenching Europe in blood" and "a nation of buccaneers, urged by sordid avarice."[144] Yet a triangular war seemed out of the question. "We resist the enterprises of England first," Jefferson observed, "because they first come vitally home to us."[145] French outrages occurred in European waters. British press gangs roamed just off American shores, and British officers—not French—were thought to be stirring up the Indians. The United States could deal with Napoleon *after* it captured Canada. "As to France," the hawkish Henry Clay explained, "we have no complaint . . . but of the past. Of England we have to complain in all the tenses."[146]

Madison well understood the potential advantages of cobelligerency with France. Napoleon's forces could keep the British bogged down in Spain. The French invasion of Russia, which began a week after the U.S. declaration of war, might bring about the full application of the Continental System, thus putting added pressure on Britain. American cruisers and privateers, meanwhile, could use French ports to refit and sell their prizes. American military weakness dictated this posture, reminiscent of American dependence on France during the Revolutionary War. But Madison shunned any formal alliance with France. Even in going to war with England, he tried to make the most of an independent foreign policy.

Wartime Diplomacy and the Peace of Ghent

"At the moment of the declaration of war, the President regretted the necessity which produced it, looked to its termination, and provided for it."[147] Thus did Secretary Monroe write to chargé d'affaires Russell, with instructions to seek an armistice, provided that England agreed to end impressment and revoke its orders in council. Several weeks after the American war declaration, news reached Washington of the British repeal of the orders in council. Hopes for a quick peace evaporated, however, when the British held stubbornly to their policy of impressment. "The Government could not consent to suspend the exercise of a right," Foreign Secretary Castlereagh told Russell, "upon which the naval strength of the empire mainly depends."[148] The Americans also remained stubborn about impressment. Two years of war followed.

The next hint of peace came from St. Petersburg in the winter of 1812–1813. The Russian foreign minister offered mediation to U.S. envoy John Quincy Adams, an offer that President Madison grasped eagerly. Without waiting for formal British agreement, Madison appointed Federalist James Bayard and Treasury Secretary Albert Gallatin to join Adams as peace commissioners in the Russian capital. British prime minister Lord Liverpool complained that "the Emperor of Russia is half an American." [149] In fact, Tsar Alexander's potential friendliness to the United States gained impetus from many "extremely affable chats" with Louisa Catherine Adams, whose personal popularity at the Russian court greatly facilitated her husband's formal diplomacy.[150] Not wanting to offend their powerful continental ally and alert to the mutual interest of Russia and the United States in defending neutral rights, the British, in the historian Norman Saul's phrase, avoided mediation by "prevarication."[151] The British told the Russians that they had no objection to treating directly with the Americans, but no one bothered to tell the three plenipotentiaries in St. Petersburg. Not until January 1814 did Castlereagh formally propose direct negotiations to the United States, and even then he remained imprecise as to time and place.

In North America during these months the war sputtered. Master Commandant Oliver Hazard Perry's "signal" victory on Lake Erie, the recapture of Detroit, and the death of Tecumseh in 1813 effectively "frustrated" British and Indian efforts to roll back American expansion in the Old Northwest and upper Louisiana.[152] Elsewhere U.S. forces found themselves constantly on the defensive. The conquest of Canada, contrary to Madison's expectation, was not accomplished with a single "rapier thrust."[153] American generals displayed incompetence, state militia units performed erratically, and the Canadians fought loyally under British command. The Madison administration shuddered at the prospect of British reinforcements, soon to be shipped to North America after the defeat of Napoleon. At sea the Americans fared better, with swift Yankee frigates winning several ship-to-ship duels with British men-of-war, and numerous American privateers waging war against British maritime trade. All told, the Americans captured 1,408 British prizes. But even on the oceans British supremacy began to assert itself by 1814 against the puny American navy. The British blockade remained strong, and naval convoys kept commerce destruction to a tolerable minimum. The Royal Navy showed in 1814 that it could land troops almost anywhere on American shores, and in August, the island of Nantucket actually signed a separate peace with the British. Little wonder, then, that Madison welcomed Castlereagh's offer to negotiate. The president shrewdly added Jonathan Russell and Henry Clay to the three peace commissioners already in Europe. The appointment of Clay, the loudest "war hawk" of all, was calculated to provide insurance with Congress in case the peace treaty did not obtain the war goals of 1812.

A diplomatic retreat seemed unavoidable. On June 27, 1814, just prior to the embarrassing British burning of Washington, D.C., and a few weeks before peace negotiations began in Belgium, Secretary Monroe instructed the plenipotentiaries to "omit any stipulation on the subject of impressment," if such action would facilitate a peace settlement.[154] The American peacemakers paced for six weeks in the picturesque Flemish village of Ghent in Belgium before the British delegation finally arrived in early August. Castlereagh had stalled sending his commissioners. Preoccupied by European negotiations at the "Great Congress" in Vienna (which

Castlereagh attended in person), the foreign secretary thought that news of British military successes in North America would simplify diplomacy at the "little Congress" in Ghent.[155] Meanwhile, like thoroughbred horses, the American delegates chafed and snapped at each other. The acerbic John Quincy Adams often found fault with his colleagues. Clay's predilection for poker, brandy, and cigars irritated the doughty New Englander, whose stoic regimen commenced each dawn with an hour of Bible study. Adams's icy reserve gradually melted, however, warmed by Clay's affability, Gallatin's tactful urbanity, and Bayard's good-humored patriotism. "We appear all to be animated by the same desire of *harmonizing* together," Adams wrote to his wife.[156]

The British peace proposals sorely tested American unity. By asking for the formation of a separate Indian buffer state in the Old Northwest, some adjustment in the Canadian–American boundary south of the Great Lakes, and a quid pro quo for renewing American fishing rights (which London claimed had lapsed during the war), the British nearly ended negotiations at the start. Of the Americans, only Clay, a self-proclaimed expert at "holding your hand, with a solemn and confident phiz, and outbragging" an opponent, thought the British were bluffing.[157] He proved right. After a few weeks the Indian issue gradually disappeared. The British still insisted on boundary changes, direct access to the Mississippi, and compensation for fishing privileges. John Quincy Adams experienced a sense of déjà vu. "The situation in which I am placed," he wrote to his father in Massachusetts, "often brings to mind that in which you were situated in the year 1782. . . . I am called upon to support the same interests, and in many respects, the same identical points and questions. . . . It is the boundary, the fisheries, and the Indian savages."[158]

Next came a British demand for *uti possidetis,* or peace based on the war map of the moment, meaning that the English would continue to hold eastern Maine and portions of American territory south of the Great Lakes. The Americans insisted on the 1783 boundary. News finally reached Ghent in late October that the British invasion of the Hudson Valley had been stopped dead at Plattsburgh, New York, and Americans had repelled the amphibious attack on Baltimore with the loss of one of England's best generals. Worse yet for Britain, President Madison had rallied support (even among New England Federalists) by violating diplomatic etiquette and publishing the initial British peace demands. "Mr. Madison has acted most scandalously," sniffed Lord Liverpool.[159]

Great Britain had a choice—continue the war or accept a peace without territorial gain. Castlereagh was having a difficult time in Vienna, where the Prussians were hungrily eyeing Saxony and the Russians demanding all of Poland. The British cabinet thereupon turned for advice to the Duke of Wellington, then in command of occupied and unruly Paris. The Iron Duke said that he would lead His Majesty's troops in America, if ordered, but it would be better, after the defeat at Plattsburgh, to negotiate peace on the terms *status quo ante bellum.* Lord Liverpool agreed, advising Castlereagh on November 18, 1814, to seek peace without territorial additions. European trouble once again served the American cause.

Another month of speedy negotiations settled all remaining questions. During this last phase the one serious disagreement arose among the American delegates.

The British, still hoping for a quid pro quo in return for American fishing rights, asked for access to the Mississippi River. When Adams, ever the protector of Yankee fishermen, seemed favorably disposed, Russell accused him of trying to "barter the patriotic blood of the West for blubber, and exchange ultra-Allegheny scalps for codfish."[160] Gallatin smoothed over the contretemps by suggesting that any reference to the Mississippi and the fisheries be omitted from the final treaty. The British delegation agreed. And so, on the night before Christmas 1814, in the residence of the British commissioners at Ghent, the treaty of peace was signed, reaffirming the *status quo ante bellum*. "I hope," said Adams, "it will be the last treaty of peace between Great Britain and the United States."[161]

The pact was received with great rejoicing when it reached Washington. On February 11, 1815, the Senate voted approval 35 to 0, despite the fact that the treaty addressed none of the ostensible causes of the war. Partly responsible for the euphoric atmosphere was the *previous* arrival of news concerning Andrew Jackson's smashing victory over the British at New Orleans on January 8. Many Americans believed erroneously that Jackson's achievement influenced the Ghent treaty, and the Madison administration did not regret ending what had been an unpopular war in a blaze of military glory. News of Ghent and New Orleans also undermined any impact that delegates from the Hartford Convention might have had on American diplomacy. Composed of New England Federalists who opposed Madison's war against England, the Hartford Convention had sent delegates to Washington with proposals to amend the Constitution (the suggestions included a sixty-day limit on embargoes and a two-thirds vote of Congress for war). Madison snubbed the New Englanders, who slunk home in disgrace.

The Legacy of an Unwon War

The Peace of Ghent, coinciding with the end of the Napoleonic wars in Europe, marked the culmination of an important phase of American foreign relations. The United States, after 1793, had reacted to Europe's wars by trying to expand its commerce as a neutral carrier and enlarge its territory by playing on European rivalries. American diplomats sought these goals without war or European entanglements until 1812, when the accumulation of grievances against America's neutral rights and a traditional interest in territorial gains catapulted an unprepared country into a second war of independence against Great Britain. The end of that Anglo-American conflict, combined with peace in Europe, made questions of maritime rights academic. For the next thirty years or so, American relations with Europe focused mainly on the matter of territorial expansion in the Western Hemisphere. A biographer of Madison has written, "The red sea of British dead created by the fire of Jackson's men [at New Orleans] dramatically and finally underscored American possession of the Western empire."[162]

By twentieth-century standards the War of 1812 seems inexpensive—2,260 battle deaths and $158 million in direct costs, including veterans' benefits (the last veteran died in 1905, the last pensioner in 1946). Yet its consequences were large. Henry Clay thought that the country had gained "respectability and character abroad—security and confidence at home. . . . [O]ur character and Constitution are placed on a solid basis, never to be shaken."[163] Albert Gallatin offered a more balanced accounting: "The War has been productive of evil & good," he wrote, "but I think the good preponderates. . . . Under our former system we were become too selfish. . . . The people . . . are more Americans: they feel & act more as a Nation, and I hope that the permanency of the Union is thereby better secured."[164] So impressed was the French minister in Washington that he characterized the naval victories of the Americans as "a prelude to the lofty destiny to which they are called," and concluded that "the war has given the Americans what they so essentially lacked, a national character founded on a glory common to all."[165]

This sense of national confidence and glory rested partly on illusion. Jackson's heroics at New Orleans caused people to forget the burning of Washington, to forget that the war was a draw at best, hardly a spectacular success. The view arose, not easily dispelled, that "citizen soldiers" could defend against European professionals, and that frontier captains outperformed West Point graduates. Many forgot the lack of preparedness. John Quincy Adams spoke only for himself in hoping that the United States would learn "caution against commencing War without a fair prospect of attaining its objects."[166] The revulsion against the Federalists, furthermore, for their apparent lack of patriotic fervor, provided an ominous precedent for future opponents of American wars. Forgotten, too, was the probability that, with more patience on the part of the Madison administration, and less haughtiness and more attentiveness to American issues on the part of the British, the War of 1812 need never have been fought.

The naval successes of the war, if limited, had a more enduring effect, as much of the wartime navy remained in service after 1815. In the ensuing decades naval officers gained fame as advance agents of American empire. But even in naval matters Americans remembered the limits of power less than the superpatriotism of Captain Stephen Decatur's famous toast: "Our country! In her intercourse with foreign nations may she always be in the right; but our country, right or wrong."[167]

Even if the peace settled no major issues by treaty, the United States, with its population doubling every twenty-three years, profited. In Henry Adams's words, "they gained their greatest triumph in referring all their disputes to be settled by time, the final negotiator, whose decision they could safely trust."[168] However much the United States took great risks by going to war in 1812, the paradoxical effect of that war was to increase American self-confidence and to ensure European respect. The young republic still had not reached the rank of a great power by Europe's standards, but the war with England had shown that in North America the United States could not be treated like Geneva or Genoa. America's economic independence seemed achieved and its territorial integrity defended.

Native Americans in the trans-Allegheny west came to know U.S. power only too well. The unity that the Prophet and Tecumseh had worked to build collapsed when General William Henry Harrison's forces killed Tecumseh at the Battle of the Thames in 1813. In an even bloodier campaign against Pan-Indian opposition in the South in 1814, Andrew Jackson's troops turned "much of Upper Creek country into a charnel house, destroying towns, killing men, sparing some women and children but forcibly relocating them," all culminating in the "dreadful victory" at Horseshoe Bend in present-day Alabama, where some 800 Indians perished.[169] The subsequent Treaty of Fort Jackson forced the Creeks to cede two-thirds of their lands. After Castlereagh's diplomats failed to obtain an Indian buffer state at the Ghent negotiations, Native Americans could no longer rely on British protection against white encroachment. By 1817 the U.S. War Department reported that the Indians had "ceased to be an object of terror, and have become that of commiseration."[170]

The legacy of 1812 significantly influenced Anglo-American relations. Even if the British refused to revoke impressment in theory, the end of the war brought the release of hundreds of U.S. citizens from British ships and prisons. Never again would the forceful abduction of U.S. citizens on the high seas be a problem in Anglo-American relations. Engaged in a life-or-death struggle with Napoleon, Britain found the United States a tough adversary. As the Duke of Wellington recognized, Canada was useless as an offensive base and could be defended only with the greatest difficulty. Postwar British exports to America rose substantially, thus presaging a commercial interdependence that served to promote peaceful Anglo-American relations. Rivalry between the two English-speaking nations did not end in 1815, of course, and Great Britain still stood as a barrier to U.S. expansion. So did Canada. The War of 1812 gave impetus to *Canadian* nationalism, causing American expansion to move south and west rather than north. In the West, the United States would again collide with British interests. Still, after 1815, Britain chose to settle differences with the United States at the negotiating table, not on the battlefield. When the British West Indies finally opened to American trade in 1830, an aging James Madison predicted that England could "no longer . . . continue mistress of the seas" and the "Trident must pass to this hemisphere."[171] And eventually it did.

FURTHER READING FOR THE PERIOD 1789–1815

General histories include Reginald Horsman, *The Diplomacy of the New Republic, 1776–1815* (1985); Michael H. Hunt, *Ideology and U.S. Foreign Policy* (1987); Lawrence S. Kaplan, *Colonies into Nation* (1972); Ralph Ketcham, *Presidents Above Party: The First American Presidency, 1789–1829* (1984); Daniel G. Lang, *Foreign Policy in the Early Republic* (1985); Peggy Liss, *Atlantic Empires* (1983); William N. Parker, *Europe, America, and the Wider World*, vol. 2 (1991); Bradford Perkins, *The Creation of a Republican Empire, 1776–1865* (1993); Jacques Portes, ed., *Europe and America: Criss-Crossing Perspectives, 1788–1848* (1987); Marshall Smelser, *The Democratic Republic, 1801–1815* (1968); and Paul A. Varg, *Foreign Policies of the Founding Fathers* (1970) and *New England and Foreign Relations, 1784–1850* (1983).

For George Washington and 1790s issues, see William H. Adams, *The Paris Years of Thomas Jefferson* (1997); John R. Alden, *George Washington* (1984); Harry Ammon, *The Genet Mission* (1973); Joyce Appleby, *Capitalism and a New Social Order* (1984); Samuel Flagg Bemis, *Jay's Treaty* (1962) and *Pinckney's Treaty* (1960); Julian P. Boyd, *Number 7* (1964); Joseph Charles, *The Origins of the American Party System* (1956); Jerald A. Combs, *The Jay Treaty* (1970); Alexander DeConde, *Entangling Alliance* (1958); Stanley Elkins and Eric McKittrick, *The Age of Federalism* (1993); Gilbert Lycan, *Alexander Hamilton and American Foreign Policy* (1970); Conor Cruise O'Brien, *The Long Affair* (1996) (Jefferson and the French Revolution); Glenn A. Phelps, *George Washington and American Constitutionalism* (1993); Charles R. Ritcheson, *Aftermath of Revolution* (1969); James Roger Sharp, *American Politics in the Early Republic* (1993); Matthew Spalding and Patrick J. Garrity, *A Sacred Union of Citizens* (1996) (Farewell Address); and Arthur P. Whitaker, *The Spanish-American Frontier, 1783–1795* (1927).

For the Adams presidency, see Albert H. Bowman, *The Struggle for Neutrality* (1974); Ralph A. Brown, *The Presidency of John Adams* (1979); Alexander DeConde, *The Quasi-War* (1966); Joseph J. Ellis, *Passionate*

Sage (1993); Lawrence S. Kaplan, *Entangling Alliances with None* (1987); Stephen Kurtz, *The Presidency of John Adams* (1957); and William Stinchombe, *The XYZ Affair* (1981).

Jefferson and his vision of empire are studied in Lance Banning, *The Jeffersonian Persuasian* (1978); Alexander DeConde, *This Affair of Louisiana* (1976); Joseph J. Ellis, *American Sphinx* (1997); Robert M. Johnstone, Jr., *Jefferson and the Presidency* (1978); Lawrence S. Kaplan, *Thomas Jefferson* (1998); Dumas Malone, *Jefferson the President* (1970); Drew R. McCoy, *The Elusive Republic* (1980); Merrill Peterson, *Thomas Jefferson and the New Nation* (1970); Norman K. Risjord, *Thomas Jefferson* (1994); Malcolm J. Rohrbough, *The Trans-Appalachian Frontier* (1978); Robert W. Tucker and David C. Henrickson, *Empire of Liberty* (1990); and Arthur P. Whitaker, *The Mississippi Question, 1795–1803* (1934).

Studies of the Lewis and Clark Expedition include John L. Allen, *Passage Through the Garden* (1975); Stephen E. Ambrose, *Undaunted Courage* (1996); Gunther Barth, ed., *The Lewis and Clark Expedition*(1998); and David Lavender, *The Way to the Western Sea* (1988).

The foreign-policy ideas and record of James Madison are treated in Irving Brant, *James Madison* (1941–1961); Ralph Ketchum, *James Madison* (1971); and Robert A. Rutland, *James Madison* (1987) and *The Presidency of James Madison*(1990).

Issues leading to the War of 1812 are traced in Roger Brown, *The Republic in Peril: 1812* (1934); Clifford L. Egan, *Neither Peace nor War: Franco-American Relations, 1803–1812* (1983); Richard J. Ellings, *Embargoes and World Power* (1985); Ronald L. Hatzenbuehler and Robert L. Ivie, *Congress Declares War* (1983); Reginald Horsman, *The Causes of the War of 1812* (1962); Julius Pratt, *Expansionists of 1812* (1925); Bradford Perkins, *The First Rapprochement* (1955) and *Prologue to War* (1961); Burton Spivak, *Jefferson's English Crisis* (1979); J. C. A. Stagg, *Mr. Madison's War* (1983); Spencer C. Tucker and Frank T. Reuter, *Injured Honor* (1996) (*Chesapeake-Leopard*); Steven Watts, *The Republic Reborn: War and the Making of a Liberal America, 1790–1820* (1987); and J. Leitch Wright, Jr., *Britain and the American Frontier, 1783–1815* (1975).

For wartime questions and Ghent peacemaking, see James Banner, *To the Hartford Convention* (1970); Pierre Berton, *The Invasion of Canada, 1812–1813* (1980); Harrison Bird, *War for the West, 1790–1813* (1971); Fred L. Engleman, *The Peace of Christmas Eve* (1962); Kenneth J. Hagan, *This People's Navy* (1991); Donald R. Hickey, *The War of 1812* (1989); Bradford Perkins, *Castlereagh and Adams* (1964); and Patrick C. T. White, *A Nation on Trial* (1965).

For aspects of expansionism, see Robert J. Allison, *The Crescent Obscured: The United States and the Muslim World, 1776–1815* (1995); James C. Bradford, ed., *Command Under Sail* (1985); Jonathan Goldstein, *Philadelphia and the China Trade, 1682–1846* (1978); David F. Long, *Nothing Too Daring: A Biography of Commodore David Porter, 1780–1843* (1970); Frank L. Owsley, Jr., and Gene A. Smith, *Filibusters and Expansionists* (1997); James P. Ronda, *Astoria and Empire* (1990); Henry Savage, Jr., *Discovering America, 1700–1875* (1979); and Reginald C. Stuart, *United States Expansionism and British North America, 1775–1871* (1988).

Borderlands isues and relations with Native Americans are discussed in John F. Bannon, *The Spanish Borderlands Frontier* (1970); Gregory Evans Dowd, *A Spirited Resistance* (1992); Dorothy V. Jones, *License for Empire* (1982); James E. Lewis, Jr., *The American Union and the Problem of Neighborhood* (1998) (U.S.–Spain); John Sugden, *Tecumseh* (1998); and David J. Weber, *The Spanish Frontier in North America* (1992) and ed., *New Spain's Far Northern Frontier* (1988).

To the biographical studies listed above and in Chapter 1, add Harry Ammon, *James Monroe* (1971); Samuel Flagg Bemis, *John Quincy Adams and the Foundations of American Foreign Policy* (1949); George A. Billias, *Elbridge Gerry* (1979); Gerald H. Clarfield, *Timothy Pickering and the American Republic* (1981); Jacob E. Cooke, *Alexander Hamilton* (1982); Robert Hendrickson, *The Rise and Fall of Alexander Hamilton* (1981); Peter P. Hill, *William Vans Murray* (1971); Jonn C. Niven, *John C. Calhoun and the Price of Union* (1988); Robert W. Remini, *Andrew Jackson and the Course of American Empire, 1767–1821* (1977) and *Henry Clay* (1991); Raymond Walters, Jr., *Albert Gallatin* (1957); and Martin R. Zahniser, *Charles Cotesworth Pinckney* (1967).

See also the General Bibliography, the notes below, and Richard Dean Burns, ed., *Guide to American Foreign Relations Since 1700* (1983).

For comprehensive coverage of foreign-relations topics, see the articles in the four-volume *Encyclopedia of U.S. Foreign Relations* (1997), edited by Bruce W. Jentleson and Thomas G. Paterson.

NOTES TO CHAPTER 2

1. Quoted in Henry Adams, *History of the United States During the Administrations of Jefferson and Madison* (New York: Charles Scribner's Sons, 1889–1891; 9 vols.), IV, 11.
2. Barron quoted in Spencer C. Tucker and Frank T. Reuter, *Injured Honor* (Annapolis: Naval Institute Press, 1996), p. 4.
3. Quoted in Adams, *History*, p. 13.
4. Quoted *ibid.*, p. 14.
5. Quoted *ibid.*, pp. 15–16.
6. Quoted in Tucker and Reuter, *Injured Honor*, p. 124.
7. Quoted in Dumas Malone, *Jefferson and His Time* (Boston: Little, Brown, 1948–1974; 5 vols.), V, 401.
8. Adams, *History*, IV, 27.
9. Quoted in Tucker and Reuter, *Injured Honor*, pp. 105, 108.
10. Quoted in Reginald Horsman, *The Causes of the War of 1812* (Philadelphia: University of Pennsylvania Press, 1962), p. 169.
11. Quoted in Adams, *History*, IV, 33.
12. Bradford Perkins, *Prologue to War* (Berkeley: University of California Press, 1961), p. 144.
13. Quoted in Paul A. Varg, *Foreign Policies of the Founding Fathers* (Baltimore: Penguin Books, 1970), p. 192.
14. Quoted in John C. Niven, *John C. Calhoun and the Price of Union* (Baton Rouge: Louisiana State University Press, 1988), p. 42.
15. Henry Cabot Lodge, ed., *The Works of Alexander Hamilton* (New York: G. P. Putnam's Sons, 1904; 12 vols.), X, 357.
16. Quoted in Samuel Flagg Bemis, *Jay's Treaty* (New Haven: Yale University Press, 1962; rev. ed.), p. 372.
17. Quoted in Jerald A. Combs, *The Jay Treaty* (Berkeley: University of California Press, 1970), p. 76.
18. Quoted in Noble E. Cunningham, Jr., *In Pursuit of Reason* (Baton Rouge: Louisiana State University Press, 1987), p. 172.
19. A. A. Lipscomb, ed., *Writings of Thomas Jefferson* (Washington, D.C.: Jefferson Memorial Association, 1903–1904; 19 vols.), IX, 10.
20. Joyce Appleby, *Capitalism and a New Social Order* (New York: New York University Press, 1984), p. 57.
21. Quoted in Walter A. McDougall, *Promised Land, Crusader State* (Boston: Houghton Mifflin, 1997), p. 29.
22. Worthington C. Ford, ed., *Writings of Thomas Jefferson* (New York: G. P. Putnam's Sons, 1892–1899; 10 vols.), VI, 278.
23. Quoted in Conor Cruise O'Brien, *The Long Affair: Thomas Jefferson and the French Revolution* (Chicago: University of Chicago Press, 1996), p. 241.
24. Appleby, *Capitalism*, p. 203.
25. Quoted in Harry Ammon, *The Genet Mission* (New York: Norton, 1973), p. 86.
26. Quoted in Claude G. Bowers, *Jefferson and Hamilton* (Boston: Houghton Mifflin, 1925), p. 229.
27. Quoted in Stanley Elkins and Eric McKittrick, *The Age of Federalism* (New York: Oxford University Press, 1993), p. 351.
28. Grenville quoted in Peter Jupp, *Lord Grenville, 1759–1834* (London: Oxford University Press, 1985), p. 162.
29. Quoted in Dorothy V. Jones, *License for Empire* (Chicago: University of Chicago Press, 1982), p. 174.
30. John E. Crowley, *The Privileges of Independence* (Baltimore: Johns Hopkins University Press, 1993), p. 168.
31. Quoted in Robert A. Rutland, *James Madison* (New York: Macmillan, 1987), p. 140.
32. Quoted in Elkins and McKittrick, *Federalism*, p. 441.
33. Joseph J. Ellis, *American Sphinx* (New York: Knopf, 1997), p. 159.
34. Quoted in Michael H. Hunt, *Ideology and U.S. Foreign Policy* (New Haven: Yale University Press, 1987), p. 25.
35. Quoted in John Garry Clifford, "A Muddy Middle of the Road: The Politics of Edmund Randolph, 1790–1795," *Virginia Magazine of History and Biography*, LXXX (July 1972), 306.
36. Bernard Mayo, ed., "Instructions to the British Ministers to the United States, 1791–1812," *Annual Report of the American Historical Association for 1936* (Washington, D.C.: Government Printing Office, 1941; 3 vols.), III, 83.
37. Quoted in John A. Carroll and Mary W. Ashworth, *George Washington* (New York: Charles Scribner's Sons, 1957), p. 294.
38. Quoted in Combs, *Jay Treaty*, p. 184.
39. Jonathan Dayton quoted in Elkins and McKittrick, *Federalism*, p. 448.
40. Arthur P. Whitaker, *The Spanish-American Frontier, 1783–1795* (Boston: Houghton Mifflin, 1927), p. 220.
41. Quoted in David J. Weber, *The Spanish Frontier in North America* (New Haven: Yale University Press, 1992), p. 290.
42. Samuel Flagg Bemis, *Pinckney's Treaty* (New Haven: Yale University Press, 1960; rev. ed.), p. vii.
43. Quoted in Henry Blumenthal, *France and the United States: Their Diplomatic Relations, 1789–1914* (Chapel Hill: University of North Carolina Press, 1970), p. 14.
44. James D. Richardson, ed., *A Compilation of the Messages and Papers of the Presidents, 1789–1901* (Washington, D.C.: Government Printing Office, 1896–1914; 10 vols.), I, 221–223.
45. Quoted in A. H. Bowman, *The Struggle for Neutrality* (Knoxville: University of Tennessee Press, 1974), pp. 268–269.
46. Quoted in Alexander DeConde, *The Quasi-War* (New York: Charles Scribner's Sons, 1966), p. 3.
47. Quoted in Roger G. Kennedy, *Orders from France* (New York: Knopf, 1989), p. 102; and in William Stinchombe, "Talleyrand and the American Negotiations of 1797–1798," *Journal of American History*, LXII (December 1975), 578.
48. Quoted in Bowman, *Struggle for Neutrality*, p. 277.
49. Quoted in Elkins and McKittrick, *Federalism*, p. 566.
50. Walter Lowrie and Matthew St. Clair Clarke, eds., *American State Papers, Foreign Relations* (Washington, D.C.: Gales and Seaton, 1832–1859; 6 vols.), II, 161.
51. Quoted in DeConde, *Quasi-War*, p. 52.
52. Quoted in Lawrence S. Kaplan, *Colonies into Nation* (New York: Macmillan, 1972), p. 276.
53. Quoted in Elkins and McKittrick, *Federalism*, p. 577.
54. Richardson, *Messages of the Presidents*, I, 256.
55. Quoted in O'Brien, *Long Affair*, p. 246.
56. Quoted in DeConde, *Quasi-War*, p. 99.
57. Quoted in Elkins and McKittrick, *Federalism*, p. 606.
58. Quoted *ibid.*, pp. 645–646.
59. Quoted in Thomas K. McCraw, "The Strategic Vision of Alexander Hamilton," *American Scholar*, LXIII (Winter 1994), 39.
60. Quoted in Kaplan, *Colonies into Nation*, p. 282.
61. Bradford Perkins, *The First Rapprochement* (Philadelphia: University of Pennsylvania Press, 1955).
62. Lowrie and Clarke, *Foreign Relations*, II, 242.
63. Quoted in Page Smith, *John Adams* (Garden City, N.Y.: Doubleday, 1962; 2 vols.), II, 995.

64. Quoted *ibid., II,* 1000.
65. Theodore Sedgewick quoted in James Rogers Sharp, *American Politics in the Early Republic* (New Haven: Yale University Press, 1993), p. 212.
66. Quoted in Phyllis Lee Levin, *Abigail Adams* (New York: St. Martin's Press, 1987), p. 371.
67. Quoted in Bradford Perkins, *The Creation of a Republican Empire, 1776–1865* (New York: Cambridge University Press, 1993), p. 109.
68. Quoted in Kennedy, *Orders from France,* p. 305.
69. Quoted in Elkins and McKittrick, *Federalism,* p. 680.
70. Quoted in Alan Schom, *Napoleon Bonaparte* (New York: HarperCollins, 1997), p. 225.
71. Quoted in Ralph Ketcham, *Presidents Above Party* (Chapel Hill: University of North Carolina Press, 1984), p. 94.
72. Richardson, *Messages of the Presidents, I,* 323.
73. Lipscomb, *Writings of Jefferson, X,* 296.
74. Adams, *History, I,* 340.
75. Quoted in Marshall Smelser, *The Democratic Republic, 1801–1815* (New York: Harper and Row, 1968), p. 87.
76. Quoted in Tim Matthewson, "Jefferson and Haiti," *Journal of Southern History, LXI* (May 1995), 215, 229.
77. Gaillard Hunt, ed., *The Writings of James Madison* (New York: G. P. Putnam's Sons, 1900–1910; 9 vols.), *VI,* 462.
78. Quoted in Robert M. Johnstone, Jr., *Jefferson and the Presidency* (Ithaca: Cornell University Press, 1978), p. 69.
79. Quoted in Malone, *Jefferson and His Time, IV,* 277.
80. Quoted in Albert H. Bowman, "Pichon, the United States, and Louisiana,"*Diplomatic History, I* (Summer 1977), 266.
81. Quoted in Theodore J. Crackel, *Mr. Jefferson's Army* (New York: New York University Press, 1987), p. 102.
82. Quoted in E. W. Lyon, *Louisiana in French Diplomacy* (Norman: University of Oklahoma Press, 1934), p. 194.
83. Smelser, *Democratic Republic,* p. 94.
84. Quoted in Eugene V. Rostow, *A Breakfast for Bonaparte* (Washington, D.C.: National Defense University Press, 1991), p. 119.
85. Quoted in Alexander DeConde, *This Affair of Louisiana* (New York: Charles Scribner's Sons, 1976), p. 174.
86. Quoted in François de Barbé-Marbois, *History of Louisiana* (Philadelphia: Lippincott, 1830), pp. 310–311.
87. Quoted in Lyon, *Louisiana in French Diplomacy,* p. 206.
88. Quoted in Malone, *Jefferson and His Time, IV,* 297.
89. Quoted *ibid.,* p. 316.
90. Albert Gallatin quoted in Weber, *Spanish Frontier,* p. 292.
91. Samuel Smith quoted in Reginald Horsman, "The Dimensions of an 'Empire for Liberty,'" *Journal of the Early Republic, IX* (Spring 1989), 11.
92. Quoted in David J. Weber, *The Mexican Frontier, 1821–1846* (Albuquerque: University of New Mexico Press, 1982), p. 279.
93. Peggy K. Liss, *Atlantic Empires* (Baltimore: Johns Hopkins University Press, 1983), p. 122
94. James P. Ronda, "Dreams and Discoveries: Exploring the American West, 1760–1815," *William and Mary Quarterly, XLVI* (January 1989), 145–146.
95. Quoted in Ellis, *American Sphinx,* pp. 201–202.
96. William H. Adams, *The Paris Years of Thomas Jefferson* (New Haven: Yale University Press, 1997), p. 166.
97. Quoted in James P. Ronda, *Astoria and Empire* (Lincoln: University of Nebraska Press, 1990), p. 44.
98. Ellis, *American Sphinx,* p. 212.
99. Lipscomb, *Writings of Jefferson, XII,* 277.
100. Quoted in James R. Sofka, "The Jeffersonian Idea of National Security," *Diplomatic History, XXI* (Fall 1997), 538.
101. Quoted in Kenneth J. Hagan, *This People's Navy* (New York: Free Press, 1991), p. 60.
102. Quoted in Robert J. Allison, *The Crescent Obscured* (New York: Oxford University Press, 1995), p. 65.
103. *Ibid.,* p. xvii.
104. Quoted in Clifford L. Egan, *Neither Peace nor War* (Baton Rouge: Louisiana State University Press, 1983), p. 27.
105. Smelser, *Democratic Republic,* p. 148.
106. Charles F. Adams, ed., *Memoirs of John Quincy Adams* (Philadelphia: Lippincott, 1874–1877; 12 vols.), *II,* 92.
107. Quoted in Perkins, *Prologue to War,* p. 41.
108. Varg, *Foreign Policies,* p. 173.
109. Quoted in Perkins, *Prologue to War,* p. 89.
110. Quoted in Varg, *Foreign Policies,* p. 182.
111. Robert A. Rutland, *Madison's Alternatives* (Philadelphia: Lippincott, 1975), p. 5.
112. Lipscomb, *Writings of Jefferson, XI,* 274.
113. Quoted in Horsman, *Causes of the War of 1812,* p. 59.
114. James A. Field, Jr., "1778–1820: All Economists, All Diplomats," in William H. Becker and Samuel F. Wells, Jr., eds., *Economics and World Power* (New York: Columbia University Press, 1984), p. 32.
115. Walter W. Jennings, *The American Embargo, 1807–1809* (Iowa City: University of Iowa, 1921), p. 231.
116. Quoted in Perkins, *Prologue to War,* p. 163.
117. Robert H. Ferrell, ed., *Foundations of American Diplomacy, 1775–1872* (New York: Harper and Row, 1968), p. 6.
118. Quoted in Perkins, *Prologue to War,* p. 161.
119. Doron S. Ben-Atar, *The Origins of Jeffersonian Commercial Policy and Diplomacy* (New York: St. Martin's Press, 1993), p. 253.
120. Quoted in Richard Mannix, "Gallatin, Jefferson, and the Embargo of 1808," *Diplomatic History, III* (Spring 1979), 168.
121. Burton Spivak, *Jefferson's English Crisis* (Charlottesville: University Press of Virginia, 1979), p. 203.
122. Quoted in Perkins, *Prologue to War,* p. 220.
123. Quoted in Smelser, *Democratic Republic,* p. 194.
124. Quoted in Ralph Ketcham, *James Madison* (New York: Macmillan, 1971), p. 496.
125. Rutland, *Madison's Alternatives,* p. 25.
126. Adams, *History, V,* 103.
127. Quoted in Horsman, *Causes of the War of 1812,* p. 155.
128. Quoted in Rutland, *Madison's Alternatives,* p. 27.
129. Quoted in Roger H. Brown, *The Republic in Peril: 1812* (New York: Columbia University Press, 1964), p. 23.
130. Quoted in Varg, *Foreign Policies,* p. 286.
131. Quoted in Gregory Evans Dowd, *A Spirited Resistance* (Baltimore: Johns Hopkins University Press, 1992), pp. 140, 142.
132. Quoted in Perkins, *Prologue to War,* p. 283.
133. Quoted in Donald R. Hickey, *The War of 1812* (Urbana: University of Illinois Press, 1989), p. 46.
134. Richardson, *Messages of the Presidents, II,* 484–490.
135. Quoted in Varg, *Foreign Policies,* p. 292.
136. *Annals of Congress,* December 12, 1811, p. 482.
137. Quoted in Perkins, *Prologue to War,* p. 359.
138. Reginald C. Stuart, *United States Expansionism and British North America, 1775–1871* (Chapel Hill: University of North Carolina Press, 1988), p. 76.
139. Quoted in Horsman, *Causes of the War of 1812,* p. 182.
140. J. C. A. Stagg, *Mr. Madison's War* (Princeton: Princeton University Press, 1983), p. 46.

141. Norman K. Risjord, "1812: Conservatives, War Hawks, and the Nation's Honor," *William and Mary Quarterly*, XVII (April 1961), 200.

142. Quoted *ibid.*, p. 205.

143. Steven Watts, *The Republic Reborn* (Baltimore: Johns Hopkins University Press, 1987), p. 242.

144. Jefferson quoted in Ben-Atar, *Origins*, p. 171.

145. Quoted in Lawrence S. Kaplan, "France and Madison's Decision for War," *Mississippi Valley Historical Review, L* (March 1964), 658.

146. J. F. Hopkins, ed., *The Papers of Henry Clay* (Lexington: University of Kentucky Press, 1959–1973; 5 vols.), *I*, 674.

147. Lowrie and Clarke, *Foreign Relations, III*, 585–586.

148. *Ibid., III*, 589–590.

149. Quoted in Bradford Perkins, *Castlereagh and Adams* (Berkeley: University of California Press, 1965), p. 14.

150. Quoted in Catherine Allgor, "'A Republican in a Monarchy': Louisa Catherine Adams in Russia," *Diplomatic History, XXI* (Winter 1997), 26.

151. Normal E. Saul, *Distant Friends* (Lawrence: University Press of Kansas, 1991), p. 72.

152. David Curtis Skaggs and Gerald T. Altoff, *A Signal Victory: The Lake Erie Campaign, 1812–1813* (Annapolis: Naval Institute Press, 1997), p. 183.

153. Quoted in Robert A. Rutland, *The Presidency of James Madison* (Lawrence: University Press of Kansas, 1990), p. 108.

154. Lowrie and Clarke, *Foreign Relations, III*, 704.

155. Quoted in Michael Dunne, "The Treaty of Gent [*sic*]: The British Perspective," in *Overdruk uit Handelingen der Maatschappij voor Geschiedenis en Oudheidkunde te Gent Nieuwe Reeks, dl. XLIV* (Gent, 1990), 37.

156. Quoted in Bradford Perkins, *Castlereagh and Adams*, (Berkeley: University of California Press, 1965), p. 49.

157. Quoted in Robert V. Remini, *Henry Clay* (New York: Norton, 1991), p. 117.

158. Quoted in Samuel Flagg Bemis, *John Quincy Adams and the Foundations of American Foreign Policy* (New York: Knopf, 1949), p. 196.

159. Quoted in Perkins, *Castlereagh and Adams*, p. 113.

160. Quoted *ibid.*, p. 124.

161. Quoted in Bemis, *John Quincy Adams*, p. 218.

162. Ketcham, *James Madison*, p. 596.

163. Quoted in Perkins, *Castlereagh and Adams*, p. 150.

164. Quoted in Raymond Walters, Jr., *Albert Gallatin* (New York: Macmillan, 1957), p. 288.

165. Quoted in Ketcham, *James Madison*, pp. 597–598.

166. Quoted in Perkins, *Castlereagh and Adams*, p. 151.

167. Quoted in Charles J. Peterson, *The American Navy* (Philadelphia: James B. Smith, 1858), p. 287.

168. Adams, *History, IX*, 53.

169. Dowd, *Spirited Resistance*, p. 187.

170. Quoted in Hickey, *War of 1812*, p. 304.

171. Quoted in Stagg, *Mr. Madison's War*, p. 517.

3

Extending and Preserving the Sphere, 1815–1848

U.S. Forces Enter Mexico City, 1847. *General Winfield Scott triumphantly parades in the plaza as an American flag flies above. One Mexican, at the left with stone in hand, did not appreciate the ceremonies. (Library of Congress)*

❖

DIPLOMATIC CROSSROAD

Mexican-American War on the Rio Grande, 1846

The momentous order to march to the Rio Grande reached "Old Rough and Ready" General Zachary Taylor on February 3, 1846. Planning and reconnoitering took several weeks, so the first infantry brigades did not tramp out from Corpus Christi until March 9. The army averaged ten miles a day, through suffocating dust, across sunbaked soil, through ankle-deep sands, past holes of brackish water, into grasslands capable of supporting vegetation. Deer, ducks, rabbits, tarantulas, and rattlesnakes crossed the soldiers' path. Near a wide, marshy stream called the Arroyo Colorado, U.S. troops nearly tangled with a Mexican cavalry unit, but the numerically superior U.S. forces managed to cross unmolested. Late in the morning of March 28, Taylor's army reached the north bank of the Rio Grande in disputed Texas territory. Across the 200 yards of mud-colored river stood the Mexican town of Matamoros and its well-armed garrison of some 3,000 men. Taylor encamped, set up earthworks (Fort Texas), and waited. "The attitude of the Mexicans is so far decidedly hostile," Taylor informed his superiors.[1]

The next three weeks passed nervously but peacefully. More than a dozen U.S. enlisted men deserted, lured by pretty señoritas and promises of 320 acres of Mexican land if they crossed the river. Such enticements "have met with considerable success," Taylor reported.[2] The general had to conduct his initial parley with the Mexicans in French because no American officer could speak Spanish and none of the Mexicans present had mastered English. Taylor assured the Mexicans that his advance to the Rio Grande was neither an invasion of Mexican soil nor a hostile act. The suspicious Mexicans reinforced their garrison with 2,000 additional troops. Then, on April 24, Major General Mariano Arista notified Taylor that hostilities had begun. A force of Mexican cavalry, 1,600 strong, crossed the river at La Palangana, fourteen miles upstream from Matamoros. Taylor sent a detachment of dragoons to investigate, but they returned having seen nothing. That same evening, April 24, Taylor ordered out another cavalry force under Captain Seth B. Thornton. This time the Americans rode into an ambush. Thornton tried to fight his way free but lost eleven men. The Mexicans took the rest of his sixty-three-man contingent captive. "We have vengeance to take on Mexico for more than one man's blood, and our boys . . . feel so indignant at the rascality of the brutes," one U.S. officer wrote home.[3] News of the fight reached Taylor at reveille on April 26. "Hostilities may now be considered as commenced," he immediately alerted Washington, D.C.[4] His dispatch, which had to travel overland, took two weeks to reach the capital.

A stiff, angular man, with sharp gray eyes set in a sad, thin face, President James K. Polk met with his cabinet on May 9. The chief executive was looking for an ex-

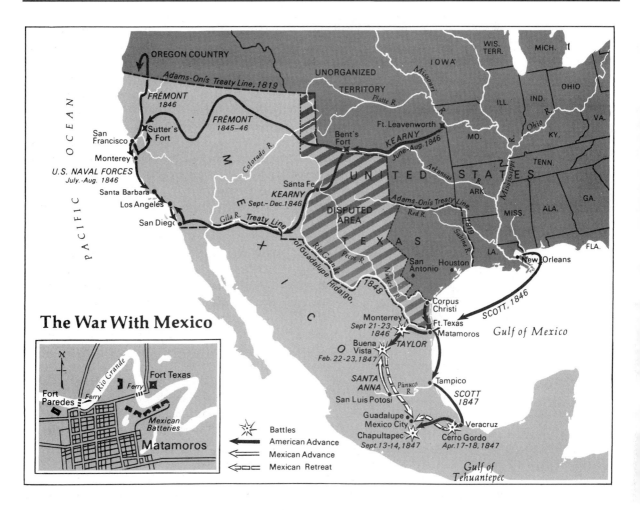

The War With Mexico

Battles
American Advance
Mexican Advance
Mexican Retreat

cuse to declare war on Mexico. Reviewing the diplomacy of the past year, which included U.S. annexation of Texas, suspension of relations with Mexico, and abortive attempts to solve boundary disputes and to purchase California and New Mexico, Polk self-righteously told his cabinet that "in my opinion we had ample cause of war, and that it was impossible that we could stand in *statu quo,* or that I could remain silent much longer."[5] He hoped that the Mexicans would commit an act of aggression against Taylor's army, but as yet nothing had happened. Polk polled the cabinet. All agreed that he should soon send a war message to Congress, although Secretary of the Navy George Bancroft thought it would be better if some hostile act on the border occurred first. The meeting adjourned, and Polk began to compose the war message.

At six o'clock that evening the news about the Rio Grande skirmish reached the White House. The cabinet hastily reconvened and reached a unanimous decision: Submit a war message as quickly as possible. All day May 10, except for two hours at church, Polk anxiously labored over his statement, conferring with cabinet colleagues, military advisers, and congressional leaders. At noon the next day he sent the message to Congress. "The cup of forbearance has been exhausted," Polk wrote. "After reiterated menaces, Mexico has passed the boundary of the United States, has invaded our territory and shed American blood upon American soil." War existed, and "notwithstanding all our efforts to avoid it, exists by the act of Mexico herself." A bill accompanied the war message authorizing the president to accept militia and volunteers for military duty. The bill did not specifically declare war but rather asked Congress to recognize that "by the act of . . . Mexico, a state of war exists between the government and the United States."[6]

A disciplined Democratic majority responded swiftly. Debate in the House was limited to two hours. Angry Whigs asked for time to examine 144 pages of documents that Polk sent with his message. Denied. The Speaker of the House repeatedly failed to recognize members who wanted to ask detailed questions about how the war started. Only by resorting to a parliamentary trick—by demanding permission to explain why they wanted to be excused from voting—did two dissenters gain the floor and denounce Polk's war message as falsehood. The House vote of 174 to 14 represented a victory for stampede tactics. In the Senate the following day, the vote was even more decisive in favor of the war bill, 40 to 2. Whigs and dissident Democrats, remembering the political fate of Federalists who had opposed the War of 1812, either voted aye or did not vote. Democratic senator John C. Calhoun of South Carolina, who "opposed the conquest of a people who were alien to American culture and whose ruling classes opposed slavery," later insisted that fewer than 10 percent of his colleagues would have voted for the war bill if Polk had presented the issue fairly.[7] Nonetheless, Calhoun abstained when his name was called.

Thus began the War with Mexico, a conflict that lasted nearly two years and added to the United States a vast domain, which included the present-day states of New Mexico, Arizona, California, Nevada, and Utah. Contemporaries called it "Mr. Polk's War," a most appropriate appellation. Despite backing from a unanimous cabinet and an overwhelming congressional declaration, the Tennesseean made the crucial decisions for war. It was Polk who unilaterally defined the geographic limits of Texas as including disputed land between the Nueces River and the Rio Grande. Polk, as commander in chief, ordered General Taylor to the Rio Grande. Polk decided that Mexico had fired the first shot. Polk presented Congress with an accomplished fact.

Despite congressional authorization, the presidential war did not go unchallenged. Representative John Quincy Adams, then in the last year of his distinguished life and himself once an advocate of expansion, was among the few who voted against an "unrighteous" war to extend slavery.[8] "It is now established as an irreversible precedent," Adams lamented, "that the President of the United States has but to declare that War exists . . . and the War is essentially declared."[9] Because of their own aggressive behavior in the acquisition of Florida a generation earlier, of course, both Calhoun and Adams, as the historian William Earl Weeks has noted, "knew well how easy it was to stampede the Congress into supporting executive actions of dubious legitimacy."[10] It was "Mr. Polk's War," but the president could bring it off successfully because his aims reflected the grand hopes of expansionist America.

Expanding the Sphere: Manifest Destiny

The War on the Rio Grande came at a critical juncture and dramatized the expansionist themes that dominated American foreign relations after the War of 1812. At the very time Taylor's troops were fighting Mexicans in the Southwest, Polk was quietly settling a dispute with England over control of the Pacific Northwest. By dividing Oregon at 49° north latitude in June 1846, Polk temporarily abated the rivalry with England over the territory and commerce of North America. The anti-British fervor of the Revolutionary era remained strong in the 1830s and 1840s, and the fear of British encroachment in Texas and California contributed to the outbreak of war against Mexico. That the United States fought Mexico and not Britain in 1846 illustrated another theme: American expansionists behaved more aggressively against weaker peoples such as Spaniards, Mexicans, and Indians than against the stronger Britishers. According to the expansionist ideology, those peoples who neither improved the land they held nor developed effective political institutions had to make way for those who could. The lands Polk wanted from Mexico had sparse populations that could easily assimilate American institutions, or so he assumed. England, with greater power and similar traditions, could be a rival but not a victim. Indeed, as Polk moved toward war in winter 1845–1846, he invoked the Monroe Doctrine in warning England against further expansion in North America, thus making explicit what had been implicit in 1823—that Europeans could not seize territory in the Western Hemisphere, but the United States could. Moreover, Polk sincerely believed that Mexico fired the first shot on the Rio Grande, just as many Americans sincerely believed that God had destined the United States to control the entire continent. The sincerity of such beliefs in American exceptionalism did not stop expansionism from being both racist and imperialistic.

Continental expansion became the watchword in the three decades after 1815. Having defended their territorial integrity during the second war with Great Britain, American nationalists proceeded to acquire Florida, Texas, Oregon, and the Mexican cession, some 1,263,301 square miles. Population nearly trebled, from 8,419,000 in 1815 to 22,018,000 in 1848. American commerce expanded into new channels, notably Latin America and Asia, with total exports climbing from $53 million in 1815 to $159 million in 1847. The gross output of farm production increased from $338 million in 1820 to $904 million thirty years later. Cotton production, a vital ingredient in Anglo-American relations, rose from 209,000 bales in 1815 to 2,615,000 bales in 1847. The construction of canals and railroads created a transportation and market revolution that quickened U.S. growth. It became the purpose of U.S. diplomacy during these years to facilitate this expansion. *"On s'agrandit toujours un peu, dans ce monde"* ("Everyone always grows a little in this world"), said Tsar Alexander I of Russia after John Quincy Adams told him of the American acquisition of West Florida.[11]

Makers of American Foreign Relations, 1815–1848

Presidents	Secretaries of State
James Madison, 1809–1817	James Monroe, 1811–1817
James Monroe, 1817–1825	John Quincy Adams, 1817–1825
John Quincy Adams, 1825–1829	Henry Clay, 1825–1829
Andrew Jackson, 1829–1837	Martin Van Buren, 1829–1831
	Edward Livingston, 1831–1833
	Louis McLane, 1833–1834
Martin Van Buren, 1837–1841	John Forsyth, 1834–1841
William H. Harrison, 1841	Daniel Webster, 1841–1843
John Tyler, 1841–1845	Abel P. Upshur, 1843–1844
	John C. Calhoun, 1844–1845
James K. Polk, 1845–1849	James Buchanan, 1845–1849

The roots of expansion were many—historical, economic, demographic, intellectual, strategic. It does not suffice to say that the United States, like Topsy, "just grew." To be sure, "extending the sphere" (in Madison's phrase) was nothing new, and much that occurred after 1815 derived from earlier decisions.[12] Part of the rationale for acquiring East Florida in 1819 followed the example of Louisiana: Just as New Orleans under foreign control had blocked navigation of the Mississippi, so too did Spanish sovereignty over the mouths of the Pearl, Perdido, and Chattahoochee Rivers make it difficult for American farmers upstream to get their produce to market. Florida, moreover, just like New Orleans, might be ceded by Spain to a more dangerous power, hence the argument for possessing it before England or France could grab it. Memories of the Revolution of 1776, combined with opportunities for Latin American markets, helped prompt the Monroe Doctrine of 1823. By stipulating that Europe and the Americas had distinctly different political systems, Monroe's message recalled the isolationist principles of Paine's *Common Sense* and Washington's Farewell Address.

Echoes of the past reverberated in the Anglo-American trade rivalry in Latin America and in the attempts to gain equal access to the British West Indian trade in the 1820s. A more explicit reference to earlier concerns about neutral rights came in 1831 when President Andrew Jackson negotiated an agreement whereby France promised to pay an indemnity of 25 million francs for illegal seizures of American shipping in the years 1805–1812. When the French defaulted on an installment in 1834, Jackson reportedly shouted: "I know them French. They won't pay unless they are made to."[13] The French paid the debt. Jackson's pugnacity undoubtedly reflected sound electioneering instincts, but it also served notice that the United States would insist on the right to expand its carrying trade in the event of another European conflagration.

"The Way They Go to California."   Nathaniel Currier's lithograph captures the American expansionist frenzy—in this case for California after the War with Mexico. (Library of Congress)

An important element in expansion after 1815 derived from the growing vision of what was possible. Despite treaties in 1818 and 1819 that established a firm claim to the Pacific coast, most Americans still thought of the Rocky Mountains as a "natural" boundary. Oregon seemed far away. It had taken Lewis and Clark eighteen months to travel to the Pacific from St. Louis. A sea voyage from Boston to the Pacific coast lasted six to eight months, depending on the weather. Even Senator Thomas Hart Benton of Missouri, who would catch the Oregon "fever" with a vengeance in the 1840s, went on record in 1825 in favor of the Rocky Mountain limitation. "Along the back of this ridge," he intoned, "the Western limit of the republic should be drawn, and the statue of the fabled god, Terminus, should be raised upon its highest peak, never to be thrown down."[14] Within a generation, in the scholar John Seelye's phrase, the Rocky Mountains became "less terminus than pivot to empire."[15]

Technology shrank geography and expanded horizons. Steamboats, canals, and railroads stimulated imaginations as well as commerce. Although fewer than 5,000 miles of railroad track existed in the United States in 1845, plans for constructing transcontinental lines had already reached the drawing boards. The development of

"Manifest Destiny."   John Gast's painting captures the ebullient spirit of the trek westward. Pioneers relentlessly move on, attracting railroads and driving out Native Americans, as "Columbia" majestically pulls telegraph wires across America. "Neither accidental nor innocent," writes the historian Thomas Hietala, "the expansion to the Pacific represented not manifest destiny, but manifest design." (Collection of Harry T. Peters, Jr.)

high-speed printing presses gave rise in the early 1840s to mass circulation newspapers, which in turn trumpeted expansionist rhetoric to a larger foreign-policy public. Samuel Morse's invention of the telegraph, first put into operation in 1844, came at an opportune time. "The magnetic telegraph," boasted the editor John L. O'Sullivan in 1845, "will enable the editors of the 'San Francisco Union,' the 'Astoria Evening Post,' or the 'Nootka Morning News,' to set up in type the first half of the President's Inaugural before the echoes of the latter half shall have died away beneath the lofty porch of the Capitol, as spoken from his lips."[16]

The same O'Sullivan, editor of the *Democratic Review,* gave the expansionist process a name in the summer of 1845. The United States, according to O'Sullivan, had the "manifest destiny to overspread the continent allotted by Providence to the free development of our yearly multiplying millions."[17] Although the geographical limits of the Temple of Freedom were not always clear—the Pacific? the continent? the hemisphere?—most believers in Manifest Destiny followed John Quincy Adams's notion, expressed in 1819, that the United States and North

America were identical. Manifest Destiny meant republicanism, religious freedom, states' rights, free trade, inexpensive land. It appealed to the individualistic ideology of Jacksonianism, which one scholar has described as "opportunity and expansion for everyone amid minimal or no government regulation, a rhetoric of republican equality that actually masked a profoundly unequal society."[18]

Manifest Destiny in its purest form did not envisage acquisition of territory by force. Peaceful occupation of uninhabited wilderness, followed by self-government on the American model and eventual annexation by mutual consent—this was the ideal. Neighboring peoples of Spanish and Indian heritage, given time and the American example, might qualify for peaceful incorporation. The process seemed almost automatic. "Go to the West," said an Indiana member of Congress in 1846,

> and see a young man with his mate of eighteen; and [after] a lapse of thirty years, visit him again, and instead of two, you will find twenty-two. That is what I call the American multiplication table. We are now twenty millions strong; and how long, under this process of multiplication, will it take to cover the continent with our posterity, from the Isthmus of Darien to Behring's straits?[19]

Reality did not match the ideal, as "Polk's War" on the Rio Grande sadly attested. Racism inevitably infused Manifest Destiny. The racial thinking of the time posited Anglo-Saxon superiority as a proven scientific fact and thus denigrated groups that resisted the inexorable march of democratic institutions. Protestant missionaries who sought to assimilate Indians into white society, according to the historian Robert Berkhofer, firmly believed that "any right-thinking savage should be able to recognize the superiority of Christian society," and thus any failures in the acculturation process were attributed to the victims.[20] Just as the negative stereotype of African Americans in the nineteenth century justified slavery in the South and unequal treatment of freedmen in the North, and as the prevailing image of the Indians as savages justified their subjugation, so too did expansionists project their notions of racial superiority against Mexicans who were allegedly too cowardly to fight or too treacherous to win if they did fight. In the historian Thomas Hietala's words, "manifest destiny, or rather manifest design, offered nothing to nonwhite peoples . . . but inevitable decline, expulsion, or final extinction."[21]

Indian relocation became official federal policy under President Andrew Jackson. When the Supreme Court ruled in 1831 that Indian tribes held unquestionable rights to their lands and that whites could not intrude without permission or treaty privilege, Jackson reportedly declared: "[Chief Justice] John Marshall has made his decision: now let him enforce it."[22] In the Removal Act of 1830 Congress gave Jackson the money and authority to impose new treaties and forcibly resettle 85,000 Indians of the five "civilized nations" from the southeastern states—Cherokee, Choctaw, Creek, Chickasaw, and Seminole—across the Mississippi. The French visitor Alexis de Tocqueville, stopping in Memphis during the winter of 1831–1832, described Choctaws crossing the great river: "the wounded, the sick, newborn babies, and the old men on the point of death . . . the sight will never fade from my memory."[23] Even the most assimilated Native Americans, such

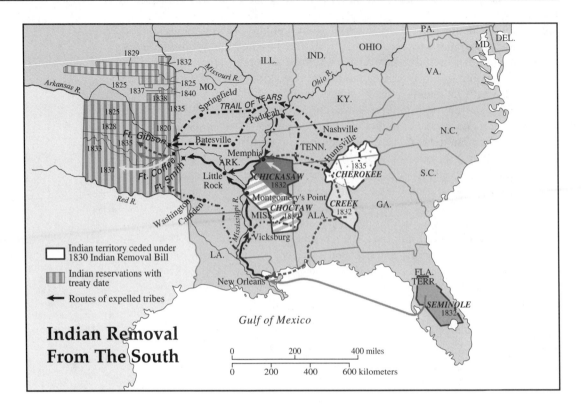

as the economically self-sufficient and self-governing Cherokees, had to relocate. According to Secretary of War Lewis Cass, removal offered the only hope for Indians to survive because "a barbarous people . . . cannot live in contact with a civilized community."[24] In a larger context, the government's treatment of Native Americans became "part of a global pattern of intensified conflict" during the nineteenth century wherein European-style imperialism expanded at the expense of indigenous populations, including the British subjugations of the Maori in New Zealand and the Xhosa in South Africa.[25]

Yet in some ways American expansion seemed a natural, organic process. Americans always sought greater productivity through the cultivation of new lands. Problems generating from increased population, inadequate transportation, depressed agricultural prices, and general hard times also caused periodic migrations into new areas. Whether emigrants moved into American territory beyond the Alleghenies or into fertile lands under alien rule, they retained their distinctly Yankee customs; if under foreign rule, they rejected alien political and social institutions and virtually established American "colonies." Friends, relatives, and politicians at home directed U.S. foreign policy toward the "protection" of their compatriots. Thus came the rhetoric of Manifest Destiny—the spread-eagle appeals to national prestige, the glittering description of natural resources and arable lands. As the American enclaves grew in size, so too did fears increase that some

European power, probably perfidious England, would snatch the potential prize. If politicians exaggerated the extent to which England meddled in California, Oregon, and Texas, the fact of a British presence contributed to the expansionist momentum.

Population movements tended to come on the heels of economic downturns. The Panic of 1819, combined with Mexico's generous land policies, encouraged the first flood of immigration into Texas in the 1820s. Similarly, the severe economic depression in 1837–1842 stimulated more western farmers and southern planters to migrate westward. The population of Texas ballooned to 100,000 by 1845, and in far-off Oregon some 5,000 Americans had crossed the Rockies. As one resident of California put it: "Once let the tide of emigration flow toward California, and the American population will soon be sufficiently numerous to play the Texas game."[26] This organic, seemingly inevitable process of agrarian migration prompted Calhoun in 1843 to advocate a "wise and masterly inactivity" on the part of the U.S. government.[27] Whigs especially believed that "whenever and wherever expansion came, it must be peaceful, [and] must proceed gradually with the consent of the governed."[28] God and the passage of time would smile benevolently on American expansion. Force did not seem necessary—at least not in theory.

Commercial Ambitions in the Pacific

Heightened interest in the commercial potential of the Pacific also fueled expansion. Trade with Latin America increased, and merchants plying the west coast of South America made profits that could be used to purchase the products of East Asia. "The North American road to India" was Senator Benton's description of the Columbia River Valley during the 1840s.[29] Whaling, salmon fisheries, furs, the fabled China trade, commercial rivalry with Britain and Russia—all were stressed from the 1820s onward by publicists seeking to colonize Oregon as a means to commercial expansion.

Just as the first wave of settlers reached Oregon in 1843, the British, victorious in the Opium War (1839–1842), were breaking down Chinese trade barriers. By the Treaty of Nanjing in 1842, Britain forced China to open five new coastal ports (Guangzhou, Xianen, Ningbo, Fuzhou, and Shanghai) and grant broad rights of extraterritoriality (legal trials for foreigners in special courts of their own nationality). This British success prompted Americans to obtain their own treaty for trade purposes. Already American clipper ships carried cotton to China and returned with tea. Already U.S. merchants used Cantonese middlemen to sell Turkish opium in the land of Confucianism. President John Tyler entrusted Massachusetts Whig Caleb Cushing with the mission to negotiate with the Chinese. Cushing, whose family engaged in the China trade, bought a special uniform of white pantaloons with gold stripes, white vest, blue coat with gilt buttons, and plumed headpiece, all presumably calculated to overawe the Chinese. His Treaty of Wangxia (1844) gained for the United States the same rights, on an unconditional most-favored nation basis, that England had won in the Opium War. The ensuing influx of and cooperation among Yankee traders, missionaries, and diplomats created what the historian Michael Hunt has called an "open door constituency" committed to "penetrating China and propagating at home a paternalistic vision . . . of defending and reforming China."[30]

The American navy's Asiatic Squadron sometimes used force to protect the China trade in the 1840s—as "the Society for the Diffusion of Cannon Balls," in one missionary's quaint phrase.[31] The navy's chief contribution came in the exploratory expeditions sponsored by Matthew Maury and led by Charles Wilkes. Charting coastlines, publicizing points of commercial and strategic interest, enlightening Washington about the Pacific, these naval explorers became, in the historian Geoffrey Smith's words, "'maritime frontiersmen,' mirror images of the thousands of mountain men, traders, pioneers, adventurers, and army surveyors who trekked westward to the Pacific."[32] A key stimulus for expansion appeared with the publication in 1842 of Wilkes's *Narrative of the United States Exploring Expedition,* which provided accurate data about the Pacific coast from Vancouver Island to Baja California. "These shores which were hitherto little more than myths," as the historian Hubert Howe Bancroft later wrote, "were now clothed in reality."[33] Wilkes's unqualified praise for San Francisco and the Strait of Juan de Fuca contrasted sharply with his dismissal of the Columbia River, with its shifting sandbars, as a viable entrepôt. American diplomats, particularly Daniel Webster, stepped up efforts thereafter to acquire one or both of these harbors. The main reason Americans pressed so hard for the triangle of Oregon between the Columbia and the strait was the need for a deepwater port. Only seven Americans lived north of the Columbia River in 1845.

Commercial empire became even more exclusively the object in Mexico's California. When a British naval officer entered San Francisco Bay in 1845, he exclaimed: "D——n it! is there nothing but Yankees here?"[34] The Americans were connected primarily with the Boston trading company of Bryant & Sturgis. Having pioneered the otter trade in the Pacific and opened an office in Portuguese Macao, Bryant & Sturgis began in the 1820s to shift from furs to hides ("California bank notes"), which it bought cheaply from Catholic missions and rancheros.[35] The firm established an office in Santa Barbara in 1829, moving a few years later to Monterey. Thomas O. Larkin, later appointed the first American consul to California and a crucial figure in the diplomacy of 1845–1846, worked for Bryant & Sturgis, as did Richard Henry Dana, author of the epic narrative *Two Years Before the Mast* (1840), depicting a voyage to California around Cape Horn. Altogether, some 25,000 persons lived in California in 1845, including 800 Americans. Its link with Mexico City, more than 1,500 miles away, was weak. Overland communications were extremely difficult, and courts, police, schools, and newspapers scarcely existed. American merchants, whalers, and sailors competed ardently with their British counterparts.

Commercial opportunities also beckoned in Hawai'i, which by the 1840s resembled New England in the mid-Pacific. "Honolulu," the scholar Samuel Eliot Morison has written, "with merchant sailors rolling through its streets, shops fitted with Lowell shirtings, New England rum and Yankee notions, orthodox missionaries living in frame houses brought around the Horn, and a neo-classic meeting house built out of coral rocks, was becoming as Yankee as New Bedford."[36] Whaling ships still frequented the islands, and sugar plantations were spreading across fertile land. By the early 1840s, Protestant missionaries, finding Hawai'i more hospitable than China, had established seventy-nine mission stations, six schools, and two printing houses to spread the gospel. In 1842 President John Tyler informed Congress that U.S. stakes in Hawai'i had become so impressive that any attempt by another nation "to take possession of the islands, colonize them, and subvert the native Government" would meet U.S. opposition.[37] Although this Tyler Doctrine endorsed Hawai'i's independence, the United States declared its special interest in the archipelago and warned other powers away.

The Pacific and beyond yielded more than profits, as mariners and missionaries brought back by the 1820s enough artifacts to start museums such as the East India Marine Society of Salem, Massachusetts. Straight-laced Yankee merchants left diaries that described "Manila girls" as the "handsomest in the world" with whom "a small puff of wind would discover their nakedness." A catalogue noted that a "Sash" constituted "the entire dress of females in the Fegee [Fiji] Islands."[38] Although apparently less interested in erotica than New Englanders, entrepreneurs in the Midwest sought to link maritime trade to agrarian migration. Farmers moving to Oregon had in mind an expanded market for their products in Asia, as did some southerners, who saw the Chinese as potential buyers of cotton and tobacco. Politicians such as Stephen Douglas, an agrarian spokesman, embraced projects linking the Mississippi Valley with the Pacific via a transcontinental railroad. Indeed, in January 1845, Asa Whitney, a prospering New York merchant engaged in the China trade, first proposed the idea of government land grants to any group undertaking to build a railroad from the Great Lakes to Oregon. Such schemes did not reach fruition until after the Civil War, but their existence in the era of Manifest Destiny testifies to the dual nature (maritime and agrarian) of continental expansion.

John Quincy Adams, the Floridas, and the Transcontinental Treaty

Following the Louisiana Purchase of 1803, American diplomats had tried to obtain some of the large tropical peninsula of Florida by arguing that it had always been a part of Louisiana. The Spanish rejected such notions. The first U.S. bite out of the territory did not come until September 1810, when a group of American settlers revolted against Spanish rule, captured the fortress at Baton Rouge, and proclaimed the "Republic of West Florida." A blue woolen flag with a single silver star replaced the Bourbon banner. President James Madison immediately proclaimed West Florida part of the United States, although he actually sent troops to occupy an area only to the Pearl River. During the War of 1812 American soldiers occupied Mobile and all of West Florida to the Perdido River—the only tangible addition of territory resulting from that war.

It fell to the Monroe administration (1817–1825) and Secretary of State John Quincy Adams to complete the absorption. Spanish minister Don Luis de Onís proved himself a dogged, skillful advocate of a hopeless cause. Adams took the diplomatic offensive, arguing that Spain should cede East Florida to the United States because Spanish authorities had not prevented Indians from raiding American territory (as required by Pinckney's Treaty of 1795). Adams also blamed the

Spanish for not returning thousands of escaped slaves and accused them of cooperating with British forces during the War of 1812. Indeed, a continuing alliance between fugitive blacks and Seminoles, as well as a "Negro fort" on the Apalachicola River, made the acquisition of Florida imperative for those Americans who could not "tolerate a southern sanctuary from slavery."[39] Onís said he would cede East Florida, but he wanted a quid pro quo. Faced with revolts in its South American empire, Spain wanted a promise from the United States neither to assist the revolutionaries nor to recognize their declared independence. Madrid also instructed Onís to settle the disputed western boundary of Louisiana, and only to cede Florida in exchange for the best frontier that circumstances would admit. Adams, delighted to negotiate this second issue, urged that the boundary be set well southwest at the Rio Grande, or at least the Colorado River of Texas. After first insisting on the Mississippi, Onís moved grudgingly to the Mermentau and Calcasieu rivers in the middle of present-day Louisiana. The negotiators were far apart. "I have seen slippery diplomatists," Adams later observed, "but Onís is the first man I ever met who made it a point of honor to pass for more of a swindler than he was."[40]

The man who would break the impasse bivouacked with 3,000 troops at Big Creek, near the Georgia-Florida boundary in early 1818. General Andrew Jackson, the hero of New Orleans, comprised a volatile mixture of frontier passion and calculating ambition. Ostensibly under orders to pursue and punish Seminole Indians and runaway slaves who had been using Spanish Florida as a base from which to raid American settlements, Jackson had suggested in a secret letter to Monroe that "the whole of East Florida [be] seized and held as indemnity for the outrages of Spain upon the property of our Citizens."[41] No scholar has determined conclusively whether Monroe or Secretary of War John C. Calhoun explicitly approved Jackson's proposal. Jackson claimed they had; both denied it. In any case, neither Monroe nor Calhoun ever told Jackson *not* to cross the border. To the pugnacious Tennessean, this silence from Washington constituted tacit agreement that the Spanish were every bit as much the enemy as were the Seminoles.

"Old Hickory" burst across the border in late March 1818. On April 6 the Spanish garrison at St. Marks surrendered, and inside Jackson found "the noted Scotch villain Arbuthnot."[42] Alexander Arbuthnot, in actuality, was a kindly, seventy-year-old British subject whose commercial dealings with the Indians had become so scrupulously honest that his profit-minded superiors in England had grown annoyed with him. Convinced that Arbuthnot was in cahoots with the Seminoles, Jackson plunged into the jungle swamps looking for the main Indian camp. He found the camp but not the Indians. He seized another Englishman, Robert C. Ambrister, formerly of the British Royal Colonial Marines. Returning to St. Marks, Jackson convened a court-martial, hanged Arbuthnot, and shot Ambrister, not at all concerned that he was administering American "justice" on Spanish soil to two British subjects. "Old Hickory" next turned west toward Pensacola, where he felt certain that the Spanish governor was supplying the "Red Sticks." Pensacola capitulated on May 28, and Jackson promptly replaced the governor with one of his own colonels and declared in force the revenue laws of the United States, all of which he justified as "absolutely necessary to put down the Indian war."[43] In two short months, although he had killed or captured very few Indians, Jackson had occupied every important Spanish post in Florida except St. Augustine.

When news of Jackson's deeds became known, Onís roused Secretary Adams from his morning Bible study and demanded an indemnity, as well as punishment of Jackson. Calhoun and other cabinet members suggested a court-martial for the rambunctious general. Monroe, who disapproved less of what Jackson had done than the way he did it, quietly agreed to return the captured posts to Spain. But he did not censure Jackson and even offered to falsify some of the general's dispatches so that the invasion would appear in a more favorable light. Congress launched an investigation. Only Adams stoutly defended Jackson.

When the British did not protest the murders of Arbuthnot and Ambrister, Monroe gave his secretary of state full backing. As usual, Adams thought that the best defense was a good offense. He drew up a memorable reply to Onís's demands for censure and indemnity. If Spain could not restrain its Indians, the United States would in self-defense. A bit embarrassed by the lack of precedents in international law, Adams boldly claimed that the right of defensive invasion was "engraved in adamant on the common sense of mankind." Charging the Spanish with "impotence" rather than perfidy, the secretary demanded that "Spain must immediately make her election, either to place a force in Florida adequate at once to the protection of her territory and to the fulfillment of her engagements, or cede to the United States a province, of which she retains nothing but the nominal possession, but which is, in fact, a derelict, open to the occupancy of every enemy, civilized or savage, of the United States, and serving no other earthly purpose than as a post of annoyance to them."[44] Onís made no effective rejoinder, and his superiors in Madrid reacted to Jackson's forays with instructions to cede Florida quickly and retreat to the best possible boundary between Louisiana and Mexico.

More negotiations followed, culminating in the Adams-Onís Treaty (or Transcontinental Treaty), signed in Washington on February 22, 1819. The United States acquired East Florida, tacit recognition that previously occupied West Florida had come with the Louisiana Purchase, and a new boundary line that began at the mouth of the Sabine River, moved stairstep fashion along various rivers in a north-westerly direction to the forty-second parallel, and then went straight west to the Pacific. The secretary of state took the initiative of extending the boundary to the Pacific entirely on his own. "I closed the day with ejaculations of fervent gratitude," Adams noted in his diary, because "a definite line of boundary to the South Sea forms a great *epocha* in our history"[45] (see map on page 119).

In return for these gains, Adams surrendered vague U.S. claims to Texas arising from the Louisiana Purchase. In fact, Onís had instructions to retreat even on the Sabine boundary, but Monroe and the cabinet thought Florida more important than Texas and did not press the matter. The United States also agreed to assume the claims of its own citizens against Spain, some $5 million resulting from Franco-Spanish seizures of American shipping during the undeclared war of 1798–1800. The Transcontinental Treaty said nothing about U.S. recognition of Spain's rebellious colonies. Adams staunchly resisted any hand-tying nonrecognition pledge. Partly because of this silence, and partly because of personal intrigues over royal land grants in Florida, Madrid dragged its feet over ratification. Two years passed before ratifications were exchanged in 1821.

Perhaps the importance of the Adams-Onís Treaty lay not in what it acquired in 1819 but in what it foreshadowed. Just as in his diplomacy with England in the

John Quincy Adams (1767–1848). This photograph taken in 1843, near the end of Adams's career as diplomat, secretary of state, president, and congressman from Massachusetts, demonstrates well his austere and gloomy countenance. "My natural disposition," Adams once wrote, "is of an over-anxious cast, and my struggles to accommodate myself to circumstances . . . have given my constitution in less than fifty years the wear and tear of seventy." Ralph Waldo Emerson wrote that Adams "must have sulphuric acid in his tea." (National Portrait Gallery, Smithsonian Institution/Art Resource, N.Y.)

Convention of 1818 (see p. 106), Adams was projecting a continental vision. It did not matter if he and Onís were drawing lines across deserts that did not exist or around mountains that were not where maps said they should be. The negotiators engaged in "a battle between two kinds of imagination," the historian George Dangerfield has written. Onís was defending "a moribund, revolted, and helpless empire." As for Adams, he was "thinking and dreaming of an America of the future whose westward movement, in those days before the railroad, was hardly calculable."[46] Although no one coined the actual phrase until the 1840s, Manifest Destiny coursed through the language of John Quincy Adams. The world "should be familiarized with the idea of considering our proper dominion to be the continent of North America," he told the cabinet in 1819.[47]

A second, more disturbing aspect was the way in which Jackson's invasion of Florida had buttressed diplomacy. Spain's willingness to yield Florida, combined with Britain's refusal to question the executions of Ambrister and Arbuthnot, minimized diplomatic repercussions. Nevertheless, as the congressional investigation revealed, Monroe and Jackson had virtually waged war without the approval of Congress. Henry Clay believed that Monroe had assured the Congress that no Spanish forts would be seized if Jackson crossed the border in pursuit of Seminoles, but this was precisely what had occurred. Since neither Monroe nor Jackson had "the power to authorize hostility," Clay urged Congress not "to shrink from our duty. Let us assert our constitutional powers, and vindicate the instrument from military violation."[48] Because Clay wanted to become president, some contemporaries viewed the investigation as an attack on Clay's chief rival, Jackson. On February 8, 1819, after a twenty-seven-day debate, the four congressional resolutions condemning Jackson went down to defeat by comfortable margins. Appreciative that the headstrong general had facilitated expansion of the national domain, Congress accepted a precedent of unilateral executive military action that would repeat itself some 200 times in American history. By endorsing the administration's undeclared war, Congress voted to acquiesce in its own subordination in the checks-and-balances system of the U.S. government.

The Monroe Doctrine Targets Europe and the Western Hemisphere

The next notable milestone for expansion came with the Monroe Doctrine of 1823. At first glance, that statement of American diplomatic principles appears entirely anti-imperialist in intent—a stern warning to reactionary Europe not to interfere with revolutions in the New World, a gesture of solidarity and sympathy with the newly independent republics to the south. Monroe's declaration was indeed a warning and a gesture, but its motives were hardly selfless. In saying "Thou Shalt Not" to Europe, James Monroe and John Quincy Adams carefully exempted the United States. By facilitating commercial expansion into Latin America and landed expansion across the North American continent, the Monroe Doctrine became, in the historian Richard Van Alstyne's words, "an official declaration fencing in the 'western hemisphere' as a United States sphere of influence."[49]

The Latin American revolutions (1808–1822) had a magnetic effect on the United States. The exploits of such Latin American leaders as Simón Bolívar, José San Martín, and Bernardo O'Higgins rekindled memories of 1776. Henry Clay, in a famous oration in 1818, claimed the Latin leaders had "adopted our principles, copied our institutions and . . . employed the very language and sentiments of our revolutionary papers."[50]

That the United States did not heed popular enthusiasms and immediately recognize the Latin American republics owed mainly to the calculating diplomacy of John Quincy Adams. Cynical and cautious, Adams "wished well" to the new nations but doubted that they could "establish free or liberal institutions of government. . . . Arbitrary power, military and ecclesiastical, was stamped upon their education, upon their habits, and upon all their institutions. Civil dissension was infused into all their seminal principles."[51] Adams carefully avoided recognition, thereby easing negotiations with Spain over the Transcontinental Treaty. After signing, he worried that Onís would jettison the treaty if the United States recognized the new Latin American states. Adams also warned that U.S. meddling in independence struggles might drain the country's resources and nurture such ambitions to use force that the United States "would no longer be the ruler of her own spirit." So the secretary of state proclaimed on July 4, 1821: "Wherever the standard of freedom and independence has or shall be unfurled, there will her [the U.S.] heart, her benedictions, and her prayers be. But she goes not abroad in search of monsters to destroy."[52] Not until spring 1822, after the expulsion of Spanish armies from the New World, and following a sharp rise in U.S. trade with Latin America, did President Monroe extend formal recognition to the new governments of La Plata, Peru, Colombia, and Mexico. Adams instructed U.S. diplomats to focus their energies on obtaining favorable trading rights. He feared that the new "republics" were exchanging Spanish political sovereignty for British commercial domination.

Additional European threats loomed. Following Napoleon's final defeat, European statesmen had endeavored to restore order and legitimacy to an international system thrown out of kilter by the French Revolution and the conquests of the Corsican usurper. Conservatism became the watchword, and by the Treaty of Paris of 1815 the members of the Quadruple Alliance (Austria, Prussia, Russia, and Britain) bound themselves to future diplomatic congresses for the maintenance of peace and the status quo. A penitent France formally joined the "Concert of Europe" in 1818, and the Quadruple Alliance turned into the Quintuple Alliance. The allies also organized in 1815 the new Holy Alliance. By 1819–1820 the Austrian foreign minister, Prince Klemens von Metternich, enthusiastically supported by Tsar Alexander I of Russia, had transformed both alliances into instruments for suppressing revolutions. At the Congress of Troppau in 1820 the Holy Allies agreed that if internal revolutions posed threats to neighboring states, "the powers bind themselves, by peaceful means, or if need be by arms, to bring back the guilty State into the bosom of the Great Alliance."[53]

In 1821, Austrian armies put down uprisings in Naples and Piedmont. The following year a French army marched across the Pyrenees in support of Spain's unstable Ferdinand VII, who was then resisting a liberal constitutionalist government.

The Holy Allies also gave diplomatic support to Ottoman Turkey in its attempt to snuff out a national revolution in Greece. With Americans particularly incensed at the betrayal of freedom in Greece, John Quincy Adams feared that any gesture on behalf of the Greeks would get the United States "encumbered with a quarrel with all of Europe."[54] He also wondered: Would the Holy Alliance's zeal for putting down revolutions everywhere lead to the restoration of imperial rule over the insurrectionist colonies of Spain in the New World?

British diplomacy during these years played an ambivalent and tortuous role. Foreign Secretary Castlereagh wanted very much to support the system devised at the Congress of Vienna and to preserve the grand coalition that had defeated Napoleon. The British had little sympathy for revolution. Confident of the stability of their own political institutions, and guarded by the English Channel and the Royal Navy, many Britons nonetheless came to see the use of French and Austrian troops to suppress foreign revolts as upsetting the balance of power. When the Congress of Verona (1822) sanctioned the deployment of French military forces in Spain, something the British had fought the long and bitter Peninsular War (1809–1814) to prevent, England's withdrawal from the Holy Alliance became inevitable. Castlereagh's successor, George Canning, promised a return to isolation from continental entanglements.

Also influencing Canning was Great Britain's position "at the top of the wheel of fortune."[55] Enjoying global economic hegemony and naval supremacy, the British eyed ever-expanding commercial opportunities—and threats to them. British merchants had captured the lion's share of trade with rebellious Spanish ports in the New World. These lucrative commercial dealings, however, had not overcome London's antipathy to revolution so as to bring about formal recognition, although the British did fear that return of Spanish America to Ferdinand VII might curtail British trade. As Canning later boasted, "I resolved that if France had Spain, it should not be Spain 'with the Indies.' I called the New World into existence to redress the balance of the old."[56]

Canning's determination to prevent any restoration in Latin America led, in August 1823, to a remarkable conversation with U.S. minister Richard Rush. In discussing the progress of French armies in Spain, Rush casually mentioned that the British would never permit France to interfere with the independence of Latin America or to gain territory there by conquest or cession. Canning listened intently. What, he asked Rush, would the U.S. government say to going hand in hand with England in such a policy? No concerted action would be necessary; if they simply told the French that the United States and Britain held the same opinions, would that not deter them? Both nations would also disavow any intention of obtaining territories for themselves. Four days later, Canning wrote Rush: "There has seldom, in the history of the world, occurred an opportunity, when so small an effort of two friendly Governments, might produce so unequivocal a good and prevent such extensive calamities."[57] Intrigued but cautious, Rush referred the matter to Washington, D.C.

Rush's dispatch arrived in early October and sparked one of the most momentous discussions in American history. Monroe sought the advice of Thomas Jefferson and James Madison. These two elder Virginians agreed with the president that he should accept the British proposal. Jefferson's reply recalled 1803, when the French seemed ready to take New Orleans. "Great Britain," he wrote, "is the nation which can do us the most harm of any one, or all on earth; and with her on our side we need not fear the whole world."[58] Madison also counseled that "with British cooperation we have nothing to fear from the rest of Europe."[59] Madison even suggested a joint statement with the British on behalf of Greek independence. Armed with these opinions, Monroe called a cabinet meeting on November 7, fully prepared to embrace British cooperation.

John Quincy Adams, however, fought vigorously for a unilateral course. Adams did not trust the British. Hoping to compete successfully for Latin American markets, and not wanting to tie U.S. hands in some future acquisition of, say, Texas or Cuba, the secretary of state argued that it would be more dignified and candid to make an independent declaration of principles to the Holy Alliance than "to come in as a cockboat in the wake of the British man-of-war."[60] In this and subsequent meetings Adams gradually won Monroe over. Complications arose when another dispatch from Rush reported that Canning had mysteriously lost interest in a joint declaration. Rush did not know that Canning, on October 9, had made an agreement with the French, the so-called Polignac Memorandum, whereby the French disclaimed "any intention or desire" to act against the former Spanish colonies in Latin America.[61] News also arrived of the French capture of Cadiz, Spain, along with rumors that a French fleet might soon embark for the New World. Secretary of War Calhoun was "perfectly moonstruck" by the French threat and, according to Adams, "has so affected the President that he appeared entirely to despair of the cause of South America." Adams remained optimistic. He detected competing national interests within the Holy Alliance, noted England's stake in Latin America, and sarcastically told Calhoun that "I no more believe that the Holy Allies will restore the Spanish dominion on the American continent than that the Chimborazo [a mountain in Ecuador] will sink beneath the ocean."[62] Adams won his point. Monroe followed his secretary's advice.

Next came the official declaration. Monroe's original draft followed Adams's previous arguments in the cabinet, but it also included a ringing indictment of the French intervention in Spain and a statement favoring the independence of revolutionary Greece. Adams opposed both points. However much he deplored events in Spain and Greece, the secretary advocated isolation from European embroilments. He urged the president "to make an American cause and adhere inflexibly to that."[63] Monroe excised the offending passages. The Monroe Doctrine then became part of the president's message to Congress of December 2, 1823. It contained three essential points: noncolonization, "hands off" the New World, and American noninvolvement in European quarrels.

Noncolonization focused specifically on Russia and responded to the tsar's announcement in 1821 that Russian dominion extended southward from Alaska along the Pacific to the fifty-first parallel. Adams had protested to the Russian minister in summer 1823, so Monroe simply reiterated the axiom that "the American continents, by the free and independent condition which they have assumed and

James Monroe (1758–1831).   Before becoming president in 1817, the distinguished Virginian served as secretary of state (1811–1817). Sharing John Quincy Adams's nationalist perspective, Monroe helped shape his namesake doctrine against European intrusions into Latin America. (Library of Congress)

maintain, are henceforth not to be considered as subjects for future colonization by any European powers." By implication, the noncolonization principle also applied to England and the Holy Alliance.

Monroe's second principle, "hands off," posited the notion of two different worlds. He observed that the monarchical system of the Old World "is essentially different from that of America" and warned that "any attempt" by the European powers to "extend their system to any portion of this hemisphere" or to oppress the newly independent governments would be regarded as "dangerous to our peace and safety" and as "an unfriendly disposition toward the United States." As for the final principle, abstention, Monroe echoed Washington's Farewell Address: "In the wars of the European powers in matters relating to themselves we have never taken any part, nor does it comport with our policy to do so."[64]

An implicit corollary to the Monroe Doctrine, although not mentioned in the address, was the principle of "no transfer." Earlier that same year, in response to reports that Britain might try to negotiate the cession of Cuba from Spain, Adams had informed both the Spaniards and the Cubans that the United States opposed British annexation. "Cuba," Adams wrote in April 1823, "forcibly disjoined from its own unnatural connection with Spain, and incapable of self-support, can only gravitate towards the North American Union, which by the same law of nature cannot cast her off from its bosom."[65] Thus, when read in the context of Adams's concern over Cuba, the noncolonization principle in the Monroe Doctrine also warned Spain against transferring its colony to England or to any other European power.

The immediate effect of Monroe's message was hardly earthshaking. Brave words, after all, would not prevent the dismemberment of Latin America. The Polignac Memorandum and the British navy actually took care of such a contingency. The Holy Allies sneered, calling Monroe's principles "haughty," "arrogant," "blustering," and "monstrous." Metternich ignored the "indecent declarations," as did the tsar, who thought "the document in question . . . merits only the most profound contempt."[66] Pleased at first, Canning soon realized that Monroe and Adams might steal his thunder and turn Latin gratitude into Yankee trade opportunities. Canning thereupon rushed copies of the Polignac Memorandum to Latin American capitals, where they learned that England, not the upstart Yankees, had thwarted "any project of bringing back the late Spanish colonies under the dominion of the mother country by foreign aid."[67] Latin Americans at first received the Monroe Doctrine cordially. When Washington refused to negotiate military alliances with Colombia and Brazil, however, disillusionment quickly set in. At home, most Americans, as the British minister reported, applauded Monroe's message for its "explicit and manly tone," which "has evidently found in every bosom a chord which vibrates in strict unison with the sentiments so conveyed."[68] In France, the Marquis de Lafayette called it "the best little bit of paper that God ever permitted any man to give to the World."[69]

Adams knew that the United States lacked the power to back up the words with deeds. The United States would defend its own territory, of course, but how could it guarantee republican governments in other countries, including those in Latin America? Later generations talked less about matching commitment and power and more about Monroe's words as justifying U.S. expansion in the name of hemispheric solidarity. Indeed, from the beginning, Monroe's message—"a vague statement of policy, a lecture, a doctrine, an ideal," in the scholar John J. Johnson's words—pledged the United States "only to its own self-interest."[70]

Trade, Canada, and Other Anglo-American Intersections

For years after the Monroe Doctrine, because of commercial rivalry in Latin America, squabbles over West Indian trade, politics in Canada, boundary disputes, and British attempts to suppress the international slave trade, most Americans continued to regard Britain as *the* principal threat to the national interest. As co-occupant of the North American continent, supreme naval power in the world, and commercial giant, only England could block U.S. expansion.

Still, just as in the 1790s, the intertwining of the two economies helped to countervail impulses toward war. In 1825, for example, the United States exported $37 million in goods to England, out of total exports valued at $91 million; by 1839 the figures stood at $57 million and $112 million. The burgeoning British textile industry came to depend on American cotton. Imports from Britain during the 1820s and 1830s fluctuated between one-half and one-third of total U.S. imports. In 1825, 18 percent of total British exports went to the United States; in 1840, 10 percent. In those same years England received 13 percent and 27 percent of its total imports from America.

These figures, combined with the British decision in 1830 to open the West Indies to direct trade with the United States, reflected a growing British trend toward free trade, which in the 1840s meant dismantling imperial "preferences," repealing protective tariffs, and concentrating on manufactured exports. Anglo-American economic interdependence, although hardly a guarantee against war, acted as a brake against military hostilities. Expanding foreign trade created intense commercial rivalry, but Britons and Yankees sometimes cooperated to reduce costs. In faraway ports such as Singapore and Hong Kong, American merchants relied on British bills of exchange and letters of credit and on the services of British agents. "Wherever English enterprise goes, ours is quickly alongside it," remarked an American diplomat who understood both the competitive and cooperative features of the relationship.[71]

The years immediately following the War of 1812 marked a high point in Anglo-American relations, thanks largely to the conciliatory diplomacy of John Quincy Adams and Lord Castlereagh. After signing the Treaty of Ghent, Adams, Albert Gallatin, and Henry Clay went directly to London and negotiated a commercial treaty with the British Board of Trade in 1815. A reciprocal trade agreement, it repeated the terms of Jay's Treaty with respect to commercial intercourse between America and Great Britain. The treaty also forbade discriminatory duties by either country against the ships or commerce of the other, thus tacitly conceding the failure of Jefferson's "peaceable coercions." The accord said nothing about impressment or neutral rights. The two nations renewed this commercial convention in 1818 for ten more years.

War's end also found the British and Americans engaged in feverish warship construction on the Great Lakes, the beginnings of a naval race that neither London nor Washington could afford. Confident that the United States could build vessels quickly in a crisis, the Monroe administration proposed a standstill agreement to the British. Much to the dismay of the Canadians, Castlereagh agreed. By the Rush-Bagot agreement, negotiated in Washington in April 1817, each country pledged to maintain not more than one armed ship on Lake Champlain, another on Lake Ontario, and two on all the other Great Lakes. The Rush-Bagot accord applied only to warships and left land fortifications intact. Although the "unguarded frontier" between Canada and the United States did not become reality until the Treaty of Washington in 1871 (see page 180), the Rush-Bagot agreement ranks as one of the world's first successful disarmament treaties.

The Convention of 1818, negotiated in London by Richard Rush and Albert Gallatin, dealt with the fisheries and the northwestern boundary. In an effort to settle the vaguely defined limits of the Louisiana Purchase, the Americans initially proposed to extend the Canadian-American boundary westward from Lake of the Woods to the Pacific Ocean along the line of 49° north latitude. Because Britain refused to abandon its claims to the Columbia River Basin, the convention stipulated that the boundary should run from Lake of the Woods to the "Stony Mountains" along the forty-ninth parallel. Beyond the Rockies, for a period of ten years, subject to renewal, the Oregon territory should remain "free and open" to both British and American citizens.

As for the vexatious matter of the Atlantic fisheries, the 1818 agreement won confirmation of the "liberty" to fish "for ever" along specific stretches of the Newfoundland and Labrador coasts, as well as to dry and cure fish along other areas of the same coastline.[72] The vague phrasing caused controversy in later decades, but Secretary John Quincy Adams accepted the agreement as vindication of his family's honor. Not for nothing was the motto on the Adams family seal *Piscemur, venemur ut olim* ("We will fish and hunt as heretofore").

The fisheries question did not see resolution until 1910 in an arbitration before the Hague Court. Technically, the issue stood as the the most complicated in nineteenth-century American diplomatic history. According to a story at Harvard University, the humorist Robert Benchley once had to answer an examination question on the North Atlantic fisheries in a course on American foreign policy. Benchley knew nothing about the fisheries. Undaunted, he wrote: "This question has long been discussed from the American and British points of view, but has anyone considered the viewpoint of the fish?"[73] Benchley proceeded to analyze the codfish question and earned, appropriately enough, the grade of C.

After the Monroe Doctrine, Canning hoped to avoid unnecessary friction with Washington. "Let us hasten settlement, if we can," he wrote, "but let us postpone the day of difference, if it must come."[74] Yet a series of crises heightened differences. Most important was the Canadian rebellion of 1837, led by William Lyon Mackenzie. Some Americans cheered the Canadian quest for self-government and volunteered. Coming a year after the Texas war for independence, the Canadian rebellion also revived expansionist visions of 1812. Rensselaer Van Rensselaer, son of an American general, tried to become a Canadian version of Sam Houston, leading a motley group of Canadian rebels and American sympathizers on raids into Canada from New York.

In December 1837 pro-British Canadians struck Van Rensselaer's stronghold on Navy Island in the Niagara River, hoping to capture the rebel supply ship *Caroline.* The troops crossed to the American shore, found the forty-five-ton *Caroline,* set it afire, and cast it adrift to sink a short distance above the great falls. During the fracas an American, Amos Durfee, died. Outrage gripped Americans along the border. Durfee's body was displayed before 3,000 mourners at Buffalo city hall. Demonstrators in Lewiston, New York, made a bonfire of books by British authors. In May 1838 some Americans boarded the Canadian steamboat *Sir Robert Peel,* plying the St. Lawrence River. They burned and looted the vessel, all the while shouting "Remember the *Caroline!*" Raids and counterraids continued through 1838. Authorities in Washington maintained their equilibrium. President Martin Van Buren sent General Winfield Scott to the New York–Ontario border to restore quiet. Scott brooked no nonsense. "Except if it be over my body," he shouted to an unruly crowd, "you shall not pass this line—you shall not embark."[75] When Mackenzie and Van Rensselaer fled to the American border, local authorities quickly arrested them, and the rebellion petered out.

A new crisis flared up in February 1839 in northern Maine. The vast timberlands spanning the Maine–New Brunswick border had long provoked diplomatic dispute because of cartographic errors in the 1783 peace treaty. In the mid-1830s, settlers moved to the fertile Aroostook Valley. Rival claims and occasional brawls ensued. Soon axe-wielding lumberjacks became embroiled in the "Aroostook War." Maine mobilized its militia that winter, as did New Brunswick, and Congress appropriated some $10 million for defense. It seemed an opportunity to whip the "Warriors of Waterloo."[76] As the "Maine Battle Song" had it: "Britannia shall not rule the Maine, / Nor shall she rule the water; / They've sung that song full long enough, / Much longer than they oughter."[77] The "war" did not last long. General Scott again rushed to the scene, and after a few tense weeks the British minister and Secretary of State John Forsyth negotiated a temporary armistice pending a final boundary settlement. The only American death came at the very end when a Maine militiaman, firing his musket in celebration of the peace, accidentally killed a farmer working his field.

Any possibility that Americans would forget the *Caroline* affair soon disappeared in November 1840, when a Canadian grocer named Alexander McLeod allegedly bragged in a Niagara, New York, saloon that he personally had killed Amos Durfee. New York State authorities quickly arrested McLeod and charged him with murder and arson. British foreign secretary Lord Palmerston fulminated that McLeod's execution "would produce . . . a war of retaliation and vengeance."[78] Judging the *Caroline* raid "a necessity of self-defense, instant, overwhelming, leaving no choice of means, and no moment for deliberation," Secretary of State Daniel Webster regretted that the federal government did not have jurisdiction in the case.[79] Anglo-American amity nonetheless survived this crisis. McLeod produced credible witnesses who swore that the Canadian grocer had not participated in the *Caroline* raid. The Utica jurors believed the witnesses, and McLeod went free.

Within a month of McLeod's acquittal, another crisis erupted. In November 1841, a cargo of slaves being transported from Hampton Roads to New Orleans mutinied and took control of the American vessel *Creole,* killing one white man in the process. The slaves sought refuge at Nassau in the Bahamas, where British authorities liberated all but the actual murderers. Southerners demanded retribution. The Supreme Court recently had passed judgment on the similar case of the Spanish slaver *Amistad,* in which fifty-three African captives, led by Joseph Cinque, killed the captain and crew in Cuban waters in 1839 and then attempted unsuccessfully to sail to Africa. U.S. authorities seized the *Amistad* off Long Island and jailed the Africans in New Haven, Connecticut. Despite Spain's demand for the return of "property" under existing treaties, John Quincy Adams, acting as a private attorney with strong backing from northern abolitionists, won freedom for the *Amistad* blacks on the basis of their natural rights as "kidnapped Africans" since Spain had outlawed the African slave trade in 1820.[80] Nonetheless, the *Creole* affair seemed more explosive because it involved legal American slaves freed by the British, whose efforts to suppress the international slave trade often collided with America's refusal to permit its vessels to be searched. Southern outrage at the loss of honor and slaves forced Secretary Webster to demand, as a matter of "comity and discretion," the return of *Creole* mutineers to stand trial.[81] As the U.S. minister to

France pointedly asked: Who made John Bull the "great Prefect of police on the ocean?"[82]

As the year 1842 approached, a long list of troubles beset Anglo-American relations. The northeastern boundary remained in contest. Britain had not apologized for the *Caroline* affair. British interest in Oregon and Texas worried Americans, who disliked British snobbery. British visitors, most notably Charles Dickens, wrote scathingly of American manners and morals. But the time seemed ripe for the settlement of many of these issues. A new Tory government took office in September 1841, and Lord Aberdeen, a conciliatory man and protégé of Castlereagh, replaced the cantankerous Palmerston at the Foreign Office. Aberdeen appointed as a special envoy to Washington the accommodating Lord Ashburton. Only recently retired from the great financial house of Baring Brothers, Ashburton had married an American, and he became so "zealous" in behalf of Americans that he opposed British maritime restrictions before the War of 1812.[83] Beetle-browed Daniel Webster reciprocated Ashburton's amicability. The secretary of state had known Ashburton for some years. Indeed, Webster had long acted as the American legal agent for the Baring firm, often earning a good salary through British commissions. Three years earlier the erudite and eloquent orator, then at the peak of his political career, had toured England, dined with Queen Victoria, and won wide acclaim. The two diplomats met leisurely for several weeks in the summer of 1842, feasted on Maine salmon, Virginia terrapin, Maryland crabs, and Chesapeake duck, and produced the Webster-Ashburton Treaty, signed and approved in August.

The Anglo-American agreement drew a new Maine boundary. Far enough south to allow a military road the British wanted to build between New Brunswick and Quebec, the border was still considerably north of Britain's maximum demand. The United States received approximately 7,000 of the 12,000 square miles under dispute, although this was some 893 square miles less than the king of the Netherlands had awarded in 1831 in his abortive attempt to arbitrate the controversy. Farther west Webster won most of the disputed territory near the headwaters of the Connecticut River, as well as a favorable boundary from Lake Superior to Lake of the Woods. Included in the latter acquisition, but largely unbeknownst at the time to the negotiators, was the valuable iron ore of the Mesabi Range in Minnesota. Although not part of the treaty per se, notes expressing mutual regrets over the *Caroline* and *Creole* affairs were exchanged by the diplomats, and in 1853 a joint claims commission awarded $110,330 to owners of the freed slaves.

Characterized by compromise and cordial personal relations, Webster's discussions with Ashburton seemed simple compared with his diplomacy with Maine and Massachusetts. The Bay State had retained half ownership in Maine's public domain after the latter had become a separate state in 1820, and so Webster had to persuade both states to approve the new boundary with Canada. The secretary resorted to some dubious cartographic persuasion. One of Webster's friends was Jared Sparks, a historian who later became president of Harvard. Sparks had been researching the diplomacy of the American Revolution in the British archives, and he told Webster he had seen the original map on which Benjamin Franklin had drawn a strong red line delineating the northeast boundary. From memory Sparks reproduced the line on a nineteenth-century map, and it corresponded closely to British claims. A

Daniel Webster (1782–1852).
A famed constitutional lawyer from Massachusetts, Webster served as a member of Congress (1823–1827), a U.S. senator (1827–1841), and secretary of state (1841–1843). He helped settle the northeastern boundary dispute. As a senator again in 1845–1850, he opposed the acquisition of Texas and the War with Mexico. From 1850 until his death, this imposing political figure sat once more as secretary of state. (National Portrait Gallery, Smithsonian Institution)

Thomas Hart Benton (1782–1858). Rugged and rambunctious, a Missouri senator from 1821 to 1851, this splashy orator championed westward expansion. But he accepted the forty-ninth-parallel compromise boundary for Oregon and only reluctantly voted for war with Mexico because he considered the Nueces the true boundary. Some expansionists opposed a field command for Benton during the war because they believed, correctly, that he would oppose a large territorial grab from Mexico. (Library of Congress)

second map turned up, older but still not genuine, also supporting the British position. Accepting both spurious maps as genuine, Webster sent Sparks to Augusta and Boston with this new "evidence" to persuade local officials to accept the treaty before the British decided to back out of the agreement. Webster also offered each state $150,000. Maine and Massachusetts then endorsed the Webster-Ashburton Treaty.

The original maps used in the 1782 peace negotiations actually did have lines that supported American boundary claims. Palmerston had found one such authentic map in 1839 but said nothing. A second map showed up in the Jay family papers in 1843. But the lines on these maps seemed preliminary rather than definitive, as Webster later recognized, not at all "drawn for the purpose of shewing [*sic*] on the map, a boundary which had been agreed on."[84] Thus only by reasonable compromise did 3,207,680 acres of Maine woodland become part of Canada.

Contest over the Oregon Country

The Webster-Ashburton negotiations did not settle the question of the "Oregon country"—that great wilderness west of the Rocky Mountains and between the forty-second parallel in the South and 54°40′ in the North. Webster proposed yielding territory north of the Columbia River if the British would, first, offer a quadrilateral tract of land adjoining the Strait of Juan de Fuca, which Webster believed had the best deepwater ports in the disputed territory, and, second, persuade Mexico to sell Upper California. Ashburton declined.

That same year, 1842, saw the beginning of "Oregon fever," as farmers began to arrive in the lush Willamette Valley. Oregon suddenly became controversial. In 1843 the Senate passed a bill calling for the construction of forts along the Oregon route, but the House demurred. When rumors leaked of Webster's offer to surrender some of Oregon, numerous "Oregon conventions" met, especially in the Midwest, to reassert America's claim to 54°40′. "Let the emigrants . . . carry their rifles," boomed Senator Thomas Hart Benton. "Thirty thousand rifles in Oregon will annihilate the Hudson's Bay Company, drive them off our continent."[85] The Democratic party platform of 1844 called for the "reoccupation" of Oregon, and the party's candidate, James K. Polk, vowed to effect it. At stake was not only the fate of U.S. citizens living in the contested lands but also the availability of ports for ships plying waters to Asian markets, especially after the Treaty of Wangxia opened more of China to American merchant vessels.

In actuality, war over Oregon lacked urgency. The American population in Oregon, although increasing every year, still numbered only 5,000 people in 1845, and all but a handful lived south of the Columbia River. In contrast, the 700-odd trappers and traders associated with the Hudson's Bay Company all lived north of the river. Four times, in 1818, 1824, 1826, and 1844, the British had proposed the Columbia as the boundary. Each time the United States had countered with 49°. The dispute centered on the triangle northwest of the Columbia, including the deepwater Strait of Juan de Fuca. Notwithstanding shouts of "Fifty-four forty or fight" from such ultras as Democratic senators Edward Hannegan of Indiana and William Allen of Ohio, only a minority of the Democratic party, mainly midwesterners, seemed eager to challenge England. Southern Democrats cared more for Texas than for Oregon. A few Whigs, such as Webster, wanted Pacific ports, but not at the risk of war. Even though Polk had won election on an expansionist platform, the new president had ample opportunity to settle the Oregon boundary through diplomacy.

Polk began badly. Bound by the Democratic platform to assert full U.S. claims, he announced in his inaugural address of March 4, 1845, that the American title to the whole of Oregon was "clear and unquestionable."[86] This claim, coming in an official state paper, raised British hackles. Polk, it seems, was talking more for domestic consumption, for in July he had Secretary of State James Buchanan propose the forty-ninth parallel (including the southern tip of Vancouver Island) as a fair compromise. Buchanan explained that the president "found himself embarrassed, if not committed, by the acts of his predecessors."[87] Buchanan's offer, however, did not include free navigation of the Columbia River, and this omission, coupled with Polk's earlier blustering about 54°40′, caused British minister Richard Pakenham to reject the proposal. Polk waited several weeks. Then, on August 30, after rejecting the advice of Buchanan—who wanted to temporize because of tensions with Mexico over Texas—the president withdrew his offer and reasserted American claims to 54°40′.

Polk increased the pressure further in his annual message to Congress of December 1845. Again claiming all of Oregon, he urged giving Britain the necessary year's notice for ending joint occupation and hinted at military measures to protect Americans in Oregon. Polk also made specific reference to the Monroe Doctrine: "The United States cannot in silence permit any European interference on the North American continent, and should any such interference be attempted [the United States] will be ready to resist it at any and all hazards."[88] Polk had Texas and California in mind, in addition to Oregon, but he was pointedly warning Britain.

For the next five months, while Congress debated ending joint occupation, Polk remained publicly adamant for 54°40′. Twice London offered to arbitrate; each time Washington refused. Lord Aberdeen sincerely wanted a settlement but could not afford to retreat in the face of Yankee braggadocio. Moving carefully, the foreign secretary already had begun a propaganda campaign in the London *Times* designed to prepare public opinion for the loss of the Columbia River triangle. It helped when the Hudson's Bay Company, faced with the flood of American settlers into the Willamette Valley, decided in 1845 to abandon the "trapped-out" southern part of Oregon and move its main depot from Fort Vancouver on the Columbia River north to Vancouver Island. Still, the British diplomat told the U.S. government that he would no longer oppose offensive military preparations in Canada, including the immediate dispatch of "thirty sail of the line." When this news reached Washington in late February 1846, Polk replied that if the British proposed "extending the boundary to the Pacific by the forty-ninth parallel and the Strait of Fuca," he would send the proposition to the Senate, "though with reluctance."[89]

The British proposal came in early June, but because it guaranteed free navigation of the Columbia to the Hudson's Bay Company, Polk found it distasteful. On the advice of his cabinet and Senator Benton, however, he decided on an unusual

Oregon Forest.   Images of massive trees in the Oregon country's bountiful environment, such as this 1844 engraving by William E. Tucker, helped inflame the "Oregon fever" that drew Americans west. (Library of Congress)

procedure. Before signing or rejecting the treaty, he submitted it to the Senate for *previous* advice. This procedure placed responsibility for the settlement squarely on the Senate and absolved Polk for his retreat from 54°40′. The Senate advised Polk, by a vote of 38 to 12, to accept the British offer. On June 15 the president formally signed the treaty, which the Senate then approved, 41 to 14, three days later. Polk and the Senate compromised so willingly, of course, because war with Mexico had begun some six weeks earlier.

The Texas Revolution and Annexation

The acquisition of Texas impelled the United States and Mexico toward war. The United States had confirmed Spanish claims to this northernmost province of Mexico in the Adams-Onís Treaty of 1819, but the self-denial was only temporary. After Mexico won independence from Spain in 1821, two American envoys attempted to purchase the area. The first, South Carolinian Joel Poinsett, involved himself in local politics in the late 1820s and tried to work through friendly liberals in the Mexican congress. His successor, Anthony Butler, an unscrupulous crony of Andrew Jackson, tried bribery. Both efforts came to naught. As in the case of Oregon and Florida, transborder migration became the chief engine of U.S. expansion.

Large-scale American settlement did not begin until the 1820s. Spanish authorities, in 1821, hoping to build up Texas as a buffer against U.S. expansion, had encouraged immigration through generous grants of land. Moses Austin, a Connecticut Yankee from Missouri, and his son Stephen became the first empresarios by pledging to bring in 300 families, who, in turn, would swear allegiance to Spain and the Catholic faith. In 1821, the new Mexican government confirmed these grants and issued others. Within a decade, more than 20,000 Americans had crossed into Texas seeking homesteads—more people than had settled in the previous three centuries. "A gentle breeze shakes off a ripe peach," wrote Stephen Austin. "The more the American population is increased," the more "the peach will be ripe."[90] Most of the "G.T.T."(Gone to Texas) were slaveholders seeking the fertile delta soil along the Gulf coast to grow cotton. Under such circumstances, according to the historian Gene M. Brack, "it did not take long for Mexicans to discern the similarity of American attitudes towards blacks, Indians, and Mexicans."[91]

Friction soon came. The newcomers, required by law to become Roman Catholics and Mexican citizens, remained predominantly Protestant and never ceased to think of themselves as Americans. Sporadic trouble erupted over immigration, tariffs, slavery, and Mexican army garrisons. Finally, General Antonio López de Santa Anna seized dictatorial power in 1834 and attempted to establish a strong centralized government in Mexico City. Regarding this change as a violation of their rights under the Mexican Constitution of 1824, Texans submitted a "Declaration of Causes" that resembled the "Declaration of Rights and Grievances" of 1775. By autumn 1835, Texans had skirmished with local Mexican soldiers, set up a provisional government, and begun raising a rebel army under Sam Houston.

Santa Anna responded by leading a huge force north across the Rio Grande. At the old Alamo mission in San Antonio, some 200 Texans stood off 1,800 Mexicans for nearly two weeks. Then, on March 6, 1836, with Mexican bugles sounding "no quarter," Santa Anna's forces broke through the Alamo's defenses and killed every resister, including the legendary Davy Crockett and James Bowie. Three weeks later another Texan force, swelled by recent volunteers from the United States, surrendered at Goliad. The Mexicans promptly executed more than three hundred. These atrocities enraged North Americans, hundreds of whom joined Houston's army, which retreated eastward. The showdown came on April 21, 1836, when Houston's force, now numbering 800, turned and attacked the Mexican military near the San Jacinto River, not far from present-day Houston, Texas. Yelling "Remember the Alamo," the Texans charged across an open field, and routed the Mexicans, killing about 630. Taken by surprise when the Texans attacked during afternoon siesta, Santa Anna was found hiding in a clump of long grass. Instead of hanging Santa Anna from the nearest tree, Houston extracted a treaty from the Mexican leader that recognized Texas's independence and set a southern and western boundary at the Rio Grande. Mexico repudiated this agreement after Santa Anna's release, but the Battle of San Jacinto ensured Texas's independence.

Texas sought immediate annexation to the United States. Houston's good friend President Jackson certainly wanted Texas and had tried to purchase the territory from Mexico, but by 1836 Texas had become a political hot potato. The problem was slavery. Fervent continentalists such as John Quincy Adams saw as never before that expansion westward also meant the expansion of slavery. The balance in 1836 stood at thirteen slave states and thirteen free states. An alert politician, "Old Hickory" tiptoed. Not until the last days of his administration, some eleven months after San Jacinto, did Jackson even recognize Texas's independence.

Texas Banner. Evoking memories of the American Revolution, Texans seeking independence carried this banner of a lady of liberty in 1836. (Archives Division, Texas State Library)

Jackson's chosen successor, Martin Van Buren, also refused to consider annexation "out of deference to the [anti-slavery] prejudices of the North."[92] The annexation issue slumbered until 1843, when unpopular President John Tyler, having everything to gain and nothing to lose, seized on Texas as a vehicle for lifting his political fortunes. He successfully negotiated an annexation treaty with the Texans and submitted it to the Senate in April 1844, just prior to the presidential nominating conventions.

Tyler, and later Polk, hoped to gain support for the absorption of Texas by playing on fears of British intrusion. Having recognized Texan independence in 1840, Britain had developed a clear interest in maintaining that independence, hoping that an independent Texas would block American expansion. Further, Texas could offer an alternative supply of cotton for England's textile factories. A low-tariff Lone Star Republic might grow into a large British market and, by example, stimulate southern states to push harder in Washington for tariff reduction. Certain Britishers also hoped that they could persuade Texas to abolish slavery, a prospect that Texan leaders manipulated to gain British support against Mexico. England did arrange a truce between Mexico and Texas in 1842, and two years later Lord Aberdeen toyed with the idea of an international agreement whereby Mexico would extend diplomatic recognition to Texas, and England, France, and, he hoped, the United States would guarantee the independence and existing borders of both Texas and Mexico. The scheme collapsed when Mexico stubbornly refused any dealings with Texas. Not until May 1845, after a resolution for annexation had already passed the U.S. Congress, did Mexico agree to recognize Texas. Too late.

Those British maneuvers, however legal and aboveboard, alarmed American expansionists. By nurturing such anxieties, the Tyler administration might have achieved annexation in 1844 had not Secretary of State John C. Calhoun injudiciously boasted that annexation would guard against the danger of abolition of slavery under British tutelage. Calhoun went on to defend slavery as "essential to the peace, safety, and prosperity" of the South, using pseudoscientific arguments that offended the British far less than they antagonized abolitionists and free soilers in the North.[93] When the Senate took its final vote on June 8, 1844, the tally was 35 to 16, a two-thirds majority *against* annexation.

Texas and annexation became a central feature of the 1844 presidential campaign. Nominating James K. Polk of Tennessee, a disciple of Jackson, the Democrats fervently embraced expansion. The party platform promised the "reoccupation of Oregon and the re-annexation of Texas," giving rise to the myth that somehow the United States once owned Texas. The Whigs chose Henry Clay, who opposed taking Texas if it meant war. After a fierce campaign, Polk won by a close margin: 1,337,000 to 1,299,000 in the popular vote and 170 to 105 in the electoral college. Although people at the time considered the Democratic victory a mandate for expansion, other factors, including an abolitionist third-party candidate who took votes from Clay in the decisive state of New York, help explain Polk's victory. Whatever the reasons for their choice, the voters, in one of the rare presidential elections in which foreign-policy issues predominated, had elected the candidate who would bring war. If Clay had won in 1844, he almost certainly would have kept peace with Mexico.

Even before Polk took office, the annexationists acted. The lame-duck Tyler suggested annexation by joint resolution (simple majorities of both houses). Opponents howled, demanding a two-thirds vote for a treaty in the Senate. Albert Gallatin called it "an undisguised usurpation of power," and John Quincy Adams grumbled that the Constitution had become a "monstrous trap."[94] But the annexationists had the votes—120 to 98 in the House, 27 to 25 in the Senate—and on March 1, 1845, three days before leaving office, Tyler signed the fateful measure. Five days later the Mexican envoy in Washington asked for his passport and went home.

Polk did not inherit an inevitable conflict with Mexico. Rather, the president made decisions and carried them out in ways that exacerbated already existing tension and made war difficult to avoid. Mexico had stated unequivocally that it would sever diplomatic relations if the United States annexed Texas, but Polk compounded the problem by supporting Texas's flimsy claim to the Rio Grande as its southern and western boundary. Except for the treaty extracted from Santa Anna in 1836, the Nueces River had always stood as the accepted boundary, and during the nine years of independence Texas made no move to occupy the disputed territory south of Corpus Christi (see page 87). During the negotiations to complete annexation in summer 1845, however, Polk's emissaries apparently urged Texas president Anson Jones to seize all territory to the Rio Grande. Polk's orders to U.S. military and naval forces, although couched in defensive terms, intended to prevent any Mexican retaliation. At this time, too, the president sent secret orders to Commodore John D. Sloat of the Pacific Squadron to capture the main ports of California in the event that Mexico attacked Texas. Whether Polk actively sought to provoke war or merely used force to buttress diplomacy, he was making unilateral decisions that disregarded Mexican sensibilities and ignored congressional prerogatives.

When Mexico failed to retaliate, Polk again turned to diplomacy. He had received word from the U.S. consul in Mexico City that the government, although furious at annexation, did not want war and would receive a special emissary to discuss Texas. Polk sent John Slidell, a Louisiana Democrat, as a full minister plenipotentiary empowered to reestablish formal relations and to negotiate issues other than Texas. California now loomed large in Polk's mind, even larger than Texas. No sooner had the president instructed Slidell to purchase New Mexico and California for $25 million (Slidell could go as high as $40 million) than a report arrived from Consul Thomas Larkin in Monterey describing in lurid terms British machinations to turn California into a protectorate. Since Polk had no way of knowing that Larkin was reporting false rumors and exaggerating British activities, this information only increased his resolve to obtain California. The president instructed Larkin to inspire Californians "with a jealousy of European dominion and to arouse in their bosoms that love of liberty and independence so natural to the American Continent."[95] A copy of these orders reached Lieutenant John C. Frémont, head of a U.S. Army exploring party in eastern California. Frémont, son-in-law of Senator Benton, interpreted the instructions as a command to foment insurrection among American settlers—"the first step in the conquest of California."[96] This he proceeded to do in the summer of 1846.

Slidell's mission, meanwhile, failed. When he reached Mexico City in early December 1845, officials refused to receive him because, they said, his title of minister plenipotentiary suggested prior acceptance of Texas's annexation. Even if Slidell had made the monetary offer for California, no Mexican leader could sell territory to the United States without inviting charges of treason. Too many Mexicans remembered the bizarre incident in 1842, when Commodore Thomas ap Catesby Jones, mistakenly believing that war had broken out, sailed into Monterey harbor and forced the astonished authorities to surrender. Jones discovered his error, apologized, and sailed away, leaving the Mexicans understandably angry. Any offer to purchase California, coming so closely on the heels of Texas's annexation, seemed out of the question. War seemed preferable. Some Mexican leaders thought that their large professional army stood an excellent chance of beating corrupt, land-grabbing Yankees. "Be assured that nothing is to be done with these people," Slidell arrogantly reported, "until they have been chastised."[97]

Polk responded on January 13, 1846, as we have seen, by ordering General Taylor to move south from Corpus Christi and occupy the left bank of the Rio Grande. Even though Polk initially regarded this action as added pressure on Mexico to negotiate, Mexicans interpreted it as heralding a war of aggression. Taylor blockaded Matamoros, itself an act of war under international law. The Mexicans retaliated. The first clash occurred on April 24, and Polk could present Congress with a fait accompli.

The War with Mexico and the Treaty of Guadalupe Hidalgo

Polk gambled on a short war. California and the Rio Grande boundary were his principal objectives, and he was willing to explore diplomatic alternatives. Shortly after hostilities broke out, the president conferred with an emissary of Santa Anna, then living in exile in Havana, Cuba. Santa Anna promised that if the United States helped him return to Mexico he would help Polk get the territory he desired. After apparently agreeing to terms, Santa Anna in August 1846 slipped through the American naval blockade and landed at Veracruz. A revolution propitiously occurred in Mexico City and Santa Anna became president. Instead of making peace, however, the self-proclaimed Napoleon of the West organized an army and marched north to fight General Taylor. More than a year passed before Polk understood that Santa Anna had conned him. As late as General Scott's campaign to capture Mexico City in autumn 1847, Polk was still hoping to bribe Santa Anna into a settlement. The Mexican kept fighting.

An even more bizarre diplomatic opportunity presented itself in November 1846 in the persons of Moses Y. Beach and Jane McManus Storms. Beach, the Democratic editor of the *New York Sun* and a chief drumbeater for Manifest Destiny, had contacts in the Mexican army and the Mexican Catholic hierarchy. He persuaded Polk to appoint him a confidential agent to Mexico, empowered to negotiate a peace that would include, in addition to Texas and California, the right to build a canal across the Isthmus of Tehuantepec. Polk thought it would be a "good joke" if Beach succeeded.[98] Beach then journeyed to Veracruz and Mexico City,

James K. Polk (1795–1849).
Tennessean, graduate of the University of North Carolina, and Democratic expansionist, Polk cast his eyes on Mexican lands and sparked war with Mexico to obtain them. John Quincy Adams once called Polk "an Anglo-Saxon, slave-holding exterminator of Indians." (P1981.65.12, artist unknown, c.1847–1849. Daguerrotype with applied color, 1/6 plate. Courtesy Amon Carter Museum, Fort Worth, Texas.)

accompanied by Mrs. Storms, a journalist whose friendships with prominent Texans, fluency in Spanish, and personal contacts with the Polk administration made her "the author of the entire episode."[99] Described by Thomas Hart Benton as having "a masculine stomach for war and politics," Storms won renown as publicist, lobbyist, political fixer, and participant in various expansionist projects from the 1830s to the 1860s.[100] Once in Mexico City, however, she and Beach rashly joined a clerical uprising against Santa Anna. The rebellion collapsed, along with hopes for a quick peace. The two Americans fled to the cover of U.S. forces in Tampico.

President Polk finally decided in spring 1847 to send an accredited State Department representative along with Scott's army. He selected Nicholas P. Trist, chief clerk of the State Department, a man of impeccable Democratic credentials (he had once been Andrew Jackson's private secretary and had married a granddaughter of Thomas Jefferson). Polk thought he could easily manage Trist, who could also keep a watchful eye on the politically ambitious Scott, a Whig. The president immediately regretted his choice. In May Trist reached the U.S. army, then marching

Abraham Lincoln (1809–1865).
As a one-term Whig member of
Congress from Illinois, Lincoln
strongly opposed the extension of
slavery into new territories and believed that President Polk had provoked Mexico into war. Lincoln
dismissed Polk's attempt to blame
the war on Mexico as the "half insane mumbling of a fever-dream."
This 1846 daguerreotype photo by
N. H. Shepherd is the earliest
known of Lincoln. (Library of
Congress)

toward the plain of central Mexico. He soon quarreled furiously with General Scott, who resented Trist's power to decide when hostilities should cease. The two men did not speak to one another for six weeks, communicating only through vituperative letters. Then Trist fell ill, and Scott chivalrously sent a box of guava marmalade to speed his recovery. The diplomat whom Scott had called "the personification of Danton, Marat, and St. Just" suddenly became "able, discreet, courteous, and amiable," as the two prickly prima donnas resolved to work together.[101]

By this time, September 1847, Scott's troops had battered their way to Mexico City, and the diplomat and warrior were trying to conclude peace with any Mexican faction that would treat. Polk, suspicious at the political implications of the Scott-Trist entente and angry that Trist had forwarded to Washington a Mexican peace proposal that still insisted on the Nueces as the Texas boundary, summarily recalled his unruly representative. The president now seemed in no hurry to conclude peace. Military successes had made it possible to obtain more territory than he had originally sought—perhaps Lower as well as Upper California, the Isthmus of Tehuantepec, and Mexico's northern provinces. Polk even contemplated the absorption of all Mexico. Lewis Cass, a Michigan Democrat, grandly declared that trying to prevent Americans from taking possession of Mexico would be as futile as attempting "to stop the rushing of the cataract of Niagara."[102] As for the inhabitants of Mexico, one colonel commented: "They are all semi-Indians and must in a short time give place to the civilization of North America."[103]

Trist next took an extraordinary step. He refused his own recall. Trist believed deeply in the promise of Manifest Destiny, "confident that Mexico, left to herself, would someday enter the temple of freedom."[104] But such a process could not be forced. Reconciliation had to come first. Any peace that demanded too much would violate this canon. Even before he received his recall notice, Trist had begun negotiations with a moderate faction that had come to power. These Mexicans urged him to remain. Scott concurred. "I will make a treaty," Trist vowed.[105] He thereupon informed Polk, in a bristling sixty-five-page letter, that he was continuing peace talks under his original instructions. Polk grew splenetic. "I have never in my life felt so indignant," he told his diary.[106]

Trist negotiated his peace treaty, signed on February 2, 1848, at Guadalupe Hidalgo, near Mexico City. Mexico ceded California and New Mexico to the United States and confirmed the annexation of Texas with the Rio Grande as the boundary. In return, the United States paid $15 million and assumed the claims of U.S. citizens totaling another $3.25 million. When the treaty arrived in Washington, the president reluctantly submitted it to the Senate, notwithstanding that "Mr. Trist has acted very badly." The territorial gains comprised all he had empowered Slidell to obtain in his 1845–1846 mission. "If I were now to reject a treaty," Polk explained, "made upon my own terms . . . with the unanimous approbation of the Cabinet, the probability is that Congress would not grant either men or money to prosecute the war."[107] The Whig-dominated Senate had just passed a resolution praising General Taylor's victories in "a war unnecessarily and unconstitutionally begun by the President of the United States." Despite their distaste for territory by conquest, as one Whig noted, the choice was "between the continuance of an expensive & unfortunate war & a *bad* treaty—the people want peace."[108] The treaty thereupon

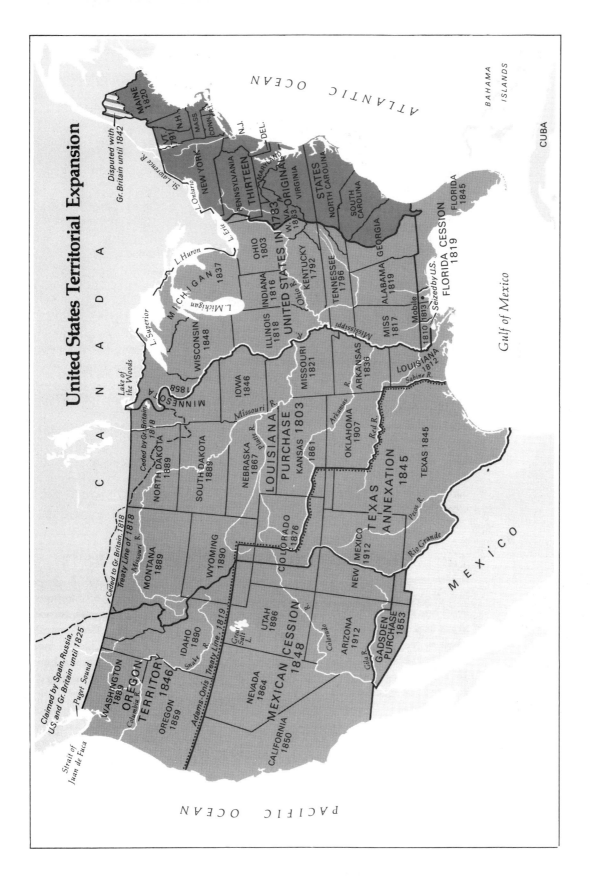

United States Territorial Expansion

CANADA

ATLANTIC OCEAN

BAHAMA ISLANDS

CUBA

Gulf of Mexico

MEXICO

PACIFIC OCEAN

Strait of Juan de Fuca

Claimed by Spain, Russia, U.S. and Gr. Britain until 1825

Puget Sound

WASHINGTON 1889

OREGON TERRITORY 1846

OREGON 1859

Columbia R.

Snake R.

IDAHO 1890

MONTANA 1889

Missouri R.

Ceded to Gr. Britain, 1818

Treaty Line of 1818

Adams-Onis Treaty Line, 1819

NEVADA 1864

CALIFORNIA 1850

UTAH 1896

MEXICAN CESSION 1848

Great Salt L.

Colorado R.

ARIZONA 1912

Gila R.

WYOMING 1890

COLORADO 1876

NEW MEXICO 1912

GADSDEN PURCHASE 1853

Rio Grande

NORTH DAKOTA 1889

SOUTH DAKOTA 1889

NEBRASKA 1867

Platte R.

KANSAS 1861

LOUISIANA PURCHASE 1803

OKLAHOMA 1907

Arkansas R.

Red R.

TEXAS ANNEXATION 1845

TEXAS 1845

Pecos R.

Ceded by Gr. Britain, 1818

MINNESOTA 1858

Lake of the Woods

L. Superior

IOWA 1846

Missouri R.

MISSOURI 1821

ARKANSAS 1836

LOUISIANA 1812

Sabine R.

WISCONSIN 1848

MICHIGAN 1837

L. Michigan

L. Huron

L. Erie

ILLINOIS 1818

INDIANA 1816

OHIO 1803

KENTUCKY 1792

Ohio R.

TENNESSEE 1796

MISS. 1817

Mississippi R.

ALABAMA 1819

Mobile

1810 1813

Seized by U.S.

FLORIDA CESSION 1819

UNITED STATES IN 1783

THIRTEEN ORIGINAL STATES

NEW YORK

PENNSYLVANIA

MARYLAND

W. VA. 1863

VIRGINIA

NORTH CAROLINA

SOUTH CAROLINA

GEORGIA

FLORIDA 1845

St. Lawrence R.

L. Ontario

Disputed with Gr. Britain until 1842

MAINE 1820

VT. 1791

N.H.

MASS.

CONN. R.I.

N.J.

DEL.

passed the Senate, 38 to 14, on March 10, 1848. A Whig critic cynically commented that the peace "negotiated by an unauthorized agent, with an unacknowledged government, submitted by an accidental President, to a dissatisfied Senate, has, notwithstanding these objections in form, been confirmed."[109]

War with Mexico swelled the membership of pacifist organizations such as the American Peace Society, which offered a $500 prize for the best essay analyzing the war. The Unitarian minister Theodore Parker denounced the "war for slavery, a mean and infamous war, an aristocratic war, a war against the best interests of mankind."[110] Yet the antiwar forces in Congress, consisting largely of Whigs and Calhoun Democrats, made little impact. The opposition lost its most effective leader in early 1848 when the octogenarian John Quincy Adams, after voting against a resolution thanking generals for their victories in Mexico, collapsed on the floor of Congress and later died. Opponents at first criticized the questionable way in which Polk had begun the war, but soon they shifted to attempts to bar slavery from any territorial gains. After Scott's victorious march to the Halls of Montezuma, critics worked against any administration effort to take "All Mexico." The Wilmot Proviso galvanized war protest. Attached as a rider to the war appropriation bill of August 1846 by Democrat David Wilmot of Pennsylvania, the proviso held that none of the territory acquired from Mexico should be open to slavery. Its supporters comprised almost exclusively northerners, and a coalition of southern Whigs and administration Democrats sufficed to defeat it. Nonetheless, the Wilmot Proviso was introduced again and again, never passing but sparking ever-increasing debate, causing southerners such as Calhoun to despair of the Union. Polk struck back at his critics by suggesting that they were aiding the enemy, a stinging charge using the Constitution's definition of treason. Few critics chose to risk voting against military supplies. As one Whig put it: "We support the war, though we condemn those who have brought us into it."[111] A war, right or wrong, which Congress had voted, had to be upheld.

The Lessons and Costs of Expansion, 1815–1848

The United States acquired more than 500,000 square miles of territory in the war against Mexico, which young Representative Abraham Lincoln labeled "a war of conquest."[112] Polk did not obtain "All Mexico," but he had taken what he wanted: Texas and California. The casualties: 1,721 Americans killed in battle and 11,550 deaths from other causes, mainly disease. At least 50,000 Mexicans died.

The war brought other ugly consequences not so easily quantified. The arrogant rationalizations for expansion appalled an old Jeffersonian such as Albert Gallatin, who noted: "All these allegations of superiority of race and destiny neither require nor deserve any answer; they are pretences [*sic*] . . . to disguise ambitions, cupidity, or silly vanity."[113] Ralph Waldo Emerson had predicted in 1847 that the United States would gobble Mexican territory "as the man swallows arsenic, which brings him down in turn."[114] Indeed, debates over the Wilmot Proviso raised the all-important question whether the new territories would become free or slave. It took two more decades and a bloody civil war to answer the question. In fact, the

"The Trail of Tears."   Robert Lindneux's poignant painting of Indian removal illustrates a tragic consequence of U.S. expansion. Of the 100,000 Indians transported beyond the Mississippi between 1824 and 1845, perhaps one-fourth to one-third died during or shortly after the forced marches. Why did not white Americans strip Indians of their names? asked one foreign visitor to the United States during this period. "They have robbed the Indians of everything else." (From the original oil painting at Woolaroc Museum, Bartlesville, Oklahoma)

issue of race in the 1850s blocked any possibility that the United States might acquire additional territories in the Caribbean or Pacific. Such potential prizes as Cuba or Hawai'i had racially mixed populations and thus seemed less adaptable to American settlers and institutions than did the more lightly populated prairies of North America.

The American Indian became a casualty of westward expansion. "Land enough—Land enough! Make way, I say, for the young American Buffalo!" shouted one fervent orator for Manifest Destiny in 1844.[115] It was the Native American who had to give way. While white Americans in the 1820s and 1830s sought fertile lands in Texas and Oregon, other farmers were encroaching on Indian lands east of the Mississippi. Despite treaties that one governor called "expedients by which ignorant, intractable, and savage people were induced without bloodshed to yield up what civilized peoples had a right to possess," the federal government removed most Native Americans in the Old Northwest and Southwest to new reservations in Oklahoma and Missouri.[116] It became a brutal process—a "trail of tears." Indians were forced to march thousands of miles, robbed by federal and state officials, ravaged by disease. Some resisted, as evidenced by the Black Hawk War of 1832 and the guerrilla warfare waged by the Seminoles in the Everglades for nearly a decade. The Seminole War finally ended in 1842 with the order: "Find the enemy, capture, or exterminate."[117] In the case of the Creeks, the population in 1860 comprised only 40 percent of what it had been thirty years earlier. Other Indians suffered similar losses. Native Americans beyond the Mississippi would feel the crunch of empire after 1848.

As for Mexico, the loser in a disastrous war, it relinquished more than half of its national territory and saw large amounts of real estate, foodstuffs, art treasures, and livestock destroyed by the invading armies. One Mexican statesman blamed defeat on the fact that "there has not been, nor could there have been, a national spirit, for there is no nation."[118] A Mexican scholar, Jorge Castañeda, has suggested that Mexico, by waging war rather than ceding half the national patrimony to John Slidell, ultimately kept Sonora, Chihuahua, and Baja California from becoming American, and thus "fighting and losing proved to be a better deal than selling and perhaps losing far more."[119]

The American invaders treated Mexicans as they did the Indians—as racial inferiors. General John Quitman, temporarily the governor of Mexico City, called Mexico's 8 million inhabitants "beasts of burden, with as little intellect as the asses whose burdens they share."[120] The multi-racial, multicultural Hispanic "frontier of inclusion" that had welcomed American settlers gave way to an Anglo-American "frontier of exclusion."[121] Mexicans who had lived in Texas lost most of their lands through fraud and outright confiscation, and the *corridos* (folk ballads) of the border region excoriated the Texas Rangers as *"los tejanos sangrientes"* ("bloody Texans")— killers of Mexicans "who shot first and asked questions later."[122] Then, too, Mexican politics, stormy since independence, grew even more tumultuous, and the country had to endure another twenty-five years of rebellion, civil war, and European intervention before attaining a degree of national unity under the authoritarian regime of Porfirio Díaz. The war increased the disparity in size, power, and population between the United States and Mexico, creating longstanding attitudes of suspicion, distrust, and prejudice on both sides of the border.

The success of continental expansion left one obvious imprint on the United States—that of increased power. No country had grown so fast as the United States, "the *wunderkind* nation of the nineteenth century."[123] True, the War with Mexico did not propel the United States into great-power status; it would take another half-century, industrialization, and a war with Spain to achieve such ranking. Still, the nation had grown from a third-rate to a second-rate power, capable of challenging any of the European giants within the hemisphere. The evolution of the Monroe Doctrine mirrored this growth. President Monroe had hurled his defiant message in 1823 without the power to enforce it. When Britain seized the Falkland Islands in 1833 and the French bombarded Mexican ports in 1838, U.S. leaders did nothing. In 1842, however, President Tyler specifically warned England and France against annexing Hawai'i. Three years later Polk arrogantly invoked the Monroe Doctrine in proclaiming U.S. rights to Texas, California, and Oregon. As American power continued to increase after 1848, as economic interests began to focus on the Caribbean and the possibility of an isthmian canal, U.S. diplomats would repeatedly invoke the Monroe Doctrine. The same mixture of motives that operated in the 1820s would continue—namely, a studied desire to forestall European interference, combined with a wish to extend U.S. influence throughout the hemisphere.

Polk told one member of Congress in 1846 that "the only way to treat John Bull was to look him straight in the eye."[124] Polk's confrontational style seemed successful with both Britain and Mexico. Polk himself thought the war had boosted national prestige abroad by demonstrating that a democracy could prosecute a foreign war "with all the vigor" usually associated with "more arbitrary forms of government."[125] The Tennessean's "lessons" for later American diplomats take on added importance when one considers his high reputation in the twentieth century.

Theodore Roosevelt saw in Polk a model for reasserting strong executive leadership in foreign policy. In 1919 Justin H. Smith published his Pulitzer Prize–winning history of the War with Mexico, defending Polk at every turn. Polls of historians continue to rank Polk among the top ten presidents.

In fact, Polk was lucky. Unlike John Quincy Adams, whose forceful diplomacy against Spain and the Holy Alliance rested on a shrewd understanding of international power realities, Polk moved inexpertly against Mexico and Britain. Regarding Oregon, his initial call for 54°40′ unnecessarily heightened jingo fevers on both sides of the Atlantic and postponed any settlement until spring 1846. In view of the concurrent crisis with Mexico, such a delay invited the disastrous possibility of a war on two fronts. British conciliation owed more to troubles at home—potato famine in Ireland, tensions with France, political turmoil over repeal of the Corn Laws—than to U.S. bravado. Aberdeen's sobering presence also helped. Had Palmerston become foreign secretary (as he very nearly did, in January 1846), Polk's "eyeball" tactics might have meant war. Given the flood of American immigration into the Pacific Northwest in 1844–1846, Calhoun's policy of "masterly inactivity" almost certainly would have produced a favorable settlement without risking war. Polk apparently had not heard what Castlereagh said a generation earlier: "You need not trouble yourselves about Oregon, you will conquer Oregon in your bedchambers."[126]

"Masterly inactivity" might have worked with Mexico as well. Polk did not want war so much as he desired the fruits of war. He wanted California, New Mexico, and the Rio Grande boundary; and he hurried because he suspected British intrigues. Slidell's offer to purchase the territory was genuine and, in Polk's narrow mind, generous, but it completely disregarded Mexican nationalist sensibilities. Keeping Taylor's army at Corpus Christi would have protected Texas with little provocation to Mexico. Negotiations could resume when tempers cooled. Whether Mexico would have ever released the territories is, of course, an open question. As for California, Polk should have understood, after a careful reading of all diplomatic correspondence, that England had no serious intention of seizing that lucrative prize.

The president might have chosen to wait, to see if the influx of American settlers would make California another Texas or Oregon. Annexation might have come peacefully—perhaps, as the historian David Pletcher has suggested, during some subsequent European crisis such as the Crimean War. As it turned out, Polk's decision for war in the spring of 1846 was reckless, coming as it did while tensions with England remained so acute. War risked all the expansionist goals. A major Mexican victory (Santa Anna nearly won the battle of Buena Vista) might have brought a European loan to Mexico, military stalemate, and possible British mediation. He might have lost California. Polk was also lucky that his repudiated agent, Trist, made a treaty of peace when he did. The capture of Mexico City and the successful negotiations that quickly followed obscured the fact that insistence on "All Mexico" might have led to the kind of protracted guerrilla war against U.S. occupation forces that Mexicans waged against French armies twenty years later (see Chapter 4). Overall, if Polk truly believed in Manifest Destiny, he should not have risked what Americans had long deemed inevitable. But because Polk ultimately succeeded in pushing American borders to the Pacific, the blemishes in his diplomatic record will probably continue to be covered with the cosmetic cream of national celebration.

FURTHER READING FOR THE PERIOD 1815–1848

For Manifest Destiny and expansionism, see Kinley J. Brauer, *Cotton Versus Conscience: Massachusetts Whig Politics and Southwestern Expansion, 1843–1848* (1967); George Dangerfield, *The Awakening of American Nationalism, 1815–1828* (1965); Richard Drinnon, *Facing West* (1980); Daniel Feller, *The Jacksonian Promise* (1995); Norman Graebner, ed., *Manifest Destiny* (1968); Thomas R. Hietala, *Manifest Design* (1985); Reginald Horsman, *Race and Manifest Destiny* (1981); Howard Jones, *Mutiny on the* Amistad (1987); Howard Kushner, *Conflict on the Northwest Coast: American-Russian Rivalry in the Pacific Northwest, 1790–1867* (1975); Frederick Merk, *Manifest Destiny and Mission in American History* (1963); Christopher Morris and Sam W. Haynes, eds., *Manifest Destiny and Empire* (1997); Michael A. Morrison, *Slavery and the American West* (1997); Gregory H. Nobles, *American Frontiers* (1997); Paul Pappas, *The United States and the Greek War for Independence, 1821–1828* (1985); Bradford Perkins cited in Chapter 2; Michael Rogin, *Fathers and Sons: Andrew Jackson and the Subjugation of the American Indian* (1975); Malcolm J. Rohrbough, *The Trans-Appalachian Frontier* (1978); Charles Sellers, *The Market Revolution: Jacksonian America, 1815–1846* (1991); Richard Slotkin, *Regeneration Through Violence* (1996); Anders Stephanson, *Manifest Destiny* (1995); William Earl Weeks, *Building the Continental Empire* (1996); Albert Weinberg, *Manifest Destiny* (1935); and Valarie H. Ziegler, *The Advocates of Peace in Antebellum America* (1992).

Leaders in this period are featured in Irving H. Bartlett, *John C. Calhoun* (1993); K. Jack Bauer, *Zachary Taylor* (1985); John M. Belohlavek, *"Let the Eagle Soar!"* (1985) (Jackson); Noble E. Cunningham, *The Presidency of James Monroe* (1996); John Eisenhower, *Agent of Destiny* (1997) (Scott); Harlan Hague and David J. Langum, *Thomas O. Larkin* (1990); Timothy D. Johnson, *Winfield Scott* (1998); Willard C. Lunder, *Lewis Cass and the Politics of Moderation* (1996); John Niven, *John C. Calhoun and the Price of Union* (1988); Norma Lois Peterson, *The Presidencies of William Henry Harrison and John Tyler* (1989); Robert Remini, *Andrew Jackson and the Course of American Freedom* (1981) and *Henry Clay* (1991); Andrew Rolle, *John Charles Frémont* (1991); and Major L. Wilson, *The Presidency of Martin Van Buren* (1984). For John Quincy Adams and Daniel Webster, see below.

For the U.S. Navy and explorations, see Kenneth J. Hagan, *This People's Navy* (1991); Vincent Ponko, *Ships, Seas, and Scientists* (1974); Henry Savage, Jr., *Discovering America, 1700–1875* (1978); John H. Schroeder, *Shaping a Maritime Empire* (1985); William Stanton, *The Great United States Exploring Expedition of 1838–1842* (1975); and Herman Viola and Carolyn Margolis, eds., *Magnificent Voyages* (1985).

John Quincy Adams is treated in Samuel Flagg Bemis, *John Quincy Adams and the Foundations of American Foreign Policy* (1949); Mary Hargreaves, *The Presidency of John Quincy Adams* (1985); Walter LaFeber, ed., *John Quincy Adams and American Continental Empire* (1965); Paul C. Nagel, *John Quincy Adams* (1997); Lynn Hudson Parsons, *John Quincy Adams* (1998); Leonard Richards, *The Life and Times of Congressman John Quincy Adams* (1986); Greg Russell, *John Quincy Adams and the Public Virtues of Diplomacy* (1995); and William E. Weeks, *John Quincy Adams and American Global Empire* (1992).

For the Floridas, the Adams-Onís Treaty, Latin America, and the Monroe Doctrine, see Philip C. Brooks, *Diplomacy and the Borderlands* (1939) (Adams-Onís); John J. Johnson, *A Hemisphere Apart* (1990); Lester D. Langley, *The Americas in the Age of Revolution* (1996); Ernest R. May, *The Making of the Monroe Doctrine* (1975); Bradford Perkins, *Castlereagh and Adams* (1964); and Dexter Perkins, *The Monroe Doctrine, 1823–1826* (1927) and *A History of the Monroe Doctrine* (1963).

Daniel Webster is studied in Irving Bartlett, *Daniel Webster* (1978); Maurice G. Baxter, *One and Inseparable* (1984); Robert Remini, *Daniel Webster* (1997); and Kenneth Shewmaker, ed., *Daniel Webster* (1990). Shewmaker and his coeditors provide analysis with documents in *The Papers of Daniel Webster: Diplomatic Papers* (1983, 1987).

Anglo-American issues, including Oregon and Canada, appear in Ray A. Billington, *Far Western Frontier* (1956); Charles C. Campbell, *From Revolution to Rapprochement* (1974); Norman A. Graebner, *Empire on the Pacific* (1955); Howard Jones, *To the Webster-Ashburton Treaty* (1977); Howard Jones and Donald Rakestraw, *Prologue to Manifest Destiny* (1997); Wilbur D. Jones, *Lord Aberdeen and the Americas* (1958) and *The American Problem in British Diplomacy, 1841–1861* (1974); Frederick Merk, *The Oregon Question* (1967); Kenneth R. Stevens, *Border Diplomacy: The Caroline and McLeod Affairs in Anglo-American-Canadian Relations, 1837–1842* (1989); and Reginald C. Stuart, *United States Expansionism and British North America, 1775–1871* (1988).

Texas, California, the War with Mexico, and President Polk are explored in Paul H. Bergeron, *The Presidency of James K. Polk* (1987); Gene Brack, *Mexico Views Manifest Destiny* (1975); William C. Davis, *Three Roads to the Alamo* (1998): Marshall De Bruhl, *Sword of San Jacinto* (1993) (Houston); Janice T. Driesbach et al., *Art of the Gold Rush* (1998); John D. Eisenhower, *So Far from God* (1989) (War with Mexico); Richard Griswold del Castillo, *The Treaty of Guadalupe Hidalgo* (1990); Neal Harlow, *California Conquered* (1982); Robert W. Johannsen, *To the Halls of Montezuma* (1985); Paul D. Lack, *The Texas Revolutionary Experience* (1992); Ernest M. Lander, Jr., *Reluctant Imperialists: Calhoun, the South Carolinians, and the Mexican War* (1980); Dean Mahin, *Olive Branch and Sword* (1997); Timothy R. Matouina, *The Alamo Remembered* (1995); James F. McCaffrey, *Army of Manifest Destiny* (1992); Anna K. Nelson, *Secret Agents: President Polk and the Search for Peace with Mexico* (1988); Wallace Ohrt, *Defiant Peacemaker* (1998) (Trist); David M. Pletcher, *The Diplomacy of Annexation* (1973); W. Dirk Raat, *Mexico and the United States* (1992); Cecil Robinson, *The View from Chapultepec* (1981); Malcolm J. Rohrbough, *Days of Gold* (1997) (California gold rush); Pedro Santoni, *Mexicans at Arms* (1996); John H. Schroeder, *Mr. Polk's War* (1973); Charles G. Sellers, *James K. Polk* (1966); David J. Weber, *The Mexican Frontier, 1821–1846* (1982); and Richard B. Winders, *Mr. Polk's Army* (1997).

For encounters with Asia—especially China—see Warren I. Cohen, *America's Response to China* (1990); Jacques M. Downs, *The Golden Ghetto* (1997) (U.S.–China); John K. Fairbank, *Trade and Diplomacy on the China Coast* (1953), and ed., *The Missionary Enterprise in China and America* (1974); Jonathan Goldstein, *Philadelphia and the China Trade, 1682–1846* (1978); Jonathan Goldstein et al., eds., *America Views China* (1991); Edward V. Gulick, *Peter Parker and the Opening of China* (1973); Curtis Henson, Jr., *Commissioners and Commodores: The East India Squadron and American Diplomacy in China* (1982); Michael Hunt, *The Making of a Special Relationship* (1983); Thomas N. Layton, *The Voyage of the "Frolic": New England Merchants and the Opium Trade* (1997); John C. Perry, *Facing West* (1994); and James Thomson et al., *Sentimental Imperialists* (1981).

See also the General Bibliography, the following notes, and Richard Dean Burns, ed., *Guide to American Foreign Relations Since 1700* (1983).

For comprehensive coverage of foreign-relations topics, see the articles in the four-volume *Encyclopedia of U.S. Foreign Relations* (1997), edited by Bruce W. Jentleson and Thomas G. Paterson.

NOTES TO CHAPTER 3

1. Quoted in K. Jack Bauer, *Zachary Taylor* (Baton Rouge: Louisiana State University Press, 1985), p. 145.
2. Quoted in Dean B. Mahin, *Olive Branch and Sword* (Jefferson, N.C.: McFarland, 1997), p. 66.
3. Quoted in Robert H. Ferrell, ed., *Monterrey Is Ours!* (Lexington: University Press of Kentucky, 1990), p. 48.
4. Quoted in David M. Pletcher, *The Diplomacy of Annexation* (Columbia: University of Missouri Press, 1973), p. 377.
5. Milo M. Quaife, ed., *The Diary of James K. Polk, 1845–1849* (Chicago: McClurg, 1919; 4 vols.), *I*, 384.
6. James D. Richardson, ed., *A Compilation of the Messages and Papers of the Presidents, 1789–1897* (Washington, D.C.: Government Printing Office, 1897–1900; 9 vols.), *IV*, 442.
7. John Niven, *John C. Calhoun and the Price of Union* (Baton Rouge: Louisiana State University Press, 1988), p. 304.
8. Quoted in Leonard L. Richards, *The Life and Times of Congressman John Quincy Adams* (New York: Oxford University Press, 1986), p. 190.
9. Quoted in Arthur M. Schlesinger, Jr., *The Imperial Presidency* (Boston: Houghton Mifflin, 1973), pp. 41–42.
10. William Earl Weeks, *John Quincy Adams and American Global Empire* (Lexington: University Press of Kentucky, 1992), p. 196.
11. Quoted in Charles F. Adams, ed., *Memoirs of John Quincy Adams* (Philadelphia: Lippincott, 1874–1877; 12 vols.), *II*, 261.
12. Jacob E. Cooke, ed., *The Federalist* (Middletown, Conn.: Wesleyan University Press, 1984), p. 64.
13. Quoted in John M. Belohlavek, *"Let the Eagle Soar!"* (Lincoln: University of Nebraska Press, 1985), p. 115.
14. Quoted in Frederick Merk, *Albert Gallatin and the Oregon Problem* (Cambridge: Harvard University Press, 1950), p. 13.

15. John Seelye, *Beautiful Machine* (New York: Oxford University Press, 1991), p. 224.
16. *Democratic Review, XVII* (July–August 1845), 9.
17. *Ibid.*, p. 5.
18. Anders Stephanson, *Manifest Destiny* (New York: Hill & Wang, 1995), p. 30.
19. *Congressional Globe*, January 10, 1846, p. 180.
20. Robert F. Berkhofer, Jr., *Salvation and the Savage* (New York: Knopf, 1976), p. 14.
21. Thomas R. Hietala, *Manifest Design* (Ithaca: Cornell University Press, 1985), p. 172.
22. Quoted in Robert V. Remini, *Andrew Jackson and the Course of American Freedom, 1822–1832* (New York: Harper and Row, 1981), p. 276.
23. J. P. Mayer and Max Lerner, eds., Alexis de Tocqueville, *Democracy in America* (New York: Harper and Row, 1966), pp. 298–299.
24. Quoted in Willard Carl Lunder, *Lewis Cass and the Politics of Moderation* (Kent, Ohio: Kent State University Press, 1996), p. 51.
25. James O. Gump, "A Spirit of Resistance," *Pacific Historical Review, LXVI* (February 1997), 25.
26. Quoted in Norman A. Graebner, ed., *Manifest Destiny* (Indianapolis: Bobbs-Merrill, 1968), p. xxxvii.
27. *Congressional Globe*, January 4, 1843, p. 139.
28. Michael A. Morrison, *Slavery and the American West* (Chapel Hill: University of North Carolina Press, 1997), p. 73.
29. Quoted in William H. Goetzmann, *When the Eagle Screamed* (New York: Wiley, 1966), pp. xvii, 43.
30. Michael H. Hunt, *The Making of a Special Relationship* (New York: Columbia University Press, 1983), p. xi.
31. *Ibid.*, p. 36.
32. Geoffrey S. Smith, "Charles Wilkes and the Growth of American Naval Diplomacy," in Frank J. Merli and Theodore A. Wilson, eds., *Makers of American Diplomacy* (New York: Charles Scribner's Sons, 1974), p. 143.
33. Quoted in Raymond G. O'Connor, "The Navy on the Frontier," in James P. Tate, ed., *The American Military on the Frontier* (Washington, D.C.: Government Printing Office, 1978), p. 46.
34. Quoted in Norman A. Graebner, *Empire on the Pacific* (New York: Ronald Press, 1955), p. 79.
35. Quoted in Walter A. McDougall, *Let the Sea Make a Noise* (New York: Basic Books, 1993), p. 198.
36. Samuel Eliot Morison, *Maritime History of Massachusetts, 1783–1860* (Boston: Houghton Mifflin, 1923), p. 264.
37. Quoted in Kenneth E. Shewmaker, "Forging the 'Great Chain,'" *Proceedings of the American Philosophical Society, CXXIX* (September 1985), 232.
38. Quoted in James M. Lindgren, "'That Every Mariner May Possess the History of the World,'" *New England Quarterly, LXVIII* (June 1995), 196.
39. Gregory Evans Dowd, *A Spirited Resistance* (Baltimore: Johns Hopkins University Press, 1992), p. 188.
40. W. C. Ford, ed., *The Writings of John Quincy Adams* (New York: Macmillan, 1913–1917; 7 vols.), VII, 167.
41. John S. Bassett, ed., *Correspondence of Andrew Jackson* (Washington, D.C.: Carnegie Institution, 1926–1935; 6 vols.), II, 346.
42. Quoted in Marquis James, *The Life of Andrew Jackson* (Indianapolis: Bobbs-Merrill, 1938) p. 288.
43. Quoted in Noble E. Cunningham, Jr., *The Presidency of James Monroe* (Lawrence: University Press of Kansas, 1996), p. 60.
44. Quoted in Samuel Flagg Bemis, *John Quincy Adams and the Foundations of American Foreign Policy* (New York: Knopf, 1949), p. 327.
45. Quoted in McDougall, *Let the Sea*, pp. 163–164.
46. George Dangerfield, *The Awakening of American Nationalism* (New York: Harper and Row, 1965), p. 66.
47. Quoted in Cunningham, *Monroe*, p. 151.
48. Quoted in Robert V. Remini, *Henry Clay* (New York: Norton, 1991), p. 165.
49. Richard Van Alstyne, *The Rising American Empire* (Chicago: Quadrangle, 1965), p. 99.
50. *Annals of Congress*, March 1818, II, 1482.
51. Adams, *Memoirs of John Quincy Adams, V*, 325.
52. Quoted in William H. Seward, *Life and Public Services of John Quincy Adams* (Auburn, N.Y.: Derby, Miller, 1849), p. 132.
53. Quoted in Charles K. Webster, *The Foreign Policy of Castlereagh* (London: G. Bell and Sons, 1963), p. 295.
54. Quoted in Lawrence S. Kaplan, "The Monroe Doctrine and the Truman Doctrine: The Case of Greece," *Journal of the Early Republic, XIII* (Spring 1993), 13.
55. Paul Kennedy, *The Rise and Fall of the Great Powers* (New York: Random House, 1987), p. 158.
56. Quoted in Harold Temperley, *The Foreign Policy of Canning* (London: G. Bell and Sons, 1925), pp. 380–381.
57. Quoted in Dangerfield, *Awakening*, p. 177.
58. Paul L. Ford, ed., *The Works of Thomas Jefferson* (New York: G. P. Putnam's Sons, 1904–1905; 12 vols.), XII, 319.
59. *Letters and Other Writings of James Madison* (Philadelphia: Lippincott, 1865; 4 vols.), III, 339.
60. Quoted in Paul C. Nagel, *John Quincy Adams* (New York: Knopf, 1997), p. 270.
61. Quoted in Wendy Hindle, *George Canning* (New York: St. Martin's Press, 1974), p. 351.
62. Adams, *Memoirs of John Quincy Adams, VI*, 186.
63. *Ibid.*, VI, 198.
64. Richardson, *Messages of the Presidents*, II, 209, 217–219.
65. Ford, *Writings of John Quincy Adams, VI*, 371–372.
66. Quoted in Dexter Perkins, *The Monroe Doctrine, 1823–1826* (Cambridge: Harvard University Press, 1927), pp. 166–168.
67. Quoted in Hindle, *Canning*, p. 355.
68. Quoted in Cunningham, *Monroe*, p. 161.
69. Quoted in Daniel Feller, *The Jacksonian Promise* (Baltimore: Johns Hopkins University Press, 1995), p. 9.
70. John J. Johnson, *A Hemisphere Apart* (Baltimore: Johns Hopkins University Press, 1990), p. 86.
71. Quoted in Kinley J. Brauer, "1820–1860," in William H. Becker and Samuel F. Wells, Jr., eds., *Economics and World Power* (New York: Columbia University Press, 1984), p. 68.
72. Quoted in Bemis, *John Quincy Adams*, p. 291.
73. Quoted in Richard M. Dorson, *American Folklore* (Chicago: University of Chicago Press, 1959), pp. 256–257.
74. Quoted in Bradford Perkins, *Castlereagh and Adams* (Berkeley: University of California Press, 1964), p. 346.
75. Quoted in Howard Jones, *To the Webster-Ashburton Treaty* (Chapel Hill: University of North Carolina Press, 1977), p. 30.
76. Quoted in Howard Jones, "Anglophobia and the Aroostook War," *New England Quarterly, XLVII* (December 1975), 527.
77. Quoted in John F. Sprague, *The Northeastern Boundary Controversy and the Aroostook War* (Dover, Maine: Observer Press, 1910), pp. 110–111.
78. Quoted in Charles Campbell, *From Revolution to Rapprochement* (New York: Wiley, 1974), pp. 56–57.
79. Quoted in Kenneth R. Stevens, *Border Diplomacy* (Tuscaloosa: University of Alabama Press, 1989), p. 103.

80. Quoted in Howard Jones, *Mutiny on the Amistad* (New York: Oxford University Press, 1987), p. 190.
81. Webster quoted in Robert Remini, *Daniel Webster* (New York: Norton, 1997), p. 542.
82. Lewis Cass quoted in Howard A. Jones and Donald A. Rakestraw, *Prologue to Manifest Destiny* (Wilmington, Del.: Scholarly Resources, 1997), p. 70.
83. Quoted *ibid.*, p. 104.
84. Quoted *ibid.*, p. 147.
85. Quoted in McDougall, *Let the Sea*, p. 224.
86. Richardson, *Messages of the Presidents, IV*, 381.
87. Quoted in Campbell, *From Revolution*, p. 66.
88. Richardson, *Messages of the Presidents, IV*, 398.
89. Quoted in Campbell, *From Revolution*, p. 70.
90. Quoted in David J. Weber, *The Mexican Frontier, 1821–1846* (Albuquerque: University of New Mexico Press, 1982), p. 178.
91. Gene M. Brack, *Mexico Views Manifest Destiny* (Albuquerque: University of New Mexico Press, 1975), p. 170.
92. Quoted in Major L. Wilson, *The Presidency of Martin Van Buren* (Lawrence: University Press of Kansas, 1984), p. 151.
93. Quoted in Michael F. Holt, *Political Parties and American Political Development* (Baton Rouge: Louisiana State University Press, 1992), p. 62.
94. Quoted in Greg Russell, *John Quincy Adams* (Columbia: University of Missouri Press, 1995), p. 63.
95. Quoted in Harlan Hague and David J. Langum, *Thomas O. Larkin* (Norman: University of Oklahoma Press, 1990), p. 114.
96. Quoted in Andrew Rolle, *John Charles Frémont* (Norman: University of Oklahoma Press, 1991), p. 78.
97. Quoted in Mahin, *Olive Branch*, p. 61.
98. Quaife, *Diary of James K. Polk, II*, 477.
99. Anna Kasten Nelson, "Mission to Mexico," *New York State Historical Quarterly, LIX* (July 1975), 230.
100. Quoted in Anna Kasten Nelson, "Jane Storms Cazneau," *Prologue, XVIII* (April 1986), 27.
101. Quoted in John Eisenhower, *Agent of Destiny* (New York: Free Press, 1997), p. 267.
102. *Congressional Globe,* December 30, 1847, p. 79.
103. Quoted in Richard B. Winders, *Mr. Polk's Army* (College Station: Texas A & M University Press, 1997), p. 184.
104. Frederick Merk, *Manifest Destiny and Mission* (New York: Vintage, 1963), p. 181.
105. Quoted in Mahin, *Olive Branch*, p. 147.
106. Quaife, *Diary of James K. Polk, III*, p. 201.
107. *Ibid.,* pp. 346–351.
108. Daniel Berringer quoted in Morrison, *Slavery*, p. 83.
109. Bayard Tuckerman, ed., *The Diary of Philip Hone* (New York: Dodd, Mead, 1889; 2 vols.), II, 347.
110. Quoted in Valarie H. Ziegler, *The Advocates of Peace in Antebellum America* (Bloomington: Indiana University Press, 1992), p. 112.
111. Daniel Bernard quoted in Morrison, *Slavery*, p. 71.
112. Quoted in Ramón E. Ruíz, "A Commentary on Morality," *Journal of the Illinois State Historical Society, LXIX* (February 1976), 29.
113. Quoted in Reginald Horsman, "Scientific Racism and the American Indian in the Mid-Nineteenth Century," *American Quarterly, XXVII* (May 1975), 168.
114. Quoted in John H. Schroeder, *Mr. Polk's War* (Madison: University of Wisconsin Press, 1973), p. 117.
115. Quoted in Albert K. Weinberg, *Manifest Destiny* (Baltimore: Johns Hopkins University Press, 1935), p. 119.
116. Quoted in Stephanson, *Manifest Destiny*, p. 26.
117. Quoted in William B. Skelton, *An American Profession of Arms: The Army Officer Corps, 1784–1861* (Lawrence: University Press of Kansas, 1992), p. 321.
118. Mariano Otero quoted in Pedro Santoni, *Mexicans at Arms* (Fort Worth: Texas Christian University Press, 1996), p. 232.
119. Robert A. Pastor and Jorge G. Castañeda, *Limits to Friendship* (New York: Knopf, 1988), p. 35.
120. Quoted in Blanche Wiesen Cook, "American Justification for Military Massacres from the Pequot War to Mylai," *Peace and Change, III* (Summer–Fall 1975), 9.
121. Weber, *Mexican Frontier*, p. 278.
122. Quoted in W. Dirk Raat, *Mexico and the United States* (Athens: University of Georgia Press, 1992), p. 74.
123. James McPherson, *The Battle Cry of Freedom* (New York: Ballantine Books, 1989), p. 6.
124. Quaife, *Diary of James K. Polk, I*, 155.
125. Quoted in Robert W. Johannsen, *To the Halls of Montezuma* (New York: Oxford University Press, 1985), p. 309.
126. Quoted in Pletcher, *Diplomacy of Annexation*, p. 103.

CHAPTER

❖ **4** ❖

Expansionism, Sectionalism, and Civil War, 1848–1865

"Black Ship."   *In 1853 and 1854 Commodore Matthew C. Perry entered Tokyo Bay with a fleet that included two coal-powered, steam-driven side-wheelers, the* Susquehanna *and the* Mississippi. *Both ships later served in the Civil War blockade against the Confederacy. Here one of the ships is sketched as a dragonlike vessel billowing the black smoke that so alarmed this Japanese artist and his compatriots. (Courtesy, The Mariners' Museum, Newport News, Virginia)*

❖

DIPLOMATIC CROSSROAD

Commodore Perry's "Opening" of Japan, 1853–1854

On July 14, 1853, as the early morning sun burned the summer haze off the Bay of Yedo (Tokyo), Commodore Matthew C. Perry paid careful attention to combing his dark, curly hair. An unsmiling person with scowling, bushy eyebrows, Perry grew anxious as he pulled on his uncomfortable full dress uniform. On the beach, five to seven thousand Japanese troops awaited him. Perry armed every man in his landing party, including the forty musicians, with swords, pistols, or muskets. He sternly warned the flag bearer not to let the Japanese capture the American ensign. Perry had already positioned his ships across the bay with loaded guns aimed at surrounding forts. With all precautions taken and spirits running high, Perry, accompanied by fifteen launches and cutters, began the short journey in his official barge over smooth water to the shore. Dour as always, the commodore looked nonetheless resplendent in gold braid, bright buttons, and ceremonial sword. All the trappings were "but for effect," he noted.[1]

For Perry, appearances counted. He came from a long line of successful naval officers. His older brother, Oliver Hazard Perry, had gained a national reputation during the War of 1812. Matthew was noted for spending hours grooming himself and surrounding himself with bodyguards, secretaries, and aides. An unrelenting disciplinarian, he thought flogging a proper punishment. "Old Bruin," like most seasoned officers, had wanted to command the prestigious and salubrious Mediterranean Squadron. In early 1852, however, he was ordered to command the East India Squadron. Disappointed but loyal, Perry took the command seriously. He was an expansionist, and expansion into Asia came logically on the heels of the victory over Mexico, the absorption of California, and the Oregon settlement. The Orient was nearer to America than ever before, and it seemed inevitable that Americans would penetrate it. "Our people must naturally be drawn into the contest for empire," Perry wrote in 1852.[2]

The fifty-seven-year-old officer's special assignment was the "opening" of Japan to Westerners. The United States sought trading and coaling ports and the protection of American sailors shipwrecked from whaling vessels. Whalers, steamship company owners, shipbuilders, and merchants, especially the New York commission merchant Aaron H. Palmer, had lobbied Washington for years.

Perry read everything he could about Japan. Like most Americans, he thought the Japanese "a weak and semi-barbarous people" who might have to be "severely chastised" if they did not accede to American requests.[3] Except for a single port, Nagasaki, where the Dutch traded, few Westerners were welcome in a Japan governed by feudal lords bent on maintaining their isolation from "barbarian" whites. Herman Melville in *Moby Dick* called Japan the "double-bolted land."[4] American

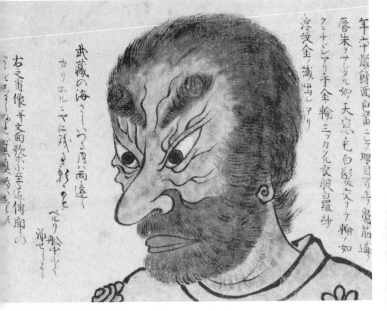

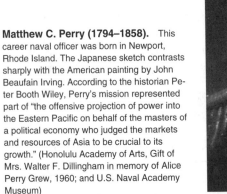

Matthew C. Perry (1794–1858). This career naval officer was born in Newport, Rhode Island. The Japanese sketch contrasts sharply with the American painting by John Beaufain Irving. According to the historian Peter Booth Wiley, Perry's mission represented part of "the offensive projection of power into the Eastern Pacific on behalf of the masters of a political economy who judged the markets and resources of Asia to be crucial to its growth." (Honolulu Academy of Arts, Gift of Mrs. Walter F. Dillingham in memory of Alice Perry Grew, 1960; and U.S. Naval Academy Museum)

commodore James Biddle, commanding two warships, had tried to open negotiations in 1846 only to have Japanese officials treat him rudely and warn him "never again to appear on the Japanese coast."[5] Perry would tolerate no such indignities.

Perry had a distinct psychological advantage. Two of his four warships were steam powered, belching clouds of black smoke. The Japanese had never seen such vessels before, and when the two steamers appeared on the horizon, in July 1853, the Japanese thought them afire, "a conflagration on the sea."[6] One feared that Japan was being invaded by "barbarians . . . in floating volcanoes."[7] For a week, in early July, the terrifying "black fleet" reconnoitered in the Bay of Yedo. The commodore, as if to illustrate his exalted importance, remained secluded on his flagship, the U.S.S. *Susquehanna,* allowing no Japanese on board. He sent word that he would meet only with the highest officials and threatened to sail directly to Tokyo. Also admirers of pomp and ceremony, the Japanese prepared a polite but cool reception for the imposing American.

On July 14, accompanied by a thirteen-gun salute, some 250 sailors and marines carrying dress swords and Colt revolvers, two heavily armed bodyguards, and a band playing "Hail, Columbia!," Perry landed from his barge and handed Japanese officials a document from President Millard Fillmore. "Our steamships can go from California to Japan in eighteen days," Fillmore's letter boasted. "I am desirous that our two countries should trade with each other." He told the Japanese to revise their laws to permit American trade and to treat shipwrecked American seamen "with kindness," adding, "we are very much in earnest in this." Finally, he asked for coaling stations for American ships. The Japanese sternly replied that they accepted the impertinent letter "in opposition to Japanese law" and that Perry could now "depart." Perry remarked that his fleet would leave in a few days, but he would return next year for an answer to the letter. When asked if he would bring all four vessels, he replied, "All of them and probably more."[8] Although he accomplished little by his bluster, Perry was satisfied that he had not suffered any indignities.

Perry's second ceremonial landing, on March 8, 1854, impressed onlookers. This time three steamers in a total of eight warships anchored in the bay. One American watched as his well-armed compatriots set off in boats "like a battalion on a parade field."[9] Perry disembarked to a seventeen-gun salute and the playing of the national anthem by three fully armed bands. Five hundred sailors marched with him. Although the Japanese had delayed negotiations for two weeks, they received the commodore courteously. Banquets, sumo wrestling, and an American minstrel entertained guests and hosts. One U.S. officer recorded that the Japanese "by the most unmistakable signs invited intercourse with their women."[10] The Japanese offered precious art objects; the Americans, reflecting their burgeoning industrial economy at home, provided the curious Japanese with a quarter-scale railroad train and a telegraph system, which they conspicuously set up on shore. According to the official narrative, the berobed Japanese asked questions that "showed them not to be entirely ignorant of the facts connected with the material progress of our country."[11] The commodore also handed over a bound history of the War with Mexico, which included dramatic sketches of the American fleet bombarding Veracruz, 100 gallons of Kentucky bourbon whiskey, and four volumes of John James Audubon's *Birds of America.* A jovial Japanese official embraced Perry, exclaiming: "Nippon and America, all the same heart."[12]

Although instructed to negotiate an expansion of commercial relations, Perry settled for less. The Japanese said they did not need foreign products. "You are right," said Perry. "Commerce brings profits to a country, but it does not concern human life. I shall not insist upon it."[13] The Treaty of Kanagawa, signed on March 31, 1854, guaranteed protection for shipwrecked American crews, opened up two ports for obtaining coal and other supplies, and established consular privileges at these ports. But the treaty had shortcomings. The two ports, Shimoda and Hakodate, were relatively inaccessible and unimportant. Although Japan granted the

United States most-favored-nation treatment, the treaty contained no binding provision for beginning trade. Perry had fallen short of his instructions; he had "opened up" Japan only slightly.

One member of the expedition wrote that the Perry mission marked "the beginning of American interference in Asia," and another began his diary with these pompous words: "The American Eagle allows little birds to sing."[14] The hero's welcome accorded Perry in the United States in April 1855 evoked similar chauvinism. The New York Chamber of Commerce presented him with a 381-piece silver dinner service, Boston merchants pinned a medal on him, and Congress voted him a bonus of $20,000. Rumors even hinted at a presidential candidacy. The Senate approved the treaty unanimously. Apparently everybody thought Perry had opened Japan to trade, but he himself later admitted that his treaty was not a "commercial compact." Commerce would come, he said, only if the United States followed up with "corresponding acts . . . of national probity."[15]

Perry saw his Japan expedition as but one step toward a U.S. empire in the Pacific. He wished to seize Okinawa and the Bonin Islands as coaling stations for a projected Pacific steamship line. He envisaged American settlements on the "magnificent island" of Formosa, and he urged U.S. military intervention in the internal affairs of Asian states because of the "responsibilities which our growing wealth and power must inevitably fasten upon us."[16] Anticipating competition from an expanding Russia in East Asia, he wrote: "The Saxon and Cossack will meet once more, in strife or friendship."[17] The commodore wanted the United States to "extend the advantages of our national friendship and protection" to Siam, Indochina, and the East Indies.[18] Eventually, the commodore prophesied, the American people would "extend their dominion and their power, until they shall have brought within their mighty embrace the Islands of the great Pacific, and place the Saxon race upon the eastern shores of Asia."[19]

Sectionalism and Sputtering Expansionism

Perry's excursion to Japan grew out of the 1840s' spirit of expansionism that had generated the Oregon settlement, the War with Mexico, and visions of a Pacific empire. With California firmly a part of the Union and with a long Pacific coastline, expansionists dreamed of strengthening links with Asia. With new and faster steamships, with the valuable ports of San Diego and San Francisco, with already existing commercial and religious missionary ties, with prospects of a canal across Central America and a transcontinental railroad to reduce the travel time between New York City and San Francisco, with the population of San Francisco ballooning (in part because of the gold rush of 1849)—with all of these changes and aspirations, American interest in Asia flamed anew after 1848. Lieutenant John Rodgers, who headed the U.S. Surveying Expedition to the North Pacific Ocean in 1853–1856, predicted great trade with the Chinese: "We shall carry to Europe their teas and silks. . . . The results are so vast as to dazzle sober calculation."[20]

This interest in Asia was nothing new. The first American ship to China sailed in the 1780s, and American merchants and missionaries had been active for decades.

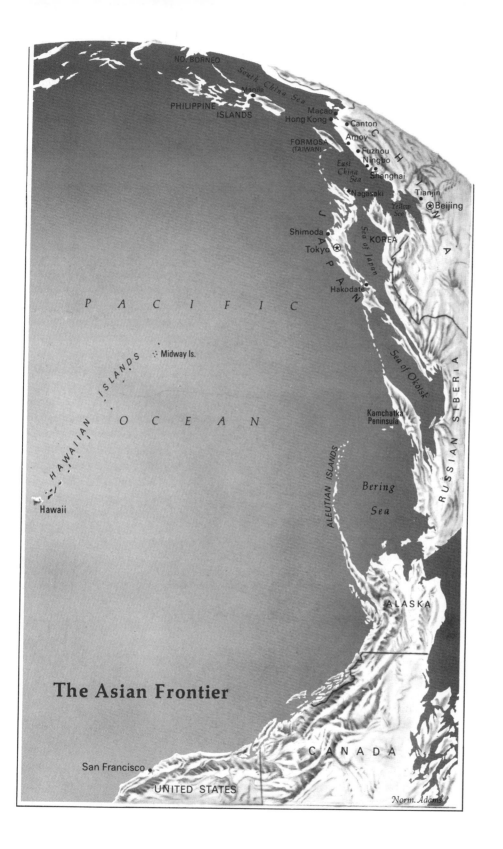

The Asian Frontier

NO. BORNEO

South China Sea

Manila

PHILIPPINE
ISLANDS

Macao
Hong Kong

Canton
Amoy

FORMOSA
(TAIWAN)

Fuzhou
Ningbo

East
China
Sea

Shanghai

Nagasaki

Tianjin

Beijing

Yellow
Sea

Shimoda

KOREA

Tokyo

Sea of Japan

J A P A N

Hakodate

P A C I F I C

HAWAIIAN ISLANDS

Midway Is.

O C E A N

Sea of Okhotsk

Kamchatka
Peninsula

R U S S I A N   S I B E R I A

Hawaii

ALEUTIAN ISLANDS

Bering
Sea

ALASKA

C A N A D A

San Francisco

UNITED STATES

Norm. Adams

Caleb Cushing, the first American commissioner to China, had secured trading privileges in five ports from China in 1844. John Quincy Adams regarded the treaty as a "nest egg" for much greater trade with Asia, including Japan.[21] By the early 1850s Americans carried about one-third of China's trade with the West. The United States did not play a major role in Asian politics, however. As junior partners, Americans usually trailed behind the British, who were not averse to using military force to build up imperial privileges, as in the Opium War. The Americans, complained a Chinese official, "do no more than follow in England's wake and utilize her strength."[22] Putting it somewhat differently, American missionary-diplomat Peter Parker advocated "a '*concurrent*' policy with England and France in China, not an *alliance*, but independent and distinct action yet similar, harmonious, and simultaneous."[23] Although the United States proved much less warlike than the other Western powers in Asia and did not gobble up territory as did Britain (India), the Netherlands (East Indies), and Portugal (Macao), Asians could only view America as another nation of grasping foreigners who denied them their sovereignty and dignity.

In 1858, during a civil war called the Taiping Rebellion, France and Britain further gouged China by opening ten new treaty ports. Once again practicing what some historians call "hitchhiking imperialism," the United States gained access to eleven more ports and low tariffs in the dictated Treaty of Tianjin (Tientsin). In Japan, where the United States in 1856 sent Townsend Harris as consul to capitalize on Perry's expedition, the gains were less impressive but nonetheless important. Isolated at the post of Shimoda, Harris patiently waited for an opportunity to negotiate a commercial treaty. Lacking the naval power exerted by the Westerners in China and displayed by Perry in 1854, Harris could not threaten Japanese leaders, who resented his very presence; but he pressed his case in another classic example of "personal diplomacy." In 1858 his tenacity paid off in a treaty wherein Japan opened other ports, provided for freedom of trade, and created a tariff schedule. The next year Harris became minister to Japan and established an American legation in Tokyo. The intrepid diplomat did not gain lasting fame until a century later when John Wayne portrayed him in the motion picture *The Barbarian and the Geisha* (1958).

Despite these evidences of American expansion in the 1850s, writes the historian Charles E. Neu, "Asia remained an abstract idea, a distant area that was only one part of a worldwide commercial empire."[24] The euphoria following Perry's drama soon evaporated. The State Department gave little guidance to its representatives in Asia, who therefore often acted on their own. In 1856, for example, Commodore James Armstrong's ships destroyed five Chinese forts near Guangzhou (Canton) after a cannon fired on an American vessel. President Franklin Pierce thereupon reprimanded the naval officer. As another example of America's secondary interest in Asia, Rodgers of the North Pacific Surveying Expedition found on returning to San Francisco in 1856 that he could not complete his survey of trade routes because his funds had run out.

This relative inattention to Asian affairs coincided with the general waning of American expansionism and Manifest Destiny after the War with Mexico. Talk of annexing Canada subsided. Even in Latin America, an area of prime focus, expansionist ventures flickered and imperial ambitions went awry. Attempts to grab Cuba collapsed and cries for acquiring more territory from Mexico became muffled. Notions of planting an American colony in slaveholding Brazil enjoyed some currency after an exploration inspired by Lieutenant Matthew F. Maury, but nothing came of the schemes. More than most southern expansionists, Maury, a future Confederate naval officer, emphasized the commercial goals of empire, citing "the Pacific railroad and a commercial thoroughfare across the Isthmus as . . . necessary fully to develop the immense resources of the Mississippi valley" and to "place the United States on the summit level of commerce" with respect to "the markets of six hundred millions of people."[25] Washington did persuade Mexico to negotiate the Gadsden Purchase of 1853, which added 29,640 square miles to the United States at a cost of $10 million for a potential railroad route to the Pacific coast—the only land acquired by the United States in the period from the War with Mexico to the end of the Civil War. Yet trade continued to expand abroad, sustaining faltering hopes for an ever-growing empire. "There is not in the history of the Roman Empire," asserted Senator William H. Seward of New York in 1850, "an ambition for aggrandizement so marked as that which has characterized the American people."[26]

Yet such passions went unfulfilled in the 1850s and early 1860s. The reason lay at home in the heated sectional debates over chattel slavery that drew the nation into the Civil War. The divisive issue of slavery curbed northern appetites for ventures into Latin America, where the "peculiar institution" might flourish and slave states might arise to vote with the South. Many southerners, having beaten back restrictions such as the Wilmot Proviso, continued the cry for empire, hoping to enhance their declining political status and mollify the threat to slavery, "the cornerstone of their way of life."[27] Northern leaders regretted that Manifest Destiny had fallen victim to the crude aspirations of slavemasters. Slavery, former member of Congress and Illinois attorney Abraham Lincoln remonstrated in 1854, "deprives our republican example of its just influence in the world—enables the enemies of free institutions to taunt us as hypocrites."[28] Divided at home by insistent northern abolitionists and southern "fire-eaters," the United States could not successfully undertake further bold schemes in international affairs, because it could not reach a foreign-policy consensus. Intensely preoccupied by the Compromise of 1850, Kansas-Nebraska Act, Fugitive Slave Act, "bleeding Kansas," *Dred Scott* decision, commercial and financial panic of 1857, Lincoln-Douglas debates, John Brown's raid, demise of the national Whig party and formation of the new Republican party, and the 1860 election of Abraham Lincoln, Americans gave less and less attention to foreign-policy questions.

Some Americans, however, tried to harmonize the sectional discord by trumpeting the nationalist "Young America" movement. They identified the revolutions of 1848 in Europe as evidence of New World, republican influences on the Old, and applauded Camillo Bensi di Cavour, Giuseppe Mazzini, and Giuseppe Garibaldi of Italy and Lajos Kossuth of Hungary, whose short-lived rebellions against entrenched conservatism and monarchy kindled American sympathies. In late 1850 Whig secretary of state Daniel Webster, for example, lectured the Hapsburg government, claiming that, compared to the mighty United States, Austria was "but a patch on the earth's surface."[29] Concerned about bitter division at home over

James Buchanan (1791– 1868). Member of Congress, senator, minister to Russia and England, secretary of state, and fifteenth president of the United States, the Pennsylvania-born Buchanan brought diplomatic experience and expansionist zeal to the White House. Called a "dough-face" because of his desire to appease southern slaveholders, Buchanan preferred expansion into what he called the "vacant lands" of Oregon, California, northern Mexico, and Alaska; he also sought to acquire more populous regions of mixed races in the belief that American settlers would bring the blessings of democracy and economic growth to the inhabitants. He tried to purchase Cuba to prevent its "Africanization" because he feared that the South could not survive with another black-ruled Haiti so near. Although he disdained Mexicans as an "inferior, indolent, mongrel" race, Buchanan sought unsuccessfully to buy Baja California and territories north of the Sierra Madre that would have brought a substantial Mexican population into the Union as free citizens. Buchanan's failed presidency helped bring on the Civil War. (Library of Congress)

slavery, he hoped his public rebuke to the government that had crushed the Hungarian revolution would "touch the national pride, and make a man feel *sheepish* and look *silly* who should speak of disunion."[30] When Kossuth excited the United States in 1851–1852 during a rousing visit, Webster once again stirred nationalist sentiment by rejoicing "to see our American model upon the lower Danube."[31] Webster's rhetoric notwithstanding, if Kossuth had asked for U.S. intervention on behalf of Hungary, the secretary promised to "have ears more deaf than adders."[32] In the 1852 Democratic party platform, the rallying cry was "Young America." The following year, "Young America" advocate and Democratic secretary of state William Marcy ordered a new dress code for American diplomats; they should wear the "simple dress of an American citizen" to reflect "republican institutions."[33]

"Young America" tried, in effect, to pour "the old wine of Jefferson and Jackson—a broad, nationally based republicanism of slavery and territorial aggrandizement—into new bottles."[34] Enthusiasts such as Democratic senator Stephen A. Douglas of Illinois exulted that "the more degrees of latitude and longitude embraced beneath our Constitution, the better." He urged Democrats and Young Americans to "come together upon the basis of *entire silence on the slavery question.*"[35] Yet the belief that expansion would subsume sectional differences over slavery proved illusory. Popular sovereignty, wherein settlers themselves voted whether territories should be free or slave, as in the Kansas-Nebraska Act of 1854, seemed a contradiction in terms—in Abraham Lincoln's view, a "deceitful pretense for the benefit of slavery."[36] In the opinion of many opponents, "Young America" expansionists were hypocrites who claimed to champion liberty abroad but denied it to black human beings at home by extending slavery into new lands.

Most scholars have rated American political leaders between the War with Mexico and Civil War as mediocre. The contemporary historian George Bancroft thought them "feeble and incompetent."[37] The presidents and secretaries of state conducted a blustering foreign policy, often playing to domestic political currents through bombastic rhetoric. Although both James Buchanan and Lewis Cass had extensive service as diplomats in Europe, neither had acquired much finesse. Nonetheless, "directed by a sot or a simpleton," America "will continue to grow and expand by a law of nature and a decree of Providence," claimed one writer in 1853.[38] An opponent mocked Stephen Douglas for thinking "he can bestride this continent with one foot on the shore of the Atlantic, the other on the Pacific. But he can't do it—he can't do it. His legs are too short."[39] Inept leaders muddled relations with Spain, crudely grasped at an elusive Cuba, permitted filibusters to alienate Latin America, squabbled clumsily with Britain in Central America, meddled with emotion but without power in European revolutions, followed the British in humiliating the Chinese, and gave halfhearted attention to Japan after "opening" it. President Lincoln and his expansionistic secretary of state, William H. Seward, certainly raised the level of competence in Washington, despite Seward's suggestion in 1861 that the United States provoke a foreign dispute to rally nationalism at home and forestall southern secession. The two managed to win the Civil War and contain it as a "localized" conflict, avoiding the world war it might have become. In doing so they preserved American power, thereby permitting the United States to resume its expansionist course after the fratricidal conflict.

Lewis Cass (1782–1866). Governor of Michigan Territory, secretary of war, minister to France, U.S. senator, Democratic presidential candidate in 1848, and secretary of state (1857–1860) under James Buchanan, Cass believed that it was the nation's destiny to spread democratic institutions throughout the Western Hemisphere. An intense Anglophobe who fought in the War of 1812, the Michigan politician supported Indian removal, backed the "All Mexico" movement during the War with Mexico, and advocated "popular sovereignty" to decide the fate of slavery in the new territories. He resigned as secretary of state when South Carolina seceded. (National Portrait Gallery, Smithsonian Institution/Art Resource, N.Y.)

Makers of American Foreign Relations, 1848–1865

Presidents	Secretaries of State
James K. Polk, 1845–1849	James Buchanan, 1845–1849
Zachary Taylor, 1849–1850	John M. Clayton, 1849–1850
Millard Fillmore, 1850–1853	Daniel Webster, 1850–1852
	Edward Everett, 1852–1853
Franklin Pierce, 1853–1857	William L. Marcy, 1853–1857
James Buchanan, 1857–1861	Lewis Cass, 1857–1860
	Jeremiah S. Black, 1860–1861
Abraham Lincoln, 1861–1865	William H. Seward, 1861–1869

The South's Dream of Empire: Filibustering and Slave Expansion

Many southern leaders tried to exploit Manifest Destiny for territorial conquest in the Caribbean. They failed largely because they provoked domestic opposition by insisting that slavery be permitted in new lands. In the 1850s most northern expansionists parted company with southern sectionalists and steadfastly opposed ventures into Latin America that might add slave territories to the Union. At the same time, some northern expansionists, such as Seward—then senator from New York— hoped that the abolition of slavery would eliminate northern opposition to expansion into the Caribbean and Mexico. Paradoxically, Southern expansionists sought a larger empire for the United States while they denigrated the supremacy of the federal government itself during the heated debates of the 1850s that led to the Civil War. "You are looking toward Mexico, Nicaragua, and Brazil," member of Congress Thomas Corwin of Ohio lectured his southern colleagues, "while you are not sure you will have a government to which these could be ceded."[40]

For southerners, expansion seemed essential. Since the Missouri Compromise of 1820, they had witnessed a profound shift in political and economic balance to the North, the free states. Under the Compromise of 1850, the territories seized from Mexico received instructions: California would enter the Union as a free state, and the rest of the Mexican cession could determine whether it wished to be slave or free (the concept of "popular sovereignty"). "'Compromise,' or 'Armistice,' or 'Sellout,' call this settlement what you will," the historian William Freehling writes, "it everywhere failed to defuse explosive questions."[41] A strong majority of southern members of Congress voted against the compromise bill.

Fearing that slavery could not adapt to the arid regions of the West, southern expansionists looked elsewhere to redress the balance. Tropical states where black slaves could toil under white mastery had long piqued the southern imagination,

The Southern Perspective
on Expansion

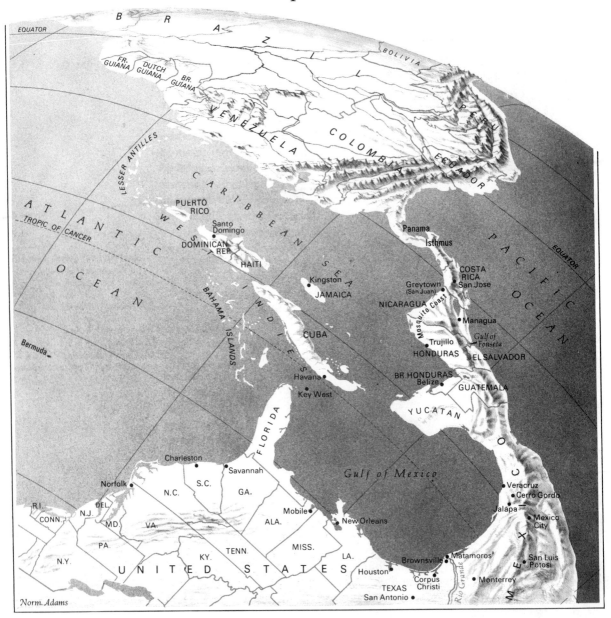

Norm. Adams

but now, in the 1850s, the matter became urgent. Shouting the message were such belligerent voices as those of James D. E. B. DeBow, in his widely read *DeBow's Review,* and the Knights of the Golden Circle, a secret society of several thousand members, many of them prominent politicians pledged to tropical expansion. The Gulf of Mexico, DeBow opined, comprised the "great *Southern sea.*"[42] Even after the Kansas-Nebraska Act in 1854 opened the territories to slavery through popular sovereignty, expansionists preferred Central America, Mexico, and Cuba, where the South, declared one southerner, would acquire "more power & influence than would a dozen wild deserts" in the American West.[43] Some white southerners thought they could carve as many as seven states out of Cuba and Puerto Rico and twenty-five out of Mexico. "I want them all for the same reason—for the planting or spreading of slavery," a Mississippi senator declared.[44]

Diplomacy could not satisfy southern desires quickly enough. Stymied by the northern rejection of their proslave imperialist aspirations, many southerners supported the filibusters (a derivative of the Dutch *vrijbuiter,* meaning pirate or "freebooter"), those soldiers of fortune who attempted to grab territories through unauthorized and illegal attacks on sovereign nations. Although often backed by financial interests in New York, and cheered by the penny press and such northern expansionists as John L. O'Sullivan and Jane Storms Cazneau, most filibuster bands originated in New Orleans, became thoroughly "southern" in goals and personnel, and employed the rhetoric of Manifest Destiny for sectional purposes. Narciso López, John A. Quitman, and William Walker led the ill-fated ventures.

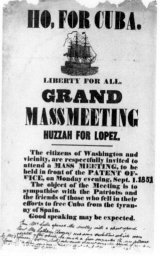

Broadside, 1851. Supporters of Narciso López, the notorious filibuster who failed to detach the Caribbean island of Cuba from the Spanish empire and attach it to the expanding U.S. empire, urged the people of the Washington, D.C., area to attend a rally to celebrate him. On September 1, 1851, Spanish authorities in Cuba executed the adventurer. (Library of Congress)

Venezuelan by birth, General Narciso López had careers as a Spanish military officer and Cuban businessman before his attempted invasion of Cuba in 1849. Married into a proslave aristocratic Cuban family, he came to see himself as the island's savior from the perfidies of imperial Spain. He wished to free Cuba and annex it to the United States. Using New York City and New Orleans as bases, López sought supporters. He enlisted some adventurous veterans from the War with Mexico, promising them "plunder, women, drink, and tobacco"; each soldier would receive a $1,000 bonus and 160 acres of Cuban land if the expedition succeeded.[45] López gathered his several hundred mercenaries at Round Island, off the Louisiana coast, but in September 1849 the U.S. Navy blockaded the isle and foiled his plans.

López reached for support elsewhere in the South. He won over southern expansionists such as John A. Quitman, a wealthy sugar and cotton planter, former general in the War with Mexico, and governor of Mississippi (1850–1851); the editor of the *New Orleans Delta,* Laurence J. Sigur; a former senator and cotton planter from Mississippi, John Henderson; and editor John L. O'Sullivan of Manifest Destiny fame. In May 1850, disguised as emigrants to California, the filibusters of the López expedition departed New Orleans for Cuba. Upon landing, they suffered sixty-six casualties to superior Spanish forces and attracted little Cuban support. López and most of his followers fled to Key West with a Spanish warship in hot pursuit. "I have nabbed López," Secretary of State John Clayton boasted to President Zachary Taylor.[46] López, Quitman, Henderson, Sigur, and O'Sullivan, among others, stood trial in New Orleans for violating the Neutrality Act of 1818, which forbade military operations from American soil against countries at peace with the United States. Southern juries soon acquitted the filibusters.

López launched another attack against Cuba in August 1851 with 500 "freebooters, pirates, and plunderers," as the black abolitionist Frederick Douglass called them.[47] Federal officials in New Orleans obligingly looked the other way. The mustachioed López invoked American icons, telling his followers: "We are sons of Washington . . . come to free a people" and "to add another glorious star to the banner which already waves . . . over 'The land of the Free.'"[48] This time López met his doom, as Spanish authorities captured most of his ragtag army. Tried by a

William Walker (1824–1860).
The most infamous of American filibusters terrorized Latin American nations, ruled Nicaragua for a short time, and flouted U.S. law—all by the age of thirty-six. He fell before a firing squad and remains buried in an unmarked grave in Honduras. The journalist Horace Greeley called him the "Don Quixote of Central America." (Smithsonian Institution)

military court, López and fifty of his mercenaries, including William Crittenden, nephew of the U.S. attorney general, were executed.

Undeterred by the López debacle, DeBow proclaimed that the American "lust for dominion" over Cuba remained.[49] An angry mob broke into the Spanish consulate in New Orleans, defaced portraits of the Spanish queen, and shredded the Spanish flag. Secretary of State Daniel Webster apologized in early 1852 and paid Spain $25,000 in damages. Quitman, who had resigned his governorship in 1851 because of the filibustering flap, grew apoplectic. He detested the Compromise of 1850 and feared that Spain might free slaves in Cuba. Only filibustering offered a quick means to avert "Africanization" and to guarantee "safety to the South & her institutions."[50] The filibusters could conquer Cuba, proclaim an independent republic on the Texas model, prevent emancipation, and insist on slave status as a condition of annexation to the United States. When a group calling itself the Cuban Junta offered Quitman "all of the powers and attributes of dictatorship," he organized an expedition of 3,000 men, but financial shortages, lack of support in Cuba, and warnings that President Franklin Pierce had "determined to prevent any expedition" forced Quitman to abandon the filibuster in April 1855.[51]

Then came William Walker, the "grey-eyed man of destiny."[52] Restless and reckless, Tennessean Walker earned a physician's degree from the University of Pennsylvania, studied medicine in Paris, practiced law in Louisiana, and edited a southern journal before he embarked on schemes in Mexico and Nicaragua. Attracted to California in 1850 by the gold rush, Walker hatched plans for an invasion of Lower California, indisputably Mexican territory. In 1853, this young man of small figure and simple dress marched into Mexican lands and captured the territorial capital of La Paz. In little time, however, the expedition collapsed from discontent among his followers and faulty organization. Tried for violating the Neutrality Act, Walker won acquittal from an admiring San Francisco jury.

"Once more aiding the stars," Walker next eyed Nicaragua, then a country often mentioned as a route for an isthmian canal.[53] Hardly the agent of benevolent, democratic Manifest Destiny that his admirers attempted to portray, he became a "freckle-faced despot," as one filibuster described him.[54] He sought to subjugate Nicaragua in 1855, 1857, 1858, and 1860. He plundered and killed. In the first expedition, leading men whom he described as "tired of the humdrum of common life," he proclaimed himself president of the country.[55] Apparently under the influence of Louisiana's proslave politician Pierre Soulé, he decreed the legal return of slavery. The American minister in Nicaragua, North Carolina slaveholder John Hill Wheeler, abetted Walker, because he believed that the "rich soil so well adapted to the culture of cotton, sugar, rice, corn, cocoa, indigo, etc. can never be developed without slave labor."[56] Walker dreamed beyond Nicaragua; he wanted to build a Central American federation (his slogan: "Five or none!") and then attack Cuba.[57] Finding no other Nicaraguan government in existence, President Franklin Pierce officially recognized Walker's regime in 1856. For the Maryland expansionist Anna Ella Carroll, Walker's triumph meant that "our stars and stripes will yet float over the Pacific gate of the Nicaraguan transit" on the road to the China market.[58] But the filibuster soon wobbled. Walker alienated Nicaraguans through pillaging and dictatorial orders, and his soldiers fell victim to frequent drunkenness and disease. He then antagonized transportation magnate Cornelius Vanderbilt, who had interests in Nicaragua; the influential Vanderbilt "declared war by proxy" in backing Honduras, Guatemala, San Salvador, and Costa Rica when they took up arms against the intruding adventurer.[59] In May 1857 Walker fled to the United States.

The famed filibuster returned to Nicaragua in November 1857, but marines from the U.S.S *Wabash* forced his surrender. The "lion-hearted devil," when captured, "wept like a child," and escaped prosecution.[60] Walker's third effort, in 1858, ended ingloriously near British Honduras, where his ship went aground on a coral reef. Still president of Nicaragua, the irrepressible Walker headed for his adopted country once again in spring 1860. This time he attacked Honduras first. Honduran troops inflicted heavy casualties, and Walker soon surrendered. "Will the South stand by and permit him to be shot down like a dog?" exhorted one southern woman. "If so, let her renounce forever her reputation for chivalry, valor, policy, or pride!"[61] Such appeals went unheeded, and Walker died before a firing squad on September 12, 1860.

Walker, like the other filibusters, aroused considerable enthusiasm in the South among prominent politicians, planters, and editors. Two Americans who at one point assisted Walker in his Nicaraguan venture were the redoubtable journalist Jane McManus Storms and her new husband, the Texas entrepreneur William Cazneau. Cazneau himself had special plans for the Dominican Republic, a country that occupied the eastern two-thirds of the island of Hispaniola which it shared with Haiti. Through his wife's contacts with Secretary of State Marcy, Cazneau wangled an appointment in 1854 as a commissioner to investigate trade opportunities. The Cazneaus described the country's resources in glowing terms, recommending immediate diplomatic recognition and acquisition of the strategic harbor of Samaná Bay. As with Cuba, racism influenced U.S. policy, for expansionists emphasized the lighter complexions of Dominicans in contrast to their black Haitian neighbors—"the more ardently expansionist the report, the lighter the portrayal of the Dominican people."[62] The Dominicans, following the advice of British and French diplomats, attached amendments to Cazneau's proposed treaty that made it unacceptable to Washington.

Recalled in late 1854, the Cazneaus embarked on a second mission in 1859–1860. Because of Washington's preoccupation with the pressing sectional crisis, however, their pleas for a "free commercial entrepôt at the gates of the Gulf of Mexico and Caribbean Sea" and their warnings that the debt-ridden Dominican government might seek reannexation to Spain brought no response.[63]

As for William Walker, for a time he became "an icon of contemporary popular culture" with the opening of a new musical, *Nicaragua, or General Walker's Victories,* at New York's Pardy's National Theater in 1856.[64] In the Hollywood film *Walker* (1988), actor Ed Harris's performance in the title role reminded audiences of Lieutenant Colonel Oliver North, a more contemporary American who also meddled in Nicaragua. In the end Walker symbolized for many the survival of slavery and the southern way of life. In his quest for adventure and glory, Walker mastered the rhetoric of southern expansion, especially in his presidential decree reinstituting slavery in Nicaragua in 1856, which he called an act of "benevolence and philanthropy" for "inferior" blacks, "half-castes," and Indians.[65] Southern "fire-eaters" took heart. Hindered by northern opponents from territorial gains through diplomacy or war, the ardent defenders of the "peculiar institution" turned to the illegal machinations of the filibusters. They would also turn to civil war in 1861. "As dream and reality met," the historian Robert E. May has written, "the South's grandiose vision of empire dissolved in the blood of war."[66]

The Cuba–United States Nexus

The Carribbean island of Cuba lay too close to the United States to escape the latter's expansionist urges. As the U.S. minister to England put it: "We want Cuba, Sir, and we must have it."[67] Indeed, as the historian Michael H. Hunt has noted, expansionists "liked to picture the Latino as a white maiden passively awaiting salvation or seduction."[68] One southerner waxed erotic: "the Queen of the Antilles [Cuba] . . . sits on her throne, upon the silver waves, breathing her spicy, tropic breath, and pouting her rosy, sugared lips. Who can object? None. She is of age— take her, Uncle Sam."[69]

Spain once called Cuba the "Ever Faithful Isle" because, unlike other Spanish possessions in the New World, Cuba did not revolt against Madrid in the stormy decades of the early nineteenth century. After 1818, with the opening of the island to world trade, a Cuba–U.S. commercial nexus began to replace the connection with Spain. "The trade of this country is falling into the hands of . . . Americans from the States," the British novelist Anthony Trollope wrote from Cuba in 1859. "Havana will soon become as much American as New Orleans."[70] Cuba's rich sugar production attracted North American entrepreneurs, slaveholders, engineers, and machinists. (Cubans, and many other Latin Americans, referred and refer to U.S. citizens as North Americans.) The new order also included the growth of Protestantism in the predominantly Catholic island.

Slave revolts in the 1830s and 1840s, as well as anticolonial rebellions in the following decade, aroused North Americans, especially Southerners who feared the abolition of slavery (45 percent of the island's population of 1 million were slaves). Slaveholders in Cuba had a reputation as cruel masters, and they participated in an illicit slave trade. A corrupt and inept Spanish administration exacerbated Cuba's plight and tugged at North American sympathies. Expansionists believed that inevitably, by "natural growth," Cuba would be taken under their eagle's outstretched wings.[71] Or, to use a metaphor of the times: "The fruit will fall into our hands when it is ripe, without an officious shaking of the tree. Cuba will be ours, and Canada and Mexico, too—if we want them—in due season, and without the wicked imperative of a war."[72] In Cuba itself, members of the Creole elite (Spaniards born in Cuba) increasingly made the case for annexation because, as part of the United States, "their sugar would be given preferential treatment and their slave property would be secure."[73]

In 1848 President Polk, looking for other fruits to match Oregon and the Mexican cession, contemplated purchasing Cuba from Spain for $100 million. But Spanish refusal and the adamant opposition of France and Britain blocked him.

Even though President Zachary Taylor warned Spain in August 1849 that the cession of Cuba to England would be an "instant signal for war," he and his successor Millard Fillmore had little interest in purchasing Cuba and worked to prevent filibustering.[74] In 1852 Britain and France asked the United States to join them in a three-power statement to disavow "all intention of obtaining possession" of Cuba.[75] Unwilling to sign such a self-denying agreement, Fillmore replied that "this question would fall like a bomb in the midst of the electoral agitation for the presidency" and divide North from South.[76] Secretary of State Edward Everett informed London and Paris that the United States did not "covet" Cuba, but the status of the island was nonetheless "mainly an American question."[77] He went on to extoll the island's strategic and commercial value, deprecating at the same time the Cuban slave trade. By quoting Washington's Farewell Address and Jefferson's aversion to "entangling alliances," Everett shunned any pact with European nations. Most important, the United States would not permit the transfer of Cuba to any other power.

Lord Palmerston, ever mindful that British colonies in the West Indies lay in the path of U.S. growth, angrily berated colleagues who thought that Britain should concede Cuba to the United States. No, that "would be like propitiating an animal of Prey by giving him one of one's Travelling Companions. It would increase his desire for similar food and spur him on to obtain it."[78]

President Pierce wanted Cuba. He pointedly had his own vice president, William R. King, sworn in by the U.S. consul in a ceremony at King's estate in Matanzas, Cuba. Backed by the expansionists Secretary of State William L. Marcy, minister to Britain James Buchanan, minister to Spain Pierre Soulé, and minister to France John Y. Mason, Pierce played to the Cuban fancies of southern Democrats. Soulé was impetuous, stubborn, and vain. Born in France, schooled as a lawyer, and elected U.S. senator from Louisiana, he became a central figure in the North American quest for Cuba. Within weeks of his arrival in Madrid, Soulé wounded the French ambassador in a duel. Fearful that "the fruit [Cuba] might become spoiled" through slave rebellion if the United States waited too long to pick it, this misplaced "diplomat" seemed to take every opportunity to irritate Spanish court officials.[79] Marcy believed that Spain would perceive the wisdom of selling its troublesome colony, so he instructed Soulé to inquire discreetly about sale. "Discreetly," however, did not exist in Soulé's vocabulary.

In February 1854, Havana authorities seized the American merchant ship *Black Warrior* for allegedly violating port regulations. Apparently seeing an opportunity to force Cuba from Spain through a threat of war, President Pierce demanded a $100,000 indemnity (raised to $300,000 soon after) and heated up American fevers for revenge by sending a belligerent anti-Spanish message to Congress. Pierce thus fed Soulé's intemperance. The haughty envoy demanded an apology from the Spanish government for an affront to the U.S. flag. The Spanish agreed to restore the ship to its owner and pay a smaller indemnity, even though Marcy found the Spanish reply full of "evasions."[80]

The *Black Warrior* affair soon became overshadowed by a new, rash attempt to annex Cuba. Because Spanish authorities had ended the slave trade and were arming free blacks to defend against filibusters, panicky U.S. consuls in Cuba predicted "a fearful revolution" and "a disastrous bloody war of the races."[81] Marcy thereupon instructed Soulé in April 1854 to try to buy Cuba for $130 million or less. Failing that, "you will then direct your efforts to the next desirable object which is to detach that island from the Spanish dominion and from all dependence on any European power."[82] Then, in August, the secretary told Soulé to meet with ministers Buchanan and Mason to discuss annexation. The three expansionists relished the chance; they met in October at Ostend, Belgium, and then at Aix-la-Chapelle in Rhenish Prussia, where they created the remarkable confidential document known as the Ostend Manifesto. The three emissaries recommended the purchase of Cuba for no more than $120 million. But if Madrid refused to sell, "by every law, human and divine, we shall be justified in wresting it from Spain if we possess the power."[83]

The manifesto arrived in Washington on election day, November 1854, and was leaked to the press. Just at that time, the Kansas-Nebraska Act had "sadly shattered our party in all the free states and deprived it of that strength which was needed & could have been much more profitably used for the acquisition of Cuba," as Marcy put it.[84] Opponents of the Kansas-Nebraska Act now accused the Pierce administration of propagating a slave conspiracy to annex Cuba, characterizing the manifesto as "the highwayman's plea, that might makes right."[85] Grasping for a scapegoat, Pierce and Marcy reprimanded Soulé, who resigned in indignation. The indefatigable Marcy then instructed Soulé's successor to encourage Spain to grant independence to Cuba. Madrid refused.

One author of the Ostend Manifesto, James Buchanan, became president in 1857. "If I can be instrumental in settling the slavery question . . . , and then add Cuba to the Union, I shall be willing to give up the ghost," he remarked.[86] In December 1858, "Old Buck" praised the commercial and strategic virtues of Cuba, urged its purchase, and asked Congress to appropriate a large sum for this purpose. The Senate Foreign Relations Committee then issued a favorable report that declared the "law of our national existence is growth. We cannot if we would, disobey it."[87] If the United States did not act, a European power might. The report also recommended $30 million—some of it no doubt for bribes of Spanish public officials. But antislavery Republicans who opposed annexation delayed action until Congress adjourned. A slow learner, Buchanan futilely appealed to Congress to pass the "Thirty Million Dollar Bill" in his annual messages of 1859 and 1860. Abraham Lincoln's election as president in 1860 frustrated any further attempts to embrace Cuba.

Anglo-American Détente, an Isthmian Canal, and Central America

Great Britain kept a worried eye on U.S. attempts, official and unofficial, to expand in the Caribbean and Central America. At the close of the War with Mexico, Anglo-American relations seemed tranquil. In 1842 Webster and Ashburton had drawn the Maine boundary and a line from Lake Superior to Lake of the Woods, and in 1846 President Polk had compromised on Oregon. As the danger of war over the Canadian-American border declined, the "Atlantic economy" revived.[88]

In the mid-1840s the growth of trade between the United States and Britain had resumed after a decade of sluggishness; by the 1850s the United States supplied Great Britain with 50 percent of its imports and 80 percent of its raw cotton, the basis of England's largest export industry. Forty percent of all U.S. imports originated in Great Britain, and America's expanding economy attracted British capital, especially during the railroad building boom of the 1840s. "Increased Commercial Intercourse may add to the Links of mutual Interest," Lord Palmerston observed. But he also warned acidly that "commercial Interest is a Link that snaps under the Pressure of National Passions."[89]

A treaty negotiated with New Granada (later Colombia) in 1846 and ratified in 1848 granted the United States transit rights across the Isthmus of Panama, a promising railroad and canal route. Alarmed by this intrusion on their maritime supremacy in the Caribbean, the British struck back. In January 1848 they seized a Nicaraguan town, which they renamed Greytown. This port controlled the most feasible transisthmian canal route, given the technology of the time. When added to the British protectorate over the Mosquito Indians inhabiting Nicaragua's eastern coast, possession of Belize (later British Honduras) and the Bay Islands, and the Royal naval base at Jamaica, Greytown accorded Great Britain a substantial position in Central America.

Lord Palmerston (1784–1865) Henry John Temple, 3d Viscount Palmerston, dominated English politics as foreign secretary (1830–1834, 1835–1841, 1846–1851) and prime minister (1855–1858, 1859–1865). "His dominance," the biographer Donald Southgate has written, "coincided with Britannia ruling the waves and London ruling the exchanges." "Old Pam" bristled against Americans who eyed British interests in the Western Hemisphere. (Mansell Collection, Ltd.)

In the same month that the British took Greytown, John Marshall discovered gold at Sutter's mill in California. The great gold rush soon swelled California's population by 100,000 and led to admission of the Golden State to the Union in 1850. Most of the "forty-niners" reached San Francisco by steamship. The trip included arduous overland travel through Nicaragua or Panama. Some adventurers made their long way to the West Coast by taking clipper ships from the eastern seaboard around the southern tip of the hemisphere at treacherous Cape Horn. Construction of an isthmian canal or railway became a matter of urgency. But the conspicuous British presence in Central America precluded unilateral U.S. action. Whig secretary of state John M. Clayton therefore proposed "a great highway" across the isthmus, "to be dedicated especially by Great Britain and the United States, to the equal benefit and advantage of all nations of the world."[90]

Foreign Secretary Palmerston, or Lord "Pumicestone," thought "these Yankees are most disagreeable Fellows to have to do with about any American Question," yet he respected the ability of the "ingenious Rogues" to deny to his Canadian provinces their much desired commercial reciprocity."[91] Thus he told Clayton that Britain had "no selfish or exclusive views" about the isthmus. Like Clayton, he hoped "that any undertaking of this sort . . . should be generally open to and available to all the nations of the world."[92] To confirm this understanding, he sent Sir Henry Bulwer to Washington in December 1849. The Clayton-Bulwer Treaty of April 19, 1850, stipulated that neither Great Britain nor the United States alone would ever monopolize or fortify a canal in Central America, and that neither would "colonize, or assume, or exercise any dominion over . . . any part of Central America."[93]

This obscure language invited conflicting interpretations, as became apparent during the exchange of ratifications. Bulwer soon informed Clayton that Britain did not believe the treaty included "whatever is Her Majesty's settlement at Honduras, nor whatever are the Dependencies of that settlement."[94] Having deftly exempted Belize and the Bay Islands from the terms of the Clayton-Bulwer Treaty, Britain thereafter excluded the Mosquito protectorate and Greytown, arguing that the treaty referred only to the acquisition of *new* territory. Despite London's verbal agility, the treaty in effect meant that "Britain could hardly turn around in Central America without being charged by Americans with violating its provisions."[95] As Bulwer perceived, however, the self-denying clause at the same time seemed "to bind the United States against further annexation."[96]

The isthmian canal would have to await the twentieth century, but American enterprise soon began to saturate Central America. Cornelius Vanderbilt organized an interoceanic steamship and railroad connection through Nicaragua, and other entrepreneurs completed a railroad across Panama in 1855. But the flag did not follow investors into Central America. The deepening domestic crisis over slavery prevented Presidents Pierce and Buchanan from doing much more than nipping verbally at the heels of the gradually retreating British. For his part, Palmerston continued to berate the "vulgar minded Bullies" of North America, from whom "nothing is gained by submission to Insult & wrong."[97] When the U.S.S. *Cyane* bombarded Greytown in 1854 in reprisal for an insult to an American diplomat, Pierce refused to disavow the attack. Despite their determination to "stick there till doomsday sooner than be evicted by the Yankees," the British quietly let the matter drop.[98]

The costly Crimean War (1854–1856), which pitted England and France against Russia, also made a showdown with the United States over Central America unthinkable. As British soldiers fell from bullets and disease before Sebastopol in the Crimea, the English government sent agents to the United States to recruit replacements, causing Secretary Marcy to dismiss the popular British envoy, John Crampton, and to send home three British consuls for violating U.S. neutrality laws. Even Palmerston recognized his country's precarious position and recommended "some little Flourish" addressed to the "free, enlightened and Generous Race . . . of the great North American Union" as a means of dampening Marcy's "Bunkum vapouring."[99]

Marcy had encouraged Palmerston's restraint by negotiating a long-desired reciprocity treaty in 1854. In 1852 the British had begun to interpret the Convention of 1818 very strictly and along the maritime provinces of Canada had seized some American fishing vessels. After Secretary Webster vowed to protect American fishing interests "hook and line, and bob and sinker," and Matthew C. Perry steamed north in the *Mississippi,* President Fillmore announced his willingness to settle the outstanding issues of fishing rights, navigation on the St. Lawrence, and reciprocity with Canada.[100] In 1854, London sent the governor-general of Canada, Lord Elgin, to negotiate with Marcy. His lordship was shrewd and the environment highly congenial. "Lord Elgin pretends to drink immensely," his secretary recorded, "but I watched him [at a party], and I don't believe he drank a glass between two and twelve. He is the most thorough *diplomat* possible,—never loses sight for a moment of his object, and while he is chaffing the Yankees and slapping them on the back, he is systematically pursuing that object."[101] In the Marcy-Elgin Treaty of June 5, 1854, Americans could navigate the St. Lawrence without restriction and fish within three miles of British North America, and Canadians could send duty-free a wide variety of agricultural products into the United States. U.S. consul Israel Andrews thought reciprocity might lead to U.S.-Canadian "convergence" wherein "under different governments we shall be one people, laboring hand in hand to accomplish the high destiny of the North American continent."[102] The Marcy-Elgin Treaty, like the Webster-Ashburton Treaty and the Oregon settlement, contributed to tranquility along the northern border of the United States.

That Anglo-American relations in the 1850s ended with a whimper and not a bang owed mainly to the worsening American crisis over the expansion of slavery. A British reappraisal following the Crimean War also facilitated Anglo-American détente. Always the bellwether of official British opinion, Lord Palmerston wrote in December 1857, in regard to Central America, that the Americans "are on the Spot, strong, deeply interested in the matter, totally unscrupulous and dishonest and determined somehow or other to carry their Point. We are far away, weak from Distance, controlled by the Indifference of the Nation . . . and by its Strong commercial Interest in maintaining Peace with the United States."[103] When he became prime minister in June 1859, Palmerston relinquished the Bay Islands to Honduras and the Mosquito Coast to Nicaragua. The new foreign secretary, Lord Malmesbury, allowed that "all the Southern part of North America must come under this Government of the United States; that he had no objection to what seemed the inevitable course of things."[104]

The American Civil War and International Relations

On April 12, 1861, at Charleston, South Carolina, Brigadier General Pierre G. T. Beauregard's Provisional Forces of the Confederate States opened fire on the federal garrison barricaded in Fort Sumter. With this defiant act the rebellious South forced Abraham Lincoln to choose between secession and civil war. Sworn to defend the Constitution, and conscious that his task was "greater than that which rested upon [George] Washington," the new Republican president called for 75,000 militiamen to suppress the insurrection.[105]

For support, Lincoln leaned on a factious cabinet of politically ambitious men, headed by a secretary of state who thought himself far abler than his chief. Convinced that his superior wisdom entitled him to act as prime minister to a hesitant president, William Henry Seward concocted plans to "wrap the world in flames" in order to melt domestic disunity in the furnace of foreign war.[106] On April 1 he sent Lincoln a memorandum titled "Some Thoughts for the President's Consideration," which proposed hostility or war against Britain, France, Russia, and Spain. The next day Seward responded to Spain's reannexation of the Dominican Republic with a threat of war. Spain ignored the bombastic secretary of state, and Lincoln proclaimed that he himself would formulate policy with the "advice of all the Cabinet."[107]

Scarcely deterred, Seward challenged Britain's interpretation of international maritime law. He successfully urged Lincoln to proclaim a blockade of the southern ports as a matter of domestic policy. Britain quite properly interpreted the

William H. Seward (1801–1872). Union College graduate, U.S. senator (1849–1861), and secretary of state (1861–1869), Seward spent the Civil War years trying to preserve the Union by keeping the European powers neutral. A British journalist described Seward as a "subtle, quick man not quite indifferent to kudos." (D. C. Heath Company)

"King Cotton Bound; or, the Modern Prometheus." In Greek mythology, Prometheus was the creator and savior of humankind whom Zeus chained to a mountain peak. In this rendition by the British humor magazine, *Punch,* the northern eagle picks at the Confederate "King Cotton," manacled by the naval blockade. Although the mythical character was later freed, in this cartoon the monarch appears doomed. In the end, northern exports of wheat ("King Corn") to Britain proved more important than southern cotton. (*Punch,* 1861)

Union blockade as the act of a nation at war, insisted that the blockade must effectively close southern harbors to be legally binding on neutral shippers, and recognized the belligerent status of the Confederacy. With equal logic, Confederate president Jefferson Davis met Lincoln's blockade by calling for privateers, a historic mode of American naval warfare.

In the 1856 Declaration of Paris following the Crimean War, Britain and France had codified the rules of maritime warfare and outlawed privateering. The United States had refused to sign away a favorite naval strategy, but the Confederacy's resort to privateering impelled Seward to inform the British minister, Lord Richard Lyons, that he wished belatedly to initial the covenant. Lyons welcomed U.S. adherence but noted Washington's inability to obligate the South. To Seward's claim that the South had no independent status, Lyons cooly replied: "Very well. If they are not independent then the President's proclamation of blockade is not binding. A blockade, according to the convention, applies only to two nations at war." Seward retorted: "Europe must interpret the law our way or we'll declare war, [and] commission enough privateers to prey on English commerce on every sea."[108] The secretary's intemperance caused Palmerston to see him as a "vapouring, blustering, ignorant Man" who "may drive us into a quarrel without intending it."[109]

Seward spoke from weakness, and the British knew it. The Union had twice the population of the South and produced 92 percent of all goods manufactured in the United States. But the North faced the difficult military task of subduing 9 million hostile people and sealing off innumerable harbors strung along a 3,500-mile coastline. To blockade this coast, the U.S. Navy could muster only forty-two operational warships, and of these only eight were in home waters. To win, "Confederate armies did not have to invade and conquer the North; they needed only to hold out long enough to force the North to the conclusion that the price of conquering the South and annihilating its armies was too high, as Britain had concluded in 1781 and as the United States concluded with respect to Vietnam in 1972."[110] British officials, especially Lyons, thought it implausible that Lincoln could reconstruct the Union against such odds.

The economic balance sheet also seemed to work against the North. Prior to the Civil War, British subjects invested widely in American securities, sent at least 25 percent of their annual exports to the United States, and depended on America for 55 percent of all foodstuffs imported each year. But these economic ties favoring the industrial North and farming West paled beside the South's share of three quarters of the British market for raw cotton, the staple undergirding an industrial and commercial empire employing between 4 and 5 million people. Stop the cotton trade and England's economy would allegedly collapse. As a southern politician bragged, cotton was "the king who can shake the jewels in the crown of Queen Victoria."[111]

President Jefferson Davis moved quickly to convert the Confederacy's economic advantage into political impregnability. In March he despatched three ministers to Europe to seek full diplomatic recognition, or even intervention, in exchange for an uninterrupted supply of cotton, free trade with the Confederacy, and expansion of European power throughout the Western Hemisphere.

Charleston, South Carolina. Its wharves piled with cotton for export, this southern city governed by wealthy planters and gentlemen relied heavily on the cotton trade for prosperity. In 1860 Charleston ranked third behind New Orleans and Mobile as a cotton-exporting port. (Library of Congress)

To parry this diplomatic thrust, Seward sped Charles Francis Adams to the Court of St. James's. "The Archbishop of antislavery," Adams was the son of the author of the Monroe Doctrine and grandson of the diplomat who had negotiated the 1783 peace with England.[112] Serenely confident that his appointment would lead him to the presidency, Adams ultimately insulated London from Seward's highly charged flashes without deviating from the secretary's goals. The historian Jay Monaghan has compared Adams to British foreign secretary Russell: "The two men were equally cold: formal, diplomatic, and almost equally British. A diamond come to cut a diamond."[113]

Adams arrived in London on May 14, 1861, dismayed to learn that England had proclaimed itself neutral and had recognized Confederate belligerency. Although he also heard some good news—the British government had forbidden its subjects to supply ammunition or privateers to either side—Russell had received but not officially met with Confederate commissioners. Adams's secretary and son, Henry Adams, saw sufficient grounds for severing diplomatic relations, but he and his father rejected such action as the "extreme of shallowness and folly," because a war with England, added to the Civil War, "would grind us all into rags in America."[114]

A process of amelioration then began on both sides of the Atlantic. In late May, Seward drafted a hostile dispatch for Adams, threatening to declare war if Britain recognized Confederate independence, only to have Lincoln pencil out the most bellicose phrases and send it for Adams's guidance rather than as an ultimatum to Russell. Even when toned down, Dispatch No. 10 struck Adams's son Henry as "so arrogant in tone and so extraordinary and unparalleled in its demands that it leaves no doubt in my mind that our Government wishes to face a war with all Europe."[115] As Adams quietly pocketed the diplomatic bombshell, reverses at the front rendered the secretary's threats of war with Europe ridiculous. On July 21, 1861, at Manassas Junction, Virginia, Confederate troops stampeded a Union army into full retreat north.

The summer and fall of 1861 brought further encouragement to Confederate officials. In England James D. Bulloch, head of the Confederacy's overseas secret service, contracted for the construction of two sloops. Disguised as merchant ships until their departure from British waters in order to circumvent the neutrality proclamation, the *Florida* and *Alabama* promised to play havoc with northern commerce. In August the *Bermuda,* a blockade runner laden with war matériel for Savannah, dashed from the Thames. Russell deflected Adams's protest with an invitation to sign the Declaration of Paris. To exploit this favorable drift of events, President Davis sent two fresh and aggressive ministers to Europe, the aristocratic James M. Mason of Virginia and John Slidell, the political boss of Louisiana and Polk's emissary to Mexico in 1845. On October 11, they boarded the Confederate steamer *Nashville* at Charleston to begin their journey.

Hoping to avoid capture by crossing the Atlantic under a neutral flag, Mason and Slidell transferred to the British mail steamer *Trent* in Havana. Captain Charles Wilkes, one of the U.S. Navy's most audacious officers, learned of their plans and intercepted the *Trent* as it left Cuban waters on November 8, 1861. Since the British vessel carried Confederate mail, Wilkes could have seized it as a prize. Instead, he hauled Mason and Slidell aboard the U.S.S. *San Jacinto* and allowed the *Trent* to continue its voyage, an act reminiscent of British impressment before the War of 1812. Ecstatic Washington crowds cheered Wilkes, and Congress voted him a gold medal. European ministers in the capital city unanimously decried the illegality of the seizure, and the chair of the Senate Foreign Relations Committee, Charles Sumner, urged immediate release of the two Confederates. Lincoln himself feared Mason and Slidell might become "white elephants" but doubted he could free the prisoners without inviting overwhelming popular disapproval.[116]

News of Wilkes's deed reached London on November 27, igniting a panic on the stock exchange and fanning fears of war. Palmerston began emergency cabinet meetings on November 29, reportedly opening one with, "You may stand for this but damned if I will."[117] The British government instructed Lyons to demand the release of Mason and Slidell and a formal apology "for the insult offered to the British flag." Prince Albert, a staunch advocate of Anglo-American peace, devised a loophole allowing the U.S. government, if it wished, to deny that Wilkes had acted under instructions, "or, if he did, that he misapprehended them." Russell then directed Lyons "to abstain from anything like menace" when insisting on freedom for Mason and Slidell and "to be rather easy about the apology."[118]

As the watered-down ultimatum crossed the Atlantic, British merchants profiting from trade with the Union joined Manchester liberals in an effort to quiet popular indignation. British officials tempered their enthusiasm for war because of their concern over the vulnerability of Canada. They also feared marauding Yankee cruisers that might prey on British shipping. Albert's death from typhoid on

December 14 further sobered the national mood. Two days later, Russell advised restraint: "I do not think the country [Britain] would approve an immediate declaration of war."[119]

Lyons made "the pill as easy to swallow as possible" when he delivered the message on December 19.[120] While the president and secretary of state considered their response, pressure mounted for U.S. capitulation. From London, Charles Francis Adams warned of implacable British determination to see Mason and Slidell free. The French minister in Washington advised that the Franco-American tradition of neutrality guaranteed safe passage for enemy civilians aboard neutral vessels. Charles Sumner chastised irresponsible war hawks who seemed willing to invite the shelling of American cities by British guns. Seeing the folly of "two wars . . . at a time," Lincoln and Seward thereupon decided to defuse the crisis.[121] Characterized by the historian Gordon Warren as "a monument to illogic," Seward's reply to Lord Lyons defended Wilkes's right to stop, search, and seize the *Trent* but admitted that the American naval officer had erred in not taking the vessel into port for hearings before a legal tribunal. The secretary thus disavowed Wilkes, congratulated the British for accepting American views on impressment, and "cheerfully liberated" the two Confederates.[122] Clever or not, Seward's settlement of the *Trent* affair "further embittered the opinion of this people toward Great Britain," the Mexican envoy Matías Romero reported from Washington. War, he predicted, "is not a remote possibility."[123]

Just prior to the *Trent* crisis, Britain, France, and Spain had landed troops at Veracruz, Mexico, ostensibly to compel payment on a $65 million foreign debt. Lord Russell had cautiously invited U.S. participation in this intervention. Seward declined, but he acknowledged the right of the powers to collect debts forcibly, provided they did not harbor political or territorial ambitions in Mexico. U.S. fears of European plots to implant a monarchical government in Latin America were realistic. In early 1862, Prime Minister Palmerston thought "the monarchy scheme . . . would be a great blessing for Mexico. . . . It would also stop the North Americans . . . in their absorption of Mexico."[124]

In April 1862, Britain and Spain settled their Mexican debts and withdrew from the joint venture. They left French troops to inch their way westward toward Mexico City, where Napoleon III hoped to install a puppet government under Archduke Ferdinand Maximilian, brother of the Austrian emperor. Fierce Mexican resistance delayed French occupation of the capital city until June 1863. This entrapment forced Napoleon to follow Britain's lead in Civil War diplomacy, despite his own bias in favor of the South. Seward and Lincoln watched these machinations without protest. "Why should we gasconade about Mexico," Seward explained, "when we are engaged in a struggle for our own life?"[125]

British "Lookers On" Across the Atlantic

In 1862, along the southern coast, the Union's tightening blockade locked up Confederate privateers and drove neutral shipping to uneconomical, shallow-draft steamers. In Tennessee an unknown general, Ulysses S. Grant, chased the rebels from Forts Donelson and Henry. Admiral David G. Farragut captured New Orleans in April, opening the Mississippi River to a campaign that would finally sever Texas, Arkansas, and Louisiana from the rest of the Confederacy. Neither North nor South, however, could score a decisive victory in the critical eastern theater. Union general George B. McClellan faltered and retreated outside Richmond in July 1862, just as Virginia's Robert E. Lee pulled back after the bloodletting at Antietam two months later. Always mindful of the vulnerability of Canada, and convinced that southern separation was an accomplished fact, the British government watched and waited. Britain prudently acquiesced in the Union blockade, accumulating precedents useful for future conflicts when once again England would be a belligerent and the United States neutral.

Cotton did not drive British policy—at least not at first. During the first year of the blockade, in fact, England did not crave raw cotton. The bumper American crop of 1860 provided 1.6 million bales for the saturated Lancashire mills in 1861, and production of cotton textiles far exceeded demand. Anticipating an early end to the Civil War, British cotton manufacturers complacently counted on their stockpiled raw cotton to carry them through a short-term crisis, which they alleviated by laying off workers and curtailing inflated production. As the military deadlock deepened in 1862, the textile producers feared future shortages and developed alternative sources, notably in Egypt and India. These new fields began to yield amply by 1863. In France, mill owners proved less resourceful, but Napoleon's insistence on following British policy toward the Civil War prevented the Confederacy from capitalizing on discontent in the French cotton industry. As the historian Thomas Schoonover has concluded: "The Confederacy exaggerated the power of cotton in the world system and misunderstood its own subordinate role in it. Cotton was not king, and it never had been."[126]

The Confederacy fared better in maritime Liverpool. Contemptuous of the blockade and the queen's neutrality proclamation, Liverpool shipping interests sought to recoup from the costly disruption of trade with the South by building blockade runners, commerce raiders, and rams for the South's agent James D. Bulloch. The blockade runners returned high profits to builders, skippers, and crews. Of 2,742 runs attempted during the war, steam-driven runners completed 2,525, or 92 percent, mainly during the ineffective first year of the blockade. Greed for profits, moreover, induced many southern shippers to import luxury items rather than military matériel, thus wasting precious cargo space and scarce southern capital.

Commerce raiders presented a greater threat to the Union. Bulloch contracted for these vessels and disguised them as cargo ships during construction in order to circumvent the British neutrality proclamation, which forbade outfitting warships for either belligerent. In March 1862 the *Oreto,* renamed *Florida* once at sea, slipped from Liverpool. Adams protested vainly and pleaded with Russell to detain a larger second vessel, "Number 290," then nearing completion. On July 31, Russell grudgingly concluded that the new rover was intended to be a Confederate commerce raider, but his order to seize it arrived a day after the "290," an alias for *Alabama,* had sailed. In the Azores, the eight-gun ship was armed and outfitted. In August 1862 the C.S.S. *Alabama* set out to destroy Union commerce. Under the command of the South's most gifted naval officer, Raphael Semmes, the raider sank nineteen Union merchant vessels in its first three months at sea. Together with the *Florida* and lesser raiders, it preyed on Union commerce worldwide, driving northern merchants to flags of foreign registry and sharply accelerating a scarcely noticed prewar decline in the American merchant marine.

Two months after the *Alabama*'s escape, awed by the Confederate victory at the Second Battle of Bull Run and the endless rivers of blood irrigating America, Russell proposed to Palmerston an Anglo-French mediation "with a view to the recognition of the independence of the Confederates."[127] Cotton shortages—the worst of the war—and fear of riots by unemployed Lancashire operatives added impetus to Russell's proposal, and William E. Gladstone, a member of the cabinet, declared publicly that Jefferson Davis had "made a nation."[128] Caught in a cabinet crisis over Mexico, however, the French hesitated, and from St. Petersburg came a resounding endorsement of "the maintenance of the American Union as one indivisible nation," which the tsar favored as a check on British supremacy in the Atlantic.[129] News of Lee's reversal at Antietam in September finally inclined Palmerston to "continue to be lookers on till the war shall have taken a more decided turn."[130] This repudiation on October 22, 1862, of both mediation and recognition of Confederate independence remained British policy until the end of the war.

Lincoln did all he could to ensure continued European neutrality. Alert to Britain's antipathy toward slavery, he issued the Emancipation Proclamation on September 22. This historic gesture set January 1, 1863, as the date for freedom of slaves in areas not controlled by the Union—in short, only in districts still in rebellion. Palmerston dismissed the proclamation as "trash," and Russell cynically noted that "the right of slavery is made the reward of loyalty."[131] Within months Henry Adams reported, however, that "the Emancipation Proclamation has done more for us here than all our former victories and all our diplomacy. It has created an almost convulsive reaction in our favor."[132]

As 1863 opened, a Polish uprising against Russian rule threatened general war and destruction of the critical European balance of power. Charles Francis Adams welcomed such continental distractions and waited impatiently for Union victories to give him diplomatic clout. In March, Henry Adams wrote his brother in the Union army that the diplomats needed encouragement from "military heroes," so that "we should be the cocks of the walk in England. . . . Couldn't some of you give us just one leetle sugar-plum? We are shocking dry."[133] Then in July came the good news: The northern armies had held at Gettysburg, and Grant had won control of the Mississippi River at Vicksburg.

As Confederate bonds plummeted thirty-two points on the London market, Minister Adams pressed Lord Russell to seize two ironclad, steam-driven vessels nearing completion at the Laird yards in Liverpool. These shallow-draft warships mounted seven-foot iron rams, theoretically an ideal weapon for piercing the wooden hulls of the Union's blockaders. Bulloch had ordered the Laird rams but so cleverly covered his tracks that the Pasha of Egypt seemed their legal owner. Since the rams lacked guns and the Crown lacked proof of Confederate ownership, Russell's law officers could not find them in violation of British neutrality. Russell,

Charles Francis Adams (1807–1886). Son of John Quincy Adams, graduate of Harvard, and Republican member of Congress from Massachusetts before Lincoln appointed him minister to Great Britain (1861–1868), the suave diplomat labored diligently to keep London neutral during the Civil War. (National Portrait Gallery, Smithsonian Institution/Art Resource, N.Y.)

however, dared not disregard Adams's increasingly shrill warnings, nor the Union's midsummer military victories. Nor was it in Britain's national interest to encourage the precedent of weak naval powers constructing warships in neutral shipyards during wartime. On September 3, 1863, he prudently detained the rams, telling Palmerston that "neutral hostility should not be allowed to go on without some attempt to stop it."[134]

Unaware of the foreign secretary's concession, Adams on September 5 penned a scathing note warning that if the rams were not halted, "it would be superfluous in me to point out to your lordship that this is war!"[135] Palmerston bridled at Adams's "insolent threats of war" and thought Russell should "say to him in civil terms, 'You be damned.'"[136] Such private pique did not detract from Adams's successful elimination of the Confederacy's last threat to the blockade.

Northern morale received a boost from the visit of the Russian Baltic and Pacific squadrons to New York and San Francisco in September and October of 1863. Fearful of war with England and France over Poland, Russia sent its ships in the hope that they could operate against the Royal Navy from ice-free American ports. One Russian officer predicted that if France recognized the Confederacy and Polish belligerency, "the Russian eagle might extend its talon to the American eagle to give a joint shake to the Gallic cock not only in words."[137] As Russian sailors marched down Broadway past a large Russian flag suspended at Tiffany's, northerners wishfully interpreted the visit as a sign of St. Petersburg's support for their cause. Secretary of the Navy Gideon Welles thought "our Russian friends are rendering us a great service."[138]

In 1863, too, the troops of Napoleon III finally fought their way into Mexico City. In July, the victorious French emperor proclaimed a Mexican monarchy under Austrian archduke Maximilian. Seward denied recognition to Maximilian when the aspiring royal arrived in Mexico in July 1864. By then General William T. Sherman was marching through Georgia and Grant crept bloodily toward Richmond. The apparently inevitable Union triumph would place a huge army and one of the world's largest navies along the border of Napoleon's puppet state. Napoleon began to scale down his commitment, intending to remove all but 20,000 French troops from Mexico by 1867. He also curried favor with Washington by directing Maximilian not to receive Confederate ministers, and he seized two Confederate rams under construction at Nantes in May 1864. A month later the U.S.S. *Kearsarge* sank the C.S.S. *Alabama* within sight of Cherbourg.

The diplomatic and naval isolation of the Confederacy became complete. "King Cotton" had failed. Confederate diplomacy, lacking decisive support from the battlefield, did not win European capitals to its cause. The "War Between the States" had remained just that.

War as Catalyst

When the guns of the Civil War finally quieted at Appomattox in April 1865, more than 600,000 Americans lay dead, and hundreds of thousands nursed disfiguring wounds. The war cost at least $20 billion in destroyed property and expenditures.

The American merchant marine lay in shambles. U.S. commerce was badly disrupted. The eleven Confederate states suffered heavy economic losses, as a dislocated population and labor force, including 4 million former slaves, worked in trampled and denuded agricultural fields and burned-out cities. Although the Union became whole once again, regional bitterness persisted. The wrenching Civil War experience and the necessity of postwar reconstruction suggested that sectionalism would continue to impede U.S. expansion abroad.

Countervailing evidence, however, indicated that the expansionism that had flourished in the 1840s and slowed in the 1850s would enjoy a rebirth. The United States, after all, had become an economic power before the Civil War. Although trade had stalled, northern commerce in grain with England expanded greatly during the war, and prospects for a renewal of the cotton trade were good. Even during the French occupation of Mexico (1862–1867), U.S. investors expanded into mining, petroleum, and agriculture south of the border.

During the war northern politicians established high tariffs to protect their own manufacturers, stabilized the banking system, passed the Homestead Act to settle western lands and the Morrill Act to build land-grant colleges, and provided for the construction of a transcontinental railroad. Large federal expenditures of about $2 million a day generated capital accumulation and stimulated some industries. The Civil War thus helped spur the American "industrial revolution" of the late nineteenth century, which increasingly shifted the character of the nation's foreign trade from agricultural to industrial goods and necessitated the sale of surplus production overseas. As the historian Thomas Schoonover has written, the North, "a semi-peripheral state" that acted as "both exploiter and exploited in the world system" had triumphed over the "peripheral" South with its one-crop economy, and the restored Union could grow to "metropole" status.[139]

The victory of Republican principles had global ramifications and elevated America's international status. Despite taunts and gibes about the American "smashup" from foreign critics, the Lincoln administration had won the war, freed the slaves, and preserved federal institutions. The Italian patriot Giuseppe Mazzini blessed the victorious people "who have done more for us in four years than fifty years of teaching, preaching, and writing from all your European brothers." None other than Karl Marx hailed the triumph of free labor over slave: "As . . . the American War of Independence sounded the tocsin for the European middle class, so . . . the American Civil War sounded it for the working class."[140] Indeed, as one historian has noted: "Before 1861 the two words 'United States' were generally regarded as a plural noun: 'the United States *are* a republic.' The war marked the transition of the United States to a singular noun."[141] Simply put, "the vision of a voluntary union of the states" had given way to "the imperatives of nation and empire, from which there could be no withdrawal."[142]

Once freed from the constraints of war, Secretary Seward envisioned a larger U.S. empire. A noted expansionist before the Civil War, Seward in 1865 turned his attention southward, intent on driving the French and Maximilian from Mexico, annexing territories, expanding trade, and building naval bases in the Caribbean. Santo Domingo, which Spain ruled from 1861 to mid-1865, became one of Seward's first targets. Moreover, Lincoln's diplomatic recognition of the free black countries of Haiti and Liberia in 1861, heretofore blocked by southern opposition, suggested that racism might prove less inhibiting to American expansion after the war.

The British in particular had good reason to be sensitive about the United States. Northerners angrily remembered the depradations of the *Alabama* and the seeming British tolerance of southern secession. Also, Anglo–American competition in Central America and the Caribbean joined competition in the Pacific and Asia to propel London and Washington along a contentious course. Reciprocity with Canada was breaking down (the Agreement of 1854 was abrogated in 1866). A new generation of American Anglophobes vowed to twist the British lion's tail, with some insisting that London cede Canada to atone for its sins. Indeed, formation of the Dominion of Canada, accomplished in 1867, may have been the "most tangible international repercussion of the American Civil War."[143]

If the British reaped intense American hostility, they also carried away from the contest some welcome precedents in international law. The seafaring British acquiesced in the tortuous U.S. rendering of maritime rights during the Civil War. While the Confederacy relied futilely on such honored American policies as embargoes and the destruction of commerce, the Lincoln administration reversed the traditional U.S. view of neutral rights and adopted what had been the British position. Seward insisted that the war was a *domestic* conflict, yet the United States declared a paper-thin blockade under *international* law. Not only did this behavior constitute a glaring contradiction; it also violated international law, for blockades must be effective. Seward even reversed the hallowed American doctrine that neutral shipping was immune to capture when traveling between neutral ports, regardless of the ultimate destination of the cargo. In 1863 he implicitly approved the capture of the *Peterhoff,* a British steamer loaded with Confederate goods en route to Matamoros, Mexico, suggesting that the cargo's ultimate destination made the voyage "continuous." During the period of American neutrality in the First World War (1914–1917), the British dusted off their history tomes and reminded Washington of Seward's Civil War policies. The legacy of the Civil War had a long reach indeed.

FURTHER READING FOR THE PERIOD 1848–1865

For the 1850s, Latin America, and the coming of the Civil War, see Frederick M. Binder, *James Buchanan and the American Empire* (1994); James C. Bradford, ed., *Captains of the Old Steam Navy* (1986) (U.S. Navy); Charles H. Brown, *Agents of Manifest Destiny* (1980) (filibusters); E. Bradford Burns, *Patriarch and Folk* (1991) (Nicaragua); Tom Chaffin, *Fatal Glory* (1996) (López); Amos A. Ettinger, *The Mission to Spain of Pierre Soulé, 1853–1855* (1932); John E. Findling, *Close Neighbors, Distant Friends* (1987) (Central America); William H. Freehling, *The Road to Disunion* (1990); Larry Gara, *The Presidency of Franklin Pierce* (1991); Kenneth J. Hagan, *This People's Navy* (1991); Michael H. Hunt, *Ideology and U.S. Foreign Policy* (1987); Robert W. Johannsen, *The Frontier, the Union, and Stephen A. Douglas* (1989) and *Lincoln, the South, and Slavery* (1991); Lester D. Langley, *Struggle for the American Mediterranean: United States–European Rivalry in the Gulf-Caribbean, 1776–1894* (1976); Luis Martínez-Fernández, *Torn Between Empires* (1994) (Spanish Caribbean); Robert E. May, *The Southern Dream of a Caribbean Empire, 1854–1861* (1973) and *John A. Quitman* (1985); Michael A. Morrison, *Slavery and the American West* (1997); Louis A. Pérez, Jr., *Cuba and the United States* (1997); Bradford Perkins cited in Chapter 2; Dexter Perkins, *The Monroe Doctrine, 1826–1867* (1933); Thomas D. Schoonover, *The United States in Central America* (1991); John Schroeder, *Shaping a Maritime Empire* (1985) (U.S. Navy); Joel H. Silbey, *The Partisan Imperative: The Dynamics of American Politics Before the Civil War* (1985); Elbert Smith, *The Presidencies of Zachary Taylor and Millard Fillmore* (1988) and *The Presidency of James Buchanan* (1975); and James T. Wall, *Manifest Destiny Denied* (1982).

For key characters, see K. Jack Bauer, *Zachary Taylor* (1985); Samuel Flagg Bemis, ed., *The American Secretaries of State and Their Diplomacy* (1927–1960); David Donald, *Charles Sumner and the Rights of Man* (1970); Robert W. Johannsen, *Stephen A. Douglas* (1973); Philip S. Klein, *President James Buchanan* (1962); William C. Klunder, *Lewis Cass and the Politics of Moderation* (1996); Jay Monaghan, *Diplomat in Carpet Slippers* (1945) (Lincoln); Roy F. Nichols, *Franklin Pierce* (1958); John Niven, *Gideon Welles* (1973); Ernest N. Paolino, *The Foundations of the American Empire* (1973) (Seward); and Glyndon G. Van Deusen, *William Henry Seward* (1967). See Chapter 3 for studies of Daniel Webster.

For Japan and Asian issues, see Warren I. Cohen, *America's Response to China* (1990); Foster R. Dulles, *Yankee and Samurai* (1965); Peter Duus, *The Japanese Discovery of America* (1996); John K. Fairbank, *Trade and Diplomacy on the China Coast* (1953); Fumiko Fujita, *American Pioneers and the Japanese Frontier* (1994); Arrell M. Gibson, *Yankees in Paradise* (1993); Gerald S. Graham, *The China Station* (1978); Curtis T. Henson, Jr., *Commissioners and Commodores: The East India Squadron and American Diplomacy in China* (1982); Michael Hunt, *The Making of a Special Relationship* (1983) (China); Walter LaFeber, *The Clash* (1997); Walter A. Mc-Dougall, *Let the Sea Make a Noise* (1993); Samuel E. Morison, *"Old Bruin"* (1967); Charles Neu, *The Troubled Encounter* (1975) (Japan); William L. Neumann, *America Encounters Japan* (1963); Robert A. Rosenstone, *Mirror in the Shrine* (1988) (Japan); Arthur Walworth, *Black Ships off Japan* (1946); and Peter Booth Wiley, *Yankees in the Land of the Gods* (1991) (Perry).

Anglo-Canadian-American relations are examined in Kenneth Bourne, *Britain and the Balance of Power in North America* (1967); Charles S. Campbell, *From Revolution to Rapprochement* (1974); Martin Crawford, *The Anglo-American Crisis of the Mid-Nineteenth Century* (1987); Wilbur D. Jones, *The American Problem in British Diplomacy* (1974); H. G. Nicholas, *The United States and Britain* (1975); Lester B. Shippee, *Canadian-American Relations, 1849–1874* (1939); Reginald C. Stuart, *United States Expansionism and British North America, 1775–1871* (1988); Donald Warner, *The Idea of Continental Union* (1960) (annexation of Canada); and Robin Winks, *Canada and the United States* (1960).

For European questions, see Henry M. Adams, *Prussian-American Relations, 1775–1871* (1960); Henry Blumenthal, *A Reappraisal of Franco-American Relations, 1830–1871* (1959) and *France and the United States* (1970); Alan Dowty, *The Limits of American Isolation* (1971) (Crimean War); James A. Field, Jr., *America and the Mediterranean World, 1776–1882* (1969); Normal Saul, *Distant Friends* (1991) (Russia); and Donald M. Spencer, *Louis Kossuth and Young America* (1977).

For Union and Confederate foreign policies, especially naval issues and maritime rights, see works cited above and Stuart L. Bernath, *Squall Across the Atlantic: American Civil War Prize Cases and Diplomacy* (1970); Eugene H. Berwanger, *The British Foreign Service and the American Civil War* (1994); Gabor S. Boritt, ed., *Why the Confederacy Lost* (1992); Kinley J. Brauer, "The Slavery Problem in the Diplomacy of the American Civil War," *Pacific Historical Review* (1977); Lynn M. Case and Warren F. Spencer, *The United States and France* (1970); Adrian Cook, *The Alabama Claims* (1975); David P. Crook, *Diplomacy During the American Civil War* (1975) and *The North, the South, and the Powers, 1861–1865* (1974); Charles P. Cullop, *Confederate Propaganda in Europe* (1969); David H. Donald, *Lincoln* (1995) and ed., *Why the North Won the Civil War* (1996); Norman B. Ferris, *The Trent Affair* (1977) and *Desperate Diplomacy: William H. Seward's Foreign Policy, 1861* (1975); Charles M. Hubbard, *The Burden of Confederate Diplomacy* (1998); Brian Jenkins, *Britain and the War for the Union* (1974–1980); Howard Jones, *Union in Peril: The Crisis over British Intervention in the Civil War* (1992); Robert E. May, ed., *The Union, the Confederacy, and the Atlantic Rim* (1995); James M. McPherson, *Battle Cry of Freedom* (1989) and *Ordeal by Fire* (1982); Frank J. Merli, *Great Britain and the Confederate Navy* (1970); Frank L. and Harriet Owsley, *King Cotton Diplomacy* (1959); Philip S. Paludan, *"A People's Contest"* (1988) and *The Presidency of Abraham Lincoln* (1994); Charles M. Robinson III, *Shark of the Confederacy* (1995) (*Alabama*); Warren F. Spencer, *The Confederate Navy in Europe* (1983); Emory M. Thomas, *The Confederate*

Nation, 1861–1865 (1979); Gordon H. Warren, *Fountain of Discontent* (1981) (*Trent*); and Robert W. Young, *Senator James Murray Mason* (1998).

For Mexico and the French intervention, see Alfred J. Hanna and Kathryn A. Hanna, *Napoleon III and Mexico* (1971); Donathon C. Olliff, *Reforma Mexico and the United States* (1981); W. Dirk Raat, *Mexico and the United States* (1992); and Thomas D. Schoonover, *Dollars over Dominion* (1978).

See also the General Bibliography, the following notes, and Richard Dean Burns, ed., *Guide to American Foreign Relations Since 1700* (1983).

For comprehensive coverage of foreign-relations topics, see the articles in the four-volume *Encyclopedia of U.S. Foreign Relations* (1997), edited by Bruce W. Jentleson and Thomas G. Paterson.

NOTES TO CHAPTER 4

1. Quoted in Arthur Walworth, *Black Ships off Japan* (New York: Knopf, 1946), p. 96.
2. Quoted in William L. Neumann, *America Encounters Japan* (Baltimore: Johns Hopkins University Press, 1963), p. 30.
3. Quoted in Henry F. Graff, *Bluejackets with Perry in Japan* (New York: New York Public Library, 1952), p. 68.
4. Quoted in Shunsuke Kamei, "The Sacred Land of Liberty: Images of America in Nineteenth Century Japan," in Akira Iriye, ed., *Mutual Images* (Cambridge: Harvard University Press, 1975), p. 55.
5. Quoted in Arrell M. Gibson, *Yankees in Paradise* (Albuquerque: University of New Mexico Press, 1993), p. 333.
6. Quoted in Oliver Statler, *The Black Ship Scroll* (Tokyo: John Weatherhill, 1963), p. 8.
7. Quoted in Walworth, *Black Ships off Japan*, p. 71.
8. Francis L. Hawks, ed., *Narrative of the Expedition of an American Squadron to the China Seas and Japan* (Washington, D.C.: Senate Printer, 1856; 3 vols.), I, 256–257, 261, 263.
9. William Heine, *With Perry to Japan* (Honolulu: University of Hawaii Press, 1990), p. 124.
10. Quoted in Walter LaFeber, *The Clash* (New York: Norton, 1997), p. 13.
11. Quoted in Fumiko Fujita, *American Pioneers and the Japanese Frontier* (Westport, Conn.: Greenwood, 1994), p. 5.
12. Quoted in Walter A. McDougall, *Let the Sea Make a Noise* (New York: BasicBooks, 1993), p. 276.
13. Quoted in Samuel Eliot Morison, *"Old Bruin"* (Boston: Little, Brown, 1967), p. 371.
14. Quoted in Neumann, *America Encounters Japan*, p. 40, and Graff, *Bluejackets with Perry*, p. 68.
15. Quoted in Morison, *"Old Bruin,"* pp. 417, 425.
16. Quoted in John Schroeder, *Shaping a Maritime Empire* (Westport, Conn.: Greenwood, 1985), pp. 158–159.
17. Quoted in McDougall, *Let the Sea*, p. 272.
18. Quoted in Peter Booth Wiley, *Yankees in the Land of the Gods* (New York: Viking Penguin, 1991), p. 489.
19. Quoted in Kenneth J. Hagan, *This People's Navy* (New York: Free Press, 1991), p. 149.
20. Quoted in Richard Van Alstyne, *The Rising American Empire* (New York: Norton, 1974 [1960]), p. 175.
21. Quoted in Michael A. Morrison, *Slavery and the American West* (Chapel Hill: University of North Carolina Press, 1997), p. 15.
22. Quoted in Warren I. Cohen, *America's Response to China* (New York: Wiley, 1990; 3rd ed.), p. 19.
23. Quoted in Kinley J. Brauer, "1820–1860," in William Becker and Samuel F. Wells, Jr., eds., *Economics and World Power* (New York: Columbia University Press, 1984), p. 89.
24. Charles E. Neu, *The Troubled Encounter* (New York: Wiley, 1975), p. 9.
25. Quoted in Thomas Schoonover, "Napoleon Is Coming," in Robert E. May, ed., *The Union, the Confederacy, and the Atlantic Rim* (West Lafayette, Ind.: Purdue University Press, 1995), p. 109.
26. Quoted in Richard Van Alstyne, "Empire in Midpassage, 1845–1867," in William A. Williams, ed., *From Colony to Empire* (New York: Wiley, 1972), p. 119.
27. Eugene D. Genovese, *The Political Economy of Slavery* (New York: Vintage Books, 1967), p. 270.
28. Quoted in Eric Foner, *Free Labor, Free Soil, Free Men* (New York: Oxford University Press, 1970), p. 72.
29. Quoted in Kenneth E. Shewmaker, "Daniel Webster and the Politics of Foreign Policy, 1850–1852," *Journal of American History*, LXIII (September 1976), 308.
30. Quoted in George T. Curtis, *Life of Daniel Webster* (New York: Appleton, 1870; 2 vols.), II, 537.
31. Quoted in Elbert B. Smith, *The Presidencies of Zachary Taylor and Millard Fillmore* (Lawrence: University Press of Kansas, 1988), p. 232.
32. Quoted in Robert V. Remini, *Daniel Webster* (New York: Norton, 1997), p. 702.
33. Quoted in Robert R. Davis, Jr., "Diplomatic Plumage," *American Quarterly*, XX (Summer 1968), 173.
34. Tom Chaffin, *Fatal Glory* (Charlottesville: University Press of Virginia, 1996), p. 10.
35. Quoted in Robert W. Johannsen, *Stephen A. Douglas* (New York: Oxford University Press, 1973), p. 347.
36. Quoted in Robert W. Johannsen, *Lincoln, the South, and Slavery* (Baton Rouge: Louisiana State University Press, 1991), p. 89.
37. Quoted in Russell B. Nye, *George Bancroft* (New York: Knopf, 1944), p. 205.
38. Quoted in Albert K. Weinberg, *Manifest Destiny* (Chicago: Quadrangle Books, 1963 [1935]), pp. 201–202.
39. Quoted in Robert W. Johannsen, *The Frontier, the Union, and Stephen A. Douglas* (Urbana: University of Illinois Press, 1989), p. 87.

40. Quoted in David Potter, *The Impending Crisis, 1848–1861* (New York: Harper and Row, 1976), p. 198.

41. William H. Freehling, *The Road to Disunion* (New York: Oxford University Press, 1990), p. 510.

42. Quoted in Robert F. Durden, "J. D. B. DeBow," *Journal of Southern History, XVII* (November 1951), 450.

43. James W. McDonald quoted in Robert E. May, *John A. Quitman* (Baton Rouge: Louisiana State University Press, 1985), p. 278.

44. Albert Gallatin Brown quoted in Luis Martínez-Fernández, *Torn Between Empires* (Athens: University of Georgia Press, 1994), p. 37.

45. Quoted in Philip S. Foner, *A History of Cuba and Its Relations with the United States* (New York: International Publishers, 1962–1963; 2 vols.), II, 43.

46. Quoted in K. Jack Bauer, *Zachary Taylor* (Baton Rouge: Louisiana State University Press, 1985), p. 280.

47. Quoted in Foner, *History of Cuba*, II, 64.

48. Quoted in Tom Chaffin, "Sons of Washington," *Journal of the Early Republic, XV* (Spring 1995), 89.

49. Quoted in Durden, "DeBow," p. 451.

50. Quoted in May, *Quitman*, p. 278.

51. Quoted in Robert E. May, "The Slave Power Conspiracy Revisited," in David W. Blight and Brooks Simpson, eds., *Union and Emancipation* (Kent, Ohio: Kent State University Press, 1997), p. 17.

52. Quoted in William H. Goetzmann, *When the Eagle Screamed* (New York: Wiley, 1966), p. 87.

53. Quoted in Roy F. Nichols, *Franklin Pierce* (Philadelphia: University of Pennsylvania Press, 1931), p. 459.

54. Quoted in William Earl Weeks, *Building the Continental Empire* (Chicago: Ivan R. Dee, 1996), p. 159.

55. Quoted in Robert E. May, *The Southern Dream of a Caribbean Empire, 1854–1861* (Baton Rouge: Louisiana State University Press, 1973), p. 91.

56. Quoted in Randall O. Hudson, "The Filibuster Minister," *North Carolina Historical Review, XLIX* (July 1972), 295.

57. Quoted in E. Bradford Burns, *Patriarch and Folk* (Cambridge: Harvard University Press, 1991), p. 195.

58. Quoted in Janet L. Coryell, "Duty with Delicacy," in Edward E. Crapol, ed., *Women and American Foreign Policy* (Westport, Conn.: Greenwood, 1992; 2nd ed.), p. 52.

59. Quoted in Burns, *Patriarch*, p. 202.

60. Quoted in Kenneth Stampp, *America in 1857* (New York: Oxford University Press, 1990), p. 296.

61. Quoted in May, *Southern Dream*, pp. 131–132.

62. Luis Martínez-Fernández, "Caudillos, Annexationism, and the Rivalry Between Empires," *Diplomatic History, XVII* (Fall 1993), 579.

63. Quoted in Robert E. May, "'Plenipotentiary in Petticoats,'" in Crapol, *Women and American Foreign Policy*, p. 33.

64. John E. Findling, *Close Neighbors, Distant Friends* (Westport, Conn.: Greenwood, 1987), p. 28.

65. Quoted in Burns, *Patriarch*, p. 208.

66. May, *Southern Dream*, p. 244.

67. James Buchanan quoted in Frederick Moore Binder, "James Buchanan and the Earl of Clarendon," *Diplomacy & Statecraft, VI* (July 1995), 333.

68. Michael H. Hunt, *Ideology and U.S. Foreign Policy* (New Haven: Yale University Press, 1987), p. 60.

69. Quoted in May, *Southern Dream*, p. 7.

70. Quoted in Louis A. Pérez, Jr., *Cuba and the United States* (Athens: University of Georgia Press, 1991), p. 14.

71. Quoted in Weinberg, *Manifest Destiny*, p. 190.

72. Parke Goodwin in Norman A. Graebner, ed., *Manifest Destiny* (Indianapolis: Bobbs-Merrill, 1968), p. lxiv.

73. Anton L. Allahar, "Sugar, Slaves, and the Politics of Annexation," *Colonial Latin American Historical Review, III* (Summer 1994), 285.

74. Quoted in Smith, *Presidencies of Taylor and Fillmore*, p. 87.

75. Quoted in John A. Logan, Jr., *No Transfer* (New Haven: Yale University Press, 1961), p. 227.

76. Quoted in Basil Rauch, *American Interest in Cuba, 1848–1855* (New York: Columbia University Press, 1948), p. 176.

77. John Bassett Moore, *A Digest of International Law* (Washington, D.C.: Government Printing Office, 1906; 8 vols.), VI, 462.

78. Quoted in Gavin B. Henderson, "Southern Designs on Cuba, 1854–1857 and Some European Opinions," *Journal of Southern History, V* (August 1939), 385.

79. Quoted in Martínez-Fernández, *Torn Between Empires*, p. 38.

80. Quoted in Amos A. Ettinger, *The Mission to Spain of Pierre Soulé* (New Haven: Yale University Press, 1932), p. 378.

81. Quoted in Martínez-Fernández, *Torn Between Empires*, p. 37

82. Quoted in Henry B. Learned, "William Learned Marcy," in Samuel Flagg Bemis, ed., *American Secretaries of State and Their Diplomacy* (New York: Cooper Square Publishers, 1963: 18 vols.), VI, 193.

83. Ruhl J. Bartlett, ed., *The Record of American Diplomacy* (New York: Knopf, 1960; 3rd ed.), p. 241.

84. Quoted in Larry Gara, *The Presidency of Franklin Pierce* (Lawrence: University Press of Kansas, 1991), p. 152.

85. Quoted in Henderson, "Southern Designs," p. 374.

86. Quoted in Philip S. Klein, *President James Buchanan* (University Park: Penn State University Press, 1962), p. 324.

87. Quoted in Graebner, *Manifest Destiny*, p. 298.

88. Quoted in H. G. Nicholas, *The United States and Britain* (Chicago: University of Chicago Press, 1975), p. 22.

89. Quoted in Philip Guedalla, *Gladstone and Palmerston* (New York: Kraus Reprint, 1971 [1928]), p. 208.

90. U.S. Senate, Executive Doc. 27 (1853), 32 Cong., 2 Sess., p. 30.

91. Quoted in Kenneth Bourne, *The Foreign Policy of Victorian England* (Oxford: Clarendon Press, 1970), p. 334.

92. Quoted in Wilbur D. Jones, *The American Problem in British Diplomacy, 1841–1861* (Athens: University of Georgia Press, 1974), p. 75.

93. Hunter Miller, ed., *Treaties and Other International Acts of the United States of America* (Washington D.C.: Government Printing Office, 1931–1948; 8 vols.), V, 672.

94. *Ibid.*, p. 685.

95. Jones, *American Problem*, p. 88.

96. Quoted in Richard Van Alstyne, "The Clayton-Bulwer Treaty," *Journal of Modern History, XI* (June 1939), 156.

97. Quoted in Kenneth Bourne, *Britain and the Balance of Power in North America, 1815–1908* (London: Longmans, Green, 1967), p. 182.

98. Quoted in Binder, "Buchanan and Clarendon," 333.

99. Quoted *ibid.*, p. 189.

100. Quoted in Kenneth E. Shewmaker, "'Hook and line, and bob and sinker': Daniel Webster and the Fisheries Dispute of 1852," *Diplomatic History, IX* (Spring 1985), 123.

101. Quoted in Margaret O. W. Oliphant, *Memoir of the Life of Laurence Oliphant and of Alice Oliphant, His Wife* (Edinburgh: Blackwood, 1891; 2 vols.), I, 120.

102. Quoted in Reginald C. Stuart, *United States Expansionism and British North America, 1775–1871* (Chapel Hill: University of North Carolina Press, 1988), p. 209.

103. Quoted in H. C. Allen, *Great Britain and the United States* (New York: St. Martin's Press, 1955), p. 423.

104. Quoted in Paul A. Varg, *United States Foreign Relations 1820–1860* (East Lansing: Michigan State University Press, 1979), p. 233.

105. Quoted in Allan Nevins, *The Coming Fury* (Garden City, N.Y.: Doubleday, 1961), p. 217.

106. Jay Monaghan, *Diplomat in Carpet Slippers* (Indianapolis: Charter, 1945), p. 58.

107. Quoted in John G. Nicolay and John Hay, *Abraham Lincoln* (New York: Century, 1890; 10 vols.), *III*, 445–449.

108. Quoted in Monaghan, *Diplomat in Carpet Slippers*, p. 82.

109. Quoted in Jones, *American Problem*, pp. 199–200.

110. James M. McPherson, "American Victory, American Defeat," in Gabor S. Boritt, ed., *Why the Confederacy Lost* (New York: Oxford University Press, 1992), p. 21.

111. S. R. Cockerill quoted in Frank L. Owsley and Harriet C. Owsley, *King Cotton Diplomacy* (Chicago: University of Chicago Press, 1959; rev. ed.), p. 19.

112. Quoted in Monaghan, *Diplomat in Carpet Slippers*, p. 26.

113. *Ibid.*, p. 100.

114. Worthington C. Ford, ed., *Letters of Henry Adams* (Boston: Houghton Mifflin, 1930–1938; 2 vols.), *I*, 92.

115. Quoted *ibid.*, p. 93.

116. Quoted in Allan Nevins, *The War for the Union* (New York: Charles Scribner's Sons, 1959–1971; 4 vols.), *I*, 392.

117. Quoted in James M. McPherson, *Battle Cry of Fredom* (New York: Ballantine Books, 1989), p. 390.

118. Quoted in David P. Crook, *The North, the South, and the Powers* (New York: Wiley, 1974), pp. 133–134.

119. Quoted *ibid.*, pp. 147, 140.

120. James J. Barnes and Patience Barnes, eds., *Private and Confidential: Letters from British Ministers in Washington* (Selinsgrove, Pa: Susquehanna University Press, 1993), p. 274.

121. Quoted in David H. Donald, *Lincoln* (New York: Simon & Schuster, 1995), p. 323.

122. Gordon H. Warren, *Fountain of Discontent* (Boston: Northeastern University Press, 1981), p. 184.

123. Quoted in Thomas Schoonover, ed., *A Mexican View of America in the 1860s* (Rutherford, N.J.: Fairleigh Dickinson University Press, 1991), p. 91.

124. Quoted in Crook, *North, South, and Powers*, pp. 93, 184.

125. Quoted in Philip S. Paludan, *"A People's Contest"* (New York: Harper and Row, 1988), p. 275.

126. Thomas D. Schoonover, *The United States in Central America* (Durham, N.C.: Duke University Press, 1991), p. 26.

127. Quoted in Emory M. Thomas, *The Confederate Nation, 1861–1865* (New York: Harper and Row, 1979), p. 179.

128. Quoted in Philip Shaw Paludan, *The Presidency of Abraham Lincoln* (Lawrence: University Press of Kansas, 1994), p. 218.

129. Quoted in Normal Saul, *Distant Friends* (Lawrence: University Press of Kansas, 1991), p. 333.

130. Quoted in Norman A. Graebner, "European Interventionism and the Crisis of 1862," *Journal of the Illinois State Historical Society*, *LXIX* (February 1976), 43.

131. Quoted in Robert H. Jones, *Disrupted Decades* (New York: Charles Scribner's Sons, 1973), p. 376, and Crook, *North, South, and Powers*, p. 238.

132. Quoted in James M. McPherson, "The Whole Family of Man," in May, *The Union*, pp. 144–145.

133. Ford, *Letters of Henry Adams, I*, 96.

134. Quoted in Monaghan, *Diplomat in Carpet Slippers*, p. 328.

135. Quoted in Frank J. Merli, *Great Britain and the Confederate Navy* (Bloomington: Indiana University Press, 1970), p. 201.

136. Quoted in Owsley and Owsley, *King Cotton*, p. 402.

137. Quoted in Robert Ivanov, "Russian Warships in North America," *International Affairs*, August 1988, p. 138.

138. Quoted in Howard K. Beale, ed., *Diary of Gideon Welles* (New York: W. W. Norton, 1960; 3 vols.), *I*, 484.

139. Schoonover, *United States in Central America*, p. 15.

140. Quoted in McPherson, "Whole Family," p. 46.

141. McPherson, *Battle Cry*, p. 859.

142. William Earl Weeks, "American Nationalism, American Imperialism," *Journal of the Early Republic*, *XIV* (Winter 1994), 493.

143. Robert E. May, "Introduction," in May, *The Union*, p. 10.

Global Rivalry and Regional Power, 1865–1895

Annexation Demonstration, Dominican Republic. *James Taylor's watercolor of a Dominican rally in favor of the nation's annexation to the United States captured the moment but did not move the question. (Library of Congress)*

❖

DIPLOMATIC CROSSROAD

The Foiled Grab of the Dominican Republic, 1869–1870

President Ulysses S. Grant salivated over his pet project as he walked from the White House across Lafayette Park to the elegant brick home of the chair of the Senate Foreign Relations Committee, Charles Sumner. The flattery of senatorial egos sometimes brought fruitful results, and in this case Grant sought a two-thirds vote. On that evening of January 2, 1870, in Washington, Sumner was offering good food and conversation to two politicos when Grant appeared uninvited and unexpected. Several awkward moments passed before the president revealed his mission. Would the Massachusetts senator support an annexation treaty for the Dominican Republic? Grant seemed impatient and only briefly sketched his case for this imperialistic scheme. "Mr. President," said Sumner, "I am an Administration man, and whatever you will do will always find in me the most careful and candid consideration."[1] The president left, satisfied that this polite remark signaled senatorial backing for the project. An American land grab seemed imminent—or so Grant thought.

The Dominican Republic, which shared the island of Hispaniola with Haiti, had a stormy history. Formerly part of both the French and the Spanish empires, the Dominicans declared independence from Spain in 1821 only to be occupied by Haiti from 1822 to 1844. República Dominicana then won its independence, but from 1861 to 1865 Spain reestablished rule over the strife-torn nation. Often known at the time by the name of its capital, Santo Domingo, the Dominican Republic suffered rule by the unscrupulous. Dominican president Buenaventura Báez, "an active intriguer of sinister talents," seemed eager to sell his country.[2]

The Dominican Republic had long held a place in the vision of U.S. expansionists. The U.S. Navy coveted the harbor at Samaná Bay, a choice strategic site in the Caribbean. The country's raw materials, especially timber and minerals, and its undeveloped status invited the attention of foreign entrepreneurs; others thought of Santo Domingo as a potential sanitarium for isthmian canal workers struck by yellow fever. The Caribbean, in any case, seemed destined to come under U.S. hegemony.

In July 1869, Grant's personal secretary, General Orville Babcock, had visited Santo Domingo to reconnoiter this "Gibraltar of the New World." Later exposed as a member of the Whiskey Ring, which defrauded the U.S. Treasury of millions of dollars, Babcock was also looking for personal profit in this Caribbean land. He befriended William and Jane Cazneau and Joseph Fabens, American speculators and sometime diplomatic agents who owned key Dominican mines, banks, and port facilities, including the frontage to Samaná Bay. Helped by Jane Cazneau's political connections with expansionists such as William Seward, the trio also represented a steamship company that sought traffic between New York and the island. With the

Cazneaus and Fabens in the wings, and warning that any attack "upon Dominicans
. . . will be considered an act of hostility to the Flag of the United States," Babcock
and Báez struck a deal in two treaties signed on November 29, 1869.[3] In the first,
the United States agreed to annex the Dominican Republic and assume its national
debt of $1.5 million. The second treaty promised that if the U.S. Senate refused to
take all of the country, Washington could buy Samaná Bay for $2 million. After the
signing, Babcock prematurely hoisted the American flag at Samaná.

Grant began to lobby for annexation. His visit to Sumner's house was a calculated step to build support. Yet the independent-minded Sumner remained noncommittal for months. The more Sumner and his colleagues heard, the more they
recoiled from the untidy affair. When the U.S. Navy intervened to prevent rebels
from toppling the corrupt, money-grabbing Báez, Republican senator Carl Schurz
of Missouri claimed that Grant "did usurp the warmaking power of Congress."[4]
Sumner's friend, the Massachusetts pacifist-abolitionist Lydia Maria Child, called
Dominican annexation "a real filibustering project, twin brother to our taking
Texas from the Mexicans."[5] Babcock, moreover, had acted as a presidential agent,
not as an accredited diplomat. Along with Fabens and the Cazneaus, he saw a lucrative opportunity and had enthralled the gullible Grant with a best-case Dominican scenario. Finally, Haiti seemed poised to join Báez's opponents and invade
Santo Domingo, especially when Grant talked loosely about purchasing "that island."[6] Sumner grumbled about these unsavory facts. Other skeptics sniffed another
scandal like that which had tarnished the Alaska purchase in 1867.

**Ulysses S. Grant
(1822–1885).** Graduate of
the U.S. Military Academy,
soldier in the War with Mexico, and Civil War general before becoming president,
Grant failed to annex the Dominican Republic. The historian William J. Nelson calls
Grant "a North American
caudillo trapped in a political
system that demanded alternative forms of persuasion."
(Library of Congress)

Grant grew annoyed with Sumner's inertia and worked vigorously for the treaty
by personally lobbying senators. He warned reluctant cabinet members to back the
treaty or resign. The indignant but cautious secretary of state, Hamilton Fish, whose
department Grant had bypassed in the rush to get the Dominican Republic, threatened to quit, but a sense of loyalty and Grant's personal appeal kept him at his post.
Fish opposed annexation but favored American hegemony over the country in the
form of a "protectorate." He could not persuade the stubborn president, who
seemed bent on total victory or total defeat. On March 15, 1870, the Foreign Relations Committee, by a 5 to 2 vote, with Sumner in the lead, disapproved the treaty.
Days later, Sumner disparaged annexation but favored a "free confederacy" in the
West Indies where the "black race should predominate" under U.S. protection.[7]

Annexationists countered that the absorption of the island would ensure a
steady flow of raw materials to the United States. They displayed pieces of Dominican hemp to prove their point, and two senators performed an impromptu tug-
of-war to demonstrate the fiber's strength. Another predicted that the spindles of
New England textile mills would whirl once the Dominicans began to buy American cotton goods. Anti-imperialists retorted that the Dominican populace consisted of two-thirds "native African"and one-third "Spanish Creole," a mixture
"still more barbaric and savage than the pure African"; that annexation would spur
the building of a larger navy, which would in turn entangle the United States in
foreign troubles; that Americans were acting too much like colonizing Europeans;
and that Congress had a constitutional duty to check such presidential schemes.[8]

To regain the offensive, Grant on May 31 sent a special message to Congress
extolling the virtues of the tiny island nation. It read like an expansionist's shopping

Charles Sumner (1811–1874). Harvard graduate, lawyer, abolitionist, critic of the War with Mexico, senator from Massachusetts, and chair of the Foreign Relations Committee (1861–1871), the strong-willed Sumner blocked attempts to annex the Dominican Republic and harassed England over the *Alabama* claims. (National Portrait Gallery, Smithsonian Institution)

list: raw materials from mines and forests, excellent harbors, a naval base, national security, a market for American products, and a site from which to help settle the revolution raging in Cuba. The United States had to keep its word as recorded by the two treaties. Without evidence, the president warned that if the United States did not take Santo Domingo, "a first class European power stands ready now to offer $2,000,000 for Samaná Bay," thus violating the Monroe Doctrine.[9] He even had the audacity to report the result of a farcical rigged plebiscite in which the Dominicans registered their support for selling themselves to the United States by the highly suspicious vote of 15,169 to 11.

Sumner would not budge. Personal feuding complicated this issue. Described by a British diplomat as "the most uncouth man I ever met," Grant had an almost visceral loathing for the urbane Sumner, who seemed an arrogant Yankee rival.[10] Unenthusiastic about Grant's nomination in 1868, Sumner had opposed some of the president's appointees and belonged to the radical wing of the Republican party—a faction to which Grant never warmed. Grant also felt betrayed, remembering that night in January when he believed Sumner had given his word of support. Stung by Sumner's charges of corruption, Babcock denounced him as a "liar and coward" and "poor *sexless* fool."[11] Sumner, for his part, had little respect for the intellectually inferior Grant and probably felt pique at not having been named to the post of secretary of state. Sumner's explosive temper, florid rhetoric, and intellectual certitude sparked obstinacy, anger and contempt in Grant, noted Charles Francis Adams. The editor E. L. Godkin of *The Nation* remarked that Sumner "works his adjectives so hard that if they ever catch him alone, they will murder him."[12] The Dominican treaty brought these personal antagonisms and different styles to the forefront.

In June, the Senate voted 28 to 28 on the treaty of annexation, well short of the two-thirds vote required for approval. "I will not allow Mr. Sumner to ride over me," Grant fumed.[13] The president and loyal Republicans vowed to strip Sumner of his leadership of the Foreign Relations Committee. Sumner began to lose support among his colleagues when he refused even to approve a commission to study Dominican annexation. The senator denounced it as a trick, a "dance of blood," in his dramatic "Naboth's Vineyard" speech (referring to the biblical story of King Ahab, who coveted his neighbor's vineyard). Delivered to the Senate on December 21, 1870, this intense oration reminded listeners of those pre–Civil War days when Sumner had blasted the defenders of slavery. Now Sumner scorned the Cazneaus and Fabens as "political jockeys" who had "seduced" Babcock. Santo Domingo, he insisted, belonged to the "colored" Dominicans and "our duty is as plain as the Ten Commandments. Kindness, beneficence, assistance, aid, help, protection, all that is implied in good neighborhood, these we must give freely, bountifully, but their independence is as sacred to them as ours is to us."[14]

The Senate nonetheless voted 32 to 9 to establish the commission (it issued a favorable report in early 1871). Many senators voted aye not because they supported annexation but because the commission provided a face-saving device for Grant and a rebuke to the carping Sumner. In March 1871, the Republican caucus voted 26 to 21 to remove Sumner altogether from the Foreign Relations Committee. Sumner, ill and irascible, still savored his victory over the Dominican land-grab scheme.

The Culture of Expansionism and Imperialism

The foiled grab of Santo Domingo, coming so soon after the Civil War, suggests that the sectional conflict only briefly interrupted the continuity of expansion. To be sure, most Americans in the late 1860s were not thinking about the Caribbean or other foreign-policy issues, preoccupied as they were with healing the wounds of war, reconstructing a fractured nation, and settling the trans-Mississippi West. And, although the soaring oratory of "Manifest Destiny" sounded again through the late nineteenth century, the United States lacked well-defined, sustained foreign "policies" and only haltingly promoted overseas expansion and empire. As the Dominican episode illustrates, domestic politics, personal whims and antagonisms, and tensions between the executive and legislative branches could intrude. Indeed, the historian Paul Holbo, in comparing Grant's failure to Woodrow Wilson's defeat over the League of Nations in 1919, has suggested that the Dominican debacle, "like Wilson's fifty years later, affected the course of American . . . foreign policy for the subsequent two decades."[15] Uncertainties and hesitancies abounded, too, because strong anti-imperialist sentiment warned that an overseas empire would undermine institutions at home, invite perpetual war, and violate honored principles such as self-determination. Also, the United States simply lacked the power to work its will in some parts of the world. American diplomats, consuls, and naval officers remained active on a global scale, but U.S. power largely confined itself to the Western Hemisphere and parts of the Pacific.

Still, the direction of U.S. foreign policy after the Civil War quickly became unmistakable: Americans intended to exert their influence beyond the continental United States. The more concerted, less restrained, and less erratic foreign policy that emerged in the 1890s consummated an imperial trend evident intermittently but persistently since the 1860s—what one scholar has called "an accumulation of calculated decisions."[16] Before the Civil War, American expansion had both commercial and territorial goals. The commercial expansion became global and largely maritime; the territorial expansion was regional and limited to areas contiguous to the United States (see Chapters 3 and 4). After the Civil War, in the historian Thomas Schoonover's words, "land was no longer the prime objective; it was replaced by investment, exploitation, and commercial goals."[17] As Secretary of State James G. Blaine said, the United States showed more interest in the "annexation of trade" than in the annexation of territory.[18] The United States did seek and take a few territories in the 1865–1895 period, of course. Unlike the pre–Civil War additions, these annexed territories were noncontiguous to the United States, and they remained in a long-term colonial status.

Although most Americans applauded economic expansion, many felt uneasy with overseas imperialism—the imposition of control over other peoples, denying them the freedom to make their own choices, undermining their sovereignty. The critical factor in empire-building was power—the power to make others move the way the imperial state dictated. Imperialism took several forms, both formal (annexation, colonialism, or military occupation) and informal (the threat of intervention or economic or political manipulation). For example, the American economic domination of a country through trade and investment constituted informal imperialism, even though the United States did not officially annex the territory and make it a colony. The United States never formally acquired the Dominican Republic, to cite a case, but by the early twentieth century, after years of private American economic expansion into the island, it had become subservient to the United States and hence part of the informal U.S. empire. There was a significant difference between imperialism and expansionism. The latter referred only to the outward movement of goods, dollars, ships, people, and ideas. In the period after the Civil War, the United States was demonstrably expansionist. In some instances, this expansion became imperialism.

An intertwined set of ideas infused post–Civil War expansion: nationalism, capitalism, exceptionalism, Social Darwinism, paternalism, and the categorization of foreigners in dismissive age-, race-, and gender-based language. Fear and prejudice also influenced American attitudes toward the world and "the Other"—fear of revolutionary disorder, fear of economic depression, fear of racial and ethnic mixing, fear of women's emancipation, fear of a closed frontier, fear of declining international stature. To assuage these fears and promote American values, it seemed necessary to remake other societies in the image of the United States.

A reinvigorated nationalism fueled the expansionist impulse. After the Civil War, national leaders sought to narrow sectional divisions. The 1876 centennial celebration emphasized national unity. Confederate and Union soldiers met on former battlefields to exchange flags. New patriotic associations emerged to champion nationalism: Colonial Dames of America (1890), Daughters of the American Revolution (1890), and Society of Colonial Wars (1893). World's fairs such as Chicago's Columbian Exposition of 1893 aimed to "teach not only to our people, but to the world, what a young republic . . . has done in its brief past, is doing in the present, and hopes to do in the greater future for its people and for mankind."[19] Americans thought themselves a special people, even God-favored, who had attained impressive material success and as an industrial power would soon surpass Great Britain and Germany. As emissaries of Christ, representatives of the Young Women's Christian Association helped indigenous women in India and China, for example, by trying to end such practices as footbinding, child marriage, and suttee (widow immolation). Although many such YWCA women "preached against war and imperialism," their "very presence depended on both."[20] Reformers in the Women's Christian Temperance Union (WCTU) spread the gospel in "heathen" lands and competed against other Anglo-Saxons who exported another "kind of American dream"—alcoholic beverages.[21]

The prevalence of Social Darwinist thought—that by the natural order of things some people were meant to survive and others to fail—encouraged notions of racial and national superiority. In their sense of racial hierarchy, Americans placed "uncivilized" people of black color and Indians at the bottom. As the Reverend Josiah Strong put it, "to be a Christian and an Anglo-Saxon and an American . . .

"The Stride of a Century." This Currier & Ives print captured the centennial spirit of 1876, which generated American nationalism and a celebration of the "progress" of the United States. (Library of Congress)

is to stand at the very mountaintop of privilege."[22] Slightly lower on the ladder, Americans ranked European peoples—"aggressive" Germans followed by "peasant" Slavs, "sentimental" French and Italians, and "Shylock" Jews. The middle rank comprised Latinos, the Spanish-speaking peoples of Latin America. Often disparaging Latinos as "dagoes" and "half-castes" unable to govern themselves, North American imperialists also portrayed Latin Americans as distressed damsels in need of manly rescue, as sister republics amenable to avuncular advice, and as squabbling children requiring paternalistic supervision. After a visit to Honduras, the journalist Richard Harding Davis, author of *Three Gringos in Venezuela and Central America* (1896), depicted Central Americans as "a gang of semi-barbarians."[23] Also in middle rank stood the peoples of East Asia, the "Orientals" or "Mongolians" whom Americans perceived as crafty, inscrutable, somnolent, and immoral, albeit in the case of the Japanese sometimes capable of regeneration with outside assistance.

A masculine ethos also shaped American conceptions of foreigners. Words such as "manliness" and "weakling" coursed through the language of American leaders. The naval historian Theodore Roosevelt, who as president would celebrate the "strenuous life," often described other nations as weak and effeminate—unable, in contrast to a virile Uncle Sam, to cope with the imperatives of world politics.[24] Roosevelt also castigated anti-navalists and anti-imperialists as "flapdoodle pacifists and mollycoddlers."[25] The gendered imagery prevalent in U.S. foreign relations joined race thinking to place women, people of color, and nations weaker than the

"The Mexican Wild Man."   Among the exhibits at American fairs were "freak shows," where people of color from abroad were displayed in exaggerated ways to suggest exotic, untamed, and uncivilized characteristics. Sometimes whites dressed up in animal skins as "wild men" and "wild women." Here, George Stall does so in the early 1890s. Such images reflected negative American views of foreign peoples of color and helped condition the environment in which U.S. leaders made decisions. In his book on U.S. relations with Central America, *Beneath the United States* (1998), the scholar Lars Schoultz argues that North American perceptions of Latin Americans as fundamentally inferior and underdeveloped consistently drove U.S. policy to a "civilizing mission." (Photo by Charles Eisenmann, Becker Collection, Syracuse University Library)

United States lowest in the hierarchy of power, and, hence, in a dependent status justifying American hegemony.

The magazine *National Geographic,* which first appeared in 1888, chronicled with photographs America's growing overseas interests. The editors chose pictures that underscored American ethnocentric notions about foreigners. Even when smiling faces predominated, the image reflected that of strange, exotic, premodern people who had not yet become "Western." Emphasizing this perspective, *National Geographic* regularly carried photographs of bare-breasted women. Fairs, too, stereotyped other peoples as falling short of "civilized." Not only did fair managers tout the technological wonders of "Western civilization," but they also put people of color on display in the "freaks" or "midway" sections. At the 1895 Atlanta and 1897 Nashville fairs, exhibits of Cubans and Mexicans in primitive village settings stood next to bearded women and the world's fattest man. P. T. Barnum's display of four reputed Fijian cannibals in 1872 spawned a small industry for the sale of cannibal forks (*"iculunibakola"*).[26]

Religious zeal also gave impetus to imperialist attitudes. "Don't stay in this country theorizing, when a hundred thousand heathen a day are dying without hope because we are not there teaching the Gospel to them," boomed the traveling secretary of the Student Volunteer Movement, founded by college students in the late 1880s.[27] However benevolent their intentions, missionaries often carried chauvinistic prejudices abroad. This missionary "Mother Goose" rhyme betrayed traces of cultural imperialism: "Ten little heathen standing in a line;/One went to mission school, then there were but nine. . . ./Three little heathen didn't know what to do;/One learned our language, then there were two./Two little heathen couldn't have any fun/One gave up idols, then there was but one./One little heathen standing all alone;/He learned to love our flag, then there were none."[28] Said the Reverend Josiah Strong, author of the influential book *Our Country* (1885): "As America goes, so goes the world."[29]

The multiple arguments for expansion and empire seemed all the more urgent when Americans anticipated the closing of the frontier at home. In 1893 Professor Frederick Jackson Turner postulated his thesis that an ever-expanding continental frontier had shaped the American character. Now that "frontier has gone, and with its going has closed the first period of American history." Turner did not explicitly say that Americans had to find a new frontier overseas, but he doubted that "the expansive character of American life has now entirely ceased. Movement has been its dominant fact, and, unless this training has no effect upon a people, the American energy will continually demand a wider field for its exercise."[30]

The dying frontier did regenerate itself, figuratively speaking, in Europe when Colonel William F. ("Buffalo Bill") Cody toured with his famed Wild West Show to England, France, Germany, Spain, Italy, and Austria-Hungary, beginning in 1887. Replete with bronco-riding, steer-roping, trick shooting, and a reenactment of General Custer's Last Stand, the stylized pageant celebrated the defeat of the primitives and "glorified the march of civilization across the American landscape" wherein the dignified, buckskin-clad Cody comported himself like "a knight of the plains" with "a chivalric past."[31] The inevitable triumph of "nature's nobleman," so one historian writes, "provided ritualistic catharsis."[32]

Of course, the "Anglo-centered" Turner thesis that American distinctiveness derived from exploiting "virgin soil" in "unoccupied territory" rhetorically relegated Native Americans "to the edge of significance."[33] So too did official policy work to remove Indians in the post–Civil War era, pushing tribes into smaller reservations, taking lands for the railroad, killing buffalo, fighting military campaigns against the Sioux, Nez Percé, and Utes in the 1870s and against the Apache a decade later, culminating in the massacre at Wounded Knee, South Dakota, in January 1890, when U.S. Army units killed 146 men, women, and children of the Sioux. The Indians' victory over General George A. Custer's troops at the Little Big Horn in Montana in 1876 proved Pyrrhic and transient, similar to temporary Zulu success against British forces in South Africa in 1879—minor reverses in the inexorable contest between "western powers and less technologically developed peoples."[34]

By 1868 the Supreme Court ruled that Congress could override old treaties by passing new statutes without the consent of the Indians, and three years later Congress forbade further Indian treaties. The Dawes Severalty Act of 1887 ended communal ownership of Indian lands and granted land allotments to individual Native American families, promising citizenship (after a twenty-five-year waiting period) to those who accepted allotments. Thus did the government, in the historian Walter Williams's words, pursue a "clear pattern of colonialism toward Native Americans" by the 1890s that set a "precedent for imperialist domination" of Filipinos and other peoples after the Spanish-American-Cuban-Filipino War.[35]

Economic Expansion and International Rivalry

The dynamics of the international system favored the United States. Victorian England, heretofore the dominant power with advantages over its rivals in wealth, production, colonies, and naval strength, started to suffer relative decline. "The Weary Titan staggers under the too vast orb of its fate," as one diplomat put it.[36] In the 1870s, European imperialists began to carve up Asia and Africa into colonies and exclusive spheres of influence. Old empires slumped and new empires grew. With the world divided into "living"and "dying powers," a British official noted that "the successful powers will be those who have the greatest industrial base."[37] When the American economy surged after the Civil War and the United States, unburdened by large defense expenditures, overtook Britain as the world's foremost industrial power in the 1890s, success seemed assured.

When nationalistic Americans boasted about their country, they especially celebrated its economic achievements. After the Civil War the United States enjoyed unprecedented economic growth. Railroads knit the nation together, creating a coast-to-coast marketplace. Bold entrepreneurs such as John D. Rockefeller and Andrew Carnegie built huge corporations whose assets and incomes dwarfed those of many of the world's nations. In the process of industrialization, inventors such as Thomas Edison and George Westinghouse pioneered whole new enterprises—in their case, electricity. The advent and spread of the telegraph and telephone linked Americans together in a national communications network. Sprawling, busy cities became the centers of rapidly expanding manufacturing production. The federal government, through subsidies, land grants, loans, tariffs, and tax relief, stimulated the growth of American business. Not all went well, of course. Economic instability (major depressions in 1873–1878 and 1893–1897), the financial insolvency of railroads, farm indebtedness, inhumane working conditions, child labor, political corruption, business abuses necessitating antitrust and regulatory measures, discriminatory wages favoring men over women in the same jobs, and the failure of consumption to keep pace with production in the age of the "robber barons" tarnished the American record. Still, the United States by 1900 had become an economic giant surpassing Great Britain and Germany. Steel production increased from 77,000 tons in 1870 to 11,227,000 tons in 1900; wheat and corn output more than doubled in the same period. From the early 1870s to 1900 the gross national product more than doubled. Proud Americans preferred to emphasize this impressive data and to hide the embarrassing blemishes.

Foreign trade constituted an important part of the nation's economic growth. American exports expanded from $234 million in 1865 to $1.5 billion in 1900. Most American goods went to Europe, Britain, and Canada, but a slight shift toward Latin America and Asia took place through the late nineteenth century. Although exports of manufactured items increased, becoming predominant for the

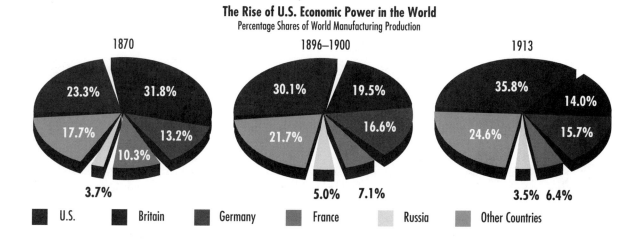

The Rise of U.S. Economic Power in the World
Percentage Shares of World Manufacturing Production

1870 — 23.3% / 31.8% / 17.7% / 13.2% / 10.3% / 3.7%

1896–1900 — 30.1% / 19.5% / 21.7% / 16.6% / 5.0% / 7.1%

1913 — 35.8% / 14.0% / 24.6% / 15.7% / 3.5% / 6.4%

■ U.S.   ■ Britain   ■ Germany   ■ France   ■ Russia   ■ Other Countries

first time in 1913, agricultural goods (cereals, cotton, meat, and dairy products) accounted for about three-quarters of the total in 1870 and about two-thirds in 1900. From 1874 until 1934, with the one exception of 1888, the United States enjoyed a favorable balance of trade (exports exceeded imports).

Growing American productive efficiency, a decline in prices that made American goods less expensive in the world market, the high quality of American products, and improvements in transportation (steamships and the Suez Canal) help explain this impressive upturn in foreign trade. Improvements in communications also facilitated economic expansion. In 1866, through the persevering efforts of Cyrus Field, an underwater transatlantic cable linked European and American telegraph networks. James A. Scrymser, backed by J. P. Morgan's capital, connected the U.S. telegraph system with Latin America. He first wired Florida to Havana, Cuba, and then, in 1881, Galveston, Texas, to Mexico City. By 1883 Americans could communicate directly with Brazil; in 1890 Scrymser's lines reached Chile. By hooking into British cables, Americans could "talk" with Asian cities as well. Whereas the transfer of information had once taken days and weeks, it could now flow around the world more cheaply and securely in hours. Business leaders, diplomats, naval officers, and journalists worked the new communications system to seize opportunities. Nellie Bly, a reporter for the *New York World,* completed a trip around the world in seventy-two days in early 1890, and showed how much technology had shrunk the globe.

Although exports represented a very small percentage (between 6 and 7 percent) of the gross national product, and although most American businesses concentrated on the domestic market, American prosperity and key segments of the economy came to rely on foreign sales. It became popular to think that surplus production, or the "glut," had to be exported to avert economic calamity at home. "We have advanced in manufactures, as in agriculture," Secretary of State William M. Evarts remarked in 1880, "until we are being forced outward by the irresistible pressure of our internal development."[38] America must open new foreign markets, the economist David A. Wells warned, or "we are certain to be smothered in our own grease."[39]

The glut thesis appealed particularly to farmers, for the American marketplace could not absorb their bounty. Producers of cotton, tobacco, and wheat counted on foreign markets. Over half of the cotton crop was exported each year, and wheat growers in the period 1873–1882 received about a third of their gross annual income from exports. Wisconsin cheesemakers shipped to Britain; the Swift and Armour meat companies sold refrigerated beef in Europe; and Quaker oats became an international food. To sell American grain in Asia, James J. Hill of the Great Northern Railroad distributed cookbooks translated into several languages.

American business leaders like Hill looked to foreign markets for profits. Rockefeller's Standard Oil sold abroad, notably in Germany, England, Cuba, and Mexico. By the 1890s about half of all American petroleum was exported. By the mid-1880s one-third of the New York Life Insurance Company's business lay outside the United States and Canada. Cyrus McCormick of International Harvester sent his "reaper kings" into Russian fields, and by the turn of the century his company's foreign sales accounted for about 20 percent of its business. The same company established "an informal empire" over the henequin fiber market of Yucatan after 1880, controlling 99.8 percent of all production by 1910.[40] Metal-products firms such as National Cash Register and Remington became active globally. Alexander Graham Bell and Thomas Edison collaborated in 1880 to install England's first telephone system. By the turn of the century, 50 percent of America's copper and 15 percent of its iron and steel were sold abroad, making many workers in those industries dependent on exports. Singer's sewing machines seemed to be everywhere, from Scandinavia to Russia to Latin America. In 1879 Singer sold more machines overseas than at home. In the 1890s Singer ran more than forty large retail stores in Russia alone and dominated world markets. Some Europeans warned against an American "commercial invasion."[41]

Official Washington subsidized American exhibitions in foreign trade fairs and assisted business in other ways to expand abroad. Consular service officers prepared reports on commercial prospects, and naval officers scouted markets and protected merchants. The government provided help in expanding the telegraph, negotiated reciprocity treaties to open trade doors, and kept up the drumbeat of patriotic rhetoric about the wonders of the export market.

But the government had a mixed record. Until the 1890s, economic expansion derived primarily from the activities of private companies and individuals, not from governmental policies. Washington neglected the merchant marine, letting it decline so that by 1900 American ships carried only 10 percent of U.S. trade. And Congress was slow to improve the navy (see pp. 174–176). The diplomatic corps and consular service were bespotted by the spoils system; too many political hacks rather than professionals filled their ranks. The writer Ambrose Bierce quipped that "American diplomats were failed politicians who were finally chosen for office, on condition that they leave the country."[42] Washington also maintained a high-tariff policy, with rates reaching a peak in the 1890 McKinley Tariff (average duties of 49 percent). This exclusionist policy may have slowed the pace of economic ex-

ZULULAND

COPYRIGHT 1892, BY THE SINGER MANUFACTURING CO.

Singer Sewing Machine in Zululand. The Singer Manufacturing Company distributed this promotional postcard at the 1893 Columbian Exposition in Chicago. Three-quarters of all sewing machines sold in world markets were Singers. This machine was sold in South Africa, where, the company advised, the "Zulus are a fine warlike people" moving toward "civilization" with Singer's help. (Neg. #WHi [X3] 48814, State Historical Society of Wisconsin)

pansion by stimulating foreign retaliatory tariffs against American products. The United States could nonetheless successfully pursue protection at home and commercial expansion abroad because England, still the world's leading economic power (or "hegemon"), maintained a liberal trade strategy and welcomed American exports. In effect, Washington was "free riding on free trade."[43]

How significant were foreign commerce and investments (American capital invested abroad equaled $700 million in 1897) to the U.S. economy? The statistics presented above tell only part of the story. The rest lies in perception—what prominent Americans *believed*. They believed that the economic health of the nation depended on selling their surplus production in foreign markets. During depressions especially, goods stacked up at home could be peddled abroad, thus stimulating the American economy and perhaps even heading off the social and political unrest that feeds on economic crisis. How, then, did foreign trade and this belief in its necessity and significance affect American foreign policy? Hypothetically, even if only 1 percent of American goods sold abroad and exports represented only 1 percent of the gross national product, foreign trade would be inescapably intertwined with foreign policy and thus a factor of importance. Anticipating conflicts and wars, the navy's policy board in 1890 concluded: "In the adjustment of our trade with a neighbor we are certain to reach out and obstruct the interest of foreign nations."[44] And even if all the efforts to expand trade delivered minimal results, the quest itself would necessitate naval and diplomatic activity.

Why did American leaders believe foreign trade so important? First, exports meant profits. That was the pocketbook issue. Second, exports might relieve social unrest at home caused by overproduction and unemployment. Third, economic ties could lead to political influence (as in Hawai'i and Mexico) without the formal necessity of military occupation and management. Fourth, foreign trade, hand in hand with religious missionary work, could promote "civilization" and human uplift. Fifth, economic expansion helped spread the American way of life, creating a world more hospitable to Americans. Sixth and last—to return to the theme of nationalism—foreign trade, if it conquered new markets abroad and helped bring prosperity to the United States, enhanced national pride at a time of international rivalry. Foreign trade, then, held an importance beyond statistics. It became an intricate part of American "greatness"; leaders believed it vital to the national interest.

Toward Command of the Seas: The New Navy

In the late nineteenth century a popular doctrine gradually fixed itself in American thinking: to protect overseas commerce, deemed vital to America's well-being, the nation had to build a larger navy. As Commodore Robert W. Shufeldt explained in popular terms, the navy acted as "the pioneer of commerce."[45] To fuel and repair ships in distant waters, naval stations and colonies had to be acquired. To ensure that foreigners did not endanger American merchants, property, investments, and trade, U.S. warships had to go on patrol, ready to use force to protect U.S. interests and prestige in an era of intense international rivalry. "The trader," Shufeldt told a member of Congress, "deals with barbarous tribes—men who appreciate only the argument of physical force. . . . The man-of-war precedes the merchantman and impresses rude people."[46] The commodore's graphic depiction of "showing the flag" bespoke historical experience. Since the end of the War of 1812, the United States had been stationing warships in Latin America, Africa, and Asia to protect the American merchant marine and merchants. New to the 1880s and 1890s was the shrinking theater of free operations, as European imperialists hastened to seize colonies and close out other foreigners. For the U.S. Navy, then, the next enemy might be an imperial European navy rather than a truculent "mob" in an Asian port. The need for new strategies and technologies became obvious.

By European standards, the American military before the 1890s was small. The army demobilized after the Civil War, then killed or tamed Indians on the frontier under a strategy of "annihilation," and shrank to below 30,000 troops.[47] The navy concentrated on defending the long American coastline and protecting American life and property abroad. For these tasks, the U.S. military seemed adequate. The nation was, after all, basically secure. The European powers, feuding in the Old World, did not threaten America. Even the most bellicose European militarist would have been deterred by the difficulties of transporting forces across the Atlantic and then supplying them in the United States, whose tremendous size and fiercely independent population could swallow alien armies. The navy, however diminutive in European eyes, could punish unarmed peoples, chase pirates, protect missionaries and traders, and chart unexplored regions. Until the United States could acquire faraway fueling stations for taking on coal, having a fleet of long-range, steam-driven, blue-water vessels did not make much sense. The brown-water ships designed for coastal defense and riverine operations seemed adequate.

In the 1880s and 1890s, as U.S. expansionism and imperialism accelerated and overseas commitments increased, a bigger, modern navy became imperative.

Young naval officers—"armed progressives"—joined politicians, shipbuilders, armaments manufacturers, and commercial expansionists to lobby for an expanded fleet.[48] The navy had not kept pace with European technological advances in hulls, engines, and guns. Dominated by the political spoils system, government-operated shipyards had become corrupt and ineffeicient. Naval leaders lobbied for higher appropriations to launch significant naval improvements. As the Europeans built fast, heavily armed, well-armored battleships, America's slower, wooden cruisers and gunboats became laughably obsolete—mere floating museums, snickered European officers. Because foreign-born sailors comprised more than half of the navy's enlisted personnel in the 1870s, recruiters increasingly sought "boys who . . . have no old world allegiance or affiliations. We want the brawn of Montana, the fire of the South and the daring of the Pacific slope."[49]

Rear Admiral Stephen B. Luce, father of the modern U.S. Navy, became an effective naval politician. He founded the Naval War College in 1884, instilled greater professionalism, and encouraged officers such as Captain Alfred T. Mahan to disseminate their ideas. Essentially summarizing the thinking of others, Mahan earned an international reputation for popularizing the relationship between a navy and expansion. An instructor at the Naval War College, Mahan published his lectures in 1890 as *The Influence of Sea Power upon History*. British, German, and Japanese leaders read the book, but, most important, it became a treasured volume in the libraries of American imperialists such as Henry Cabot Lodge and Theodore Roosevelt. Mahan posited a simple thesis: A nation's greatness depended on its sea power. Victory in war and a vigorous foreign trade, two measurements of greatness, depended on an efficient and strong navy. Ships of war, in turn, required fueling stations or "resting places" and colonies, which would further enhance foreign commerce and national power.[50] The loop closed: Great navies required colonies; colonies begat great navies. The United States could not stand aloof from the international race for greatness.

The American naval revival began in earnest during the 1880s. The navy evolved from sail-driven and wooden-hull ships to steam-powered and steel-clad vessels. Its mission ultimately shifted from coastal defense to command of the seas. In 1883 Congress funded the *Atlanta, Boston,* and *Chicago*—steel-hull, steam-powered cruisers. Between 1884 and 1889, money was appropriated for thirty more vessels, including the battleship *Maine*. Secretary of the Navy Benjamin F. Tracy (1889–1893) wanted seagoing battleships for this "New Navy." Soon the fast armor-plated *Oregon, Indiana, Massachusetts,* and *Iowa* joined the fleet bearing the names of states to rally public support for naval expansion. The sleek battleship designs, especially featuring modern armored turrets and jutting guns, so impressed the editors of *Scientific American* that they reproduced them in seventeen cover engravings in 1887, thus projecting an allure that one scholar has called "battleship envy."[51] In the process, the government, military, and industry forged a partnership that would grow through the twentieth century.

By 1893 the navy ranked seventh in the world. Anti-imperialists presciently warned that this large navy would propel Americans into a larger empire. "New Navy" ships in fact figured in the imperialist ventures of the 1890s: the *Boston* and its crew helped attach Hawai'i to the United States; the destruction of the *Maine* in

Alfred Thayer Mahan (1840–1914). Graduate of the U.S. Naval Academy, this bookish officer, historian, and respected naval politician articulated the necessity for overseas expansion and a large navy. He became world famous for his writings. Oxford and Cambridge universities gave him honorary degrees, and German and Japanese leaders read his many statements. (*American Review of Reviews,* 1894)

the harbor of Havana helped move the United States toward war with Spain; the 14,000-mile race of the battleship *Oregon* from the Pacific coast to Cuba in 1898 fired desire for a canal across Central America; and the cruiser *Olympia* carried Commodore George Dewey into Manila Bay to help seize the Philippines from Spain. Secretary Tracy predicted: "The sea will be the future seat of empire. And we shall rule it as certainly as the sun doth rise."[52]

Secretary William H. Seward Eyes the Future

As secretary of state from 1861 to 1869, William Henry Seward provided a connection between prewar and postwar expansionism. During the Civil War he had to prevent European powers from interfering in the internecine crisis (see Chapter 4). But after the war, this vain, confident, and intelligent Republican leader avidly redirected foreign policy toward his vision of a U.S. empire. The secretary foresaw a coordinated empire tied together by superior American institutions and commerce. Latin America, the Pacific islands, Asia, and Canada, Seward prophesied, would eventually gravitate toward the United States because of the contagion of American greatness and because of some immeasurable will of God. He believed that "commerce has largely taken the place of war" and that trade would produce "influence" and bind distant areas together.[53] Seward once speculated that Mexico would be an appropriate location for the new imperial capital. He indicated the means for acquiring this empire: improved foreign trade, immigration to provide cheap labor for productive American factories, high tariffs for the protection of American industry, liberal federal land policies to open the American West to economic development, globe-circling telegraph systems, transcontinental railroads, a Central American canal, and, of course, the annexation of noncontiguous territories.

In 1865 Seward began negotiations with Denmark to purchase the Danish West Indies (Virgin Islands), whose excellent harbors offered potential naval stations for defending the Caribbean and Gulf. Two years later the islanders voted for American annexation. Seward raised his offer to $7.5 million for two of the islands, St. Thomas and St. John, but a combination of bad weather and heated politics undercut the treaty Seward signed with Copenhagen in October 1867. When a hurricane and tidal wave wracked St. Thomas, critics poked fun at Seward's request for "footholds." The treaty reached the Senate at the very time that President Andrew Johnson faced impeachment, and Seward himself lost credit with the Senate by supporting Johnson's unpopular Reconstruction policies. Incoming President Grant shelved the treaty, and the Virgin Islanders had to wait until 1917 for American overlordship.

Seward also wanted a piece of the Dominican Republic. In 1866 he offered $2 million for Samaná Bay, but the proposed deal remained open when he left office. Seward's vision encompassed Haiti (which he thought of annexing outright), some small Spanish, French, and Dutch islands in the Caribbean, revolution-torn Cuba, Iceland and Greenland (both of which he hoped to buy), Honduras's Tigre Island, and Hawai'i, fast becoming Americanized as more sugar was planted and more

Makers of American Foreign Relations, 1865–1895

Presidents	Secretaries of State
Andrew Johnson, 1865–1869	William H. Seward, 1861–1869
Ulysses S. Grant, 1869–1877	Elihu B. Washburne, 1869
	Hamilton Fish, 1869–1877
Rutherford B. Hayes, 1877–1881	William M. Evarts, 1877–1881
James A. Garfield, 1881	James G. Blaine, 1881
Chester A. Arthur, 1881–1885	Frederick T. Freylinghuysen, 1881–1885
Grover Cleveland, 1885–1889	Thomas F. Bayard, 1885–1889
Benjamin Harrison, 1889–1893	James G. Blaine, 1889–1892
	John W. Foster, 1892–1893
Grover Cleveland, 1893–1897	Walter Q. Gresham, 1893–1895
	Richard Olney, 1895–1897

churches were built. Seward's imperialist ambitions went unfulfilled in his day, but the secretary did achieve two real estate transactions. One minor acquisition occurred in August 1867 when Captain William Reynolds of the U.S.S. *Lackawanna* formally claimed the Midway Islands, some 1,000 miles northwest of Hawai'i. Most Americans never heard again about these tiny imperial outposts until the great American-Japanese naval battle there in 1942.

More significant, attractive, and controversial was Seward's purchase of Alaska. Russia had put Alaska up for sale because it no longer remained profitable as colonial property, and because the tsar feared that Britain would seize the undefended territory in a future war. Then, too, Russia seemed resigned to the inevitable. "The ultimate rule of the United States over the whole of America is so natural," the governor of eastern Siberia told the tsar, "that we must ourselves sooner or later recede."[54] Edouard de Stoeckl, the Russian minister to the United States who negotiated the transfer, later agreed: "In American eyes this continent is their patrimony. Their destiny (manifest destiny as they call it) is to always expand."[55] American fur traders, whalers, and fishermen had been exploiting the area's natural resources for decades. Why not cultivate a "friend" and sell the 591,000 square miles (twice the size of Texas) to the United States? Seward moved quickly. "Why wait until tomorrow, Mr. Stoeckl? Let us make the treaty tonight," he said.[56]

The cabinet and president remained largely ignorant of the talks until Seward presented them and the Congress with a hastily drawn treaty and a bill for $7.2 million—no small sum in March 1867. One Treasury official estimated that the United States actually paid $43.4 million: $7.2 million in principal, $12.5 million in army and navy expenses, and $23.7 million in lost interest on the principal had the money remained in the Treasury for twenty-five years. Alaska, nevertheless, constituted a substantial bargain.

William H. Seward (1801–1872). Once freed from the restraints of the Civil War, Secretary of State Seward vigorously pursued a larger U.S. empire. Asked in 1870 about his greatest achievement, Seward answered: "The purchase of Alaska! But it will take people a generation to find that out." (National Archives)

Contemporary critics howled anyway, especially because Seward had ignored Congress. Although critics such as the editor Horace Greely joked about "Walrussia" as a worthless acquisition, Seward astutely won over Charles Sumner, who applauded Alaska's commercial potential and natural resources.[57] Sumner's influence; a vigorous propaganda program, in which Seward compared Alaska to the Louisiana Purchase; the Russian minister's hiring of lobbyists and distributing $100,000 in bribes to key members of Congress; and the exhilaration over expanding American boundaries—all combined to carry the treaty through the Senate only ten days after it was signed. The House stalled, delaying fifteen months before voting the funds, but by then Seward had already ordered the Stars and Stripes raised over his imperial catch.

Seward acquired fewer territories than he desired, largely because of domestic obstacles. A Republican supporter of Democratic President Johnson, Seward evinced little sympathy for the plight of freed blacks in the South. Displaying their disapproval, angry Radical Republicans called for Seward's ouster from the cabinet and helped block his imperialistic schemes. Some people soured on expansion because of the corruption attending the annexation of Alaska. Reconstruction, railroad growth, an inflated economy, landless freedmen, a recalcitrant South—such issues compelled many Americans to look inward and to skimp on foreign adventures that cost money. A nation that had just freed its slaves after a bloody civil war had little interest in acquiring Cuba, in which slavery flourished. Seward could only lament "how sadly domestic disturbances of ours demoralize the National ambition."[58]

The secretary's ambition misfired, too, because articulate anti-imperialists such as Senator Justin Morrill (Vermont), the author Mark Twain, and the editor E. L. Godkin spoke out. They called for the development of America's existing lands and for an American showcase of domestic social, political, and economic improvements as the best way to persuade other people to adopt American institutions. Whereas some imperialists were racists who wanted to subjugate "inferior" people, some anti-imperialists made racist arguments against adding more nonwhites to the American population. Godkin opposed the annexation of the Dominican Republic, because that country harbored tens of thousands of Catholic, Spanish-speaking blacks who might seek U.S. citizenship. Other anti-imperialists insisted that colonialism violated the principle of self-government and increased the threat of foreign wars. Such critics and ideas, joined to the partisan struggle over Reconstruction, helped thwart Seward's efforts to create a larger empire. He moved too fast for most Americans.

Great Britain, Canada, and North American Disputes

Anglo-American and Canadian-American tensions, so evident before and during the Civil War, persisted in the 1865–1895 period. Union leaders remained irate over Britain's favoritism toward the South during the Civil War, especially the outfitting of Confederate vessels in British ports. At the end of the war, Seward filed damage claims against the British, even proposing at one point that Britain cede to the United States British Columbia or the Bahama Islands in lieu of a cash settlement. The secretary also grew annoyed that British officials would not permit American soldiers to pursue the destitute Sioux Indians into Canadian territory. Canadians and Americans squabbled over the Fenian raids, tariffs, boundaries, fishing rights in the North Atlantic, and seal hunting. The neighbors to the north bristled at arrogant predictions that the United States would one day absorb Canada.

Although annexationist rhetoric echoed throughout the United States, only the hottest heads urged employing force to attach Canada to the Union. Pure Manifest Destiny doctrine, after all, prescribed patience until the inevitable "Americanization" of Canadians. And while Americans were busy settling their own West, there seemed no hurry. A military attack would no doubt have precipitated war with Great Britain, and even though "twisting the Lion's tail" proved popular politics in the United States, few politicians wanted to invite British naval assaults on the Gulf and East coasts.

The resistance of infant Canadian nationalism offered another reason for not "taking" Canada. Disputing William Seward, Canadians did not consider themselves a mere gap in the U.S. empire. Canadian nationalists such as John A. Macdonald actually thought of themselves as British North Americans. They recoiled from the political scandals, racial and ethnic prejudices, and flashy materialism of Gilded Age America. Macdonald became his nation's first prime minister when the Dominion of Canada came into being on July 1, 1867, as a confederation of provinces. Free homesteads under the Dominion Lands Act of 1872 and construction of the Canadian Pacific Railway facilitated settlement of Canada's prairie provinces and ensured that the dominant culture would remain "Protestant, conservative, and very British."[59] The movement toward nationhood had received major stimulus from the annexationist rumblings in the United States, for the Dominion was Canada's way of resisting the American challenge. Before long, Americans viewed Canada less as "a northern enemy base" and more as "a brother government soon to adopt the republican principles America held dear."[60]

In the late nineteenth century, Anglo-Canadian-American relations moved from crisis to crisis. In 1866, armed forces of the Fenian Brotherhood, an Irish-American society of some 10,000 members organized to promote Irish independence from Britain, attacked Canada from Vermont. Seward wanted Canada, but not through such methods. He sent troops to the border to squelch further skirmishes, but both London and Ottawa believed he had acted too slowly.

Canada soon became entangled in another Anglo-American dispute: the question of the English-built Confederate ships (especially the *Alabama*) that had disrupted Union shipping during the Civil War. The irrepressible Charles Sumner added the naval damages to indirect damages that he derived by calculating that the Civil War was protracted for two years by British material help to and sympathy for the South; he totaled up a bill of $2.125 billion. One British diplomat shamelessly explained that Sumner "was fool enough some year or so ago to marry a young and pretty widow. She found that he was not gifted with 'full powers' and has left him. . . . He therefore makes up by vigour of tongue for his want of capacity in other organs."[61] Some Americans thought the transfer of Canada to the United States would erase the debt. A Joint High Commission convened in Washington from February to May 1871; it produced the Washington Treaty dated May 8. The British expressed regret for the actions of British-built Confederate raiders, and the signatories agreed to establish a tribunal in Geneva, Switzerland, to determine damages and claims. That commission finally issued its decision in December 1872: Britain must pay the United States $15.5 million. "As the price of conciliating the United States, and protecting British naval interests," the historian David P. Crook has written, "it was a bargain."[62]

The Washington Treaty attempted to settle two other Anglo-American disputes. Nestled between Vancouver Island (British Columbia) and territorial Washington in the Strait of Juan de Fuca were the San Juan Islands, claimed by both the United States and Britain on the basis of confusing geographical language in the Treaty of 1846. The Treaty of Washington provided for arbitration by the German emperor, who decreed in 1872 that the islands belonged to the United States.

Another longstanding dispute proved more rancorous and more serious—the rights of American fishermen in North Atlantic waters. The Washington Treaty gave permission to Yankee fishermen to cast their nets in Canadian waters and allowed Canadians to fish the coastal regions of the United States above 39° north latitude. Macdonald grumbled that the British were conceding too much to the Americans. But the prime minister recognized Canadian weakness—the federation had not yet "hardened from gristle into bone."[63] In 1877 a fisheries commission ruled that the United States should pay $5.5 million for the privilege of fishing in Canadian waters. The United States paid, but in 1885, in protest against the award, it reactivated the fish war by unilaterally abrogating that part of the Washington Treaty dealing with fishing rights. The Canadians thereupon began seizing American vessels. New negotiations became testy. A British diplomat denounced Americans as "a bunch of dishonest tricksters."[64] An Anglo-American fisheries treaty of 1888 never passed the Senate, and President Grover Cleveland threatened an economic embargo of Canada, but an interim agreement cooled tempers.

About the same time, British minister Sir Lionel Sackville-West committed a sin of the first order for a diplomat—he intruded into American politics. When in 1888 a Republican pretending to be a former Englishman asked Sackville-West whether he should vote for the Republican candidate Benjamin Harrison or the Democrat Grover Cleveland, the careless diplomat recommended Cleveland as the politician more friendly to Britain. Gleeful Republicans printed and distributed copies of Sackville-West's indiscreet letter. Cleveland sent Sackville-West packing just before the president lost his reelection bid. The prime minister, Lord Salisbury, pointedly did not send a new envoy until March of the next year.

Anglo-American rivalry next flared over seals in the Bering Sea near Alaska. "Amphibious is the fur seal, ubiquitous and carnivorous, uniparous, gregarious and withal polygamous," the historian Samuel Flagg Bemis has written.[65] Most of the seal herds lived in the Pribilof Islands near the Aleutians. American law forbade the killing of female or young seals and limited the slaughter of males. Yet foreign hunters slaughtered at will when the animals wandered on the high seas in search of food. In 1889 President Harrison warned Canadians against "pelagic" sealing (killing animals in ocean waters). When U.S. cutters seized several Canadian sealing boats in international waters, London and Ottawa protested. In mid-1890 the

British sent four warships to the disputed region as Canadian sealers shot seals to death. American captains made no arrests this time. In 1891 diplomats struck a temporary agreement halting pelagic sealing for a year, and after another dispute the next year, London and Washington agreed to create an arbitral tribunal. In 1893 the arbiters handed Americans a defeat, for it permitted pelagic sealing within prescribed limits. The furry mammals continued their numerical decline until 1911, when the United States, Britain, Russia, and Japan finally banned pelagic sealing altogether and limited land kills. The seal population soon rejuvenated, thus marking an early example of U.S. and international environmental regulation.

Americans in Asia: China, Japan, and Korea

With its vast territory, huge population, and tributary states, China attracted foreigners eager to sell, buy, invest, convert, and dominate. Although some Chinese leaders considered Americans less bullying than British gunboat diplomatists, the Chinese viewed all Westerners as "barbarians." One diplomat regretted having to meet with his Western counterparts, for it was like "associating with dog and swine—a misfortune in a man's life."[66] And any more favorable images of Americans steadily diminished, because the United States demanded the same privileges China granted to other nations: open ports, low tariffs, protection for missionaries, and extraterritoriality (the exemption of foreigners from the legal jurisdiction of the country in which they resided). Before the 1890s the United States largely followed the British lead. Americans protested gunboat diplomacy—evident, for example, in 1860 when British and French forces occupied Beijing (Peking), but, practicing "hitchhiking" or "jackal" diplomacy, they seized opportunities created by the guns of other Westerners to expand trade and missionary work. Americans were not passive. The Asiatic Squadron, for example, cruised the seas and visited ports to protect American lives and commerce.

In 1870, fifty American companies operated in China, but that number dropped to thirty-one a decade later as some of the great merchant houses closed. American exports to China slumped to $1 million in 1880; and although they rose to $3 million in 1890 and $15 million in 1900, trade with China claimed a minuscule part of American overseas commerce. Cotton goods and kerosene constituted the largest exports. "It is my dream," vowed the governor of Georgia in 1878, to see "in every valley . . . a cotton factory to convert the raw material of the neighborhood into fabrics which shall warm the limbs of Japanese and Chinese."[67] Cheap, coarse cloth from U.S. mills soon undercut finer British textiles and came to dominate the Chinese market and to account for about half of the American industry's foreign sales. Kerosene also became big business in China; Standard Oil of New York advertised widely and, to improve sales, introduced small, inexpensive lamps. American investments in China remained modest, growing to less than $20 million by 1900.

Protestant missionaries, another American presence in China, steadily expanded their work, moving from treaty ports to the interior. They first visited China in the 1830s; by 1889 five hundred of them, mostly women, carried Christian teachings to "the heathen Chinee." By 1900 their number had grown to more than a thousand. They not only gained converts; they also helped promote American products simply by using them in front of curious Chinese. In some cases, religious missionaries and economic expansionists joined hands, as when Singer executives and missionaries championed the "civilizing medium" of the sewing machine.[68] "Fancy what would happen to the cotton trade if every Chinese wore a shirt!" remarked Charles Denby, who represented the State Department in China in 1885–1898. "Well, the missionaries are teaching them to wear shirts."[69] Before the mid-1890s, however, American commercial and missionary activities in China never matched such inflated rhetoric.

Between 1850 and 1900 about half a million Chinese, mostly males, emigrated to the United States. Many returned home after several years, and most sent money home after first paying travel debts. They mined, built railroads, farmed, and laundered. By the mid-1870s about 150,000 Chinese resided in the United States, with the largest percentage in the San Francisco area. Wherever they settled, the Chinese formed close-knit communities, or "Chinatowns." Many joined secret societies and maintained their cultural identity. Sinophobia on the West Coast wreaked hatreds and violence on the expatriate Chinese and created laws to exclude Asian immigrants. Americans in California called the Chinese "coolies" (*koo lee,* or "hired muscle") and spawned myths about filthy, rat-eating, opium-drunk "Mongolians" who threatened American culture by refusing to assimilate. Especially in times of economic bust in a frontier setting, Sinophobia flourished. White laborers complained that Chinese workers ate little and depressed wages. Anti-coolie clubs formed, and in the 1870s the Irish immigrant Dennis Kearney's Workingmen's party became an instrument for Sinophobia. Anti-Chinese violence flared through the 1860s and 1870s; riots rocked Los Angeles in 1870 and San Francisco seven years later. One U.S. senator called Chinese immigrants "a cold pebble in the public stomach which cannot be digested."[70] In October 1880, 3,000 white men attacked the Chinese district in Denver, killing one resident, beating others, destroying property.

Five years later at Rock Springs, in the Wyoming Territory, white miners invaded Chinatown during labor and ethnic unrest in the area. The Chinese workers fled, but many were shot; others burned to death in fires set to raze the Chinese community. At least twenty-five mutilated Chinese bodies lay in the debris. The Chinese minister to the United States protested the massacre, calling the local judicial proceedings, in which all rioters won acquittal, a "burlesque."[71] President Cleveland, who had dispatched federal troops to the scene to restore order, called the result a "ghastly mockery of justice."[72] Congress eventually paid an indemnity of $148,000 to Chinese who had lost property.

Washington strongly lectured the western states against violence but informed Chinese diplomats that the federal government had no legal jurisdiction. At the same time, U.S. officials petitioned Beijing to protect Americans in China against multiplying antiforeign acts. As symbols of outside assaults on China's integrity, missionaries received the brunt of nativist hostility and violence. By undermining the authority of local elites and by seeking Christian converts who fractured the local society, missionaries became subversive "foreign devils" around whom circled myths about exotic sexual and medical practices. Antimissionary riots erupted in the 1880s and 1890s, prompting religious elders to appeal for official U.S. protection.

"Pacific Chivalry." How Californians handled the Chinese. (*Harper's Weekly,* 1869)

Washington and Beijing became preoccupied with threats to one another's nationals, and with Chinese immigration to the United States. Anson Burlingame, U.S. minister to China (1861–1867), went to work for the Chinese government after his retirement with an assignment to reduce Western intrusions. With Secretary Seward he negotiated the 1868 Burlingame Treaty, providing for free immigration between the two nations and the stationing of Chinese consuls in the United States (to look after Chinese subjects). Seward welcomed the pact as a step toward improved trade.

Sinophobic politicians from the West lobbied hard for laws to restrict Chinese immigration. In 1879, Congress legislated that only fifteen Chinese could arrive on any one ship in the United States. President Rutherford B. Hayes vetoed the measure as a violation of the Burlingame Treaty. A new immigration treaty negotiated with China in 1880 permitted the United States to suspend, but not prohibit, Chinese immigration. Two years later Congress suspended Chinese immigration for ten years and denied Chinese immigrants U.S. citizenship. Congress would renew these provisions again and again. China could neither protect its people in the United States nor challenge American immigration policy.

In 1863–1864, despite the Civil War, the U.S. Navy deployed one armed warship alongside British, French, and Dutch vessels to punish the Japanese for their antiforeign riots and harassment of merchant ships. At Shimonoseki this firepower destroyed forts and boats, opening the strait to trade once again. Internally divided and militarily weak, the Japanese could not resist the $3 million indemnity forced on them by the Western powers. (The United States received its share, $780,000, but returned it to Japan in 1883.) Then, in the Convention of 1866, Japan reluctantly bestowed low tariffs on the Western nations. By the late 1890s, America's trade with Japan surpassed its trade with China but still constituted only about 2 percent of total U.S. foreign commerce. Soon the Japanese consciously adopted a policy of "westernization" (which included learning American baseball), persuading some Americans that the Japanese, unlike the Chinese, had become "civilized."

American Sailor and Geisha. Although official Japanese-American relations remained cool for much of the nineteenth century, U.S. ships increasingly traded with the once isolated island-nation. The inevitable intermingling of cultures occurred. This woodcut by Yoshitora Utagawa depicts an American sailor in the company of a geisha, a Japanese hostess hired to entertain. (Library of Congress)

Korea became one of Japan's victims. This kingdom, called the "hermit nation" because of its self-imposed isolation, remained technically a dependency of China—a tributary state that relied on Beijing to handle its external relations. But China's weakness denied Korea any protection from the predatory Japanese and Westerners, including the French, who used gunboats in the 1860s to punish Korea's mistreatment of missionaries. Secretary Seward hoped to trade with the kingdom, but the fate of the merchant ship *General Sherman* revealed obstacles. In 1866, without Korean permission, the trading schooner pushed upriver. Its captain became embroiled in a dispute with villagers, who burned the ship and killed all aboard. The following year, Commodore Shufeldt investigated; he recommended a punitive force to teach Korea the lesson "taught to other Eastern nations, that it can no longer maintain that contemptuous exclusiveness."[73] Not until 1871 did the United States retaliate. That year a mission, headed by the American minister to China and buttressed by five warships, sought not only to deal with the *General Sherman* incident but also to establish commercial relations and to guarantee the protection of shipwrecked Americans. When the fleet sailed up the Han River, Koreans fired on the advance party, whereupon American guns bombarded their forts, killing at least 300 defenders. "Every urchin in our kingdom [will] spit at and curse you," and the whole world "will indignantly sympathize with us," said the Koreans as they again rejected any treaty.[74]

Japan battered Korea's gates open by imposing a treaty in 1876 that recognized Korean independence from China. The Chinese then encouraged Western contacts with Korea to thwart the Japanese—"to play off the foreign enemies one against the other," reasoned China's chief diplomat.[75] In 1882 a Korean-American treaty provided for American diplomatic representation (a legation in Seoul) and trade relations; the Treaty of Chemulpo passed the Senate the following year. Throughout the 1880s American business people built trade links; even Thomas Edison signed a contract for the installation of electric lights in the royal residence. For the United States, however, Korea constituted a peripheral interest, and Washington could not prevent it from moving into Japan's orbit. As China seemed increasingly prostrate, Japan took advantage. In the Sino-Japanese War of 1894–1895 Japanese forces crushed the Chinese. The United States remained neutral. Americans, including the missionaries, seemed to favor a Japanese triumph to force China into the modern age. Victorious Japan soon dominated Korea, and China lay humiliated, all the more vulnerable to Western and Japanese imperialists. In the late 1890s, to protect their interests in China, Americans turned to the Open Door policy (see Chapter 6).

Pacific Prizes: Hawai'i and Samoa

Hawai'i, that commercial and naval jewel of eight major islands in the Pacific, was linked in the American mind to Asia. The Hawaiian (or Sandwich) Islands sat as convenient stations on the way to Asian markets. The undeveloped port of Pearl Harbor was an admiral's dream, and sugar had become big business. American missionaries acquired converts and property. The United States had repeatedly emphasized that, although not yet ready to annex the islands, it would permit no other power to do so. In 1875, the United States virtually bound Hawai'i to the American economy through a reciprocity treaty. This arrangement allowed Hawaiian sugar to enter the United States duty free, provided Hawai'i did not grant territory to another country. Secretary of State James G. Blaine in 1881 warned the British to stay out of Hawai'i, "essentially a part of the American system of states, and a key to the North Pacific trade."[76] In the 1880s, Americans in Hawai'i organized secret clubs and military units to contest the government of King Kalakaua. In 1887, the conspirators forced the native monarch to accept a new constitution—the so-called Bayonet Constitution—which granted foreigners the right to vote and shifted decisionmaking authority from the throne to the legislature. The same year, Hawai'i granted the United States naval rights to Pearl Harbor, prompting Britain to call futilely for Hawaiian neutrality and equal commercial accessibility for all nations. Nor did Japan, whose 12,000 nationals made up about 14 percent of the islands' population, look kindly on American advances.

Reflecting the longstanding American interest in Hawai'i, Secretary Blaine noted that "Hawaii may come up for decision at any unexpected hour, and I hope we shall be prepared to decide it in the affirmative."[77] Like the expansionists of the 1840s, Americans hurried the hour. The McKinley Tariff of 1890 eliminated Hawaiian sugar's favored status in the United States by admitting all foreign sugar duty free. The measure also provided a bounty of two cents a pound to domestic U.S. growers, making it possible for them to sell their sugar at a price lower than that charged for foreign sugar. Sugar shipments to the United States soon declined. Hawaiian producers screamed in economic pain and plotted revolution against Queen Lili'uokalani, who became monarch in 1891. "They were lying in wait," she remembered.[78] Organized into the subversive Annexation Club, the revolutionaries came from the ranks of influential white American lawyers, merchants, and sugar planters, many of them the sons of Protestant missionaries. They composed a distinct minority of the population (2,000 of a total of 90,000), but they owned a major part of the islands' wealth. One of them, Sanford B. Dole, who became Hawai'i's first president, called the queen inept and corrupt (she favored the legalization of opium and a lottery to raise revenues). He and other plotters also feared that as a Hawaiian nationalist she would roll back the political power of the *haole* (foreigners). One consiprator likened the queen to a "slumbering volcano, which one morning will spew out blood and destroy us all."[79] At the root of the conspiracy, of course, lay the desire to annex Hawai'i to the United States so that Hawaiian sugar would be classified as domestic rather than foreign.

On January 16, 1893, the conspirators bloodlessly toppled the queen and proclaimed a provisional government. Surrendering in protest to what she acknowledged as the "superior force" of the United States, Queen Lili'uokalani endured confinement for several months.[80] After gaining her freedom, she continued to speak out, making the Hawaiian nationalist case against annexation in *Hawaii's Story by Hawaii's Queen* (1898). The revolution could not have succeeded without the assistance of American minister John L. Stevens and the men of the U.S.S. *Boston*. An active partisan for annexation, Stevens sent 164 armed bluejackets from the U.S. cruiser into Honolulu. They did not bivouac near American property to protect it, the announced pretext for landing, but quickly deployed near the monarch's

Queen Lili'uokalani of Hawai'i (1838-1917). Outspoken and tenacious, this Hawaiian nationalist sought to stem the growing economic and political power of foreigners in her island nation. Eager to take Hawai'i back for her people when she inherited the throne in 1891, she could not prevent the white Annexation Club's conspiracy to overthrow her in 1893. Hawai'i, which the United States had recognized as an independent nation in 1849, became a U.S. territory on July 7, 1898, and a state on August 21, 1959. (Library of Congress)

palace. Sipping lemonade while at the same time brandishing Gatling guns and cannon, the troops by their very presence forced the queen to give up. Stevens recognized the provisional government, declared an American protectorate, and warned Washington that the "Hawaiian pear is now fully ripe, and this is the golden hour for the United States to pluck it."[81] Native Hawaiians, making up some 53 percent of the population, never voted on whether they wished to be absorbed by the United States.

Although President Harrison had not authorized Stevens to intervene so directly, he accepted the result and in February signed a treaty of annexation with a "Hawaiian" commission (four Americans and one Englishman). Before the Senate could act, Grover Cleveland had replaced Harrison in the White House. Cleveland soon withdrew the treaty for reflection and ordered an investigator, former member of congress James H. Blount, to the islands. Blount's report confirmed that most native Hawaiians opposed the coup and that "the American Minister [Stevens] and the revolutionary leaders had determined on annexation to the United States, and agreed on the part each was to act to the very end."[82] Although a commercial expansionist, Cleveland opposed taking colonies. He also worried about some prickly questions. What would southern Democrats think of incorporating a multiracial population in the Union? Could Hawai'i, an overseas territory, ever become a state? What if native Hawaiians revolted against their white rulers? Why stir up another heated issue when the United States was already beset at home by Chinese immigration, agricultural depression, and labor protests? Cleveland killed the treaty, but he did not restore the queen, who urged beheading the usurpers and confiscating their property. The white leaders in Hawai'i thus had to wait for a more friendly president in Washington and for more propitious world events for the United States to annex the islands (see Chapter 6).

Other imperialistic nations had cast longing eyes on Hawai'i, and international rivalry increased throughout the Pacific. Germany, Britain, and the United States collided in Samoa, a group of fourteen volcanic islands lying 4,000 miles from San Francisco along the trade route between the United States and Australia. American whalers had long been stopping there, and in 1839 Charles Wilkes of the U.S. Navy had surveyed the islands as part of his exploring expedition in the Pacific. After the American Civil War, nationals of the three great powers scrambled for privileges and exploited the chaotic and often violent tribal politics of the islets. At stake were coconut plantations, national pride stimulated by the three-cornered rivalry, and coaling stations. In 1872 a tribal chief granted the United States naval rights at Pago Pago, the "most perfect land-locked harbor . . . in the Pacific."[83] This pact died because the Senate took no action and Grant, timid after the defeat of his Dominican scheme, did not push it. In 1878 American agents for the Central Polynesian Land and Commercial Company accompanied the Samoan chief Le Mamea to Washington and negotiated a new treaty. It gave Americans privileges at Pago Pago and provided for U.S. good offices in disputes between Samoa and outside nations, which were also collecting treaties of privilege.

In 1885–1886, after years of German intrigue, Secretary of State Thomas F. Bayard launched a more active American diplomacy toward Samoa. He protested

"Two Good Old Friends." In this German cartoon, John Bull (Britain) and Uncle Sam try to balance their Pacific interests in Samoa and Hawai'i while native inhabitants feel the imperial weight. (*Kladderadatsch* in *Review of Reviews*, 1893)

to Berlin that "the United States had assumed the position of a benevolent protector, and the German intervention would mean the virtual displacement of the United States from that preferred status."[84] In 1887 Bayard convened a three-power Washington Conference, but it could not reach agreement. When Germany landed marines on Samoa, Washington dispatched a warship. The British and Americans refused to pay taxes to the German-dominated government. German chancellor Otto von Bismarck vowed to "show sharp teeth."[85] Eager for a "bit of a spar with Germany," Theodore Roosevelt admitted that the Germans might burn New York City.[86] (Americans had other grievances against Germany; a German ban on American pork products was hamstringing trade. The Harrison administration used retaliatory threats to reach a favorable settlement in 1891.) In early 1889 Congress authorized half a million dollars to protect Americans and their Samoan property and another $100,000 to build a naval station at Pago Pago. Whether boldness or bluff, this American action prodded Bismarck to seek peace. A typhoon that devastated Samoa and sank all German and American warships also facilitated peace. After that disaster, nobody had the weapons in Samoa to fight a war.

At the Berlin Conference of 1889, the three powers carved Samoa into a tripartite protectorate (the United States got Pago Pago) and forced an unpopular king on the Samoans. The writer Robert Louis Stevenson, a prominent resident of the islands, protested this violation of native sovereignty, this "Triple-Headed Ass."[87] Ten years later, in the aftermath of the Spanish-American-Cuban-Filipino War, the United States and Germany formally partitioned Samoa into colonies, with Britain compensated by other Pacific acquisitions.

Probing Africa

Before the Civil War, American ships and merchant traders, especially from Salem, Massachusetts, frequented Africa's coast. But conflict disrupted old trading patterns, lower transportation costs made European goods less expensive in African markets, and discriminatory trade practices stymied Yankee competition. As a result, the American presence on the continent shrank in the late nineteenth century. American adventurers, explorers, mining engineers, and traders, and a few naval officers dispatched to identify prospects for foreign commerce, kept some U.S. interest in Africa alive. The navy's ships patrolled along the African coast to protect American lives and property. But official Washington took few steps to advance U.S. interests in the vast land that the European powers were rushing to conquer.

American tobacco, kerosene, and rum nevertheless continued to claim a good share of African markets. Zanzibar preferred American cotton goods; in exchange, East African gum copal and ivory were shipped to New England factories. When, in the early 1880s, tribal warfare in Tanganyika (present-day Tanzania) interrupted the ivory trade, Connecticut plants had to shut down. In west Africa, where Americans had once participated in the slave trade and where many consular agents had long handled American commercial interests, British tariffs hurt American trade— for example, tobacco and rum on the Gold Coast and Sierra Leone. Higher tariffs in French West Africa also diminished American commerce. By the end of the century, American trade with the continent had become inconsequential.

Such a decline might not have occurred had Washington heeded Commodore Shufeldt's recommendations. In 1878 the State and Navy departments ordered him to sail the U.S.S. *Ticonderoga* to Africa and Asia for "the encouragement and extension of American commerce."[88] Shufeldt wrote detailed reports on economic opportunities, port facilities, and laws. He introduced American products to Africans and negotiated trade treaties. For American surplus goods, he advised, "Africa with its teeming population presents a tempting field."[89] He warned that the British and other imperialists were working to drive Americans from the continent. Washington officials read and listened but took no action.

Americans nonetheless became fascinated with black Africa because individuals bent on adventure, fame, and wealth popularized it. Foremost among them was Henry M. Stanley, an immigrant from Wales who claimed U.S. citizenship. While working for the *New York Herald,* after stints in both the Confederate and the Union armies, Stanley was directed by the newspaper's owner to depart for Africa and find Dr. David Livingstone, the missionary-explorer who in 1866 had disappeared into central Africa while searching for the Nile's source. Stanley arrived in Zanzibar in 1871 and began to write dramatic stories about Africa. With an American flag at the head of his large expedition, he cut across Tanganyika and found Livingstone, who

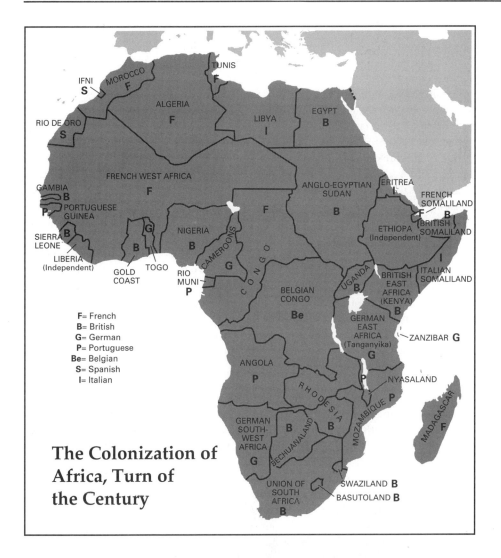

F= French
B= British
G= German
P= Portuguese
Be= Belgian
S= Spanish
I= Italian

The Colonization of Africa, Turn of the Century

appreciated Stanley's supplies and medicine but insisted on continuing his quest for the great river's headwaters. Three years later Stanley led another venture into the African interior; in his 999-day trek through the wilderness he battled hostile Africans, mapped the territory, disparaged natives as "wooly-headed rabble . . . unchecked and uncurbed by the hand of law," and made the Congo Basin and himself internationally famous.[90] Congress even voted him a resolution of thanks.

King Leopold II of Belgium saw in Stanley an instrument to bring his small nation a large empire. Unable to compete with the more powerful European imperialists, Leopold formed an organization whose announced philanthropic purpose was ending the slave trade and protecting legitimate commerce, but whose real objective was obtaining an imperial foothold for Belgium in the Congo. The king hired Stanley, who negotiated with African leaders in the region to gain their allegiance to the international organization. Leopold also secured the services of Henry S. Sanford, a former American minister to Belgium who sought personal commercial gain from enlarged U.S. trade in the region. Working to thwart the encroaching Europeans, Sanford lobbied in Washington for American support of the principle of free trade in the Congo. In 1884 Sanford succeeded when the United States recognized the *Association Internationale du Congo* as sovereign over the area.

The United States then found itself in the midst of an international dispute, for other European nations claimed parts of the Congo. To head off a clash, the European rivals convened in Berlin in fall 1884. Washington sent two delegates, one of them Sanford; Stanley advised the American diplomats. The conferees signed an agreement that recognized the international association's (and hence Leopold's) authority over the Congo and ensured an open trade door. The new president, Grover Cleveland, avoiding entanglements with Europeans, withdrew the accord from the Senate. Still, the United States abided by its terms and in 1890 sent representatives to another Congo conference. This time, the conferees in Brussels closed the commercial door by permitting Leopold to levy import duties in the Congo ostensibly to eradicate the slave trade. "Easily hoodwinked," American leaders inadvertently helped the Belgian monarch take over a million and a half square miles of African territory and create "a gigantic trading monopoly behind a smokescreen of philanthropy and altruism."[91] Two years later the United States ratified the accord.

American Christian missionaries also entered Africa. By the end of the century the American Board of Commissioners for Foreign Missions had built schools, hospitals, and a seminary for training an African clergy. Its missionaries established stations in South Africa, Mozambique, and Angola, and translated the Bible into Zulu. Baptists sought converts in Nigeria, and Lutherans opened missions in Madagascar. The African Methodist Episcopal Church, a major black church in the United States, sought converts in Liberia, Sierra Leone, and South Africa. In the 1890s, one of its bishops, black nationalist Henry Turner, urged segregated and disenfranchised American blacks to emigrate to Africa. "I would make Africa a place of refuge," Turner declared, "because I see no other shelter from the stormy blast, from the red tide of persecution, from the horrors of American prejudice."[92] Hundreds of African Americans heeded his call, but the back-to-Africa movement remained peripheral to the experience of most blacks in the United States. Most white Americans, ignorant of African diversity, viewed the continent through a racist prism: A black African was "either an obedient, childlike servant accompanying white hunters or explorers, or a practically naked savage bent on cannibalism."[93]

American prospectors and mining engineers flocked to the gold and diamond regions of South Africa. One fortune seeker, Jerome L. Babe, arrived in 1870 as a salesman for the Winchester Repeating Arms Company and reporter for the *New York World*. He stayed on to invent a screening apparatus for diamond mining and to buy and sell the precious stones. A self-taught engineer from Kentucky, Hamilton Smith wrote glowing reports on gold that attracted large investments from the European bank of Rothschild. An unusual group of Americans, over twenty in number, became soldiers of fortune for Egypt before Britain occupied the country in 1882.

Americans knew more about Liberia than about any other African area. Settled in 1821 and governed by American blacks under the auspices of the American Colonization Society, Liberia suffered internal strife and French and British nibblings at its territory. The United States, in 1875 and again in 1879, displayed its warships to help the Americo-Liberians quell rebellions by indigenous Africans. In the 1880s and 1890s British and French forces coerced Liberia into ceding land.

Calling Liberia "an offshoot of our own system" and deploring "encroachment" on the vulnerable nation's land, President Cleveland declared that the United States had a "moral right and duty" to protect Liberia.[94] Washington appealed for imperial restraint but refused to employ its meager power in the area to halt imperial ambitions. Perhaps America's patronage, however minimal, forestalled full-scale European domination of that African nation.

With the United States as an interested observer, whites carved up Africa—the British took Egypt, Sierra Leone, and the Gold Coast; the Germans feasted on Tanganyika (East Africa) and Southwest Africa; the French grabbed Tunis and West Africa; the Portuguese absorbed Angola and Mozambique; and the Belgians gained the Congo (see map on page 189). By 1895 imperialists had partitioned most of Africa. Washington worried, as always, that the colonial enclaves would close their doors to American trade. As at the Berlin conference more than a decade earlier, U.S. officials constantly reminded the European imperialists to keep the doors open to honor the principle of equal trade opportunity.

Latin America Moves into the Yankee Vortex

During this period the United States was more active in Latin America than in any other part of the world. Americans challenged European interests, expanded trade and investment links, intervened in inter-American disputes and revolutions, deployed warships in troubled waters to "show the flag," tried to annex territories, sought canal routes across Central America, lectured everybody about the supremacy of the Monroe Doctrine, and organized the Pan American movement.

European competitors persisted in meddling in Latin American affairs, but when the French in 1861 intervened militarily in Mexico and placed the young Archduke Ferdinand Maximilian of Austria on a Mexican throne, the Civil War–wracked United States pursued what Seward called "a patient policy of persuasion" (see Chapter 4).[95] The intervention seemed to threaten U.S. security and expansion and to hurl a blatant challenge at the Monroe Doctrine. Seward first sent arms to the forces of former Mexican president Benito Juárez. After the Civil War, President Andrew Johnson ordered 52,000 American soldiers to Texas. Under the command of General Philip Sheridan, the troops staged military maneuvers along the Mexican border to buttress Washington's diplomatic demands for a French exit. In early 1866 Seward firmly asked Napoleon III when the French military would withdraw. Facing opposition at home and Prussian competition in Europe, harassed by guerrillas in Mexico, and confronted by a noisy, well-armed, and victorious United States, the emperor decided to recall his troops. The hapless and abandoned

Hamilton Fish (1808–1893).
Graduate of Columbia University
and lawyer, Fish served as a U.S.
senator from New York
(1851–1857) and opposed the expansion of slavery in the 1850s.
More patient and tactful than President Grant, he served as secretary of state, 1869–1877.
(*Harper's Weekly*, 1869)

"archdupe" Maximilian fell in 1867 before a Mexican firing squad. Americans believed, much too simply, that they had forced France out and that the Monroe
Doctrine, although not mentioned by name in this crisis, had gained new vigor.

Another, but quite different, challenge sprang from Cuba, the Spanish colony
that many North Americans believed would one day become part of the U.S. empire. From 1868 to 1878, a Creole-led rebellion bloodied the island. With annexationist sentiment strong among the Creoles, they petitioned Washington for
admission to the Union. During the Ten Years' War, U.S. officials rejected Cuban
independence, urged Spain to introduce reforms, and explored possibilities of buying the island. When Secretary Fish characterized the rebels as deserving the "con-
demnations of all honest citizens," President Grant denounced any recognition of
Cuban independence as impractical and indefensible.[96] The Creoles' defense of
slavery posed a major obstacle to U.S. alignment in any form with Cuba. Fish also
doubted that a mixed population of Spaniards, Africans, and Indians could govern
itself. Someday, Fish remarked in 1869, Spanish rule would collapse and "civilized
nations" would "all be glad that we should interpose and regulate the control of the
Island."[97]

The *Virginius* affair of 1873 entangled the United States in the rebellion. That
Cuban-owned, gun-running vessel was captured by the Spanish, who shot as "pirates" fifty-three of the passengers and crewmen, some of them U.S. citizens. As
Americans shouted for revenge, the levelheaded Fish demanded and received an
apology and indemnity from Madrid of $80,000. In view of the "hundreds of thou-
sands of children who might have been made orphans, in an *unnecessary* war undertaken for a dishonest vessel," Fish worked "to avoid the terrible evil."[98] Cuba
continued to bleed until 1878, when the rebellion ended and slavery was abolished.
From then until 1895, when a new revolution erupted, islanders and exiles still
cried for *Cuba Libre*.

Cubans turned more and more toward the United States. Cuban dependence
on U.S. markets and capital grew when beet-sugar growers in Europe cut into
Cuban sales and threw the island economy into chaos. North American investors
seized opportunities to obtain plantations across Cuba. Boston banker Edwin Atkins
became one of the island's largest landowners, displacing planters of the Creole
elite. "Cuba is already inside the commercial union of the United States," a U.S.
consul reported in 1882.[99] Cubans played the American game of baseball, forming
their first professional league in 1878. Expatriates in Tampa and Key West donated
baseball gate receipts to the cause of Cuban independence. *Béisbol*, according to the
historian Louis A. Pérez, Jr., became "an expression of change and an agent of
change," as Cubans "celebrated the modernity and progress implied in baseball, associated with the United States, and denounced the inhumanity and backwardness
suggested by bullfighting, associated with Spain."[100] Further evidence of cultural
fusion became evident in the flow of people back and forth between Cuba and the
United States. Wealthy Creoles sent their children to American colleges, married
North American spouses, took North American names, and jettisoned Catholicism
for Protestant denominations.

American economic interests provided an important source of U.S. influence
in Cuba and elsewhere in Latin America. American investments in and trade with

Latin American countries expanded dramatically—in Cuba (sugar and mines), Guatemala (the United States handled 64 percent of the country's trade by 1885), and Mexico (railroads and mines). Many of Mexico's provinces were "pulled into the Yankee vortex" by U.S. investors and developers.[101] American capitalists built railroads, dug copper ore, and developed ports. By the early 1890s, the United States was buying 75 percent of Mexico's exports and supplying about 50 percent of its imports. The long and stable regime of the Mexican dictator Porfirio Díaz (1876–1910) invited this foreign economic penetration. By 1890, American citizens had invested some $250 million in Latin America. Still, the region took just 5 percent of total American exports that year. Most U.S. trade remained with Europe. Although these economic ties with Latin America comprised a small part of total U.S.-world economic relationships, for countries like Cuba and Mexico such links became vital and brought the United States into the internal affairs of these countries. American economic interests also drew the United States into a Brazilian civil war in 1893–1894, where Washington sent the South Atlantic Squadron to break a rebel blockade of Rio de Janeiro.

James G. Blaine (1830–1893). Republican representative and senator from Maine and secretary of state (1881, 1889–1892), Blaine expanded U.S. interests in Latin America. (Library of Congress)

Central America attracted considerable American interest because of prospects for an isthmian canal linking the Pacific Ocean and the Gulf of Mexico, thereby greatly reducing commercial and naval travel time between the eastern seaboard and Asian markets. The gala opening of the Suez Canal in 1869 spurred American canal enthusiasts, most notably the irascible Senator John Tyler Morgan of Alabama, an ardent expansionist who hoped to convert "the Gulf of Mexico into an American Mediterranean and Mobile into a flourishing international port."[102] Panama and Nicaragua seemed possible sites. The problem was the Clayton-Bulwer Treaty (1850), which held that a Central American canal had to be jointly controlled by Britain and the United States. Washington resented this limitation on American expansion, and when President Rutherford Hayes learned in 1880 that Ferdinand de Lesseps, builder of the Suez Canal, would attempt to construct a canal through Panama, he sent two warships to demonstrate U.S. concern. "A canal under American control, or no canal," exclaimed Hayes.[103]

In 1881 Secretary Blaine forcefully but futilely asked the British to abrogate the Clayton-Bulwer Treaty, claiming that the United States "with respect to European states, will not consent to perpetuate any treaty that impeaches our right and long-established claim to priority on the American continent."[104] Three years later, in overt violation of the treaty, the United States signed a canal treaty with Nicaragua, although President Cleveland withdrew the offending pact when he took office. The movement led by naval officers, business leaders, and diplomats for an exclusive U.S. canal had begun nonetheless. In Panama in 1873 and 1885, U.S. troops went ashore to protect American property threatened by civil war. In the latter year an American warship under the command of Alfred Thayer Mahan displayed U.S. power to Guatemala, whose invasion of El Salvador threatened American-owned property, including James A. Scrymser's Central and South American Telegraph Company.

The convocation of the first Pan American Conference in Washington in 1889 bore further witness to the growing U.S. influence in Latin America. Secretary Blaine, hoping to expand American trade and boost his presidential aspirations, had first recommended such a conference in 1881, but his departure in that year from the cabinet left the question open until his return (1889–1892). The conference attracted representatives from seventeen countries. Six of the ten U.S. delegates were business people. After a grand tour of industrial sites in forty-one cities, the conferees assembled in Washington to hear Blaine's appeal for "enlightened and enlarged intercourse."[105] Unlike similar conferences in the twentieth century, the United States could not dictate the results of the conclave. Argentina stood as a tenacious opponent of hemispheric union; the Argentines saw Pan Americanism as a U.S. ruse to gain commercial domination. Although the Pan American conferees rejected Blaine's proposals for a low-tariff zone and for compulsory arbitration of political disputes, they did organize the International Bureau of American Republics (later called the Pan American Union) and encouraged reciprocity treaties to expand hemispheric trade. The conference also promoted inter-American steamship lines and railroads and established machinery to discuss commercial questions.

The Pan American Union amounted to little in its early days. It had its most conspicuous impact on the Washington landscape, where, with major financial help from the steel baron Andrew Carnegie, the Pan American Union put up an impressive building in the nation's capital. Pan Americanism did not mean hemispheric unity; rather it represented growing U.S. influence among neighbors to the south. For that reason European powers eyed the new organization with suspicion.

Crises with Chile in 1891 and with Venezuela in 1895 (see Chapter 6) demonstrated U.S. determination to dominate the Western Hemisphere. Chilean-American relations steadily deteriorated, in part because the United States had clumsily attempted to end the War of the Pacific (1879–1883), in which Chile battled Bolivia and Peru to win nitrate-rich territory. Then, at the Pan American Conference, Chile had stood as a fearless critic of the United States. When civil war ripped through Chile in early 1891, the United States backed the sitting government, which had tried to assume dictatorial powers. The U.S. Navy seized arms purchased in the United States and destined for the rebels. When the victorious revolutionary Congressionalists took office, President Benjamin Harrison at first withheld recognition, muttering haughtily that "sometime it may be necessary to instruct them" on "how to use victory with dignity and moderation."[106] The United States had sided with the losers; anti-Yankeeism flourished in the winners. To make matters worse, Washington suspected that Britain, ever the competitor in Latin America, was cementing close ties with the new Chilean regime.

An incident in October 1891, after the end of the civil war, nearly exploded into a Chilean-American war. At Valparaiso, a major port for North American traders, one of the ships of the Pacific Squadron, the heavily armed *Baltimore,* anchored in the harbor. "She can whip any that can catch her and run away from any that can whip her," bragged Secretary of the Navy Tracy.[107] Commanded by Captain Winfield S. Schley, who had attended the Naval Academy with Mahan and George Dewey, the ship had orders to protect American interests during the civil war. On October 16 its crew went ashore on liberty. The exuberant sailors gave local taverns and brothels considerable business. Outside the True Blue Saloon, rum-drunk Americans and anti-Yankee Chileans quarreled, fists flew, and knives slashed. Two Americans died, others suffered wounds, and some were arrested.

STATE DEPARTMENT, WASHINGTON, D.C.

Punishment for Chile, 1891.
An angry Uncle Sam is about to administer U.S. retribution to Chile after the *Baltimore* affair. The historian Joyce Goldberg has written that "the narrow-minded nationalism and diplomatic bullying demonstrated in the *Baltimore* affair annoyed the very powers the United States wanted to impress. They interpreted it as rude, unnecessarily belligerent, and undignified behavior." (*Harper's Weekly*, 1891)

President Harrison reacted bitterly against this affront to the American uniform, especially when the Chilean government did not hurry to apologize. Captain Robley D. ("Fighting Bob") Evans of the *Yorktown* replaced Schley and warned Chileans that "if they could not control their people . . . I should arm my boats and shoot any and every man who insulted me or my men or my flag in any way."[108] A British diplomat observed: "The President and the Secretary of the Navy wish for war; one to get re-elected, the other to see his new ships fight and get votes for more."[109] After a change in the Chilean cabinet in early 1892, the cautious South Americans expressed regret and paid an indemnity of $75,000 in gold. The Yankee Goliath had humbled Chile, and Latin Americans had to wonder what Pan Americanism really meant. Advocates of the expanding U.S. Navy cheered the "victory" over Chile, but a British official thought the incident created a "passionate sense of hatred toward the United States, which will take a long time to remove."[110]

Senator George Shoup of Iowa drew a different lesson from the Chilean episode: "The American Republic will stand no more nonsense from any power, big or little."[111] Indeed, by the mid-1890s, the United States had become far more self-confident and certainly cockier than it had been in 1865, and far more willing to exert the power it had built over the last few decades, especially in Latin America. The anti-imperialist sentiments that had spoiled earlier imperial ventures had weakened by the 1890s, undercut by chauvinistic nationalism, international rivalry, the glut thesis, the depression of the 1890s, and the relentless U.S. expansion that had put Iowa farmers' cereals in England, missionaries in China, Wild West shows in Europe, cans of Armour corned beef in India, Singer sewing machines in the Caroline Islands, McCormick reapers in Russia, warships in Korea and Brazil, explorers in Africa, sugar growers in Hawai'i, baseball in Cuba, mining companies in Mexico, rollicking sailors in Chile, and Nellie Bly "girdling" the globe.[112] All demonstrated the transformation of the United States from a regional to a global power.

FURTHER READING FOR THE PERIOD 1865–1895

General and presidential studies include Robert L. Beisner, *From the Old Diplomacy to the New* (1986); Charles W. Calhoun, ed., *The Gilded Age* (1995); Charles S. Campbell, *The Transformation of American Foreign Relations, 1865–1900* (1976); Justus D. Doenecke, *The Presidencies of James A. Garfield and Chester A. Arthur* (1981); John A. S. Grenville and George B. Young, *Politics, Strategy, and American Diplomacy* (1967); David Healy, *U.S. Expansionism* (1970); Ari Hoogenboom, *The Presidency of Rutherford B. Hayes* (1988) and *Rutherford B. Hayes* (1995); Rhodri Jeffreys-Jones, ed., *Eagle Against Empire* (1983); Paul A. Koistinen, *Mobilizing for Modern War: The Political Economy of American Warfare, 1865–1916* (1997); Walter LaFeber, *The American Search for Opportunity, 1865–1913* (1993) and *The New Empire*, new ed. (1998); Henry E. Mattox, *The Twilight of Amateur Diplomacy* (1989) (foreign service); Tennant S. McWilliams, *The New South Faces the World* (1988); Milton Plesur, *America's Outward Thrust* (1971); David M. Pletcher, *The Awkward Years* (1962); Serge Ricard, ed., *La république impérialiste* (1987); Homer E. Socolofsky and Allan B. Spetter, *The Presidency of Benjamin Harrison* (1987); Richard E. Welch, *The Presidencies of Grover Cleveland* (1988); Robert Wiebe, *The Search for Order* (1967); and William A. Williams, *The Roots of the Modern American Empire* (1969) and *The Tragedy of American Diplomacy* (1962).

For explanations of shifting power in the international system of the late nineteenth century and for comparative studies, see Philip Darby, *Three Faces of Imperialism: British and American Approaches to Asia and Africa, 1870–1970* (1987); Aaron L. Friedberg, *The Weary Titan: Britain and the Experience of Relative Decline, 1895–1905* (1988); Daniel R. Headrick, *The Invisible Weapon: International Communications and International Politics, 1851–1945* (1991); Paul Kennedy, *The Rise and Fall of the Great Powers* (1987); and Anne Orde, *The Eclipse of Great Britain* (1996). See also works cited in Chapters 6 and 7.

Biographical studies include William M. Armstrong, *E. L. Godkin and American Foreign Policy* (1957); Charles W. Calhoun, *Gilded Age Cato* (1988) (Gresham); Michael Devine, *John W. Foster* (1980); David Donald, *Charles Sumner and the Rights of Man* (1970); Joseph A. Fry, *Henry S. Sanford* (1982) and *John Tyler Morgan and the Search for Southern Automony* (1992); William S. McFeely, *Grant* (1981); Allan Nevins, *Hamilton Fish* (1937); Ernest N. Paolino, *The Foundations of the American Empire* (1973) (Seward); Hans L. Trefousse, *Carl Schurz* (1982); and Glyndon C. Van Deusen, *William Henry Seward* (1967).

For cultural and ideological influences, including American images of foreign peoples, see Nancy Boyd, *Emissaries* (1996) (YWCA); Alexander DeConde, *Ethnicity, Race, and American Foreign Policy* (1992); Patricia Hill, *The World Their Household* (1985) (women missionaries); Richard Hofstadter, *Social Darwinism in American Thought* (1955); Michael H. Hunt, *Ideology and U.S. Foreign Policy* (1987); Amy Kaplan and Donald E. Pease, eds. *Culture of United States Imperialism* (1993); R. Kroes et al., eds., *Cultural Transformations and Receptions* (1993); Catherine A. Lutz and Jane L. Collins, *Reading National Geographic* (1993); Emily S. Rosenberg, *Spreading the American Dream* (1982); David Spurr, *The Rhetoric of Empire* (1993); Robert W. Rydell, *All the World's a Fair* (1985), ed., *Fair Representations* (1994), and *World of Fairs* (1993); Anders Stephanson, *Manifest Destiny* (1995); Ian Tyrrell, *Women's World/Women's Empire* (1991) (WTCU); and Rubin F. Weston, *Racism in United States Imperialism* (1972). See also works cited in Chapters 6 and 7.

Economic questions are treated in Beisner, Campbell, LaFeber, and Williams above and in William H. Becker, *The Dynamics of Business-Government Relations* (1982); Vincent P. Carosso, *The Morgans* (1987); Fred V. Carstensen, *American Enterprise in Foreign Markets* (1984); Robert B. Davies, *Peacefully Working to Conquer the World* (1976); David A. Lake, *Power, Protection, and Free Trade* (1988); David Pletcher, *The Diplomacy of Trade and Investment* (1998) and *Rails, Mines, and Progress* (1958) (Mexico); Howard B. Schonberger, *Transportation to the Seaboard* (1971); Tom Terrill, *The Tariff, Politics, and American Foreign Policy, 1874–1901* (1973); and Mira Wilkins, *The Emergence of the Multinational Enterprise* (1970).

The transformation of the U.S. Navy is discussed in Benjamin F. Cooling, *Benjamin Franklin Tracy* (1973) and *Gray Steel and Blue Water Navy* (1979); Frederick C. Drake, *The Empire of the Seas* (1984) (Shufeldt); Kenneth J. Hagan, *American Gunboat Diplomacy and the Old Navy, 1877–1889* (1973), ed., *In Peace and War* (1984), and *This People's Navy* (1991); Walter R. Herrick, *The American Naval Revolution* (1966); Peter Karsten, *The Naval Aristocracy* (1972); David F. Long, *Gold Braid and Foreign Relations* (1988); Robert Seager, *Alfred Thayer Mahan* (1977); Mark R. Shulman, *Navalism and the Emergence of American Sea Power* (1995); Harold and Margaret Sprout, *The Rise of American Naval Power, 1776–1918* (1966); and William N. Still, Jr., *American Sea Power in the Old World* (1980).

For the Great Britain–Canada–U.S. relationship, see Kenneth Bourne, *Britain and the Balance of Power in North America, 1815–1908* (1967); Robert C. Brown, *Canada's National Policy, 1883–1900* (1964); Charles S. Campbell, *From Revolution to Rapprochement* (1974); Adrian Cook, *The Alabama Claims* (1975); Edward P. Crapol, *America for Americans: Economic Nationalism and Anglophobia* (1973); Brian Jenkins, *Fenians and Anglo-American Relations During Reconstruction* (1969); Lawrence Martin, *The Presidents and the Prime Ministers* (1982); W. S. Neidhardt, *Fenianism in North America* (1975); Richard A. Preston, *The Defense of the Undefended Border* (1977); Lester B. Shippee, *Canadian-American Relations, 1849–1874* (1939); and Reginald C. Stuart, *United States Expansionism and British North America, 1775–1871* (1988).

U.S. relations with Latin America are discussed in Richard H. Bradford, *The Virginius Affair* (1980); Jules Davids, *American Political and Economic Penetration of Mexico, 1877–1920* (1976); Joyce S. Goldberg, *The Baltimore Affair* (1986); Alfred J. Hanna and Kathryn A. Hanna, *Napoleon III and Mexico* (1971); José M. Hernández, *Cuba and the United States* (1993); Lester D. Langley, *Struggle for the American Mediterranean* (1976); Luis Martínez-Fernández, *Torn Between Empires* (1994) (Spanish Caribbean); Louis A. Pérez, Jr., *Cuba and the United States* (1997) and *Cuba Between Empires* (1982); Dexter Perkins, *The Monroe Doctrine, 1867–1907* (1937); Frederick B. Pike, *Chile and the United States, 1880–1962* (1963); W. Dirk Raat, *Mexico and the United States* (1992); Ramón E. Ruíz, *The People of Sonora and Yankee Capitalists* (1988); William F. Sater, *Chile and the United States* (1990); Karl M. Schmitt, *Mexico and the United States, 1821–1973* (1974); Thomas D. Schoonover, *Dollars over Dominion* (1978) (Mexico) and *The United States in Central America, 1860–1911* (1991); Lars Schoultz, *Beneath the United States* (1998); Joseph Smith, *Illusions of Conflict: Anglo-American Diplomacy Toward Latin America, 1865–1896* (1979); Charles C. Tansill, *The United States and Santo Domingo, 1798–1873* (1938) and Steven C. Topik, *Trade and Gunboats* (1996) (Brazil).

For Hawai'i, see Helena G. Allen, *Sanford Ballard Dole* (1988) and *The Betrayal of Queen Liliuokalani* (1982); Ralph S. Kuykendall, *The Hawaiian Kingdom, 1874–1893* (1967); W. A. Russ, Jr., *The Hawaiian Revolution, 1893–94* (1959); and Merze Tate, *The United States and the Hawaiian Kingdom* (1965).

For Asian-American relations, see David L. Anderson, *Imperialism and Idealism* (1985); Gunther Barth, *Bitter Strength: A History of the Chinese in the United States, 1850–1870* (1964); Jerome Ch'en, *China and the West* (1979); Warren I. Cohen, *America's Response to China* (1990); John K. Fairbank, ed., *The Missionary Enterprise in China and America* (1974); Wayne Flynt and Gerald W. Berkley, *Taking Christianity to China* (1997); Gael Graham, *Gender, Culture, and Christianity* (1995) (missionaries in China); Fred Harvey Harrington, *God, Mammon, and the Japanese* (1944) (Korea); Michael Hunt, *The Making of a Special Relationship* (1983) (China); Akira Iriye, *Across the Pacific* (1967); Paul M. Kennedy, *The Samoan Tangle* (1974); Yur-Bok Lee, *Diplomatic Relations Between the United States and Korea, 1866–1887* (1970); Charles J. McClain, *In Search of Equality* (1994) (Chinese in United States); Robert McClellan, *The Heathen Chinee* (1971); Stuart C. Miller, *The Unwelcome Immigrant* (1969) (Chinese); Craig Storti, *Incident at Bitter Creek* (1991); Shih-shan Henry Tsai, *China* and the Overseas Chinese in the United States, 1868–1911 (1983); and Thomas A. Tweed, *The American Encounter with Buddhism, 1844–1912* (1992).

Alaska and Russian-American relations are discussed in James T. Gay, *American Fur Seal Diplomacy* (1987); Paul S. Holbo, *Tarnished Expansion* (1983); Ronald J. Jensen, *The Alaska Purchase and Russian-American Relations* (1975); Howard I. Kushner, *Conflict on the Northwest Coast* (1975); Norman E. Saul, *Concord & Conflict* (1996); and Frederick F. Travis, *George Kennan and the American-Russian Relationship, 1865–1924* (1990).

U.S. interest in Africa is studied in Edward W. Chester, *Clash of Titans* (1974); Clarence Clendenen, Robert Collins, and Peter Duignan, *Americans in Africa, 1865–1900* (1966); Sybil E. Crowe, *The Berlin West African Conference, 1884–1885* (1942); Peter Duignan and L. H. Gann, *The United States and Africa* (1987); Thomas Pakenham, *The Scramble for Africa* (1991); Edwin S. Redkey, *Black Exodus: Black Nationalist and Back-to-Africa Movements, 1890–1910* (1969); Elliott P. Skinner, *African Americans and U.S. Policy Toward Africa, 1850–1924* (1992); and Walter L. Williams, *Black Americans and the Evangelization of Africa, 1877–1900* (1982).

See also the General Bibliography, the following notes, and Richard Dean Burns, ed., *Guide to American Foreign Relations Since 1700* (1983).

For comprehensive coverage of foreign-relations topics, see the articles in the four-volume *Encyclopedia of U.S. Foreign Relations* (1997), edited by Bruce W. Jentleson and Thomas G. Paterson.

NOTES TO CHAPTER 5

1. Quoted in William S. McFeely, *Grant* (New York: Norton, 1981), p. 341.
2. Charles C. Tansill, *The United States and Santo Domingo* (Baltimore: Johns Hopkins Press, 1938), p. 134.
3. Admiral Charles Poor quoted in David Long, *Gold Braid and Foreign Relations* (Annapolis: Naval Institute Press, 1988), p. 348.
4. Quoted in Hans L. Trefousse, *Carl Schurz* (Knoxville: University of Tennessee Press, 1982), p. 195.
5. Quoted in Edward P. Crapol, "Lydia Maria Child," in Crapol, ed., *Women and American Foreign Policy* (Westport, Conn., Greenwood, 1992; 2nd ed.), p. 13.
6. Quoted in William J. Nelson, *Almost a Territory* (Newark: University of Delaware Press, 1990), p. 102.
7. Quoted in David Donald, *Charles Sumner and the Rights of Man* (New York: Knopf, 1970), p. 443.
8. Fernando Wood quoted in Luis Martínez-Fernández, *Torn Between Empires* (Athens: University of Georgia Press, 1994), p. 166.
9. John Y. Simon, ed., *The Papers of Ulysses S. Grant* (Carbondale: Southern Illinois University Press, 1967– ; 20 vols. to date), XX, 155.
10. Quoted in McFeely, *Grant*, p. 335.
11. Simon, *Grant Papers*, XX, 164n.
12. Rollo Ogden, ed., *Life and Letters of Edwin Lawrence Godkin* (New York: Macmillan, 1907; 2 vols.), I, 304–305.
13. Quoted in Allan Nevins, *Hamilton Fish* (New York: Dodd, Mead, 1937), p. 372.
14. *The Works of Charles Sumner* (Boston: Lee and Shepard, 1870–1883; 15 vols.), XIV, 94–124.
15. Paul Holbo, *Tarnished Expansion* (Knoxville: University of Tennessee Press, 1983), p. 91.
16. Edward P. Crapol, "Coming to Terms with Empire," *Diplomatic History*, XVI (Fall 1992), 593–594.
17. Thomas D. Schoonover, *Dollars over Dominion* (Baton Rouge: Louisiana State University Press, 1978), p. 249.
18. Quoted in Walter LaFeber, *The New Empire* (Ithaca: Cornell University Press, 1963), p. 106.
19. Quoted in Robert W. Rydell, *All the World's a Fair* (Chicago: University of Chicago Press, 1984), p. 7.
20. Nancy Boyd, *Emissaries* (New York: Woman's Press, 1986), p. 52.
21. Ian Tyrrell, *Woman's World/Woman's Empire* (Chapel Hill: University of North Carolina Press, 1991), p. 4.
22. Quoted in Alexander DeConde, *Ethnicity, Race, and American Foreign Policy* (Boston: Northeastern University Press, 1992), p. 54.
23. Quoted in David Spurr, *The Rhetoric of Empire* (Durham, N.C.: Duke University Press, 1993), p. 31.
24. Theodore Roosevelt, *The Strenuous Life* (New York: Century, 1900).
25. Quoted in Mark R. Shulman, *Navalism and the Emergence of American Sea Power, 1882–1893* (Annapolis: Naval Institute Press, 1995), p. 157.
26. Robert W. Rydell, ed., *Fair Representations* (Amsterdam: Vu University Press, 1994), p. 42.
27. Quoted in Emily S. Rosenberg, *Spreading the American Dream* (New York: Hill & Wang, 1982), p. 29.
28. Quoted in William R. Hutchinson, *Errand to the World* (Chicago: University of Chicago Press, 1987), p. 123.
29. Quoted in Milton Plesur, *America's Outward Thrust* (DeKalb: Northern Illinois University Press, 1971), p. 26.
30. Frederick J. Turner, "The Significance of the Frontier in American History," *Annual Report of the American Historical Association, 1893* (Washington, D.C.: Government Printing Office, 1894), p. 227.
31. John F. Sears, "Bierstadt, Buffalo Bill, and the Wild West in Europe," in R. Kroes et al., eds., *Cultural Transformations and Receptions* (Amsterdam: Vu University Press, 1993), pp. 11, 19.

32. Rosenberg, *American Dream*, p. 35.

33. Patricia Nelson Limerick, "A Panel of Appraisal," *Western Historical Quarterly*, XX (August 1989), 317.

34. James O. Gump, *The Dust Rose like Smoke* (Lincoln: University of Nebraska Press, 1994), p. 137.

35. Walter L. Williams, "United States Indian Policy and the Debate over Philippine Annexation," *Journal of American History*, LXVI (March 1980), 810–812.

36. Quoted in Aaron L. Friedberg, *The Weary Titan* (Princeton: Princeton University Press, 1988), p. vii.

37. Quoted in Paul Kennedy, *The Rise and Fall of the Great Powers* (New York: Random House, 1987), p. 196.

38. Quoted in David M. Pletcher, "Economic Growth and Diplomatic Adjustment, 1861–1898," in William H. Becker and Samuel F. Wells, Jr., eds., *Economics and World Power* (New York: Columbia University Press, 1984), pp. 124–125.

39. Quoted in David M. Pletcher, "Rhetoric and Results," *Diplomatic History*, V (Spring 1981), 95.

40. Gilbert M. Joseph, *Revolution from Without* (Cambridge, Eng.: Cambridge University Press, 1982), p. 43.

41. Quoted in Plesur, *America's Outward Thrust*, p. 33.

42. Quoted in Henry E. Mattox, *The Twilight of Amateur Diplomacy* (Kent, Ohio: Kent State University Press, 1989), p. x.

43. David A. Lake, *Power, Protection, and Free Trade* (Ithaca: Cornell University Press, 1988), p. 117.

44. Quoted in David Healy, *U.S. Expansionism* (Madison: University of Wisconsin Press, 1970), p. 44.

45. Quoted in Lance C. Buhl, "Maintaining 'An American Navy,' 1865–1889," in Kenneth J. Hagan, ed., *In Peace and War* (Westport, Conn.: Greenwood, 1984; 2nd ed.), p. 167.

46. Quoted in Kenneth J. Hagan, *American Gunboat Diplomacy and the Old Navy* (Westport, Conn.: Greenwood, 1973), p. 37.

47. Russell F. Weigley, *The American Way of War* (New York: Macmillan, 1973), p. 153.

48. Peter Karsten, "Armed Progressives," in Jerry Israel, ed., *Building the Organizational Society* (New York: Free Press, 1972), pp. 196–232.

49. Commander F. J. Higgenson quoted in Shulman, *Navalism*, p. 41.

50. Quoted in Kenneth J. Hagan, "Alfred Thayer Mahan," in Frank Merli and Theodore A. Wilson, eds., *Makers of American Diplomacy* (New York: Charles Scribner's Sons, 1974), p. 290.

51. Shulman, *Navalism*, p. 38.

52. Quoted in Allen Millett and Peter Maslowski, *For the Common Defense* (New York: Free Press, 1984), p. 252.

53. Quoted in Anders Stephanson, *Manifest Destiny* (New York: Hill & Wang, 1995), p. 62.

54. Quoted in Oleh W. Gerus, "The Russian Withdrawal from Alaska: The Decision to Sell," *Revista de historia de America*, LXXV–LXXVI (December 1973), 162.

55. Quoted in Ronald J. Jensen, *The Alaska Purchase and Russian-American Relations* (Seattle: University of Washington Press, 1975), p. 55.

56. Quoted in Milton O. Gustafson, "Seward's Bargain," *Prologue*, XXVI (Winter 1994), 263.

57. Quoted in Norman E. Saul, *Concord & Conflict* (Lawrence: University Press of Kansas, 1996), p. 3.

58. Quoted in Ernest N. Paolino, *The Foundations of the American Empire* (Ithaca: Cornell University Press, 1973), p. 207.

59. Walter Nugent, *Crossings* (Bloomington: Indiana University Press, 1992), p. 144.

60. Reginald C. Stuart, *United States Expansionism and British North America, 1775–1871* (Chapel Hill: University of North Carolina Press, 1988), p. 261.

61. Quoted in Adrian Cook, *The Alabama Claims* (Ithaca: Cornell University Press, 1975), p. 89.

62. Quoted in David P. Crook, *Diplomacy During the American Civil War* (New York: Wiley, 1975), p. 131.

63. Quoted in Gerald M. Craig, *The United States and Canada* (Cambridge: Harvard University Press, 1968), p. 149.

64. Quoted in Lawrence Martin, *The Presidents and the Prime Ministers* (Toronto: Doubleday Canada, 1982), p. 42.

65. Samuel Flagg Bemis, *A Diplomatic History of the United States* (New York: Holt, Rinehart and Winston, 1965; 5th ed.), p. 413.

66. Quoted in Michael H. Hunt, *The Making of a Special Relationship* (New York: Columbia University Press, 1983), p. 115.

67. Quoted in William A. Williams, *The Roots of the Modern American Empire* (New York: Random House, 1969), p. 219.

68. Quoted in Robert B. Davies, "Peacefully Working to Conquer the World," *Business History Review*, XLIII (Autumn 1969), 323.

69. Quoted in David L. Anderson, *Imperialism and Idealism* (Bloomington: Indiana University Press, 1985), pp. 3–4.

70. Quoted in DeConde, *Ethnicity*, p. 50.

71. Quoted in Shih-shan Henry Tsai, *China and the Overseas Chinese in the United States, 1868–1911* (Fayetteville: University of Arkansas Press, 1983), p. 75.

72. Quoted in Craig Storti, *Incident at Bitter Creek* (Ames: Iowa State University Press, 1991), p. 156.

73. Quoted in Frederick C. Drake, *The Empire of the Seas* (Honolulu: University of Hawaii Press, 1984), p. 105.

74. Quoted in Long, *Gold Braid*, p. 379.

75. Quoted in Hunt, *Making of a Special Relationship*, p. 128.

76. Quoted in David M. Pletcher, *The Awkward Years* (Columbia: University of Missouri Press, 1962), p. 70.

77. Quoted in Julius W. Pratt, *Expansionists of 1898* (Chicago: Quadrangle, [1936], 1964), p. 25.

78. Quoted in Helena G. Allen, *Sanford Ballard Dole* (Glendale, Calif.: Arthur H. Clark, 1988), p. 149.

79. Quoted in Walter A. McDougall, *Let the Sea Make a Noise* (New York: BasicBooks, 1993), p. 380.

80. Quoted in Ralph S. Kuykendall, *The Hawaiian Kingdom* (Honolulu: University of Hawaii Press, 1967), p. 603.

81. Quoted in Merze Tate, *The United States and the Hawaiian Kingdom* (New Haven: Yale University Press, 1965), p. 210.

82. Quoted in Tennant S. McWilliams, *The New South Faces the World* (Baton Rouge: Louisiana State University Press, 1988), p. 34.

83. Quoted in Long, *Gold Braid*, p. 391.

84. Quoted in Paul M. Kennedy, *The Samoan Tangle* (New York: Barnes & Noble, 1974), p. 53.

85. Quoted *ibid.*, p. 76.

86. Quoted in Healy, *U.S. Expansionism*, p. 118.

87. Quoted in Jon D. Holstine, "Vermonter in Paradise," *Vermont History*, XLIII (Spring 1975), 140.

88. Quoted in Drake, *Empire of the Seas*, p. 177.

89. Quoted *ibid.*, p. 185.

90. Quoted in Spurr, *Rhetoric*, p. 80.

91. Quoted in Thomas Pakenham, *The Scramble for Africa, 1876–1912* (New York: Random House, 1991), pp. 246–248.

92. Quoted in Elliott P. Skinner, *African Americans and U.S. Policy Toward Africa, 1850–1924* (Washington, D.C.: Howard University Press, 1992), p. 134.

93. Thomas Borstlemann, *Apartheid's Reluctant Uncle* (New York: Oxford University Press, 1993) pp. 8–9.

94. Quoted *ibid.*, p. 117.

95. Quoted in Stephen J. Vallone, "'Weakness Offers Temptation,'" *Diplomatic History, XIX* (Fall 1995), 586.

96. Quoted in Martínez-Fernández, *Between Empires*, p. 169.

97. Quoted in Louis A. Pérez, Jr., *Cuba and the United States* (Athens: University Press of Georgia, 1997; 2nd ed.), p. 59.

98. Quoted in Richard H. Bradford, *The* Virginius *Affair* (Boulder: Colorado Associated University Press, 1980), p. 134.

99. Quoted in Pérez, *Cuba and the United States*, p. 61.

100. Louis A. Pérez, Jr., "Between Baseball and Bullfighting," *Journal of American History, LXXX* (September 1994), 505.

101. Ramón Eduardo Ruíz, *The People of Sonora and Yankee Capitalists* (Tucson: University of Arizona Press, 1988), p. 1.

102. Joseph A. Fry, *John Tyler Morgan and the Search for Southern Autonomy* (Knoxville: University of Tennessee Press, 1992), p. xii.

103. Quoted in Ari Hoogenboom, *Rutherford B. Hayes* (Lawrence: University Press of Kansas, 1995), p. 419.

104. Quoted in Richard Van Alstyne, *The Rising American Empire* (New York: Norton [1960], 1974), p. 163.

105. Quoted in Alice Felt Tyler, *The Foreign Policy of James G. Blaine* (Minneapolis: University of Minnesota Press, 1927), p. 178.

106. Quoted in Robert L. Beisner, *From the Old Diplomacy to the New, 1865–1900* (Arlington Heights, Ill.: Harlan Davidson, 1986; 2nd ed.), p. 102.

107. Quoted in Joyce S. Goldberg, "Consent to Ascent," *Americas, XLI* (July 1984), 22.

108. Quoted in Shulman, *Navalism*, p. 92.

109. Quoted in Kenneth J. Hagan, *This People's Navy* (New York: Free Press, 1991), p. 199.

110. Quoted in William F. Sater, *Chile and the United States* (Athens: University of Georgia Press, 1990), p. 67.

111. Quoted in Ernest R. May, *Imperial Democracy* (New York: Harper and Row [1961], 1973), p. 10.

112. Brook Kroeger, *Nellie Bly* (New York: Times Books, 1994), p. 177.

Imperialist Leap, 1895–1900

"If There Must Be War."   Lord Salisbury and President Grover Cleveland slug it out during the Venezuelan crisis of 1895. According to the historian Richard E. Welch, Jr., Cleveland's "innate talent to identify his personal judgment with righteousness and truth encouraged him to confuse compromise with surrender." (Life, 1896)

❖

DIPLOMATIC CROSSROAD

The Venezuelan Crisis, 1895

Grover Cleveland felt pleased. On July 7, 1895, the day his third daughter was born, he wrote an enthusiastic note to Secretary of State Richard Olney. Just a few days before, Olney had personally delivered a 12,000-word draft document to the president on the Venezuelan boundary dispute. A successful corporate lawyer and former attorney general, Olney fretted and fidgeted. He knew that Cleveland wanted the dispute cleared up, and Olney himself liked to keep his desk tidy. The president's note arrived bearing laudatory words: "It's the best thing of the kind I ever read." Cleveland suggested "a little more softened verbiage here and there," and he directed Olney to send the document to London, which he did on July 20, 1895. Cleveland later christened it Olney's "twenty-inch gun." It was as much Cleveland's weapon as Olney's.[1]

They aimed the gun at Great Britain, which for decades had haggled with Venezuela over the boundary separating that country and British Guiana. A Britisher, Robert Schomburgk, had drawn a line in the 1840s, but nobody liked it. Both sides made claims that went deep into the other's territory. In the 1880s, the discovery of gold in the disputed region—including the largest nugget ever found, 509 ounces—heightened competition. At stake, too, was control of the mouth of the Orinoco River, gateway to the potential trade of northern South America, which U.S. entrepreneurs were beginnning to turn into a "commercial battle-ground."[2] In the 1870s Venezuela had begun to appeal to the United States for help, arguing that the poaching British violated the Monroe Doctrine. Washington repeatedly asked the British to submit the issue to arbitration but met constant rebuff. In December 1894, Cleveland renewed the call for arbitration. After another British refusal, the impatient president ordered the State Department to prepare a report on the boundary question. The "twenty-inch gun" sounded Olney's memorable answer.

Why did Cleveland and Olney become so agitated about the Venezuelan boundary question? First, the political dimension: In the early 1890s the Venezuelan government hired William L. Scruggs, a former U.S. minister to Caracas, to propagandize its case before the American public. His widely circulated pamphlet, *British Aggressions in Venezuela, or the Monroe Doctrine on Trial* (1895), aroused considerable sympathy for the South American nation. Olney himself read it before preparing his blast of July 20. American sentiment soon congealed: The land-grabbing British were robbing a poor hemispheric friend of the United States. A unanimous congressional resolution of February 1895, calling for arbitration, reflected growing U.S. concern. Cleveland listened attentively to such expressions, because his Democratic party had lost badly in the 1894 congressional elections and Republicans were attacking his administration as pusillanimous for not annexing

Hawai'i and for doing nothing when the British briefly landed troops in Nicaragua in April 1895. Cleveland could deflect criticism and recoup Democratic losses by bold action. As one Democrat advised the president: "Turn this Venezuela question up or down, North, South, East or West, and it is a 'winner.'"[3]

The president did not need such partisan inducements. He leaned toward action anyway because of momentous events in the 1890s, the golden age of European imperialism, when the powers were carving up territories in Asia, the Near East, and Africa. The British, already holding large stakes in Latin America, seemed intent on enlarging them. Their recent intervention in Nicaragua looked ominous, like the French intervention in Mexico a generation earlier. "Palpably unjust," as Olney's predecessor Walter Q. Gresham described it, Britain's claim against Venezuela became a symbol of European intrusion into the Western Hemisphere.[4]

The American depression of the 1890s also helped fix attention on Venezuela. Many, including Cleveland, thought that overproduction had caused the slump and expanding foreign trade could cure it. Might the British close off the Orinoco River and hence the markets of the area? At that time, American economic activity in Venezuela was ripening. For example, the National Association of Manufacturers, organized in 1895 to expand exports, chose Caracas as the site for its first permanent overseas display of American products. In short, international competition and economic woes suggested that Venezuela's dispute with Britain threatened U.S. interests.

Cleveland's own character and style colored his response. He did not like bullies. He had already rejected Hawaiian annexation in part because he thought that Americans had bullied the Hawaiians. Now Britain seemed to be arrogantly manhandling the Venezuelans. Seeking an intellectual peg on which to hang their case, the president and Olney found it in a refurbished Monroe Doctrine. Olney's "twenty-inch gun" of July 20, 1895, invoked that venerable principle in bumptious and unvarnished language. The brash message noted that the British claim had grown larger and larger, cutting deeper and deeper into Venezuela, possibly leading to political control. Olney warned that the European partition of Africa might repeat itself in Latin America. The "safety," "honor," and "welfare" of the United States were at stake, and the Monroe Doctrine forbade European intervention leading to control in the Western Hemisphere. He asserted that "any permanent political union between a European and an American state [was] unnatural and inexpedient."

Driven by its national interest, the United States had to intervene in the dispute. "The states of America, South as well as North, by geographical proximity, by natural sympathy, by similarity of governmental constitutions, are friends and allies, commercially and politically, of the United States. To allow the subjugation of any one of them by a European power is, of course, to completely reverse that situation and signifies the loss of all the advantages incident to their natural relations with us." The forceful overriding theme of Olney's proclamation addressed an international audience: "To-day the United States is practically sovereign on this continent, and its fiat is law upon the subjects to which it confines its interposition." And more: The United States's "infinite resources combined with its isolated position render it master of the situation and practically invulnerable as against any or

"The Real British Lion."   A popular American depiction of the British global presence during the crisis over Venezuela. A few years later, President Cleveland himself recalled British behavior as "mean and hoggish." (*New York Evening World,* 1895)

all other powers."[5] Olney, finally, demanded arbitration, vaguely threatened U.S. intervention, and requested a British answer before the president's annual message to Congress in December.

Ambassador to England Thomas Bayard delivered the document to the giant of European diplomats, Lord Salisbury, then doubling as the British prime minister and foreign secretary. The bearded sixty-five-year-old Salisbury struck an imposing figure—intelligent, aristocratic, cautious, well read. He received the missive with some surprise and sent it to the Foreign Office for study. Distracted by crises elsewhere (especially in Africa), Salisbury saw no urgency. In the late nineteenth century American Anglophobic bombast was not unusual. The issue, he thought, would probably fizzle out once American politics calmed down. Nor did he relish arbitrating any question that might weaken the British Empire. The British reply did not arrive until after Cleveland's annual message (actually tame on the Venezuelan controversy). Salisbury's note, which smacked of "the peremptory schoolmaster trying—with faded patience—to correct the ignorance of dullards in Washington," denied the applicability of the Monroe Doctrine and dismissed any U.S. interest in the dispute.[6]

Cleveland, all 250 pounds of him, was duck-hunting in North Carolina when the British response reached Washington. On his return he read it and became "mad clean through."[7] Now what? War? Retreat? Olney struggled for alternatives and finally selected one that left some maneuvering room, kept diplomacy in the hands of the executive branch, and avoided war or backstepping: an American study commission appointed by the president. Cleveland's special message to Congress on December 17 rang the alarm bell. England must arbitrate; the United States would create an investigating commission to set the true boundary line; and then American action would follow. Most observers labeled the message an ultimatum, with the possibility of war lurking throughout.

The nation buzzed in anticipation. Congress appropriated funds for the investigating commission. Irish-Americans volunteered to fight the hated British. Both Republicans and Democrats lined up behind the president, and Senator Henry Cabot Lodge noted with approval that "Jingoes are plenty enough now."[8] New York City police commissioner Theodore Roosevelt boomed: "Let the fight come if it must; I don't care whether our sea coast cities are bombarded or not; we would take Canada."[9] Many business leaders rallied behind the administration, with Whitelaw Reid, editor of the *New York Tribune,* hyperbolically declaring that "this is the golden opportunity of our merchants to extend our trade to every quarter of Central and South America."[10] British ambassador Sir Julian Pauncefote reported: "Nothing is heard but the voice of the Jingo bellowing defiance to England."[11]

Jingo fevers subsided rapidly in early 1896. Many bankers and business people became alarmed when the stock market plummeted, in large part because British investors were pulling out. Joseph Pulitzer's *New York World* put out a special Christmas issue with portraits of the Prince of Wales and Lord Salisbury under the headline "PEACE AND GOOD WILL," implying that a war was unconscionable with Britain, a country so close in race, language, and culture.[12] Critics such as E. L. Godkin, editor of *The Nation,* and respected international law specialist John Bassett Moore pointed out how haughtily Cleveland and Olney had acted. Even Ambassador Bayard feared that the president had been "too *precipitate,* for I do not see why he should abandon suddenly his attitude of conservatism and go apparently into the camp of aggressiveness."[13] But Cleveland never wanted war. He wanted peace on U.S. terms.

What followed seemed anticlimactic. The British cabinet, on January 11, 1896, instructed Salisbury to seek an "honourable settlement" with the United States.[14] A new dispute with Germany over South Africa necessitated retreat. England needed friends now, not enemies. British troops could not defend Canada, and the Admiralty thought that the Royal Navy was outgunned in the North Atlantic and Caribbean. Formal talks continued until November 1896, when Britain and the United States agreed to set up a five-person arbitral board to define the boundary, with each to name two members, who would in turn select the fifth. Finally, in October 1899, the tribunal reached a decision that rejected the extreme claims of each party and generally followed the Schomburgk line. The pivotal Point Barima at the mouth of the Orinoco went to Venezuela, which came out of the dispute pretty well, considering that neither the United States nor Great Britain cared much about *Venezuela*'s national interest.

In fact, the United States negotiated directly with Britain without ever consulting Venezuela. Both parties excluded Venezuela's duly accredited minister in Washington from the talks. Olney never even gave the Venezuelans a copy of his "twenty-inch gun" (they eventually read it in the newspapers); and when they balked over the 1896 Anglo-American agreement, he curtly made one concession: Venezuela could name one of the five members of the arbitration board—so long as that person was not a Venezuelan. Lobbyist William Scruggs complained that the

United States sought to "*bull-doze* Venezuela."[15] He had it right, but Washington's vigorous diplomacy targeted others besides that South American nation. The overweening theme of Olney's "twenty-inch gun" merits repeating: "To-day the United States is practically sovereign on this continent, and its fiat is law upon the subjects to which it confines its interposition."

Men of Empire in the 1890s

The Venezuelan crisis punctuated an era of imperialist competition when, as one senator grandly put it: "The great nations are rapidly absorbing . . . all the waste areas of the earth. It is a moment which makes for civilization and the advancement of the race."[16] Cleveland and Olney helped move the United States toward world-power status. As an example of forceful, even aggressive, American diplomacy, the Venezuelan controversy accelerated important trends. Besides ignoring the rights and sensibilities of small nations, it revealed a United States more sure of itself, more certain about the components of its "policy," and willing to lecture others. The episode stimulated what critics at the time called "jingoism." The Monroe Doctrine gained new stature as a warning to European nations to curb their activities in the Western Hemisphere. The executive branch kept the Venezuelan issue in *its* hands, thereby strengthening the foreign-policy power of the president by going to the brink of war without consulting Congress.

Other ramifications became evident. Latin Americans learned once again that the United States intended to establish supremacy in the Western Hemisphere and would intervene when it saw fit. The United States had always kept an eye on the Caribbean, but the Venezuelan crisis and the outbreak of revolution in Cuba in 1895 intensified North American interest, a significant dimension of which was economic. The Venezuelan issue and the disposition of the Orinoco River also brought more attention to the theory of overproduction as a cause of depression, which exports could allegedly cure. Commercial expansion, always a trend in American history, received another boost.

The discord with Britain over Venezuela helped foster Anglo-American rapprochement. Cooperation and mutual interest increasingly characterized relations between Washington and London. British diplomats sought U.S. friendship as a possible counterweight to growing German power, and Britain's willingness to permit the United States to govern Caribbean affairs facilitated the emerging entente.

One way, the chief way, the United States could manage events in that area was through naval power. The Venezuelan crisis, joined by crises in Asia and the belief that naval construction would employ those idled by depression, stimulated additional American naval expansion. The Navy Act of 1896, for example, provided for three new battleships and ten new torpedo boats. All told, then, the Venezuelan boundary dispute advanced the United States along the path of expansion.

That path, by the end of the decade, led to new U.S. colonies in the Pacific, Asia, and the Caribbean, a firm hold on independent Cuba, and Europe's recognition of U.S. hegemony in the Caribbean. By 1900, too, the United States had pledged itself to preserve the "Open Door" in China; it had built a navy that had

"Either Caesar or Nothing!" Uncle Sam protests against imperialism but refuses to return to his cramped log cabin now that he has taken up "skyscraper" diplomacy, according to this German cartoon. (*Kladderadatsch,* 1899)

just annihilated the Spanish fleet and ranked sixth in the world; and it had developed an export trade amounting to $1.5 billion. Steel and iron production exemplified its industrial might, which almost equaled that of Britain and Germany combined. U.S. acquisition of new colonies after the Spanish-American-Cuban-Filipino War suggests that *only then,* about 1898, did the United States become an imperialist world power. But what actually happened, one scholar writes, was a "culmination" not an "aberration."[17] Having taken halting steps toward a larger empire before the depression of the 1890s, the United States then took the leap.

Assistant Secretary of the Navy Theodore Roosevelt described the anti-imperialists in 1897 as "men of a by-gone age" and "provincials."[18] Indeed, anti-imperialism waned through the late nineteenth century. Increasing numbers of educated, economically comfortable Americans made the case for formal empire (colonies or protectorates) or informal empire (commercial domination). Naval officers, diplomats, politicians, farmers, skilled artisans, business leaders, and clergy made up what political scientists call the "foreign-policy public." Better read than

Grover Cleveland (1837–1908).
This portrait of the two-term president, overweight from frequenting saloons as a young man, exhibits the gruff American attitude toward Britain during the Venezuelan crisis. The historian Dexter Perkins wrote that Cleveland was "so honest, so brave, so independent . . . , but also so rigid and inflexible in his thinking, so unimaginative, so dogmatic." (Library of Congress)

most Americans and having access to lecterns to disperse their ideas, this "elite" helped move America to war and empire. Neither "public opinion," nor the jingoistic "yellow press," nor the "people" in the 1890s compelled the United States to war. Rather, two key elements stand out: a McKinley administration very much in charge of its diplomacy through skillful maneuvering, and a majoritarian view within the articulate "foreign-policy public" in favor of a vigorous outward thrust.

Analysis of the phrase "public opinion" helps explain the *hows* as distinct from the *whys* of decisionmaking. One often hears that "public opinion" or "the man in the street" influenced a leader to follow a certain course of action. But "public opinion" did not comprise a unified, identifiable group speaking with one voice. Further, political leaders and other articulate, knowledgeable people often shaped the "public opinion" they wanted to hear by their very handling of events and their control over information—that is, leaders *led*. In trying to determine who the "people" are and what "public opinion" is, social-science studies demonstrate that in the 1890s the people who counted, the people who expressed their opinion publicly in order to influence policy, numbered no more than 1.5 million to 3 million, or between 10 and 20 percent of the voting public. This percentage—upper- and middle-income groups, educated, active politically—constituted the "foreign-policy public." As Secretary of State Walter Q. Gresham put it in 1893: "After all, public opinion is made and controlled by the thoughtful men of the country."[19] The "public opinion" the president heard in the 1890s did not come from the "people," but rather from a small, articulate segment of the American population alert to foreign-policy issues. Although this educated public counted anti-imperialists among them, including substantial numbers of women activists, the "foreign-policy public" leaned heavily toward the side of imperialism.

The president, as a consummate politician and good tactician, often dominates policymaking, even thwarting the advice of the "foreign-policy public" itself. President Cleveland, for example, successfully resisted pressure to annex Hawai'i and withdrew the treaty from the Senate, and he never let Congress or influential public opinion set the terms of his policy toward the Venezuelan crisis. Pressures from jingoes in Congress and a sensationalist press intruded in the 1890s, but the initiative in foreign affairs, unlike in the 1860s and 1870s, remained largely in the hands of the men in the executive branch. In most historical periods, the public *reacts* to *immediate* events; the executive *acts* and *manages* with *long-term* policy considerations.

Cleveland Confronts *Cuba Libre*, 1895–1897

The year 1895 brought momentous events. The Venezuelan crisis, Japan's defeat of China in the Sino-Japanese War, and the outbreak of revolution in Cuba—all carried profound meaning for U.S. foreign relations. The sugar-rich island of Cuba, since the close of its unsuccessful war for independence (1868–1878), suffered political repression and poverty. After that war Cuban nationalists prepared for a new assault on their Spanish overlords. From 1880 to 1895, Cuban national hero José Martí plotted from exile in the United States. In 1892 he organized the Cuban Revolutionary party, using U.S. territory to recruit men and money. Martí's op-

Makers of American Foreign Relations, 1895–1900

Presidents	Secretaries of State
Grover Cleveland, 1893–1897	Walter Q. Gresham, 1893–1895
	Richard Olney, 1895–1897
William McKinley, 1897–1901	John Sherman, 1897–1898
	William R. Day, 1898
	John Hay, 1898–1905

portunity came when Cuba's economy fell victim in 1894 to a new U.S. tariff, which raised duties on imported sugar and hence reduced Cuban sugar shipments to the United States. On February 24, 1895, with cries of "*Cuba Libre*," the rebels opened their drive for independence.

Cuban revolutionaries kept a cautious eye on the United States, well known for its relentless interest in the island, and thus feared an ultimate U.S. attempt to control their nation's destiny. José Martí's fifteen-year stay in the United States had turned him into a critic of what he called "the monster"—an "aggressive" and "avaricious" nation "full of hate" and "widespread spiritual coarseness." And he warned against a U.S. "conquering policy" that "arrogantly" treated Latin American countries as "dependencies."[20] On May 19 Martí died in action.

Cuban and Spanish military strategies produced destruction and death. Led by General Máximo Gómez, a veteran of the 1868–1878 war, the *insurrectos* burned cane fields, blew up mills, and disrupted railroads, with the goal of rendering Cuba an economic liability to Spain. "The chains of Cuba have been forged by her own richness," Gómez proclaimed, "and it is precisely this which I propose to do away with soon."[21] Although outnumbered (about 30,000 Cuban troops fought 200,000 Spanish) and lacking adequate supplies, the insurgents, with the sympathy of the populace, wore the Spanish down through guerrilla tactics. Journalists covering this phase of the war included the young Briton Winston S. Churchill, who reported the thrill of being "shot at without result."[22] By late 1896 rebels controlled about two-thirds of the island, with the Spanish concentrated in coastal and urban regions. That year, to break the rebel stronghold in the rural areas, Governor-General Valeriano y Nicolau Weyler instituted the brutal reconcentration program. He divided the island into districts and then herded a half-million Cubans into fortified camps, where frightful sanitation conditions, poor food, and disease contributed to the death of perhaps 200,000 people. Weyler's soldiers regarded any Cubans outside the camps as rebels and hence targets for death; they also killed livestock, destroyed crops, and polluted water sources. This effort to starve the insurgents and deprive them of physical and moral support, combined with the rebels' destructive behavior, made a shambles of Cuba's society and economy.

The Cleveland administration faced several alternatives. It could recognize Cuban belligerency. But such an act, Olney noted, would relieve Spain of any responsibility for paying claims filed by Americans for properties destroyed in Cuba.

Cleveland and Olney found recognition of Cuban independence even less appetizing, for they believed the Cubans incapable of self-government and feared anarchy and even racial war. That course might also arouse a Spanish declaration of war or force U.S. belligerency because, logically, a Spanish attempt to conquer an "independent" Cuba would constitute a violation of the Monroe Doctrine. Olney toyed with buying the island at one point. The Cleveland administration settled on a dual policy of hostility to the revolution and pressure on Spain to grant some autonomy. Diplomacy and lecturing to a foreign government seemed to work in the Venezuelan crisis; perhaps it would work with Cuba.

Prodded by a Republican Congress (it passed a resolution in April 1896, urging the president to recognize Cuban belligerency), by continued evidence of wholesale destruction, and by Spanish obstinacy in refusing reforms and adhering to force, Olney sent a note to Spain in April 1896. He urged a political solution that would leave "Spain her rights of sovereignty . . . yet secure to the [Cubans] all such rights and powers of local self-government as they [could] ask."[23] Spain should initiate reforms short of independence. Olney showed particular concern for the interests of Americans, not those of the Cubans. With American property estimated at $50 million, the decline in sugar production wrought disaster to Cuban-American trade relations. In 1892 Cuba had shipped to the United States goods worth $79 million; by 1898 that figure had slumped to $15 million.

When Spain rejected Olney's advice, the Cleveland administration seemed stymied. It did not desire war, but it meant to protect U.S. interests. Congress kept asking for firm action. And in Havana, hotheaded American consul-general Fitzhugh Lee clamored for U.S. annexation. Cleveland did not feel he could fire Lee, nephew of General Robert E. Lee, because the incumbent president needed political friends at a time when Democrats were dumping him in favor of William Jennings Bryan. Consul-General Lee also warned that "there may be a revolution within a revolution," noting that Cuban insurgents vowed to redistribute property, which U.S. officials (and Creole elites) would not tolerate.[24] It further nettled Cleveland and Olney that Spain had approached the courts of Europe for diplomatic support, with the argument that the Monroe Doctrine threatened all European powers. Spain's appeal went unheeded, but leaders in Washington still worried about possible European intrusion in Cuba.

British ambassador to Spain H. Drummond Wolff accurately claimed that for Cuba the United States wanted "peace with commerce."[25] In December 1896, Cleveland reported that neither the Spanish nor the Cuban rebels had established their authority over the island. Americans felt a humanitarian concern, he said, and their trade and investments ("pecuniary interest") faced destruction. Further, to maintain its neutrality, the United States had to police the coastline to intercept unlawful expeditions. Spain must grant autonomy or "home rule," but not independence, to "fertile and rich" Cuba to end the bloodshed and devastation. Otherwise, the United States, having thus far acted with "restraint," might abandon its "expectant attitude."[26]

But Cleveland had more bark than bite. Through Olney he successfully buried a Senate resolution urging recognition of Cuban independence and contented himself with some limited Spanish reforms of February 1897. Thereafter he let the Cuban issue fester, bequeathing it to the incoming McKinley administration.

McKinley's Road to War, 1897–1898

A veteran Republican politician and deft manager of people, President William McKinley had defeated William Jennings Bryan in the election of 1896. The tee-totaling Ohioan seemed a stable, dignified figure in a time of crisis. He projected deep religious conviction, personal warmth, sincerity, commitment to economic development and the revival of business, party loyalty, and support for expansion abroad. Yet McKinley often gave the appearance of being a pliant follower, a mind-less flunky of the political bosses. One joke went: "Why is McKinley's mind like a bed?" Answer: "Because it has to be made up for him every time he wants to use it." Plucky Theodore Roosevelt allegedly remarked that McKinley had "no more backbone than a chocolate éclair."[27] Such an image was created in large part by bel-licose imperialists who believed that McKinley was not moving fast enough and by critics of domestic policy such as Bryan who saw McKinley as clay in the hands of big business and party machines. Certainly a party regular and friend of large cor-porations, the president was no lackey. A manager of diplomacy, who wanted ex-pansion and empire without war and a settlement of the Cuban question without U.S. military intervention, McKinley acted as his own man.

McKinley shared America's image of itself as an expanding, virile nation of su-perior institutions and as a major power in Latin America. He agreed that the United States must have a large navy, overseas commerce, and foreign bases. He be-lieved strongly that America must export its surplus goods. As a tariff specialist, he favored high tariffs on manufactured goods, low tariffs on raw materials, and reci-procity agreements. Although McKinley uttered almost nothing about foreign is-sues in the campaign of 1896, the Republican party platform overflowed with expansionist rhetoric. It urged American control of Hawai'i, a Nicaraguan canal run by the United States, an enlarged navy, purchase of the Virgin Islands, and Cuban independence. Between election and inauguration, however, McKinley quietly joined Cleveland and Olney in sidetracking a Senate resolution for recognition of Cuba. He wanted a free hand, and he did not believe that Cubans could govern themselves. His appointment of the old and ailing Senator John Sherman as secre-tary of state suggested further that McKinley would take charge of his own diplo-macy. His inaugural address vacuously urged peace, never mentioning the Cuban crisis.

McKinley's first tilt with Congress came in March 1897. Resolutions on Cuba sprang up repeatedly, but the president managed to kill them. He did satisfy impe-rialists by sending a Hawaiian annexation treaty to the Senate. The president was preparing for his own nonpublic diplomatic assault on Spain. In June, Madrid re-ceived an American reprimand for Weyler's uncivilized warfare and for his disrup-tion of the Cuban economy. Spain, however, showed no signs of tempering its military response to the insurrection. American citizens languished in Spanish jails;

William McKinley (1843–1901). A Civil War vet-eran and long-time member of Congress, the twenty-fifth presi-dent displayed supreme political skills in his quest for empire. An aide wrote in his diary in 1898 that McKinley "is the strong man of the Cabinet, the dominating force; but with it all are such gentleness and graciousness." An assassin killed him in Buffalo, New York. (Library of Congress)

American property continued to be razed. Fitzhugh Lee, who remained at his post in Havana, bellowed for U.S. intervention. In July, McKinley instructed the new American minister to Spain, Stewart L. Woodford, to demand that the Spanish stop the fighting. Increasingly convinced that the Cuban *insurrectos* would not compromise, the president implored Spain to grant autonomy. A new Spanish government soon moderated policy by offering Cuba a substantial degree of self-government. Even more, it removed the hated Weyler and promised to end reconcentration. Never fully implemented, these reforms did not end the fighting, because the Cuban junta demanded full independence.

McKinley's December 6, 1897, annual message to Congress discussed the Cuban insurrection at great length. Voicing the "gravest apprehension," McKinley rejected annexation as "criminal aggression." He argued against recognition of belligerency, because the rebels hardly constituted a government worthy of recognition. And he ruled out intervention as premature at a time when the Spanish were traveling the "honorable paths" of reform. He asked for patience to see if Spanish changes would work, but he hinted that the United States would keep open all policy options, including intervention "with force."[28]

By mid-January evidence had poured into Washington proving that the reforms had not moderated the crisis; in fact, insurgents, conservatives, and the Spanish army all denounced them. Antireform Spaniards rioted in Havana. The United States ordered the warship *Maine* to Havana on January 24, 1898, to protect American citizens and demonstrate concern. On February 9, the State Department received a copy of a private letter written in late 1897 by Spanish minister to the United States Enrique Dupuy de Lôme and sent to a senior Spanish politician touring Cuba. Intercepted in Cuba by a rebel sympathizer who forwarded it to the Cuban junta in New York City. Not only did it reach the State Department, but William Randolph Hearst's flamboyant *New York Journal* published it that day with the banner headline: "Worst Insult to the United States in its History." De Lôme labeled McKinley "weak," a "bidder for the admiration of the crowd," and a "would-be politician."[29] McKinley, along with most Americans, found de Lôme's remarks infuriating. The administration particularly resented another statement that suggested that Spain did not take its reform proposals seriously and would persist in fighting to defeat the rebels. Spain, it appeared, had tricked the United States. De Lôme's hasty recall hardly salved the hurt.

Trying to avoid war, a restless McKinley nevertheless recognized the dangerous trend. On occasion in early 1898 he had to take drugs to sleep. The rush of events did not improve his demeanor. Less than a week after the de Lôme episode, on February 15, explosions ripped through the *Maine,* anchored conspicuously in Havana harbor. Two hundred sixty-six of 354 U.S. officers and crew died as the 6,700-ton vessel sank quickly. With no evidence but with considerable emotion many Americans assumed that Spain had committed the dastardly deed. McKinley ordered an official investigation and decided to try diplomacy and threat again. In early March, Woodford protested strongly to the Spanish government about the de Lôme incident and the *Maine.* The "grave" Cuban crisis had to be resolved. On March 6 the president met with Joe Cannon, chair of the House Committee on Appropriations, and urged him to present a bill providing $50 million for arms. "It

The U.S.S. *Maine* Before and After.
Part of the battleship was raised in 1911, investigated, and sunk at sea with flag flying. The investigators concluded that an external explosion of unknown origins destroyed the vessel. Notwithstanding a 1976 navy study by Admiral Hyman G. Rickover that blamed the sinking on an internal accident, the historians Harold and Peggy Samuels, in *Remembering the* Maine (1995), argue anew that the ship exploded because of an external mine, most likely planted by Spanish zealots. (Before—*Harper's Weekly,* 1888; after—National Archives)

seemed as though a hundred Fourths of July had been let loose in the House," a clerk noted, as Congress enthusiastically obliged three days later.[30] Spain, Woodford reported, was stunned by the appropriation.

In mid-March Senator Redfield Proctor of Vermont, a friend of McKinley reportedly opposed to war, graphically told his colleagues about his recent trip to Cuba. He recounted ugly stories about the reconcentration camps. "Torn from their homes, with foul earth, foul air, foul water, and foul food or none, what wonder that one-half died and that one-quarter of the living are so diseased that they cannot be saved?"[31] Shortly after this moving speech, which convinced many members of Congress and business leaders that Spain could not bring order to Cuba, the American court of inquiry on the *Maine* concluded that an external mine of unknown origins had destroyed the vessel. A Spanish commission at about the same time attributed the disaster to an internal explosion. In 1898 vocal Americans pinned the crime squarely on Spain. "Remember the *Maine,* to hell with Spain" became the popular chant.

Such events inexorably narrowed options. The president did explore the possibility of purchasing Cuba for $300 million—or some other means "by which Spain can part with Cuba without loss of respect and with certainty of American control."[32] But a jingo frenzy had seized the Congress. Following one stormy Senate session, Vice President Garrett Hobart warned McKinley: "They will act without you if you do not act at once." "Say no more," McKinley responded.[33] On March 27 Washington cabled the U.S. demands; an armistice, Cuban-Spanish negotiations to secure a peace, McKinley's arbitration of the conflict if there was no peace by October, termination of the reconcentration policy, and relief aid to the Cubans. Implicit was the demand that Spain grant Cuba its independence under U.S. supervision. As a last-ditch effort to avoid American military intervention, the ultimatum had little chance of success. Spain's national pride and interest precluded surrender. Madrid's answer showed promise: It had already terminated reconcentration, would launch reforms, and would accept an armistice if the rebels did so first. By refusing McKinley's mediation and Cuban independence, the Spanish reply did not satisfy the president or Congress. McKinley began to write a war message in early April. On the ninth, Spain made a new concession, declaring a unilateral suspension of hostilities "for such length of time" as the Spanish commander "may think prudent."[34] Too qualified, the declaration still sidestepped Cuban independence and U.S. mediation. Any chance of European intervention ended when the British told Washington that they would "be guided [on Cuban issues] by the wishes of the President."[35]

Why War: Exploiting Opportunity

On April 11 McKinley asked Congress for authority to use armed force to end the Cuban war. Since neither Cubans nor Spaniards could stem the flow of blood, Americans would do so because of the "cause of humanity" and the "very serious injury to the commerce, trade, and business of our people, and the wanton destruction of property." And, citing the *Maine,* McKinley described the conflict as "a constant menace to our peace." At the very end of the message, noting that Spain had recently offered an armistice, the president asked Congress to give this new information "your just and careful attention."[36]

As Congress debated an armistice that the Cubans themselves rejected, McKinley beat back a Senate attempt to recognize the rebels. He strongly believed that Cuba needed American tutelage to prepare for self-government. Indeed, as the historian Louis A. Pérez, Jr., has argued, McKinley's decision for war may have been "directed as much against Cuban independence as it was against Spanish sovereignty."[37] Congress did endorse the Teller Amendment, which disclaimed any U.S. intention of annexing the island. Some who voted for the amendment feared that annexation would commit the United States to assume Cuba's large bond debt. On April 19 Congress proclaimed Cuba's independence (but without recognizing the Cuban junta), demanded Spain's evacuation from the island, and directed the president to use force to ensure these results. Spain, on April 21, broke diplomatic relations. On the twenty-second, American ships began to blockade Cuba; two days later Spain declared war. On the twenty-fifth, Congress declared that a state of war had existed from the twenty-first.

Because of the Teller Amendment, the decision for war seemed selfless and humanitarian, and for many Americans it undoubtedly was. But the decision had more complex motives. Different people endorsed war for different reasons. McKinley himself cited humanitarian concern, property, commerce, and the removal of an annoyance. Politics also mattered. Senator Lodge, among others, told the White House that "if the war in Cuba drags on through the summer . . . we [Republicans] shall go down to the greatest defeat ever known."[38] Important business leaders, initially hesitant, shifted in March and April to demand an end to Cuban disorder. Farmers and business leaders interested in Asian and Latin American markets thought victory against Spain might open new trade doors by eliminating a colonial power. Many highly moralistic Americans simply felt compelled to end the bloodshed. Republican senator George F. Hoar of Massachusetts, later an anti-imperialist, could not "look idly on while hundreds of thousands of innocent human beings . . . die of hunger close to our doors. If there is ever to be a war it should be to prevent such things."[39] Lyman Abbott, well-known pastor of Plymouth Church in Brooklyn, thought war the "answer to America to the question of its own conscience: Am I my brother's keeper?"[40] Ending Spanish rule in Cuba, declared a Catholic priest, would get rid of all that "is old and vile and rotten and mean and cruel and false."[41] Church missionaries dreamed of new opportunities to convert the "uncivilized." Imperialists hoped war would add new territories to the United States and encourage the growth of a larger navy. "Warriors" differed from "imperialists" in that some people opposed empire and sincerely thought war would halt the long conflict in Cuba, whereas the imperialists seized on war as an opportunity to expand the American empire.

Emotional nationalism also mattered. The de Lôme and *Maine* incidents stimulated a national anger already infused with notions of American superiority, racial and otherwise. Imperialist senator Albert Beveridge waxed ebullient: "At last, God's hour has struck. The American people go forth in a warfare holier than liberty—holy as humanity."[42] The journalist Finley Peter Dunne's popular Irish-American characters provided a fitting summary: "'We're a gr-reat people,' said Mr. Hennessy, earnestly. 'We ar-re,' said Mr. Dooley. 'We ar-re that. An' th best iv it is, we know we ar-re.'"[43] Excited statements by people such as Roosevelt, who looked on war as he looked on horseback riding and cowboying in the Dakotas— a sport, a game, fun—aroused martial fevers. Newspapers of the "yellow press" variety, such as Hearst's *New York Journal* and Pulitzer's *New York World*, sensationalized stories of Spanish atrocities. Others proudly compared the Cuban and American revolutions. The American people, already steeped in a brash nationalism and prepared by earlier aggressive diplomatic triumphs, reacted favorably to this hyperbole.

"Cuba Reconciling the North and South."   Captain Fritz W. Guerin's 1898 photograph trumpeted nationalism in the Spanish-American-Cuban-Filipino War. Golden-haired Cuba, liberated from her chains by her North American heroes, oversees the reconciliation of the Union and Confederacy in a splashy display of patriotism. (Library of Congress)

Both Washington and Madrid had tried diplomacy, but their diplomatic paths never crossed. McKinley wanted "peace" and independence for Cuba under U.S. tutelage. The first Spain could not deliver because the Cuban rebels had become entrenched and bent on independence and Spanish forces remained weak. The second Spain could not grant immediately for fear that ultranationalists might overthrow the Bourbon constitutional monarchy. Spain said it would fight the war more humanely and grant autonomy, but McKinley and Congress wanted more, and they believed they had the right and duty to judge the affairs of Spain and Cuba.

Critics said America might have been less haughty, letting the Cubans and Spaniards settle their own affairs. McKinley's actions in dispatching the *Maine* and asking Congress for $50 million probably encouraged the Cuban rebels to resist any compromise. He might have given Spain a bit more breathing space. Spain, after all, did fire Weyler, terminate reconcentration, and approve an armistice; most important, Madrid did grant partial autonomy, which ultimately might have led to independence. Some critics said the president should have recognized the Cuban insurgents and covertly aided them, and then American soldiers would not necessarily have had to fight in Cuba, the Philippines, and Puerto Rico. American matériel, not men, in other words, might have liberated Cuba from Spanish rule. McKinley wanted to avoid war, and he only reluctantly chose it after trying other options. That he adamantly refused to recognize the insurgency or the republic suggests also that the president did not endorse outright Cuban independence. He probably had two goals in 1898: to remove Spain from Cuba and to control Cuba in some manner yet ill defined. When the Spanish balked at a sale and both belligerents rejected compromise, McKinley opted for war—the only means to oust Spain *and* to control Cuba.

The Spanish-American-Cuban-Filipino War

Americans flocked to recruiting stations and enlisted in what they trumpeted as a glorious expedition to demonstrate U.S. right and might. They were cocky. Young author Sherwood Anderson joked that fighting Spain would be "like robbing an old gypsy woman in a vacant lot at night after a fair."[44] U.S. ambassador to England John Hay called it a "splendid little war," and Theodore Roosevelt, who resigned as assistant secretary of the navy to lead the flashy but overrated Rough Riders, remarked that "it wasn't much of a war, but it was the best war we had."[45] It was a short war, ending August 12, but 5,462 Americans died in it—only 379 of them in combat. Most of the rest met death from malaria and yellow fever. As hundreds of disease-wracked men came home to be quarantined on the tip of Long Island, a surgeon wrote: "The pale faces, the sunken eyes, the staggering gait and the emaciated forms" marked some as "wrecks for life" and others as "candidates for a premature grave."[46]

Led by officers seasoned in the Civil War and in campaigns against Native Americans, the new imperial fighters embarked from Florida in mid-June. Seventeen thousand men, clutching their Krag-Jörgensen rifles, crammed into the flotilla for a week. They ate hardtack and tasteless canned beef, drank bitter coffee, waited anxiously, and got seasick. On June 22 they disembarked on Cuban soil, finding no Spanish resistance. Cuban insurgents met with American officers, and they agreed to help one another against Spanish forces.

Yet the big news had already arrived from the Philippine Islands, Spain's major colony in Asia. Only days after the American declaration of war, Commodore George Dewey sailed his Asiatic Squadron from Hong Kong to Manila Bay, where he smashed the Spanish fleet with the loss of one sailor. Slipping by the Spanish guns at Corregidor, Dewey entered the bay at night. Early in the morning of May 1 his flagship *Olympia* began to demolish the ten incompetently handled Spanish ships. With his laconic order, "You may fire when ready, Gridley," Dewey quickly became a first-line hero. Some people, ignorant of American interests in the Pacific, the beckoning China market, and the feebleness of Spanish rule over the Philippines, wondered how a war to liberate Cuba saw its first action in Asia. Although probably few Americans knew the location of the Philippines, naval officials had pinpointed them in contingency plans as early as 1896. Often credited alone with ordering Dewey on February 25, 1898, to attack Manila if war broke out, Assistant Secretary of the Navy Theodore Roosevelt actually set in motion preexisting war plans already known and approved by the president. After the war, when the Navy Department balked at revealing its advance preparations, Roosevelt was "naturally delighted at shouldering the responsibility."[47]

By late June, U.S. troops in Cuba had advanced toward Santiago, where dispirited Spanish soldiers manned antique guns. Joined by experienced Cuban rebels, the North Americans on July 1 battled for San Juan Hill. American forces, spearheaded by the Rough Riders and the black soldiers of the Ninth Cavalry, finally captured the strategic promontory overlooking Santiago after suffering heavy casualties. Two days later the Spanish fleet, penned in Santiago harbor for weeks by U.S. warships, made a desperate daylight break for open sea. Some U.S. vessels nearly collided as they hurried to sink the helpless Spanish craft, which went down with 323 dead. Its fleet destroyed, Spain entered its imperial death throes. Santiago soon surrendered.

U.S. troops also invaded another Spanish colony, Puerto Rico, which expansionists such as Roosevelt coveted as a Caribbean base for a "proper navy" and a strategic post that might help protect a Central American canal.[48] In nineteen days General Nelson A. Miles, losing only three soldiers, captured the sugar- and coffee-exporting island. At least at first, the Puerto Rican elite welcomed their new North American masters as an improvement over their Spanish rulers.

Manila capitulated in mid-August, after the Spanish put up token resistance in a deal with Dewey that salvaged Spanish pride and kept Filipino nationalist Emilio Aguinaldo from the walled city. Washington soon ordered Aguinaldo and other Filipino rebels, who had fought against the Spanish for independence since 1896 and had surrounded Manila for weeks, to remain outside the capital and to recognize the authority of the United States.

In July, to ensure uninterrupted reinforcement of Dewey, the United States officially absorbed Hawai'i, where ships took on coal en route to Manila. From 1893 to 1897, when Cleveland refused annexation, politics in Hawai'i had changed little. The white revolutionaries clung to power. Once elected, McKinley proclaimed: "We need Hawai'i . . . a good deal more than we did California. It is manifest destiny."[49] After negotiating a new treaty with the white-led Hawaiian government, he adopted the ploy of asking for a joint resolution. On July 7, 1898, Congress passed the resolution for annexation by a majority vote (290 to 91 in the House and 42 to 21 in the Senate), thereby formally attaching the strategically and commercially important islands to the United States.

Peace and Empire: The Debate in the United States

Spain sued for peace, and on August 12 the belligerents proclaimed an armistice. To negotiate with the Spanish in Paris, McKinley appointed a "peace commission" loaded with imperialists and headed by Secretary of State William R. Day, friend and follower of the president's wishes. As negotiations continued into autumn, and after McKinley tested public opinion by touring the Midwest, he chose to demand all of the Philippines, the island of Guam in the Marianas, and Puerto Rico, as well as to make Cuba independent. Articulate Filipinos pleaded for their country's freedom but met a stern U.S. rebuff. Spanish diplomats accepted this American land grab after the United States offered $20 million as compensation. In early December, U.S. delegates signed the treaty and walked out of the elegant French conference room with the Philippines, Puerto Rico, and Guam.

"Hurrah for Imperialism." This anti-imperialist cartoon expressed the fear that the United States was walking blindly along a disastrous path of empire. Anti-imperialists lost the debate in part because Uncle Sam knew where he was going in adding new territories to the U.S. domain. (*Life,* 1898)

Anti-imperialists howled in protest. They had organized the Anti-Imperialist League in Boston in November 1898, but they never acted in unison. They counted among their number such unlikely bedfellows as steel magnate Andrew Carnegie, labor leader Samuel Gompers, agrarian spokesman William Jennings Bryan, Massachusetts senator George Hoar, Harvard president Charles W. Eliot, and the humorist Mark Twain—people who had often disagreed on domestic issues. Some anti-imperialists took inconsistent positions. Hoar, the most outspoken senator against the treaty, had voted for war and annexation of Hawai'i. An expansionist, Carnegie apparently would accept colonies if they could be taken without force. He even offered to write a personal check for $20 million to buy the independence of the Philippines. And the anti-imperialists could not overcome the *fait accompli,* possession and occupation of territory, handed them by McKinley. After all, argued the president, could America really let loose of this real estate so nobly taken in battle?

The anti-imperialists denounced the thesis that greatness lay in colonies. Some of them wanted trade too, but not at the cost of subjugating other peoples. The anti-imperialist David Starr Jordan, president of Stanford University, spoke of the "peaceful conquest" of Mexico by trade rather than by annexation.[50] Quoting the Declaration of Independence and Washington's Farewell Address, these critics recalled America's tradition of self-government and *continental* expansion. Some anti-imperialists insisted that serious domestic problems demanded attention and resources first. And one senator, opposed to annexation, depicted the Philippines as a racial "witches' cauldron" and chanted: "Black spirits and white,/Red spirits and gray,/Mingle, mingle, mingle,/You that mingle may."[51] Mark Twain wrote a scathing parody of the *Battle Hymn of the Republic*: "Mine eyes have seen the orgy of the launching of the Sword;/He is searching out the hoardings where the

George F. Hoar (1826–1904).
Graduate of Harvard, this Republican became a U.S. senator in 1877. He urged Cuban independence and opposed the annexation of the Philippines. He praised the Filipinos for their written constitution and ability to govern themselves. He compared the lynching of African Americans in the U.S. South to the "lynching" of the Filipino people. (Library of Congress)

strangers' wealth is stored;/ He has loosed his fateful lightning, and with woe and death has scored;/His lust is marching on."[52]

Prominent women also participated in the debate, hoping to build a distinct foreign-policy constituency out of existing networks of women's clubs and organizations. The New Hampshire pacifist Lucia True Ames Mead pronounced it immoral for "any nation . . . which buys or takes by conquest another people, and dominates them without promise of granting them independence."[53] The social reformer Jane Addams saw children playing war games in the streets of Chicago. The kids were *not freeing Cubans,* she protested, but rather *slaying Spaniards* in their not-so-innocent play. Although unsuccessful in the fight against empire, tens of thousands of women became activists over the next decade. "Never before," writes the historian Judith Papachristou, "had American women involved themselves in foreign affairs in such a way and to such an extent."[54]

The imperialists, led by Senators Henry Cabot Lodge and Nelson Aldrich, Roosevelt, and McKinley, and backed strongly by business leaders, engaged their opponents in vigorous debate in early 1899. These empire builders stressed pragmatic considerations, although they communicated common ideas of racial superiority and national destiny to civilize the savage world. "We are a conquering race," boasted Senator Albert Beveridge, and "we must obey our blood and occupy new markets, and, if necessary, new lands."[55] The Philippines provided stepping-stones to the rich China market and strategic ports for the expanding navy that protected American commerce and demonstrated U.S. prestige. International competition also dictated that the United States keep the fruits of victory, argued the imperialists; otherwise, a menacing Germany or expansionist Japan might pick up what America discarded. Few believed that the United States should relinquish territory acquired through blood. National honor demanded retention, or so the annexationists argued. Roosevelt, countering the charge that no one had asked the Filipinos if they desired annexation to the United States, delighted in telling Democratic anti-imperialists that President Thomas Jefferson took Louisiana without a vote by its inhabitants. McKinley put it simply: "Duty determines destiny."[56] Duty, destiny, defense, and dollars became the alliterative imperialist litany.

Pro-imperialist Senator Lodge described the treaty fight as the "closest, most bitter, and most exciting struggle I . . . ever expect to see in the Senate."[57] Shortly before the upper house took action, word reached Washington that Filipino insurrectionists and American soldiers had begun to fight. The news apparently stimulated support for the Treaty of Paris. Democrats tended to be anti-imperialists and Republicans imperialists, yet enough of the former endorsed the treaty on February 6, 1899, to pass it, just barely, by the necessary two-thirds vote, 57 to 27. William Jennings Bryan, believing that rejection of the treaty would prolong the war and that the Philippines could be freed after terminating the hostilities with Spain, urged an aye vote on his anti-imperialist friends. The Republicans probably had enough votes in reserve to pass the treaty even if Bryan had opposed it. Eight days later, the tie-breaking vote of the vice president killed a Senate resolution providing for Philippine independence as soon as the Filipinos established a stable government.

Imperial Collisions in Asia: The Philippine Insurrection and the Open Door in China

Controlling, protecting, and expanding the enlarged U.S. empire became a major chore. The Filipinos proved the most obstructionist. By the end of the war, Aguinaldo and rebel forces controlled most of the islands, having routed the Spanish and driven them into Manila. Aguinaldo had arrived from exile in a U.S. warship and believed that American leaders, including Dewey, had promised his country independence if he joined U.S. forces in defeating the Spanish. Ordered out of Manila by U.S. authorities after the Spanish-American armistice, he and his cohorts had to endure racial insults, including "nigger" and "goo goo." American soldiers considered the Filipinos inferior, the equivalent of Indians and blacks at home. Although one Methodist missionary boasted that the Americans had found Manila "a pesthole, and made it a health resort," critics claimed that imperialism exported the worst in American life.[58] The Treaty of Paris angered the Filipinos, as did McKinley's decree asserting the supreme authority of the United States in the Philippines. In open defiance of Washington, Aguinaldo and other prominent Filipinos organized a government at Malolos, wrote a constitution, and proclaimed the Philippine Republic in late January 1899.

Although American anti-imperialist critics did not err in calling the Filipino government as virtuous as that of Chicago, McKinley believed his new subjects to

Emilio Aguinaldo (1869–1964). Of mixed Chinese and Tagalog ancestry, this Filipino nationalist was exiled by the Spanish from his country in 1897. He returned with American forces and later clashed with them when he declared independence for the Philippines. Captured in 1901, he then declared allegiance to the United States. During World War II, however, he favored the Japanese, who occupied the islands, and American authorities briefly imprisoned him in 1945 when they reestablished U.S. power over Manila. (Library of Congress)

be ill fitted for self-government. In February 1899 the Filipinos began fighting better-armed American troops. After bloody struggles, Aguinaldo was captured in March 1901. Before the insurrection collapsed in 1902, some 4,165 Americans and more than 200,000 Filipinos died. One hundred twenty-five thousand American troops quelled the insurrection, which cost the United States at least $160 million. In Batangas province south of Manila, General J. Franklin Bell drove insurrectionists into the hills and killed their livestock. Then malaria-transmitting mosquitoes "were forced to get their meals from people" instead of cattle. The result: an "epidemiological catastrophe" wherein the Batangas population declined by 90,000 (one-quarter of the people) over a six-year period.[59] Anti-imperialist William James, distinguished Harvard University philosopher, poignantly summarized the impact of U.S. intervention: "We are destroying the lives of these islanders by the thousands, their villages and their cities. . . . Civilization is, then, the big, hollow, resounding, corrupting, sophisticating, confusing torrent of mere brutal momentum and irrationality that brings forth fruits like this!"[60]

One of the ugliest wars in American history, this contest saw both sides commit atrocities. After Filipinos massacred an American regiment on Samar and stuffed molasses into disemboweled corpses to attract ants, General Jacob Smith told his officers: "I want no prisoners. I wish you to kill and burn, the more you kill and burn the better you will please me."[61] Americans burned *barrios* to the ground, placing villagers in reconcentration camps like those that had defaced Cuba. To get information, Americans administered the "water cure," forcing prisoners to swallow gallons of water and then punching the swollen stomach to empty it quickly. General Arthur MacArthur viewed his task as "conquering eight millions of recalcitrant, treacherous, and sullen people."[62] Racist notions of white superiority surfaced. Army captain Frank R. McCoy could not comprehend the Muslim Moros who refused American medical treatment. "You mention Cholera to them," he wrote, "and they throw up their hands [saying,] 'God has given and God has taken away.'"[63] For most soldiers, an army song had it right: "Civilize 'em with a Krag."[64] The civil governor of the Philippines from 1901 to 1904, William Howard Taft, put the question less crudely when he described the American mission as to "teach those people individual liberty, which shall lift them up to a point of civilization . . . , and which shall make them rise to call the name of the United States blessed."[65] In fact, Taft administered a sedition act that sought to suppress criticism of the United States. His authorities censored newspapers and jailed dissenters.

For years, the Moros would not submit to American rule. One military expert predicted that "the Moro question will eventually be settled in the same manner as the Indian question, that is by gradual extermination."[66] In a June 1913 battle on the island of Jolo, U.S. forces killed 500 Moros. The army's premier "guerrilla warrior," General John J. Pershing, called that bloody encounter "the fiercest [fighting] I have ever seen."[67] Until 1914, moreover, the followers of Artemio Ricarte harassed the U.S. military with their hit-and-run tactics. Ricarte himself, imprisoned from 1904 to 1910 and then deported to Hong Kong and Japan, refused allegiance to the United States and set up a government-in-exile that demanded "immediate and complete independence and the equalization of wealth."[68]

William Howard Taft (1857–1930) and Animal. The first U.S. civil governor of the Philippines, Taft weighed more than 300 pounds. He once proudly reported to Washington that he had ridden twenty-five miles to a high mountain spot. Secretary of War Elihu Root replied: "HOW IS HORSE?" (U.S. Army Military History Institute)

The carrot joined the stick to pacify the Philippines. Local self-government, social reforms, and American schools, which taught Filipinos of all social classes English and arithmetic, helped win over elites and key minorities. "We'll larn ye our language," said the inimitable Mr. Dooley, "because 'tis easier to larn ye ours thin to larn ourselves ye'ers."[69] A general amnesty proclaimed by President Theodore Roosevelt on July 4, 1902, also encouraged accommodation. By restricting suffrage at the outset to Filipinos with wealth, education, and previous government service, U.S. administrators successfully wooed Filipino elites, including former revolutionaries. American roads, bridges, port improvements, and sanitation projects soon followed. At the St. Louis World's Fair in 1904, a thousand Filipinos were put on display as "living exhibits," and photographs and dioramas depicted their "rapid social, educational and sanitary development" under "the kindly tutelage of the United States."[70] In 1916, the Jones Act promised Philippine independence but set no date. Thirty years later the Philippines became an independent nation allied with the United States.

Proximity to China made the Philippines especially valuable to U.S. leaders who predicted lucrative markets for American products. In early 1898 business

"The Metamorphosis of a Bontoc Igorot."   Dean Worcester, an American zoology professor who served as the U.S. secretary of the interior for the Philippines from 1900 to 1913, included these two photographs of "Pit-a-pit," a Bontoc Igorot, in his 1914 book to illustrate his conclusion that U.S. policies and programs had a civilizing effect on Filipinos. The two pictures were taken nine years apart. Worcester classified the islands' population of 8 million into eighty-four tribes, including the Bontoc Igorot. At the 1904 St. Louis World's Fair, the village of three Igorot tribes (Bontoc, Syoc, and Benguet) became one of the most popular exhibits, to which visitors flocked because of the popularized image of the Igorot as head-hunters and dog-eaters. As the scholar Eric Breitbart writes in his book, *A World on Display 1904* (1997), this image "symbolized the gulf between 'savagery' and 'civilization'" and between "clothed and naked," confirming the "otherness" of native peoples abroad. (Dean Worcester, *The Philippines Past and Present* [New York: Macmillan Company, 1914], vol. 2, frontispiece)

leaders organized the American Asiatic Association to stimulate public and governmental concern to protect and enlarge U.S. interests in China. Treasury official Frank Vanderlip typically lauded the Philippines as the "pickets of the Pacific, standing guard at the entrances to trade with the millions of China."[71] Although China attracted only 2 percent of U.S. foreign commerce, American traders had long dreamed of an unbounded China market, and missionaries romanticized a Christian kingdom. These ambitions remained dreams more than reality. Yet dreams spurred action, and during the 1890s the United States, despite limited power, sought to defend its Asian interests, real and imagined.

In that decade the European powers and Japan were dividing China, rendered helpless in 1895 after the Sino-Japanese War, into spheres of influence and establishing discriminatory trading privileges in their zones. The McKinley administration in early 1898 watched anxiously as Germany grabbed Jiaozhou (Kiaochow) and Russia gained a lease at Port Arthur on the Liaodong Peninsula. France, already ensconced in Indochina, leased Guangzhou Bay in southern China in April of that year. Japan already had footholds in Formosa and Korea. The British in March 1898 suggested a joint Anglo-American declaration on behalf of equal commercial opportunity in China. In the midst of the Cuban crisis, Washington gave little attention to the request. Britain, which already had Hong Kong, then forced China to give up part of the Shandong Peninsula.

American economic and religious interests in China seemed threatened. The American Asiatic Association and missionary groups appealed to Washington for

American Cigarettes in China. An American soldier in China peddles cigarettes. After the invention of the cigarette machine in 1881, the tobacco tycoon James B. Duke asked to see an atlas. Leafing through the pages, he noticed China's large population of 430 million. "That," he said, "is where we are going to sell cigarettes." Nine years later came the first exports; by 1916 Duke and other American entrepreneurs were selling 12 billion cigarettes in China. (Edward J. Parrish Papers, Duke University Library)

help. Drawing on recommendations from William W. Rockhill, adviser on Asian policy, who in turn consulted his British friend and officer of the Chinese customs service, Alfred Hippisley, Secretary of State John Hay tried words. Even though President McKinley seemed "to want a slice" of China, Hay sent an "Open Door" note on September 6, 1899, to Japan, Germany, Russia, Britain, France, and Italy, asking them to respect equal trade opportunity for all nations in their spheres.[72] It was, of course, a traditional American principle. Noncommittal replies trickled back, but Hay read into them what he wanted and proclaimed definitive acceptance of the Open Door proposal.

Although frail, the Open Door policy carried meaning. Americans knew they had less leverage than the other imperialists in Asia, but they also noted that a delicate balance of power existed there that the United States could unbalance. The European powers and Japan might hesitate to exclude American commerce altogether from China, for fear that the United States would tip that balance by joining one of the powers against the others. They also feared that a world war might erupt from competition in Asia. Americans hoped the Open Door policy would serve their goals in an area where they had little military power. The United States wanted the commercial advantages without having to employ military force, as it

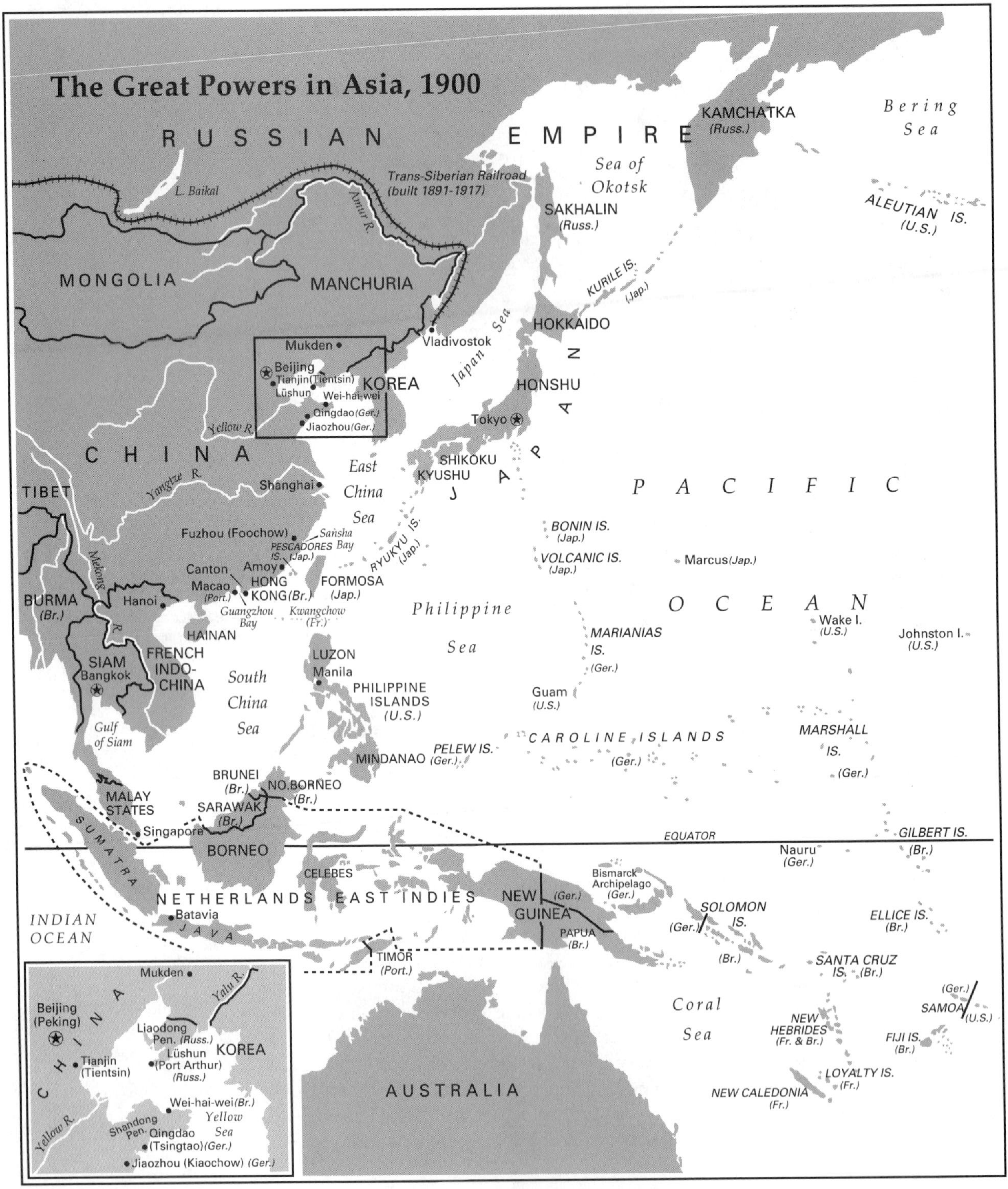
The Great Powers in Asia, 1900
RUSSIAN EMPIRE
KAMCHATKA (Russ.)
Bering Sea
Sea of Okotsk
L. Baikal
Trans-Siberian Railroad (built 1891-1917)
Amur R.
SAKHALIN (Russ.)
ALEUTIAN IS. (U.S.)
KURILE IS. (Jap.)
MONGOLIA
MANCHURIA
HOKKAIDO
Vladivostok
Japan Sea
Mukden
Beijing
Tianjin(Tientsin)
Lüshun
Wei-hai-wei
Qingdao (Ger.)
Jiaozhou (Ger.)
KOREA
HONSHU
Tokyo
JAPAN
Yellow R.
CHINA
SHIKOKU
KYUSHU
East China Sea
Yangtze R.
Shanghai
TIBET
PACIFIC OCEAN
Fuzhou (Foochow)
Sansha Bay
PESCADORES IS. (Jap.)
RYUKYU IS. (Jap.)
BONIN IS. (Jap.)
VOLCANIC IS. (Jap.)
Marcus (Jap.)
Canton
Amoy
Macao (Port.)
HONG KONG (Br.)
FORMOSA (Jap.)
Mekong
BURMA (Br.)
Hanoi
Guangzhou Bay
Kwangchow (Fr.)
Philippine Sea
Wake I. (U.S.)
Johnston I. (U.S.)
MARIANIAS IS. (Ger.)
HAINAN
SIAM
Bangkok
FRENCH INDO-CHINA
South China Sea
LUZON
Manila
PHILIPPINE ISLANDS (U.S.)
Guam (U.S.)
Gulf of Siam
MINDANAO
PELEW IS. (Ger.)
CAROLINE ISLANDS (Ger.)
MARSHALL IS. (Ger.)
BRUNEI (Br.)
NO. BORNEO (Br.)
MALAY STATES
SARAWAK (Br.)
Singapore
SUMATRA
BORNEO
EQUATOR
GILBERT IS. (Br.)
Nauru (Ger.)
CELEBES
NETHERLANDS EAST INDIES
NEW GUINEA
(Ger.)
Bismarck Archipelago (Ger.)
PAPUA (Br.)
SOLOMON IS.
(Ger.)
(Br.)
ELLICE IS. (Br.)
Batavia
JAVA
INDIAN OCEAN
TIMOR (Port.)
SANTA CRUZ IS. (Br.)
SAMOA
(Ger.)
(U.S.)
Coral Sea
NEW HEBRIDES (Fr. & Br.)
FIJI IS. (Br.)
LOYALTY IS. (Fr.)
NEW CALEDONIA (Fr.)
AUSTRALIA
Mukden
Yalu R.
Beijing (Peking)
CHINA
Liaodong Pen. (Russ.)
Lüshun (Port Arthur) (Russ.)
KOREA
Tianjin (Tientsin)
Wei-hai-wei (Br.)
Yellow Sea
Shandong Pen.
Qingdao (Tsingtao) (Ger.)
Jiaozhou (Kiaochow) (Ger.)
Yellow R.

did in Latin America. The policy did not always work, but it fixed itself in the American mind as a guiding principle for Chinese affairs.

The Open Door note notwithstanding, the Manchu dynasty (1644–1912) neared death, unable to cope with the foreign intruders. Resentful nationalistic Chinese, led by a secret society called *Yihequan* ("Righteous and Harmonious Fists," or the "Boxers"), undertook in 1900 to throw out the imperialist aggressors. The Boxers murdered hundreds of Christian missionaries and their Chinese converts, and laid siege to the foreign legations in Beijing (Peking). "If we die we die in peace," one missionary woman wrote just before she was murdered.[73] To head off a complete gouging of China by vengeful Europeans and Japanese, McKinley, without consulting Congress, sent 2,500 American troops to Beijing from the Philippines to join 15,500 soldiers from other nations to lift the siege. And Hay, without consulting the Chinese government, issued another Open Door note on July 3, 1900. He defined U.S. policy as the protection of American life and property, the safeguarding of "equal and impartial trade," and the preservation of China's "territorial and administrative entity."[74] In short, keep the trade door open by keeping China intact.

Certainly these actions did not save China from continued incursion (it had to pay more than $300 million for the Boxers' damages). The United States itself even asked for a territorial concession in late 1900 at Sansha Bay, Fujian Province. The Japanese, catching Hay red-handed, politely reminded him of his notes, and he shelved the request. Thereafter Washington buttressed its support for the Open Door by increasing the Asiatic Squadron to forty-eight warships and earmarking army forces in the Philippines for future emergency deployment in China.

The Elbows of a World Power, 1895–1900

Venezuela, Cuba, Hawai'i, the Philippines, Open Door notes—together they meant an unprecedented set of commitments and responsibilities for the United States. Symbolic of this thrust to world-power status was the ascendancy of the imperialists' imperialist, Theodore Roosevelt, to the presidency in 1901. Peering into the twentieth century, Roosevelt warned Americans to avoid "slothful ease and ignoble peace." Never "shrink from the hard contests"; "let us therefore boldly face the life of strife."[75] Indeed, many diplomats looked back on the triumphs of the 1890s as a testing time when the United States met the international challenge and rightfully asserted its place as a major world power. Europeans watched anxiously. Some, especially Germans, spoke of the "American peril."[76] Russia, however, supported U.S. annexation of Hawai'i because it prevented this "Malta of the Pacific" from becoming Japanese.[77] The United States, European leaders pointed out, had become a factor in the "balance of power." With whom would the nation ally itself?

The odds seemed to favor Great Britain, although the Anglo-American courtship would be prolonged and marriage something for the future. Ever since the eye-opening Venezuelan crisis, the British, in Colonial Secretary Joseph Chamberlain's words, had applauded Washington for "entering the lists and sharing the task which might have proved too heavy for us alone" and pursued what one

John M. Hay (1838–1905). The author of the Open Door notes graduated from Brown University and served as one of President Abraham Lincoln's secretaries. He became a newspaper editor and diplomat and, in 1897, ambassador to Great Britain. The following year McKinley named him secretary of state, a post he held until his death. The historian Christopher Thorne has described the Open Door policy as a "singular blend of evangelicalism, political calculation, benevolent imperialism, and crude self-interest." (National Portrait Gallery, Smithsonian Institution)

Pears Soap advertisement.
This unusual mixture of commercial and diplomatic advertising salutes Anglo-American rapprochement. (*Life*, 1898)

historian has called the "great rapprochement."[78] Looking for support against an expansionist Germany, John Bull thought Uncle Sam a fit partner. During the Spanish-American-Cuban-Filipino War the British conspicuously tilted toward the American side and encouraged the subsequent U.S. absorption of Spanish colonies. American leaders, in turn, sympathized with the British suppression of the Boer Republics in South Africa during 1899–1902, comparing that struggle to their own war with the Filipinos. Articulate Americans welcomed Britain's implicit acceptance of their imperialism. "Germany, and not England, is the power with whom we are apt to have trouble over the Monroe Doctrine," wrote Roosevelt in 1898.[79] Vague Anglo-Saxonism and cultural ties joined British recognition of the power of the United States to forge more amicable relations. Anglophobes continued to twist the lion's tail and commercial competition remained intense, but Anglo-American relations moved from being "cool, grudging, and occasionally hostile" to tolerant and cordial.[80]

Britain still ranked first in naval power, but in the late 1890s the United States was growing, standing sixth by 1900. In 1898 alone, spurred by the war with Spain, the United States added 128 vessels to its navy, at a cost of $18 million. At the 1898 American Historical Association meeting, Professor Edwin A. Grosvenor of Amherst College caught the new times in his address: "Barriers of national seclusion are everywhere tumbling like the great wall of China. Every nation elbows other nations to-day."[81] The steel magnate Andrew Carnegie boasted that "the old nations of the earth creep at a snail's pace," but the United States "thunders past with the rush of the express."[82] Many commentators reported that the United States, although still divided North and South on many issues, had united as never before. Southern racists and northern imperialists now had something in common: the need to keep inferior peoples in their place. Befitting their new imperial status, U.S. leaders often used gendered and age-based language that presumed superiority over peoples deemed "emotional, irrational, irresponsible, unbusinesslike, unstable, childlike."[83] If Americans played "the part of China, and [were] content to rot by inches in ignoble ease within our borders," warned Roosevelt, they will "go down before other nations which have not lost the manly and adventurous qualities."[84] As one college professor expostulated in 1898: "We must govern as those who learn; and they must obey as those who are in tutelage. They are children and we are men in these deep matters of government and justice."[85]

The events of the 1895–1900 period further altered the process of decision-making. Both Cleveland and McKinley conducted their own foreign policies, often thwarting or manipulating Congress. "Expansion and disorder abroad equaled centralization at home," one historian has written.[86] In 1907, looking back on the days of 1898, Woodrow Wilson, then president of Princeton University, recorded the historical impact: "The war with Spain again changed the balance of powers. Foreign questions became leading questions again, as they had been in the first days of the government, and in them the President was of necessity leader. . . . The nation has risen to the first rank in power and resources. . . . Our President must always, henceforth, be one of the great powers of the world."[87] Wilson exaggerated America's power, for that strength still largely centered in the Western Hemisphere, but for the United States, as the *Washington Post* editorialized in 1898, "the policy of isolation is dead. . . . A new consciousness seems to have come upon us—the consciousness of strength, and with it a new appetite, a yearning to show our strength. . . . Ambition, interest, land-hunger, pride, the mere joy of fighting, whatever it may be, we are animated by a new sensation. . . . The taste of empire is in the mouth of the people, even as the taste of blood in the jungle."[88] After 1900 the task of managing the expansive empire and the global responsibilities that came with it preoccupied U.S. leaders.

FURTHER READING FOR THE PERIOD 1895–1900

For the 1890s push for empire and the coming and waging of the Spanish-American-Cuban-Filipino War, see Edward J. Berbusse, *The United States and Puerto Rico, 1898–1900* (1966); Charles H. Brown, *The Correspondents' War* (1967); Richard Challener, *Admirals, Generals,* and *American Foreign Policy, 1898–1914* (1973); Graham A. Cosmas, *An Army for Empire* (1971); Willard B. Gatewood, Jr., *Black Americans and the White Man's Burden, 1898–1903* (1975); Kristin L. Hoganson, *Fighting for American Manhood: How Gender Politics Provoked the Spanish–American and Philippine–American Wars* (1998); John M. Kirk, *José Martí* (1983); Gerald F. Linderman, *The Mirror of War* (1974); Ernest R. May, *Imperial Democracy* (1961); Joyce Milton, *The Yellow Kids* (1989) (journalists); Ian Mugridge, *The View from Xandu* (1995) (Hearst); Ivan Musicant, *Empire by Default* (1998); John L. Offner, *An Unwanted War* (1992); Louis A. Pérez, Jr., *The War of 1898* (1998), *Cuba and the United States* (1997), and *Cuba Between Empires, 1878–1902* (1983); Julius Pratt, *Expansionists of 1898* (1938); Hyman G. Rickover, *How the Battleship Maine Was Destroyed* (1976); Emily Rosenberg, *Spreading the American Dream* (1982); Göran Rystad, *Ambiguous Imperialism* (1981); Peggy Samuels and Harold Samuels, *Remembering the Maine* (1995); David F. Trask, *The War with Spain in 1898* (1981); and Paul Wolman, *The Republican Revisionists and U.S. Tariff Policy, 1897–1912* (1992).

For U.S. leaders, see Howard K. Beale, *Theodore Roosevelt and the Rise of America to World Power* (1956); John Braeman, *Albert J. Beveridge* (1971); H.W. Brands, *T.R.* (1997); Charles W. Calhoun, *Gilded Age Cato* (1988) (Gresham); Kenton J. Clymer, *John Hay* (1975); Gerald Eggert, *Richard Olney* (1973); Lewis L. Gould, *The Presidency of William McKinley* (1981); William Harbaugh, *The Life and Times of Theodore Roosevelt* (1975); Margaret Leech, *In the Days of McKinley* (1959); Nathan Miller, *Theodore Roosevelt* (1992); H. Wayne Morgan, *William McKinley and His America* (1963); Edmund Morris, *The Rise of Theodore Roosevelt* (1979); Ronald Spector, *Admiral of the New Empire* (1974) (Dewey); Richard E. Welch, Jr., *The Presidencies of Grover Cleveland* (1988); and William C. Widenor, *Henry Cabot Lodge and the Search for an American Foreign Policy* (1980).

Anti-imperialism is treated in William N. Armstrong, *E. L. Godkin and American Foreign Policy* (1957); Robert L. Beisner, *Twelve Against Empire* (1968); Kendrick A. Clements, *William Jennings Bryan* (1983); Paolo E. Coletta, *William Jennings Bryan* (1964–1969); John C. Farrell, *Beloved Lady* (1967) (Addams); Thomas J. Osborne, *"Empire Can Wait": American Opposition to Hawaiian Annexation, 1893–1898* (1981); E. Berkeley Tompkins, *Anti-Imperialism in the United States* (1970); Hans L. Trefousse, *Carl Schurz* (1982); and Joseph F. Wall, *Andrew Carnegie* (1970).

The Open Door policy and Asia are discussed in Thomas A. Breslin, *China, American Catholicism, and the Missionary* (1980); Charles S. Campbell, *Special Business Interests and the Open Door Policy* (1951); Sherman Cochran, *Big Business in China* (1980) (cigarette industry); Michael Hunt, *Frontier Defense and the Open Door* (1973) and *The Making of a Special Relationship* (1983); Akira Iriye, *Across the Pacific* (1967); Robert McClellan, *The Heathen Chinee* (1971); Thomas McCormick, *China Market* (1967); Valentin H. Rabe, *The Home Base of American China Missions, 1880–1920* (1978); and Marilyn Blatt Young, *The Rhetoric of Empire* (1968). For Hawai'i, see works listed in Chapter 5.

The Philippine rebellion and the American debate receive scrutiny in Teodoro Agoncillo, *Malolos* (1960); A. J. Bacevich, *Diplomat in Khaki* (1989) (General Frank McCoy); Kenton J. Clymer, *Protestant Missionaries in the Philippines, 1898–1916* (1986); John M. Gates, *Schoolbooks and Krags* (1973); Stanley Karnow,

In Our Image (1989); Brian M. Linn, *Guardians of Empire* (1997) and *The U.S. Army and Counterinsurgency in the Philippine War, 1899–1902* (1989); Glenn A. May, *Battle for Batangas* (1991) and *Social Engineering in the Philippines* (1980); Stuart C. Miller, *"Benevolent Assimilation"* (1982); Daniel B. Schirmer, *Republic or Empire* (1972); Peter Stanley, *A Nation in the Making* (1974), and ed., *Reappraising an Empire* (1984); and Richard E. Welch, *Response to Imperialism* (1979).

For the Venezuelan crisis and Anglo-American relations, see Stuart Anderson, *Race and Rapprochement* (1981); Charles S. Campbell, *From Revolution to Rapprochement* (1974); Judith Ewell, *Venezuela and the United States* (1996); Richard B. Mulanax, *The Boer War in American Politics and Diplomacy* (1994); R. G. Neale, *Great Britain and United States Expansion, 1800–1900* (1966); Thomas J. Noer, *Briton, Boer, and Yankee* (1978); Bradford Perkins, *The Great Rapprochement* (1968); Serge Ricard and Hélène Christol, eds., *Anglo-Saxonism in U.S. Foreign Policy* (1991); and Joseph Smith, *Illusions of Conflict: Anglo-American Diplomacy Toward Latin America, 1865–1896* (1979).

See also the General Bibliography, the following notes, and Richard Dean Burns, ed., *Guide to American Foreign Relations Since 1700* (1983).

For comprehensive coverage of foreign-relations topics, see the articles in the four-volume *Encyclopedia of U.S. Foreign Relations* (1997), edited by Bruce W. Jentleson and Thomas G. Paterson.

NOTES TO CHAPTER 6

1. Quoted in Gerald G. Eggert, *Richard Olney* (College Park: Penn State University Press, 1974), p. 208.
2. U.S. Consul Eugene Plumacher quoted in Judith Ewell, *Venezuela and the United States* (Athens: University of Georgia Press, 1996), p. 69.
3. Quoted in Ernest R. May, *Imperial Democracy* (New York: Harper and Row, [1961], 1973), p. 33.
4. Quoted in Charles W. Calhoun, *Gilded Age Cato* (Lexington: University Press of Kentucky, 1988), p. 217.
5. *Foreign Relations, 1895,* Part I (Washington, D.C.: Government Printing Office, 1896), pp. 545–562.
6. Richard E. Welch, Jr., *The Presidencies of Grover Cleveland* (Lawrence: University Press of Kansas, 1988), p. 184.
7. Quoted in Robert L. Beisner, *From the Old Diplomacy to the New, 1865–1900* (Arlington Heights, Ill.: Harlan Davidson, 1986; 2nd ed.), p. 111.
8. Quoted in Howard K. Beale, *Theodore Roosevelt and the Rise of America to World Power* (New York: Collier Books, [1956], 1962), p. 60.
9. Quoted in H. W. Brands, *T.R.* (New York: BasicBooks, 1997), p. 289.
10. Quoted in Eggert, *Olney*, p. 223.
11. Quoted in Stuart Anderson, *Race and Rapprochement* (Rutherford, N.J.: Fairleigh Dickinson University Press, 1981), p. 97.
12. Quoted in Joyce Milton, *The Yellow Kids* (New York: Harper and Row, 1989), p. 27.
13. Quoted in Allan Nevins, *Grover Cleveland* (New York: Dodd, Mead, 1932), p. 644.
14. Quoted in Joseph Smith, *Illusions of Conflict* (Pittsburgh: University of Pittsburgh Press, 1979), p. 207.
15. Quoted in George Young, "Intervention Under the Monroe Doctrine," *Political Science Quarterly,* LVII (June 1942), 277.
16. Henry Cabot Lodge quoted in Fredrick B. Pike, *The United States and Latin America* (Austin: University of Texas Press, 1992), pp. 158–159.

17. Joseph A. Fry, "From Open Door to World Systems," *Pacific Historical Review,* LX (May 1996), 282.
18. Quoted in Richard E. Welch, Jr., *George Frisbie Hoar and the Half-Breed Republicans* (Cambridge: Harvard University Press, 1971), p. 209.
19. Walter Q. Gresham to Carl Schurz, October 6, 1893, Walter Q. Gresham Papers, Library of Congress, Washington, D.C.
20. Quoted in Louis A. Pérez, Jr., *Cuba and the United States* (Athens: University of Georgia Press, 1997; 2nd ed.), p. 80; and John M. Kirk, *José Martí* (Gainesville: University Presses of Florida, 1983), pp. 52, 56, 58, 90, 118.
21. Quoted in Philip S. Foner, *The Spanish-Cuban-American War and the Birth of American Imperialism* (New York: Monthly Review Press, 1972; 2 vols.), I, 21.
22. Quoted in William Manchester, *The Last Lion* (Boston: Little, Brown, 1983), p. 228.
23. Quoted in John L. Offner, *An Unwanted War* (Chapel Hill: University of North Carolina Press, 1992), p. 26.
24. Quoted in Walter LaFeber, *The American Search for Opportunity 1865–1913* (New York: Cambridge University Press, 1993), p. 132.
25. Quoted in Eggert, *Olney*, p. 265.
26. James D. Richardson, ed., *A Compilation of the Messages and Papers of the Presidents, 1789–1897* (Washington, D.C.: Government Printing Office, 1896–1899; 10 vols.), IX, 716–722.
27. Quoted in Edmund Morris, *The Rise of Theodore Roosevelt* (New York: Coward, McCann, & Geoghegan, 1979), p. 610.
28. *Congressional Record, XXXI* (December 6, 1897), 3–5.
29. *Foreign Relations, 1898* (Washington D.C.: Government Printing Office, 1901), pp. 1007–1008.
30. Quoted in Offner, *Unwanted War*, p. 129.
31. *Congressional Record, XXXI* (March 17, 1898), 2916–2919.
32. Quoted in Louis A. Pérez, Jr., *Cuba Between Empires, 1878–1902* (Pittsburgh: University of Pittsburgh Press, 1983), p. 172.
33. Quoted *ibid.*, p. 174.
34. *Foreign Relations, 1898*, p. 746.

35. Quoted in LaFeber, *American Search*, p. 143.

36. *Congressional Record, XXXI* (April 11, 1898), 3699–3702.

37. Pérez, *Cuba Between Empires*, p. 178.

38. Quoted *ibid.*, p. 174.

39. Quoted in H. Wayne Morgan, *America's Road to Empire* (New York: Wiley, 1965), p. 63.

40. Quoted in Winthrop Hudson, "Protestant Clergy Debate the Nation's Vocation, 1898–1899" (unpub. ms., 1974).

41. Rector of Catholic University quoted in Pike, *United States and Latin America*, p. 168.

42. Quoted in John Braeman, *Albert J. Beveridge* (Chicago: University of Chicago Press, 1971), p. 23.

43. Finley Peter Dunne, *Mr. Dooley in Peace and War* (Boston: Small, Maynard, 1899), p. 9.

44. Quoted in Gerald F. Linderman, *The Mirror of War* (Ann Arbor: University of Michigan Press, 1974), p. 125.

45. Quoted in Louis A. Pérez, Jr., "The Meaning of the *Maine*," *Pacific Historical Review, LVIII* (August 1989), 320.

46. Quoted in Frank Freidel, *The Splendid Little War* (Boston: Little, Brown, 1958), p. 295.

47. Quoted in John A. S. Grenville and George B. Young, *Politics, Strategy, and American Diplomacy* (New Haven: Yale University Press, 1966), p. 278.

48. Quoted in Raymond Carr, *Puerto Rico* (New York: Vintage Books, 1984), p. 25.

49. Quoted in Walter A. McDougall, *Promised Land, Crusader State* (Boston: Houghton Mifflin, 1997), pp. 111–112.

50. Quoted in Robert L. Beisner, "1898 and 1968," *Political Science Quarterly, LXXV* (June 1970), 200.

51. Senator John Daniel quoted in H. W. Brands, *Bound to Empire* (New York: Oxford University Press, 1992), p. 30.

52. Quoted in Hugh Deane, *Good Deeds & Gunboats* (San Francisco: China Books and Periodicals, 1990), p. 65.

53. Quoted in John M. Craig, "Lucia True Ames Mead," in Edward P. Crapol, ed., *Women and American Foreign Policy* (Westport, Conn.: Greenwood, 1992; 2nd ed.), p. 72.

54. Judith Papachristou, "American Women and Foreign Policy, 1898–1905," *Diplomatic History, XIV* (Fall 1990), 493.

55. Quoted in Anders Stephanson, *Manifest Destiny* (New York: Hill & Wang, 1995), p. 98.

56. Quoted *ibid.*, p. 87.

57. Quoted in H. Wayne Morgan, *William McKinley and His America* (Syracuse: Syracuse University Press, 1963), p. 422.

58. Quoted in Kenton J. Clymer, *Protestant Missionaries in the Philippines, 1898–1916* (Urbana: University of Illinois Press, 1986), p. 159.

59. Glenn A. May, *Battle for Batangas* (New Haven: Yale University Press, 1991), pp. 267, 291.

60. *Boston Evening Transcript*, March 1, 1899.

61. Quoted in Stanley Karnow, *In Our Image* (New York: Random House, 1989), p. 191.

62. Quoted in Brian M. Linn, *Guardians of Empire* (Chapel Hill: University of North Carolina Press, 1997), p. 19.

63. Quoted in A. J. Bacevich, *Diplomat in Khaki* (Lawrence: University Press of Kansas, 1989), p. 29.

64. Quoted in John M. Gates, *Schoolbooks and Krags* (Westport, Conn.: Greenwood, 1973), p. vii.

65. Henry F. Graff, ed., *American Imperialism and the Philippine Insurrection* (Boston: Little, Brown, 1969), p. 36.

66. Benjamin Foulois quoted in Linn, *Guardians*, p. 36.

67. Quoted in Donald Smythe, *Guerrilla Warrior* (New York: Charles Scribner's Sons, 1973), p. 198.

68. Quoted in Reynaldo C. Ileto, "Orators and the Crowd," in Peter W. Stanley, ed., *Reappraising an Empire* (Cambridge: Harvard University Press, 1984), p. 103.

69. Quoted in Karnow, *In Our Image*, p. 201.

70. Robert W. Rydell, *World of Fairs* (Chicago: University of Chicago Press, 1993), pp. 75–76.

71. Quoted in Thomas J. McCormick, *China Market* (Chicago: Quadrangle, 1967), p. 119.

72. Quoted in Louis L. Gould, *The Presidency of William McKinley* (Lawrence: University Press of Kansas, 1981), p. 222.

73. Eva Jane Price, *China Journal, 1899–1900* (New York: Charles Scribner's Sons, 1989), p. 232.

74. *Foreign Relations, 1901* (Washington, D.C.: Government Printing Office, 1902), Appendix, p. 12.

75. Quoted in Beale, *Theodore Roosevelt*, p. 84.

76. Quoted in Fareed Zakaria, *From Wealth to Power* (Princeton: Princeton University Press, 1998), p. 133.

77. Mikhail Murav'ev quoted in Normal Saul, *Concord and Conflict* (Lawrence: University Press of Kansas, 1996), p. 438.

78. Quoted in Anderson, *Race and Rapprochement*, p. 127.

79. Quoted in Edward P. Crapol, "From Anglophobia to Fragile Rapprochement," in Hans-Jürgen Schröder, ed., *Confrontation and Cooperation* (Providence, R.I.: Berg, 1993), p. 21.

80. Paul M. Kennedy, *The Rise and Fall of the Great Powers* (New York: Random House, 1987), p. 251.

81. American Historical Association, *Annual Report, 1898* (Washington, D.C.: Government Printing Office, 1899), p. 288.

82. Quoted in Smith, *Illusions of Conflict*, p. 40.

83. Emily S. Rosenberg, "Walking the Borders," in Michael J. Hogan and Thomas G. Paterson, eds., *Explaining the History of American Foreign Relations* (New York: Cambridge University Press, 1991), p. 33.

84. Quoted in Gail Bederman, *Manliness & Civilization* (Chicago: University of Chicago Press, 1995), p. 193.

85. Woodrow Wilson quoted in Tony Smith, *America's Mission* (Princeton: Princeton University Press, 1994), p. 63.

86. LaFeber, *American Search*, p. 117.

87. Quoted in Arthur Link's essay in *Wilson's Diplomacy* (Cambridge: Schenkman, 1973), p. 6.

88. *Washington Post*, June 2, 1898.

CHAPTER

❖ **7** ❖

Managing, Policing, and Extending the Empire, 1900–1914

"The Thirteenth Labor of Hercules." With this official poster by Perham Nahl, the Panama-Pacific Exposition in San Francisco in 1915 celebrated the opening of the Panama Canal. The artist commemorates the ten-year construction project using symbols that reflect the empire-building and male hegemony of the era: A powerful, muscular Hercules (the United States) forcibly parts the land (a yielding Panama) to make space for the canal. (Library of Congress)

❖

DIPLOMATIC CROSSROAD

Severing Panama from Colombia for the Canal, 1903

"Revolution imminent" warned the cable from the American consul at Colón, a normally quiet Colombian seaport on the Atlantic side of Panama. Acting Secretary of State Francis B. Loomis bridled his curiosity for an hour. Then he fired off an inquiry to the U.S. consul at Panama City, on the Pacific slope: "Uprising on Isthmus reported. Keep Department promptly and fully informed." The response came back in four hours: "No uprising yet. Reported will be in the night. Situation is critical." Loomis's anxiety soon increased when he learned that an "important message" intended for the U.S.S. *Nashville* anchored at Colón had miscarried and troops of the Colombian government had landed in the city.

At the Department of State it was now 8:20 P.M., November 3, 1903. As far as Loomis knew, a revolution had not yet broken out on the isthmus. Nonetheless, he hurriedly drafted instructions for the consuls at Panama and Colón. "Act promptly" to convey to the commanding officer of the *Nashville* this order: "In the interests of peace make every effort to prevent [Colombian] Government troops at Colón from proceeding to Panama [City]." Loomis agonized for another hour. Finally, a new cable arrived in Washington, D.C.: "Uprising occurred to-night . . . no bloodshed. . . . Government will be organized to-night." Loomis had done his part to ensure success in the scheme to acquire a canal controlled by the United States.

If November 3 was busy for Loomis, it was far more hectic for José Augustín Arango and his fellow conspirators in Panama. The tiny band of Panamanians and Americans living on the isthmus had actively plotted revolution since August, when the Colombian congress rejected the treaty that would have permitted the United States to construct an isthmian canal. By late October, they had become convinced that the North American colossus, frustrated in its overtures to Colombia, would lend them moral and physical support. Confident that U.S. naval vessels would be at hand, they selected November 4 as the date of their coup d'état. To their dismay, however, the Colombian steamer *Cartagena* disembarked about 400 troops at Colón early on November 3. Because the "important message" directing him to prevent the "landing of any armed force . . . either Government or insurgent at Colón" had not reached him, Commander John Hubbard of the *Nashville* did not interfere with the landing.

Forced to rely on their own wits, the conspirators made good use of the transisthmian railroad. They deviously separated the Colombian commanding general from his troops, lured him aboard a train, and sped him across the isthmus to Panama City. At 6:00 P.M. on the third, the revolutionaries arrested their guest, formed a provisional government, and paraded before a cheering crowd at the Cathedral Plaza. But the revolution would remain perilously unfinished so long as armed Colombian soldiers occupied Colón. Too weak to expel the soldiers by

Theodore Roosevelt the Pirate. The Colombian minister called the United States a "pirate." When Roosevelt justified to his cabinet the actions he had taken toward Panama in 1903, Secretary of War Elihu Root observed: "You have shown that you have been accused of seduction and you have conclusively proved that you were guilty of rape." Michael C. C. Adams, author of *The Great Adventure: Male Desire and the Coming of World War I* (1990), reads Roosevelt differently, comparing him to Peter Pan, "the boy who would not grow up." (Frank Nankivell, Swann Collection of Caricature and Cartoon)

force, the insurgents gave the colonel in charge $8,000 in gold, whereupon he ordered his troops aboard a departing steamer. The U.S. consul at Panama City cabled: "Quiet prevails." At noon the next day, Secretary of State John Hay recognized the sovereign Republic of Panama.

The frantic pace of isthmian diplomacy continued. The new Panamanian government appointed as its minister plenipotentiary a Frenchman, Philippe Bunau-Varilla, an engineer of an earlier failed Panama canal project. With Gallic flourish, Bunau-Varilla congratulated Secretary Hay for rescuing Panama "from the barbarism of unnecessary and wasteful civil wars to consecrate it to the destiny assigned to it by Providence, the service of humanity, and the progress of civilization."[1] John Hay thoroughly understood Bunau-Varilla's rhetoric and eagerly negotiated the treaty both men wanted. On November 18, 1903, less than two weeks after U.S. recognition of Panama, they signed the Hay–Bunau-Varilla Treaty, by which the United States would build, fortify, and operate a canal linking the Atlantic and Pacific oceans. Washington also guaranteed the "independence of the Republic in Panama," thereby ensuring Panama's national survival against any threat from Colombia.[2]

Hay had at last achieved a goal set by his chief, President Theodore Roosevelt, several years earlier. "I do not see why we should dig the canal if we are not to fortify it," Roosevelt had remarked in 1900. If an unfortified, neutral canal had existed in Central America during the recent war with Spain, Roosevelt argued, the United States would have spent most of the war in "wild panic," fearful that the Spanish fleet would slip through the waterway and rush to the Philippines to attack Commodore Dewey. The obvious lesson: "Better to have no canal at all, than not give us the power to control it in time of war," Roosevelt expostulated.[3]

The Clayton-Bulwer Treaty of 1850, stipulating joint Anglo-American control of any isthmian canal, seemed to block the way. In December 1898, flushed with victory over Spain, President William McKinley had directed Secretary Hay to modify that agreement with the British ambassador, Sir Julian Pauncefote. The Hay-Pauncefote Treaty of February 1900 permitted the United States to build a canal but forbade its fortification, much to the dismay of Roosevelt, then governor of New York. He spearheaded an attack that defeated the treaty in the Senate, forcing renegotiation. On November 18, 1901, with Roosevelt now president, Hay and Pauncefote signed a new pact satisfactory to the Rough Rider.

Then began the complex process of determining the route. In November 1901, after a two-year investigation, the Walker Isthmian Canal Commission reported in favor of Nicaragua. The decisive criterion—cost—seemed exorbitant for Panama because of the obduracy of the New Panama Canal Company, a French-chartered firm that held the Colombian concession for canal rights. The company estimated its assets on the isthmus at $109 million—machinery, property, and excavated soil left by the defunct de Lesseps organization after its failure to cut through Panama in 1888. Purchase of the company's rights and holdings would make a Panama canal prohibitively expensive although technologically easier. For these reasons, the House of Representatives on January 8, 1902, passed the Hepburn Bill authorizing a canal through Nicaragua.

The New Panama Canal Company's American lawyer, William Nelson Cromwell, a partner in the prestigious New York law firm of Sullivan and

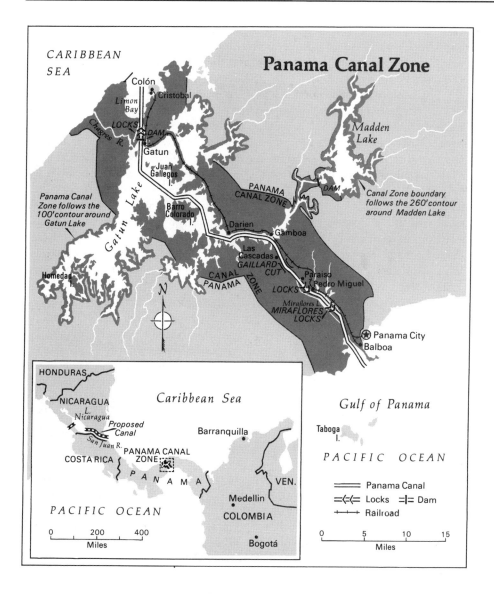

Panama Canal Zone

CARIBBEAN SEA

Colón

Cristobal

Limon Bay

LOCKS

Chagres R.

DAM

Gatun

Juan Gallegos I.

Gatun Lake

Barro Colorado I.

Panama Canal Zone follows the 100' contour around Gatun Lake

Homedad

Darien

Gamboa

Madden Lake

DAM

PANAMA CANAL ZONE

Canal Zone boundary follows the 260' contour around Madden Lake

Las Cascadas

GAILLARD CUT

Paraiso

Pedro Miguel

CANAL ZONE

PANAMA

Miraflores L.

MIRAFLORES LOCKS

LOCKS

Panama City

Balboa

N

HONDURAS

NICARAGUA

L. Nicaragua

Proposed Canal

San Juan R.

COSTA RICA

PANAMA CANAL ZONE

P A N A M A

Caribbean Sea

Barranquilla

VEN.

Medellin

COLOMBIA

Bogotá

PACIFIC OCEAN

Gulf of Panama

Taboga I.

PACIFIC OCEAN

Panama Canal

Locks   Dam

Railroad

0   200   400
Miles

0   5   10   15
Miles

Cromwell, schemed to sell the assets of his French client for the highest possible price. The attorney began to pull strings. Lobbying hard, Bunau-Varilla even exposed the unsuitability of Nicaraguan terrain by deluging Congress with Nicaraguan postage stamps that depicted a belching volcano.

On January 18, 1902, the Walker Commission reversed itself and decided for the technologically preferable Panama passage, citing the company's willingness to sell out for the reduced sum of $40 million. Guided by Roosevelt and Cromwell, Congress five months later chose the Panama route. The State Department soon opened negotiations with Colombia. The annual rent became a stumbling block, which Hay removed only by delivering an ultimatum to the Colombian chargé d'affaires, Tomás Herrán, in January 1903. On January 22 he and Hay signed a treaty granting Colombia an initial payment of $10 million and $250,000 annually. The United States would control the six-mile-wide canal zone for one hundred years, a privilege renewable at the "sole and absolute option" of the North American republic.[4]

The U.S. Senate approved the Hay–Herrán Treaty on March 17, 1903, but the Colombian government attempted to extract a $10 million payment from the New Panama Canal Company for permitting the transfer of its assets to the U.S. government. Cromwell promptly cried foul, whereupon Secretary Hay bluntly announced that any payment by the company to Colombia was "not permissible."[5] The Colombians next tried to raise the initial American cash payment from $10 million to $15 million. Roosevelt exploded against "those contemptible little creatures in Bogotá."[6] The president believed that "you could no more make an agreement with the Colombian rulers than you could nail currant jelly to the wall."[7] TR's intransigence and Hay's extraordinary intercession on behalf of a privately owned foreign corporation increased Colombians' resentment against U.S. infringement on their sovereignty over Panama. The Colombian congress unanimously defeated the treaty on August 12, 1903.

Bogotá's rejection did not catch Roosevelt napping. As early as March 30, U.S. minister Arthur N. Beaupré had warned that "without question public opinion is strongly against its ratification," and Roosevelt had begun to ponder undiplomatic alternatives.[8] On June 13 the ubiquitous Cromwell had met with Roosevelt and then planted a story in the *New York World* reporting that, if Colombia rejected the treaty, Panama would secede and grant to the United States "the equivalent of absolute sovereignty over the Canal Zone," and that "President Roosevelt is said to strongly favor this plan."[9] By now the president was peppering his correspondence with contempt for Colombian "jack rabbits," "foolish and homicidal corruptionists," and "cat-rabbits."[10] Even the usually urbane Hay denounced "the government of folly and graft that now rules at Bogotá."[11]

Roosevelt now considered two options: seizure of Panama by force, or instant recognition and support for any revolutionary regime in Panama. The president inclined sharply toward the latter course after a meeting with Bunau-Varilla on October 10, during which the Frenchman predicted an uprising. When Bunau-Varilla asked what the United States would do, TR replied: "Colombia by her action has forfeited any claim upon the U.S. and I have no use for a government that would do what that government has done."[12] One week later, on October 16, Secretary Hay informed Bunau-Varilla that American naval vessels were heading toward the isthmus. Calculating the steaming time, Bunau-Varilla cabled the revolutionaries waiting on the isthmus that American warships would arrive by November 2. Early that evening the U.S.S. *Nashville* dropped anchor at Colón as predicted. Although the *Nashville* landed troops to keep order *after* the Panamanian junta had gained control, a Colombian diplomat rightfully complained: "The Americans are against us. What can we do against the American Navy?"[13]

In his annual message to Congress after the Panamanian revolution, Roosevelt urged swift ratification of the Hay–Bunau-Varilla Treaty, claiming that Colombia had forced the United States "to take decisive steps to bring to an end a condition of affairs which had become intolerable."[14] When critics complained about his

Panama Canal. The U.S.S. *Ohio* passes through the Culebra Cut (now called the Gaillard Cut) of the Panama Canal about a year after the canal opened to traffic—both warships and commercial vessels. (Library of Congress)

"Bowery-boy" behavior toward Colombia, Roosevelt denounced the "small body of shrill eunuchs who consistently oppose" his "righteous" policies.[15] On February 23, 1904, the Senate approved the treaty by a vote of 66 to 14. The treaty granted the United States "power and authority" within the zone "in perpetuity" as "if it were the sovereign of the territory."[16] Later, in 1911, TR reportedly boasted that "I took the Canal Zone and let Congress debate; and while the debate goes on the Canal does also."[17]

Construction began in mid–1904, and the fifty-mile-long canal opened on August 15, 1914. During the first year of operation alone, 1,058 merchant vessels slid through the locks, while the Atlantic and Pacific fleets of the U.S. Navy freely exchanged ships. In 1922 the United States paid "conscience money" or "canalimony" of $25 million to Colombia but did not formally apologize for having taken the canal zone. Although Roosevelt's handling of the Panama issue constitutes "one of the ineradicable blots on his record," most Americans have applauded his bold meddling in the internal affairs of Colombia.[18] Roosevelt himself ranked it alongside the Louisiana Purchase and the acquisition of Texas.

The Conservative Shapers of Empire

The taking of Panama symbolized the new activism characteristic of American foreign policy after the Spanish-American-Cuban-Filipino War, and construction of the canal ensured the United States virtual hegemony over Latin America. It also

Makers of American Foreign Relations, 1900–1914

Presidents	Secretaries of State
Theodore Roosevelt, 1901–1909	John Hay, 1898–1905
	Elihu Root, 1905–1909
	Robert Bacon, 1909
William Howard Taft, 1909–1913	Philander C. Knox, 1909–1913
Woodrow Wilson, 1913–1921	William Jennings Bryan, 1913–1915

intensified Washington's participation in the global contest for empire among the great powers. "The United States will be attacked as soon as you are about to complete the canal," Germany's Kaiser Wilhelm II predicted to an American diplomat in 1907, identifying Japan as the most likely culprit.[19] Britain, which had the power to challenge U.S. preeminence in the hemisphere, chose to acquiesce in the face of a growing political and naval threat from Germany. In turn, the vigorous German Empire, having expanded its markets and investments in Central and South America to more than 2 billion marks by 1900, seemed "desirous of obtaining a foothold in the Western Hemisphere," as the General Board of the U.S. Navy put it.[20] The kaiser boasted: "We will do whatever is necessary for our navy, even if it displeases the Yankees. Never fear."[21] Revolutionary upheavals in Russia, China, and Mexico produced further shifting in the international balance of power. As European alliances consolidated and lurched toward a world war, it became the task of President Roosevelt and his successors to defend, develop, and enlarge the new U.S. empire in an era of tumultuous transformation.

In the late nineteenth century, Roosevelt had associated closely with the most vocal pressure group agitating for an American canal, the uniformed "professors of war" at the Naval War College.[22] He corresponded regularly with Alfred Thayer Mahan, the navalist who tirelessly explained the strategic advantages of a canal. During the war of 1898, the warship *Oregon* dashed at full speed from San Francisco around South America to Cuba in time to help destroy the Spanish fleet off Santiago. The race of more than 14,000 miles fired American imaginations, but it also consumed sixty-eight days and underscored the need for an interoceanic canal across Central America.

Roosevelt's sense of isthmian strategic necessity reflected a broad worldview he shared with many "progressives" in the early twentieth century. A conservative patrician reformer motivated by noblesse oblige, he "feared that unrest caused by social and economic inequities would impair the nation's strength and efficiency."[23] He saw a similar danger to American interests in unrest abroad, and he sought to exert U.S. influence to create order on a global scale through "proper policing."[24] A quintessential chauvinist, Roosevelt talked about doing the "rough work of the world" and about the need to "speak softly and carry a big stick."[25] Imbibing Darwinist doctrines of "natural selection," Roosevelt proclaimed "our duty toward the people living in barbarism to see that they are freed from their chains, and we can free them only by destroying barbarism itself."[26] For Roosevelt in particular, Anglo-Saxon superiority was best expressed in war. "All the great masterful races have been fighting races," he lectured.[27] Not all Progressive-era reformers joined Roosevelt in advocating a vigorous activism abroad. Wisconsin's Senator Robert M. La Follette, for example, opposed imperialism and contended that the same corporate monopolists they battled at home were dragging the United States into perpetual intervention overseas. Activists in women's organizations bemoaned the "present intoxication with the hashish of conquest" as they urged "women's values" on a male government so as to rein in the "champing steeds" of American militarism and expansion.[28]

Roosevelt vigorously debated his critics and added his unique personal characteristics to American foreign policy. Exuberant and calculating, he centralized foreign-policy decisionmaking, frequently bypassed Congress, and believed "the people" so ignorant about foreign affairs that they should not direct an informed president like himself. At the same time, he kept favorite journalists and other "intelligent observers sufficiently enlightened to prevent their going wrong."[29] Seeking world stability, Roosevelt advocated "minimizing the chances of war among civilized people" and "multiplying the methods and chances of honorably avoiding war in the event of controversy."[30] Indeed, he won the Nobel Peace Prize in 1906 for his mediating effort at the Portsmouth Conference (see pages 252–253). The robust president disliked pomp and ceremony and once broke up a state luncheon by demonstrating jujitsu holds on the Swiss minister. "The biggest matters," this progenitor of the imperial presidency later wrote, "such as the Portsmouth peace, the acquisition of Panama, and sending the fleet around the world, I managed without consultation with anyone; for when a matter is of capital importance, it is well to have it handled by one man only."[31]

Roosevelt and other shapers of American foreign policy before World War I were members of an American quasi aristocracy and sure-footed devotees of "order." Most had graduated from prestigious eastern colleges and distinguished themselves in high political office or in the professions. They moved comfortably in the affluent, cosmopolitan, upper-class society of the Atlantic seaboard. Roosevelt, a graduate of Harvard College and prolific author, had served as assistant secretary of the navy and governor of New York. His successor, Ohioan William Howard Taft, a graduate of Yale, had served as a federal circuit court judge, governor of the Philippines (1901–1904), and secretary of war (1904–1908). Woodrow Wilson earned a Ph.D. from Johns Hopkins, wrote books on government and history, presided over Princeton, and governed New Jersey before entering the White House.

Their secretaries of state, with one exception, belonged to the same elite. John Hay, secretary from 1898 to 1905, was born in Indiana and educated at Brown University. A poet, novelist, biographer, and editor of the *New York Tribune,* the wealthy Hay had served as Lincoln's personal secretary during the Civil War and later as McKinley's ambassador to Great Britain. A chief architect of the Anglo-American rapprochement, Hay regarded "a firm understanding with England" as the "indispensable feature of our foreign policy."[32] His successor, Elihu Root (1905–1909), was born in upstate New York, graduated from Hamilton College, took a law degree at New York University, and became one of America's most successful corporation lawyers. As secretary of war from 1899 to 1904, he created mechanisms, such as the Platt Amendment for Cuba, for managing the American empire. Like TR, he believed that the "main object of diplomacy is to keep the country out of trouble" and maintain order abroad.[33] Philander C. Knox (1909–1913) followed Root. A corporation lawyer born in Pennsylvania, Knox served as attorney general and U.S. senator before entering the State Department. He liked to play golf at Chevy Chase, spend summers with his trotters at his Valley Forge Farms estate, vacation in Florida in the winter, and delegate departmental work to subordinates. He advocated "dollar diplomacy" as a means of creating order in revolution-prone areas—that is, using private financiers and business leaders to promote foreign policy, and using diplomacy to promote American commerce and investment abroad. As his *second* secretary of state President Wilson named New Yorker Robert Lansing (1915–1920), a graduate of Amherst College, son-in-law of a former secretary of state, and practitioner of international law. Reserved and conservative, Lansing also abhorred disorder in the U.S. sphere of Latin America.

William Jennings Bryan, Wilson's *first* appointment (1913–1915), lacked such conservative elite status. The "boy orator" of Nebraska could mesmerize crowds by decrying the "cross of gold" on which eastern capitalists were crucifying western and southern farmers, but he could not win a presidential election (he ran in 1896, 1900, and 1908). The "Great Commoner" languished for years as the most prominent has-been of the Democratic party until Wilson named him secretary of state as a reward for support at the convention of 1912. The president let Bryan appoint "deserving Democrats" to diplomatic posts and indulge his fascination with peace or "cooling off" treaties, but Wilson bypassed him in most important diplomatic decisions, even to the point of composing overseas cables on his own White House typewriter.

These conservative managers of American foreign policy believed that a major component of national power was a prosperous, expanding economy invigorated by a healthy foreign trade. The principle of the "Open Door"—to keep open trade and investment opportunities—became a governing tenet voiced globally, if often tarnished in application. Mahan believed that commerce acted as the "energizer of material civilization," and Roosevelt declared that "America has only just begun to assume that commanding position in the international business world which we believe will more and more be hers."[34] In 1900 the United States exported goods valued at $1.5 billion. By 1914 that figure stood at $2.5 billion. Exports to Latin America increased markedly from $132 million at the turn of the century to $309 million in 1914. Investments there in sugar, transportation, and banking shot up. By 1913 the United Fruit Company, the banana empire, had some 130,000 acres in cultivation in Central America, a fleet of freighters, and political influence as well. By 1914 U.S. entrepreneurs dominated nickel mining in Canada and sugar production in Cuba, and total American investments abroad equaled $3.5 billion.

But those statistics meant more than contributions to pocketbooks. Americans believed that economic expansion also carried abroad the best of "Americanism," the core values of industriousness, honesty, morality, and private initiative. Thus Yale University-in-China and the Young Men's Christian Association (YMCA) joined Standard Oil Company and Singer Sewing in China as advance agents of civilization. And Taft said about the Chinese: "The more civilized they become the more active their industries, the wealthier they become, and the better market they will become for us."[35] President Wilson, who added missionary paternalism to the quest for order, said simply that he would "teach the South American Republics to elect good men."[36] Some foreign observers did not appreciate American benefi-cence. The typical "Yankee," one German wrote in 1904, was "a boorish fellow . . . who pursued the dollar and sensation, a barbarian in science and art, a bigoted, sanctimonious hypocrite who chewed tobacco and whose chief amusement was found in lynchings."[37] Whatever Americans' intentions or habits, their compulsion to shape the lives of other peoples while denying any desire to dominate brought mixed results.

Cuba's Limited Independence Under the Platt Amendment

In December 1898, President William McKinley promised Cuba "free and inde-pendent" status once the American military occupation had achieved "complete tranquility" and a "stable government" on the island.[38] Two months later the Philip-pine insurrection erupted, and Secretary of War Elihu Root, charged with formu-lating Cuban occupation policy, feared that in Cuba the United States stood "on the verge daily of the same sort of thing that happened to us in the Philippines."[39]

To accelerate Cuban democracy and stability, Root appointed General Leonard Wood the military governor of the island. A Harvard graduate with a de-gree in medicine, Wood was a friend of the adventurous Roosevelt. Wood favored outright annexation of Cuba, but he loyally carried out the administration's policy of patrician tutelage. During his tenure as military governor (1899–1902), he worked to eradicate yellow fever, Americanize education, construct highways, and formulate an electoral law guaranteeing order. He even added "before" and "after" photos of public toilets in his reports. The general defined his objectives conserva-tively: "When money can be borrowed at a reasonable rate of interest and when capital is willing to invest in the Island, a condition of stability will have been reached."[40] Given the war-ravaged Cuban economy, only the North Americans had the resources to generate reconstruction. Those Cuban elites who spoke Eng-lish and knew American ways could serve as local managers, traders, agents, and ad-visers. The occupation thus stressed the teaching of English in the public schools because, according to one official, "the Cuban people will never understand the people of the United States until they appreciate our institutions."[41] Many Cubans realized that "to be educated by the people who had conquered them was the ex-tension of conquest, only by another name."[42]

Root began construction of a Cuban-American political relationship designed to weather the storms of independence. Working closely with Senator Orville Platt, Root fashioned the Platt Amendment to the Army Appropriation Bill of 1901. By the amendment's terms, Cuba could not make a treaty with any nation that might impair its independence. Should Cuban independence ever be threatened, or should Cuba fail to protect adequately "life, property, and individual liberty," the

"If General Wood Is Unpopular with Cuba, We Can Guess the Reason." General Leonard Wood (1860–1927), before serving as military governor of Cuba (1899–1902), was a surgeon who entered the army in 1886 and earned a Congressional Medal of Honor for capturing Indian leader Geronimo. He also commanded the Rough Riders at San Juan Hill during the Spanish-American-Cuban-Filipino War. Later he helped govern the Philippines. (*Minneapolis Tribune* in *Literary Digest,* 1901)

United States had the right to intervene. For these purposes, Cuba would cede to the United States "lands necessary for coaling or naval stations."[43]

Cubans howled. On Good Friday 1901, the front page of Havana's *La Discusión* carried a cartoon of "The Cuban Calvary" depicting the Cuban people as Christ and Senator Platt as a Roman soldier. Anti-imperialist critics charged that the amendment extinguished Cuban independence. Root piously denied any "intermeddling or interference with the affairs of a Cuban government," but General Wood privately conceded that "little or no independence [was] left Cuba under the Platt Amendment."[44] A reluctant Cuban convention adopted the measure as an amendment to the new constitution on June 12, 1901, and the two governments signed a treaty embodying the Platt Amendment on May 22, 1903. That same year the U.S. Navy constructed a naval base at Guantánamo Bay; "Gitmo," as the marines christened it, was leased to the United States in perpetuity for a small annual fee. With North American investments pouring into capital-starved Cuba, extending control over sugar, tobacco (the new Tobacco Trust exported 90 percent of Havana cigars by 1902), mining, transportation, utilities, and cattle ranching, the Reciprocity Treaty of 1902 permitted Cuban products to enter the United States at specially reduced tariff rates, thereby further interlocking the economies of the two countries.

The first president of the Republic of Cuba, Tomás Estrada Palma, acted "more plattish than Platt himself."[45] Following his rigged reelection and second inauguration, discontented Cuban nationalists revolted. In September 1906, the U.S. consul general in Havana reported Estrada Palma's inability to quell the rebellion or "protect life and property."[46] President Roosevelt immediately ordered the cruiser *Denver* to Havana, whereupon a battalion of sailors landed at Estrada Palma's request. Roosevelt summarily ordered the men back aboard ship. "I am so angry with that infernal little Cuban republic," exploded the Rough Rider, "that I would like to wipe its people off the face of the earth." All he wanted from the Cubans was that "they should behave themselves."[47]

Into this turmoil stepped the portly secretary of war, William Howard Taft, whom Roosevelt sent to mediate between the warring factions. Estrada Palma resigned, permitting Taft to establish a new government with himself as governor. Taft soon lectured students in Havana that Cubans needed a "mercantile spirit," a "desire to make money, to found great enterprises."[48] He returned home in mid-October, leaving behind a government headed by an American civilian, administered by U.S. Army officers, and supported by more than 5,000 American soldiers. For twenty-eight months Governor Charles E. Magoon attempted to reinstate Leonard Wood's electoral and humanitarian reforms, while Roosevelt publicly scolded the Cubans that if their "insurrectionary habit" persisted, it would be "absolutely out of the question that the Island should continue independent."[49]

Under his successor Taft, and under Taft's successor Woodrow Wilson, U.S. policy toward Cuba reflexively supported existing governments, by force if necessary. Taft and Wilson made no serious effort to reform Cuba in the North American image. Through "dollar diplomacy," the United States sought order in Cuban politics and security for investments and commerce, particularly in sugar. The $50 million invested by Americans in 1896 jumped to $220 million in 1913. By 1920 American-owned mills produced about half of Cuba's sugar. Cuban exports to the United States in 1900 equaled $31 million, by 1914 $131 million, and by 1920 $722 million. U.S. entrepreneurs helped establish missionary schools (such as the Candler school in Havana, named after the founder of Coca-Cola) that, in effect, trained Cubans for employment in North American companies. When revolution threatened these interests, as in May 1912 and February 1917, marines went ashore. After Havana followed Washington's lead and declared war against Germany in April 1917, some 2,500 American troops went to the island, ostensibly to protect the sugar plantations that helped feed the Allied armies.

The Constable of the Caribbean: The Roosevelt Corollary, Venezuela, and the Dominican Republic

President Theodore Roosevelt pondered that most hallowed of American doctrines, the one enunciated by James Monroe in 1823. In his first annual message, on December 3, 1901, Roosevelt called the doctrine "a guarantee of the commercial independence of the Americas." The United States, however, as protector of that independence, would "not guarantee any state against punishment if it misconducts itself, provided that punishment does not take the form of the acquisition of territory by any non-American power."[50] If a Western Hemispheric country misbehaved toward a European nation, Roosevelt would "let the European country spank it."[51]

The president was thinking principally of Germany and Venezuela. Under the rule of Cipriano Castro, an unsavory dictator whom Roosevelt once labeled an "unspeakable villainous monkey," Venezuela perpetually deferred payment on bonds worth more than $12.5 million and held by German investors.[52] Berlin became impatient. Britain also rankled at Venezuelan defaults to British creditors. In December 1902, after clearing the way with Washington, Germany and Britain delivered an ultimatum demanding immediate settlement of their claims, seized several Venezuelan vessels, bombarded two forts, and blockaded all ports. To all of this Roosevelt initially acquiesced, despite the doctrine of Argentina's Foreign Minister Luis M. Drago that "the public debt cannot occasion armed intervention . . . by a European power."[53]

In mid-January 1903, the German navy bombarded two more forts. "Are the people in Berlin crazy?" asked TR.[54] This time the president delivered a quiet warning to desist. He also sent Admiral George Dewey on naval maneuvers in the Caribbean, which were intended, Dewey later boasted, as "an object lesson to the Kaiser."[55] TR privately mused: "The only power which may be a menace to us in anything like the immediate future is Germany."[56] Impressed by the U.S. reaction, Kaiser Wilhelm II replaced his ill-informed ambassador with Hermann Speck von Sternburg, an old friend of Roosevelt. The president urged on him a quick settlement. Thereupon, Britain and Germany in early February lifted the blockade and submitted the dispute to the Permanent Court at The Hague. Prime Minister Arthur Balfour calmed troubled waters by announcing that "the Monroe Doctrine has no enemies in this country."[57] Speck von Sternburg also averred that the kaiser "would no more think of violating that [Monroe] doctrine than he would of colonizing the moon."[58] When the Hague arbiters found in favor of Germany and England in early 1904, a State Department official complained that this decision put "a premium on violence" and made likely similar European interventions in the future.[59]

TR also worried increasingly about the Dominican Republic, revolution-torn since 1899 and seemingly vulnerable to German interests. "I have about the same desire to annex it," Roosevelt said privately, "as a gorged boa constrictor might have to swallow a porcupine wrong-end to."[60] An American firm claimed damages of several million dollars, and European creditors demanded action by their governments. The president prayed that the Dominicans "would behave so that I would not have to act in any way." By spring 1904 he thought he might have to do "what a policeman has to do."[61] If he said "'Hands off' to the powers of Europe, then sooner or later we must keep order ourselves," he told Root.[62]

On December 6, 1904, Roosevelt described to Congress his conception of the United States as hemispheric policeman. "Chronic wrongdoing, or an impotence which results in a general loosening of the ties of civilized society," he proclaimed, "may in America, as elsewhere, ultimately require intervention by some civilized nation, and in the Western Hemisphere the adherence of the United States to the Monroe Doctrine may force the United States, however reluctantly, in flagrant cases of such wrongdoing or impotence, to the exercise of an international police power."[63] With this statement the twenty-sixth president added to the Monroe Doctrine his own corollary, which fundamentally transformed that prohibition on European meddling into a brash promise of U.S. regulation of the Americas.

The Rough Rider soon donned his constable's badge. He assigned a U.S. collector of Dominican customs. "The Constitution," Roosevelt later explained, "did not explicitly give me the power to bring about the necessary agreement with Santo Domingo. But the Constitution did not forbid me."[64] Yet "policing" and "civilizing" the Dominican Republic by presidential order provoked nationalist resentment from Dominicans who, as one naval officer reported in 1906, "are quieting their children with the threat 'There comes an American. Keep quiet or he will kill you.'"[65] Taft's secretary of state, Philander C. Knox, applauded the customs receivership in the Dominican Republic because it denied to rebels the funds they so eagerly "collected" through the capture of customshouses, thus curing "century-old evils."[66] The assassination of the Dominican president in November 1911 suggested that Knox spoke prematurely. And in 1912 revolutionaries operating from contiguous Haiti marauded throughout the Dominican Republic, forcing the closure of several customshouses. To restore order, Taft in September 1912 sent a commission backed by 750 marines. The commissioners redefined the Haitian-Dominican border, forced the corrupt Dominican president to resign, and avoided direct interference in a new election.

His denunciation of "dollar diplomacy" notwithstanding, Woodrow Wilson had written in 1907 that "concessions obtained by financiers must be safeguarded by ministers of state, even if the sovereignty of unwilling nations be outraged in the process."[67] No wonder that President Wilson's search for stability in Latin America retraced familiar steps. When, in September 1913, revolution again threatened the Dominican government, Secretary Bryan promised "every legitimate means to assist in the restoration of order and the prevention of further insurrections."[68] When Wilson ordered naval intervention after further Dominican disorders in May 1916, he said: "If a man will not listen to you quietly in a seat, sit on his neck and make him listen."[69] As the 400 marines of Admiral William Caperton's landing force entered the city of Santo Domingo at dawn on May 15, they found empty streets, bolted doors, shuttered windows, and Dominican flags festooned with black crepe—a "*duelo publico* (public mourning)."[70] A new treaty gave the United States full control over Dominican finances. In November, as U.S. participation in the European war became increasingly probable, Wilson proclaimed the formal military occupation of the Dominican Republic, ostensibly to curtail the activities of revolutionaries suspected of a pro-German bias. Despite an insurgency by peasants in the eastern region of the Dominican Republic, who waged hit-and-run guerrilla warfare, the U.S. Navy formally governed the country until 1922. The main legacy of the occupation, in the historian Bruce Calder's terse judgment, was "a strong anti-U.S. feeling" among the Dominican people.[71]

The Quest for Order in Haiti and Nicaragua

The Dominican Republic shares the island of Hispaniola with Haiti, where revolution became an increasingly popular mode of changing governments. American investments in Haiti were limited to ownership of a small railroad and a one-third share in the Haitian National Bank. Nationals of France and Germany controlled the bank, and disorder thus could give either European nation a pretext for intervention. After the outbreak of World War I, the Wilson administration worried about "the ever present danger of German control" of Haiti and Haiti's deepwater harbor of Môle Saint Nicolas.[72] The Navy Department, content with bases in Cuba and Puerto Rico, nonetheless remembered the German cruiser *Panther*'s sinking a Haitian gunboat in 1902. The State Department sought to buy the Môle "to take it out of the market."[73] To impose order on Haiti, Wilson pressed for an American customs receivership on the Dominican model.

The Haitians resisted successfully until July 1915, when the regime of Guillaume Sam fell in an orgy of grisly political murders. Wilson could stomach no more, and he ordered the navy to invade Haiti. After 2,000 marines imposed martial law and the State Department took over the customshouses, Admiral William B. Caperton reported that "only a government superimposed by the firm hand and supervised under the watchful eye of the United States . . . could ever rescue that unhappy republic from her beastly national sins."[74] Subsequent fighting between occupiers and native guerrillas, which critics perceived as "a racial war of extermination," killed more than 2,250 Haitians compared to 16 marine casualties.[75] An American military regime ruled Haiti until 1934.

The United States also intervened, virtually at will, in Nicaragua. For Theodore Roosevelt, Nicaragua held importance primarily as a potential canal route, a rivalry decided in Panama's favor in 1903. He manifested interest in Nicaragua only briefly thereafter, during 1907, when he and Mexico's president jointly proposed a peace conference to end the incessant warfare among Central American states. As Secretary Root explained, their conduct mattered because the Panama Canal put them "in the front yard of the United States."[76] When President José Santos Zelaya solicited funds to build a second interoceanic canal, especially from Germany (whose capital investments stood three times greater than U.S. properties in Nicaragua), Washington turned against a leader whom some Nicaraguans had compared to Roosevelt himself. For Zelaya's crime of seeking a "better economic position for Nicaragua outside the U.S. economic subsystem," as one historian has written, North Americans labeled him "a tyrannical, self-serving, brutal, greedy disturber of Central American peace, an enemy of U.S. businessmen, and an opponent of all reasonable diplomatic objectives."[77]

After Zelaya "yanked Mr. Taft by the ear" by executing two Americans for aiding rebels, Washington broke diplomatic relations in November 1909, threatened naval intervention, and forced Zelaya into exile.[78] Secretary Knox then negotiated a treaty with the victorious conservatives led by Adolfo Díaz, providing for U.S. control of the customs service and an American loan. Instead of gratitude, "the natural sentiment of an overwhelming majority of Nicaraguans is antagonistic to the United States," the U.S. envoy reported.[79] Rebuffed by the U.S. Senate, Knox and a group of bankers simply went ahead without a treaty. In September 1912, the administration ordered Major Smedley D. Butler and 354 marines into battle on behalf of the Díaz regime, which the State Department deemed representative "of an educated, property-owning and civilized small minority . . . , [and] the ablest people of the country."[80] After tipping the scales against the newest revolutionary army, the leathernecks returned home, leaving one hundred behind as a legation guard in

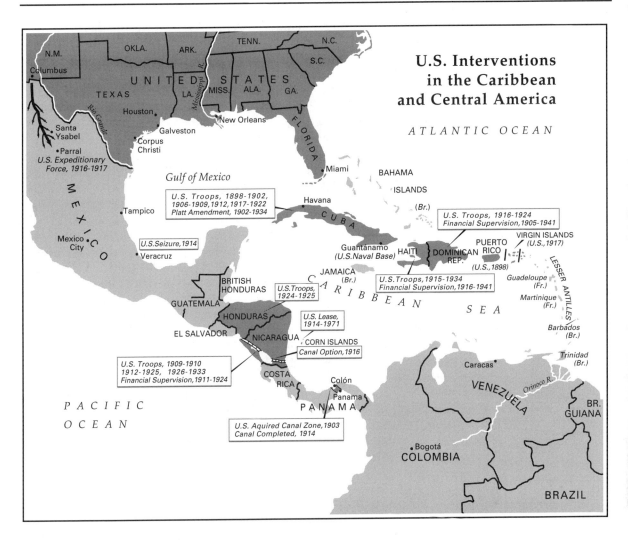

U.S. Interventions
in the Caribbean
and Central America

ATLANTIC OCEAN

U.S. Troops, 1898-1902,
1906-1909, 1912, 1917-1922
Platt Amendment, 1902-1934

U.S. Troops, 1916-1924
Financial Supervision, 1905-1941

U.S. Seizure, 1914

U.S. Troops, 1915-1934
Financial Supervision, 1916-1941

U.S. Troops,
1924-1925

U.S. Lease,
1914-1971

CORN ISLANDS
Canal Option, 1916

U.S. Troops, 1909-1910
1912-1925, 1926-1933
Financial Supervision, 1911-1924

U.S. Aquired Canal Zone, 1903
Canal Completed, 1914

Managua. The marines could prevent a coup d'état, but "*keeping* a surrogate in power in Central America was often as problematical as *putting* him in power."[81]

Bryan in spring 1913 dusted off a shelved draft treaty granting the United States a canal option in Nicaragua in exchange for $3 million. He hoped that this money would "give sufficient encouragement" to American bankers to lend Díaz more.[82] The secretary also added a clause similar to the Platt Amendment before sending the Bryan-Chamorro Treaty to the Senate. When the upper house balked, Bryan had to delete the U.S. right of intervention. Ratification in February 1916 did help Nicaragua's finances. The treaty also effectively excluded European powers from naval bases in the Gulf of Fonseca, and to make that point stick, Wilson ordered U.S. warships to cruise offshore during the 1916 Nicaraguan presidential campaign. Although nominally independent, Nicaragua remained a U.S. protectorate until 1933.

The Mexican Revolution Threatens U.S. Interests

Mexico changed governments with uncharacteristic frequency after the outbreak of revolution in 1910. In 1911 Francisco I. Madero toppled Porfirio Díaz, the aged dictator who had maintained order, personal power, and a healthy environment for North American investments since the late 1870s. U.S. citizens owned more than 40 percent of Mexico's property, and Mexico had become the world's third largest oil producer, thanks to Standard Oil Company, Texas Oil Company (Texaco), and other firms. The revolution thus inevitably took on an anti-Yankee tinge. Despite the threat to American lives and property, Taft determined to "sit tight on the lid and it will take a good deal to pry me off."[83] In February 1913, U.S. ambassador Henry Lane Wilson encouraged one of Madero's trusted generals, Victoriano Huerta, to overthrow the revolutionary nationalist. Indeed, Huerta had Madero shot and then set about to consolidate his own power. The German ambassador called these events "the usual American policy of replacing hostile regimes with pliable ones through revolutions without taking official responsibility for it."[84] But one of the state governors, Venustiano Carranza, organized the "Constitutionalist" revolt on February 26. When American residents became caught in the crossfire, the departing Taft administration refused recognition until Huerta punished the "murderers of American citizens" and ended "discriminations against American interests."[85]

Appalled by Madero's murder, President Wilson vowed not to recognize a "government of butchers."[86] He denounced Huerta as a "diverting brute! . . . seldom sober and always impossible."[87] Seemingly unconcerned about private American properties in Mexico worth some $1.5 billion, Wilson refused to act as "the servant of those who wish to enhance the value of their Mexican investments."[88] When Ambassador Wilson, whom the president suspected of complicity in Madero's ouster, continued to advocate recognition of Huerta to protect those American interests, Washington recalled the U.S. envoy in July 1913 and dismissed him from the diplomatic corps. The president thereafter treated with Mexico through special emissaries, only one of whom spoke fluent Spanish.

In August one such representative, John Lind, arrived in Mexico City. A rabid anti-Catholic and former governor of Minnesota without diplomatic experience, Lind delivered Wilson's proposal for an armistice between Huerta's federalist troops and all revolutionary groups, "an early and free election," and Huerta's promise not to run for president. In exchange, the United States pledged recognition and aid to "the administration chosen and set up . . . in the way and on the conditions suggested." With sublime arrogance, Woodrow Wilson wondered, "can Mexico give the civilized world a satisfactory reason for rejecting our good offices?"[89] Mexican foreign minister Federico Gamboa ridiculed Wilson's "counsels and advice (let us call them thus)," for no Mexican government would ever accept a "veto of any President of the United States."[90] After this snub, Woodrow Wilson announced a restrained policy of "watchful waiting."[91]

Undeterred, Huerta in October dissolved an unruly legislature, arrested its members, and held a special election, which returned an entirely submissive congress ready to extend his presidency indefinitely. Wilson then turned to Carranza in northern Mexico, sending the same proposal Huerta's foreign minister had rejected

William Jennings Bryan (1860–1925), Woodrow Wilson (1856–1924), and Franklin D. Roosevelt (1882–1945), 1913. President Wilson, in white trousers and dark jacket, speaks while Secretary of State Bryan, to the president's right, and Assistant Secretary of the Navy Roosevelt, at the far right of the picture, look on. Wilson spoke proudly of his "missionary diplomacy," for he believed that "every nation needs to be drawn into the tutelage of America." Latin Americans resisted such U.S. paternalism. (Franklin D. Roosevelt Library)

in August. Equally nationalistic, Carranza contemptuously refused Wilsonian mediation and rejected any solution short of his own triumph. Wilson informed the other powers on November 24 of his policy "to isolate General Huerta entirely . . . and so to force him out." If such pressure failed to induce Huerta's retirement, "it will become the duty of the United States to use less peaceful means to put him out."[92]

Most European powers, especially Germany, had recognized Huerta in defiance of Wilson. "Good. Finally unity against the Yankee," the kaiser had noted in July 1913.[93] The British, however, their capital investments in Mexico ranking second only to those of the United States and their navy relying on Mexican oil as a backup to Middle East sources, did not want to antagonize Wilson when tensions were mounting in Europe. The British Foreign Office therefore notified Huerta that it would not support him against the United States, urged him to resign, and recalled Minister Sir Lionel Carden, whose alleged influence over Huerta had provoked American antipathy—all the while viewing Wilson's policies as "most impractical and unreasonable."[94]

With British compliance assured, Wilson lifted the U.S. arms embargo in February 1914 and permitted large quantities of arms to flow to both factions. As Carranza's resupplied forces pushed south, the president sent U.S. naval vessels to the oil-producing town of Tampico on the Gulf of Mexico. On April 9, at Tampico, Huerta's troops arrested several American sailors loading gasoline aboard a whaleboat docked provocatively near the Mexican outpost. The Mexican colonel in charge quickly disavowed the arrests, freed the sailors, and apologized orally. The hotheaded U.S. squadron commander, Rear Admiral Henry T. Mayo, demanded a formal twenty-one-gun salute because Mexico had insulted the flag—"a hostile act, not to be excused."[95] Using Huerta's rejection of the Mayo ultimatum as justification, the president undertook to drive the Mexican leader from power. On April 20, Wilson requested congressional approval to use armed force "to obtain from General Huerta and his adherents the fullest recognition of the rights and dignity of the United States."[96] Rather than protect American-owned oil fields at Tampico, Wilson ordered U.S. warships to the port of Veracruz to stop a German arms shipment intended for Huerta.

On April 21, 1914, 800 American sailors and marines landed. Huerta's troops withdrew from the city, but cadets from the naval academy, joined by prisoners liberated from jails and other irregulars, put up a bloody resistance. Nineteen Americans and several hundred Mexicans died. An anguished Wilson bemoaned that "it was I who ordered those young men to their deaths."[97] Although calculated to undermine Huerta, the historian Ramón E. Ruíz has written, "the capture of Veracruz nearly united Mexicans behind him . . . [because] Mexicans, believing their independence endangered, rushed to enlist in Huerta's army."[98] Rejecting advice from his military advisers, who wanted to march to Mexico City, Wilson accepted mediation when proposed by Argentina, Brazil, and Chile (the ABC powers) on April 25.

A month later, representatives of the United States, Huerta, and the ABC powers met on the Canadian side of Niagara Falls. Intransigence doomed the mediation. Wilson refused to discuss the evacuation of Veracruz or Tampico, a major reason for convening the conference. He sought instead "the entire elimination of General Huerta."[99] But Carranza indignantly boycotted any foreign meeting dealing with Mexico's internal affairs. On July 2 the jilted mediators adjourned, two weeks later Huerta fled to Europe, and on August 20 a triumphant Carranza paraded before enthusiastic throngs in Mexico City.

The Constitutionalist triumph did not last. One of Carranza's northern generals, Francisco (Pancho) Villa, soon broke from the ranks, marched south, and in December occupied Mexico City. Wilson saw Villa as a Robin Hood "robbing the rich in order to give to the poor," a potential client who could be "the sword of the revolution" while Wilson offered "capable and disinterested advice."[100] Because Villa had not criticized Veracruz, the president eased arms exports to him and refused to recognize Carranza. To prevent a military clash with any Mexican faction, all American troops withdrew from Veracruz on November 23, 1914. Once again, Wilson watched and waited.

Relations remained tense during early 1915. Carranza's forces gradually drove Villa north, but in the process Mexico City became a no-man's-land, with bread riots and starvation threatening its inhabitants, including 2,500 Americans and 23,000 other foreign residents. Further complications arose along the Mexico-U.S. borderland, especially in southern Texas, where the massive influx of refugees and revolutionaries exacerbated local tensions between Anglos and *Tejanos*. The Plan of San Diego, an anarchist manifesto in early 1915, demanded return of all lands "robbed in a most perfidious manner," execution of every North American "over sixteen years of age," restoration of Indian lands, and sovereign territory for blacks.[101] The ensuing raids and counterraids turned south Texas into a war zone as vigilantes and

Texas rangers killed at least 150 Mexicans. A new verb—"rangered"—described summary treatment of suspects by Texas authorities.[102] Preoccupied by the *Lusitania* crisis with Germany after May 1915 (see page 268), Wilson reluctantly concluded that "Carranza will somehow have to be digested."[103] With American oil fields under Carranza's protection, Wilson extended de facto recognition to the Constitutionalist regime in June 1915, permitted arms exports (while banning them to opponents), and beefed up the U.S. military presence along the border.

Egged on by German agents who envisaged a Mexican-American war as "a noose . . . to tie the United States to the American continent," Villa denounced *Carranzistas* as "vassals" of the United States.[104] In the predawn hours of March 9, 1916, Villa led a band of *Villistas* across the border into Columbus, New Mexico, initiating a bloody battle that left seventeen Americans and more than a hundred Mexicans dead. Within hours of the attack, Wilson unleashed the Punitive Expedition of 7,000 soldiers, commanded by General John J. Pershing, which penetrated 350 miles into Mexico in a vain search for Pancho Villa. Even though, as Pershing reported, "the natives are not generally arming to oppose us," a clash with *Carranzista* troops occurred at Carrizal in June 1916.[105]

Carranza kept up drumfire demands for U.S. withdrawal, but Wilson hesitated for fear of appearing weak during a presidential election year. Just prior to Germany's resumption of unrestricted submarine warfare, however, Wilson ordered Pershing's troops to disengage; all left Mexico by February 5, 1917. In late February, the secret Zimmermann telegram, proposing an anti-American alliance between Germany and Mexico (and possibly including Japan), came into the hands of the State Department, courtesy of British intelligence. This German ploy accelerated Wilson's movement toward full diplomatic relations with Carranza's government. The United States extended de jure recognition on August 31, 1917, in order to ensure Mexican neutrality during the fight against Germany. After four futile years, Wilson had finally given up trying to tutor the Mexicans. Carranza "may not have fulfilled the social goals of the revolution," as one scholar has written, "but he kept the gringos out of Mexico City."[106]

Francisco (Pancho) Villa (1878–1923). The intelligent, dedicated revolutionary nationalist bedeviled both Mexico and the United States. His daring raid on an American town was calculated to outrage President Wilson, whom he mocked as "an evangelizing professor of philosophy who is destroying the independence of a friendly people." (W. H. Horne postcard. Southwest Collection, El Paso Public Library)

Japan, China, and Dollar Diplomacy in Asia

Managing Asian affairs proved even more difficult. Secretary of State John Hay's Open Door notes did not prevent the further emasculation of China. During the Boxer Rebellion Russia stationed 175,000 troops in Manchuria and demanded exclusive rights from China, including a commercial monopoly. Roosevelt and Hay acquiesced because the Open Door had "always recognized the exceptional position of Russia" in Manchuria and had merely sought the commercial freedom "guaranteed to us by . . . the whole civilized world."[107] Washington retreated because Roosevelt realized that the American people would not fight for nebulous principles of Chinese integrity in Manchuria. He thought it futile "to play the role of an Asian power without military power."[108]

Japan viewed the question quite differently. Russia blocked Japanese economic expansion into Manchuria, posed a potential naval menace, and endangered the

"Spread-eagleism" in China. The missionary teacher Grace Roberts teaches a Bible class in 1903 in Manchuria. Americanism and religious work, flag and missionary, became partners. The mission force was feminized—the majority of missionaries were women. (By permission of the Houghton Library, Harvard University)

Japanese position in Korea. Tokyo covered its flanks with an Anglo-Japanese Alliance in 1902 and prepared for war. On February 8, 1904, the Japanese navy destroyed Russia's Asian fleet in a surprise attack at Port Arthur. At first Roosevelt cheered privately, "for Japan is playing our game," but as the enormity of Japanese victories became apparent he hoped for peace "on terms which will not mean the creation of either a yellow peril or a Slav peril."[109] By spring 1905, Japanese soldiers had triumphed at Mukden, where Russia lost 97,000 men. Revolutionary stirrings had hit St. Petersburg, and Admiral Nakagori Togo had sunk the Russian Baltic fleet. "The Russian bubble has been pretty thoroughly pricked," TR noted.[110] On May 31, Japanese envoy Kogoro Takahira requested Roosevelt "directly and entirely of his own motion and initiative to invite the two belligerents to come together" for direct peace negotiations.[111]

Hoping to balance the belligerents "so that each may have a moderative action on the other" and thus protect American interests in the Pacific and Asia, the president invited Japanese and Russian representatives to meet at Portsmouth, New Hampshire, on August 9, 1905.[112] The Japanese delegates demanded Russia's leasehold on the Liaodong Peninsula and the railroad running from Harbin to Port Arthur, evacuation of Russian troops from Manchuria, and Japan's control of Korea. The Russians quickly conceded these points but rejected additional Japanese requests for an indemnity and cession of the island of Sakhalin. Roosevelt broke the deadlock by proposing division of Sakhalin and agreement "in principle" on an indemnity. Tsar Nicholas II agreed to partition the island but "not a kopeck of compensation."[113] Japan yielded and in late August signed a peace treaty. Roosevelt had earned the Nobel Peace Prize.

The Roosevelt administration's search for equipoise in East Asia neither began nor ended at Portsmouth. As early as March 1904, TR had conceded to Japan a relationship with Korea "just like we have with Cuba."[114] Secretary of War Taft reaffirmed the concession with Prime Minister Taro Katsura on July 27, 1905. In the Taft-Katsura "agreed memorandum of conversation," the prime minister denied Japanese designs on the Philippines, and Taft, in the words of the historian John Wilz, put an American "seal on the death warrant of an independent Korea."[115] A year later the Japanese reopened southern Manchuria to foreign and American trade but discouraged foreign capital investments. Japan formally annexed Korea in 1910.

Elihu Root (1845–1937). Root served as secretary of state (1905–1909). He helped devise methods for managing the American empire. (Library of Congress)

This studied attempt to balance interests augured well for a continuation of traditional Japanese-American cordiality, until a local dispute in California abruptly undercut Rooseveltian diplomacy. On October 11, 1906, the San Francisco School Board created a special "Oriental Public School" for all Japanese, Chinese, and Korean children. Japan immediately protested, and Theodore Roosevelt denounced the "infernal fools in California" whose exclusion of Japanese from all other public schools was "as foolish as if conceived by the mind of a Hottentot."[116] Given existing federal-state jurisdictions, however, he could do little more than rail against the recalcitrant school board, apply political pressure to the California legislature to prevent statewide discriminatory measures, and propose legislation to naturalize Japanese residing permanently in the United States. Defending segregation, the *San Francisco Examiner* editorialized: "Californians do not want their growing daughters to be intimate in daily school contact with Japanese young men. Is this remarkable?"[117] Always the political realist, Roosevelt accepted what he personally disliked and sought accommodation with Japan. In February 1907, he reached a "Gentlemen's Agreement" with Tokyo, sharply restricting Japanese immigration on a voluntary basis.

Because "the Japanese jingoes are . . . about as bad as ours," the president shrewdly pressed for more battleships and fortification of Hawai'i and the vulnerable Philippines, now America's "heel of Achilles," so that the United States would "be ready for anything that comes."[118] He also dramatized the importance of a strong navy to Congress and to Japan by ordering the battle fleet to the Pacific and around the world. The armada of sixteen battleships steamed out of Hampton Roads, Virginia, on December 16, 1907. Germany's kaiser predicted that U.S. warships in the Pacific "will upset all British and Japanese calculations."[119] Just after the "Great White Fleet" visited Tokyo in October 1908, Ambassador Takahira received instructions to reach an agreement with the United States recognizing the Pacific Ocean as an open avenue of trade, pledging the integrity of Japanese and American insular possessions in the Pacific, and promising equal opportunity in China. The ensuing Root-Takahira declaration of November 30, 1908, seemed to restore Japanese-American harmony.

Conflicting Japanese-American goals toward China spoiled the new epoch. Despite John Hay's Open Door notes, American commerce with China stalled during the Roosevelt era, in part because of resurgent nationalism. When Congress barred Chinese immigration in 1904, the Chinese staged a short-lived boycott of American goods and revoked a railroad franchise held by financier J. P. Morgan. As the historian Eileen Scully has noted, moreover, prostitution flourished in China's treaty ports, conducted by "American sex workers and their male compatriots." This illegitimate China trade ("deeply corrupt, overtly predatory, transnational, transracial, conducted without regard to a 'national interest'") undercut the gains of legitimate American commerce in China.[120] Because Roosevelt viewed the Chinese as opulent and effete, "sunk in Oriental stagnation and corruption," he placed strategic interests first and refused to antagonize Japan over China.[121]

Taft thought otherwise. Instead of a decrepit China in decay, Taft envisaged expanded trade with a "young China, rousing from a centuries-old slumber and rubbing the sand of its past from its eyes."[122] During a 1905 trip to East Asia, Taft met the impressive, intensely anti-Japanese American consul general in Mukden, Willard Straight. Two years later Straight proposed the creation of a Manchurian bank, to be financed by the American railroad magnate E. H. Harriman. He condemned the Root-Takahira agreement as "a terrible diplomatic blunder," because it accepted Japan's exploitative position in Manchuria.[123] Under Taft, Straight and the State Department quickly inspired several New York banks to form a combination, headed by J. P. Morgan, to serve as the official agency of American railroad investment in China. As acting chief of the department's new Far Eastern Division, Straight demanded admission of the American bankers into a European banking consortium undertaking construction of the Huguang Railway linking Beijing and Guangzhou (Canton). Straight then resigned from the State Department to become the Morgan group's roving representative.

In November 1909, Washington had proposed to Britain the neutralization of Manchurian railroads through a large international loan to China for the purchase of the lines. Britain, however, joined both Japan and Russia to reject the proposal. Instead of an open door in Manchuria, Secretary of State Knox had "nailed that door closed with himself on the outside."[124] In fall 1910, an agreement expanded the Huguang Railway consortium to include American bankers, but the Chinese Revolution broke out in May 1911 against the Manchu dynasty and foreign interests and delayed railroad construction until 1913. "Dollar diplomacy," Willard Straight ruefully admitted, "made no friends in the Hukuang matter."[125] "We're goin' to give ye [Chinese] a railroad so ye can go swiftly to places that ye don't want to see," observed Finley Peter Dunne's Mr. Dooley.[126]

Hoping to reap tangible benefits by dissociating from the other powers, President Wilson and Secretary Bryan repudiated American participation in the international consortium on March 18, 1913. Failure to cancel the loan, Wilson believed, would have cost the United States "the proud position . . . secured when Secretary Hay stood for the open door in China after the Boxer Uprising." Wilson became the first to extend formal diplomatic recognition to the Chinese Republic on May 6.[127] He had thereby renewed America's commitment to the political integrity of China, a goal pragmatically abandoned by Roosevelt, unsuccessfully resuscitated by Taft, and consistently opposed by Japan.

Events at home soon made Wilson's Asian policy resemble Taft's more than Roosevelt's. In April 1913, Democratic and Progressive politicians placed before the California legislature a bill denying residents "ineligible to citizenship" the right to own land. The measure struck directly at the 50,000 Japanese living in California. Racist passions erupted, with one farmer recoiling from the prospect of racial intermarriage: "What is that baby? It isn't a Japanese. It isn't white. It is a germ of the mightiest problem . . . that will make the black problem of the South look white."[128] Basically sharing the Californians' anti-Japanese prejudices, and philosophically sensitive to states' rights, Wilson sent Bryan to Sacramento to beg for a euphemistic statute. But the California legislature passed the offensive bill on May 3, 1913. When Japan protested the "unfair and intentionally racially discriminatory" measure, Wilson and Bryan lamely argued that one state's legislation did not constitute a "national discriminatory policy."[129]

Wilson's antipathy toward Japan reappeared in fall 1914 when Japan declared war on Germany, seized the German Pacific islands north of the equator, and swept across China's Shandong Peninsula to capture the German leasehold of Jiaozhou. "When there is a fire in a jeweller's shop," a Japanese diplomat theorized, "the neighbours cannot be expected to refrain from helping themselves."[130] Tokyo immediately followed with the Twenty-One Demands of January 18, 1915, creating a virtual protectorate over all of China. Despite stout resistance by Beijing, Japan emerged with extensive political and economic rights in Shandong, southern Manchuria, and Mongolia. Preoccupied with Mexico and the *Lusitania* crisis, the Wilson administration refused to recognize Japan's gains, which amounted to a repudiation of the Open Door policy.

Wilson's nonrecognition policy ran counter to secret treaties in which the European Allies promised to support Japan's conquests at the peace conference after World War I. The United States soon compromised. In an agreement with Viscount Kikujiro Ishii, signed November 2, 1917, Secretary Lansing admitted that "territorial propinquity creates special relationships between countries, and consequently . . . Japan has special interests in China," while Ishii pledged his nation's dedication to the Open Door and integrity of China.[131] The Wilson administration also revived the international banking consortium as the only way to check further unilateral Japanese economic penetration of China proper. The wheel had turned full circle for Wilson. Like Taft before him, Wilson failed to protect China's fragile sovereignty without conciliating or blocking Japan.

Anglo-American Rapprochement and Empire-Building

American policies toward Asia and Latin America often fell short of their proclaimed goals because of the pseudoscientific race thinking of the early twentieth century. Americans viewed Asians as "inscrutable and somnolent," depicted Latin Americans as black children or alluring maidens, imagined Africa as the "dark continent" of "savage beasts and beastly savages," and referred to Filipinos as "our little brown brothers," and these biased stereotypes inevitably impeded statecraft and aroused resentment from Bogotá to Beijing, from Managua to Manila.[132] Yet such Darwinist racial attitudes also facilitated much closer relations between the United States and Great Britain. As the historian Michael H. Hunt has written about the ideology of the time, victory "in the international competition among the races . . . might not go to the refined and peaceful peoples but rather to the amoral, the cunning, the fecund, and the power hungry." Thus "Anglo-Americans might then need to cultivate a sense of solidarity and a capacity for cooperation."[133] Theodore Roosevelt certainly thought so when he claimed that "together . . . , the two branches of the Anglo-Saxon race . . . can whip the world."[134] So too did the British, as evidenced by their retreat after the Venezuelan crisis of 1895 and their willingness to accept exclusive American control of a canal in Panama. Also prompted by Britain's search for allies against Germany (evidenced in the Anglo-Japanese Alliance of 1902 and the Entente Cordiale with France in 1904), London's pursuit of what future prime minister Herbert H. Asquith called "the most cordial and constant cooperation" with the United States led to a celebrated "great rapprochement."[135]

The new Anglo-American affinity, however, nearly dissolved in 1903 when the Alaska boundary controversy, which stemmed from Canadian claims to large areas of the Alaskan panhandle, strained relations. As the power responsible for the Dominion's foreign relations (Canada did not establish a foreign office until 1909), Britain found itself backing Ottawa's dubious contention that much of the panhandle's coastline actually belonged to Canada. Roosevelt thought Canada had less right "than the United States did to Cornwall or Kent."[136] The president refused arbitration and sent 800 soldiers to Alaska to awe his opponents. London finally agreed in January 1903 to an American proposal for a mixed boundary commission composed of six "impartial jurists," three from each side.[137] Taking no chances, Roosevelt appointed Senator Henry Cabot Lodge and Secretary Root, hardly disinterested judges, to the commission. He informally warned London he would run the line himself if the commissioners failed to agree. One British commissioner sided with the Americans, and on October 20, 1903, by a vote of 4 to 2, the commission officially decided for the United States. The British "made the inevitable choice to please a power ten times the size of Canada and with more than ten times the wealth."[138]

Canadian-American relations did improve with the Migratory Bird Treaty of 1916. Conservationists and scientists, alarmed by a decline in North American birds caused by reckless sport and commercial hunting, pressed for this agreement under the principle of "common property resources." The death of the last passenger pigeon, in the Cincinnati Zoo in 1914, symbolized the crisis. Because the treaty restricted hunting, especially during the mating season, it sparked some opposition in the United States. Member of Congress John Tillman, a Democrat from Arkansas who defended duck hunting in gendered terms, cried that the accord "should be bedecked with skirts" because it "would feminize our boys."[139] The bird population increased, and such wildlife protection, also evident in the Inland Fisheries

John Bull in Need of Friends. Battered by criticism over its war against the Boers in South Africa and challenged by a rising Germany, Great Britain found a new friend in the United States. Not all Britons embraced Anglo-American affinity. "Only 1/4 of the population of the United States are what you might call natives," wrote a British admiral in 1901, "the rest are Germans, Irish, Italians, and the scum of the earth! all of them hating the English like poison." (*Des Moines Leader* in *Literary Digest,* 1901)

Treaty (1908) and the North Pacific Fur Seal Convention (1911), became landmarks in international environmental history.

Anglo-American entente also characterized the settlement of the North Atlantic fisheries dispute. Since 1782, American fishermen had insisted on retaining their pre-Revolutionary privileges off Canada's Newfoundland. Indeed, "a gilded wooden cod" still hung from the ceiling of the Massachusetts State House.[140] The modus vivendi of 1888, under which they had fished for several years, collapsed in 1905 when Newfoundland placed restrictions on American fishing vessels. Senator

Lodge cried for warships to protect his constituents' livelihood. To avoid a heated quarrel, Roosevelt proposed, and London accepted, arbitration at The Hague Tribunal. In 1910 the tribunal ruled that Britain could oversee fishing off Newfoundland if it established reasonable regulations, that a fisheries commission would hear cases, and that Americans could fish in large bays if they remained three miles from shore. This compromise defused the oldest dispute in American foreign relations and symbolized London's political withdrawal from the Western Hemisphere.

The naval retreat had occurred earlier, when the Admiralty abolished the North Atlantic station based at Jamaica. After 1902 the Royal Navy patrolled the Caribbean only with an annual visit by a token squadron of cruisers. Admiral Sir John Fisher, who oversaw this historic retrenchment, wanted to concentrate his heavy ships in the English Channel and North Sea as monitors of the growing German navy. He regarded the United States as "a kindred state with whom we shall never have a parricidal war."[141]

Even the aggressive hemispheric diplomacy of Taft and Wilson did not undermine Anglo-American rapprochement. Britain criticized dollar diplomacy in Latin America, and Wilson's quixotic efforts to dislodge Huerta from the presidency of Mexico met with little sympathy in England. But Foreign Secretary Sir Edward Grey tersely laid to rest all talk of a challenge: "His Majesty's Government cannot with any prospect of success embark upon an active counterpolicy to that of the United States, or constitute themselves the champions of Mexico or any of these republics against the United States."[142] In reciprocation, Wilson protected British oil interests and made it a "point of honor" to eliminate the one potentially dangerous British grievance inherited from his predecessor.[143] Late in the Taft administration, Congress had exempted American intercoastal shippers from payment of Panama Canal tolls. British opinion condemned this shifting of canal maintenance costs to other users. Because it unfairly discriminated against foreign shipping, Wilson persuaded Congress to revoke the law in June 1914.

In the end, rapprochement meant mutual respect for each other's empires. Roosevelt, for example, encouraged London to frustrate native aspirations for independence in India, while the British accepted the American suppression of the Filipinos and U.S. hegemony in Latin America. American leaders usually spoke favorably of independence for colonial peoples—but independence only after long-term tutelage to make them "civilized" enough to govern. In 1910 in Egypt, where Roosevelt applauded Britain's "great work for civilization," the ex-president even lectured Muslim nationalists about Christian respect for womanhood.[144] In unstable Liberia, where the United States in 1912 instituted a financial receivership in the African nation like that in the Dominican Republic, the British encouraged Washington to use a strong hand in what London called America's "protectorate."[145]

While building an empire, policymakers largely adhered to the tradition of aloofness from continental European political and military affairs. Even Roosevelt overtly tampered only once with Europe's balance of power. In 1904 France acquiesced in British control of Egypt in exchange for primacy in Morocco. A year later, Germany decided to test the solidity of the new Anglo-French entente by challenging France's claims in Morocco. Speaking at Tangier, the kaiser belligerently demanded a German political role in Morocco, which France at once refused. After a brief European war scare, in which Britain stood by its ally, Germany asked Roosevelt to induce France and England to convene a conference to settle Morocco's future. Worried about Kaiser Wilhelm's "violent and often wholly irrational zigzags," Roosevelt accepted the personal invitation only after assuring Paris that he did not act on Berlin's behalf.[146] During the conference, held in early 1906 at Algeciras, Spain, Roosevelt devised a pro-French compromise and persuaded the kaiser to accept it. This political intervention isolated Germany and reinforced the Anglo-French entente, but it generated criticism at home. Roosevelt's successors made sure they did not violate the American policy of nonentanglement with Europe during the more ominous second Moroccan and Balkan crises preceding the First World War.

Nonentanglement also doomed the sweeping arbitration treaties that Secretary Hay negotiated with several world powers. When the Senate attached crippling amendments, Roosevelt withdrew the treaties because they did "not in the smallest degree facilitate settlements by arbitration."[147] After 1905 Secretary Root persuaded Roosevelt to accept watered-down bilateral arbitration treaties, and Secretary Bryan later negotiated a series of supplementary "cooling-off" treaties by which nations pledged to refrain from war during international investigations of serious disputes. None of these arrangements, however, effectively bound signatories, and like the Permanent Court of Arbitration at The Hague, they represented a backwater in international diplomacy. Ambassador Whitelaw Reid compared U.S. participation in the Hague Peace Conference of 1907 to a farmer taking his hog to market: "That hog didn't weigh as much as I expected he would, and I always knew he wouldn't."[148]

The mainstream of American foreign policy between 1900 and 1914 flowed through the Panama Canal, a momentous political, military, and technological achievement. The United States became the unchallenged policeman of the Caribbean region, empowering Washington, in Taft's words, "to prevent revolutions" so that "we'll have no more."[149] Although the German authorities thought that the canal, once completed, would shift American priorities to Asia and "today's Atlantic fleet will become the Pacific fleet," the United States still lacked the power to challenge Japan or Britain.[150] As Roosevelt understood, the Open Door "completely disappears as soon as a powerful nation determines to disregard it."[151] One military officer told Congress in 1910: "We have grown from a little frontier army to one spread all over the world—in America, Porto Rico, Hawai'i, Alaska, the Philippines, and sometimes in Cuba—and we have not got the officers and men to do it."[152]

American insensitivity to the nationalism of other peoples became another imperial legacy. Filipino resistance to American domination, Cuban anger against the Platt Amendment, Colombian outrage over Panama, and Mexican rejection of Wilsonian intervention bore witness to the depth of nationalistic sentiments. Like the European powers who were carving up Asia, Africa, and the Middle East, the United States was developing its empire and subjugating peoples and compromising their sovereignty in Latin America and the Pacific. As a Panamanian diplomat

Naval Arms Race. The international naval competition in the early twentieth century was foreboding. Disarmament talks at The Hague Conferences and arbitration treaties did not curb the arms buildup. Roosevelt's decision to send the "Great White Fleet" around the world in 1907–1908 may have encouraged both Japan and Germany to speed up their naval programs. (*Detroit News* in *Literary Digest*, 1904)

later explained: "When you hit a rock with an egg, the egg breaks. Or when you hit an egg with a rock, the egg breaks. The United States is the rock. Panama is the egg. In either case, the egg breaks."[153] With the exception of the Virgin Islands, purchased from Denmark for $25 million in 1917 to forestall any wartime German seizure, the empire grew little from outright territorial gains. It was, instead, an informal empire administered by troops, financial advisers, and reformers who showed contempt for native peoples' culture, politics, and economies through a paternalistic discourse. The U.S. Army marching song—"The Monkeys Have No Tails in Zamboanga"—expressed soldierly disdain for the Filipino populace.

"There is something pathetic and childlike about the people," Roosevelt wrote condescendingly of the Puerto Ricans.[154] Under the Foraker Act (1900), Puerto Rico and its naval base on Culebra became a "new constitutional animal"—an "unincorporated territory" subject to the will of the U.S. Congress and governed by the War Department (until 1934).[155] In a series of decisions called the Insular Cases (1901–1904), the Supreme Court upheld the Foraker Act, providing Washington with a means to govern people it did not wish to organize as a state. In March 1917, Congress granted Puerto Ricans U.S. citizenship just in time for them to be drafted into the U.S. armed forces in the war against Germany. To this day, Puerto Rico remains a colony, or "commonwealth," and Puerto Ricans remain divided in their views about statehood, independence, and commonwealth status.

The adventures of American foreign relations under an imperial ideology and the male ethos in the years 1900–1914 attracted many capable, well-educated young men to diplomatic service. "It was TR's call to youth which lured me to Washington," future under secretary of state William Phillips recalled.[156] Career ambassador Joseph C. Grew first gained presidential favor by shooting a tiger in China. Several of these young foreign-service professionals, virtually all graduates of Ivy League colleges, including Phillips, Grew, Willard Straight, former Rough Rider Henry P. Fletcher, and soldier-diplomat Frank R. McCoy, lived in an exclusive bachelors' townhouse at 1718 H Street during their Washington service. Known among themselves as "the Family," these youthful professionals blended camaraderie with careers and "became the elite or legendary 'inner circle' of the State Department" for the next forty years.[157] The New York attorney Henry L. Stimson, himself a protégé of Elihu Root, served as secretary of war under Taft (1911–1913) and continued this tradition of recruiting some of the brightest public servants in a succession of high-level posts through the end of World War II.

Cultural or public foreign relations also flourished during these years. Just as Buffalo Bill Cody's Wild West Show had "hyped" American cultural myths abroad since the 1890s, Wilbur Wright's airplane tour of Europe in 1908 set records, thrilled crowds, and impressed military strategists.[158] The cruise of the "Great White Fleet" provided as much pageantry as statecraft—"a feast, a frolic, or a fight," as Admiral Robley D. Evans put it.[159] Colonial subjects became popular on college campuses, as anthropologists and ethnographers offered courses on "Savage Childhood" and "Peoples of the Philippines."[160] When academic exchanges with European universities expanded after 1900, Harvard University commemorated its new Germanic Museum by bestowing an honorary doctorate on Prince Henry of Prussia (the kaiser's brother)—"a simple, natural person who got used in a day to our troublesome democratic ways."[161]

Thousands of wealthy Americans traveled abroad clutching their Baedeker guidebooks, spending American dollars, and sometimes acquiring foreign titles through marriage, as in the case of Jennie Jerome and Lord Randolph Churchill, whose son Winston valued Anglo-American partnership. Civic leaders took pride in hosting the Olympic Games in St. Louis in 1904, hailed an American victory in the 1908 Round-the-World Automobile race, became "weekend frontiersmen" after organizing the Boy Scouts of America in 1910, and cheered the gold medals won by Native American Jim Thorpe at the Stockholm Olympics in 1912.[162] Just as they seemed to take up the great game of empire from Great Britain, so too did Americans become proficient in that most diplomatic of athletic competitions, the royal and ancient Scottish sport of golf. For some Americans, true Anglo-American entente did not occur until young Francis Ouimet bested British champions Harry Vardon and Ted Ray in the U.S. Open at Brookline, Massachusetts, in 1913.

Yet beneath the glitter lurked danger. Winston Churchill later wrote of living in two different worlds: "the actual, visual world with its peaceful activities" and "a hypothetical world 'beneath the threshold'"—"a world at one moment utterly fantastic, at the next seeming to leap into reality—a world of monstrous shadows moving in convulsive combination through vistas of fathomless catastrophe."[163] Once the world started spinning around Sarajevo, Bosnia, it became impossible for the growing American empire to escape the maelstrom of world war.

FURTHER READING FOR THE PERIOD 1900–1914

See studies listed in the last two chapters and Michael C. C. Adams, *The Great Adventure: Male Desire and the Coming of World War I* (1990); A. J. Bacevich, *Diplomat in Khaki* (1989) (General Frank McCoy); William H. Becker, *The Dynamics of Business-Government Relations: Industry and Exports, 1893–1921* (1982); Gail Bederman, *Manliness & Civilization* (1995); Lester H. Brune, *The Origins of American Security Policy* (1981); Richard D. Challener, *Admirals, Generals, and American Foreign Policy, 1898–1914* (1973); Kendrick A. Clements, *William Jennings Bryan* (1982); Kurkpatrick Dorsey, *The Dawn of Conservation Diplomacy: U.S.–Canadian Wildlife Protection Treaties in the Progressive Era* (1999); Lloyd C. Gardner, *Safe for Democracy: The Anglo-American Response to Revolution, 1913–1923* (1984); Robert C. Hilderbrand, *Power and the People: Executive Management of Public Opinion in Foreign Affairs, 1897–1921* (1981); E. Berkeley Tompkins, *Anti-Imperialism in the United States* (1970); Richard H. Werking, *The Master Architects* (1977) (foreign service); Rachel West, *The Department of State on the Eve of the First World War* (1978); Rubin F. Westin, *Racism in United States Imperialism* (1972); William C. Widenor, *Henry Cabot Lodge and the Search for an American Foreign Policy* (1980); and Mira Wilkins, *The Emergence of Multinational Enterprise: American Business Abroad from the Colonial Era to 1914* (1970).

Theodore Roosevelt is the subject of Howard K. Beale, *Theodore Roosevelt and the Rise of America to World Power* (1956); John M. Blum, *The Republican Roosevelt* (1954); H. W. Brands, *T.R.* (1997); David H. Burton, *Theodore Roosevelt* (1968); Richard H. Collin, *Theodore Roosevelt: Culture, Diplomacy, and Expansion* (1985); John M. Cooper, Jr., *The Warrior and the Priest: Woodrow Wilson and Theodore Roosevelt* (1983); Thomas G. Dyer, *Theodore Roosevelt and the Idea of Race* (1980); Raymond A. Esthus, *Theodore Roosevelt and the International Rivalries* (1970); Lewis L. Gould, *The Presidency of Theodore Roosevelt* (1991); William H. Harbaugh, *The Life and Times of Theodore Roosevelt* (1975); Frederick W. Marks, *Velvet on Iron* (1979); Natalie A. Naylor et al., eds., *Theodore Roosevelt* (1992); and William N. Tilchin, *Theodore Roosevelt and the British Empire* (1997).

For the Taft administration, see Paolo E. Coletta, *The Presidency of William Howard Taft* (1973); Ralph E. Minger, *William Howard Taft and American Foreign Policy* (1975); and Walter V. Scholes and Marie V. Scholes, *The Foreign Policies of the Taft Administration* (1970).

For Wilson policies, see the next chapter and Frederick S. Calhoun, *Power and Principle: Armed Intervention in Wilsonian Foreign Policy* (1986) and *Uses of Force and Wilsonian Foreign Policy* (1993); Kendrick A. Clements, *The Presidency of Woodrow Wilson* (1990); Edward S. Kaplan, *U.S. Imperialism in Latin America* (1997) (on Bryan's policies); and John M. Mulder, *Woodrow Wilson: The Years of Preparation* (1978).

U.S. relations with Latin America are examined in José A. Cabranes, *Citizenship and the American Empire* (1979) (Puerto Rico); Bruce J. Calder, *The Impact of Intervention* (1984) (Dominican Republic); Raymond A. Carr, *Puerto Rico* (1984); Arturo M. Carrión, *Puerto Rico* (1983); Mark T. Gilderhus, *Pan American Visions* (1986) (Wilson); David Healy, *Drive to Hegemony* (1989) and *Gunboat Diplomacy in the Wilson Era* (1976) (Haiti); Warren G. Kneer, *Great Britain and the Caribbean, 1901–1913* (1975); Walter LaFeber, *Inevitable Revolutions* (1993) (Central America); Lester D. Langley, *Struggle for the American Mediterranean* (1976), *The United States and the Caribbean, 1900–1970* (1980), and *The Banana Wars* (1983); Lester D. Langley and Thomas Schoonover, *The Banana Men* (1995); Dana Munro, *Intervention and Dollar Diplomacy* (1964); Thomas F. O'Brien, *The Revolutionary Mission: American Business in Latin America* (1996); Dexter Perkins, *The Monroe Doctrine, 1867–1907* (1937); Fredrick B. Pike, *The United States and Latin America* (1992); Brenda G. Plummer, *Haiti and the United States* (1992) and *Haiti and the Great Powers, 1902–1915* (1988); Hans Schmidt, *The United States Occupation of Haiti, 1915–1934* (1971); Thomas D. Schoonover, *The United States in Central America, 1860–1911* (1991); and Lars Schoultz, *Beneath the United States* (1998).

For the Panama Canal, see Richard H. Collin, *Theodore Roosevelt's Caribbean* (1990); Michael L. Conniff, *Panama and the United States* (1992); Richard L. Lael, *Arrogant Diplomacy* (1987); Walter LaFeber, *The Panama Canal* (1989); John Major, *Prize Possession* (1993); David McCullough, *The Path Between the Seas* (1977); and Stephen J. Randall, *Colombia and the United States* (1992).

U.S. hegemony in Cuba is discussed in David Healy, *The United States in Cuba, 1898–1902* (1963); José M. Hernández, *Cuba and the United States* (1993); James H. Hitchman, *Leonard Wood and Cuban Independence, 1898–1902* (1971); Allan R. Millett, *The Politics of Intervention* (1968); and Louis A. Pérez, Jr., *Cuba and the United States* (1997) and *Cuba Under the Platt Amendment, 1902–1934* (1986).

Relations with Mexico are treated in Jonathan C. Brown, *Oil and Revolution in Mexico* (1993); Clarence C. Clendenen, *Blood on the Border* (1969); Jules Davids, *American Political and Economic Penetration of Mexico, 1877–1920* (1976); Joseph M. Gilbert, *Revolution from Without* (1982); Mark T. Gilderhus, *Diplomacy and Revolution* (1977); Kenneth J. Grieb, *The United States and Huerta* (1969); John M. Hart, *Revolutionary Mexico* (1988); Larry D. Hill, *Emissaries to a Revolution: Woodrow Wilson's Executive Agents in Mexico* (1973); Friedrich Katz, *The Life and Times of Pancho Villa* (1998) and *The Secret War in Mexico* (1981); Alan Knight, *U.S.–Mexican Relations, 1910–1940* (1987); Daniel Nugent, ed., *Rural Revolt in Mexico and U.S. Intervention* (1988); Robert E. Quirk, *An Affair of Honor* (1962) (Veracruz); Ramón E. Ruíz, *The Great Rebellion* (1980); Karl M. Schmitt, *Mexico and the United States, 1821–1973* (1974); Paul J. Vanderwood and Frank N. Samponaro, *Border Fury* (1988); and Josefina Vázquez and Lorenzo Meyer, *The United States and Mexico* (1985).

For America's interactions with Asia and China, see William R. Braisted, *The United States Navy in the Pacific, 1897–1909* (1958) and *1909–1922* (1971); Jongsuk Chay, *Diplomacy of Asymmetry* (1990) (Korea); Warren I. Cohen, *America's Response to China* (1990); Daniel M. Crane and Thomas A. Breslin, *An Ordinary Relationship: American Opposition to Republican Revolution in China* (1986); Jonathan Goldstein et al., eds., *America Views China* (1991); Robert A. Hart, *The Great White Fleet* (1965); Michael H. Hunt, *The Making of a Special Relationship* (1983); Akira Iriye, *Across the Pacific* (1967); Delber L. McKee, *Chinese Exclusion Versus the Open Door Policy, 1900–1906* (1976); Dennis L. Noble, *The Eagle and the Dragon* (1990); and Noel H. Pugach, *Paul S. Reinsch* (1979).

Japanese-American relations are studied in Burton F. Beers, *Vain Endeavor: Robert Lansing's Attempt to End the American-Japanese Rivalry* (1962); Roger Daniels, *The Politics of Prejudice* (1962) (anti-Japanese sentiment); Raymond A. Esthus, *Double Eagle and Rising Sun* (1988) (Portsmouth) and *Theodore Roosevelt and Japan* (1966); Akira Iriye, *Pacific Estrangement* (1972); Walter LaFeber, *The Clash* (1997); Charles E. Neu, *An Uncertain Friendship* (1967) and *The Troubled Encounter* (1975); and E. P. Trani, *The Treaty of Portsmouth* (1969).

American missionaries, especially in Asia, are covered in Kenton J. Clymer, *Protestant Missionaries in the Philippines, 1898–1916* (1986); Gael Graham, *Gender, Culture, and Christianity* (1995); Patricia R. Hill, *The World Their Household* (1985) (women); Jane Hunter, *The Gospel of Gentility* (1984) (women in China); Xi Lian, *The Conversion of Missionaries* (1997); and James Reed, *The Missionary Mind and American East Asia Policy, 1911–1915* (1983).

U.S. relations with Europe and Great Britain, and rivalry with Germany, are discussed in Stuart Anderson, *Race and Rapprochement* (1981); A. E. Campbell, *Great Britain and the United States, 1895–1903* (1960); Charles S. Campbell, *Anglo-American Understanding, 1898–1903* (1957); David Dimbleby and David Reynolds, *An Ocean Apart* (1989); Holger H. Herwig, *Politics of Frustration: The United States in German Naval Planning, 1889–1941* (1976); Manfred Jonas, *The United States and Germany* (1984); B. J. C. McKercher and Lawrence Aronson, eds., *The North Atlantic Triangle in a Changing World* (1996); Bradford Perkins, *The Great Rapprochement* (1968); Stephen R. Rock, *Why Peace Breaks Out* (1989); Hans-Jürgen Schröder, ed., *Confrontation and Cooperation* (1993) (Germany); and Frederick F. Travis, *George Kennan and the Russian-American Relationship, 1865–1924* (1990).

The peace movement and the role of The Hague are discussed in Peter Brock, *Pacifism in the United States* (1968); Charles Chatfield, *The American Peace Movement* (1992); Merle E. Curti, *Peace or War* (1936); Calvin Davis, *The United States and the First Hague Conference* (1962) and *The United States and the Second Hague Peace Conference* (1975); Charles DeBenedetti, *The Peace Reform in American History* (1980); Sondra R. Herman, *Eleven Against War* (1969); Charles F. Howlett and Glen Zeitzer, *The American Peace Movement* (1985);

C. Roland Marchand, *The American Peace Movement and Social Reform, 1898–1918* (1973); and David S. Patterson, *Toward a Warless World* (1976).

See also the General Bibliography, the following notes, and Richard Dean Burns, ed., *Guide to American Foreign Relations Since 1700* (1983).

For comprehensive coverage of foreign-relations topics, see the articles in the four-volume *Encyclopedia of U.S. Foreign Relations* (1997), edited by Bruce W. Jentleson and Thomas G. Paterson.

NOTES TO CHAPTER 7

1. All quotations from U.S. Congress, *Diplomatic History of the Panama Canal*, Senate Doc. 474 (1914), pp. 345–363.
2. Quoted in John Major, *Prize Possession* (New York: Cambridge University Press, 1993), p. 45.
3. Elting E. Morison, ed., *The Letters of Theodore Roosevelt* (Cambridge: Harvard University Press, 1951–1954; 8 vols.), II, 1185–1187.
4. *Diplomatic History of the Canal*, p. 261.
5. Quoted in Dwight C. Miner, *The Fight for the Panama Route* (New York: Columbia University Press, 1940), p. 275.
6. Quoted in Henry F. Pringle, *Theodore Roosevelt* (New York: Harcourt, Brace, 1931), p. 311.
7. Quoted in Howard K. Beale, *Theodore Roosevelt and the Rise of America to World Power* (Baltimore: Johns Hopkins Press, 1956), p. 33.
8. Quoted in David McCullough, *The Path Between the Seas* (New York: Simon & Schuster, 1977), p. 333.
9. *New York World*, June 14, 1903.
10. Quoted in Pringle, *Roosevelt*, p. 311.
11. Quoted in Tyler Dennett, *John Hay* (New York: Dodd, Mead, 1933), p. 377.
12. Quoted in Thomas Schoonover, "Max Farrand's Memorandum on the U.S. Role in the Panamanian Revolution of 1903," *Diplomatic History*, XII (Fall 1988), 505.
13. Quoted in Stephen J. Randall, *Colombia and the United States* (Athens: University of Georgia Press, 1992), p. 88.
14. Quoted in Lewis L. Gould, *The Presidency of Theodore Roosevelt* (Lawrence: University Press of Kansas, 1991), p. 98.
15. C. F. Adams to Moorfield Story, December 9, 1903, Moorfield Story Papers, Massachusetts Historical Society, Boston; Roosevelt quoted in H. W. Brands, *T.R.* (New York: BasicBooks, 1997), p. 487.
16. Quoted in Walter LaFeber, *The Panama Canal* (New York: Oxford University Press, 1989; updated ed.), pp. 225–226.
17. *New York Times*, March 25, 1911.
18. William H. Harbaugh, *The Life and Times of Theodore Roosevelt* (New York: Oxford University Press, 1975; rev. ed.), p. 197.
19. Quoted in Wayne A. Wiegand, *Patrician in the Progressive Era* (New York: Garland, 1988), p. 120.
20. Quoted in Stephen R. Rock, *Why Peace Breaks Out* (Chapel Hill: University of North Carolina Press, 1989), p. 132.
21. Quoted in Holger H. Herwig, *Politics of Frustration* (Boston: Little, Brown, 1976), p. 67.
22. Ronald H. Spector, *Professors of War* (Newport, R.I.: Naval War College Press, 1977).
23. John Milton Cooper, Jr., "Progressivism and American Foreign Policy," *Mid-America*, LI (October 1969), 261.
24. Quoted in John Morton Blum, *The Republican Roosevelt* (New York: Atheneum [1954], 1973), p. 127.
25. Quoted in Beale, *Theodore Roosevelt*, p. 77; G. Wallace Chessman, *Theodore Roosevelt and the Politics of Power* (Boston: Little, Brown, 1969), p. 70.
26. Quoted in Frank Ninkovich, *Modernity and Power* (Chicago: University of Chicago Press, 1994), p. 6.
27. Quoted in Beale, *Theodore Roosevelt*, p. 140.
28. Quoted in Judith Papachristou, "American Women and Foreign Policy, 1896–1905," *Diplomatic History*, XIV (Fall 1990), 499, 501, 509.
29. Quoted in Frederick F. Travis, *George Kennan and the Russian-American Relationship, 1865–1924* (Athens: Ohio University Press, 1990), p. 266.
30. Quoted in Ninkovich, *Modernity*, p. 13.
31. Quoted in John Milton Cooper, Jr., *The Warrior and the Priest* (Cambridge: Harvard University Press, 1983), p. 75.
32. Quoted in Foster Rhea Dulles, "John Hay," in Norman A. Graebner, ed., *An Uncertain Tradition* (New York: McGraw-Hill, 1961), p. 24.
33. Quoted in Richard W. Leopold, *Elihu Root and the Conservative Tradition* (Boston: Little, Brown, 1954), p. 50.
34. Quoted in David H. Burton, *Theodore Roosevelt* (Philadelphia: University of Pennsylvania Press, 1968), p. 97; *Congressional Record, XXXV* (December 3, 1901), 82–83.
35. Quoted in Ralph E. Minger, *William Howard Taft and United States Foreign Policy* (Urbana: University of Illinois Press, 1975), p. 179.
36. Quoted in Ray S. Baker, *Woodrow Wilson* (Garden City, N.Y.: Doubleday, Doran, 1927–1939; 8 vols.), IV, 289.
37. Quoted in Rock, *Why Peace*, p. 142.
38. *Foreign Relations, 1898* (Washington, D.C.: Government Printing Office, 1901), pp. lxvi–lxvii.
39. Quoted in Philip C. Jessup, *Elihu Root* (New York: Dodd, Mead, 1938; 2 vols.), I, 286–287.
40. Quoted in David F. Healy, *The United States in Cuba, 1898–1902* (Madison: University of Wisconsin Press, 1963), p. 133.
41. U.S. Commissioner Robert P. Porter quoted in Louis A. Pérez, Jr., *Cuba and the United States* (Athens: University of Georgia Press, 1997, 2nd ed.), p. 127.
42. *Ibid.*, p. 128.
43. *Congressional Record, XXXIV* (February 26, 1901), 3036.
44. Quoted in H. Hagedorn, *Leonard Wood* (New York: Harper, 1931; 2 vols.), I, 362; Healy, *United States in Cuba*, p. 178.
45. Quoted in R. H. Fitzgibbon, *Cuba and the United States, 1900–1935* (New York: Russell & Russell, 1964), p. 112.

46. Quoted in Allan R. Millett, *The Politics of Intervention* (Columbus: Ohio State University Press, 1968), p. 72.
47. Quoted in Burton, *Theodore Roosevelt*, p. 106.
48. James D. Richardson, ed., *A Compilation of the Messages and Papers of the Presidents, 1789–1897* (Washington, D. C.: Government Printing Office, 1896–1899; 10 vols.), X, 7436–7437.
49. Quoted in Minger, *William Howard Taft*, p. 136.
50. Fred L. Israel, ed., *The State of the Union Messages* (New York: Chelsea House, 1967; 3 vols.), II, 2038.
51. Morison, *Letters of Roosevelt, III,* 116.
52. *Ibid., IV,* 1156.
53. Quoted in J. Lloyd Mecham, *A Survey of United States–Latin American Relations* (Boston: Houghton Mifflin, 1965), p. 67.
54. Quoted in William N. Tilchin, *Theodore Roosevelt and the British Empire* (New York: St. Martin's Press, 1997), p. 33.
55. Quoted in John G. Clifford, "Admiral Dewey and the Germans, 1903," *Mid-America, XLIX* (July 1967), 218.
56. Quoted in Manfred Jonas, *The United States and Germany* (Ithaca: Cornell University Press, 1984), pp. 68–69.
57. Quoted in David Dimbleby and David Reynolds, *An Ocean Apart* (New York: Vintage, 1989), p. 38.
58. Quoted in Jonas, *United States and Germany*, p. 73.
59. Quoted *ibid.*, p. 420.
60. Quoted in Brands, *T.R.*, p. 524.
61. Quoted in Dexter Perkins, *The Monroe Doctrine, 1867–1907* (Baltimore: Johns Hopkins Press, 1937), p. 420.
62. Quoted in Warren G. Kneer, *Great Britain and the Caribbean, 1901–1913* (East Lansing: Michigan State University Press, 1975), p. 103.
63. Quoted in Brands, *T.R.*, p. 526.
64. Theodore Roosevelt, *An Autobiography* (New York: Charles Scribner's Sons, 1926), p. 511.
65. Quoted in Richard D. Challener, *Admirals, Generals, and American Foreign Policy, 1898–1914* (Princeton: Princeton University Press, 1973), p. 142.
66. *Foreign Relations, 1912* (Washington, D.C.: Government Printing Office, 1919), p. 1091.
67. Quoted in Lloyd C. Gardner, *Safe for Democracy* (New York: Oxford University Press, 1984), p. 41.
68. *Foreign Relations, 1913* (Washington, D.C.: Government Printing Office, 1920), p. 426.
69. Quoted in Frederick S. Calhoun, *Uses of Force and Wilsonian Foreign Policy* (Kent, Ohio: Kent State University Press, 1993), p. 53.
70. Bruce J. Calder, *The Impact of Intervention* (Austin: University of Texas Press, 1984), p. 12.
71. *Ibid.*, p. 250.
72. Quoted in Dana G. Munro, *Intervention and Dollar Diplomacy in the Caribbean* (Princeton: Princeton University Press, 1964), p. 336.
73. Quoted in Brenda G. Plummer, *Haiti and the Great Powers, 1902–1915* (Baton Rouge: Louisiana State University Press, 1988), p. 188.
74. Quoted in Calhoun, *Uses of Force*, p. 19.
75. Alexander DeConde, *Ethnicity, Race, and American Foreign Policy* (Boston: Northeastern University Press, 1993), pp. 79–80.
76. Quoted in Munro, *Intervention*, p. 155.
77. Thomas D. Schoonover, *The United States in Central America, 1860–1911* (Durham: Duke University Press, 1991), p. 130.
78. Zelaya quoted in Lester D. Langley and Thomas Schoonover, *The Banana Men* (Lexington: University Press of Kentucky, 1995), p. 89.
79. Elliott Northcott quoted in Walter LaFeber, *The American Search for Opportunity, 1865–1913* (New York: Cambridge University Press, 1993), p. 219.
80. Quoted in John E. Findling, *Close Neighbors, Distant Friends* (Westport, Conn.: Greenwood, 1987), p. 61.
81. Langley and Schoonover, *Banana Men*, p. 114.
82. Quoted in Baker, *Wilson, IV,* 436.
83. Quoted in Paolo E. Coletta, *The Presidency of William Howard Taft* (Lawrence: University Press of Kansas, 1973), p. 176.
84. Quoted in Friedrich Katz, *The Secret War in Mexico* (Chicago: University of Chicago Press, 1981), p. 113.
85. *Foreign Relations, 1912*, p. 846.
86. Quoted in Howard F. Cline, *The United States and Mexico* (New York: Atheneum, 1963; rev. ed.), p. 144.
87. Quoted in Arthur S. Link, *Wilson: The New Freedom* (Princeton: Princeton University Press, 1956), p. 360.
88. Quoted in Arthur S. Link, *Wilson: Confusions and Crises, 1915–1916* (Princeton: Princeton University Press, 1964), p. 317.
89. Quoted in Link, *Wilson: New Freedom*, p. 358.
90. Quoted *ibid.*, p. 360.
91. Quoted in Kenneth J. Grieb, *The United States and Huerta* (Lincoln: University of Nebraska Press, 1969), p. 137.
92. Quoted in Link, *Wilson: New Freedom*, pp. 386–387.
93. Quoted in Katz, *Secret War*, p. 216.
94. Quoted in Grieb, *United States and Huerta*, p. 135.
95. Quoted in Robert E. Quirk, *An Affair of Honor* (Lexington: University of Kentucky Press, 1962), p. 26.
96. Quoted in Mark T. Gilderhus, *Diplomacy and Revolution* (Tucson: University of Arizona Press, 1977), p. 11.
97. Quoted in Cary T. Grayson, *Woodrow Wilson* (New York: Holt, Rinehart and Winston, 1960), p. 30.
98. Ramón E. Ruíz, *The Great Rebellion: Mexico, 1905–1924* (New York: Norton, 1980), p. 395.
99. Quoted in Grieb, *United States and Huerta*, p. 160.
100. Quoted in Gardner, *Safe for Democracy*, p. 58.
101. Quoted in Douglas Monroy, "Fence Cutters, *Sedicioso,* and First Class Citizens: Mexican Radicalism in America," in Paul Buhle and Dan Georgakis, eds., *The Immigrant Left in the United States* (Albany: State University of New York Press, 1996), pp. 21–22.
102. Quoted in James A. Sandos, *Rebellion in the Borderlands* (Norman: University of Oklahoma Press, 1992), p. 92.
103. Quoted in Arthur S. Link, *Wilson: The Struggle for Neutrality, 1914–1915* (Princeton: Princeton University Press, 1960), p. 491.
104. Katz, *Secret War*, p. 560; Villa quoted in Friedrich Katz, "Pancho Villa and the Attack on Columbus, New Mexico," *American Historical Review, LXXXIII* (February 1978), 111, 114.
105. Quoted in Ana Maria Alonso, "U.S. Military Intervention," in Daniel Nugent, ed., *Rural Revolt in Mexico and U.S. Intervention* (San Diego: Center for U.S.–Mexican Studies, 1988), p. 217.
106. Lester Langley, *The Banana Wars* (Lexington: University Press of Kentucky, 1983), p. 114.
107. Morison, *Letters of Roosevelt, III,* 497–498.
108. Akira Iriye, *The Cold War in Asia* (Englewood Cliffs, N.J.: Prentice-Hall, 1974), p. 35.
109. Morison, *Letters of Roosevelt, IV,* 724, 761.
110. Quoted in Norman Saul, *Concord & Conflict* (Lawrence: University Press of Kansas, 1996), p. 496.
111. Quoted in Raymond A. Esthus, *Double Eagle and Rising Sun* (Durham: Duke University Press, 1988), p. 39.
112. Quoted in Brands, *T.R.*, p. 534.
113. Quoted in Saul, *Concord*, p. 504.
114. Quoted in Raymond A. Esthus, *Theodore Roosevelt and Japan* (Seattle: University of Washington Press, 1966), p. 101.

115. John Edward Wilz, "Did the United States Betray Korea in 1905?" *Pacific Historical Review, LIV* (August 1985), 252.

116. Quoted in Akira Iriye, *Across the Pacific* (New York: Harcourt, Brace & World, 1967), p. 107.

117. Quoted in Ian Mugridge, *The View from Xanadu: William Randolph Hearst and American Foreign Policy* (Montreal: McGill–Queen's University Press, 1995), p. 51.

118. Quoted in Walter A. McDougall, *Let the Sea Make a Noise* (New York: BasicBooks, 1993), p. 479; Morison, *Letters of Roosevelt, V,* 729–730, 761–762.

119. Quoted in Ute Mehnert, "German *Weltpolitik* and the American Two Front Dilemma," *Journal of American History, LXXXII* (March 1996), 1458.

120. Quoted in Eileen P. Scully, "Taking the Low Road to Sino-American Relations," *ibid., LXXXII* (June 1995), 63–64.

121. Anders Stephanson, *Manifest Destiny* (New York: Hill & Wang, 1995), p. 97.

122. Ninkovich, *Modernity*, p. 25.

123. Quoted in Herbert Croly, *Willard Straight* (New York: Macmillan, 1925), p. 276.

124. A. Whitney Griswold, *The Far Eastern Policy of the United States* (New Haven: Yale University Press, 1938), p. 157.

125. Quoted in Croly, *Straight*, pp. 392–393.

126. Quoted in Walter LaFeber, *The Clash* (New York: Norton, 1997), p. 72.

127. Quoted in Daniel M. Crane and Thomas A. Breslin, *An Ordinary Relationship* (Miami: Florida International University Press, 1986), p. 122.

128. Quoted in Roger Daniels, *The Politics of Prejudice* (New York: Atheneum, [1962], 1968), p. 59.

129. Quoted in Link, *Wilson: New Freedom*, pp. 300–301.

130. Quoted in Kendrick A. Clements, *The Presidency of Woodrow Wilson* (Lawrence: University Press of Kansas, 1990), p. 108.

131. *Foreign Relations, 1922* (Washington, D.C.: Government Printing Office, 1938; 2 vols.), II, 591.

132. Quoted in Michael H. Hunt, *Ideology and U.S. Foreign Policy* (New Haven: Yale University Press, 1987), pp. 69, 71, 79, 81.

133. *Ibid.*, p. 79.

134. Quoted in Beale, *Theodore Roosevelt*, pp. 81, 152.

135. Quoted in Rock, *Why Peace*, p. 51; Bradford Perkins, *The Great Rapprochement* (New York: Atheneum, 1968).

136. Roosevelt quoted in Frederick W. Marks, *Velvet on Iron* (Lincoln: University of Nebraska Press, 1979), p. 168.

137. Quoted in Perkins, *Great Rapprochement*, p. 168.

138. Robert Bothwell, *Canada and the United States* (New York: Twayne, 1992), p. 8.

139. Quoted in Kurk Dorsey, "Scientists, Citizens, and Statesmen," *Diplomatic History, XIX* (Summer 1995), 426.

140. Mark Kurlansky, *Cod* (New York: Walker, 1997), p. 79.

141. Quoted in Arthur Marder, *From the Dreadnought to Scapa Flow* (London: Oxford University Press, 1961–1970; 5 vols.), I, 125.

142. Quoted *ibid.*, p. 201.

143. Quoted in Link, *Wilson: New Freedom*, p. 308.

144. Quoted in Burton, *Theodore Roosevelt*, p. 190.

145. Quoted in Emily S. Rosenberg, "The Invisible Protectorate: The United States, Liberia, and the Evolution of Neocolonialism, 1909–40," *Diplomatic History, IX* (Summer 1985), 194, 198.

146. Quoted in Tilchin, *Theodore Roosevelt*, p. 67.

147. Morison, *Letters of Roosevelt, IV,* 1119.

148. Quoted in Calvin Davis, *The United States and the Second Hague Peace Conference* (Durham: Duke University Press, 1975), p. 296.

149. Quoted in Minger, *William Howard Taft*, p. 106.

150. Quoted in Mehnert, "German *Weltpolitik*," p. 1461.

151. Quoted in Jerry Israel, *Progressivism and the Open Door* (Pittsburgh: University of Pittsburgh Press, 1971), p. 96.

152. General William Carter quoted in Brian Linn, *Guardians of Empire* (Chapel Hill: University of North Carolina Press, 1997), p. 62.

153. Quoted in Michael L. Conniff, *Panama and the United States* (Athens: University of Georgia Press, 1992), p. 3.

154. Quoted in Arturo Morales Carrión, *Puerto Rico* (New York: Norton, 1983), p. 163.

155. Raymond Carr, *Puerto Rico* (New York: Vintage, 1984), p. 36.

156. William Phillips, *Ventures in Diplomacy* (Boston: Beacon Press, 1952), p. 6.

157. Quoted in A. J. Bacevich, *Diplomat in Khaki* (Lawrence: University Press of Kansas, 1989), p. 48.

158. Emily S. Rosenberg, *Spreading the American Dream* (New York: Hill & Wang, 1982), p. 35.

159. Quoted in Robert A. Hart, *The Great White Fleet* (Boston: Little, Brown, 1965), p. 45.

160. Quoted in Franklin Ng, "Knowledge for Empire," in Robert David Johnson, ed., *On Cultural Ground* (Chicago: Imprint Publications, 1994), p. 135.

161. Charles W. Eliot quoted in Frank Trommler, "Inventing the Enemy," in Hans-Jürgen Schröder, *Confrontation and Cooperation* (Providence, R.I.: Berg Publishers, 1993), p. 101.

162. Arnold Testi, "The Gender of Reform Politics," *Journal of American History, LXXXI* (March 1995), 1522.

163. Winston S. Churchill, *The World Crisis* (New York: Charles Scribner's Sons, 1927; 6 vols.), I, 18.

CHAPTER
8

War, Peace, and Revolution in the Time of Wilson, 1914–1920

Mass Grave of Lusitania Victims. *In Queenstown, Ireland, a large burial ground holds more than a hundred victims of the* Lusitania *disaster of 1915, which rudely brought World War I to American consciousness. (U.S. War Department, National Archives)*

❖

DIPLOMATIC CROSSROAD

The Sinking of the *Lusitania,* 1915

"Perfectly safe; safer than the trolley cars in New York City," claimed a Cunard Line official the morning of May 1, 1915.[1] Indeed, the majestic *Lusitania,* with its watertight compartments and swiftness, seemed invulnerable. The British government loaned Cunard the money to build this fast passenger liner, more than twice as long as an American football field. The British Admiralty dictated the coal-burning ship's specifications, so that the 30,396-ton vessel could be armed if necessary during war. "Lucy's" priority was pleasure, not war. Resplendent with tapestries and carpets, the luxurious floating palace dazzled. One impressed American politician found the ship "more beautiful than Solomon's Temple—and big enough to hold all his wives."[2]

A crew of 702 attended the 1,257 travelers who departed from New York's Pier 54 on May 1. Deep in the *Lusitania*'s storage area rested a cargo of foodstuffs and contraband (4.2 million rounds of ammunition for Remington rifles, 1,250 cases of empty shrapnel shells, and eighteen cases of nonexplosive fuses). The Cunarder thus carried, said a U.S. State Department official, both "babies and bullets."[3]

In the morning newspapers of May 1 a rather unusual announcement, placed by the Imperial German Embassy, appeared beside the Cunard Line advertisement. The German "Notice" warned passengers that the waters around the British Isles constituted a war zone wherein British vessels were subject to destruction. Only a handful of passengers canceled their bookings on the *Lusitania.* Few transferred to the *New York,* ready to sail under the American flag that same day. But the unattractive *New York* was slow and for the American "smart set" socially unacceptable. The State Department did not intercede to warn the 197 American passengers away from the *Lusitania.* Most Americans accepted the Cunard Line statement: "She is too fast for any submarine. No German war vessel can get her or near her."[4] During this very time, Secretary of State William Jennings Bryan was trying to persuade President Woodrow Wilson that Americans should be prohibited from traveling on belligerent ships. Bryan made little headway.

Captained by William T. Turner, the *Lusitania* steamed into the Atlantic at half past noon on May 1. Manned by an ill-trained crew (the best now on war duty), "Lucy" enjoyed a smooth crossing in calm water. Despite lifesaving drills, complacency about the submarine danger lulled captain, crew, and passengers alike. Passengers joked about torpedoes, played cards, consumed gallons of liquor, and listened to concerts on deck. On May 6, as the *Lusitania* neared Ireland, Turner received a warning from the Naval Centre at Queenstown: "Submarines active off south coast of Ireland."[5] The captain posted lookouts but took no other precautions, despite follow-up warnings. He had standing orders from the Admiralty to take a zigzag path, to steer a midchannel course, and to steam at full speed—all to make it difficult for lurking German submarines to zero in on their targets. But Turner proceeded straight ahead.

The *Lusitania* and *U-20*.
The majestic passenger liner was sunk by German submarine *U-20* off the coast of Ireland on May 7, 1915. "Suppose they should sink the *Lusitania* with American passengers on board," King George V had mused to Colonel Edward M. House on that fateful morning. (Peabody Museum of Salem; Bundesarchiv)

A beautiful day with unusually good visibility, recorded Lieutenant Walter Schwieger in his log on May 7. The young commander was piloting his *U-20* submarine along the southern Irish coast. That morning it had submerged because British ships capable of ramming the fragile, slender craft were passing by. Schwieger surfaced at 1:45 P.M. and soon spotted a four-funneled ship in the distance. Schwieger quickly submerged and set a track toward the *Lusitania,* eager to take advantage of this chance meeting. At 700 meters the *U-20* released a torpedo. The deadly missile dashed through the water tailed by bubbles. A watchman on the starboard bow of the *Lusitania* cried out. Captain Turner, unaccountably below

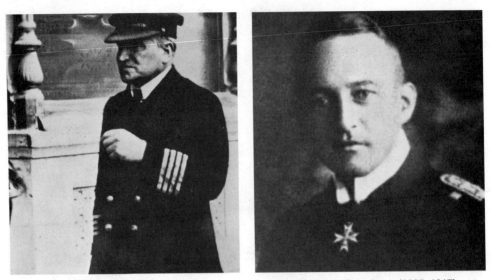

Captain William T. Turner (1856–1933). He commanded the *Lusitania* to disaster. (U.S. War Department)

Lieutenant Walter Schwieger (1885–1917). His *U–20* sank the *Lusitania*. (Bundesarchiv)

deck in those dangerous waters, did not hear the megaphone one minute before the torpedo struck. Had he heard the warning, the ship *might* have veered sharply and avoided danger. Turner felt the explosion as it ripped into the *Lusitania*. Schwieger watched through his periscope as the mighty vessel leaned on its starboard side and its bow dipped. Panic swept the passengers as they stumbled about the listing decks or groped in the darkness below. Steam whistled from punctured boilers. Less than half the lifeboats lowered; some capsized or embarked only partially loaded. Within eighteen minutes the "Queen of the Atlantic" sank, killing 1,198—128 of them Americans. A survivor said that when the *Lusitania* went down, "it sounded like a terrible moan."[6]

President Wilson had just ended a cabinet meeting in the White House when he learned of the disaster. His special assistant, Colonel Edward House, then in London, predicted: "We shall be at war with Germany within a month."[7] The pro-British House had actually sailed on the *Lusitania* in February and had witnessed, much to his surprise, the hoisting of an American flag as the ship neared the Irish coast. Fearing war, Secretary Bryan told the president that "ships carrying contraband should be prohibited from carrying passengers. . . . it would be like putting women and children in front of an army."[8] Bellicose ex-president Theodore Roosevelt soon seared the air with his declaration that "this represents . . . piracy on a vaster scale of murder than old-time pirates ever practiced."[9] American after American voiced horror, but few wanted war. Wilson secluded himself to ponder a response to this ghastly event. Just months before, he had said he would hold Berlin strictly accountable for the loss of any American ships or lives because of submarine warfare. Thereafter, Wilson found himself trying to fulfill America's "double

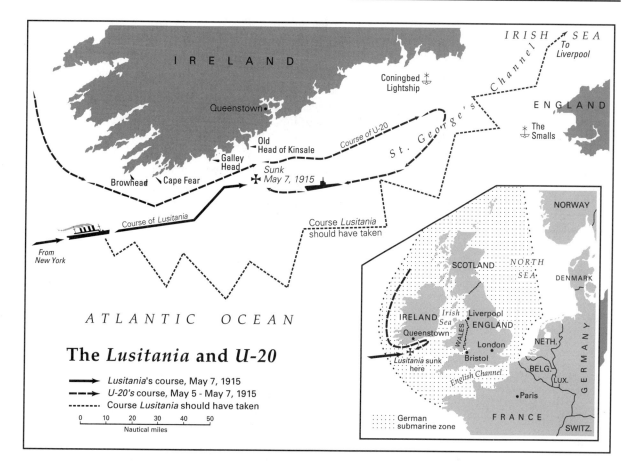

The *Lusitania* and U-20

→ *Lusitania*'s course, May 7, 1915
- - -> U-20's course, May 5 - May 7, 1915
······· Course *Lusitania* should have taken

0 10 20 30 40 50
Nautical miles

wish"—"to maintain a firm front . . . [toward] Germany and yet do nothing that might by any possibility involve us in war."[10]

After reading memoranda from Bryan warning that Americans should not travel on Allied ships carrying contraband, Wilson spoke in Philadelphia on May 10. His words, much misunderstood, suggested he had no backbone: "There is such a thing as a man being too proud to fight. There is such a thing as a nation being so right that it does not need to convince others by force that it is right."[11] When former secretary of state Elihu Root called it "incredible" that Wilson could see "no greater moral question involved," the president regretted his impromptu words.[12] Preoccupied by his intense courtship of his future second wife, Wilson did "not know just what I said in Philadelphia . . . because my heart was in such a whirl."[13] The next morning he told the cabinet that he would send a note to Berlin insisting that Americans had a right to travel on the high seas and demanding a disavowal by the German government of the inhumane acts of its submarine commanders. Bryan sadly approved this first "*Lusitania* note." Long upset about an apparent American double standard in protesting more against German than British violations of American neutral rights, the secretary pleaded for a simultaneous protest to London. But only one note went out on May 13—to Berlin: "The Imperial Government will not expect the United States to omit any word or any act necessary to the performance of its sacred duty of maintaining the rights of the United States and its citizens and of safeguarding their free exercise and enjoyment."[14] In short, end submarine warfare, or else.

The German government took much less pleasure than the German navy did in the destruction of the *Lusitania.* Chancellor Theobold von Bethmann-Hollweg had more than once chastised the navy for inviting war with the United States through submarine attacks on neutral or Allied merchant vessels. On May 28 he sent an evasive reply to Wilson's note. The *Lusitania* case could not be settled, it read, until they clarified certain questions. The German note claimed that the ship was armed, carried munitions, and had orders to ram submarines. Germany asked Washington to investigate. That same day, in a secret meeting with German ambassador Johann von Bernstorff, Wilson proposed that if Germany would settle the *Lusitania* crisis favorably, he would press the British to suspend their blockade and then call a conference of neutrals to mediate an end to the war on the following basis: "1. The status quo in Europe; 2. Freedom of the seas. . . . 3. Adjustments concerning colonial possessions."[15]

Wilson convened the cabinet on June 1. When one member recommended a strong note demanding observance of American rights, another suggested as well a note to England to protest British interference with American commerce. Debate became heated. A majority rejected simultaneous notes. Bryan called the cabinet pro-Ally. Wilson quickly rebuked him for "unfair and unjust" comments.[16] When Germany did not immediately reply to his mediation proposal, Wilson sent a second "*Lusitania* note." This note vigorously demanded an end to warfare by submarine. Wilson rejected Bryan's plea for a warning to passengers and a protest note to England. Sensing that "this will destroy me," Bryan quietly resigned on June 8.[17] Wilson went to the golf links to free himself from the blinding headaches of the past several days. "He is absolutely *sincere,*" the president said of Bryan. "That is what makes him dangerous."[18]

More correspondence on the *Lusitania* followed. The United States insisted that Germany admit it had committed an illegal act; but Germany, unwilling to abandon one of its few effective weapons against British mastery of the ocean, refused to admit wrongdoing and asked for arbitration. "Utterly impertinent," sniffed Kaiser Wilhelm II, who preferred victory to Wilson's mediation.[19] Eventually Germany sought compromise. On February 4 it expressed regret over the American deaths and offered to pay an indemnity (eventually paid in the early 1920s). Wilson accepted the German concession.

The horrible deaths from the *Lusitania* remained etched in American memories. The torpedoing of the magnificent Cunarder marked a turning point. The Germans suffered a "naval victory worse than a defeat," as Britons and Americans alike depicted the "Huns" as depraved.[20] The sinking also hardened Wilson's opinion of Germany. After Germany spurned his secret mediation offer, Wilson no longer made diplomatic life easier for the Germans by simultaneously protesting

British infractions. The British were violating property rights, but the Germans violated human rights. He also refused to warn Americans away from belligerent ships. In short, if a U-boat attacked a British ship with Americans aboard, Germany would have to take the consequences. Wilson did not spell out those consequences, but the logical implication was war—just what Bryan feared. His resignation brought pro-Ally Robert Lansing to the secretaryship of state. After the *Lusitania* crisis, Lansing believed "that we would ultimately become an ally of Great Britain."[21] The sinking of the *Lusitania* pointed up, for all to see, the complexities, contradictions, and uncertainties inherent in American neutrality during the European phase of the First World War, 1914–1917.

The Travails of Neutrality

Woodrow Wilson acted virtually as his own secretary of state during those troubled years. "Wilson makes confidant of no one. No one gets his whole mind," an aide wrote.[22] British prime minister Lloyd George put it less kindly: Wilson "believed in mankind but . . . distrusted all men."[23] The president defined the overall character of American foreign policy—what historians call "Wilsonianism." Above all else, Wilson stood for an *open* world unencumbered by imperialism, war, or revolution. Barriers to trade and democracy had to come down, and secret diplomacy had to give way to public negotiations. The right of self-determination would force the collapse of empires. Constitutional procedures would replace revolution. A free-market, humanized capitalism would ensure democracy. Disarmament programs would restrict weapons. The Open Door of equal trade and investment would harness the economic competition that led to war. Wilson, like so many Americans, saw the United States as exceptional—"a sort of pure air blowing in world politics, destroying illusions and cleaning places of morbid miasmic gasses."[24] His reformist, expansionist zeal blended with realism. The president calculated the nation's economic and strategic needs and devised a foreign policy to protect them. Yet many Americans feared that his world-reforming efforts might invite war, dissipate American resources, and undermine reform at home. Wilson led a divided nation.

Few Americans, Wilson included, desired war. Most watched in shock as the European nations savagely slashed at one another in 1914. The progressive faith in human ability to right wrongs, the belief that war belonged to the decadent past, the conviction that civilization had advanced too far for such bloodletting—all were ruthlessly challenged. Before 1914 the new machine guns, howitzers, submarines, and dreadnoughts were simply too awesome for leaders to launch them. The outbreak of World War I smashed illusions and tested innocence. The shock did not become despair, despite the news of poison gas, U-boats, and civilian casualties. The Progressive era exuded optimism, and Americans, particularly the crusading Wilson, sought to retrieve a happier past by assuming the role of civilized instructors: America would help Europe come to its senses by teaching it the rules of humane conduct. The carnage justified the mission. In 1915 alone France suffered 1.3 million

Makers of American Foreign Relations, 1914–1920

President	Secretaries of State
Woodrow Wilson, 1913–1921	William Jennings Bryan, 1913–1915
	Robert Lansing, 1915–1920
	Bainbridge Colby, 1920–1921

casualties, including 330,000 deaths. Germany suffered 848,000 casualties, 170,000 of them deaths. Britain followed with 313,000 casualties, and 73,000 deaths.

Americans had good reason, then, to believe that Europe needed help in cleaning its own house. The outbreak of the war seemed so senseless. By June 1914, the great powers had constructed two blocs, the Triple Alliance (Germany, Austria-Hungary, and Italy) and the Triple Entente (France, Russia, and Great Britain). Some called this division of Europe a balance of power, but an assassin's bullet unbalanced it. Between Austria and Serbia lay Bosnia, a tiny province in the Austro-Hungarian Empire. Slavic nationalists sought to build a greater Serbia—an independent Slavic state—by annexing Bosnia, which the Austro-Hungarian Empire had absorbed just a few years before, in 1909. A Slavic terrorist group, the Black Hand, decided to force the issue. On June 28 the heir to the Hapsburg Crown of Austria-Hungary, Archduke Franz Ferdinand, visited Sarajevo, the capital of Bosnia. As his car moved through the streets of the city, a Black Hand assassin gunned him down.

Austria-Hungary sent impossible demands to Serbia. The Serbs rejected them. Austria-Hungary had already received encouragement from Germany, and Serbia had a pledge of support from Russia, which in turn received backing from France. A chain reaction set in. On July 28 Austria-Hungary declared war on Serbia; on August 1 Germany declared "preventive" war on Russia and two days later on France; on August 4 Germany invaded Belgium, and Great Britain declared war on Germany. In a few weeks Japan joined the Allies (Triple Entente) and Turkey the Central Powers, and Italy entered on the Allied side the next year. As the German leader Otto von Bismarck had once prophesied, "some damned foolish thing in the Balkans" had started a world war.[25]

The Atlantic seemed at first an adequate barrier to insulate the United States. In early August, the U.S. ambassador to England, Walter Hines Page, wrote the president: "Be ready; for you will be called on to compose their huge quarrel. I thank Heaven for many things—first the Atlantic Ocean."[26] Wilson issued a Proclamation of Neutrality on August 4, followed days later by an appeal to Americans to be neutral in thought, speech, and action. Laced with patriotic utterances, the decree sought to cool the passions of immigrant groups who identified with the belligerents. America must demonstrate to a troubled world that it was "fit beyond others to exhibit the fine poise of undisturbed judgment, the dignity of self-control, the efficiency of dispassionate action."[27] A lofty call for restraint, an expression of

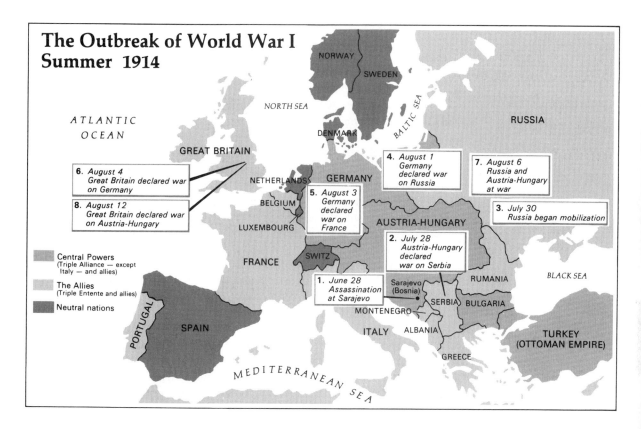

The Outbreak of World War I Summer 1914

NORWAY

SWEDEN

NORTH SEA

BALTIC SEA

RUSSIA

ATLANTIC OCEAN

DENMARK

GREAT BRITAIN

6. August 4
Great Britain declared war
on Germany

8. August 12
Great Britain declared war
on Austria-Hungary

NETHERLANDS

GERMANY

4. August 1
Germany
declared war
on Russia

7. August 6
Russia and
Austria-Hungary
at war

BELGIUM

5. August 3
Germany
declared
war on
France

3. July 30
Russia began mobilization

LUXEMBOURG

AUSTRIA-HUNGARY

2. July 28
Austria-Hungary
declared
war on Serbia

Central Powers
(Triple Alliance — except Italy — and allies)

The Allies
(Triple Entente and allies)

Neutral nations

FRANCE

SWITZ.

1. June 28
Assassination
at Sarajevo

Sarajevo
(Bosnia)

SERBIA

RUMANIA

BLACK SEA

BULGARIA

MONTENEGRO

PORTUGAL

SPAIN

ITALY

ALBANIA

TURKEY
(OTTOMAN EMPIRE)

GREECE

MEDITERRANEAN SEA

America as the beacon of common sense in a world gone mad, a plea for unity at home—but difficult to achieve.

Few Americans, including officials of the Wilson administration, proved capable of neutral thoughts and deeds. Loyalties to fatherlands and motherlands did not abate. German Americans identified with the Central Powers. Many Irish Americans, nourishing their traditional Anglophobia at a time when Ireland chafed under British rule and readied for rebellion, wished catastrophe on Britain. But Anglo-American traditions and cultural ties, as well as slogans such as "Remember LaFayette," pulled most Americans toward a pro-Allied position. Since the 1890s Anglophobia had weakened in the face of the calming Anglo-American rapprochement. Woodrow Wilson himself harbored pro-British sentiment, telling the British ambassador that "everything I love is at stake" and that a German victory "will be fatal to our form of Government and American ideals."[28] Wilson's advisers, House and Lansing, were ardently pro-British. Ambassador Page became so fiercely pro-British that he wanted Americans "to hang our Irish agitators and shoot our hyphenates and bring up our children with reverence for English history and . . . English literature."[29]

German war actions, exaggerated by British propaganda, also undermined neutrality. To Americans, the Germans, led by arrogant Kaiser Wilhelm II, became symbols of the dreaded militarism and conscription of the Old World. Even Chancellor Bethmann-Hollweg admitted that "we often got on the world's nerves."[30] Germany, too, seemed an upstart nation, an aggressive latecomer to the scramble for imperialist prizes, and a noisy intruder in the Caribbean where the British had already acknowledged U.S. hegemony. Eager to grasp world power and encouraging Austria-Hungary to war, Berlin certainly had little claim on virtue. The European powers had guaranteed Belgium neutrality by treaty, but Bethmann-Hollweg dismissed it as a "scrap of paper."[31] On August 4, 1914, hoping to get at France, the Germans attacked Belgium and, angered that the Belgians resisted, ruthlessly proceeded to raze villages, unleash firing squads against townspeople, and deport young workers to Germany. One magazine called Belgium "a martyr to civilization, sister to all who love liberty, or law; assailed, polluted, trampled in the mire, heel-marked in her breast, tattered, homeless."[32] American hearts and hands went out in the form of a major relief mission headed by a young, wealthy, and courageous mining engineer, Herbert Hoover.

American economic links with the Allies also undercut neutrality. England had always been America's best customer, and wartime conditions simply intensified the relationship. The Allies needed both war matériel and consumer goods. Americans, inspired by huge profits and a chance to pull out of a recession, obliged. In 1914 U.S. exports to England and France equaled $754 million; in 1915 the figure shot up to $1.28 billion; and in 1916 the amount more than doubled to $2.75 billion. Comparable statistics for Germany reveal why Berlin believed the United States was taking sides. In 1914 exports to Germany totaled $345 million; in 1915 they plummeted to $29 million; and in 1916 they fell to $2 million. In 1914–1917 New York's banking house of J. P. Morgan Company served as an agent for England and France and arranged for the shipment of more than $3 billion worth of goods. In April 1915, Britain ordered shells from the American Locomotive Company costing $63.7 million, and that year Bethlehem Steel contracted for some $150 million in ammunition, to cite two examples. By April 1917, British purchasing missions were spending $83 million a week for American copper, steel, wheat, oil, and munitions.

Britain and France sold many of their American securities and liquidated investments to pay for these goods. This netted them several billion dollars. Next, in appeals to prominent American bankers and State Department officials, they also sought loans. In 1914 Bryan discouraged private American loans to the belligerents, because "money is the worst of all contrabands because it commands everything else."[33] Yet in early 1915 the Wilson administration did not object to a Morgan credit to France of $50 million. With Bryan's resignation and Lansing's ascent as secretary of state, the practice became common. As Lansing told Wilson, if Americans did not extend loans to the Allies, it would invite "restriction of output, industrial depression, idle capital, idle labor, numerous failures, financial demoralization, and general unrest and suffering among the laboring classes."[34] The Wilson administration permitted loans to the Allies amounting to $2.3 billion in the years 1914–1917—a sharp contrast to loans of only $27 million to Germany. Once it joined the war as a belligerent, the American economic powerhouse became even more the dispenser of munitions, food, and money to the Allies. Indeed, as the historian Kathleen Burk has written, "the passing of hegemony from Britain to the United States . . . as the leading financial power can be seen occurring, step by step, in the negotiations between the British Treasury mission and the American government during 1917–18."[35]

Berlin protested such "unneutral" economic ties. Yet curbing trade with Britain, which ruled the seas, would have constituted unneutral behavior in favor of the Germans, for under international law a belligerent could buy, at its own risk, contraband and noncontraband goods from a neutral. Neutral or not, the United States had become the arsenal of the Allied war effort. Berlin tried to stop this trade by unleashing *unterseebooten*.

Submarines, Neutral Rights, and Mediation Efforts

To strangle Germany, the British invoked legal doctrines of retaliation and contraband without ever technically declaring a blockade. They mined the North Sea, expanded the contraband list to include foodstuffs and cotton, forced American ships into port for inspection, seized "contraband" from neutral vessels, halted American trade with Germany's neutral neighbors Denmark and Holland, armed British merchant ships, used decoy ships to lure U-boats into traps, flew neutral (often American) flags, and rammed whenever possible any U-boats that complied with international law by surfacing to warn a British merchant vessel of an imminent attack. The British "ruled the waves and waived the rules," so to speak. Defending neutral rights, the Wilson administration issued protests, some mild, some tough, against these illegalities. The Foreign Office usually paid appropriate verbal deference to neutral rights and international law and went right on with its restrictive behavior. Britain sometimes compensated U.S. businesses for damages and purchased large quantities of goods at inflated prices. Americans thus came to tolerate the indignities of British economic warfare. Britain managed brilliantly to sever American economic lines to the Central Powers without rupturing Anglo-American relations.

Germans protested vehemently against American acquiescence in the British "hunger" or "starvation" blockade. To continue the war, Germany had to have imports and had to curb the flourishing Anglo-American trade that fueled the Allied war machine. The German surface fleet, bottled up in ports, seemed inadequate for the task, so German leaders hesitantly turned to a relatively new experimental weapon of limited maneuverability, the submarine. At the start they possessed just 21 U-boats, and at peak strength in October 1917 they had but 127. Only a third of this fleet operated at sea at any one time. On February 4, 1915, Berlin announced that it was retaliating against British strangulation by declaring a war zone around Britain. All *enemy* ships in the area would be destroyed. It warned neutral ships to *stay out* of the zone because of possibly mistaken identity, a real prospect given the British practice of hoisting neutral flags. Passengers from neutral countries were urged, moreover, to *stay off* enemy passenger vessels. Six days later Wilson held Germany to "strict accountability" for the loss of American life and property.[36]

William Jennings Bryan (1860–1925). The great agrarian reformer went to Congress in 1890 as a Democrat from Nebraska. After several unsuccessful runs for the presidency, Bryan endorsed Wilson and became secretary of state in 1913. He favored the arbitration of international disputes, and he perpetuated U.S. interventionist policy in Latin America. Believing that Wilson was tilting toward the British after the *Lusitania* disaster of 1915, Bryan resigned in protest. A colleague called him "too good a Christian to run a naughty world." (National Portrait Gallery, Smithsonian Institution)

The British continued to arm their merchant vessels, which thereby became warships and theoretically ineligible to take on arms or munitions in neutral ports. But Washington invoked a fine distinction between offensive and defensive armaments and permitted such "defensively" armed British craft to carry war supplies from American ports. Crying foul, the Germans also argued that old international law, which Wilson invoked, did not fit the submarine. Rules "adopted during the sailing-ship era" held that an attacking cruiser about to sink or capture enemy merchant vessels had to give adequate warning so as to ensure the safety of passengers and crew.[37] Yet if a submarine surfaced in its sluggish fashion, the merchant ship's crew might sink it with a blast from a deck gun or even a hand grenade, or ram the slow-moving craft. Imagine the problem for Schwieger of *U-20* when he spotted the *Lusitania*. Had he surfaced to warn the ship, the *Lusitania* probably would have attempted to ram *U-20* or flee and would have sent distress signals to British warships in the vicinity. Even if the *Lusitania* had submitted to the warning, it might have taken an hour for passengers to get into lifeboats before Schwieger could torpedo the *Lusitania,* by which time British warships might have closed in. In short, from the German point of view, to comply with an international law that failed to anticipate the submarine was not possible. Wilson retorted that differences over international law could be "adjusted after the war," whereas Germany's "sheer acts of piracy on the high seas . . . might easily lead to actual hostilities."[38]

Secretary Bryan tried diplomacy in early 1915, asking Germany to give up use of unannounced submarine attacks in exchange for a British promise to disarm its merchant carriers and permit food to flow to Germany. The Germans seemed interested, but London refused to abandon its successful blockade. At this point Wilson might have pressed the belligerents to alter their naval strategies or face the prospect of U.S. warships convoying America's neutral ships. Or he might have launched a vigorous diplomatic offensive to delay explosive events on the seas. Yet American armed convoys in the Atlantic could very well draw the country into a war it did not want. A diplomatic offensive, given the intensity of war fever in Europe, seemed a long shot. In March 1915, Wilson did send Colonel House to Europe to sound out possibilities for mediation, but to no avail. Nonetheless, Wilson failed to adjust or shelve ancient international law, which had no provision for the submarine. He accepted British alterations but not German ones, for reasons of both morality and economics.

Between February and May 1915, marauding submarines sank ninety ships in the war zone. One American, on the British passenger ship *Falaba,* died in the sinking of that vessel on March 28. Then came the *Lusitania* in May. Through Wilson's many protest notes, a U.S. posture took shape: uneasy tolerance of British violations of property rights and rejection of German violations of human rights. Despite secret German orders to submarine commanders to avoid a repetition of the *Lusitania* incident, on August 19 the *Arabic,* another British liner, was torpedoed with the loss of two American lives. A worried Ambassador Bernstorff publicly pledged that U-boats would now spare passenger ships.

In early 1916, calling the United States ideally suited as the "mediating nation of the world," Wilson tried to bring the warring parties to the conference table.[39]

Colonel House talked with British officials in London but left with no promises for peace. He journeyed next to Berlin, where German leaders gave no assurances. Both sides would fight on. "Hell will break loose in Europe this spring and summer as never before," House informed Wilson.[40] House then traveled to Paris, where he rashly informed his skeptical French hosts: "If the Allies obtain a small success this spring or summer, the U.S. will intervene to promote a peaceful settlement, but if the Allies have a setback, the United States will intervene militarily and will take part in the war against Germany."[41] House did not report his prediction to the president.

House returned to London to press Sir Edward Grey, British foreign secretary, to heed Wilson's call for a peace conference. The American envoy recorded their agreements in the House-Grey Memorandum of February 22, 1916, a document loaded with "ifs." The first paragraph read: "Colonel House told me that President Wilson was ready, on hearing from France and England that the moment was opportune, to propose that a Conference should be summoned to put an end to the war. Should the Allies accept the proposal, and should Germany refuse it, the United States would probably enter the war against Germany." The record of conversation also reported that House had said that the peace conference would secure terms "not unfavourable to the Allies" and that if the conference failed to achieve peace, "the United States would leave the Conference as a belligerent on the side of the Allies, if Germany was unreasonable."[42] Wilson pronounced the memorandum a diplomatic triumph, but he clouded its meaning all the more by inserting a "probably" before the word "leave" in the sentence quoted above. He took the document much more seriously than did the British or French, who shelved it, snubbed American mediation, and vowed victory over Germany.

Edward M. House (1858–1938). This Texas "colonel" served as Wilson's trusted emissary abroad. In the House-Grey Memorandum of 1916 he showed signs of the deviousness that led to his break with the president after the Versailles conference. He misled the British by depicting the mediation overture as a pretext for America's entering the war, and he misled Wilson by reporting that the British were genuinely interested in mediation. (National Portrait Gallery, Smithsonian Institution)

As House moved among European capitals, Lansing informed the Allied governments that the United States sought a modus vivendi to defuse naval crises: The Allies would disarm merchant vessels, and the Germans would follow international law by warning enemy merchant ships. This suggestion revealed that the Wilson administration understood the German argument that armed merchant vessels actually operated as offensive craft—that is, warships. The British and Colonel House remonstrated when they received this news. The Germans seemed to endorse the proposal by declaring on February 10 that submarines would henceforth attack only *armed* merchant ships without warning. Suddenly Wilson reversed policy. He abandoned the modus vivendi in order to restore his standing with the British and sustain House's mediation efforts in London. Lansing announced, furthermore, that the United States would not ban its citizens from traveling on "defensively" armed merchant ships.

Wilson Leads America into World War

Why let one American passenger and a trigger-happy U-boat captain start a war? asked public critics such as Bryan. Why not, they inquired, keep Americans off belligerent ships and require them instead to sail on American vessels? From August

**Woodrow Wilson
(1856–1924).** Scholar, professor, university president (Princeton), and Democratic governor (New Jersey), Woodrow Wilson was usually cocksure once he made a decision. "I would rather fail in a cause that will ultimately triumph than triumph in a cause that will ultimately fail," he once said. (*Cartoons*, 1912)

1914 to mid-March 1917 only three Americans (on the oil tanker *Gulflight,* May 1, 1915) had lost their lives on an American ship torpedoed by a U-boat. In contrast, about 190 Americans, including the *Lusitania*'s 128, died on belligerent ships. After the *Falaba* was sunk, Bryan, still secretary of state, recognized that Americans had a right to travel on belligerent vessels, but he wanted Wilson to ask them to forgo that right. "I cannot see," Bryan wrote the president, "that he [an American on a belligerent ship] is differently situated from those who by remaining in a belligerent country assume risk of injury."[43] Wilson had, after all, urged Americans to leave war-torn Mexico. Ambassador James W. Gerard in Berlin wondered, "why should we enter a great war because some American wants to cross on a ship where he can have a private bathroom?"[44]

In January 1916, member of Congress Jeff McLemore of Texas, a Democrat, introduced a resolution to prohibit Americans from traveling on armed belligerent vessels. In February, Senator Thomas P. Gore of Oklahoma, another Democrat, submitted a similar resolution in his chamber. Wilson, a firm believer in presidential supremacy in decisionmaking, bristled at this challenge from Congress. He unleashed cabinet members with patronage muscle on timid legislators, suggesting that Gore-McLemore was a pro-German ploy. To halt American passage on belligerent ships, Wilson declared, would be to accept national humiliation and destruction of the "whole fine fabric of international law."[45] In short, he stuck with rigid, archaic concepts, refusing to adjust to the new factor of the submarine or to appreciate the impact on Germany of the obvious British violations of the same law. In early March, the Gore-McLemore resolution lost 68 to 14 in the Senate and 276 to 142 in the House. The resolution asked America to give up very little; despite presidential rhetoric, it did not besmudge national honor. Wilson's message to Berlin rang loud and clear: Do not use your submarines.

In March 1916, another passenger ship, another U-boat, another torpedo, more American injuries: The French ship *Sussex,* moving across the English Channel, took a hit but did not sink. Aboard was a young American scholar, Samuel Flagg Bemis, later a renowned historian of foreign relations but then fresh from archival research on Jay's Treaty. Bemis glimpsed the swirling wake of a torpedo moments before impact. "The entire bow was blown off and with it the people who were in the dining room," he recalled.[46] Although four Americans sustained injuries, a wet Bemis escaped serious harm and managed to save his little bag of note cards.

The *Sussex* attack violated the "*Arabic* pledge," even though the U-boat commander mistook the ship for a minelayer. Lansing wanted to break diplomatic relations with Berlin. Wilson decided instead on an ultimatum. He warned the Germans on April 18 that he would sever relations if they did not halt their submarine warfare against passenger and merchant vessels; he went to Congress the next day and repeated the warning. With the unsuccessful German offensive at Verdun costing more than half a million lives, Berlin did not want war with the United States. In early May Germany promised (the "*Sussex* pledge") that submarines would not attack passenger or merchant ships without prior warning. The Germans also nagged Washington to stop British infractions of international law.

The British, sensing favorable winds, clamped down even harder on trade with the Central Powers. In July, London issued a "blacklist" of more than eighty American companies that had traded with the Central Powers. Even Wilson now fumed that he was "about at the end of my patience with Great Britain and the Allies."[47] He contemplated a ban on loans and exports to them, but he did little. Many Americans also condemned the brutal British smashing of the Irish Easter Rebellion in April 1916.

Shortly after his reelection in 1916, under the slogan "He Kept Us Out of War," the president boldly asked the belligerents to state their war aims. Neither Berlin nor London, still seeking military victory, welcomed Wilson's mediation. Germany coveted Poland, Lithuania, Belgium, and the Belgian Congo; Britain sought German colonies; France wanted Alsace-Lorraine. Wilson pointedly rejected such goals on January 22, 1917, when he called for a "peace without victory" because only through a peace founded on the "equality of nations" could a lasting world order be achieved. He regarded victory as "an intoxicant that fires the national brain and leaves a craving for more."[48] The French novelist Anatole France responded cynically: "Peace without victory is bread without yeast . . . , love without quarrels, a camel without humps, night without moon, roof without smoke, town without brothel."[49]

In early 1917 crises mounted quickly. On January 31 Berlin announced that German submarines would attack without warning and sink all vessels, enemy and neutral, found near British waters. This declaration of unrestricted submarine warfare expressed Germany's calculated risk that it could defeat England and France before the United States could mobilize and send soldiers overseas. The cocky German naval minister remarked: "From a military standpoint, America's entrance is as nothing."[50] German naval officers persuaded the kaiser that the U-boats, now numbering about one hundred, could knock Britain out of the war in six months. Army officers, bogged down in trench warfare, hoped to end their costly immobility through a bold stroke.

On February 3 Washington severed diplomatic relations with Berlin. Wilson still did not want war with Germany, even though he had become incensed by Berlin's most recent decision. According to Lansing, Wilson became "more and more impressed with the idea that 'white civilization' and its domination over the world rested largely on our ability to keep this country intact, as we would have to build up the nations ravaged by the war."[51] Yet Wilson had also committed himself to stand firmly against unrestricted submarine warfare. Allied ships carrying war supplies soon suffered increasing losses, and the few American vessels carrying contraband stayed in port or shifted to trade outside the European war zones. Goods stacked up on wharves. The U.S. economy seemed imperiled.

Next came an apparent challenge to U.S. security. Washington had already endured espionage and sabotage by German agents, most notably the "thunderous" explosions at the Black Tom munitions factories across from the Statue of Liberty in July 1916.[52] In late February the British passed to Ambassador Page an intercepted telegram dated January 16 and sent to Mexico by German foreign minister Arthur Zimmermann. The message proposed a military alliance with the U.S.

**Jeannette Rankin
(1880–1973).** Native of Montana, Rankin, in 1916, became the first woman to be elected to the House of Representatives. A lifelong pacifist, she voted against war in 1917, only to lose her seat the following year. In the interwar period she lobbied for peace and was again elected to Congress in 1940. Once again she refused to send American soldiers into "the foreign slaughterhouse" and cast the only vote against war in 1941. She later marched against the Vietnam War. (Library of Congress)

neighbor. And should war with the United States break out, Germany would help Mexico "reconquer" the territory lost in 1848. Zimmermann also suggested adding Japan to the alliance "at the moment war breaks out between Mexico and the United States."[53] Although the skeptical Mexican government never took up the German offer, Wilson saw the telegram as a direct challenge. "This wd [would] precipitate a war between almost any 2 nations," Page confided to his diary.[54]

Wilson now asked Congress for authority to arm American merchant vessels. On March 1, to create a favorable public opinion for the request, he released the Zimmermann telegram to the press. But antiwar senators Robert La Follette and George Norris led a filibuster—a "little group of willful men," Wilson snarled—that killed the armed ship legislation.[55] Stubbornly ignoring the Senate, Wilson ordered the arming anyway. To no avail: during March 16–18 alone U-boats sunk the American ships *City of Memphis, Illinois,* and *Vigilancia.* Buttressed by the unanimous support of his cabinet, the president decided for war.

After several intense days writing his own speech with help from Colonel House, Wilson played golf with his new wife before addressing a special joint session of Congress on the evening of April 2. He asked for a declaration of war against Germany—a war that Berlin had "thrust" on the United States. The "unmanly business" of using submarines, he asserted, constituted "warfare against mankind." Freedom of the seas, commerce, American lives, human rights—the "outlaw" U-boats challenged all. Economic self-interest, morality, and national honor compelled Americans to fight. He characterized the German government as a menacing monster striking at the "very roots of human life." The "Prussian autocracy" stirred up trouble through spies and the Zimmermann telegram. He also hailed the Russian Revolution of March, which made Russia "a fit partner for a league of honor" in a crusade against autocracy. Then came the memorable words: "The world must be made safe for democracy."[56]

Although the oration simplified issues and promised too much for American intervention, the moment required patriotic fervor. At the end, according to one historian, most listeners "were ready to grasp the Hun by the collar, feeling that surely God was on their side, and if He was not, God this one time must be wrong."[57] By votes of 82 to 6 in the Senate on April 4 (La Follette and Norris among the dissenters) and 373 to 50 in the House on April 6 (Majority Leader Claude Kitchin and nine of Wisconsin's eleven representatives among those voting nay), Congress endorsed Wilson's call for a war for peace. In a rebuke to feminist pacifism, one senator voted for war because it required "a courage both moral and physical, a mind free from trash and slush, flexed muscles and sinews that have not been debilitated, or degenerated by sensuality, security, and luxury."[58]

Submarine warfare precipitated the American decision to enter the war. Had no submarine menaced American lives, property, and the U.S. definition of international law, no American soldiers would have gone to France. Critics have argued, however, that from the German perspective, the submarine became necessary because of the long list of unfriendly American acts: acquiescence in the British blockade, part of a general pro-British bias; huge munitions shipments to the Allies; large loans; an interpretation of neutral rights that insisted that American passengers could sail anywhere, even into a war zone. Take away those acts, which the Germans considered unneutral, and they might not have launched the U-boats. To dissenters it seemed wrong that American ideals and interests could depend so perilously on armed ships carrying contraband, heading for Britain, and steaming through a war zone. Yet Wilson and his advisers had so defined the problem.

Permeating Wilson's policies was the traditional American belief that others must conform to U.S. prescriptions and that America's ideals served as a beacon for the world. "We created this Nation," the president once proclaimed, "not to serve ourselves, but to serve mankind."[59] When the Germans defied America's rules, ideals, and property, and threatened its security through a proposed alliance with Mexico, they had to be punished. Here was an opportunity to protect both humane principles and commercial interests. When Wilson spoke passionately of the right of a neutral to freedom of the seas, he demonstrated the interconnections among American moral, economic, and strategic interests. Wilson sought the role of peace-maker and promised to remake the world in the American image—that is, to create a world order in which barriers to political democracy and the Open Door came down, in which revolution and aggression no longer disturbed world order. As the philosopher John Dewey put it, war came at a "plastic juncture" in history in which Americans could fight to reshape the world according to progressive principles.[60]

The Debate over Preparedness

Berlin's assumption that American soldiers could not reach France fast enough to reverse an expected German victory proved a gross misjudgment. American military muscle and economic power, in fact, decisively tipped the balance against Germany. Given the information available in early 1917, however, the German calculation does not seem so unrealistic. In April the United States had no capacity to send a major expedition to the western front. At that date the Regular Army counted only 130,000 officers and men, backed by 180,000 national guardsmen. Although some American officers had been seasoned by military interventions in Cuba, in the Philippines, and recently in Mexico, many soldiers lacked adequate training. Arsenals had meager supplies of such modern weapons as the machine gun. The "Air Service," then part of the army, did not have a plane of modern design with a machine gun, and some warships had never fired a gun.

An American "preparedness movement" had been under way for months, encouraged by prominent Americans such as the tough-minded Rough Rider and military evangelist General Leonard Wood, who overstated the case when he argued that America's military weakness invited attack, but rang true when he noted that the United States was not recognized as a top-notch military power. After 1914, Wood, Theodore Roosevelt, the National Security League, the Army League, and the Navy League lobbied actively for bigger military appropriations with the argument that "preparedness" offered insurance against war. When the hit pacifist song "I Didn't Raise My Boy to Be a Soldier" became "an icon of popular antiwar sentiment" in 1915, preparedness proponents countered with parodies such as "I Didn't Raise My Boy to Be a Coward."[61] One propaganda film, *The Battle*

Cry of Peace (1916), in showing spike-helmeted soldiers invading America, used gendered images of "a strong manhood ready to protect vulnerable femininity."[62] In another film, *In Again, Out Again* (1917), a virile Douglas Fairbanks ridiculed "puny, pussyfooting pacifists" for "pulling the punch out of preparedness."[63]

Wilson belatedly supported moderate preparedness. He asked Congress in December 1915 for a half-billion-dollar naval expansion program, including ten battleships and one hundred submarines.[64] The president expected the United States to surpass Britain as "incomparably the greatest navy in the world."[65] Land forces would also be enlarged and reorganized.

Perpetuating the antimilitarist tradition of great numbers of Americans, Senator La Follette, Representative Kitchin, and prominent reformers such as William Jennings Bryan, Lillian Wald, and Oswald Garrison Villard spurred a movement against these measures. These peace advocates, the Women's Peace Party, and the League to Limit Armaments argued that war would interrupt reform at home, benefit big business, and curtail civil liberties. Several peace leaders also joined the auto manufacturer Henry Ford in December 1915 as he sailed to Europe on his peace ship, *Oscar II,* to establish a Neutral Conference for Continuous Mediation—a quixotic attempt to end the war and get "the boys out of the trenches by Christmas."[66] The American Union Against Militarism agitated against preparedness with its papier-mâché dinosaur, "Jingo," whose collar read "ALL ARMOR PLATE—NO BRAINS."[67] Because his support of mediation, disarmament, and a postwar association of nations appealed to antiwar liberals and socialists ("progressive internationalists"), Wilson hoped that moderate preparedness would not alienate them.[68] Chicago's famed social reformer Jane Addams remembered "moments of uneasiness," but she and others endorsed Wilson in the 1916 presidential campaign, for it seemed "at last that peace was assured and the future safe in the hands of an executive who had received an unequivocal mandate from the people 'to keep us out of war.'"[69]

In January 1916, Wilson set out on a two-month speaking tour, often criticizing members of his own party for their opposition to a military buildup. U-boat sinkings aided the president's message. In May 1916, Congress passed the National Defense Act, increasing the Regular Army to some 200,000 men and 11,000 officers, and the National Guard to 440,000 men and 17,000 officers. The act also authorized summer training camps, modeled after one held in Plattsburg, New York, in 1915 for the social and economic elite. Despite Jane Addams's query, "Why spend $45,000,000 for warships, when they will only be reduced to scrap heap after this war," the navy bill passed in August 1916.[70] Theodore Roosevelt thought the measures inadequate, but the anarchist Emma Goldman saw no difference between Roosevelt, "the born bully who uses a club," and Wilson, "the history professor who uses the smooth polished mask."[71]

Once in the war, after learning what the Allies "want and need is men, whether trained or not," Wilson relied on the Selective Service Act of May 1917.[72] National military service, proponents believed, would not only prepare the nation for battle but also instill respect for order, democracy, and sacrifice. Thus the Wilson administration transformed the army "into a potent instrument for citizenship inculca-

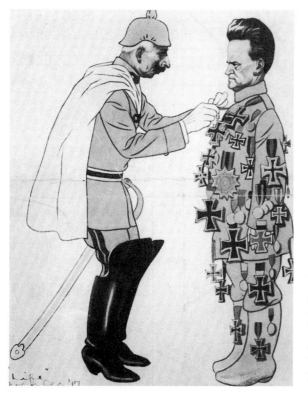

Senator Robert M. La Follette (1855–1925). This *Life* magazine cartoon depicted the antiwar, progressive reformer as a traitor. La Follette wanted a referendum on the war, certain that the American people would vote no. Some Americans thought that he should be expelled from the Senate. Others claimed that he took orders from the German kaiser, here shown pinning medals on the Wisconsin senator. La Follette withstood the intolerance of dissent and continued to speak against organized power and for the powerless, who, he said, were the people destined to do the fighting and dying abroad. (State Historical Society of Wisconsin)

tion," the historian Penn Borden has written, as "the army became sociologist, psychologist, physician, and preacher to the nation."[73] Under the selective service system, 24,340,000 men eventually registered for the draft. Some 3,764,000 men received draft notices, and 2,820,000 were inducted (the others failed preinduction tests, never showed up, or claimed conscientious objector—CO—status). Over all, 4,744,000 soldiers, sailors, and marines served. The typical serviceman was a white, single, poorly educated (most had not attended high school) draftee between twenty-one and twenty-three years of age. Officer training camps turned out "ninety-day wonders," thousands of commissioned officers drawn largely from people of elite background. Although excluded from military combat, women became navy clerks, telephone operators in the Army Signal Corps, and nurses and physical therapists to the wounded and battle-shock cases.

Right after the U.S. declaration of war, the Allies begged for soldiers. General John J. "Black Jack" Pershing, now head of the American Expeditionary Force to Europe, soon sent a "show the flag" contingent to France to boost Allied morale. Neither Wilson nor Pershing, however, would accept the European recommendation that U.S. troops be inserted in Allied units. American units would cooperate in joint maneuvers with other forces, but the U.S. Army would remain separate and independent. National pride dictated this decision, but so did the realization that

Allied commanders had for years wasted the lives of hundreds of thousands in trench warfare. Soldiers jumped out to charge German lines, also a maze of trenches. Machine guns mowed them down; chlorine gas, first used by Germany in 1915, poisoned them. Nor did Wilson wish to endorse exploitative Allied war aims. Thus did the United States call itself an "associated" rather than an "allied" power in the war.

The Doughboys Make the Difference in Europe

On July 4, 1917, General Pershing reviewed the first battalion to arrive in France, as nearly a million Parisians tossed flowers, hugged the "doughboys" (apparently so-called because their buttons resembled dumplings made of dough), and cheered wildly. Enthusiastic but ill-trained recruits, "these men couldn't even slope arms. They were even more dangerous with a loaded rifle," one company commander recalled.[74] But to the war-weary French, these fresh American troops offered inspiration.

To the dismay of American leaders, taverns and brothels quickly surrounded military camps. Alcohol and prostitution, of course, ranked as taboos in the United States during the Progressive era. "Fit to Fight" became the government's slogan, as it moved to close "red-light districts," designated "sin-free zones" around camps, and banned the sale of liquor to men in uniform. Secretary of the Navy Josephus Daniels preached that "men must live straight if they would shoot straight."[75] The YMCA and the Jewish Welfare Board sent song leaders to camps. Movies, athletic programs, and well-stocked stores sought to keep soldiers on the base by making them feel "at home."

Success against venereal disease contrasted with a major flu epidemic, which first struck camps in spring 1918. The extremely contagious flu virus cut across race, gender, and class lines. At Camp Sherman, Ohio, one of the bases hit hardest, 1,101 people died between September 27 and October 13. Whereas about 51,000 soldiers died in battle during the war, some 62,000 soldiers died from diseases. "Dough-boys" infected with the virus carried the flu with them to the European war, where it ignored national boundaries (the Germans called it *Blitzkatarrh*) and turned into a global pandemic that killed more than 21 million people by spring 1919.

Approximately 400,000 African-American troops suffered racism and discrimination during this war "to make the world safe for democracy." Camps were segregated and "white only" signs posted. In 1917 in Houston, Texas, whites provoked blacks into a riot that left seventeen whites and two blacks dead. In the army, three out of every four black soldiers served in labor units, where they wielded a shovel, not a gun, or where they cooked or unloaded supplies. African Americans endured second-class citizenship and the contradiction between America's wartime rhetoric and reality. A statistic revealed the problem: 382 black Americans were lynched in the period 1914–1920. To little effect, Germany's propagandists added a separate unit for "American race problems" to target discontented blacks in the South.[76]

Red Cross Postcard. Women served in many roles in the war. They became workers in weapons factories. They sold Liberty Bonds and publicized government mobilization programs as members of the Women's Committee of the Council of National Defense. In France, women nurses and canteen workers became envoys of the U.S. home front, representing the mothers, wives, and sisters left behind. As the historian Susan Zeiger has written, the government's sponsorship of these wartime roles for women cleverly blunted the feminist-pacifist claim that women were "inherently more peaceful than men and would oppose war out of love for their children." (Library of Congress)

The first official American combat death in Europe came only ten days after Congress declared war—that of Edmund Charles Clinton Genet, the great-great-grandson of French Revolutionary diplomat Citizen Genet and member of the famed American volunteer air squadron, the Lafayette Escadrille. Despite Allied impatience, General Pershing hesitated to commit his green soldiers to full-scale battle. As it was, great numbers of troops shipped over in British vessels and had to borrow French weapons. Disease continued to stalk U.S. forces. American reformers hoped soldiers had enough social armor not to be tempted by "sin" overseas, but the venereal-disease rate spiraled up. French premier Georges Clemenceau offered licensed—health-inspected—prostitutes. When Secretary of War Newton Baker received the Gallic proposal, he exclaimed: "For God's sake . . . don't show this to the President or he'll stop the war."[77] Prevention programs and the threat of court-martial eventually reduced the "VD" problem.

By early 1918 the Allies had become mired in a murderous strategy of throwing ground forces directly at enemy ground forces. German troops were mauling

First Division Troops Encounter German Gas Warfare, 1918. Near Soissons, France, U.S. soldiers attacked German lines through air contaminated with poisonous gas. The soldier in the foreground, wounded by fire, tore off his gas mask. (The Bettmann Archive)

Italian forces, and the French army was still suffering from mutinies of the year before. In March, after Germany swallowed large chunks of European Russia through the Brest-Litovsk Treaty, Wilson warned of a German "empire of force" out to "dominate the world itself" and urged Americans to "arm and prepare themselves to contest the mastery of the world."[78] In April he called for "Force, Force to the utmost, Force without stint or limit."[79] U.S. soldiers soon trooped into battle.

In March the German armies, swollen by forty divisions from the Russian front, launched a great offensive. Allied forces retreated, and by late May the kaiser's soldiers encamped near the Marne River less than fifty miles from Paris. Saint-Mihiel, Belleau Wood, Cantigny, Château-Thierry—French sites where U.S. soldiers shed their blood—soon became household words for Americans. In June at Château-Thierry the doughboys dramatically stopped a German advance. From May through September 1918 more than 1 million American troops went to France—2 million by the November armistice. In mid-July the Allies launched a counteroffensive; nine American divisions fought fiercely near Château-Thierry, helping to lift the German threat from Paris. In the Meuse-Argonne offensive (begun in late September), more than 1 million American soldiers joined French and British units to penetrate the crumbling German lines. "The American infantry in the Argonne [Forest] won the war," German marshal Paul von Hindenburg later commented.[80]

On October 4, the German chancellor asked Wilson for an armistice. German troops had mutinied; revolution and riots plagued German cities; Bulgaria had left the war in September. Then Turkey dropped out in late October, and Austria-Hungary surrendered on November 3. Germany had no choice but to seek terms.

The kaiser fled to Holland. On November 11, in a railroad car in the Compiègne Forest, German representatives capitulated.

Wilson Imagines a Better Future: The Fourteen Points and the Peace Conference

During the combat, President Wilson had begun to explain his plans for the peace. He trumpeted his vision most dramatically in his "Fourteen Points" speech before Congress on January 8, 1918. The first five points promised an "open" world after the war, a world distinguished by "open covenants, openly arrived at," freedom of navigation on the seas, equal trade opportunity and the removal of tariffs, reduction of armaments, and an end to colonialism. Points six through thirteen called for self-determination for national minorities in Europe. Point fourteen stood paramount: a "general association of nations" to ensure "political independence and territorial integrity to great and small states alike."[81] His Fourteen Points signaled a generous, nonpunitive postwar settlement. Pacifists felt that they had been "sent up into the very heaven of internationalism."[82] The Fourteen Points served too as effective American propaganda against revenge-fed Allied aims and Russian Bolshevik appeals for European revolution.

Leaders in France, Britain, and Italy feared that Wilson would deny them the spoils of war. In 1915 the Allies had signed secret treaties carving up German territories, including colonies in Africa and Asia. Dreaming of imperial expansion at Germany's expense, the Allies did not appreciate the "modern St. George," as the publicist Herbert Croly depicted Wilson, or his attempts to slay the "dragons of reaction" in Europe.[83] In view of the comparative wartime losses, Europeans believed that Wilson "had bought his seat at the peace table at a discount."[84] When, in September and October 1918, Wilson exchanged notes with Germany and Austria-Hungary about an armistice, the Allied powers expressed strong reservations about the Fourteen Points. General Tasker Bliss, the U.S. representative on the Supreme War Council (established in fall 1917 to coordinate the Allied war effort), despaired that "the war will accomplish more than the abolition of *German* militarism while leaving *European* militarism as rampant as ever."[85] Wilson hinted that the United States might negotiate a separate peace with the Central Powers. The president might even publicize the exploitative Allied war aims. Also facing possible reduced American shipments to Europe, London, Paris, and Rome reluctantly accepted, in the armistice of November, peace negotiations on the basis of the Fourteen Points.

Wilson relished his opportunity. "Never . . . was the world in such plastic state," one Wilsonian adviser explained.[86] The United States could now claim a major role in deciding future international relations. The pictures of dying men dangling from barbed-wire fences and the battle-shock victims who staggered home persuaded many Americans of the need to prevent another conflagration. Wilson's call for a just peace commanded the backing of countless foreigners as well. Italians hoisted banners reading *Dio di Pace* ("God of Peace") and *Redentore dell' Humanità* ("Redeemer of Humanity") to welcome Wilson to Europe.

David Lloyd George (1863–1945). "America," said the British prime minister referring to the League of Nations, "had been offered the leadership of the world, but the Senate had tossed the sceptre into the sea." (Sketch by Anthony Saris, American Heritage Publishing Company)

The president weakened his position even before the peace conference. Congressional leaders wanted him to stay home to handle domestic problems. Lansing feared that Wilson would lose his exalted image in the day-to-day conference bickering. The president would have only one vote, whereas from Washington he could symbolically marshal the votes of humankind. Wilson retorted that distance contributes to confusion and, because "England and France have not the same views with regard to peace that we have," he had to attend personally to defend the Fourteen Points.[87]

Domestic politics soon set Wilson back. In October 1918, Wilson "hurled a brick into a beehive" by asking Americans to return a Democratic Congress loyal to him.[88] Partisan Republicans, resenting Wilson's attempt to identify himself and the Democratic party with the well-being of the nation, proceeded to capture the November election and majorities in both houses of Congress; they would sit in ultimate judgment of Wilson's peacemaking. The president also made the political mistake of not appointing either an important Republican or a senator to the American Peace Commission. Wilson, House, and Lansing sat on it; so did General Bliss and Henry White, a seasoned diplomat and nominal Republican. Some concessions to his political opposition, and to senatorial prerogatives in foreign affairs, might have smoothed the path later for his peace treaty.

On December 4, with great fanfare, Wilson departed from New York aboard the *George Washington*. He settled into a quiet voyage, surrounded by advisers and nearly 2,000 reports produced by "The Inquiry," a group of scholars who had studied issues likely to arise at the peace conference. But the administration had made few plans, and the president continued to speak in vague terms. After reaching France on December 15, Wilson basked in the admiration of enthusiastic Parisian crowds, and later thousands in Italy and England cheered him with near religious fervor. Wilson assumed that this generous outpouring meant that *his* peace plan was universally popular and that *he* had a missionary duty to carry it forward. He would soon discover that such "man-in-the-street" opinion did not impress David Lloyd George, prime minister of Britain, French premier Georges Clemenceau, or Italian prime minister Vittorio Orlando, his antagonists at the peace conference.

Germany and Bolshevik Russia (see page 298) were excluded from the conference of January–May 1919, but thirty-two nations sent delegations, which essentially followed the lead of the "Big Four." Most sessions worked in secrecy, hardly befitting Wilson's first "point." Clemenceau resented Wilson's "sermonettes" and preferred to work with the more compliant Colonel House. "The old tiger [Clemenceau] wants the grizzly bear [Wilson] back in the Rocky Mountains before he starts tearing up the German Hog," commented Lloyd George, who sought to build a strong France and to ensure German purchases of British exports.[89] A fervent Italian nationalist, Orlando concerned himself primarily with enlarging Italian territory. These leaders distrusted American power and sought bigger empires. Lloyd George complained of a chameleon-like Wilson—"the noble visionary, the implacable and unscrupulous partisan, the exalted idealist and the man of rather petty personal rancour."[90] Wilson, in turn, thought the Europeans "too weatherwise to see the weather."[91]

Wilson in Dover, England, 1919. Wilson received flowers from English schoolchildren. British liberals subsequently voiced their bitter disillusionment. As the economist John Maynard Keynes wrote of Wilson: "He had no plan, no scheme, no constructive ideas whatever for clothing with the flesh of life the commandments which he had thundered from the White House. He could have preached a sermon on any of them or have addressed a stately prayer to the Almighty for their fulfillment, but he could not frame their concrete application when it came [time to act]." (U.S. Signal Corps, National Archives)

Much wrangling occurred over the disposition of colonies and the creation of new countries. Wilson had appealed for self-determination, but the belligerents had already signed secret treaties of conquest. After hard negotiating, the conferees mandated former German and Turkish colonies to the countries that had conquered them, to be loosely supervised under League of Nations auspices. Under the mandate system—a compromise between outright annexation and complete independence—France (with Syria and Lebanon) and Britain (with Iraq, Trans-Jordan, and Palestine) received parts of the Middle East. Japan acquired China's Shandong Province and some of Germany's Pacific islands. After Wilson's reluctant acceptance of the Shandong arrangement, the president lamented that it "was the best that could be had out of a dirty past."[92] Outraged Chinese students in Beijing protested by launching the May Fourth Movement, an increasingly important antiimperialist voice. France gained the demilitarization of the German Rhineland and a stake in the coal-rich Saar Basin. Italy annexed South Tyrol and Trieste from the collapsed Austro-Hungarian Empire. Some 1,132,000 square miles changed hands. Newly independent countries also emerged from the defunct Austro-Hungarian Empire: Austria, Czechoslovakia, Hungary, Romania, and Yugoslavia. The Allies further exploited nationalism to recognize a ring of hostile states already established around Bolshevik Russia: Finland, Poland, Estonia, Latvia, and Lithuania, all formerly part of the Russian empire (see map on page 293). The mandate system smacked of imperialism, in violation of the Fourteen Points, but the new states in

Europe fulfilled Wilson's self-determination pledge. To assuage French fears of a revived Germany, Britain and the United States signed a security pact with France guaranteeing its border, but Wilson never submitted it for Senate approval.

Reparations proved a knotty issue. The United States wanted a limited indemnity for Germany to avoid a harsh peace that might arouse long-term German resentment or debilitate the German economy and politics. "Our greatest error," Wilson predicted in March 1919, "would be to give her [Germany] powerful reasons for wishing one day to take revenge. Excessive demands would most certainly sow the seeds of war."[93] To cripple Germany, France pushed for a large bill of reparations. The conferees wrote a "war guilt clause," which held Germany responsible for all of the war's damages. Rationalizing that the League would ameliorate any excesses, Wilson gave in on both reparations and war guilt. The Reparations Commission in 1921 presented a hobbled Germany with a huge reparations bill of $33 billion, thereby destablizing international economic relations for more than a decade.

Wilson's primary concern, unlike that of the other participants, was the League of Nations. Drafted largely by Wilson, the League's covenant provided for an influential council of five big powers (permanent) and representatives from smaller nations (by election) and an assembly of all nations for discussion. Wilson saw the heart of the covenant as Article 10, a provision designed to curb aggression and war: "The Members of the League undertake to respect and preserve as against external aggression the territorial integrity and existing political independence of all Members of the League." In case of aggression or threat, "the Council shall advise upon the means by which this obligation shall be fulfilled."[94] Wilson persuaded the conferees to merge the League covenant and the peace terms in a package. The League charter, then, constituted the first 26 articles of a 440-article Treaty of Paris. Wilson deemed the League covenant the noblest part of all—"It is practical, and yet it is intended to purify, to rectify, to elevate."[95]

The Germans signed sullenly on June 28 in the elegant Hall of Mirrors at Versailles. By stripping Germany of 13 percent of its territory, 10 percent of its population, and all of its colonies, and by demanding reparations, the treaty humiliated the Germans without crushing them. In the historian Antony Lentin's words, the treaty contained "a witches' brew" with "too little Wilsonianism to appease, too little of Clemenceau to deter; enough of Wilson to provoke contempt, enough of Clemenceau to inspire hatred."[96] When Wilson died on February 3, 1924, the Weimar Republic in Berlin refrained from issuing an official condolence, and the German Embassy in Washington broke custom by not lowering its flag to half-mast.

Principle, Personality, Health, and Partisanship: The League Fight

Wilson spent almost six months in Europe negotiating the postwar peace. From February 24 to March 14, 1919, he returned to the United States for executive business. On arrival, he vowed not to let "minds that have no sweep beyond the nearest horizon" reject the American purpose of making people free. "I have fight-

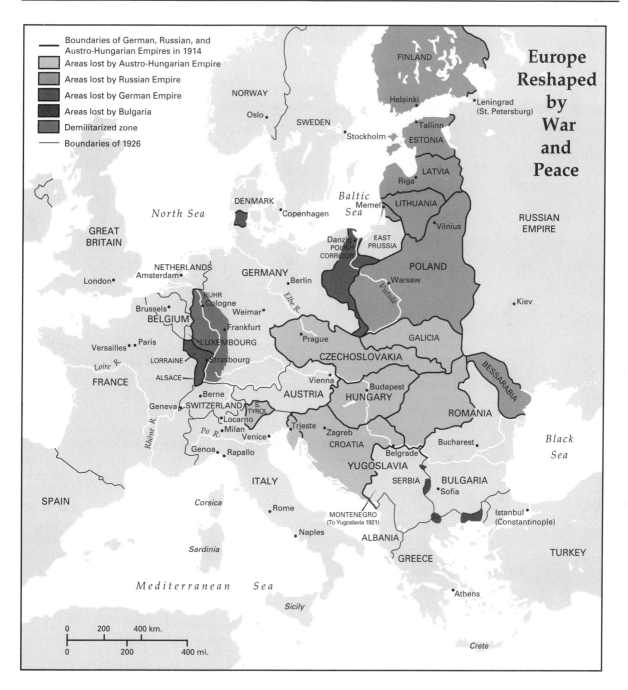

ing blood in me," he asserted.[97] In Washington, Republicans peppered Wilson with questions about the degree to which the covenant limited American sovereignty. When Wilson spoke vaguely, Senator Frank Brandegee of Connecticut felt as if he had been "wandering with Alice in Wonderland and had tea with the Mad

Georges Clemenceau (1841–1929). Auguste Rodin's bronze aptly conveys the formidable stature of "The Tiger" from France, eager for revenge against Germany. (The Rodin Museum, Philadelphia)

Hatter."[98] In early March, Republican senator Henry Cabot Lodge of Massachusetts engineered a "Round Robin," a statement by thirty-nine senators (enough to deny the treaty a two-thirds vote) that questioned the League covenant and requested that the peace treaty and the covenant be acted on separately. Many signers feared that the League would limit U.S. freedom to act independently in international affairs.

A defiant Wilson sailed again for France, determined that "little Americans," full of "watchful jealousies [and] of rabid antagonisms," would not destroy his beloved League.[99] Still, he was politician enough, and stung enough, to seek changes in Paris. He amended the covenant so that League members could refuse mandates, League jurisdiction over purely domestic issues was precluded, and the Monroe Doctrine was safeguarded against League interference. But he would not alter Article 10. When he returned to the United States in July, Wilson submitted the long Treaty of Versailles to the Senate on July 10, with an address that resembled an evangelical sermon: "The stage is set, the destiny disclosed. It has come about by no plan of our conceiving, but by the hand of God, who led us into this way."[100] Asked if he would accept senatorial "reservations" to the treaty, Wilson snapped: "I shall consent to nothing. The Senate must take its medicine."[101]

Wilson, against strong odds, gained a good percentage of his goals as outlined in the Fourteen Points. Self-determination for nationalities advanced as never before in Europe, and the League ranked as a notable achievement. But Wilson did compromise, especially when faced by formidable opposition such as that thrown up by Clemenceau. During the conference, too, both Italy and Japan had threat-

ened to walk out unless they realized some territorial goals. Still, Wilson had so
built up a case for an unselfish peace that when the conquerors' hard bargaining and
harsh terms dominated the conference, observers could only conclude that the
president had failed badly to live up to his millennial rhetoric. "How in our con-
sciences are we to square the results with the promises?" asked the journalist Walter Lippmann.[102] Some critics said that Wilson should have left Paris in protest,
refusing to sign, or that he should have threatened the European powers with U.S.
economic power by curbing postwar loans and trade. Believing desperately that the
League, with Article 10, would rectify all, Wilson instead had accepted embarrassing compromises.

He would not compromise at home, however. And he seldom provided sys-
tematic, technical analysis to treaty clauses. He simply expected the Senate dutifully
to ratify his masterwork. Yet his earlier bypassing of that body and his own partisan
speeches and self-righteousness ensured debate with influential critics. Progressive
internationalists protested that "the capitalists wanted the League as a superstate to
protect their exploitative concessions in underdeveloped countries."[103] Conservative senator Henry Cabot Lodge asked a key question: "Are you willing to put your
soldiers and your sailors at the disposition of other nations?"[104] Senator James Reed
of Missouri feared racial peril from a League initially comprising fifteen white nations and seventeen nations of "black, brown, yellow, and red races," which, he
claimed, ranked low in "civilization" and high in "barbarism."[105]

Article 10 seemed to rattle everybody. The article did not require members to
use force, but it implied they should. Senator William Borah complained that "I
may be willing to help my neighbor . . . , but I do not want him . . . [to] decide for
me when and how I shall act or to what extent I shall make sacrifice."[106] Because
Article 10 seemed to freeze the status quo against colonial rebellion, one Irish-
American editor wrote: "Were a League of Nations in existence in the days when
George Washington fought and won, . . . we would still be an English colony."[107]
The article seemed too open-ended. Yet Wilson argued that without such a commitment to halt warmakers the League would become feeble. "In effect," the historian Roland N. Stromberg has noted, "Wilson and the Democrats wanted to
accept an obligation that we might thereafter refuse, while Lodge and the Republicans wanted to refuse an obligation we might thereafter accept."[108]

Henry Cabot Lodge towered as Wilson's chief legislative obstacle. Chair of the
Senate Foreign Relations Committee, nationalist-imperialist, author, Republican
partisan, like Wilson a scholar in politics, Lodge packed his committee with anti-
League senators, dragged out hearings for weeks, kept most Republicans together
on treaty votes, and nurtured a personal animosity toward Wilson matched only by
Wilson's detestation for Lodge. Whether or not Lodge sought to kill the League in
infancy, he attacked obliquely. He proposed "reservations" to the League covenant.
Although in retrospect these reservations, intended to guard American sovereignty,
do not appear to have been death blows to the League, at the time they stirred impassioned debate. They addressed the central question of American national interest—the degree to which the United States would limit its freedom of action, the
degree to which the United States should engage in collective security. In fact,
many of the fourteen reservations stated the obvious—that Congress would retain
its constitutional role in foreign policy, for example. Others excluded the Monroe

**Henry Cabot Lodge
(1850–1924).** Wilson's partisan
rival complained that the president's
speeches in Europe "are all in the
clouds and fine sentiments that lead
nowhere." As for the League
covenant, Lodge ridiculed its scholarship. "It might get by at Princeton," Wilson's alma mater, "but
certainly not at Harvard," where the
senator had earned a Ph.D. in history. (Library of Congress)

Woodrow Wilson After His Stroke. Recent scholarly assessments of medical evidence reveal that Wilson had a long history of cerebrovascular disease. Wilson remained in the White House after his massive stroke in October 1919, while his wife and doctor tried to keep secret the severity of his physical incapacity. Dr. Edwin A. Weinstein, who has studied the relationship among Wilson's health, personality, and decision-making, has noted that the president could not maintain his train of thought and was prone to bursts of temper. (Library of Congress)

Doctrine from League oversight more explicitly than the covenant's version and denied the League jurisdiction over American domestic legislation such as immigration laws. The reservation that qualified Article 10 disclaimed any obligation to preserve the territorial integrity or political independence of another country unless authorized by Congress.

The Senate divided into four groups. Wilson counted on about forty loyal Democrats called the Non-Reservationists. Another group, the Mild-Reservationists, led by Frank B. Kellogg, numbered about thirteen Republicans. The third faction, managed by Lodge, stood together as the Strong-Reservationists—some twenty Republicans and a few Democrats. The fourth group, consisting of sixteen Irreconcilables, ardently opposed the treaty with or without reservations. Most of them were Republicans, including La Follette, George Norris of Nebraska, and Hiram Johnson of California.

Wilson met individually with some twenty-three senators over two weeks, but he suffered a minor stroke on July 19, 1919. He thereafter rigidly refused to accept any reservations. He argued that a treaty ratified with reservations would have to go back to another conference for acceptance and every nation would then rush in with its pet reservations. This argument seemed hollow after the British announced that they would accept American reservations. In September 1919, Wilson set off on a 10,000-mile train trip across the United States. Growing more exhausted with each day, suffering severe headaches and nighttime coughing spells, and showing signs of what the medical historian Bert E. Park has diagnosed as "dementia" from hypertension and cerebrovascular disease, Wilson pounded the podium in forty speeches.[109] He took the offensive, blasting his traducers as "absolute, contemptible quitters."[110] Comparing critics to radical Bolsheviks, he denounced Irish- and German-American opponents—"hyphens are the knives that are being stuck" into the treaty, he asserted.[111] He confused his audiences when he stated that Article 10 meant that the United States had a moral but not legal obligation to use armed force. But he also highlighted often neglected features of the covenant—for example, provisions for the arbitration of disputes and for an international labor conference to abolish child labor and install the eight-hour workday. On September 26, after an impassioned speech in Pueblo, Colorado, he awoke to nausea and uncontrollable facial twitching. "I just feel as if I am going to pieces," he said.[112] When his doctor ordered him to cancel the rest of his trip, Wilson wept.

After Wilson returned to Washington, a massive stroke paralyzed his left side. He lay flat in bed for six weeks and saw virtually no one except his wife and Dr. Cary Grayson. "The government," in the historian Arthur Walworth's terse phrase, "like its president, was paralyzed."[113] For months Mrs. Wilson ran her husband's political affairs, screening messages and banishing House and Lansing, among others, from presidential favor. If the president had resigned, as Dr. Grayson advised him to do, the Senate and Vice President James Marshall almost certainly would have reached some compromise agreement on admission to the League with reservations. As it was, his concentration hampered and his stubbornness accentuated by the stroke, Wilson adamantly refused to change his all-or-nothing position.

In November 1919, the Senate balloted on the complete treaty *with* reservations and rejected it, 39 to 55 (Irreconcilables and Non-Reservationists in the negative). Then it voted on the treaty *without* reservations and also rejected it, 38 to 53

(Irreconcilables and Reservationists in the negative). The president had instructed loyal Democrats not to accept any "reserved" treaty. In March 1920, another tally saw some Democrats vote in favor of reservations. Still not enough, the treaty failed, 49 to 35, short of the two-thirds majority required for approval. "It is dead," Wilson lamented to his cabinet. "Every morning I put flowers on its grave."[114] "We have torn up Wilsonianism by the roots," boasted Senator Lodge.[115] Still a fighter, the president claimed that the election of 1920 would be a "solemn referendum" on the treaty. Other questions actually blurred the League issue in that campaign, and Warren G. Harding, who as a senator had supported reservations, promptly condemned the League after his election as president. In July 1921, Congress officially terminated the war, and in August, by treaty with Germany, the United States claimed as valid for itself the terms of the Treaty of Versailles— exclusive of the League articles.

The memorable League fight had ended. The tragic denouement occurred because of political partisanship, personal animosities, senatorial resentments, the president's failing health, adherence to traditional unilateralism, and disinterest and confusion in the public, which increasingly diverted its attention to readjusting to a peacetime economy. Progressive internationalists, many of them harassed by wartime restrictions on civil liberties and disappointed by Wilson's compromises with the imperial powers, no longer backed a president they thought reactionary. "THIS IS NOT PEACE," shouted a headline in *The New Republic*.[116] Then, of course, there was Wilson himself—stubborn, pontificating, combative, and increasingly ill. But for the "marked and almost grotesque accentuation" of personality traits resulting from Wilson's cerebrovascular disease, he might have conceded that the peace had imperfections.[117] He might have provided more careful analysis of a long, complicated document. He might have remembered when he first learned of the secret treaties. He might, further, have admitted that his opponents held a respectable intellectual position. Instead, he chose often shrill rhetoric and rigid self-righteousness. Most important, he saw the difference between himself and his critics as fundamental: whether it was in America's national interest to participate in collective security or seek safety unilaterally. Traditional American nationalism and nonalignment, or unilateralism, helped decide the debate against Wilson.

Although the League came into being without the United States as a member, none of the great powers wished to bestow significant authority on the new organization. Even if Washington had joined, it most likely would have acted outside the League's auspices, especially regarding its own empire in Latin America. No international association at that time could have outlawed war, dismantled empires, or scuttled navies. Wilson overshot reality in thinking that he could reform world politics through a new international body. Certainly the League represented a commendable restraint against war, but hardly a panacea for world peace.

Red Scare Abroad: Bolshevism and Intervention in Russia

"Paris cannot be understood without Moscow [Russia]," wrote Wilson's press secretary Ray Stannard Baker.[118] Indeed, throughout the Versailles conference, "[V. I.]

"Comrade Lenin Sweeps the Globe Clean."   Vladimir Ilyich Lenin (1870–1924) is shown in this Bolshevik art as a revolutionary ridding the world of monarchs and capitalists. But Lenin also craved Western trade and investment to spur his nation's economic reconstruction. As he said in 1919: "We are decidedly for an economic understanding with America—with all countries, but especially with America." (By Mikhail Cheremnykh and Victor Deni in Mikhail Guerman, comp., *Art of the October Revolution,* Leningrad: Aurora Art Publishers, 1979)

Тов. Ленин ОЧИЩАЕТ землю от нечисти.

Lenin looms always on the horizon to the East."[119] As he traveled to France aboard the *George Washington,* President Wilson depicted Bolshevism as "the poison of disorder, the poison of revolt, the poison of chaos."[120] Revolutionary and anticapitalist, the Bolsheviks, or Communists, threw fright into the leaders of Europe and America. At home and abroad the peacemakers battled the radical left. In the United States the Wilson administration trampled on civil liberties during an exaggerated "Red Scare," which sent innocent people to jail or deported them. The fluidity of events abroad, however, and the multiplicity of American views led to a range of policy options—from recognizing and taming the Bolsheviks to overthrowing them. Wilson himself seemed to think that "the only way to kill Bolshevism is . . . to open all the doors to commerce."[121] Only belatedly, after authorizing secret aid and espionage against the "Reds," did the president openly "cast in his lot" with the other powers in a futile attempt to destroy the new revolutionary regime.[122]

Most Americans applauded the Russian Revolution of March 1917, which toppled Tsar Nicholas II. Wilson himself viewed it as a thrust against autocracy, war, and imperialism. But when the moderate Provisional government under Alexander Kerensky fell to the radical Bolsheviks in October, Americans responded first with irritation and then anger in March 1918 when the Bolsheviks signed the Brest-Litovsk Treaty with Germany and ceded Ukraine and Finland, among other territories—a total of 1,267,000 square miles, 62,000,000 people, and one-third of Russia's best agricultural land. A necessary peace for a devastated Russia from the Bolshevik perspective, the treaty seemed a stab in the back for the Allies, a decisive victory for Berlin. Because German authorities had allowed Lenin to travel to Russia via Germany in 1917, some irate American officials even considered Bolsheviks pro-German. Others recoiled after Ambassador David Francis's testimony that Bolsheviks had "nationalized women."[123]

Lenin actually treated the United States as a special, favored case, and he consistently sought accommodation with Washington. Described by the Red Cross official Raymond Robins as "heavy set, deliberate, always cool . . . , steadfast, patient, utterly courageous, fanatical and confident," Lenin (and other Soviet officials) held a series of cordial conversations from December 1917 to May 1918 with Robins, a de facto U.S. representative.[124] They reached agreements on food relief, purchase of strategic materials, and exemption of American corporations from Bolshevik nationalization decrees. Prior to Brest-Litovsk, Robins urged prompt recognition of the Bolshevik government to keep Russia in the war, but President Wilson paid more heed to Francis's prediction that the Bolshevik regime would soon collapse.

Although American officials in Russia engaged in propaganda and espionage, and cooperated with Allied and "White" agents in anti-Bolshevik activities after November 1917, Wilson knew only broad outlines of this "secret war" when he sent U.S. troops to Archangel in northern Russia in August 1918. Ordered to avoid military action in the Russian civil war, they inevitably cooperated with British and French forces in attempts to roll back Bolshevik influence. Wilson said publicly that he authorized the expedition only to prevent German seizure of military supplies and a railroad, but he had already authorized $50 million in secret payments to White armies fighting the Bolsheviks. Wilson's motives, according to the historian Robert Foglesong, were "simultaneously anti-German and anti-Bolshevik."[125] Some 5,000 American troops eventually participated. They suffered through a bitter winter of fifty-below-zero temperatures. Their morale sagged; mutiny threatened. In December 1918, Senator Hiram Johnson of California introduced a resolution to withdraw American troops from Russia. It failed by one vote. U.S. soldiers did not leave Russia until June 1919. Two hundred twenty-two American soldiers died on Russian soil.

Wilson always said that he "hoped to avoid intervention, even the appearance of intervening in Russian affairs," preferring to draw the Bolsheviks peacefully into a new world order.[126] But pressure from the deeply anticommunist French and British and expansionist Japanese and his own anti-Bolshevism inclined him to send another expedition, this time to Siberia, where many envisioned the growth of a non-Bolshevik Russian bastion. In July he approved the expedition, later officially explaining to the American people that he was sending the troops (eventually numbering 10,000) to rescue a group of 70,000 Czechs stranded in Russia. Organized earlier as part of the Tsarist Russian army to fight for a Czech homeland in Austria-Hungary, the Czech legion in 1918 was battling Bolsheviks along the Trans-Siberian Railroad in an effort to reach Vladivostok and possible transportation to the western front. Wilson's avowed purpose of evacuating the Czech legion derived also from

A. Mitchell Palmer (1872–1936). When U.S. troops were intervening in Bolshevik Russia, Wilson's attorney general, A. Mitchell Palmer, was chasing suspected radicals at home. An architect of the "Red Scare," Palmer believed that the "blaze of revolution" was "eating its way into the homes of the American workmen, its sharp tongues of revolutionary heat . . . licking the altars of the churches, leaping into the belfry of the school bell, crawling into the sacred corners of American homes, burning up the foundations of society." In January 1920, the "Palmer Raids" put 4,000 people in jail. (Library of Congress)

his "friendly feelings" for Professor Thomas Masaryk and Czechoslovakia's independence, which Wilson soon recognized in October.[127]

Despite his disingenuous official explanation, Wilson believed, as one scholar has put it, that "a limited, indirect intervention to help the Russian people overcome domination by Bolsheviks and Germans would not contradict, but rather facilitate self-determination."[128] Yet intervention in Siberia became openly anti-Bolshevik because the Czechs were fighting Lenin's forces. Once Wilson found it impossible to evacuate the Czechs in time to fight in Europe, he reluctantly bowed to Allied pressure and gave support to the anti-Bolshevik White Russian leader Admiral A. V. Kolchak in the hope that he could form a pro-Western constitutional government. Despite money and supplies from the Allies, Kolchak faltered and his armies were routed before they could reach Moscow in June 1919. American troops in Siberia finally withdrew in early 1920 after thirty-six deaths.

At the Paris peace conference, the victors tried to isolate what they considered revolutionary contagion. The organization of the Third International in Moscow in early 1919 alarmed postwar leaders, as did communist Bela Kun's successful revolution in Hungary in March 1919, which lasted only until August. At Versailles, the conferees granted territory to Russia's neighbors (Poland, Romania, and Czechoslovakia) and recognized the nations of Finland, Estonia, Latvia, and Lithuania as a ring of unfriendly states around Russia. During the conference, besides the military interventions, the Allies imposed a strict economic blockade on Russia, sent aid to the White forces, and extended relief assistance to Austria and Hungary to stem political unrest.

Even though Wilson found the Soviets distasteful for their revolutionary, anticapitalist, anticlerical, authoritarian program, he never settled on a definitive, workable policy to co-opt or smash Bolshevism. Through "a reluctant, chaotic, and capricious process," the president allowed subordinates and circumstances to determine U.S. policy toward Russia.[129] His growing estrangement at Versailles from Colonel House, a conduit for pro-Soviet liberals, meant that the interventionist Allies and the rabidly anti-Bolshevik Secretary Lansing exerted greater influence.

Wilson's one serious effort to end the civil war in Russia through diplomacy came in January 1919 when he invited the warring groups to meet on Prinkipo (Prince's) Island in the Sea of Marmara off the Turkish coast. The Bolsheviks cautiously accepted the invitation, but the anti-Bolsheviks rejected any meeting. Next, in February, House helped arrange a trip by William C. Bullitt, a member of the U.S. delegation at Versailles, and Lincoln Steffens, the radical muckraking journalist, to Russia. Wilson envisioned a fact-finding mission. The ambitious Bullitt, however, negotiated a proposal whereby the Allies would withdraw their troops, suspend military aid to the White forces, and lift the economic blockade. If the Allies accepted these terms, the Soviet government promised to initiate a ceasefire in the civil war and permit its opponents to hold the territories they occupied. Bullitt and Steffens returned to Paris convinced that their agreement would satisfy all parties. Lloyd George squelched it; Wilson ignored it. Bullitt, already disgusted by Wilson's compromises with the Allies at Paris, resigned in protest.

The Allied counterrevolution proved costly. "It intensified the civil war and sent thousands of Russians to their deaths," the British official Bruce Lockhart later wrote. "Its direct effect was to provide the Bolsheviks with a cheap victory, . . .

and to galvanize them into a strong and ruthless organism."[130] Although the Bolshevik emissary Ludwig Martens laid the foundations for future Soviet-American trade during the height of the Red Scare, Kremlin leaders nurtured long memories. "Never have any of our soldiers been on American soil," Premier Nikita S. Khrushchev lectured Americans as late as 1959, "but your soldiers were on Russian soil."[131] Participation by such young men as Allen and John Foster Dulles in Wilson's "secret war" against the Bolsheviks provided "the formative experiences that inclined [them] to rely on propaganda and covert action" when they later directed U.S. policies during the Cold War.[132] Such tactics ultimately backfired, as Wilson recognized before his death. "Bolshevism is a mistake," Wilson said. "If left alone it will destroy itself. It cannot survive because it is wrong."[133]

The Whispering Gallery of Global Disorder

More than 116,000 American soldiers died in World War I, and the conflict cost the U.S. government more than $30 billion. A third of the figure was paid through taxes; the other two-thirds represented borrowed money, which postwar generations would have to pay back. If one counts the long-term expense of veterans' benefits, the cost to the United States probably equaled three times the immediate direct costs. What President Dwight D. Eisenhower would later call the "military-industrial complex" had its origins in a high degree of government-business cooperation during that war; economic decisionmaking for the nation became centralized as never before; and the increased application of efficient methods in manufacturing contributed to American economic power.[134] The era of World War I witnessed other domestic events that impinged on foreign affairs: racial conflict, evidenced by twenty-five race riots in 1919; suppression of civil liberties under the Espionage and Sedition Acts, by which people who dissented from the war were silenced; the stunting of radical commentary (Socialist leader Eugene Debs and the pacifist Alice Paul, among others, went to jail for opposing the war) and hence the imposition of coercive consensus; and the emasculation of the reform impulse. Although Wilson tried to co-opt dissent by appointing labor leaders such as Samuel Gompers to war mobilization agencies, the historian Beth McKillen has argued that the negative response to the League of Nations among immigrants and industrial workers indicated "a revolt against corporatist wartime institutions."[135]

In foreign affairs, the White House assumed more authority in initiating policy and controlling execution. The State Department read diplomatic messages that Wilson had typed on his own machine. Wilson bypassed Congress on a number of occasions, failing to consult that body about the Fourteen Points, the goals at Versailles, and the intervention in Russia. He acted, according to his biographer Arthur S. Link, "like a divine-right monarch in the conduct of foreign relations."[136] The Senate finally rebelled by rejecting the League of Nations, but that negative decision did not reverse the trend of growing presidential power over foreign policy.

World War I took the lives of some 14,663,400 people—8 million soldiers and 6.6 million civilians (flu pandemic victims not included). Russia led with 3.7 million dead; Germany followed with 2.6 million; then came France with 1.4 million, Austria-Hungary with 950,000, and Britain with 939,000. One out of every two

"We Are Making a New World."   The British painter Paul Nash rendered this gloomy commentary on the devastation wrought by World War I. (Imperial War Museum, London)

French males between the ages of twenty and thirty-two (in 1914) died during the war. It had been a total war, involving whole societies, not merely their armies. Never before had a war left the belligerents so exhausted, so battered. New destructive weapons made their debut—tanks, airplanes, poison gas, the Big Bertha gun, and submarines—"a preview of the Pandora's box of evils that the linkage of science with industry in the service of war was to mean."[137] The war reinforced American desires to avoid foreign entanglement. Captain Harry S. Truman of Battery D of the 129th Field Artillery Regiment claimed that most soldiers "don't give a whoop (to put it mildly) whether Russia has a Red Government or no government and if the King of the Lollipops wants to slaughter his subjects or his Prime Minister it's all the same to us."[138] Disillusioned intellectuals such as Ernest Hemingway and John Dos Passos mocked the carthaginian peace. E. M. Remarque's *All Quiet on the Western Front* (1929) captured the antiwar mood: "A hospital alone shows what war is."[139]

World War I stacked the cards for the future by bequeathing an unstable international system. Empires broke up—the Turkish, Austro-Hungarian, German, and Russian—creating new and weak nations. The Europe-oriented international order of the turn of the century fragmented and left, in Thomas Masaryk's words, "a laboratory atop a vast cemetery" that included several new states in central and eastern Europe.[140] Nationalists in Asia, such as Mahatma Gandhi in British-dominated India and Ho Chi Minh in French-controlled Indochina, set goals of national liberation based in part on Wilson's ideal of self-determination. "Wilson's proposals, once set forth, could not be recalled," said Sun Zhongshan (Sun Yat-Sen) in 1924 as his China battled imperialist domination.[141] In Latin America, prewar European economic ties withered, inviting the United States to expand its interests there, where nationalists resented the greater North American presence. The rise of Bolshevism in Russia and the hostility it aroused around the world made an already fluid international system even more so. Because of fear of a revived Germany, leaders tried to strip it of power, creating bitter resentments among the German people. Facing reconstruction problems at home, the victors tagged Germany with a huge reparations bill that would disorient the world economy. Nobody seemed happy with the postwar settlement; many would attempt to recapture lost opportunities or to redefine the terms. The high-minded lessons Wilson sought to teach went unlearned. World War I had, surely, created as many problems as it had solved.

During World War I the United States became the world's leading economic power. As Wilson confidently put it: "The financial leadership will be ours. The industrial primacy will be ours. The commercial advantage will be ours."[142] During the war years, to meet the need for raw materials, American companies expanded operations in developing nations. Goodyear went into the Dutch East Indies for rubber, Swift and Armour reached into South America, tin interests tapped Bolivia, copper companies penetrated Chile, and oil firms sank new wells in Latin America and gained new concessions in the Middle East. Washington encouraged this economic expansion by building up the merchant marine, which by 1919 had grown 60 percent larger than its prewar size. By 1920, the United States produced about 40 percent of the world's coal and 50 percent of its pig iron.

Because the U.S. government and American citizens loaned heavily to the Allies during the war, the nation shifted from a debtor to a creditor, with Wall Street replacing London as the world's financial center. Whereas before the war Americans owed foreigners some $3 billion, after the conflict foreigners owed Americans and the U.S. government about $13 billion ($10 billion of this figure represented governments' debts). Americans had devised plans to seize the apparent economic opportunities given them by the war—the Edge Act to permit foreign branch banks, and the Webb-Pomerene Act to allow trade associations to continue to combine for export trading without fear of antitrust action, for example—but a key question remained: How could Europeans pay back their debt to the United States? The answer lay somewhere in a complicated tangle of loans, reparations, tariffs, and world trade. "We are on the eve of a commercial war of the severest sort," predicted Wilson in early 1920.[143]

Economic disorder and political instability thus became the twin legacies of global war. "The world is all now one single whispering gallery," Wilson asserted in September 1919. "All the impulses . . . reach to the ends of the earth; . . . with the tongue of the wireless and the tongue of the telegraph, all the suggestions of disorder are spread." More than most Americans, Woodrow Wilson understood that global interdependence exposed America to the "disorder and discontent and dissolution throughout the world."[144]

FURTHER READING FOR THE PERIOD 1914–1920

Many of the works listed in the last chapter also explore the themes, events, and personalities in the era of World War I. See also John W. Chambers, *The Tyranny of Change* (1992); Paul Fussell, *The Great War and Modern Memory* (1975); Ellis W. Hawley, *The Great War and the Search for a Modern Order* (1992); Clayton D.

James and Anne Sharp Wells, *America and the Great War* (1998); Bernadotte E. Schmitt and Harold C. Vedeler, *The World in the Crucible, 1914–1919* (1984); Tony Smith, *America's Mission* (1994); David Stevenson, *The First World War and International Politics* (1988); and Spencer C. Tucker, *The Great War* (1998).

For Woodrow Wilson and his foreign-policy views, consult Edward H. Buehrig, ed., *Wilson's Foreign Policy in Perspective* (1957); Kendrick A. Clements, *The Presidency of Woodrow Wilson* (1990) and *Woodrow Wilson* (1987); John Milton Cooper, Jr., *The Warrior and the Priest* (1983); Thomas J. Knock, *To End All Wars* (1992); Arthur S. Link, *Wilson* (1960–1965) and *Woodrow Wilson: Revolution, War, and Peace* (1979); Frank Ninkovich, *The Wilsonian Century* (1999); and Jan Willem Schulte Nordholt, *Woodrow Wilson* (1991).

Wilson's health problems and their relationship to decisionmaking are examined in Robert H. Ferrell, *Ill-Advised* (1992), and Edwin A. Weinstein, *Woodrow Wilson: A Medical and Psychological Biography* (1981). See also the essays by Dr. Bert E. Park in volumes of Arthur S. Link et al., eds., *The Papers of Woodrow Wilson*, and Park's *Ailing, Aging, and Addicted* (1993) and *The Impact of Illness on World Leaders* (1986).

Central actors in the period's drama are presented in LeRoy Ashby, *William Jennings Bryan* (1987); Kendrick A. Clements, *William Jennings Bryan* (1982); Paolo Coletta, *William Jennings Bryan* (1956–1969); John Milton Cooper, Jr., *Walter Hines Page* (1977); Ross Gregory, *Walter Hines Page* (1970); George H. Nash, *The Life of Herbert Hoover* (1996); Daniel M. Smith, *Robert Lansing and American Neutrality* (1958); Donald Smythe, *Pershing* (1986); Ronald Steel, *Walter Lippmann and the American Century* (1981); David P. Thelen, *Robert M. La Follette and the Insurgent Spirit* (1976); and William C. Widenor, *Henry Cabot Lodge and the Search for an American Foreign Policy* (1980).

For European questions and the neutrality issue on the U.S. road to World War I, see Thomas A. Bailey and Paul B. Ryan, *The Lusitania Disaster* (1975); Henry Blumenthal, *Illusion and Reality in Franco-American Diplomacy, 1914–1945* (1986); John W. Coogan, *The End of Neutrality* (1981); Patrick Devlin, *Too Proud to Fight* (1975); David M. Esposito, *The Legacy of Woodrow Wilson: American War Aims in World War I* (1996); Robert H. Ferrell, *Woodrow Wilson and World War I* (1985); Ross Gregory, *The Origins of American Intervention in the First World War* (1971); and Ernest R. May, *The World War and American Isolation, 1914–1917* (1959).

The German-American relationship is spotlighted in Reinhard R. Doerries, *Imperial Challenge* (1989); Manfred Jonas, *The United States and Germany* (1984); Hans-Jürgen Schröder, ed., *Confrontation and Cooperation* (1993); and Barbara Tuchman, *The Zimmermann Telegram* (1958).

The Anglo-American relationship is featured in Kathleen Burk, *Britain, America, and the Sinews of War, 1914–1918* (1985); G. R. Conyne, *Woodrow Wilson: British Perspectives, 1912–21* (1992); and Joyce G. Williams, *Colonel House and Sir Edward Grey* (1984).

For the peace movement, see works cited in the previous chapter and Charles DeBenedetti, ed., *Peace Heroes in Twentieth-Century America* (1986); Allen F. Davis, *American Heroine* (1974) (Addams); Barbara S. Kraft, *The Peace Ship* (1978); Erika A. Kuhlman, *Petticoats and White Feathers* (1997); and Ernest A. McKay, *Against Wilson and War* (1996).

America's preparedness and warmaking experiences are discussed in John W. Chambers, *To Raise an Army* (1987); J. Garry Clifford, *The Citizen Soldiers* (1972); Edward M. Coffman, *The War to End All Wars* (1968); Henry A. DeWeerd, *President Wilson Fights His War* (1968); Kenneth J. Hagan, *This People's Navy* (1991); Thomas C. Leonard, *Above the Battle* (1978); Bullitt Lowry, *Armistice, 1918* (1997); David F. Trask, *The AEF and Coalition Warmaking* (1993), *Captains & Cabinets: Anglo-American Naval Relations, 1917–1918* (1980), and *The United States in the Supreme War Council* (1961); and David R. Woodward, *Trial by Friendship: Anglo-American Relations, 1917–1918* (1993).

For the wartime home front, civil-liberties issues, and propaganda, see George T. Blakey, *Historians on the Homefront* (1970); Allan M. Brandt, *No Magic Bullet* (1985) (venereal disease); Alfred W. Crosby, *America's Forgotten Pandemic* (1989); David M. Kennedy, *Over Here* (1980); Seward W. Livermore, *Politics Is Adjourned* (1966); Elizabeth McKillen, *Chicago Labor and the Quest for a Democratic Diplomacy* (1995); Joseph A. McCartin, *Labor's Great War* (1998); Paul L. Murphy, *World War I and the Origin of Civil Liberties* (1979); Horace C. Peterson and Gilbert C. Fite, *Opponents of War, 1917–1918* (1957); Richard Polenberg, *Fighting Faiths* (1987); Ronald Schaffer, *America in the Great War* (1991); John A. Thompson, *Reformers and War* (1986); Stephen Vaughn, *Hold Fast the Inner Lines* (1980) (Committee on Public Information); and Neil Wynn, *From Progressivism to Prosperity* (1986).

The Versailles peacemaking and League debate are discussed in Lloyd E. Ambrosius, *Wilsonian Statecraft* (1991) and *Woodrow Wilson and the American Diplomatic Tradition* (1987); Manfred F. Boemeke et al., eds., *The Treaty of Versailles* (1998); Inga Floto, *Colonel House in Paris* (1973); Lawrence E. Gelfand, *The Inquiry* (1963); Derek Heater, *National Self-Determination* (1994); Warren F. Kuehl, *Seeking World Order* (1969); Warren F. Kuehl and Lynne K. Dunne, *Keeping the Covenant* (1997); Antony Lentin, *Lloyd George, Woodrow Wilson, and the Guilt of Germany* (1985); Herbert F. Margulies, *The Mild Reservationists* (1989); Keith Nelson, *Victors Divided: America and the Allies in Germany, 1918–1923* (1973); Stuart I. Rochester, *American Liberal Disillusionment in the Wake of World War I* (1977); Klaus Schwabe, *Woodrow Wilson, Revolutionary Germany, and Peacemaking* (1985); Alan Sharp, *The Versailles Settlement* (1991); Ralph A. Stone, *The Irreconcilables* (1970); Marc Trachenberg, *Reparations in World Politics* (1986); and Arthur Walworth, *America's Moment, 1918* (1977) and *Wilson and His Peacemakers* (1986).

The U.S. response to Bolshevism, intervention in Russia, and the Red Scare are investigated in Stanley Coben, *A. Mitchell Palmer* (1963); Victor M. Fic, *The Collapse of American Policy in Russia and Siberia, 1918* (1995); David S. Foglesong, *America's Secret War Against Bolshevism* (1995); John Lewis Gaddis, *Russia, the Soviet Union, and the United States* (1990); Lloyd Gardner, *Safe for Democracy* (1984); George F. Kennan, *Russia Leaves the War* (1956) and *The Decision to Intervene* (1958); Linda Killen, *The Russian Bureau* (1983); N. Gordon Levin, Jr., *Woodrow Wilson and World Politics* (1968); Arthur S. Link, ed., *Woodrow Wilson and a Revolutionary World, 1913–1921* (1982); Arno Mayer, *Politics and Diplomacy of Peacemaking* (1967); David W. McFadden, *Alternative Paths: Soviets and Americans, 1917–1920* (1993); Robert K. Murray, *Red Scare* (1955); William Pencak, *For God and Country* (1989) (American Legion); Benjamin D. Rhodes, *The Anglo-American Winter War with Russia, 1918–1919* (1988); Neil V. Salzman, *Reform and Revolution* (1991) (Robins); Ilya Somin, *Stillborn Crusade: The Tragic Failure of Western Intervention in the Russian Civil War* (1996); John Thompson, *Russia, Bolshevism, and the Versailles Peace* (1966); and Betty Miller Unterberger, *America's Siberian Expedition* (1956) and *The United States, Revolutionary Russia, and the Rise of Czechoslovakia* (1989).

U.S. economic expansion abroad during the war is studied in Burton I. Kaufman, *Efficiency and Expansion* (1974); Emily S. Rosenberg, *World War I and the Growth of United States Predominance in Latin America* (1987); and Jeffrey J. Safford, *Wilsonian Maritime Diplomacy, 1913–1921* (1978).

Also see the General Bibliography, the following notes, and Richard Dean Burns, ed., *Guide to American Foreign Relations Since 1700* (1983).

For comprehensive coverage of foreign-relations topics, see the articles in the four-volume *Encyclopedia of U.S. Foreign Relations* (1997), edited by Bruce W. Jentleson and Thomas G. Paterson.

NOTES TO CHAPTER 8

1. Quoted in Thomas Bailey and Paul Ryan, *The* Lusitania *Disaster* (New York: Free Press, 1975), p. 81.
2. Quoted in Edward Ellis, *Echoes of Distant Thunder* (New York: Coward, McCann & Geoghegan, 1975), p. 195.
3. Quoted in Bailey and Ryan, Lusitania *Disaster*, p. 94.
4. Quoted *ibid.*, p. 82.
5. Quoted *ibid.*, p. 133.
6. Quoted in C. L. Droste and W. H. Tantum, eds., *The* Lusitania *Case* (Riverside, Conn.: 7 C's Press, 1972), p. 172.
7. Quoted in Burton J. Hendrick, *Life and Letters of Walter Hines Page* (Garden City, N.Y.: Doubleday, Page, 1922–1925; 3 vols.), II, 2.
8. William Jennings Bryan and Mary B. Bryan, *Memoirs* (Chicago: Winston, 1925), pp. 398–399.
9. Quoted in William Harbaugh, *The Life and Times of Theodore Roosevelt* (New York: Oxford University Press, 1975), p. 448.
10. John Milton Cooper, Jr., *The Warrior and the Priest* (Cambridge: Harvard University Press, 1983), p. 288.
11. R. S. Baker and W. E. Dodd, eds., *Public Papers of Woodrow Wilson* (New York: Harper & Brothers, 1926; 2 vols.), I, 321.
12. Quoted in Priscilla Roberts, "The Anglo-American Theme," *Diplomatic History, XXI* (Summer 1997), 340.
13. Quoted in August Hecksher, *Woodrow Wilson* (New York: Charles Scribner's Sons, 1991), p. 365.
14. *Foreign Relations, 1915, Supplement* (Washington, D.C.: Government Printing Office, 1928), p. 396.
15. Quoted in Richard R. Doerries, *Imperial Challenge* (Chapel Hill: University of North Carolina Press, 1989), p. 105.
16. David F. Houston, *Eight Years with Wilson's Cabinet* (Garden City, N.Y.: Doubleday, Page, 1926), 137.
17. Quoted in LeRoy Ashby, *William Jennings Bryan* (Boston: Twayne, 1987), p. 160.
18. Quoted *ibid.*, p. 161.
19. Quoted in Doerries, *Imperial Challenge*, p. 111.
20. Bailey and Ryan, Lusitania *Disaster*, p. 340.

21. Robert Lansing, *War Memoirs* (Indianapolis: Bobbs-Merrill, 1935), p. 128.
22. Ray S. Baker quoted in Arthur S. Link et al., eds., *The Papers of Woodrow Wilson* (Princeton: Princeton University Press, 1989), *LXI*, 383.
23. Quoted in Rohan Butler, "The Peace Settlement of Versailles, 1918–1933," in C. L. Mowat, ed., *The New Cambridge Modern History*, vol. *XII* (Cambridge, Eng.: Cambridge University Press, 1968), p. 214.
24. Quoted in Frank Ninkovich, *Modernity and Power* (Chicago: University of Chicago Press, 1994), p. 42.
25. Quoted in Barbara Tuchman, *The Guns of August* (New York: Dell, [1962], 1963), p. 91.
26. Quoted in Hendrick, *Life and Letters*, I, 310.
27. Baker and Dodd, *Public Papers*, I, 157–159.
28. Cecil Spring-Rice quoting Wilson in G. R. Conyne, *Woodrow Wilson* (New York: St. Martin's Press, 1992), p. 44.
29. Quoted in Alexander DeConde, *Ethnicity, Race, and American Foreign Policy* (Boston: Northeastern University Press, 1992), p. 86.
30. Quoted in Tuchman, *Guns of August*, p. 349.
31. Quoted *ibid.*, p. 153.
32. *Life* quoted in Mark Sullivan, *Our Times* (New York: Charles Scribner's Sons, 1926–1937; 6 vols.), V, 59.
33. Quoted in Ray Stannard Baker, *Woodrow Wilson* (New York: Doubleday, Doran, 1927–1939; 8 vols.), V, 175.
34. Quoted in Paul Birdsall, "Neutrality and Economic Pressures, 1914–1917," *Science and Society*, III (Spring 1939), 221.
35. Kathleen Burk, *Britain, America, and the Sinews of War, 1914–1918* (Boston: Allen & Unwin, 1985), p. 5.
36. *Foreign Relations, 1915, Supplement*, p. 99.
37. John W. Coogan, "Submarine Warfare," in Bruce W. Jentleson and Thomas G. Paterson, eds., *Encyclopedia of U.S. Foreign Relations* (New York: Oxford University Press, 1997; 4 vols.), IV, 145.
38. Frederick Dixon quoting Wilson in Conyne, *Wilson*, p. 51.
39. Quoted in Frederick S. Calhoun, *Uses of Force and Wilsonian Foreign Policy* (Kent, Ohio: Kent State University Press, 1993), p. 100.
40. Quoted in Arthur S. Link, *Woodrow Wilson and the Progressive Era, 1910–1917* (New York: Harper and Row, 1954), p. 203.
41. French report quoted in Joyce G. Williams, *Colonel House and Sir Edward Grey* (Lanham, Md.: University Press of America, 1984), p. 83.
42. Quoted in Arthur S. Link, *Wilson: Confusions and Crises, 1915–1916* (Princeton: Princeton University Press, 1964), pp. 134–135.
43. Bryan and Bryan, *Memoirs*, p. 397.
44. *Foreign Relations, 1915, Supplement*, p. 461.
45. Link, *Papers of Wilson*, XXXVI (1981), 213–214.
46. Samuel Flagg Bemis, "A Worcester County Student in Wartime London and Paris (via Harvard): 1915–1916," *New England Galaxy*, XI (Spring 1970), 20.
47. Quoted in Patrick Devlin, *Too Proud to Fight* (New York: Oxford University Press, 1975), p. 517.
48. Quoted in Ninkovich, *Modernity and Power*, p. 50.
49. Quoted in Arthur S. Link, *Wilson: Campaigns for Progressivism and Peace, 1916–1917* (Princeton: Princeton University Press, 1965), p. 274.
50. Quoted *ibid.*, p. 289.
51. Lansing, *War Memoirs*, p. 212.
52. Jules Witcover, *Sabotage at Black Tom* (Chapel Hill, N.C.: Algonquin Books, 1989), p. 12.
53. *Foreign Relations, 1917, Supplement 1* (Washington, D.C.: Government Printing Office, 1931), p. 147.
54. Quoted in John Milton Cooper, Jr., *Walter Hines Page* (Chapel Hill: University of North Carolina Press, 1977), p. 369.
55. Quoted in Thomas W. Ryley, *A Little Group of Willful Men* (Port Washington, N.Y.: Kennikat Press, 1975), p. 2.
56. Link, *Papers of Wilson*, XLI (1983), 519–527.
57. Ross Gregory, *The Origins of American Intervention in the First World War* (New York: Norton, 1971), p. 128.
58. Henry F. Ashurst quoted in Erika A. Kuhlman, *Petticoats and White Feathers* (Westport, Conn.: Greenwood, 1997), p. 90.
59. Quoted in Robert E. Osgood, *Ideals and Self-Interest in American Foreign Relations* (Chicago: University of Chicago Press, 1953), p. 177.
60. Quoted in Michael S. Sherry, *In the Shadow of War* (New Haven: Yale University Press, 1995), p. 8.
61. Susan Zeiger, "She Didn't Raise Her Boy to Be a Slacker," *Feminist Studies*, XXII (Spring 1996), 11–12.
62. Kuhlman, *Petticoats*, p. 51.
63. Quoted in Zeiger, "Slacker," p. 18.
64. Quoted in Paolo E. Coletta, "The American Navy Leaders' Preparations for War," in R. J. Q. Adams, ed., *The Great War, 1914–18* (College Station: Texas A & M University Press, 1990), p. 170.
65. Quoted in Kenneth J. Hagan, *This People's Navy* (New York: Free Press, 1991), p. 252.
66. Quoted in Barbara S. Kraft, *The Peace Ship* (New York: Macmillan, 1978), p. 1.
67. Quoted in Thomas J. Knock, *To End All Wars* (New York: Oxford University Press, 1992), p. 63.
68. *Ibid.*, p. 50.
69. Jane Addams, *Peace and Bread in Time of War* (New York: King's Crown Press, 1945), p. 58.
70. Quoted in Kuhlman, *Petticoats*, p. 56.
71. Quoted in J. Garry Clifford, *The Citizen Soldiers* (Lexington: University Press of Kentucky, 1972), p. 123.
72. General Tasker Bliss quoted in Calhoun, *Uses of Force*, p. 114.
73. Penn Borden, *Civilian Indoctrination of the Military* (Westport, Conn.: Greenwood, 1989), p. 143.
74. Quoted in Edward M. Coffman, *The War to End All Wars* (New York: Oxford University Press, 1968), p. 4.
75. Quoted in Allen F. Davis, "Welfare, Reform, and World War I," *American Quarterly*, XIX (Fall 1967), 530.
76. Quoted in Jorg Nagler, "German Imperial Propaganda," in Hans-Jürgen Schröder, *Confrontation and Cooperation* (Providence, R.I.: Berg Publishers, 1993), p. 172.
77. Quoted in Davis, "Welfare," p. 531.
78. Quoted in Ninkovich, *Modernity and Power*, p. 52.
79. Link, *Papers of Wilson*, XLVII (1984), 270.
80. Quoted in Donald Smythe, *Pershing* (Bloomington: Indiana University Press, 1986), p. 237.
81. Link, *Papers of Wilson*, XLV (1984), 529.
82. Addams, *Peace and Bread*, p. 58.
83. Quoted in Selig Adler, *The Isolationist Impulse* (New York: Collier Books, [1957], 1961), pp. 60–61.
84. H. G. Nicholas essay in *Wilson's Diplomacy* (Cambridge: Schenkman, 1973), p. 81.
85. Quoted in David F. Trask, *The United States in the Supreme War Council* (Middletown, Conn.: Wesleyan University Press, 1961), p. 155.
86. Ray S. Baker quoted in John A. Thompson, *Reformers and War* (New York: Cambridge University Press, 1988), p. 234.
87. Quoted in James D. Startt, "American Propaganda in Britain During World War I," *Prologue*, XXVIII (Spring 1996), 20.

88. Knock, *To End All Wars*, p. 180.
89. Quoted in David W. McFadden, *Alternative Paths* (New York: Oxford University Press, 1993), p. 209.
90. Quoted in Herbert Hoover, *The Ordeal of Woodrow Wilson* (New York: McGraw-Hill, 1958), p. 254.
91. Quoted in Walter A. McDougall, *Promised Land, Crusader State* (Boston: Houghton Mifflin, 1997), p. 139.
92. Quoted in Ross Gregory, "To Do Good in the World," in Frank Merli and Theodore Wilson, eds., *Makers of American Diplomacy* (New York: Charles Scribner's Sons, 1974), p. 380.
93. Quoted in Lawrence E. Gelfand, "Where Ideals Confront Self-Interest," *Diplomatic History, XVIII* (Winter 1994), 133.
94. U.S. Congress, Senate, *Treaties*, Senate Doc. 348 (Washington, D.C.: Government Printing Office, 1923), pp. 3336–3345.
95. Link, *Papers of Wilson, LV* (1985), 177.
96. Antony Lentin, *Lloyd George, Woodrow Wilson, and the Guilt of Germany* (Baton Rouge: Louisiana State University Press, 1984), p. 132.
97. Link, *Papers of Wilson, LV* (1985), 238–245.
98. Quoted in D. F. Fleming, *The United States and the League of Nations, 1918–1920* (New York: Russell & Russell, 1968), p. 134.
99. Quoted in Beth McKillen, "The Corporatist Model, World War I, and the Debate over the League of Nations," *Diplomatic History, XV* (Spring 1991), 174.
100. Link, *Papers of Wilson, LXI* (1989), 436.
101. Quoted in Arthur S. Link, *Wilson the Diplomatist* (Chicago: Quadrangle, [1957], 1963), p. 131.
102. Quoted in Thompson, *Reformers and War*, p. 239.
103. Robert David Johnson, *The Peace Progressives and American Foreign Relations* (Cambridge: Harvard University Press, 1995), p. 102.
104. Quoted in William C. Widenor, "The United States and the Versailles Peace Settlement," in John M. Carroll and George C. Herring, Jr., eds., *Modern American Diplomacy* (Wilmington, Del.: Scholarly Resources, 1986), p. 49.
105. Quoted in Lloyd E. Ambrosius, *Woodrow Wilson and the American Diplomatic Tradition* (New York: Cambridge University Press, 1987), p. 139.
106. Quoted in Osgood, *Ideals and Self-Interest*, p. 286.
107. Quoted in McKillen, "Corporatist Model," 292.
108. Roland N. Stromberg, *Collective Security and American Foreign Policy* (New York: Praeger, 1963) p. 37.
109. Bert E. Park, "Wilson's Neurological Illness," in Link, *Papers of Wilson, LXII* (1990), 629.
110. Link, *Papers of Wilson, LXIII* (1990), 35.
111. Quoted in DeConde, *Ethnicity*, p. 97.
112. Quoted in Knock, *To End All Wars*, p. 263.
113. Arthur Walworth, *Wilson and His Peacemakers* (New York: Norton, 1986), p. 533.
114. Quoted in E. David Cronon, ed., *The Cabinet Diaries of Josephus Daniels* (Lincoln: University of Nebraska Press, 1963), p. 520.
115. Quoted in Warren F. Kuehl and Lynne K. Dunne, *Keeping the Covenant* (Kent, Ohio: Kent State University Press, 1997), p. 18.
116. Quoted in Knock, *To End All Wars*, p. 254.
117. Bert E. Park, "The Aftermath of Wilson's Stroke," in Link, *Papers of Wilson, LXIV* (1986), 525.
118. Quoted in John M. Thompson, *Russia, Bolshevism, and the Versailles Peace* (Princeton: Princeton University Press, 1966), pp. 3–4.
119. Ray S. Baker quoted in McFadden, *Alternative Paths*, p. 240.
120. Quoted in David S. Foglesong, *America's Secret War Against Bolshevism* (Chapel Hill: University of North Carolina Press, 1995), p. 25.
121. Quoted in McFadden, *Alternative Paths*, p. 247.
122. Winston Churchill quoting Wilson in Lloyd C. Gardner, *Safe for Democracy* (New York: Oxford University Press, 1984), p. 239.
123. Quoted in Foglesong, *Secret War*, p. 43.
124. Quoted in McFadden, *Alternative Paths*, p. 104.
125. Foglesong, *Secret War*, p. 77.
126. Quoted in Betty Miller Unterberger, *The United States, Revolutionary Russia, and the Rise of Czechoslovakia* (Chapel Hill: University of North Carolina Press, 1989), p. 264.
127. Betty Miller Unterberger, "Woodrow Wilson and the Russian Revolution," in Arthur S. Link, ed., *Woodrow Wilson and a Revolutionary World, 1913–1921* (Chapel Hill: University of North Carolina Press, 1982), p. 70.
128. Foglesong, *Secret War*, p. 190.
129. Victor M. Fic, *The Collapse of American Policy in Russia and Siberia, 1918* (New York: Columbia University Press, 1995), p. 141.
130. Quoted in McFadden, *Alternative Paths*, p. 154.
131. Quoted in Benjamin D. Rhodes, *The Anglo-American War with Russia, 1918–1919* (Westport, Conn.: Greenwood, 1988), p. 123.
132. Foglesong, *Secret War*, p. 296.
133. Quoted *ibid.*, p. 291.
134. Dwight D. Eisenhower, *Waging Peace, 1956–1961* (Garden City, N.Y.: Doubleday, 1965), p. 616.
135. McKillen, "Corporatist Model," 173.
136. Arthur S. Link, *The Higher Realism of Woodrow Wilson* (Nashville: Vanderbilt University Press, 1971), p. 83.
137. Quoted in Gordon A. Craig, "The Revolution in War and Diplomacy," in Jack J. Roth, ed., *World War I* (New York: Knopf, 1967), p. 12.
138. Quoted in Robert H. Ferrell, *Woodrow Wilson and World War I* (New York: Harper and Row, 1985), p. 180.
139. E. M. Remarque, *All Quiet on the Western Front* (London: Putnam, 1929), p. 224.
140. Quoted in Tony Smith, *America's Mission* (Princeton: Princeton University Press, 1994), p. 102.
141. Quoted in Hans Schmidt, "Democracy in China," *Diplomatic History, XXII* (Winter 1998), 28.
142. Link, *Papers of Wilson, LXII* (1990), 47.
143. Quoted in John A. DeNovo, "The Movement for an Aggressive American Oil Policy Abroad, 1918–1920," *American Historical Review, LXI* (July 1956), 858.
144. Quoted in Foglesong, *Secret War*, p. 1.

Appendix

Makers of American Foreign Relations

Presidents	Secretaries of State	Chairs of the Senate Foreign Relations Committee
George Washington (1789–1797)	Thomas Jefferson (1790–1793) Edmund Randolph (1794–1795) Timothy Pickering (1795–1797)	
John Adams (1797–1801)	Timothy Pickering (1797–1800) John Marshall (1800–1801)	
Thomas Jefferson (1801–1809)	James Madison (1801–1809)	
James Madison (1809–1817)	Robert Smith (1809–1811) James Monroe (1811–1817)	James Barbour (1816–1817)
James Monroe (1817–1825)	John Quincy Adams (1817–1825)	James Barbour (1817–1818) Nathaniel Macon (1818–1819) James Brown (1819–1820) James Barbour (1820–1821) Rufus King (1821–1822) James Barbour (1822–1825)
John Quincy Adams (1825–1829)	Henry Clay (1825–1829)	Nathaniel Macon (1825–1826) Nathan Sanford (1826–1827) Nathaniel Macon (1827–1828) Littleton W. Tazewell (1828–1829)
Andrew Jackson (1829–1837)	Martin Van Buren (1829–1831) Edward Livingston (1831–1833) Louis McLane (1833–1834) John Forsyth (1834–1837)	Littleton W. Tazewell (1829–1832) John Forsyth (1832–1833) William Wilkins (1833–1834) Henry Clay (1834–1836) James Buchanan (1836–1837)
Martin Van Buren (1837–1841)	John Forsyth (1837–1841)	James Buchanan (1837–1841)
William H. Harrison (1841)	Daniel Webster (1841)	William C. Rives (1841)
John Tyler (1841–1845)	Daniel Webster (1841–1843)	William C. Rives (1841–1842)

Makers of American Foreign Relations *(continued)*

Presidents	Secretaries of State	Chairs of the Senate Foreign Relations Committee
	Abel P. Upshur (1843–1844) John C. Calhoun (1844–1845)	William S. Archer (1842–1845)
James K. Polk (1845–1849)	James Buchanan (1845–1849)	William Allen (1845–1846) Ambrose H. Sevier (1846–1848) Edward A. Hannegan (1848–1849) Thomas H. Benton (1849)
Zachary Taylor (1849–1850)	John M. Clayton (1849–1850)	William R. King (1849–1850)
Millard Fillmore (1850–1853)	Daniel Webster (1850–1852) Edward Everett (1852–1853)	Henry S. Foote (1850–1851) James M. Mason (1851–1853)
Franklin Pierce (1853–1857)	William L. Marcy (1853–1857)	James M. Mason (1853–1857)
James Buchanan (1857–1861)	Lewis Cass (1857–1860) Jeremiah S. Black (1860–1861)	James M. Mason (1857–1861)
Abraham Lincoln (1861–1865)	William H. Seward (1861–1865)	Charles Sumner (1861–1865)
Andrew Johnson (1865–1869)	William H. Seward (1865–1869)	Charles Sumner (1865–1869)
Ulysses S. Grant (1869–1877)	Elihu B. Washburne (1869) Hamilton Fish (1869–1877)	Charles Sumner (1869–1871) Simon Cameron (1871–1877)
Rutherford B. Hayes (1877–1881)	William M. Evarts (1877–1881)	Hannibal Hamlin (1877–1879) William W. Eaton (1879–1881)
James A. Garfield (1881)	James G. Blaine (1881)	Ambrose E. Burnside (1881) George F. Edmunds (1881)
Chester A. Arthur (1881–1885)	Frederick T. Frelinghuysen (1881–1885)	William Windon (1881–1883) John F. Miller (1883–1885)
Grover Cleveland (1885–1889)	Thomas F. Bayard (1885–1889)	John F. Miller (1885–1887) John Sherman (1887–1889)
Benjamin Harrison (1889–1893)	James G. Blaine (1889–1892) John W. Foster (1892–1893)	John Sherman (1889–1893)
Grover Cleveland (1893–1897)	Walter Q. Gresham (1893–1895) Richard Olney (1895–1897)	John T. Morgan (1893–1895) John Sherman (1895–1897)
William McKinley (1897–1901)	John Sherman (1897–1898) William R. Day (1898) John Hay (1898–1901)	William P. Frye (1897) Cushman K. Davis (1897–1901)
Theodore Roosevelt (1901–1909)	John Hay (1901–1905) Elihu Root (1905–1909) Robert Bacon (1909)	William P. Frye (1901) Shelby M. Cullom (1901–1909)
William Howard Taft (1909–1913)	Philander C. Knox (1909–1913)	Shelby M. Cullom (1909–1913)

Makers of American Foreign Relations *(continued)*

Presidents	Secretaries of State	Chairs of the Senate Foreign Relations Committee
Woodrow Wilson (1913–1921)	William Jennings Bryan (1913–1915) Robert Lansing (1915–1920) Bainbridge Colby (1920–1921)	Augustus O. Bacon (1913–1915) William J. Stone (1915–1919) Henry Cabot Lodge (1919–1921)
Warren G. Harding (1921–1923)	Charles E. Hughes (1921–1923)	Henry Cabot Lodge (1921–1923)
Calvin Coolidge (1923–1929)	Charles E. Hughes (1923–1925) Frank. B. Kellogg (1925–1929)	Henry Cabot Lodge (1923–1924) William E. Borah (1925–1929)
Herbert C. Hoover (1929–1933)	Henry L. Stimson (1929–1933)	William E. Borah (1929–1933)
Franklin D. Roosevelt (1933–1945)	Cordell Hull (1933–1944) Edward R. Stettinius, Jr. (1944–1945)	Key Pittman (1933–1940) Walter F. George (1940–1941) Tom Connally (1941–1945)

Presidents	Secretaries of State	Chairs of the Senate Foreign Relations Committee	Secretaries of Defense	Assistants to the President for National Security Affairs
Harry S. Truman (1945–1953)	Edward R. Stettinius, Jr. (1945) James F. Byrnes (1945–1947) George C. Marshall (1947–1949) Dean G. Acheson (1949–1953)	Tom Connally (1945–1947) Arthur H. Vandenberg (1947–1949) Tom Connally (1949–1953)	James V. Forrestal (1947–1949) Louis A. Johnson (1949–1950) George C. Marshall (1950–1951) Robert A. Lovett (1951–1953)	
Dwight D. Eisenhower (1953–1961)	John F. Dulles (1953–1959) Christian A. Herter (1959–1961)	Alexander Wiley (1953–1955) Walter F. George (1955–1957) Theodore F. Green (1957–1959) J. William Fulbright (1959–1961)	Charles E. Wilson (1953–1957) Neil H. McElroy (1957–1959) Thomas S. Gates, Jr. (1959–1961)	Robert Cutler (1953–1955 & 1957–1958) Dillon Anderson (1955–1956) William H. Jackson (1956) Gordon Gray (1958–1961)
John F. Kennedy (1961–1963)	Dean Rusk (1961–1963)	J. William Fulbright (1961–1963)	Robert S. McNamara (1961–1963)	McGeorge Bundy (1961–1963)
Lyndon B. Johnson (1963–1969)	Dean Rusk (1963–1969)	J. William Fulbright (1963–1969)	Robert S. McNamara (1963–1968) Clark M. Clifford (1968–1969)	McGeorge Bundy (1963–1966) Walt W. Rostow (1966–1969)

Makers of American Foreign Relations *(continued)*

Presidents	Secretaries of State	Chairs of the Senate Foreign Relations Committee	Secretaries of Defense	Assistants to the President for National Security Affairs
Richard M. Nixon (1969–1974)	William P. Rogers (1969–1973) Henry A. Kissinger (1973–1974)	J. William Fulbright (1969–1974)	Melvin R. Laird (1969–1973) Elliot L. Richardson (1973) James R. Schlesinger (1973–1974)	Henry A. Kissinger (1969–1974)
Gerald R. Ford (1974–1977)	Henry A. Kissinger (1974–1977)	J. William Fulbright (1974–1975) John Sparkman (1975–1977)	James R. Schlesinger (1974–1976) Donald Rumsfeld (1976–1977)	Henry A. Kissinger (1974–1975) Brent Scowcroft (1975–1977)
James E. Carter (1977–1981)	Cyrus R. Vance (1977–1980) Edmund Muskie (1980–1981)	John Sparkman (1977–1979) Frank Church (1979–1981)	Harold Brown (1977–1981)	Zbigniew Brzezinski (1977–1981)
Ronald W. Reagan (1981–1989)	Alexander M. Haig, Jr. (1981–1982) George P. Shultz (1982–1989)	Charles Percy (1981–1985) Richard G. Lugar (1985–1987) Claiborne Pell (1987–1989)	Caspar Weinberger (1981–1987) Frank C. Carlucci (1987–1989)	Richard Allen (1981) William P. Clark, Jr. (1981–1983) Robert C. McFarlane (1983–1985) John M. Poindexter (1985–1986) Frank C. Carlucci (1986–1987) Colin L. Powell (1987–1989)
George H. W. Bush (1989–1993)	James A. Baker III (1989–1992) Lawrence Eagleburger (1992–1993)	Claiborne Pell (1989–1993)	Richard B. Cheney (1989–1993)	Brent Scowcroft (1989–1993)
William J. Clinton (1993–)	Warren M. Christopher (1993–1997) Madeleine K. Albright (1997–)	Claiborne Pell (1993–1995) Jesse Helms (1995–)	Les Aspin (1993–1994) William J. Perry (1994–1997) William S. Cohen (1997–)	Anthony Lake (1993–1996) Samuel R. Berger (1996–)

GENERAL BIBLIOGRAPHY

General Reference Works

See also "Overviews of Relations with Countries, Regions, and Other Places of the World" and "Overviews of Subjects," both below, and your library's computer-based sources. Comprehensive bibliographies also appear in the four volumes of Bruce W. Jentleson and Thomas G. Paterson, eds., *Encyclopedia of U.S. Foreign Relations* (1997).

Annual Surveys: *Facts on File* (1941–); *Human Development Report* (1990–); *Keesing's Record of World Events* (also titled *Keesing's Contemporay Archives*) (1931–); London Institute of World Affairs, *The Yearbook of World Affairs* (1947–); Alan F. Pater and Jason R. Pater, eds., *What They Said In . . . : The Yearbook of World Opinion* (1971–); *Political Handbook of the World* (1928–); *The Statesmen's Year-Book World Gazetteer* (1864–); United Nations, *Demographic Yearbook* (1948–); *The World Bank Atlas* (1967–); *World Development Report* (1978–). See also "Statistics."

Atlases and Gazetteers: Ewan W. Anderson and Don Shewan, *An Atlas of World Political Flashpoints* (1993); Andrew Boyd, *An Atlas of World Affairs* (1998); Anna Bramwall, *The Atlas of Twentieth Century History* (1989); Gerard Chaliand and Jean-Pierre Rageau, *Strategic Atlas* (1990); Rodger Doyle, *Atlas of Contemporary America* 1994); Robert Ferrell and Richard Natkiel, *Atlas of American History* (1987); *Hammond Atlas of the World* (1992); Eric Homberger, *The Penguin Historical Atlas of North America* (1995); Michael Kidron and Ronald Segal, *The State of the World Atlas* (1995); Catherine Mattson and Mark T. Mattson, *Contemporary Atlas of the United States* (1998); David Munro, ed., *Chambers World Gazetteer* (1988); *National Geographic Atlas of the World* (1992); Richard Natkiel et al., eds., *Atlas of the Twentieth Century* (1982); *The New York Times Atlas of the World* (1992); *Oxford Atlas of the World* (1992); Rand McNally, *Today's World* (1996); Dan Smith, *The State of War and Peace Atlas* (1997); *The Times Atlas of World History* (1993).

Bibliographies: Samuel Flagg Bemis and Grace Gardner Griffin, *Guide to the Diplomatic History of the United States, 1775–1921* (1935); Richard Dean Burns, ed. *A Guide to American Foreign Relations Since* 1700 (1982); Congressional Information Service, *American Foreign Policy Index* (1994–); Council on Foreign Relations, *Foreign Affairs Bibliography* (1933–1972); Byron Dexter, ed., *The Foreign Affairs 50-Year Bibliography* (1972); Frank Freidel, ed., *Harvard Guide to American History* (1974); Mary Beth Norton, ed., *Guide to Historical Literature* (1995); Francis P. Prucha, *Handbook for Research in American History* (1987). The journal *Diplomatic History* regularly publishes articles that review the historiography of major topics and periods and provide extensive bibliographical guidance. The *Journal of American History* regularly lists recent publications. Journals such as *Foreign Affairs* and *Political Science Quarterly* regularly publish reviews of recent books.

Biographical Aids: John S. Bowman, *The Cambridge Dictionary of American Biography* (1995); Asa Briggs, *A Dictionary of Twentieth Century World Biography* (1990); Mari Jo Buhle et al., eds., *The American Radical* (1994); David Crystal, ed., *The Cambridge Biographical Encyclopedia* (1994); *Current Biography* (1940–); *Dictionary of American Biography* (1928–); *Encyclopedia of World Biography* (1998); John A. Garraty and Mark C. Carnes, eds., *American National Biography* (1999); John Garraty and Jerome L. Stersbstin, eds., *The Encyclopedia of American Biography* (1996); *International Who's Who* (1935–); Bernard K. Johnpoll and Harvey Klehr, eds., *Biographical Dictionary of the American Left* (1986); Warren F. Kuehl, ed., *Biographical Dictionary of Internationalists* (1983); *National Cyclopedia of American Biography* (1898–); Alan Palmer, *Who's Who in Modern History* (1980); Philip Rees, *Biographical Dictionary of the Extreme Right Since 1890* (1991); Frank W. Thackery and John E. Findling, eds., *Statesmen Who Changed the World* (1993); U.S. Department of State, *Biographic Register* (1860–1974) and *Foreign Service List* (1929–); *Who Was Who in America* (1963–); *Who's Who in America* (1899–); *Who's Who in the World* (1971–).

Chronologies: Lester H. Brune, *Chronological History of U.S. Foreign Relations* (1985, 1991); Gorton Carruth, *The Encyclopedia of American Facts and Dates* (1993) and *The Encyclopedia of World Facts and Dates* (1993); Council on Foreign Relations, *Foreign Affairs Chronology, 1978–1989* (1990) and *The United States in World Affairs* (1932–

1972); Robert H. Ferrell and John S. Bowman, eds., *The Twentieth Century* (1984); Bernard Grun, *The Timetables of History* (1991); John E. Jessup, *A Chronology of Conflict and Resolution, 1945–1985* (1989); Thomas Parker and Douglas Nelson, *Day by Day: The Sixties* (1983); Royal Institute of International Affairs, *Survey of International Affairs, 1920–1963* (1972–1977); Laurence Urdang, ed., *The Timetables of American History* (1996). See also "Annual Surveys."

Documentary Collections and Series: Martin P. Claussen, ed., *The National State Papers of the United States: Texts of Documents (1789–1817)* (1980–   ); Council on Foreign Relations, *Documents on American Foreign Relations, 1938/1939–1970* (1939–1973); Royal Institute of International Affairs, *Documents on International Affairs, 1928–1963* (1929–1973); Arthur M. Schlesinger, Jr., ed., *The Dynamics of World Power: A Documentary History of U.S. Foreign Policy, 1945–1973* (1973); U.S. Congress, *American State Papers* (1852–1859); U.S. Department of State, *A Decade of American Foreign Policy: Basic Documents, 1941–1949* (1985), *American Foreign Policy: Basic Documents, 1950–1955* (1957), *American Foreign Policy: Basic Documents, 1977–1980* (1983–1986), *American Foreign Policy: Current Documents, 1956–1967* (1956–1967), *American Foreign Policy: Current Documents, 1981–*   (1984–   ), *Bulletin* (1938–   ), *Dispatch* (1990–   ), *Foreign Relations of United States, 1861–*   (1862–   ), and *Press Conferences of the Secretaries of State, 1922–1974* (n.d.); *Vital Speeches of the Day* (1934–   ).

Encyclopedias and Dictionaries: Alexander DeConde, *Encyclopedia of American Foreign Policy* (1978); Margaret Denning and J. K. Sweeney, *Handboook of American Diplomacy* (1992); John Drexel, ed., *The Facts on File Encyclopedia of the 20th Century* (1991); Graham Evans and Jeffrey Newnham, eds., *The Dictionary of World Politics* (1990); John M. Farragher, ed., *The American Heritage Encyclopedia of American History* (1998); John E. Findling, *Dictionary of American Diplomatic History* (1989); Stephen A. Flanders and Carl N. Flanders, *Dictionary of American Foreign Affairs* (1991); Charles W. Freeman, Jr., *The Diplomat's Dictionary* (1997); Jack P. Greene, ed., *Encyclopedia of American Political History* (1984); Kenneth L. Hill, *Encyclopedia of Conflicts Since World War II* (1998); Stanley Hochman, *The Penguin Dictionary of Contemporary American History* (1997); Bruce W. Jentleson and Thomas G. Paterson, eds., *Encyclopedia of U.S. Foreign Relations* (1997); Joel Krieger et al., eds., *The Oxford Companion to the Politics of the World* (1993); Stanley I. Kutler, ed., *Encyclopedia of the United States in the Twentieth Century* (1995); Richard B. Morris et al., *Encyclopedia of American History* (1996); Jack C. Plano and Ray Olton, *The International Relations Dictionary* (1988); Jack E. Vincent, *A Handbook of International Relations* (1968); *Worldmark Encyclopedia of the Nations* (1995).

Statistics: Erik W. Austin and Jerome C. Clubb, *Political Facts of the United States Since 1789* (1986); International Monetary Fund, *International Financial Statistics* (1948–   ); George T. Kurian, ed., *The Illustrated Book of World Rankings* (1996); Victor Showers, *World Facts and Figures* (1989); Ruth L. Sivard, *World Military and Social Expenditures* (1974–   ); Charles L. Taylor and David A, Jodice, *World Handbook of Political and Social Indicators* (1983); United Nations, *Demographic Yearbook* (1948–   ), *Report on the World Social Situation* (1952–   ), and *Statistical Yearbook* (1948–   ); U.S. Agency for International Development, *United States Overseas Loans and Grants and Assistance from International Organizations, July 1, 1945–Sept. 30, 1980* (1981); U.S. Bureau of the Census, *Historical Statistics of the United States* (1975) and *Statistical Abstract of the United States* (1878–   ); U.S. Central Intelligence Agency, *Handbook of International Economic Statistics* (1971–   ) and *The World Factbook* (1981–   ); World Bank, *World Tables* (1974–   ); World Resources Institute, *World Resources* (1990–   ). See also "Annual Surveys."

Overviews of Relations with Countries, Regions, and Other Places of the World, Including Atlases and Gazetteers (A), Annual Surveys and Chronologies (AS), Bibliographies (B), Biographical Aids (BA), Chronologies (C), Encyclopedias and Dictionaries (E), and Statistics (S)

Afghanistan: Anthony Arnold, *Afghanistan* (1985); Henry S. Bradsher, *Afghanistan and the Soviet Union* (1985); B. S. Gupta, *Afghanistan* (1986); M. Hassar Kakar, *Afghanistan: The Soviet Invasion and the Afghan Response* (1995); Nancy P. Newell and Richard S. Newell, *The Struggle for Afghanistan* (1981); Leon B. Poullada, *The Kingdom of Afghanistan and the United States, 1828-1973* (1995); Stanley Wolpert, *Roots of Confrontation in South Asia* (1982).

Africa: Chris Cook and David Killinway, *African Political Facts Since 1945* (1991) (E); Peter Duignan and Lewis H. Gann, *The United States and Africa* (1987); Dennis Hickey and Kenneth White, *An Enchanting Darkness* (1993); Lawrence C. Howard, *American Involvement in Africa South of the Sahara, 1800–1860* (1988); Henry F. Jackson, *From the Congo to Soweto* (1982); Zaki Laidi, *The Superpowers and Africa* (1990); Colin Legum, ed., *Africa Contemporary Record* (1968–   ) (AS); Michael McCarthy, *Dark Continent* (1983); Lysle E. Meyer, *The Farther Frontier* (1992); Thomas Noer, *Cold War and Black Liberation* (1985); Anthony G. Pazzanita and Tony Hodges, *Historical Dictionary of Western Sahara* (1994) (E); Peter J. Schraeder, *United States Foreign Policy Toward Africa* (1994); Elliot P. Skinner, *African-Americans and*

U.S. Policy Toward Africa, 1850–1924 (1992); U.S. Library of Congress, *The United States and Sub-Saharan Africa* (1984) (B). See also countries.

Alaska: Paul S. Holbo, *Tarnished Expansion* (1983); Ronald J. Jensen, *The Alaska Purchase* (1975); Walter A. McDougall, *Let the Sea Make a Noise* (1993). See also Kushner and Saul in "Russia and the Soviet Union."

Albania: William B. Bland, *Albania* (1988) (B).

Algeria: Charles-Robert Ageron, *Modern Algeria* (1992); Helen C. Metz, ed., *Algeria* (1994); Martin Stone, *The Agony of Algeria* (1997). See also "North Africa."

Angola: Richard Black, *Angola* (1992) (B); Susan H. Broadhead, *Historical Dictionary of Angola* (1992) (E); Thomas Collelo, ed., *Angola* (1990); Fernando A. Guimarães, *The Origins of the Angolan Civil War* (1998); Lawrence W. Henderson, *Angola* (1979); John A. Marcum, *The Angolan Revolution* (1969, 1978); Kenneth Mokoena and Nicole Gaymon, eds., *The Angola Crises* (1991); Inge Tvedten, *Angola* (1997). See also "Africa."

Antarctica: Peter J. Beck, *The International Politics of Antarctica* (1986); Robert Headland, *Chronological List of Antarctic Expeditions* (1989) (E and C); Christopher C. Joyner and Ethel R. Theis, *Eagle over the Ice* (1997); Frank G. Klotz, *America on the Ice* (1990); Jeffrey D. Myhre, *The Antarctic Treaty System* (1986); John Stewart, *Antarctica* (1990) (E); Gilligan D. Triggs, ed., *The Antartic Treaty Regime* (1987).

Arab World: See "Israel, Palestine, and Arab-Israeli Conflict" and "Middle East."

Arctic: Elizabeth B. Elliot-Meisel, *Arctic Diplomacy: Canada and the United States in the Northwest Passage* (1998); Clive Holland, *Arctic Exploration and Development* (1993) (E). See also "Canada."

Argentina: Alan Biggs, *Argentina* (1991) (B); Harold F. Peterson, *Argentina and the United States* (1964); David Rock, *Argentina* (1985); David Sheinin, *Searching for Authority* (1998); Joseph Tulchin, *Argentina and the United States* (1990); Arthur P. Whitaker, *The United States and the Southern Cone* (1976). See also "Latin America."

Armenia: Vrej Nerses Neressian, *Armenia* (1993) (B).

Asia and Pacific Islands: Alexander Besher, *The Pacific Rim Almanac* (1991) (E); Jessica S. Brown et al., eds., *The United States in East Asia* (1985) (B); Frederica M. Bunge and Melinda W. Cooke, eds., *Oceania* (1985); I. C. Campbell, *A History of the Pacific Islands* (1989); Sucheng Chan, *Asian-Americans* (1991); Warren I. Cohen, ed., *Pacific Passage* (1996); Donald Denoon and Stewart Firth, eds., *The Cambridge History of the Pacific Islanders* (1997); John C. Dorance, *The United States and the Pacific Islands* (1992); Norman Douglas and Ngaire Douglas, eds., *Pacific Islands Yearbook* (1932–) (AS); Arthur P. Dudden, *The American Pacific* (1992); Ainslie T. Embree, *Encyclopedia of Asian History* (1988) (E); Gerald Fry, *Pacific Basin and Oceania* (1987) (B); Roger W. Gale, *The Americanization of Micronesia* (1979); Arrell M. Gibson, *Yankees in Paradise* (1993); Akira Iriye, *Across the Pacific* (1967); Donald D. Johnson, *The United States in the Pacific* (1995); John C. Perry, *Facing West* (1994); Deryck Scarr, *The History of the Pacific Islands* (1990); Gerald Segal, *Rethinking the Pacific* (1990); David Shavit, *The United States in Asia* (1990) (E); Roger C. Thompson, *The Pacific Rim Since 1945* (1994); James C. Thomson, Jr., et al., *Sentimental Imperialists* (1981). See also countries and "Vietnam and Southeast Asia."

Australia: Glen St. John Barclay, *Friends in High Places* (1985); Philip Bell, *Implicated* (1993); Norman Harper, *A Great and Powerful Friend* (1987); Joseph Siracusa and Yeong-Han Cheong, *America's Australia, Australia's America* (1997). See also "Asia and Pacific Islands."

Austria: William Bader, *Austria Between East and West* (1966); Audrey K. Cronin, *Great Power Politics and the Struggle over Austria, 1945–1955* (1986); Barbara Jelavich, *Modern Austria* (1988); Mellany A. Sully, *A Contemporary History of Austria* (1990); Reinhold Wagnleitner, *Coca-Colonization and the Cold War* (1994). See also "Europe."

Azerbaijan: Ian Bremmer and Ray Taras, eds., *Nations and Politics in the Soviet Successor States* (1993). See also "Russia and the Soviet Union."

The Bahamas: Paul G. Boultbee, *The Bahamas* (1989) (B).

Bahrain: F. Gregory Gauss, *Oil Monarchies* (1994). See also "Middle East" and "Persian Gulf."

Baltic States: Walter C. Clemens, Jr., *Baltic Independence and Russian Empire* (1991); David Flint, *The Baltic States* (1992); Kristian Gerner, *The Baltic States and the End of the Soviet Empire* (1993); Walter R. Iwaskiw, ed., *Estonia, Latvia, and Lithuania* (1996); Anatol

Lieven, *The Baltic Revolution* (1993); Inese A. Smith and Marita V. Grunts, *The Baltic States* (1993). See also "Estonia."

Bangladesh: See Brown in "India."

Belarus: Helen Fedor, *Belarus and Moldova* (1995).

Belgium: Jonathan E. Helmreich, *United States Relations with Belgium and the Congo* (1998); Frank E. Hugget, *Modern Belgium* (1969). See also "Europe."

Belize: O. Nigel Bolland, *Belize* (1996). Also see Merrill in "Guyana."

Berlin: See "Germany and Berlin."

Bhutan: See "Nepal."

Bolivia: Rex A. Hudson and Dennis M. Haggerty, eds., *Bolivia* (1991); Waltraud Q. Morales, *Bolivia* (1992); Lawrence Whitehead, *The United States and Bolivia* (1969); J. W. Wilkie, *The Bolivian Revolution and U.S. Aid Since 1952* (1969). See also "Latin America" and Pike in "Peru."

Bosnia-Herzegovina: Noel Malcolm, *Bosnia* (1994). See also "Yugoslavia."

Brazil: Jan Black, *United States Penetration of Brazil* (1977); Elizabeth A. Cobbs, *The Rich Neighbor Policy: Rockefeller and Kaiser in Brazil* (1992); John Dickenson, ed., *Brazil* (1997) (B); Gerald K. Haines, *The Americanization of Brazil* (1989); Stanley Hilton, *Brazil and the Great Powers* (1975); Rex A. Hudson, ed., *Brazil* (1998); Frank McCann, *The Brazilian-American Alliance, 1937–1945* (1973); Joseph Smith, *Unequal Giants* (1991); Steven C. Topik, *Trade and Gunboats* (1996); W. Michael Weis, *Cold Warriors and Coups d'État* (1993). See also "Latin America."

Bulgaria: Glenn A. Curtis, ed., *Bulgaria* (1993). See also "Europe."

Burma: See "Myanmar."

Burundi: Morna Daniels, *Burundi* (1992) (B). See also "Africa."

Cambodia: MacAlister Brown and Joseph J. Zasloff, *Cambodia Confronts the Peacemakers, 1979–1998* (1998); David P. Chandler, *The Tragedy of Cambodian History* (1991); Michael Haas, *Cambodia, Pol Pot, and the United States* (1991); Henry Kamm, *Cambodia* (1998); Ben Kiernan, *How Pol Pot Came to Power* (1985) and *The Pol Pot*

Regime (1996); Russell R. Ross, ed., *Cambodia* (1990); William Shawcross, *The Quality of Mercy* (1984) and *Sideshow* (1979). See also "Southeast Asia."

Cameroon: Julius A. Amin, *The Peace Corps in Cameroon* (1992); Mark DeLancey, *Cameroon* (1986) (B); Mark DeLancey and H. Mbella Mokeba, *Historical Dictionary of Cameroon* (1990) (E). See also "Africa."

Canada: David J. Bercuson and J. L. Granatstein, *The Collins Dictionary of Canadian History* (1988) (E); Robert Bothwell, *Canada and the United States* (1992); Charles Doran, *Forgotten Partnership* (1984); Charles Doran and John H. Sigler, *Canada and the United States* (1985); William T. Fox, *A Continent Apart* (1985); J. L. Granatstein and Robert Bothwell, *Pirouette* (1990); J. L. Granastein and Norman Hillmer, *For Better or For Worse* (1992); Archie Hobson, *The Cambridge Gazetteer of the United States and Canada* (1996) (A); Lansing Lamont and Duncan Edmonds, eds., *Friends So Different* (1989); Seymour Martin Lipset, *Continental Divide* (1990); Lawrence Martin, *The Presidents and the Prime Ministers* (1982); J. F. Rooney, Jr., et al., eds., *This Remarkable Continent* (1982) (A); Denis Smith, *Diplomacy of Fear* (1988); Reginald C. Stuart, *United States Expansionism and British North America 1775–1871* (1988); John H. Thompson and Stephen J. Randall, *Canada and the United States* (1998). See also "Great Britain."

Caribbean: Charles D. Ameringer, *The Caribbean Legion* (1974); David Healy, *Drive to Hegemony* (1988); Roger Hughes, *The Caribbean* (1987) (B); Lester D. Langley, *The United States and the Caribbean, 1900–1970* (1980) and *The United States and the Caribbean in the Twentieth Century* (1989); Sandra W. Meditz and Dennis M. Hanratty, eds., *Islands of the Commonwealth Caribbean* (1989); Robert F. Smith, *The Caribbean World and the United States* (1994). See also "Central America," "Latin America," and countries.

Central African Republic: Pierre Kalck, *Historical Dictionary of the Central African Republic* (1992) (E). See also "Africa."

Central America: Tom Barry, *Central America Inside Out* (1991) (C and E); Leslie Bethel, ed., *Central America Since Independence* (1991); Morris J. Blachman et al., eds., *Confronting Revolution* (1986); John Booth and Thomas Walker, *Understanding Central America* (1993); John Coatsworth, *Central America and the United States* (1994); Kenneth M. Coleman and George C. Herring, eds., *Understanding the Central American Crisis* (1991); John E. Findling, *Close Neighbors, Distant Friends* (1987); Kenneth J. Grieb, *Central America in the Nineteenth and Twentieth Centuries* (1988) (B); Walter LaFeber, *Inevitable Revolutions* (1993); Thomas M. Leonard, *Central America and the United*

States (1991) and *Central America and U.S. Policies, 1820s–1980s* (1985) (B); Thomas D. Schoonover, *The United States in Central America, 1860–1911* (1991); Ralph L. Woodward, *Central America* (1985). See also "Caribbean," "Latin America," and individual countries.

Chad: Thomas Collelo, ed., *Chad* (1990); Samuel Decalo, *Historical Dictionary of Chad* (1987) (E). See also "Africa."

Chile: Michael Francis, *The Limits of Hegemony* (1977); Rex A. Hudson, ed., *Chile* (1990); Michael Monteon, *Chile in the Nitrate Era* (1982); Heraldo Munoz and Carlos Portales, *Elusive Friendship* (1991); Fredrick B. Pike, *Chile and the United States, 1880–1962* (1963); William F. Sater, *Chile and the United States* (1990); Paul E. Sigmund, *The United States and Democracy in Chile* (1993). See also "Latin America" and Whitaker in "Argentina."

China (and Taiwan): Gordon Chang, *Friends and Enemies* (1990); Warren I. Cohen, *America's Response to China* (1990); John K. Fairbank, *China Perceived* (1974) and *The United States and China* (1983); Rosemary Foot, *The Practice of Power* (1995); John Gittings, *The World and China, 1922–1972* (1974); Jonathan Goldstein et al., eds., *America Views China* (1991); Harry Harding, *A Fragile Relationship* (1992); Michael H. Hunt, *The Making of a Special Relationship* (1983); Arnold Xiangze Jiang, *The United States and China* (1988); Wei-cin Lee, *Taiwan* (1990) (B); Ernest R. May and John K. Fairbank, eds., *America's China Trade in Historical Perspective* (1986); Stuart C. Miller, *The Unwelcome Immigrant: The American Image of the Chinese, 1785–1882* (1969); Robert S. Ross, *Negotiating Cooperation* (1995); Michael Schaller, *The United States and China in the Twentieth Century* (1990); David Shambaugh, *Beautiful Imperialist* (1991); Henry Shih-Shan Tsai, *The Chinese Experience in America* (1986); Nancy B. Tucker, *Taiwan, Hong Kong, and the United States* (1994); Shu Guang Zhang, *Deterrence and Strategic Culture* (1992). See also "Asia and Pacific Islands."

Colombia: David Bushnell, *The Making of Modern Colombia* (1993); Robert H. Davis, *Colombia* (1990) (B); Dennis M. Hanratty and Sandra W. Meditz, eds., *Colombia* (1990); Harvey F. Kline, *Colombia* (1995); Richard L. Lael, *Arrogant Diplomacy* (1987); Stephen J. Randall, *Colombia and the United States* (1992) and *The Diplomacy of Modernization* (1977). See also "Latin America" and "Panama (and Panama Canal)."

Comoros: See "Indian Ocean."

Congo (Brazzaville): See "Africa."

Congo (Kinshasa): David N. Gibbs, *The Political Economy of Third World Intervention* (1991); Madeline G. Kalb, *The Congo Cables* (1982); Sean Kelly, *America's Tyrant: The CIA and Mobutu of Zaire* (1993); Dsandra W. Meditz and Tim Merrill, eds., *Zaire* (1994); Michael G. Schatzberg, *Mobutu or Chaos* (1991); Crawford Young and Thomas Turner, *The Rise and Decline of the Zairian State* (1985). See also "Africa" and Helmreich in "Belgium."

Costa Rica: Theodore S. Creedman, *Historical Dictionary of Costa Rica* (1991) (E); Kyle Longley, *The Sparrow and Hawk* (1997); Charles L. Stansifer, *Costa Rica* (1991) (B). See also "Central America" and "Latin America."

Cuba: Jules Benjamin, *The United States and Cuba* (1977); Leslie Bethell, ed., *Cuba* (1992); Ronald H. Chilcote and Sheryl Lutjens, eds., *Cuba, 1953–1978* (1986) (B); Juan del Aguilar, *Cuba* (1988); Jorge Domínguez, *To Make the World Safe for Revolution* (1989); Jesse J. Dossick, ed., *Cuba, Cubans, and Cuban-Americans, 1902–1991* (1992) (B); José M. Hernández, *Cuba and the United States: Intervention and Militarism, 1868–1933* (1993); Donna R. Kaplowitz, *Anatomy of a Failed Embargo* (1998); Morris H. Morley, *Imperial State and Revolution* (1987); Thomas G. Paterson, *Contesting Castro* (1994); Louis A. Pérez, Jr., *Cuba* (1995), *Cuba* (1988) (B), and *Cuba and the United States* (1997); Jaime Suchlicki, *Historical Dictionary of Cuba* (1988) (E). See also "Caribbean," "Latin America," and "Spanish-American-Cuban-Filipino War."

Cyprus: Tozun Bahcheli, *Greek-Turkish Relations Since 1955* (1990); Henry A. Richter, *Greece and Cyprus Since 1920* (1991) (B); Eric Solsten, ed., *Cyprus* (1991). See also Stearns in "Greece."

Czech Republic (and Czechoslovakia): David Short, *Czechoslovakia* (1986) (B); Gordon Skilling, *Czechoslovakia* (1991); Walter Ullmann, *The United States in Prague, 1945–1948* (1978); Betty Miller Unterberger, *The United States, Revolutionary Russia, and the Rise of Czechoslovakia* (1989). See also "Eastern Europe."

Dominican Republic: G. Pope Atkins and Larman C. Wilson, *The Dominican Republic and the United States* (1998) and *The United States and the Trujillo Regime* (1972); Ian Bell, *The Dominican Republic* (1981); Bruce J. Calder, *The Impact of Intervention* (1984); Piero Gleijeses, *The Dominican Crisis* (1978); Richard A. Haggerty, ed., *Dominican Republic and Haiti* (1991); Rayford W. Logan, *Haiti and the Dominican Republic* (1968); Eric P. Roorda, *The Dictator Next Door* (1998); Kai Schoenhals, *Dominican Republic* (1990) (B); Howard J. Wiarda, *The Dominican Republic* (1992). See also "Caribbean" and "Latin America."

Eastern Europe: Robert F. Byrnes, *U.S. Policy Toward Europe and the Soviet Union* (1989); Stephen A. Garrett, *From Potsdam to Poland* (1986); Bennett Kovrig, *Of Walls and Bridges* (1991); Geoffrey Swain and Nigel Swain, *Eastern Europe Since 1945* (1993). Also see "Russia and the Soviet Union," "Europe," and countries.

Ecuador: David Corkill, *Ecuador* (1989) (B); Dennis M. Hanratty, ed., *Ecuador* (1991); David W. Schodt, *Ecuador* (1987). See also "Latin America" and Pike in "Peru."

Egypt: Gregory L. Aftandilian, *Egypt's Bid for Arab Leadership* (1993); Geoffrey Aronson, *From Sideshow to Center Stage* (1986); William J. Burns, *Economic Aid and American Policy Toward Egypt, 1955–1981* (1985); Peter L. Hahn, *The United States, Great Britian, and Egypt, 1945–1956* (1991); Ragai N. Makar, *Egypt* (1988) (B); Helen C. Metz, ed., *Egypt* (1991); Gail E. Meyer, *Egypt and the United States* (1980); William B. Quandt, *The United States and Egypt* (1990). See also "Israel, Palestine, and Arab-Israeli Conflict" and "Middle East."

El Salvador: America's Watch, *El Salvador's Decade of Terror* (1991); Cynthia Arnson, *El Salvador* (1982); Enrique A. Baloyra, *El Salvador in Transition* (1982); Martin Diskin and Kenneth Sharpe, *The Impact of U.S. Policy in El Salvador, 1979–1986* (1986); Richard A. Haggerty, ed., *El Salvador* (1990); T. S. Montgomery, *Revolution in El Salvador* (1982); Ralph Lee Woodward, *El Salvador* (1988) (B). See also "Central America" and "Latin America."

Estonia: Toivo U. Raun, *Estonia and the Estonians* (1991). See also "Baltic States."

Ethiopia: David A. Korn, *Ethiopia, the United States, and the Soviet Union* (1986); Jeffrey S. Lefebvre, *Arms for the Horn* (1991); Harold G. Marcus, *Ethiopia, Great Britain, and the United States, 1941–1974* (1983); Thomas P. Ofcansky, ed., *Ethiopia* (1993); Chris Prouty and Eugene Rosenfeld, *Historical Dictionary of Ethiopia* (1994) (E). Also see "Africa."

Europe: Peter Coffey, *The EC and the United States* (1993); Simon W. Duke and Wolfgang Krieger, eds., *U.S. Military Forces in Europe* (1993); *The Economist Atlas of the New Europe* (1992) (A); Nicholas V. Gianaris, *The European Community and the United States* (1991); John L. Harper, *American Visions of Europe* (1994); Ethan B. Kapstein, *The Insecure Alliance: Energy Crises and Western Politics Since 1914* (1990); Geir Lundestad, *"Empire" by Integration* (1998); Jacques Portes, ed., *Europe and America* (1987); Pascaline Winand, *Eisenhower, Kennedy, and the United States of Europe* (1993). See also "Eastern Europe," "North Atlantic Treaty Organization (NATO)," countries, and wars.

Finland: Jussi M. Hanhimäki, *Containing Coexistence* (1997); Max Jacobson, *Finnish Neutrality* (1969); Robert Rinehart, ed., *Finland and the United States* (1993); Eric Solsten and Sandra W. Meditz, *Finland* (1990). See also "Europe" and "Scandinavia."

France: Henry Blumenthal, *A Reappraisal of Franco-American Relations, 1830–1871* (1959), *France and the United States* (1970), and *Illusion and Reality in Franco-American Diplomacy, 1914–1945* (1986); James A. Carr, ed., *American Foreign Policy During the French Revolution-Napoleonic Period* (1994) (B); Charles Cogan, *Oldest Allies, Guarded Friends* (1994); Frank Costigliola, *The Cold Alliance* (1992); Robert O. Paxton and Nicholas Wahl, eds., *De Gaulle and the United States, 1930–1970* (1994); Irwin M. Wall, *The United States and the Making of Postwar France* (1991); Marvin Zahniser, *Uncertain Friendship* (1975). See also "Europe."

Gabon: David E. Gardinier, *Historical Dictionary of Gabon* (1994) (E). See also "Africa."

Germany and Berlin: David E. Barclay and Elisabeth Glaser-Schmidt, eds., *Transatlantic Image and Perceptions* (1997); Dennis L. Bark and David R. Gross, *A History of West Germany* (1993); Hans W. Gatzke, *Germany and the United States* (1980); Wolfram F. Hanrieder, *Germany, America, Europe* (1989); Manfred Jonas, *The United States and Germany* (1984); Margrit Krewson, *German-American Relations* (1995) (B); Roger P. Morgan, *The United States and West Germany, 1945–1973* (1974); Frank Ninkovich, *Germany and the United States* (1995); Cathal J. Nolan and Carl C. Hodge, eds., *Shepherd of Democracy?* (1992); Hans-Jürgen Schröder, ed., *Confrontation and Cooperation* (1993); Thomas A. Schwartz, *America's Germany* (1991); Eric Solsten, ed., *Germany* (1996); Frank Trommler and Joseph McVeigh, eds., *America and the Germans* (1985); Ian Wallace, *Berlin* (1993) (B); Peter Wyden, *Wall* (1989). See also "Europe," "Holocaust," "War Crimes and Trials," "World War I," and "World War II."

Ghana: LaVerde Berry, ed., *Ghana* (1995); Daniel McFarland, *Historical Dictionary of Ghana* (1985). See also "Africa."

Great Britain: C. J. Bartlett, *"The Special Relationship"* (1992); Kenneth Bourne, *Britain and the Balance of Power in North America, 1815–1908* (1967); Charles S. Campbell, *From Revolution to Rapprochement* (1974); David Dimbleby and David Reynolds, *An Ocean Apart* (1989); Alan P. Dobson, *Anglo-American Relations in the Twentieth Century* (1995); Robert M. Hathaway, *Great Britain and the United States* (1990); David A. Lincove and Gary R. Treadway, eds., *The Anglo-American Relationship* (1988) (B); William Roger Louis and Hedley Bull, eds., *The Special Relationship* (1986); H. G. Nicholas,

The United States and Great Britain (1975); Anne Orde, *The Eclipse of Great Britain* (1996). See also "Canada" and "War of 1812."

Greece: Louis Cassimatis, *American Influence in Greece, 1917–1929* (1988); Theodore A. Couloumbis, *The United States, Greece, and Turkey* (1983); Theodore A. Couloumbis and John O. Iatrides, eds., *Greek-American Relations* (1980); Glenn E. Curtis, ed., *Greece* (1995); John O. Iatrides, ed., *Ambassador MacVeagh Reports: Greece, 1933–1947* (1980); Jon V. Kofas, *Intervention and Underdevelopment: Greece During the Cold War* (1989); Monteagle Stearns, *Entangled Allies* (1991); Lawrence S. Wittner, *American Intervention in Greece, 1943–1949* (1982). See also "Europe" and Richter in "Cyprus."

Grenada: Peter M. Dunn and Bruce W. Watson, eds., *American Intervention in Grenada* (1985); Gordon K. Lewis, *Grenada* (1987); Kai P. Schoenhals and Richard A. Melanson, eds., *Revolution and Intervention in Grenada* (1985). See also "Caribbean."

Guam: Timothy P. Maga, *Defending Paradise* (1988); Earl S. Pomeroy, *Pacific Outpost* (1951); Robert F. Rogers, *Destiny's Landfall* (1995). See also "Asia and Pacific Islands."

Guatemala: Nick Cullather, *Secret History* (1999); Paul J. Dosal, *Doing Business with the Dictators: A Political History of United Fruit in Guatemala, 1899–1944* (1993); Piero Glejeses, *Shattered Hope* (1991); Jim Handy, *Gift of the Devil* (1985); Richard Immerman, *The CIA in Guatemala* (1982); Ralph Lee Woodward, *Guatemala* (1992) (B). See also "Central America" and "Latin America."

Guyana: Tim Merrill, ed., *Guyana and Belize* (1993). See also "Latin America."

Haiti: Frances Chambers, *Haiti* (1983) (B); Rayford W. Logan, *Diplomatic Relations of the United States with Haiti, 1776-1891* (1941); David Nicholls, *From Dessalines to Duvalier* (1979); Brenda Gayle Plummer, *Haiti and the United States* (1992); Robert I. Rotberg, *Haiti* (1971). See also "Caribbean," "Latin America," and Haggerty and Logan in "Dominican Republic."

Hawai'i: Helena G. Allen, *The Betrayal of Queen Lilioukalani* (1982); Ralph S. Kuykendall, *The Hawaiian Kingdom* (1938–1967); Nancy Morris and Love Dean, *Hawai'i* (1992) (B); Merze Tate, *The United States and the Hawaiian Kingdom* (1965). See also "Asia and Pacific Islands."

Honduras: Alison Acker, *Honduras* (1988); Pamela F. Howard-Reguindin, *Honduras* (1992) (B); Harvey Meyer and Jessie Meyer,

Historical Dictionary of Honduras (1994) (E). See also "Central America."

Hong Kong: See Tucker in "China (and Taiwan)."

Hungary: Stephan R. Burant, ed., *Hungary* (1990). See also "Eastern Europe" and "Europe."

Iceland: Donald E. Neuchterlein, *Iceland* (1975). See also "Scandinavia."

India: William J. Barnds, *India, Pakistan, and the Great Powers* (1972); H. W. Brands, *India and the United States* (1990); W. Norman Brown, *The United States and India, Pakistan, and Bangladesh* (1972); Srinivas M. Chary, *The Eagle and the Peacock* (1994); Kenton J. Clymer, *Quest for Freedom* (1995); James Heitzman and Robert L. Worden, eds., *India* (1996); Gary R. Hess, *America Encounters India, 1941–1947* (1971); Harold R. Issacs, *Images of Asia* (1958); Dennis Kux, *India and the United States* (1992); Robert J. McMahon, *The Cold War on the Periphery* (1994); Dennis Merrill, *Bread and the Ballot* (1990); Norman D. Palmer, *The United States and India* (1984); Santosh C. Saha, *Indo-U.S. Relations, 1947–1988* (1990) (B); Stanley Wolpert, *Nehru* (1997). See also "Asia and Pacific Islands" and Wolpert in "Afghanistan."

Indian Ocean: Helen C. Metz, ed., *Indian Ocean: Five Island Countries* (1995). See also "Africa."

Indonesia: Paul F. Gardner, *Shared Hopes, Separate Fears* (1997); Gerald Krausse and Sylvia Krausse, *Indonesia* (1994) (B); Michael Leifer, *Indonesia's Foreign Policy* (1983); Robert J. McMahon, *Colonialism and Cold War* (1981); Robert L. Worden, ed., *Indonesia* (1993). See also "Asia and Pacific Islands."

Iran: James A. Bill, *The Eagle and the Lion* (1988); Richard W. Cottam, *Iran and the United States* (1988); Mark J. Gasiorowski, *U.S. Foreign Policy and the Shah* (1991); Sīrūs Ghanī, *Iran and the West* (1987) (B); James F. Goode, *The United States and Iran, 1946–51* (1989); Nikki R. Keddie and Mark J. Gasiorowski, eds., *Neither East nor West* (1990); Mark H. Lytle, *The Origins of the Iranian-American Alliance, 1941–1953* (1987); Rouhollah K. Ramazani, *The United States and Iran* (1982); Barry Rubin, *Paved with Good Intentions* (1980); Kuross A. Samii, *Involvement by Invitation* (1987); Abraham Yeselson, *United States–Persian Diplomatic Relations, 1883–1921* (1956). See also "Middle East" and "Persian Gulf."

Iraq: Rick Atkinson, *Crusade* (1993); Lawrence Freedman and Efraim Karsh, *The Gulf Conflict, 1990–1991* (1993); Bruce Jentleson,

With Friends like These (1994); Helen C. Metz, ed., *Iraq* (1990); William Stivers, *Supremacy and Oil* (1982). See also "Middle East" and "Persian Gulf."

Ireland: Donald H. Akenson, *The United States and Ireland* (1973); Thomas N. Brown, *Irish-American Nationalism, 1870–1890* (1966); Francis M. Carroll, *American Opinion and the Irish Question, 1910–1923* (1978); Sean Cronin, *Washington's Irish Policy, 1916–1986* (1987); Troy D. Davis, *Dublin's American Policy* (1998); Alan J. Ward, *Ireland and Anglo-American Relations, 1899–1921* (1969). See also "Europe" and "Great Britain."

Israel, Palestine, and Arab-Israeli Conflict: George W. Ball and Douglas B. Ball, *The Passionate Attachment* (1992); Abraham Ben-Zvi, *The United States and Israel* (1994); Ian J. Bickerton and Carla L. Klausner, *A Concise History of the Arab-Israeli Conflict* (1998); Peter Grose, *Israel and the Mind of America* (1983); William Roger Louis and Robert W. Stookey, eds., *The End of the Palestine Mandate* (1986); Camille Mansour, *Beyond Alliance* (1994); Donald Neff, *Fallen Pillars: U.S. Policy Towards Palestine and Israel Since 1945* (1995); Ilan Pappe, *The Israel/Palestine Question* (1999); William B. Quandt, *Peace Process* (1993); John Quigley, *Palestine and Israel* (1990); Bernard Reich, ed., *An Encyclopedia of the Arab-Israeli Conflict* (1996) (E) and *The United States and Israel* (1984); Cheryl Rubenberg, *Israel and the American National Interest* (1986); David Schoenbaum, *The United States and the State of Israel* (1993); Mohammed K. Shadid, *The United States and the Palestinians* (1981); Charles D. Smith, *Palestine and the Arab-Israeli Conflict* (1992); Steven Spiegel, *The Other Arab-Israeli Conflict* (1985); Michael W. Suleiman, ed., *U.S. Policy on Palestine* (1995); Mark Tessler, *A History of the Israeli-Palestinian Conflict* (1994); Edward Tivnan, *The Lobby* (1987). See also "Middle East."

Italy: Frank J. Coppa and William Roberts, *Modern Italian History* (1990) (B); Alexander DeConde, *Half-Bitter, Half-Sweet* (1971); H. Stuart Hughes, *The United States and Italy* (1979); James E. Miller, *The United States and Italy, 1940–1950* (1986); David F. Schmitz, *The United States and Fascist Italy, 1922–1940* (1988); Leo J. Wollemborg, *Stars, Stripes, and Italian Tricolor* (1990). See also "Europe."

Jamaica: See "Caribbean."

Japan: Sadao Asada, *Japan and the World* (1989) (B); Michael A. Barnhart, *Japan and the World Since 1868* (1995); John H. Boyle, *Modern Japan: The American Nexus* (1993); Roger Buckley, *US-Japan Alliance Diplomacy, 1945–1990* (1992); Donald E. Dolan and Robert L. Worden, eds., *Japan* (1992); John K. Emmerson and Harrison M. Holland, *The Eagle and the Rising Sun* (1988); Akira Iriye, *Pacific Estrangement: Japanese and American Expansion, 1897–1911* (1972); Wal-

ter LaFeber, *The Clash* (1997); Rita E. Neri, *U.S. and Japan Foreign Trade* (1988) (B); William R. Nester, *Power Across the Pacific* (1996); Charles E. Neu, *The Troubled Encounter* (1975); Michael Schaller, *Altered States* (1997) and *The American Occupation of Japan* (1985). See also "Asia and Pacific Islands," "War Crimes and Trials," and "World War II."

Jordan: Madiha Rashid al-Madfai, *Jordan, the United States, and the Middle East Peace Process* (1993); Helen C. Metz, ed., *Jordan* (1991). See also "Middle East."

Kazakhstan: Glenn E. Curtis, *Kazakhstan, Kyrgyzstan, Tajikistan, Turkmenistan, and Uzbekistan* (1997); Michael Mandelbaum, ed., *Central Asia and the World* (1994).

Kenya: See "Africa" and Lefebvre in "Ethiopia."

Korea and Korean War: Jongsuk Chay, *Diplomacy of Asymmetry* (1990); Bruce Cumings, *Korea's Place in the Sun* (1997) and *The Origins of the Korean War* (1981, 1990); Paul M. Edwards, *The Korean War* (1998) (B); Burton I. Kaufman, *The Korean War* (1997); Yun-Bok Lee and Wayne Patterson, eds., *Korean-American Relations, 1866–1997* (1998); Stewart Lone and Gavan McCormack, *Korea Since 1850* (1993); Donald S. Macdonald, *U.S.-Korean Relations* (1992); James I. Matray, ed., *Historical Dictionary of the Korean War* (1991) (E); Keith McFarland, *The Korean War* (1986) (B); Andrew C. Nahm, *Historical Dictionary of the Republic of Korea* (1993) (E); Don Oberdorfer, *The Two Koreas* (1997); Stanley Sandler, *The Korean War* (1995) (E); Andrea M. Savada, ed., *North Korea* (1994) and *South Korea* (1992); William Stueck, *The Korean War* (1995); Harry G. Summers, Jr., *Korean War Almanac* (1990) (C and E). See also "Asia and Pacific Islands."

Kuwait: Abdul-Reda Assiri, *Kuwaiti Foreign Policy* (1990); Jill Crystal, *Kuwait* (1992) and *Oil and Politics in the Gulf* (1995). See also "Middle East" and "Persian Gulf."

Kyrgyzstan: See "Kazakhstan."

Laos: Timothy N. Castle, *At War in the Shadow of Vietnam* (1993); Helen Cordell, *Laos* (1993) (B); Arthur J. Dommen, *Laos* (1985); Jane Hamilton-Merritt, *Tragic Mountains* (1993); Andrea M. Savada, ed., *Laos* (1995); Charles A. Stevenson, *The End of Nowhere* (1972). See also "Vietnam and Southeast Asia."

Latin America: G. Pope Atkins, *Encyclopedia of the Inter-American System* (1997) (E) and *Latin America in the International System* (1995); John A. Britton, *The United States and Latin America* (1997) (B); Peter

Calvert, *The International Politics of Latin America* (1994); David W. Dent, *U.S.–Latin American Policymaking* (1995) (B); Mark T. Gilderhus, *The Second Century* (2000); Jack W. Hopkins, ed., *Latin America and Caribbean Contemporary Record* (1983–   ) (AS); John J. Johnson, *A Hemisphere Apart* (1990); Lester D. Langley, *America and the Americas* (1989); Abraham F. Lowenthal, ed., *Exporting Democracy* (1991); Carlos Marichal, *A Century of Debt Crises in Latin America* (1988); John D. Martz, *United States Policy in Latin America* (1995); Michael C. Meyer, ed., *Supplement to a Bibliography of United States–Latin American Relations Since 1810* (1979) (B); James W. Park, *Latin American Underdevelopment* (1995); Fredrick B. Pike, *The United States and Latin America* (1992); Lars Schoultz, *Beneath the United States* (1998); David Shavit, *The United States in Latin America* (1992) (E); Joseph Smith, *Illusions of Conflict: Anglo-American Diplomacy Toward Latin America, 1865–1896* (1979); Peter H. Smith, *Talons of the Eagle* (1996); Barbara Stallings, *Banker to the Third World* (1988); Barbara A. Tenenbaum, ed., *Encyclopedia of Latin American History and Culture* (1995) (E); David F. Trask et al., *A Bibliography of United States–Latin American Relations Since 1810* (1968) (B). See also "Caribbean," "Central America," "Communications," "Monroe Doctrine," "Pan Americanism," and countries.

Latvia: See "Baltic States."

Lebanon: C. H. Bleaney, *Lebanon* (1991) (B); Thomas L. Friedman, *From Beirut to Jerusalem* (1989); Irene Gendzier, *Notes from the Minefield* (1997); Dilip Hiro, *Lebanon* (1993); Itamar Rabinovich, *The War for Lebanon, 1970–1985* (1986). See also "Middle East."

Liberia: D. Elwood Dunn, *The Foreign Policy of Liberia During the Tubman Era, 1944–1971* (1979); Katherine Harris, *The United States and Liberia* (1985); Hassan B. Sisay, *Big Powers and Small Nations* (1985); Charles M. Wilson, *Liberia* (1985). See also "Africa."

Libya: Scott L. Bills, *The Libyan Arena* (1995); Mahmoud G. El-Warfally, *Imagery and Ideology in U.S. Policy Toward Libya, 1969–1982* (1988); P. Edward Haley, *Qaddafi and the United States Since 1969* (1984); Dirk Vanderville, ed., *Qadhafi's Libya* (1995). See also "Africa" and "Middle East."

Lithuania: Saulius Sužiedelis, *Historical Dictionary of Lithuania* (1997) (E). See also "Baltic States."

Madagascar: Hilary Budt, *Madagascar* (1993) (B). See also "Africa" and "Indian Ocean."

Malaysia: James W. Gould, *The United States and Malaysia* (1969). See also "Asia and Pacific Islands."

Maldives: See "Indian Ocean."

Mauritania: Robert E. Handloff, ed., *Mauritania* (1990). See also "Africa."

Mauritius: Larry Bowman, *Mauritius* (1991). See also "Indian Ocean."

Mexico: Leslie Bethel, ed., *Mexico Since Independence* (1991); Lester D. Langley, *Mexico and the United States* (1991); David E. Lorey, ed., *United States–Mexico Border Statistics Since 1900* (1990) (S) and *The U.S.–Mexican Border in the Twentieth Century* (2000); Robert A. Pastor and Jorge G. Castañeda, *Limits to Friendship* (1988); George D. C. Philip, *Mexico* (1993) (B); W. Dirk Raat, *Mexico and the United States* (1997); Karl M. Schmitt, *Mexico and the United States* (1974); Norman E. Tutorow, ed., *The Mexican-American War* (1981) (B); Barbara G. Valk et al., *Borderline* (1988) (B); Josefina Vázquez and Lorenzo Meyer, *The United States and Mexico* (1985); David J. Weber, *The Mexican Frontier, 1821–1846* (1982); Sidney Weintraub, *A Marriage of Convenience* (1990). See also "Latin America."

Micronesia: See "Asia and Pacific Islands."

Middle East: Robert J. Allison, *The Crescent Observed: The United States and the Muslim World, 1776–1815* (1995); H. William Brands, *Into the Labyrinth* (1994); Thomas A. Bryson, *American Diplomatic Relations with the Middle East, 1784–1975* (1977) and *U.S.–Middle East Diplomatic Relations* (1979) (B); Uriel Dann, ed., *The Great Powers in the Middle East, 1919–1939* (1988); John A. DeNovo, *American Interests and Policies in the Middle East, 1900–1939* (1963); James A. Field, *America and the Mediterranean World, 1776–1882* (1969); T. G. Fraser, *The USA and the Middle East Since World War 2* (1989); Martin Gilbert, *Atlas of the Arab-Israeli Conflict* (1993) (A); Burton I. Kaufman, *The Arab Middle East and the United States* (1996); Colin Legum et al., eds., *Middle East Contemporary Survey* (1978–   ) (AS); George Lenczowski, *American Presidents and the Middle East* (1989); William R. Polk, *The Arab World Today* (1991); David Shavit, *The United States in the Middle East* (1988) (E); Sanford R. Silverburg and Bernard Reich, *U.S. Foreign Policy and the Middle East/North Africa* (1989) (B); Reeva S. Simon et al., eds., *The Encyclopedia of the Modern Middle East* (1996) (E); William Stivers, *America's Confrontation with Revolutionary Change in the Middle East, 1948–83* (1986); Alan R. Taylor, *The Superpowers and the Middle East* (1991). See also "Biological and Chemical Warfare," "Israel, Palestine, and Arab-Israeli Conflict," "Persian Gulf," and countries.

Moldova: See "Belarus."

Mongolia: Robert C. Worden and Andrea M. Savada, eds., *Mongolia* (1991).

Morocco: Leon B. Blair, *Western Window in the Arab World* (1970); Luella J. Hall, *The United States and Morocco, 1776–1956* (1961). See also "Africa" and "North Africa."

Mozambique: Mario Azevedo, *Historical Dictionary of Mozambique* (1991) (E); Maraget Hall and Tom Young, *Confronting Leviathan* (1997); Malyn Newitt, *A History of Mozambique* (1995). See also "Africa."

Myanmar: John F. Cady, *The United States and Burma* (1976); Patricia M. Herbert, *Burma* (1991) (B). See also "Vietnam and Southeast Asia."

Namibia: John J. Grotpeter, *Historical Dictionary of Namibia* (1994) (E). See also "Africa."

Nepal: Andrea M. Savada, ed., *Nepal and Bhutan* (1993).

Netherlands: Doeko Bosscher et al., eds., *American Culture in the Netherlands* (1996); Hans Loeber, ed., *Dutch-American Relations, 1945–1969* (1992); J. W. Schulte Nordholt and Robert P. Swierenga, eds., *A Bilateral Centennial: A History of Dutch-American Relations, 1783–1982* (1982); Gertrude Reichenbach-Consten and Abraham Noordergraaf, eds., *Two Hundred Years of Netherlands-American Interaction* (1985); Cornelis van Minnen, *American Diplomats in the Netherlands, 1815–50* (1993). See also "Europe."

New Zealand: See "Australia."

Nicaragua: Karl Berman, *Under the Big Stick* (1986); E. Bradford Burns, *Patriarch and Folk* (1991); Paul C. Clark, Jr., *The United States and Somoza* (1992); Peter Kornbluh, *Nicaragua* (1987); Tim L. Merrill, ed., *Nicaragua* (1994); Richard Millett, *Guardians of the Dynasty* (1977); Morris H. Morley, *Washington, Somoza, and the Sandinistas* (1994); Neil Narr, *Sandinista Nicaragua* (1990) (B); Robert Pastor, *Condemned to Repetition* (1987); Thomas W. Walker, *Nicaragua* (1991), ed., *Reagan Versus the Sandinistas* (1987), and ed., *Revolution & Counterrevolution in Nicaragua* (1991); Knut Walter, *The Regime of Anastasio Somoza* (1993); Ralph Lee Woodward, *Nicaragua* (1994) (B). See also "Central America" and "Latin America."

Nigeria: Bassey E. Ate, *Decolonization and Dependence* (1987); Helen C. Metz, ed., *Nigeria* (1992); Robert B. Shepard, *Nigeria, Africa, and the United States* (1991); Joseph E. Thompson, *American Policy and African Famine* (1990). See also "Africa."

North Africa: Charles F. Gallagher, *The United States and North Africa* (1963); Richard S. Parker, *North Africa* (1984). See also "Africa."

North Korea: See "Korea and Korean War."

Norway: Mats Berdal, *The United States, Norway, and the Cold War* (1997); Wayne S. Cole, *Norway and the United States* (1989); Ronald C. Popperwell, *Norway* (1972); Sigmund Skard, *The United States in Norwegian History* (1976); Rolf Tamnes, *The United States and the Cold War in the High North* (1991). See also "Europe" and "Scandinavia."

Oceania: See "Asia and Pacific Islands."

Oman: Joseph A. Kechichian, *Oman and the World* (1995). See also "Middle East" and "Persian Gulf."

Pacific Islands: See "Asia and Pacific Islands."

Pacific Rim: See "Asia and Pacific Islands."

Pakistan: Peter R. Blood, ed., *Pakistan* (1995); Iftikhar Malik, *U.S.–South Asian Relations, 1940–1947* (1991); Leo E. Rose and Noor A. Husain, eds., *U.S.–Pakistan Relations* (1985); Shirin Tahir-kheli, *The United States and Pakistan* (1982); David D. Taylor, *Pakistan* (1990) (B); M. S. Venkataramani, *The American Role in Pakistan, 1947–1958* (1982). See also Wolpert in "Afghanistan" and Barnds and McMahon in "India."

Palestine: See "Israel, Palestine, and Arab-Israeli Conflict."

Panama (and Panama Canal): Michael L. Conniff, *Panama and the United States* (1992); David N. Farnsworth and James W. McKenney, *U.S.-Panama Relations, 1903–1978* (1983); J. Michael Hogan, *The Panama Canal in American Politics* (1986); Walter LaFeber, *The Panama Canal* (1990); Thomas M. Leonard, *Panama, the Canal, and the United States* (1993) (B); John Major, *Prize Possession* (1993); David McCullough, *The Path Between the Seas* (1977). See also "Latin America."

Paraguay: Anibal Miranda, *United States–Paraguay Relations* (1990); Riordan Roett and Richard S. Sacks, *Paraguay* (1991). See also "Latin America" and Whitaker in "Argentina."

Persian Gulf: Bruce R. Kuniholm, *The Persian Gulf and United States Policy* (1984) (B); Charles A. Kupchan, *The Persian Gulf and the West* (1987); Helen C. Metz, ed., *Persian Gulf States* (1993); Michael

A. Palmer, *Guardians of the Gulf* (1992). See also "Middle East" and Cottam in "Iran."

Peru: James C. Carey, *Peru and the United States, 1900–1962* (1964); Lawrence A. Clayton, *Peru and the United States* (1999); Rex A. Hudson, ed., *Peru* (1993); Fredrick B. Pike, *The United States and the Andean Republics* (1977); Ronald B. St. John, *The Foreign Policy of Peru* (1992). See also "Latin America."

Philippines: Teodoro A. Agoncillo, *A Short History of the Philippines* (1969); David H. Bain, *Sitting in Darkness* (1984); Raymond Bonner, *Waltzing with a Dictator* (1987); H. W. Brands, *Bound to Empire* (1992); Nick Cullather, *Illusions of Influence* (1994); Ronald E. Dolan, ed., *Philippines* (1993); Stanley Karnow, *In Our Image* (1989); Glenn A. May, *Battle for Batangas* (1991); Jim Richardson, *Philippines* (1989) (B); Peter W. Stanley, *A Nation in the Making* (1974). See also "Asia and Pacific Islands" and "Spanish-American-Cuban-Filipino War."

Poland: Glenn E. Curtis, ed., *Poland* (1994); Richard Lukacs, *Bitter Legacy* (1982); Piotr Wandycz, *The United States and Poland* (1980). See also "Eastern Europe" and "Europe."

Portugal: Scott B. MacDonald, *European Destiny, Atlantic Transformations* (1993); Kenneth Maxwell and Michael H. Haltzel, eds., *Portugal* (1990); Eric Solsten, ed., *Portugal* (1994). See also "Europe."

Puerto Rico: Raymond Carr, *Puerto Rico* (1984); Arturo Morales Carrión, *Puerto Rico* (1984); Elena E. Cevallos, *Puerto Rico* (1985) (B); Truman B. Clark, *Puerto Rico and the United States, 1917–1933* (1975); Ronald Fernandez, *The Disenchanted Island* (1996); A. W. Maldonado, *Teodora Moscoso and Puerto Rico's Operation Bootstrap* (1997); José Trías Monge, *Puerto Rico* (1997). See also "Caribbean."

Qatar: See "Persian Gulf."

Romania: Ronald D. Bachman, ed., *Romania* (1990); Joseph F. Harrington and Bruce J. Courtney, *Tweaking the Nose of the Russians* (1991). See also "Eastern Europe."

Russia and the Soviet Union: N. N. Bolkhovitinov and J. Dane Hartgrove, *Russia and the United States* (1987) (B); Peter G. Boyle, *American-Soviet Relations* (1993); Archie Brown et. al., eds, *The Cambridge Encyclopedia of Russia and the Soviet Union* (1994) (E); Glenn E. Curtis, ed., *Russia* (1998); Philip J. Funigiello, *American-Soviet Trade in the Cold War* (1988); John Lewis Gaddis, *Russia, the Soviet Union, and the United States* (1990); Raymond L. Garthoff, *Détente and Confrontation* (1985) and *The Great Transition* (1994); Howard Kushner, *Conflict on the Northwest Coast: American-Russian Rivalry in the Pacific*

Northwest, 1790–1867 (1975); Walter LaFeber, *America, Russia, and the Cold War* (1997); James K. Libbey, *American-Russian Economic Relations* (1989) (B); J. D. Parks, *Culture, Conflict, and Coexistence: American-Soviet Cultural Relations, 1917–1958* (1983); Norman E. Saul, *Concord and Conflict: The United States and Russia, 1867–1914* (1996) and *The United States and Russia, 1763–1867* (1991); David Shavit, *United States Relations with Russia and the Soviet Union* (1993) (E). See also "Baltic States," "Cold War," "Eastern Europe," and "Europe."

Rwanda: Learthen Dorsey, *Historical Dictionary of Rwanda* (1994) (E). See also "Africa."

Samoa (American): J. A. C. Gray, *Amerika Samoa* (1960); Paul Kennedy, *The Samoan Tangle* (1974); George H. Ryden, *The Foreign Policy of the United States in Relation to Samoa* (1933). See also "Asia and Pacific Islands."

Saudi Arabia: Irvine H. Anderson, *Aramco, the United States, and Saudi Arabia* (1981); Lee Grayson, *Saudi-American Relations* (1982); David E. Long, *The United States and Saudi Arabia* (1989); Helen C. Metz, ed., *Saudia Arabia* (1993); Aaron D. Miller, *Search for Security: Saudi Arabian Oil and American Foreign Policy, 1939–1949* (1980); Nadav Safran, *Saudi Arabia* (1986). See also "Middle East."

Scandinavia: Jussi M. Hanhimäki, *Scandinavia and the United States* (1997); Geir Lundestad, *America, Scandinavia, and the Cold War* (1980); Franklin D. Scott, *Scandinavia* (1975) and *The United States and Scandinavia* (1950). See also "Europe" and countries.

Senegal: R. M. Dilley and J. S. Eades, *Senegal* (1994) (B). See also "Africa."

Serbia: See "Yugoslavia."

Seychelles: See "Indian Ocean."

Singapore: Barbara L. LePoer, ed., *Singapore* (1991).

Slovenia: See "Yugoslavia."

Somalia: John L. Hirsch and Whert B. Oakley, *Somalia and Operation Restore Hope* (1995); Helen C. Metz, ed., *Somalia* (1993). See also "Africa" and Lefebvre in "Ethiopia."

South Africa: James Barber and John Barratt, *South Africa's Foreign Policy* (1990); Thomas Borstelmann, *Apartheid's Reluctant Uncle* (1993); Rita M. Byrnes, ed., *South Africa* (1997); Christopher Coker, *The United States and South Africa, 1968–1985* (1986); Jeffrey V.

Davis, *South Africa* (1994) (B); Terrel D. Hale, *United States Sanctions and South Africa* (1993) (B); Richard W. Hull, *American Enterprise in South Africa* (1990); C. T. Keto, *American–South African Relations, 1784-1980* (1985) (B); Y. G. M. Lulat, *U.S. Relations with South Africa* (1991) (B); Robert K. Massie, *Loosing the Bonds* (1997); William Minter, *King Soloman's Mines Revisited* (1986); Thomas J. Noer, *Briton, Boer, and Yankee* (1978) and *Cold War and Black Liberation* (1985). See also "Africa."

Southeast Asia: See "Vietnam and Southeast Asia."

Spain: James W. Cortada, *Two Nations over Time* (1978), and ed., *Spain in the Twentieth-Century World* (1980); Robert W. Kern, *Historical Dictionary of Modern Spain* (1990) (E); Boris N. Liedtke, *Embracing a Dictatorship* (1998); Eric Solsten and Sandra W. Meditz, eds., *Spain* (1990). See also "Europe" and "Spanish-American-Cuban-Filipino War."

Sri Lanka: Russell R. Ross and Andrea M. Savada, eds., *Sri Lanka* (1990).

Sudan: Carolyn Fkuehr-Lobban et al., *Historical Dictionary of Sudan* (1992) (E); Helen C. Metz, ed., *Sudan* (1992); Peter Woodward, *Sudan* (1989). See also "Africa."

Sweden: Sture Kindmark and Tore Tallroth, eds., *Swedes Looking West* (1983). See also "Europe" and "Scandinavia."

Switzerland: Heinze K. Meier, *Friendship Under Stress: U.S.-Swiss Relations, 1900–1950* (1970) and *The United States and Switzerland in the Nineteenth Century* (1963). See also "Europe."

Syria: David W. Lesch, *Syria and the United States* (1992); Moshe Ma'oz, *Syria and Israel* (1995); Andrew Rathwell, *Secret War in the Middle East* (1995); Bonnie Saunders, *The United States and Arab Nationalism* (1996); Abdul Latif Tibawi, *American Interests in Syria, 1800–1901* (1965). See also "Middle East."

Taiwan (Formosa): See "China (and Taiwan)."

Tajikistan: See "Kazakhstan."

Tanzania: See "Africa."

Thailand: Richard Aldrich, *The Key to the South* (1993); Barbara L. LePoer, ed., *Thailand* (1989); Robert J. Muscat, *Thailand and the United States* (1990). See also "Vietnam and Southeast Asia."

Trieste: Bogdan C. Novak, *Trieste, 1941–1954* (1970); Roberto Rabel, *Between East and West* (1988). See also "Italy."

Trinidad and Tobago: See "Caribbean."

Tunisia: See "North Africa."

Turkey: David J. Alvarez, *Bureaucracy and Cold War Ideology* (1980); George S. Harris, *Troubled Alliance* (1972); Harry H. Howard, *Turkey, the Straits, and U.S. Policy* (1974); Helen C. Metz, ed., *Turkey* (1996). See also "Europe" and Couloumbis and Stearns in "Greece."

Turkmenistan: See "Kazakhstan."

Uganda: Rita M. Byrnes, ed., *Uganda* (1992). See also "Africa."

Ukraine: Lubomyr A. Hajda, ed., *Ukraine in the World* (1998); Steven Woehrel, *Ukraine* (1994). See also "Russia and the Soviet Union."

United Arab Emirates: See "Middle East" and "Persian Gulf."

Uzbekistan: See "Kazakhstan."

Uruguay: Kitty L. Drummond, *Relations Between Uruguay and the United States* (1936); Rex A. Hudson and Sandra W. Meditz, eds., *Uruguay* (1992); Martin Weinstein, *Uruguay* (1987). See "Latin America" and Whitaker in "Argentina."

Venezuela: Judith Ewell, *Venezuela and the United States* (1996); Richard A. Haggerty, ed., *Venezuela* (1993); Sheldon B. Liss, *Diplomacy and Independence* (1978); Stephen G. Rabe, *The Road to OPEC* (1982). See also "Latin America" and "Oil."

Vietnam and Southeast Asia: David L. Anderson, ed., *Shadow on the White House* (1993); John S. Bowman, ed., *The Vietnam War* (1986) (C); Lester H. Brune and Richard Dean Burns, eds., *America and the Indochina Wars, 1945–1990* (1991) (B); William J. Duiker, *Historical Dictionary of Vietnam* (1989) (E); Frances Fitzgerald, *Fire in the Lake* (1972); Lloyd C. Gardner, *Approaching Vietnam* (1988); George C. Herring, *America's Longest War* (1996); Gary R. Hess, *Vietnam and the United States* (1998); George Kahin, *Intervention* (1986); Stanley Karnow, *Vietnam* (1991); Gabriel Kolko, *Anatomy of a War* (1985); Stanley I. Kutler, ed., *Encyclopedia of the Vietnam War* (1995) (E); David G. Marr, *Vietnam* (1992) (B); Robert J. McMahon, *The Limits of Empire* (1999); James S. Olson, *Dictionary of the Vietnam War* (1988) (E) and *The Vietnam War* (1993) (B); Andrew J. Rotter, *The Path to Vietnam* (1987); Robert D. Schulzinger, *A Time for War* (1997); Anthony Short, *The Origins of the Vietnam War* (1989); Harry

G. Summers, Jr., *Vietnam War Almanac* (1985) (C); Marilyn Young, *The Vietnam Wars* (1991). See also "Asia and Pacific Islands," "Military, U.S. Army, and Wars," and "Peace Movements."

Virgin Islands and West Indies: William W. Boyer, *America's Virgin Islands* (1983); Cary Fraser, *Ambivalent Anti-Colonialism: The United States and the Genesis of West Indian Independence, 1940–1964* (1993); Verna P. Moll, *Virgin Islands* (1991) (B). See also "Caribbean."

Yemen: Ahmed Nomen Al-Madhaqi, *Yemen and the USA* (1994); Fred Halliday, *Revolution and Foreign Policy* (1989). See also "Middle East."

Yugoslavia: Phylis Auty, *Yugoslavia* (1965); Leonard Cohen, *Broken Bonds* (1993); John R. Lampe et al., *Yugoslav-American Relations Since World War II* (1991); Lorraine M. Lees, *Keeping Tito Afloat* (1997); Susan Woodward, *Balkan Tragedy* (1995). See also "Eastern Europe."

Zambia: See "Africa."

Zimbabwe: J. D. Omer-Cooper, *A History of Southern Africa* (1994); R. Kent Rasmussen, *Historical Dictionary of Zimbabwe* (1990) (E). See also "Africa."

Overviews of Subjects, Including Atlases (A), Annual Surveys (AS), Bibliographies (B), Biographical Aids (BA), Chronologies (C), Encyclopedias (E), and Statistics (S)

African Americans: Gerald Horne, *Black and Red* (1986); Michael L. Krenn, *Black Diplomacy* (1998); Brenda Gayle Plummer, *Rising Wind* (1996); "Symposium: African Americans and U.S. Foreign Relations," *Diplomatic History*, XX (Fall 1996); Penny von Eschen, *Race Against Empire* (1997). See also "Race and Racism" and Skinner in "Africa."

AIDS Pandemic: J. Mann, Daniel Tarantola, and T. Netter, eds., *AIDS in the World* (1992, 1996); Matthew Smallman-Raynor et al., *Atlas of AIDS* (1992). See also "Health Organizations."

Air Force and Air Power: Charles D. Bright, ed., *Historical Dictionary of the U.S. Air Force* (1992) (E); Alan P. Dobson, *Peaceful Air Warfare* (1991); Richard P. Hallion, *The Literature of Aeronautics, Astronautics, and Air Power* (1984) (B); John B. Rae, *Climb to Greatness* (1968); Michael S. Sherry, *The Rise of American Air Power* (1987); Jeffrey S. Underwood, *The Wings of Democracy* (1991); Bruce W. Wat-

son and Susan W. Watson, *The United States Air Force* (1992) (E). See also "Military, U.S. Army, and Wars" and specific wars.

Alliance for Progress: Jerome Levinson and Juan de Onís, *The Alliance That Lost Its Way* (1970); L. Ronald Scheman, ed., *The Alliance for Progress* (1988). See also "Latin America."

American Revolution: Richard Blanco, ed., *The American Revolution* (1993) (E); Mark M. Boatner III, *Encyclopedia of the American Revolution* (1974) (E); Lester J. Cappon, ed., *Atlas of Early American History: The Revolutionary Era, 1760–1790* (1976) (A); John M. Faragher, ed., *The Encyclopedia of Colonial and Revolutionary America* (1990) (E); Jack P. Greene and J. R. Pole, eds., *The Blackwell Encyclopedia of the American Revolution* (1991) (E); John W. Raimo, ed., *Biographical Directory of American Colonial and Revolutionary Governors, 1607–1789* (1980) (BA).

Anti-Americanism: "Anti-Americanism," *The Annals*, May 1988; Dan Diner, *German Anti-Americanism* (1995); Rob Kroes and Maarten van Rossem, eds., *Anti-Americanism in Europe* (1986); Denis Lacorne et al., eds., *The Rise and Fall of Anti-Americanism* (1990); Richard Pells, *Not Like Us* (1997); Alvin Z. Rubenstein and Donald E. Smith, eds., *Anti-Americanism in the Third World* (1985); David Strauss, *Menace in the West: The Rise of French Anti-Americanism in Modern Times* (1978).

Anticommunism and McCarthyism: Jeff Broadwater, *Eisenhower and the Anti-Communist Crusades* (1992); Peter H. Buckingham, *America Sees Red* (1987) (B); Richard M. Fried, *Nightmare in Red* (1990); Robert Griffith, *The Politics of Fear* (1987); John E. Haynes, *Communism and Anti-Communism in the United States* (1987) (B); Joel Kovel, *Red Hunting in the Promised Land* (1994); Stanley I. Kutler, *The American Inquisition* (1982); Richard G. Powers, *Not Without Honor* (1995); Stephen J. Whitfield, *The Culture of the Cold War* (1991). See also "Cold War."

ANZUS Pact: David W. McIntyre, *Background to the Anzus Pact* (1995). See also "Australia."

Arab-Israeli Conflict: See "Israel, Palestine, and Arab-Israeli Conflict" and "Middle East."

Arms Control: See "Disarmament and Arms Control."

Arms Sales and Trade: Michael Broszka and Thomas Ohlson, *Arms Transfers to the Third World* (1987); Michael T. Klare, *American Arms Supermarket* (1984); Edward J. Laurence, *The International Arms*

Trade (1992); Andrew J. Pierre, *The Global Politics of Arms Sales* (1982). See also "Military, U.S. Army, and Wars."

Assassination: Carl Sifakis, *Encyclopedia of Assassinations* (1991) (E).

Atlantic Charter: Douglas Brinkley and David Facey-Crowther, eds., *The Atlantic Charter* (1994); Theodore A. Wilson, *The First Summit* (1991). See also "World War II."

Biological and Chemical Warfare: G. M. Burck and Charles C. Flowerree, *International Handbook on Chemical Weapons Proliferation* (1991) (E); Anthony H. Cordesman, *Weapons of Mass Destruction in the Middle East* (1991); Stephen Endicott and Edward Hagerman, *The United States and Biological Warfare* (1999); John Norris and Will Fowler, *NBC: Nuclear, Biological, and Chemical Warfare on the Modern Battlefield* (1998) (E); Amy E. Simpson, ed., *The Chemical Weapons Convention Handbook* (1993); Victor A. Utgoff, *The Challenge of Chemical Weapons* (1991).

Bricker Amendment: Duane Tananbaum, *The Bricker Amendment Controversy* (1988). See also "Congress (House and Senate)."

Bureaucracy: Graham Allison, *Essence of Decision* (1971); I. M. Destler, *Presidents, Bureaucrats, and Foreign Policy* (1974); Louis Galambos, ed., *The New American State* (1987); Morton H. Halperin, *Bureaucratic Politics and Foreign Policy* (1974); Irving L. Janis, *Groupthink* (1983); James Q. Wilson, *Bureaucracy* (1989). See also "President (General)."

Business: See "Economic Relations and Business."

Central Intelligence Agency (CIA): See "Intelligence, CIA, and Covert Action."

Chemical Warfare: See "Biological and Chemical Warfare."

Civil War (American): Mark M. Boatner III, *The Civil War Dictionary* (1988) (E); D. P. Crook, *The North, the South, and the Powers* (1974); Richard N. Current, ed., *Encyclopedia of the Confederacy* (1993) (E); John T. Hubbell and James W. Geary, eds., *Biographical Dictionary of the Union* (1995) (BA); Howard Jones, *Union in Peril* (1992); David C. Roller and Robert W. Twyman, eds., *The Encyclopedia of Southern History* (1979) (E); Jon L. Wakelyn, ed., *Biographical Dictionary of the Confederacy* (1977) (BA); Steven E. Woodworth, ed., *The American Civil War* (1996) (B).

Cold War: Stephen Ambrose and David Brinkley, *Rise to Globalism* (1997); Thomas S. Arms, *Encyclopedia of the Cold War* (1994) (E);

Joseph L. Black, *Origins, Evolution, and Nature of the Cold War* (1986) (B); H. W. Brands, *The Devil We Knew* (1993); John Lewis Gaddis, *We Now Know All* (1997); Michael Kort, *The Columbia Guide to the Cold War* (1998) (E); Walter LaFeber, *America, Russia, and the Cold War* (1997); Thomas J. McCormick, *America's Half-Century* (1995); Thomas G. Paterson, *Meeting the Communist Threat* (1988) and *On Every Front* (1992). See also "Disarmament and Arms Control," "Nuclear Arms," "Russia and the Soviet Union," and "Threat Perception and Calculation."

Communications: James L. Baughman, *The Republic of Mass Culture* (1992); David H. Culbert, *News for Everyman* (1976) (radio); Howard H. Frederick, *Global Communications and International Relations* (1992), Julian Hale, *Radio Power* (1975); Daniel R. Headrick, *The Invisible Weapon: Telecommunications and International Politics, 1851–1945* (1991); James G. Savage, *The Politics of International Telecommunications Regulation* (1989); James Schwoch, *The American Radio Industry and Its Latin American Activities* (1990); Anthony Smith, *Geopolitics of Information* (1980); Philip M. Taylor, *Global Communications* (1997). See also "Cultural Relations."

Congress (House and Senate): Betty Austin, *J. William Fulbright* (1995) (B); Stephen G. Christianson, *Facts About the Congress* (1996); Congressional Quarterly, *Biographical Directory of the American Congress* (1997) (BA) and *Congress and the Nation, 1945–1984* (1965–1985) (E); Robert U. Goehlert and John R. Sayre, *The United States Congress* (1981) (B); Barbara Hinckley, *Less Than Meets the Eye* (1994); James M. Lindsey, *Congress and the Politics of U.S. Foreign Policy* (1994); James A. Robinson, *Congress and Foreign Policy-Making* (1967); John Rourke, *Congress and the Presidency in U.S. Foreign Policymaking* (1983); Goran Rystad, ed., *Congress and American Foreign Policy* (1982); John Spanier and Joseph Nogee, eds., *Congress, the Presidency, and Foreign Policy* (1980); U.S. Congress, *Biographical Directory of the United States Congress, 1774–1989* (1989) (BA); Gerald F. Warburg, *Conflict and Consensus* (1989); Stephen R. Weissman, *A Culture of Deference* (1995). See also "Constitution and Constitutional Interpretation," "President (General)," and "War Powers."

Conservation: See "Environment."

Constitution and Constitutional Interpretation: David G. Adler and Larry N. George, eds., *The Constitution and American Foreign Policy* (1996); Henry B. Cox, *War, Foreign Affairs, and Constitutional Power, 1829–1901* (1984); Louis Fischer, *Constitutional Conflicts Between the President and Congress* (1985); Thomas M. Franck and Michael J. Glennon, *Foreign Relations and National Security Law* (1993); Louis Henkin, *Constitutionalism, Democracy, and Foreign Affairs* (1990) and *Foreign Affairs and the Constitution* (1972); Harold Honggju Koh,

The National Security Constitution (1990); Leonard W. Levy et al., eds., *Encyclopedia of the American Constitution* (1986) (E); Gordon Silberstein, *Imbalance of Powers* (1997); Joan E. Smith, *The Constitution and American Foreign Policy* (1989); Abraham Sofaer, *War, Foreign Affairs, and Constitutional Power* (1976). See also "War Powers."

Containment: Terry L. Deibel and John Lewis Gaddis, eds., *Containment* (1986); John Lewis Gaddis, *Strategies of Containment* (1982); Charles Gati, ed., *Caging the Bear* (1974); Deborah Larson, *Origins of Containment* (1985). See also "Cold War."

Counterinsurgency: Benjamin R. Beede, *Intervention and Counterinsurgency* (1984) (B); Douglas S. Blaufarb, *The Counterinsurgency Era* (1977); Larry E. Cable, *Conflict of Myths* (1986); Michael T. Klare and Peter Kornbluh, eds., *Low-Intensity Warfare* (1988); Michael McClintock, *Instruments of Statecraft* (1992); D. Michael Shafer, *Deadly Paradigms* (1988). See also "Intelligence, CIA, and Covert Action."

Credibility: Robert J. McMahon, "Credibility and World Power," *Diplomatic History*, XV (Fall 1991), 455–471; Jonathan Mercer, *Reputation and International Politics* (1996).

Cultural Relations: Paul Braisted, ed., *Cultural Affairs and Foreign Relations* (1968); Jongsuk Chay, ed., *Culture and International Relations* (1990); Morrell Heald and Lawrence S. Kaplan, *Culture and Diplomacy* (1977); Akira Iriye, *Cultural Internationalism and World Order* (1997); Robert D. Johnson, ed., *On Cultural Ground* (1994); Gilbert M. Joseph el al., eds., *Close Encounters of Empire* (1998); Amy Kaplan and Donald E. Pease, eds., *Cultures of United States Imperialism* (1993); Frank Ninkovich, *The Diplomacy of Ideas* (1981); Emily Rosenberg, *Spreading the American Dream* (1982); Anthony Smith, *The Geopolitics of Information* (1980). See also "Communications," "Films, Television, and Cultural Expansion," "Philanthropy and Foundations," and "Propaganda and Public Diplomacy."

Decline Thesis: David P. Calleo, *Beyond American Hegemony* (1987); Paul Kennedy, *The Rise and Fall of the Great Powers* (1987); Henry Nau, *The Myth of America's Decline* (1990); Joseph P. Nye, Jr., *Bound to Lead* (1990).

Decolonization: Franz Ansprenger, *The Dissolution of Colonial Empires* (1989); Prosser Gifford and William Roger Louis, eds., *Decolonization and African Independence* (1988); D. A. Low, *Eclipse of Empire* (1991); Brian Urquhart, *Decolonization and World Peace* (1989).

Defense: See "Military, U.S. Army, and Wars," "Nuclear Arms," and particular wars.

Department of State, Foreign Service, and Diplomatic Practice: W. Wendell Blancke, *The Foreign Service of the United States* (1969); Robert U. Goehlert and Elizabeth Hoffmeister, *The Department of State and American Diplomacy* (1986) (B); Warren F. Ilchman, *Professional Diplomacy in the United States, 1779–1939* (1961); Charles S. Kennedy, *The American Consul* (1990); Henry E. Mattox, *The Twilight of Amateur Diplomacy* (1989); Robert H. Miller et al., *Inside an Embassy* (1992); Cathal Nolan, ed. *Notable U.S. Ambassadors Since 1775* (1998); Elmer Plischke, *United States Diplomats and Their Mission* (1979); Barry Rubin, *Secrets of State* (1985); Robert D. Schulzinger, *The Making of the Diplomatic Mind* (1975); Martin Weil, *A Pretty Good Club* (1978); Richard H. Werking, *The Master Architects* (1977). See also "President (General)."

Dependency: Fernando Henrique Cardoso and Enzo Faletto, *Dependency and Development in Latin America* (1979); Andre Gunder Frank, *Capitalism and Underdevelopment in Latin America* (1967); Vincent A. Mahler, *Dependency Approaches to International Political Economy* (1980); Robert A. Packenham, *The Dependency Movement* (1992). See also "World-System Analysis."

Deterrence: Alexander L. George and Richard Smoke, *Deterrence in American Foreign Policy* (1974); Ted Hopf, *Peripheral Visions* (1994); Robert Jervis et al., *Psychology and Deterrence* (1985). Also see "Cold War" and "Nuclear Arms."

Dictatorships: H. E. Chehabi and Juan J. Linz, *Sultanistic Regimes* (1998); David F. Schmitz, *Thank God They're on Our Side* (1999).

Diplomatic Immunity: Linda S. Frey and Marsha L. Frey, *The History of Diplomatic Immunity* (1999).

Disarmament and Arms Control: Sheikh Rustum Aki, *The Peace and Nuclear War Dictionary* (1989) (E); Stephen E. Atkins, *Arms Control and Disarmament* (1989) (B); Richard Dean Burns, ed., *Encyclopedia of Arms Control and Disarmament* (1993) (E); Jeffrey M. Elliot and Robert Reginald, *The Arms Control, Disarmament, and Military Security Dictionary* (1989) (E); Milton S. Katz, *Ban the Bomb* (1986); Stockholm International Peace Research Institute, *SIPRI Yearbook: International Armaments and Disarmament* (1969–   ) (AS and S); United Nations, *Disarmament Yearbook* (1976–   ) (AS); Lawrence S. Wittner, *One World or None* (1993). See also "Cold War," "Nuclear Arms," and "Peace Movements."

Dollar Diplomacy: Emily S. Rosenberg, *Dollar Diplomacy* (1999). See also "Economic Relations and Business."

Domino Theory: Frank Ninkovich, *Modernity and Power* (1994).

Drug Trafficking: Bruce M. Bagley, ed., *Drug Traffiking Research in the Americas* (1997) (B); Donald J. Mabry, ed., *The Latin American Narcotics Trade and U.S. National Security* (1989); Scott B. MacDonald and Bruce Zagaris, eds., *International Handbook on Drug Control* (1992) (E); Arnold H. Taylor, *American Diplomacy and the Narcotics Traffic, 1900–1931* (1969); William O. Walker III, *Drug Control in the Americas* (1981), ed., *Drugs in the Western Hemisphere* (1996), and *Opium and Foreign Policy* (1991).

Economic Relations and Business: William H. Becker and Samuel F. Wells, eds., *Economics and World Power* (1984); David P. Calleo, *The Imperious Economy* (1982); Alfred E. Eckes, Jr., *Opening America's Market* (1995); Michael J. Freeman, *Atlas of World Economy* (1991) (A); Carolyn Gibson, *The McGraw-Hill Dictionary of International Trade* (1994) (E); Judith Goldstein, *Ideas, Interests, and American Trade Policy* (1993); John N. Ingham, *Biographical Dictionary of American Business Leaders* (1983) (BA); John N. Ingham and Lyness B. Feldman, *Contemporary American Business Leaders* (1990) (BA); Edward S. Kaplan and Thomas W. Ryley, *Prelude to Trade Wars: American Trade Policy, 1890–1922* (1994); Diane Kunz, *Butter and Guns* (1997); Thelma Liesner, *One Hundred Years of Economic Statistics* (1989) (S); Wahib Nasrallah, *United States Corporation Histories* (1991) (B); Timothy O'Donnell et al., eds., *World Economic Data* (1991) (S); James S. Olsen, *Dictionary of American Economic History* (1992) (E); Richard Robinson, *United States Business History* (1990) (E); Joan E. Spero and Jeffrey A. Hart, *The Politics of International Economic Relations* (1997); United Nations, *International Trade Statistics Yearbook* (1985–) (AS and S), *World Economic Survey* (1955–) (AS and S), and *Yearbook of International Trade Statistics* (1950–1982) (AS and S); Herman Van Der Wee, *The Search for Prosperity: The World Economy, 1945–1977* (1977); Malcolm Warner, ed., *International Encyclopedia of Business and Management* (1996) (E); Mira Wilkins, *The Emergence of Multinational Enterprise* (1970) and *The Maturing of Multinational Enterprise* (1975); Thomas W. Zeiler, *Free Trade, Free World: The Advent of GATT* (1999). See also "Dollar Diplomacy," "Economic Sanctions and Export Controls," "Export-Import Bank," "Minerals," "North American Free Trade Agreement (NAFTA)," "Tariffs and Protectionism," and Funigiello in "Russia and the Soviet Union."

Economic Sanctions and Export Controls: Margaret P. Doxey, *Economic Sanctions and International Enforcement* (1980); Gary C. Hufbauer and Jeffrey J. Schott, *Economic Sanctions Reconsidered* (1990); William J. Long, *U.S. Export Control Policy* (1989); Donald Losman, *International Economic Sanctions* (1979); Homer E. Moyer, Jr., and Linda L. Mabry, *Export Controls as Instruments of Foreign Policy* (1988); Sidney Weintrub, ed., *Economic Coercion and U.S. Foreign Policy* (1982); Thomas G. Weiss, *Political Gain and Civilian Pain* (1998). See also "Economic Relations and Business" and "Tariffs and Protectionism."

Environment: Robert Broadman, *International Organization and the Conservation of Nature* (1981); Lester R. Brown et al., *State of the World* (1984–) (AS); Lynton K. Caldwell, *International Environmental Policy* (1990); André R. Cooper, Sr., ed., *Cooper's Comprehensive Environmental Desk Reference* (1996) (E); Kurkpatrick Dorsey, *The Dawn of Conservation Diplomacy* (1999); Fridtjof Nansen Institute (Norway), *Green Globe Yearbook* (1992–) (AS); John McCormick, *The Global Environment* (1995) and *Reclaiming Paradise: The Global Environmental Movement* (1989); Organisation for Economic Co-operation and Development, *The State of the Environment* (1991) (E and S); Robert Paehlke, ed., *Conservation and Environmentalism* (1995) (E); Kirkpatrick Sale, *The Green Revolution* (1993); World Resources Institute, *Environmental Almanac* (1992) (E); World Resources Institute (or International Institute for Environment and Development), *World Resources* (1976–). See also "Law of the Sea."

Ethics: Gerald Elfstrom, *Ethics for a Shrinking World* (1990); J. E. Hare and Carey B. Joynt, *Ethics and International Affairs* (1982); Dorothy V. Jones, *Code of Peace* (1991); Kenneth W. Thompson, ed., *Ethics and International Relations* (1985) and *Moral Dimensions of American Foreign Policy* (1984).

Ethnic Conflict: David Callahan, *Unwinnable Wars* (1997); Human Rights Watch, *Slaughter Among Neighbors* (1995); David A. Lake and Donald Rothchild, eds., *The International Spread of Ethnic Conflict* (1998). See also countries.

Ethnic Groups and Immigration: Mohammed E. Ahrari, ed., *Ethnic Groups and U.S. Foreign Policy* (1987); Gerald Chaliand and Jean-Pierre Rageau, *The Penguin Atlas of Diasporas* (1995) (A); Francesco Cordasco, ed., *Dictionary of American Immigration History* (1990) (E); Alexander DeConde, *Ethnicity, Race, and American Foreign Policy* (1992); Robert A. Divine, *American Immigration Policy, 1924–1952* (1963); Louis L. Gerson, *The Hyphenate in Recent American Politics and Diplomacy* (1964); David M. Reimers, *Still the Golden Door: The Third World Comes to America* (1992); Abdul Aziz Said, ed., *Ethnicity and U.S. Foreign Policy* (1977); Stephen Thernstrom, ed., *Harvard Encyclopedia of American Ethnic Groups* (1980) (E); Robert W. Tucker et al., eds., *Immigration and U.S. Foreign Policy* (1990). See also "Refugees."

Exceptionalism: David K. Adams and Cornelis A. van Minnen, eds., *Reflections on American Exceptionalism* (1994). See also "Ideology."

Executive Agreements: Lawrence Margolis, *Executive Agreements and Presidential Power in Foreign Policy* (1986); Wallace M. McClure, *International Executive Agreements* (1941). See also "President (General)."

Export-Import Bank: Frederick C. Adams, *Economic Diplomacy* (1976); Richard E. Feinberg, *Subsidizing Success* (1982); Rita M. Rodriquez, ed., *The Export-Import Bank at Fifty* (1987). See also "Economic Relations and Business."

Extraterritoriality: Wesley R. Fishel, *The End of Extraterritoriality* (1952); Dietr Lange and Gary Born, eds., *The Extraterritorial Application of National Laws* (1987). See also "International Law and Hague Conferences."

Films, Television, and Cultural Expansion: Clayton R. Koppes and Gregory D. Black, *Hollywood Goes to War* (1987); Thomas Doherty, *Projections of War* (1999); James F. Larson, *Global Television and Foreign Policy* (1988); Thomas J. Saunders, *Hollywood in Berlin* (1994); Kristin Thompson, *Exporting Entertainment* (1985). See also "Communications" and "Cultural Relations."

Food Diplomacy and Relief: Nicole Ball, ed., *World Hunger* (1981) (B); Raymond F. Hopkins and Donald J. Puchala, *Global Food Interdependence* (1980); Don Paarlberg, *Toward a Well-Fed World* (1988); Vernon W. Ruttan, ed., *Why Food Aid?* (1993); Hans W. Sinder et al., *Food Aid* (1987); Ross B. Talbott, *The Four World Food Agencies in Rome* (1990). See also "Foreign Aid" and "Humanitarian Relief and Intervention."

Foreign Aid: David Baldwin, *Economic Development and American Foreign Policy, 1943–1962* (1966); Herbert Feis, *Foreign Aid and Foreign Policy* (1964); David H. Lumsdaine, *Moral Vision in International Politics: The Foreign Aid Regime, 1949–1989* (1993); Robert A. Packenham, *Liberal America and the Third World* (1973); Roger Riddell, *Foreign Aid Reconsidered* (1987); Vernon W. Ruttan, *United States Development Assistance Policy* (1995). See also "Food Diplomacy and Relief."

Foreign Investment in the United States: Mira Wilkins, *The History of Foreign Investment in the United States to 1914* (1989). See also "Economic Relations and Business."

Foreign Service: See "Department of State, Foreign Service, and Diplomatic Practice."

French and Indian War: Seymour I. Schwartz, *The French and Indian War, 1854–1763* (1995) (E). See also "Military, U.S. Army, and Wars."

Fulbright Program: Walter Johnson and Francis Collegan, *The Fulbright Program* (1965); Leonard Sussman, *The Culture of Freedom* (1992). See also "Cultural Relations."

Genocide: Israel Charney, ed., *Genocide* (1988) (B); Leo Kuper, *Genocide* (1981); Lawrence J. LeBlanc, *The United States and the Geno-*cide Convention (1991); Ervin Staub, *The Roots of Evil* (1989); Charles B. Stroozier and Michael Flynn, eds., *Genocide, War, and Human Survival* (1996). See also "Holocaust," "Humanitarian Relief and Intervention," and "War Crimes and Trials."

Good Neighbor Policy: David Green, *The Containment of Latin America* (1971); Fredrick B. Pike, *FDR's Good Neighbor Policy* (1995); Bryce Wood, *The Dismantling of the Good Neighbor Policy* (1985) and *The Making of the Good Neighbor Policy* (1961). See also "Latin America."

Guano: Jimmy M. Skaggs, *The Great Guano Rush* (1994).

Health and Medical History of Leaders: Kenneth R. Crispell and Carlos F. Gomez, *Hidden Illness in the White House* (1988); Robert H. Ferrell, *Ill-Advised* (1992); Robert E. Gilbert, *The Mortal Presidency* (1992); Bert E. Park, *Ailing, Aged, Addicted* (1993) and *The Impact of Illness on World Leaders* (1986). See also "President (General)" and "President (By Administration)."

Health Organizations: Javid Siddiqi, *World Health and World Politics* (1994); Paul Weindling, ed., *International Health Organizations and Movements* (1995).

Holocaust: Richard Breitman and Alan M. Kraut, *American Refugee Policy and European Jewry* (1987); Leonard Dinnerstein, *America and the Survivors of the Holocaust* (1982); Henry L. Feingold, *Bearing Witness* (1995); Martin Gilbert, *Auschwitz and the Allies* (1981); Israel Gutman, ed., *Encyclopedia of the Holocaust* (1990) (E); Deborah E. Lipstadt, *Beyond Belief* (1993); Michael R. Marrus, *The Holocaust in History* (1987); David Wyman, *The Abandonment of the Jews* (1984) and *Paper Walls* (1968). See also "Genocide," "Germany and Berlin," "War Crimes and Trials," and "World War II."

Hostage-Taking: Russell D. Buhite, *Lives at Risk* (1995).

Humanitarian Relief and Intervention: Larry Minear and Thomas G. Weiss, *Humanitarian Politics* (1995); Robert I. Rotberg and Thomas G. Weiss, eds., *From Massacres to Genocide* (1996). See also "Ethnic Conflict," "Genocide," "Human Rights," and countries.

Human Rights: America's Watch Staff (periodic reports on Latin American countries); Amnesty International, *The Amnesty International Report* (1977–) (AS); Peter R. Baehr, *The Role of Human Rights in Foreign Policy* (1994); Jack Donnelly and Rhoda E. Howard, eds., *International Handbook of Human Rights* (1987) (E); Charles Humana, *World Human Rights Guide* (1992); Human Rights Watch, *World Report* (1983–) (AS); Natalie Kaufman, *Human Rights Treaties and the Senate* (1990); William Korey, *The Promises We Keep* (1993); Edward Lawson, *Encyclopedia of Human Rights* (1991) (E);

A. Glenn Mower, *Human Rights and American Foreign Policy* (1987) and *The United States, the United Nations, and Human Rights* (1979); A. H. Robertson and J. G. Merrills, *Human Rights in the World* (1997) (B); Lars Schoultz, *Human Rights and United States Policy Toward Latin America* (1981); Kenneth W. Thompson, ed., *The Moral Imperatives of Human Rights* (1980); Sandy Vogelgesang, *American Dream, American Nightmare* (1980). See also "Holocaust," "Humanitarian Relief and Intervention," and "War Crimes and Trials."

Ideology: Richard J. Barnet, *Roots of War* (1972); Edward M. Burns, *The American Idea of Mission* (1957); Arthur A. Ekirch, Jr., *Ideas, Ideals, and American Diplomacy* (1966); Michael H. Hunt, *Ideology and U.S. Foreign Policy* (1987); David M. Potter, *People of Plenty* (1954); E. L. Tuveson, *Redeemer Nation* (1968); William A. Williams, *The Tragedy of American Diplomacy* (1962). See also "Manifest Destiny" and "Race and Racism."

Immigration: See "Ethnic Groups and Immigration."

Imperialism: Michael B. Brown, *The Economics of Imperialism* (1974); Benjamin J. Cohen, *The Question of Imperialism* (1973); Philip Darby, *Three Faces of Imperialism* (1987); Michael Doyle, *Empires* (1986); Gabriel Kolko, *The Roots of American Foreign Policy* (1969); Tony Smith, *The Pattern of Imperialism* (1981); Richard W. Van Alstyne, *The Rising American Empire* (1960). See also "Dependency" and "World-System Analysis."

Indians (Native Americans): Brian W. Dippie, *The Vanishing American* (1982); Michael Green, *The Politics of Indian Removal* (1982); Barry Klein, ed., *Reference Encyclopedia of the American Indian* (1993) (E); Calvin Martin, ed., *The American Indian and the Problem of History* (1986); Francis Paul Prucha, *Atlas of American Indian Affairs* (1990) (A) and *The Indian in American Society* (1985); Michael Rogin, *Fathers and Sons* (1975); Paul Stuart, *Nation Within a Nation* (1987) (S); Carl Waldman, *Atlas of the North American Indian* (1985) (A); Philip Weeks, *Farewell My Nation* (1990).

Intelligence, CIA, and Covert Action: Charles D. Ameringer, *U.S. Foreign Intelligence* (1990); Christopher Andrew, *For the President's Eyes Only* (1995); Paul W. Blackstock and Frank L. Schaf, eds., *Intelligence, Espionage, Counterespionage, and Covert Operations* (1978) (B); Marjorie W. Cline et al., *Scholar's Guide to Intelligence Literature* (1983) (B); George C. Constantinides, *Intelligence & Espionage* (1983) (B); Arthur B. Darling, *The Central Intelligence Agency* (1990); Rhodri Jeffreys-Jones, *The CIA and American Democracy* (1989); Rhodri Jeffreys-Jones and Andrew Lownie, eds., *North American Spies* (1991); Loch K. Johnson, *America's Secret Power* (1989), *A Season of Inquiry* (1985), and *Secret Agencies* (1996); Stephen F. Knott, *Secret and Sanc-*

tioned (1996); Mark Lowenthal, *U.S. Intelligence* (1992); Ernest R. May, ed., *Knowing One's Enemies* (1985); Neal H. Petersen, *American Intelligence, 1775–1990* (1992) (B); Walter Pforzheimer, *Bibliography of Intelligence Literature* (1985) (B); John Prados, *The Presidents' Secret Wars* (1986); John Ranelagh, *The Agency* (1986); W. Michael Reisman and James E. Baker, *Regulating Covert Action* (1992); Frank J. Smist, Jr., *Congress Oversees the United States Intelligence Community* (1994); Jeffrey T. Richelson, *A Century of Spies* (1995) and *The U.S. Intelligence Community* (1995); Bradley F. Smith, *The Shadow Warriors* (1983); Gregory F. Treverton, *Covert Action* (1987); Bruce W. Watson et al., eds., *United States Intelligence* (1990) (E); Robin W. Winks, *Clock & Gown* (1987). See also "Assassination."

International Finance: See "International Monetary Fund and System" and "World Bank."

International Law and Hague Conferences: Robert L. Bledsoe and Boleslaw A. Boczek, *The International Law Dictionary* (1987) (E); Calvin D. Davis, *The United States and the First Hague Conference* (1962) and *The United States and the Second Hague Conference* (1976); Ingrid Delupis, ed., *Bibliography of International Law* (1975) (B); Richard Falk et al., eds., *International Law* (1985); James Fox, *Dictionary of International and Comparative Law* (1991) (E); Daniel P. Moynihan, *The Law of Nations* (1990). See also "Law of the Sea."

International Monetary Fund and System: Margaret G. DeVries, *The IMF in a Changing World* (1986); Barry Eichengreen, *Globalizing Capital* (1996); Harold James, *International Monetary Cooperation Since Bretton Woods* (1996); Mary E. Johnson, *The International Monetary Fund* (1993) (B); Robert Soloman, *Money on the Move* (1999); Brian Tew, *The Evolution of the International Monetary Fund, 1945–81* (1982).

International Organizations: Sheikh Ali, *The International Organization and World Order Dictionary* (1992) (E); George W. Baer, ed., *International Organizations, 1918–1945* (1981) (B); Edward J. Osmanczyk, *The Encyclopedia of the United States and International Organizations* (1990) (E); Hans-Albrecht Schraepler, *Directory of International Organizations* (1996); Union of International Associations, *Yearbook of International Organizations* (1948–) (AS). See also specific organizations.

Isolationism: Selig Adler, *The Isolationist Impulse* (1957); Wayne S. Cole, *Roosevelt and the Isolationists* (1983); Justus D. Doenecke, *Anti-Intervention* (1987) (B); Thomas N. Guinsburg, *The Pursuit of Isolationism in the United States Senate* (1982); Manfred Jonas, *Isolationism in America, 1935–1941* (1966).

Journalism and Media: James L. Baughman, *Henry R. Luce and the Rise of the American News Media* (1988); Bernard C. Cohen, *The Press and Foreign Policy* (1963); Joseph P. McKerns, ed., *Biographical Dictionary of American Journalism* (1989) (BA); Brigitte Lebens Nacos, *The Press, Presidents, and Crises* (1990); Johanna Neuman, *Lights, Camera, War* (1995); Michael Schudson, *The Power of News* (1995); Simon Serfaty, *The Media and Foreign Policy* (1990); Ronald Steel, *Walter Lippmann and the American Century* (1980); William H. Taft, ed., *Encyclopedia of Twentieth-Century Journalists* (1986) (BA); John Tebbel and Sarah Miles Watts, *The Press and the Presidency* (1985). See also "Film, Television, and Cultural Expansion" and "Public Opinion."

Korean War: See "Korea and Korean War."

Labor: Philip S. Foner, *U.S. Labor Movement and Latin America* (1988); Ronald Radosh, *American Labor and United States Foreign Policy* (1969); Federico Romero, *The United States and the European Trade Union Movement, 1944–1951* (1992).

Law of the Sea: Jack N. Barkenbus, *Deep Seabed Resources* (1979); Ann L. Hollick, *U.S. Foreign Policy and the Law of the Sea* (1981); D. P. O'Connell, *The International Law of the Sea* (1982); Clyde Sanger, *Ordering the Oceans* (1987); United Nations, *The Law of the Sea* (1991) (B). See also "Environment" and "International Law and Hague Conferences."

League of Nations: Denna F. Fleming, *The United States and the League of Nations* (1932); Warren F. Kuehl, *Seeking World Order* (1969); F. S. Northedge, *The League of Nations* (1986). See also "International Organizations" and "United Nations."

Low Intensity Warfare: See "Counterinsurgency."

Manifest Destiny: Norman A. Graebner, ed., *Manifest Destiny* (1968); Thomas R. Hietala, *Manifest Design* (1985); Reginald Horsman, *Race and Manifest Destiny* (1981); Robert W. Johannsen, ed., *Manifest Destiny* (1998); Anders Stephanson, *Manifest Destiny* (1995); Albert K. Weinberg, *Manifest Destiny* (1935). See also "Ideology."

Marshall Plan: Michael J. Hogan, *The Marshall Plan* (1987); Alan S. Milward, *The Reconstruction of Western Europe, 1945–51* (1984); Imanuel Wexler, *The Marshall Plan Revisited* (1983). See also "Europe" and "Foreign Aid."

Marine Corps: Allan R. Millett, *Semper Fidelis* (1980). See also "Military, U.S. Army, and Wars" and specific wars.

McCarthyism: See "Anticommunism and McCarthyism."

Media: See "Journalism and Media."

Merchant Marine: John A. Butler, *Sailing on Friday* (1997); Rene De La Pedraja, *A Historical Dictionary of the U.S. Merchant Marine and Shipping Industry* (1994) (E).

Military, U.S. Army, and Wars: William M. Arkin et al., *Encyclopedia of the U.S. Military* (1990) (E); Benjamin R. Beede, *Military and Strategic Policy* (1990) (B); Daniel K. Blewett, *American Military History* (1994) (B); John W. Chambers, *To Raise an Army* (1987); Edward M. Coffman, *The Old Army* (1986); E. Ernest Dupuy and Trevor N. Dupuy, *The Harper Encyclopedia of Military History* (1993) (E); John C. Fredriksen, *Shield of the Republic/Sword of Empire* (1990) (B); Kenneth J. Hagan and William R. Roberts, eds., *Against All Enemies* (1986); Robin Higham and Donald J. Mrozek, eds., *A Guide to the Sources of United States Military History* (1975–) (B); International Institute for Strategic Studies, *Strategic Survey* (1966–) (AS) and *The Military Balance* (1959/1960–) (AS); *International Military and Defense Encyclopedia* (1993) (E); John E. Jessup and Louise B. Ketz, eds., *Encyclopedia of the American Military* (1994) (E); Kenneth Macksey and William Woodhouse, *The Penguin Encyclopedia of Modern Warfare* (1992); Allan R. Millett and Peter Maslowski, *For the Common Defense* (1994); Jay M. Shafritz et al., eds., *Dictionary of Military Science* (1989); Roger J. Spiller and Joseph G. Dawson III, eds., *Dictionary of American Military Biography* (1984) (BA); Jerry K. Sweeney, ed., *A Handbook of American Military History* (1996) (E); Herbert K. Tillema, *International Armed Conflict Since 1945* (1991) (B); Peter G. Tsouras et al., *The United States Army* (1991) (E); U.S. Military Academy, *The West Point Atlas of American Wars, 1689–1953* (1959) (A); Cynthia Watson, *U.S. National Security Policy Groups* (1990) (E); Russell F. Weigley, *The American Way of War* (1973) and *History of the United States Army* (1984). See also "Marine Corps," "Navy and Sea Power," and wars.

Minerals: Alfred E. Eckes, *The United States and the Global Struggle for Minerals* (1979); Jordan E. Helmreich, *Gathering Rare Ores* (1986); Ronnie Lipschutz, *When Nations Clash* (1989). See also "Economic Relations and Business."

Missionaries: Henry Bowden, *Dictionary of American Religious Biography* (1993) (BA); John K. Fairbank, ed., *The Missionary Enterprise in China and America* (1974); Patricia Hill, *The World Their Household* (1985); Jane Hunter, *The Gospel of Gentility* (1984); William R. Hutchison, *Errand to the World* (1987); Paul A. Varg, *Missionaries, Chinese, and Diplomats* (1958). See also "Cultural Relations" and "Ideology."

Monroe Doctrine: Ernest R. May, *The Making of the Monroe Doctrine* (1975); Dexter Perkins, *A History of the Monroe Doctrine* (1963);

Gaddis Smith, *The Last Years of the Monroe Doctrine* (1994). See also "Latin America."

National Security Council: Gerry Andrianopoulos, *Kissinger and Brzezinski* (1991); John Prados, *Keepers of the Keys* (1991); Bromley K. Smith, *Organizational History of the National Security Council During the Kennedy and Johnson Administrations* (1988).

Navy and Sea Power: George W. Baer, *One Hundred Years of Sea Power* (1994); James C. Bradford, *Admirals of the New Steel Navy* (1990), *Captains of the Old Steam Navy* (1986), and *Command Under Sail* (1985); William B. Cogan, *Dictionary of Admirals of the United States Navy* (1989) (BA); Paolo E. Coletta, *A Selected and Annotated Bibliography of American Naval History* (1988) (B); Paolo E. Coletta et al., eds., *American Secretaries of the Navy* (1980) (BA); Michael J. Crawford and Christine F. Hughes, *The Reestablishment of the Navy, 1787–1801* (1995) (B); Kenneth J. Hagan, ed., *In Peace and War* (1984) and *This People's Navy* (1991); John B. Hattendorf and Lynn C. Hattendorf, *A Bibliography of the Works of Alfred Thayer Mahan* (1986) (B); David F. Long, *Gold Braid and Foreign Relations* (1988); Barbara A. Lynch and John E. Vajda, *United States Naval History* (1993) (B); Franklin D. Margiotta, ed., *Brassey's Encyclopedia of Naval Forces and Warfare* (1996) (E); Elmer B. Potter, ed., *Sea Power* (1981); Harold Sprout and Margaret Sprout, *The Rise of American Naval Power* (1966); Jack Sweetman, ed., *American Naval History* (1984) (C); Bruce W. Watson and Susan M. Watson, *The United States Navy* (1991) (E). See also "Military, U.S. Army, and Wars" and wars.

Neutralism and Nonalignment: H. W. Brands, *The Specter of Neutralism* (1989); K. C. Chaudhary, *Non-aligned Summitry* (1988); Steven R. David, *Choosing Sides* (1991); Richard L. Jackson, *The Non-aligned, the UN, and the Superpowers* (1983); Lawrence W. Martin, ed., *Neutralism and Nonalignment* (1962).

Nobel Peace Prize: Irwin Abrams, *The Nobel Peace Prize and the Laureates* (1988); Oaula McGuire, ed., *Nobel Prize Winners Supplement* (1992); Tyler Wasson, ed., *Nobel Prize Winners* (1987). See also "Peace Movements."

Nonproliferation (Nuclear): See "Cold War" and "Nuclear Arms."

North American Free Trade Agreement (NAFTA): Allan Metz, *A NAFTA Bibliography* (1996) (B); Jerry M. Rosenberg, *Encyclopedia of the North American Free Trade Agreement* (1984) (E). See also "Canada" and "Economic Relations and Business."

North Atlantic Treaty Organization (NATO): Timothy Ireland, *Creating the Entangling Alliance* (1981); Robert S. Jordan, Jr., ed., *Generals in International Politics* (1987); Lawrence S. Kaplan, *The Long Entanglement: NATO's First Fifty Years* (1999) and *NATO & the United States* (1994); Augustus R. Norton et al., *NATO* (1985) (B); Joseph Smith, ed., *The Origins of NATO* (1990). See also "Cold War," "Europe," and "Nuclear Arms."

Nuclear Arms: Paul Boyer, *By the Bomb's Early Light* (1985); McGeorge Bundy, *Danger and Survival* (1990); Robert A. Divine, *The Sputnik Challenge* (1993); Lawrence Freedman, *The Evolution of Nuclear Strategy* (1989); Gregg Herken, *Counsels of War* (1985); David Holloway, *The Soviet Union and the Arms Race* (1984); Fred Kaplan, *The Wizards of Armageddon* (1983); Charles R. Morris, *Iron Destinies, Lost Opportunities* (1988); John Newhouse, *War and Peace in the Nuclear Age* (1989); William G. M. Pearson, *The Nuclear Arms Race* (1989) (E); Ronald E. Powaski, *March to Armageddon* (1987); Scott D. Sagan, *The Limits of Safety* (1993); Stephen I. Schwartz, ed., *Atomic Audit* (1998); Richard Smoke, *National Security and the Nuclear Dilemma* (1987); Spencer R. Weart, *Nuclear Fear* (1988); Allan M. Winkler, *Life Under a Cloud* (1993). See also "Cold War," "Disarmament and Arms Control," and "Space and Satellites."

Oil: M. A. Adelman, *The Genie out of the Bottle* (1995); Gerald D. Nash, *United States Oil Policy, 1890–1964* (1968); David S. Painter, *Oil and the American Century* (1986); Stephen J. Randall, *United States Foreign Oil Policy, 1919–1984* (1985); Anthony Sampson, *The Seven Sisters* (1991); Michael B. Stoff, *Oil, War, and American Security* (1980); Fiona Venn, *Oil Diplomacy in the Twentieth Century* (1986); Daniel Yergin, *The Prize* (1991). See also "Mexico," "Middle East," "Minerals," "Organization of Petroleum Exporting Countries (OPEC)," "Venezuela," and Anderson and Miller in "Saudi Arabia."

Olympics: Allen Guttmann, *The Games Must Go On* (1984) and *The Olympics* (1992); Christopher R. Hill, *Olympic Politics* (1996); David Wallechinsky, *The Complete Book of the Summer Olympics* (1996) (E) and *The Complete Book of the Winter Olympics* (1993) (E). See also "Sports."

Organization of American States (OAS): David Sheinin, *The Organization of American States* (1996) (B). See also "Latin America" and "Pan-Americanism."

Organization of Petroleum Exporting Countries (OPEC): M. E. Ahrari, *OPEC* (1986); Albert L. Danielson, *The Evolution of OPEC* (1982); Ian Skeet, *OPEC* (1988). See also "Oil" and Rabe in "Venezuela."

PanAmericanism: J. Floyd Mecham, *The United States and Inter-American Security, 1889–1960* (1961); Arthur P. Whitaker, *The Western Hemisphere Idea* (1954). See also "Latin America."

Peace Corps: Fritz Fischer, *Making Them Like Us* (1998); Elizabeth Cobbs Hoffman, *All You Need Is Love* (1998); T. Zane Reeves, *The Politics of the Peace Corps & Vista* (1988); Gerald T. Rice, *Bold Experiment* (1985); Robert Ridinger, *The Peace Corps* (1989) (B): D. David Searles, *The Peace Corps Experience* (1997). See also "Cultural Relations."

Peacekeeping: Paul F. Diehl, *International Peacekeeping* (1993); William J. Durch, ed., *The Evolution of UN Peacekeeping* (1993); Alan James, *Peacekeeping in International Politics* (1990); Nathan A. Pelcovits, *The Long Armistice* (1993). See also "United Nations."

Peace Movements: Harriet Hyman Alonso, *Peace as a Women's Issue* (1993); Peter Brock, *Pacifism in the United States* (1968); Charles Chatfield, *The American Peace Movement* (1992); Charles DeBenedetti, ed., *Peace Heroes in Twentieth Century America* (1986) and *The Peace Reform in American History* (1980); Catherine Foster, *Women for All Seasons* (1989); Charles F. Howlett, *The American Peace Movement* (1990) (B); Harold Josephson et al., eds., *Biographical Dictionary of Modern Peace Leaders* (1985) (BA); Robert Kleidman, *Organizing for Peace: Neutrality, the Test Ban, and the Freeze* (1993); Elvin Laszlo and Jong Youl Yoo, eds., *World Encyclopedia of Peace* (1986) (E); Robert S. Meyer, *Peace Organizations Past and Present* (1988) (E); David S. Patterson, *Toward a Warless World* (1976); Nancy L. Roberts, *American Peace Writers, Editors, and Periodicals* (1991) (BA); Lawrence S. Wittner, *Rebels Against War* (1984) and *The Struggle Against the Bomb* (1993–); Valarie H. Ziegler, *The Advocates of Peace in Antebellum America* (1992). See also specific wars.

Pearl Harbor, 1941: Stanley L. Falk, "Pearl Harbor," *Naval History* (1988) (B); Robert W. Love, Jr., ed., *Pearl Harbor Reexamined* (1990); Martin V. Melosi, *The Shadow of Pearl Harbor* (1977); Frank P. Mintz, *Revisionism and the Origins of Pearl Harbor* (1985); James W. Morley, ed., *The First Confrontation* (1995); Gordon W. Prange, *Pearl Harbor* (1986); Myron J. Smith, Jr., *Pearl Harbor* (1991) (B). Also see "World War II."

Philanthropy and Foundations: Robert Arnove, *Philanthropy and Cultural Imperialism* (1980); Edward H. Berman, *The Influence of the Carnegie, Ford, and Rockefeller Foundations on American Foreign Policy* (1983); Marcos Cueto, ed., *Missionaries of Science: The Rockefeller Foundation and Latin America* (1994); Merle Curti, *American Philanthropy Abroad* (1963); Robert L. Daniel, *American Philanthropy in the Near East, 1820–1960* (1970); Raymond Fosdick, *The Story of the*

Rockefeller Foundation (1989). See also "Cultural Relations" and Cobbs in "Brazil."

Population: *The Encyclopedia of Global Population and Demographics* (1998) (E); William Peterson and Renee Peterson, *Dictionary of Demography* (1986) (E).

President (General): James Barber, *The Presidential Character* (1992); E. S. Corwin, *The President* (1957); Robert A. Divine, *Foreign Policy and U.S. Presidential Elections, 1940–1960* (1974); Robert U. Goehlert and Fenton S. Martin, *The Presidency* (1985) (B); George T. Kurian, *A Historical Guide to the U.S. Government* (1997) (E); Leonard W. Levy and Louis Fisher, eds., *Encyclopedia of the American Presidency* (1993) (E); Theodore Lowi, *The Personal President* (1985); John E. Mueller, *War, Presidents, and Public Opinion* (1973); Richard E. Neustadt, *Presidential Power and the Modern Presidents* (1990); Arthur M. Schlesinger, Jr., *The Imperial Presidency* (1973); Robert Sobel, ed., *Biographical Directory of the United States Executive Branch, 1774–1977* (1977) (BA). See also "Bureaucracy," "Congress (House and Senate)," "Constitution and Constitutional Interpretation," "Health and Medical History of Leaders," "Presidents (By Administration)," and "War Powers."

Presidents (By Administration): Harry Ammon, *James Monroe* (1991) (B); Peter H. Buckingham, *Woodrow Wilson* (1989) (B); Richard Dean Burns, *Harry S. Truman* (1984) (B); John Ferling, *John Adams* (1993) (B); James N. Giglio, *John F. Kennedy* (1995) (B); Otis L. Graham, Jr., and Meghan R. Wander, eds., *Franklin D. Roosevelt* (1985) (E); John R. Greene, *Gerald R. Ford* (1994) (B); Richard S. Kirkendall, ed., *The Harry S. Truman Encyclopedia* (1989) (E); Peter B. Levy, *Encyclopedia of the Reagan-Bush Years* (1996) (E); Merrill D. Peterson, *Thomas Jefferson* (1986) (E); Robert A. Rutland, ed., *James Madison and the American Nation* (1994) (E). See also "Health and Medical History of Leaders" and "President (General)."

Privateering: Donald B. Chidsey, *The American Privateers* (1962); Reuben E. Stivers, *Privateers and Volunteers* (1975); Carl E. Swanson, *Predators and Prizes* (1991). See also "Navy and Sea Power."

Propaganda and Public Diplomacy: Leo Bogart, *Premises for Propaganda* (1976) (USIA); Robert Cole, *The Encyclopedia of Propaganda* (1997) (E); Robert E. Elder, *The Information Machine* (1968); Walter Hixson, *Parting the Curtain* (1997); Alexandre Lauien, *The Voice of America* (1988); Gifford Malone, *Political Advocacy and Cultural Communication* (1988); Jarol B. Manheim, *Strategic Public Diplomacy and American Foreign Policy* (1994); Sig Mickelson, *America's Other Voice*

(1983); Michael Nelson, *War of the Black Heavens: The Battles of Western Broadcasting in the Cold War* (1997); Holly C. Shulman, *The Voice of America* (1990); Thomas C. Sorensen, *The Word War* (1968); Allen M. Winkler, *The Politics of Propaganda* (1978). See also "Communications," "Cultural Relations," and "Fulbright Program."

Public Opinion: Richard J. Barnet, *The Rockets' Red Glare* (1990); Bernard C. Cohen, *The Public's Impact on Foreign Policy* (1973); H. Schuyler Foster, *Activism Replaces Isolationism: U.S. Public Attitudes, 1940–1975* (1983); George Gallup, *The Gallup Poll: Public Opinion* (1972–) (AS and S); Ole R. Holsti, *Public Opinion and American Foreign Policy* (1996); Ralph B. Levering, *The Public and American Foreign Policy* (1978); David D. Newsom, *The Public Dimension of Foreign Policy* (1996); Melvin Small, *Democracy and Diplomacy* (1996). See also "Journalism and Media" and "President (General)."

Race and Racism: Michael L. Krenn, ed., *Race and U.S. Foreign Policy* (1998); Paul Gordon Lauren, *Power and Prejudice* (1988); Hazel M. McFerson, *The Racial Dimension of American Overseas Colonial Policy* (1997); George E. Shepherd, ed., *Racial Influence on American Foreign Policy* (1971); Jay A. Sigler, ed., *International Handbook on Race and Race Relations* (1987) (E); Rubin F. Weston, *Racism in U.S. Imperialism* (1972). See also "African Americans," "Ethnic Groups and Immigration," "Ideology," and "Manifest Destiny."

Recognition Policy: Thomas M. Franck, *The Power of Legitimacy Among Nations* (1990); L. Thomas Galloway, *Recognizing Foreign Governments* (1978).

Red Cross: Nicholas O. Berry, *War and the Red Cross* (1997); Pierre Bossier, *From Solferino to Tsushima* (1985); John F. Hutchinson, *Champions of Charity* (1996). See also "Humanitarian Relief and Intervention."

Refugees: Anna Bramwell, ed., *Refugees in the Age of Total War* (1988); Gil Loescher, *Beyond Charity* (1993); Gil Loescher and John A. Scalan, *Calculated Kindness* (1986); J. Bruce Nichols, *The Uneasy Alliance: Religion, Refugee Work, and U.S. Foreign Policy* (1988); Michael S. Teitelbaum and Myron Weiner, eds., *Threatened Peoples, Threatened Borders* (1995); U.S. Committee on Refugees, *World Refugee Survey* (1980–) (AS). See also "Ethnic Groups and Immigration," "Holocaust," and "Humanitarian Relief and Intervention."

Rivers: *Rand McNally Encyclopedia of World Rivers* (1980) (E).

Scientists and Science: Robert Gilpin and Christopher Wright, eds., *Scientists and National Policy-making* (1964); Greta Jones, *Science, Politics and the Cold War* (1988); Clarence Lasby, *Operation Paperclip*

(1971); Joseph Rotblat, ed., *Scientists, the Arms Race, and Disarmament* (1982); Alice K. Smith, *A Peril and a Hope: The Scientists' Movement in the United States, 1945–47* (1965). See also "Nuclear Arms."

Sectionalism: Peter Trubowitz, *Defining the National Interest* (1998). See also "The South (U.S.)."

Self-Determination: Antonio Cassese, *Self-Determination of Peoples* (1995); David B. Knight and Maureen Davies, *Self-Determination* (1988) (B).

Slave Trade and Slavery: Randall Miller and John Smith, eds., *Dictionary of Afro-American Slavery* (1988) (E); Junius P. Rodriguez, ed., *The Historical Encyclopedia of World Slavery* (1997) (E).

The South (U.S.): Alfred Hero, *The Southerner and World Affairs* (1965); Charles O. Lerche, *The Uncertain South* (1964); Tennant S. McWilliams, *The New South Faces the World* (1988).

Space and Satellites: William E. Burrows, *Deep Black* (1986); Walter A. McDougall, *The Heavens and the Earth* (1985); Jeffrey T. Richelson, *America's Secret Eyes in Space* (1990); Paul B. Stares, *The Militarization of Space* (1985). See also "Nuclear Arms."

Spanish-American-Cuban-Filipino War: Benjamin R. Beede, ed., *The War of 1898 and U.S. Interventions, 1899–1934* (1994) (B); James C. Bradford, ed., *Crucible of Empire* (1993); Louis A. Peréz, Jr., *The War of 1898* (1998); Anne C. Venzon, *The Spanish-American War* (1990) (B). Also see "Cuba," "Military, U.S. Army, and Wars," and "Spain."

Sports: Allen Guttmann, *Games and Empires* (1994). See also "Olympics."

Summit Conferences: Keith Eubank, *The Summit Conference* (1966); Elmer Plischke, *Diplomat in Chief* (1986) and *Summit Diplomacy* (1958); Robert D. Putnam and Nicholas Bayne, *Hanging Together: The Seven-Power Summits* (1984); Gordon R. Weihmiller and Dusko Doder, *U.S.-Soviet Summits* (1986). See also "Cold War."

Tariffs and Protectionism: David A. Lake, *Power, Protection, and Free Trade* (1988); James M. Lutz, *Protectionism* (1988) (B); Robert A. Pastor, *Congress and the Politics of U.S. Foreign Economic Policy, 1929–1976* (1980); Sidney Ratner, *The Tariff in American History* (1972); Frank W. Taussig, *Tariff History of the United States* (1931); Tom E. Terrill, *The Tariff, Politics, and American Foreign Policy, 1874–1901* (1973); Paul Wolman, *Most Favored Nation* (1992); Thomas Zeiler, *American Trade and Power in the 1960s* (1992). See also

"Economic Relations and Business" and "Economic Sanctions and Export Controls."

Telecommunications: See "Communications."

Terrorism: Martha Crenshaw and John Pimlott, eds., *Encyclopedia of World Terrorism* (1996) (E); Christopher Dobson and Ronald Payne, *The Never Ending War* (1987); Lawrence Freedman et al., *Terrorism and International Order* (1986); Robert Kumamoto, *International Terrorism and American Foreign Relations, 1945–1976* (1999); Walter Laqueur, *The Age of Terrorism* (1987); Edward F. Mickolus et al., *International Terrorism in the 1980s* (1989) (C), *Terrorism, 1988–1991* (1993) (C), and *Transnational Terrorism . . . , 1968–1979* (1980) (C); Suzanne R. Ontiveros, *Global Terrorism* (1986) (B); Barry Rubin, ed., *The Politics of Terrorism* (1990); Jeffrey D. Simon, *The Terrorist Trap* (1994); John R. Thackrah, *Encyclopedia of Terrorism and Political Violence* (1987) (E).

Threat Perception and Calculation: Noel E. Firth and James H. Noren, *Soviet Defense Spending: A History of CIA Estimates, 1950–1990* (1998); Robert H. Johnson, *Improbable Dangers* (1994). See also "Cold War."

Think Tanks: Donald E. Abelson, *American Think-Tanks and Their Role in US Foreign Policy, 1976–88* (1996); Peter Grose, *Continuing the Inquiry* (1996); David M. Ricci, *The Transformation of American Politics* (1993); Robert D. Schulzinger, *The Wise Men of Foreign Affairs: The History of the Council on Foreign Relations* (1984); Christopher Simpson, ed., *Universities and Empire: Money and Politics in the Social Sciences During the Cold War* (1999); Bruce L. R. Smith, *The Rand Corporation* (1966); James A. Smith, *The Idea Brokers* (1991); Michael Wala, *The Council on Foreign Relations and American Foreign Policy in the Early Cold War* (1994).

Tourism and Travel: James Clifford, *Routes* (1997); Foster Rhea Dulles, *Americans Abroad* (1964); Cynthia Enloe, *Bananas, Beaches, and Bases* (1990); Maxine Fieffer, *Tourism in History* (1985); Marie-Françoise Lanfant et al., *International Tourism* (1995); Sara Mills, *Discourses of Difference* (1991); David Spurr, *The Rhetoric of Empire* (1993); John Urry, *The Tourist Gaze* (1990).

Trade: See "Economic Relations and Business," "Economic Sanctions and Export Controls," "Tariffs and Protectionism," "United States Trade Representative," and "World Trade Organization (WTO)."

United Nations: Joseph P. Baratta, *Strengthening the United Nations* (1987) (B); Robert A. Divine, *Second Chance* (1967); Seymour M. Finger, *American Ambassadors at the United Nations* (1987); Thomas M. Frank, *Nation Against Nation* (1985); Max Harrelson, *Fires All Around the Horizon* (1989); Robert C. Hilderbrand, *Dumbarton Oaks* (1990); Evan Luard and Derek Herter, *The United Nations* (1993); Kumiko Matsuura et al., *Chronology and Fact Book of the United Nations, 1941–1991* (1992) (C); Edmund Jan Osmanczyk, *The Encyclopedia of the United Nations and International Relations* (1990) (E); Gary B. Ostrower, *The United States and the United Nations* (1998); William Preston, Jr., et al., *Hope and Folly* (1989) (UNESCO); Caroline Pruden, *Conditional Partners* (1998). See also "International Organizations," "League of Nations," and "Peacekeeping."

United States Trade Representative: Steve Dryden, *Trade Warriors* (1995). See also "Economic Relations and Business."

Vietnam War: See "Vietnam and Southeast Asia."

War Crimes and Trials: Richard L. Lael, *The Yamashita Precedent: War Crimes and Command Responsibility* (1982); John R. Lewis, *Uncertain Judgment* (1979) (B); Philip R. Piccigallo, *The Japanese on Trial* (1979); Telford Taylor, *Nuremberg and Vietnam* (1970); Norman E. Tutorow, ed., *War Crimes, War Criminals, and War Crimes Trials* (1986) (B). See also "Germany and Berlin," "Holocaust," "Human Rights," and "Japan."

War of 1812: John C. Fredriksen, *Free Trade and Sailors' Rights* (1985) (B); Dwight L. Smith, *The War of 1812* (1985) (B). See also "Military, U.S. Army, and Wars."

War Powers: Louis Fischer, *Presidential War Power* (1995); Christopher N. May, *In the Name of War* (1989); Gary M. Stein and Morton H. Halperin, eds., *The U.S. Constitution and the Power to Go to War* (1994); John H. Sullivan, *The War Powers Resolution* (1982); Francis D. Wormuth and Edwin B. Firmage, *To Chain the Dog of War* (1989). See also "Congress (House and Senate)," "Constitution and Constitutional Interpretation," and "President (General)."

West (U.S.) and Frontier: William A. Beck and Ynez D. Haase, *Historical Atlas of the American West* (1989) (A); William Goetzmann and Glyndwr Williams, *The Atlas of North American Exploration* (1992) (A); J. Norman Heard, *Handbook of the American Frontier* (1987) (E); Adrian Johnson, *America Explored* (1974) (E); Howard R. Lamar, ed., *The New Encyclopedia of the American West* (1998) (E); Clyde A. Milner III et al., eds., *The Oxford History of the American West* (1994) (E); Charles Phillips and Alan Axelrod, eds., *Encyclopedia of the American West* (1996) (E); Dan L. Thrapp, *The Encyclopedia of Frontier Biography* (1988–   ) (BA).

Whaling: Daniel Francis, *A History of World Whaling* (1990); Alexander Sarbuck, *History of the American Whale Fishery* (1989). See also "Environment."

World Bank: Devesh Kapur et al., *The World Bank* (1997).

World Cities: Immanuel Ness, *Encyclopedia of World Cities* (1998).

World Health Organization: See "Health Organizations."

World Trade Organization (WTO): Bernard Hoekman and Michel Kostecki, *The Political Economy of the World Trading System* (1996). Also see "Economic Relations and Business."

Women and Gender Issues: Homer L. Calkin, *Women in the Department of State* (1978); Edward P. Crapol, ed., *Women and American Foreign Policy* (1992); John A. Edens, *Eleanor Roosevelt* (1994) (B); Rebecca Grant and Kathleen Newland, eds., *Gender and International Relations* (1991); Human Rights Watch, *Global Report on Women's Human Rights* (1995); Rhodri Jeffreys-Jones, *Changing Differences* (1995); Nancy W. McGlen and Meredith Reid Sarkes, *Women in Foreign Policy* (1993). See also "Peace Movements."

World Court: Michael Dunne, *The United States and the World Court, 1920–1935* (1988); D. F. Fleming, *The United States and the World Court* (1945); Shabtai Rosenne, *The World Court* (1989) (E). See also "International Law and Hague Conferences."

World's Fairs: John E. Findling, ed., *Historical Dictionary of World's Fairs and Expositions* (1990); Robert H. Haddow, *Pavilions of Plenty* (1997); Robert W. Rydell, *All the World's a Fair* (1987) and *World of Fairs* (1993); Robert W. Rydell and Nancy Gwinn, eds, *Fair Representations* (1994). See also "Cultural Relations" and "Propaganda and Public Diplomacy."

World-System Analysis: Thomas J. McCormick, *America's Half-Century* (1995); Immanuel Wallerstein, *Geopolitics and Geoculture* (1991), *The Modern World-System* (1974), *Politics of the World-Economy* (1984), and *World Inequality* (1975). See also "Dependency."

World War I: Arthur Banks, *A Military History Atlas of the First World War* (1975) (A); Martin Gilbert, *Atlas of World War I* (1994) (A); Holger H. Herwig and Neil M. Heyman, *Biographical Dictionary of World War I* (1982) (BA); George T. Kurian, *Encyclopedia of the First World War* (1990) (E); Stephen Pope and Elizabeth-Anne Wheal, *The Dictionary of the First World War* (1995) (E); Anne C. Venzon, ed., *The United States and the First World War* (1995) (B). See also "Military, U.S. Army, and Wars."

World War II: Marcel Baudot et al., eds., *The Historical Encyclopedia of World War II* (1980) (E); David G. Chandler and James Lawton Collins, Jr., eds., *The D-Day Encyclopedia* (1983) (E); I. C. B. Dear and M. R. D. Foot, eds., *The Oxford Companion to World War II* (1995) (E); Robert Goralski, *World War II Almanac* (1981) (C); John Keegan, ed., *The Times Atlas of the Second World War* (1989) (A); Norman Polmar and Thomas B. Allen, *World War II* (1991) (E); John J. Sbrega, *The War Against Japan* (1989) (B); Ronald Spector, "The Scholarship on World War II," *Journal of Military History* (1991) (B); U.S. Military Academy, *Campaign Atlas to the Second World War* (1980) (A); Peter Young, ed., *Atlas of the Second World War* (1973) (A); David T. Zabecki, *World War II in Europe* (1997) (E). See also "Military, U.S. Army, and Wars."

Index